From a Painting by Frank Holland — Copyrighted, 1914, by G. W. Browne

GEN. GEORGE REID

VITAL RECORDS

OF

LONDONDERRY

NEW HAMPSHIRE

A FULL AND ACCURATE TRANSCRIPT OF THE BIRTHS, MARRIAGE INTENTIONS, MARRIAGES AND DEATHS IN THIS TOWN FROM THE EARLIEST DATE TO 1910

Compiled from the Town Books, Church Records, Family Records, Graveyard Inscriptions and other sources, by

DANIEL GAGE ANNIS

The Subject Matter Edited, with Introduction, Sketches and Annotations by

GEORGE WALDO BROWNE

GENEALOGICAL PUBLISHING Co., Inc

Originally published: Manchester, New Hampshire, 1914
Reprinted by Genealogical Publishing Co., Inc.
Baltimore, Maryland, 1994
Library of Congress Catalogue Card Number 94-78265
International Standard Book Number 0-8063-1415-X
Made in the United States of America

LONDONDERRY, N. H., Nov. 5, 1913.

Following is a true copy of Article 4 of the warrant for the March election in the year 1912:

"ARTICLE 4. To see if the town will vote to raise the sum of three hundred dollars ($300.00) to be expended by the Selectmen for printing the Vital Statistics (Births, Marriages and Deaths) of Londonderry from the settlement thereof, 1719, to the year 1910."

The following action was taken on the above article:

Upon motion, it was voted that the Selectmen be instructed to have the Vital Statistics printed at a cost of three hundred dollars.

LONDONDERRY, N. H., Nov. 5, 1913.

I certify that the above is a true copy of Article 4 of the Warrant for the annual meeting of 1912, and the action taken thereon.

ATTEST:

WILLIAM H. CROWELL,
Town Clerk.

LONDONDERRY, N. H., Dec. 27, 1913.

I have made what I believe to be a true copy of all the names and dates included in the following transcript of the births, marriage intentions, marriages, and deaths of Londonderry.

[Signed] DANIEL GAGE ANNIS.

Then personally appeared Mr. Daniel G. Annis and made oath to the statement above. Before me,

JOHN E. RAY,
Justice of the Peace.

CONTENTS.

Campbell, Duke of Argyle

INTRODUCTION.

It is perhaps needless to say that care has been taken in transcribing the records as given in the originals, that their value may be made certain by being accurate. Mistakes no doubt there are in names and dates, but these cannot be frequent, and in most cases are not due to the compiler. The spelling of names, as a rule, is the same as it was given in the first place. This accounts for the difference in names and the vagaries that frequently occur. It was not thought best to follow the literal wording of the original entries in the old town books, but to separate the different classes under their respective headings, Births, Marriage Intentions, Marriages and Deaths. The first of these items have been arranged alphabetically under the names of the parents, the children following in chronological order. This seemed to be easier of identification, while saving considerable space, which was a matter calling for attention. Intentions of marriages and marriages have been given under the surnames of both bride and groom. The deaths are in the alphabetical order. Occasionally this rule has been broken, especially among the births, where sometimes a marriage or death is given, as it would make more complete the item, which might not be consistently filled elsewhere.

As indicated by the title-page, the sources of information have been many, for the compiler labored zealously in his work. It was not deemed necessary to designate these sources, as that would tend to confuse the reader and add little, if any, value to the item. The abbreviations are those generally followed in works of this kind, and will be readily understood. For instance, b. stands for birth; m. for married; d. for death; dau. for daughter; s. for son; w. for wife; bur. for buried, etc.

The town has very generously made possible this publication by the payment of three hundred dollars towards the cost of production, the balance of the expense, something like two hundred dollars, being borne by the undersigned.

Above all else the thanks of every person interested in this subject are due to Mr. Annis for his patient, conscientious work in compiling these records, a task of no little magnitude, which he has performed without payment or expectation of reward. He was in every way admirably well fitted for the undertaking, and I believe he has done his work well. It is no more than justice that I should give here a brief sketch of his life.

DANIEL GAGE ANNIS.

Mr. A. L. Annis, in his compilation of the Genealogy of the Annis family, says that Charles Cumway Annis, born in Enniskillen, Ire., probably of English parentage, in 1638, was the ancestor of most, if not all, of the persons in this country bearing that surname. This Charles Annis, at the age of 28, married Sarah Chase and settled in Newbury, Mass. The descendants of this worthy couple are very numerous and are widely scattered over the United States, Canada and Nova Scotia.

Charles and Sarah (Chase) Annis had nine children, the fourth of whom, Abraham, was born April 12, 1672, and resided in Newbury, Mass. He married Hannah, daughter of Christopher and Hannah (Belknap) Osgood, born October 19, 1668. They had ten children. The second son and fourth child was named John and was born May 1, 1700. He married, December 16, 1724, Abigail Rolfe, daughter of Ezra and Sarah (Jackson) Rolfe. This couple had nine children, the third of whom was named Rolfe, born December 21, 1734; married September 1, 1757, to Sarah Rollins, daughter of Benjamin and Hannah (Annis) Rollins. This couple had two children, and probably others. Isaac, the second son, was born in November, 1759, and married Hannah Dwinnell in 1785 or 1786. He was a Revolutionary soldier. The children of Isaac and Hannah (Dwinnell) Annis, all born in Londonderry, were eight, according to the records, and the second of these, John, was born October 13, 1790, and died April 22, 1871.

Daniel G. Annis was the youngest son of a family of five sons and six daughters, the children of John and Delilah (Coburn) Annis, and was born in Londonderry, N. H., January 25, 1839. His father and grandfather both lived in Litchfield, though the former removed to a farm in north Londonderry, which he purchased in 1820. All of his children were born here. He was a member of the old Whig party and of its offshoot, the Republican party. His wife, Delilah, died in 1853, and he in 1871, April 22.

The subject of this sketch, Daniel G. Annis, received his education in No. 8 district school of Londonderry and Pinkerton Academy in Derry. Upon completing his education he taught school for several winters, and soon after reaching his majority was engaged a couple of years in the ice trade for the well-known firm of Smith & Prescott, Jamaica Plain, Mass. In the winter of 1862–63 he returned to the farm to care for his parents and look after the homestead.

During his long and useful life Mr. Annis has filled many offices of public trust to the great satisfaction of his townsmen. He served as selectman in 1867 and 1868, and was chosen again to that office in 1893 and 1894, being chairman of the board for both terms. He was town clerk from 1873 to 1882 inclusive, and town treasurer from 1874 to 1878 inclusive, and again town treasurer in 1891 and 1892. He was collector of taxes from 1874 to 1884, inclusive, and chosen again to that office from 1895 to 1911, inclusive, making his service in that capacity of twenty-eight years. He was postmaster of North Londonderry for four years, and he has held the commission of justice of the peace for thirty-three years. His long service in the different offices he has held speaks in more eloquent words than tongue of his honesty and efficiency.

Mr. Annis is a member of the Londonderry Presbyterian church, which he joined in 1863. He is a charter member of Londonderry Grange, instituted in 1875.

Mr. Annis was married June 18, 1868, to Miss Mina Alfaretta, eldest daughter of Samuel and Nancy (Proctor) Gilcreast. She died February 19, 1885, aged 37 years, leaving one son, John S., born September 24, 1871. He married, second, Miss Fannie M. Fling, December 1, 1886. She was the oldest daughter of John W. and Mary Ann (Goodwin) Fling, and died January 16, 1901, leaving no children.

The "Old Homestead Farm" was disposed of several years ago, and since then Mr. Annis has made his home in a commodious cottage near Londonderry depot. While acting as town clerk he thoroughly examined the records of the town from its settlement in 1719 and arranged in alphabetical order the vital statistics and many other important items of town record. Since then he has brought this list down to 1910, adding very much to it from other sources, until the work has grown to the size and importance of this volume of over 300 pages.

GEN. GEORGE REID.

Londonderry has furnished many men and women of prominence in the world's work outside of the town, and it would be eminently proper that sketches of these should be given here, but space forbids even the mention of anything like a full list. I cannot refrain from referring to that pioneer of Presbyterianism in this country, Rev. James McGregor; Rev. Matthew Clark, the fighting parson, who was his successor; Matthew Thornton, M. D., one of the signers of the Declaration of American Independence; Joseph McKeen, the noted Doctor of Divinity; James Wilson, the inventor of the school globe; and last, but not least, Gen. George Reid, the Revolutionary patriot.

Of General Reid by far too little has been said, and knowing of no portrait that could better grace this volume, I have been to the expense of having one painted expressly for this work. He was born in Londonderry in 1733, the son of James and Mary Reid. He seems to have been educated mostly under private tutelage, and early was imbued with a military spirit, and had a local company under organization before the news of the battle of Lexington reached his home. Immediately he called his men together and marched them to Cambridge. His company did good service under the left wing of Stark's men at Bunker Hill. The Continental Congress rewarded him for his meritorious work with the commission of captain of a company in the Fifth Regiment of infantry.

Rising rapidly in his ranking capacity as an officer, his record during the Revolution was an admirable one, noted for courage and keen foresight as a military leader. He participated with distinction in the battles of Long Island, White Plains, Trenton, Brandywine, Germantown, Saratoga, Stillwater, and experienced the hardships of the winter at Valley Forge. He, with General Cilley, served in Sullivan's famous expedition against the Six Nations. In 1785 he was made brigadier-general of the New Hampshire troops.

At the time of the threatened armed disturbance in 1786, arising from the demand of certain persons in New Hampshire asking for the issuance of paper money which could be used as legal tender in the payment of taxes and debts, General Reid was placed in command to quell the uprising. His own town had voted for this measure, so that he was in a trying situation. But he proved equal to the occasion, and owing to his prompt and decisive action the whole affair was suppressed and a settlement effected without the loss of life or prolonged disturbance of the peace. A local writer in speaking of this affair says: "So intense was the feeling against him in his own county for the part he had taken in suppressing the insurrection that his life and property were threatened. On one occasion, when an angry crowd surrounded his house at night, he appeared at the window fully armed and addressed the rioters who had come to take his life. His coolness and the force of his words alone induced them to disperse without doing him harm."

General Reid is one of the forceful characters of his day of whom too little is known. He married, in 1757, Mary Woodburn, daughter of John Woodburn and Mary Boyd. She was a most estimable woman, who possessed a vigorous intellect combined with a cheerful and happily modulated disposition, which served as a happy medium to control his more excitable nature. Her half-brother, David Woodburn, was the maternal grandfather of Horace Greeley. General Reid died in 1815, at the age of 82 years, while Mrs. Reid followed him April 7, 1823, in her eighty-eighth year. Londonderry has had no more worthy couple, and they deserve greater recognition than they have received.

I could not resist the temptation of including in these pages the romantic story of "Ocean Mary," one of the fair daughters of Londonderry, as the facts have been gathered by Mr. J. Warren Thyng and told in his inimitable way.

THE ROMANCE OF "OCEAN MARY."

Previous to 1720, the year in which the principal events of this narrative occurred, many families of Scotch peasantry crossed the North Channel and found, for a time, homes in the larger towns on or near the coast of Ireland. Thus Londonderry became the residence of a large number of Scotch yeomanry.

In those old times of slow ships and many perils of the sea, it was a far cry from Londonderry in Ireland to Londonderry in the Granite State. Still, Scotland and the Emerald Isle had already sent sturdy pioneers to the new world on the Merrimack.

Tradition, often the truer part of history, has failed to save from oblivion the name of the ship which sailed from Londonderry for Boston in July, 1720, but she is said to have been in many respects vastly superior to others of her class in those times. At any rate, long before she dropped anchor off the picturesque coast many well-to-do families had prepared for the long voyage. Of those who from the deck of the departing ship watched the green shores of Ireland fade from view, a large proportion were not only strong of limb, but thrifty and provident.

Out through Lough Foye, past Inishowen Head and far beyond Giant's Causeway, with favoring winds, sailed the fated ship.

Among the passengers were James Wilson and his young wife. A year before, Wilson married Elizabeth Fulton, and they were now on their way to Londonderry, N. H., where land had been laid out to James Wilson as one of the grantees of that town.

In the small valley settlement to which Wilson and his wife were traveling were friends under whose hands profitable harvests were sure, and a generation was springing up whose influence was to be felt long years after.

Concerning the earlier part of the voyage of the emigrant ship, tradition is nearly silent, although certain fragmentary accounts hint of a protracted calm and following storm of such violence that the vessel was driven from her course. However that may be, it is reasonably certain that the passage was about one third accomplished when events transpired that made the voyage memorable in the lives of all on board.

One sultry evening the lookout saw on the horizon a sail standing like a gray silhouette against the early rising moon. All through the hot summer night the strange craft wore nearer and nearer, and when morning came her low hull could be seen like a black shadow under her full set of canvas.

The pirate was within gunshot of the emigrant ship. To fight or run away was not to be thought of. The slow ship had not a dozen muskets. They simply waited. They had not long to wait, for boats were soon alongside and, swarming upon the deck, the robbers fell to work as men who knew how to plunder and kill. Crew and passengers were bound, and some were left lying where they were captured, and some were rolled into corners, just as suited a momentary freak of the invaders.

None were killed. Valuables were gathered into parcels convenient to be transferred to the pirate ship. The robber captain, going below to search the officers' quarters, threw open the after-cabin door with a rough hand, but seeing a woman lying in the berth, stopped.

"Why are you there?" demanded the ruffian.

"See." The terrified woman uncovered a baby's face.

Then the pirate drew near. "Is it a boy or a girl?"

"A girl."

"Have you named her?"

"No."

The pirate went to the cabin door and commanded that no man stir until further orders. Then, returning, he went close to the berth where the woman lay, and said gently, "If I may name that baby, that little girl, I will unbind your men and leave your ship unharmed. May I name the girl?"

"Yes."

Then the rough old robber came nearer still and took up the tiny, unresisting hand of the baby. "Mary," was the name the woman heard him speak. There were other words, but spoken so low she could not hear. Only his Maker and his own heart knew, but when the child drew its hand away the mother saw a tear on the pink fingers.

There have been other knights than Bayard.

As good as his word, the pirate captain ordered all captives unbound and goods and valuables restored to the places from which they had been taken. Then with his crew he left the ship and pulled to his own vessel. But the emigrant ship had scarcely got under way when a new alarm came to them. The pirate was returning.

If they were dismayed at his reappearance, they were surprised to see him come on board alone and go directly below to the cabin. There he took from a parcel a piece of brocaded silk of marvelous fineness of texture and beauty of design. Seen at a little distance, the effect of the pattern is as of a plaid, combining in wonderfully harmonized tones nameless hues of red and green, softened with lines of what evidently was once white.

Time has, perhaps, somewhat mellowed its color tone, but the richness of its quality is as the richness of pearls.

"Let Mary wear this on her wedding day," the pirate said as he laid the silk on the berth.

The pirate left the ship and was seen no more. In the fulness of time the emigrant ship reached Boston without further incident. There James Wilson died soon after landing. Elizabeth Wilson, with Mary, soon after went to live in Londonderry, where friends were waiting for them. Here the widow married James Clark, great-great-grandparent of Horace Greeley.

* * * * *

For years the people of the little hamlet religiously kept July 28, in thanksgiving for the deliverance of their friends from the hands of pirates.

Some time early in the year 1738 Thomas Wallace emigrated to America and settled in Londonderry, where, on December 18 of the same year, he was married to Ocean Mary by Rev. Mr. Davidson of that town. Her wedding gown was the pirate's silk.

A granddaughter and a great-granddaughter have also worn the same dress on like occasions.

Four sons were born to Mary Wallace, three of whom removed to Henniker. There, on a sightly hill, Robert built the house which in his day was far and away the grandest mansion in all the country around. He was a man of large hospitality and intelligent strength of character.

Here Ocean Mary lived many years, and died in 1814 at the age of ninety-four years. Her grave is in the Center burying-ground, about half way down the middle walk, a bowshot distant from the railroad station. The curious visitor may, if he choose, read the inscription on the slate: "In Memory of Widow Mary Wallace, who died Feb'y 13, A. D., 1814, in the 94th year of her age."

The likeness tradition has left of Ocean Mary is that of a woman symetrically tall, with light hair, blue eyes and a florid complexion, together with a touch of the aristocracy of nature and a fine repose of manner in her energetic, determined and kindly ways.

—*J. W. Thyng.*

ANCESTORS OF THE COLONISTS OF LONDONDERRY.

The historians of the austere Pilgrims of Plymouth and the stern Puritans of the Massachusetts Bay colony have been numerous, so that the story of the political, and more especially the religious, persecution which sent them from their native land has become a familiar subject to him who reads history. It is a story of deep wrongs and unswerving fidelity to the principles upon which they builded their code of moral philosophy.

Coming to New England almost, if not quite, contemporaneously with the two named was another class of colonists of whom far less has been written. These brave men and fearless women were from the sturdy yeomanry of northern and western England, and the founders of most of the towns in the Merrimack valley. Unlike the two mentioned first, though a God-fearing people, they did not nurture in their hearts a religious grievance, but came here with a desire to improve their condition in life. They were the progressive pioneers of New England. Scarcely a town granted in those days in New Hampshire failed to have one or more of these families. Ay, there is probably not a state in the union today whose census roll does not contain the names of some of their descendants. Many of them appear in the following pages. In the cosmopolitan make-up of the English-speaking people these colonists could claim a remote kinship with the Pilgrims and the Puritans, but far enough removed to have moulded a new type of citizenship.

While possessing as rugged virtues as either of the others, and bearing a yoke of religious persecution that made the loads of the others seem light in comparison, the colonists of Londonderry belonged to a different ancestry. In a past so remote that no historian has dared to fix the date, certain wild tribes of western Asia, belonging probably to the Scythian race, swept over Europe, scattered clans stopping by the way until the continent was dotted here and there with their camps. Some even pushed out from the mainland to the island since named Ireland. More addicted to warfare than to peaceful pursuits, they failed to formulate a form of government, and existed as hostile tribes side by side.

Possibly five hundred years since the invasion of the Scythians, or Celtics, and about eight hundred years before the reputed founding of Rome, an adventurous people belonging to the Gaelic, Milesian or Scotic race followed in the footsteps of the first, conquering the rude inhabitants of Europe, as in more recent years the Roman legions followed in their footsteps. A certain number of the Scotic race crossed over the channel from the mainland into Ireland, and, for weal or woe, pitched their tents in the midst of the race already occupying the island.

The newcomers had a decided advantage over the original colonists of Ireland inasmuch as they brought with them a good measure of the enlightenment that had established laws, morals and intelligent government in Assyria, Egypt, Babylon and other eastern countries. It was an easy matter for them to conquer or drive into the interior of the island the earlier claimants for the territory. For hundreds of years, however, these Milesian rulers of Ireland were divided among themselves, different lords, descendants of the original stock, holding petty sovereignty by might over as many followers as they could bring under their subjection. During this long interval, in which there must have been more or less mingling with the earlier race, a part of the great Scythian or Celtic family, the Romans, had invaded Great Britain and left upon its people the seal of the Church of Rome.

The uncompromising division of the inhabitants of Ireland caused certain of the nobles to push farther and farther north, until some of the most venturesome had crossed the North Channel and entered ancient Caledonia, a corruption of the Celtic term *Celyddon,* "dweller in the forest," as Scotland was then called. This country was peopled largely by a stalwart race known as the Picts, dwelling in the highlands, and another clan known as the Saxons, in the lowlands. The last had come near the middle of the fifth century, and one of their kings, Edwin, had founded Edinburgh. The pioneers from Ireland came in the beginning of the seventh century and established themselves on the western coast. They were called "Scotch-Irish," and this is the first time that name appears in history.

Naturally the Picts and Saxons looked upon the newcomers as foes, and, though they had nothing else in common, they fought with the single purpose of driving from their shores these invaders, but in vain. On common footing now the Scots united under the banner of one Kenneth, an illustrious name in Scottish history. During this period the Picts were converted to the religious belief of the conquerors. For over six hundred years this conquest went on, until there were added to the fame of Kenneth that of Alexander, Malcolm and other heroic figures. Always opposed by bitter enemies, the warfare continued until each firth and burn, glen and moor, lovely vale and grassy slope awoke to deeds of valor such as come where the genius of civilization clashes hand to hand with the nemesis of barbarism.

The name of Caledonia was succeeded by that of Scotland, but, though the Scots had been successful, a grave peril still threatened their liberty. This fell destroyer was an enemy they nurtured in their own bosoms. While, no doubt, there lingered some vague remembrance of the simpler faith of Iona, the "landscapes were covered with fair, rich and stately abbeys, and Cistercian and Benedictine friars, black or gray, consumed in opulent ease the wealth of the nation. Its bishops were temporal lords, ruling in no modest pomp over wide domains. The priests had engrossed one half of the land of a poor nation; the churches and the cathedrals glittered with the wealth that had been ravished from the cottages and hovels of the peasants, or won through the superstitions of feeble kings. Nor was there any land where the clergymen were more corrupt, or the gross manners of a depraved hierarchy less hidden by a decent veil."

The Moses to bring the light to this benighted land was Patrick Hamilton, a fair-haired student at Wurtenburg, who had listened to the inspired teachings of Luther, the great German reformer. With the courage of his convictions young

Hamilton returned to his native land to declare the doctrine of the new religion. He was given respectful attention by many, but he encountered bitter opposition from those who saw the doom of their own church in the acceptance of his. So Patrick Hamilton was seized and burned at the stake, the first victim of the Scottish Reformation. If the price paid was dear the reward was beyond his most sanguine expectations. As if by magic the ashes of Hamilton seemed scattered to the remote glens as well as to the towns. Nobles and peasants, monks and priests were awakened suddenly to the gravity of the situation. Queen Elizabeth came to the rescue, and trained soldiery that menaced the common people were driven from the field. The impetuous Knox rallied the people, and before the dazed papal heads could awaken to defend their position church and cathedral had been shorn of their images and sacred emblems, until Scotland was strewn with the wrecks of fallen monasteries and the moonlit ruins of some Melrose was to be found at night in any section. Quoting from the same authority as before: "With one vigorous exercise of latent strength the Scottish intellect had freed itself from Italian bondage and might well prepare for rapid progress in the new paths of reform. Nor could it have foreseen that pains or woes scarcely surpassed in the Vaudios valleys or in the fens of Holland were to spring from a sister church and from its native kings; that the darkest period in the history of its stern and barren land was to come from the malice of Rome disguised in the thin mask of bishops like Laud or Sharp, princes like the first and second Charles and the first and second James."

The history of the persecution of the Presbyterians of Scotland, as far as it relates to its enemies, is not pleasant to follow. One reason for the darkness of the portrayal is the fact that the Church of England had fallen into corrupt control following the excellent and liberal spirit of Elizabeth and James I. Under the dissolute princes that succeeded, the church ceased to be the friend of the common people. This was what drove the Puritan and Low Churchman to leave the country in such large numbers. It was the underlying current that impelled so many of the people to rebel against the Stuarts. In Scotland, where the new doctrine was fostered by the common people and not favored by the kings, Charles I. thought to suppress it by the arms of England.

A generation had passed since Hamilton had led in the Reformation, and at first the people awakened slowly to the threatened loss of the liberty gained by the fervid intellect and fearless defiance of their fathers. This time it took a woman to lead them out into the light. The bigoted Laud, representing the church and the king of England, had planned to install the new ritual of the popish church in place of the Presbyterian in the High Church of St. Giles at Edinburgh. When the announcement was made to the large congregation present, Jenny Geddes, rising in her righteous indigation, flung the stool upon which she had been sitting at the head of the dean, crying: "Vile wretch, will ye read mass at my lug?" Such an uproar followed this invective that priest nor bishop could silence the crowd. Nor was it stilled for more than a hundred years.

It was a stormy century that succeeded, and often the brave Presbyterians were so hard pressed that their cause seemed lost. But the fire would not be quenched, and it was no uncommon spectacle to see hundreds of the outlawed people coming out from their concealment to listen under a wide-spreading oak to the fervid pleadings of some spiritual leader upon whose head at that very moment was a heavy reward, while at any moment an officer of the rival church might seize him. In the early part of this interval a considerable number of the Scottish Covenanters returned across the channel into the north of Ireland, which had been so ravaged by the English that the land was deserted of its inhabitants. So, after more than a thousand years, the descendants of the early people of Ireland returned to the scenes of their forefathers. But there were no open arms to receive them, though they set about to repair their shattered fortunes with unfaltering courage.

In Scotland the battle waxed so fierce and strong that in 1638, with uncompromising enthusiasm, a vast congregation gathered at Greyfriar's church, Edinburgh, to pledge anew their faith in the Presbytery. A new covenant was written upon a huge parchment and signed by loyal supporters until, as big as it was, the great document could not contain all of the names of the would-be signers. This imperishable proclamation was more than a religious covenant of the faith of an awakened people, for it announced the independence of thought, the principles of liberty which were to make the thrones of kings tremble, and send to New England the tidings of Jenny Geddes. The unscrupulous Laud fell under the storm that assailed the prelatical régime. In November, 1640, the king of England convened that memorable parliament that reëstablished the Presbyterian church in Scotland and established it in England. Thus the stern decree signed upon the tombstone at Edinburgh was made supreme from the Orkneys to the English Channel.

Unfortunately, the Scots forgot some of the wrongs done them by the Stuarts, and with honest loyalty, now that they had gained their ends, espoused the cause of Charles II. This brought upon them the enmity of Cromwell, which should not have been. Still this opposition did not rise to persecution, and during the period from 1640 to 1660 the Presbyterians enjoyed comparative peace. When Charles II. came back to the throne, among the foremost to welcome him was the stalwart Scotchman, Archibald Campbell, Marquis of Argyle, who had placed the crown upon him as a prince and now hastened to London with his glad greeting. The ungrateful Stuart, remembering only the just criticism Argyle had once uttered against his vices but had long since overlooked, arrested the Scot and threw him into the tower. Later he was sent to Edinburgh doomed to the headsman's block. "I could die like a Roman," said the marquis to his friends, "but I would rather die like a Christian." Then, donning his cloak and hat, he walked calmly down the street to where the scaffold awaited him, accompanied by several of his weeping comrades. Ascending the steps without a tremor, he offered a short prayer, himself gave the signal, and became the first victim of the new and most infamous persecution.

Again Scotland was to be deluged in blood and the best and bravest of her people slaughtered like beasts of prey or sent into an exile more horrible in its sufferings than death. The brave clergy resolutely dared the hatred of their persecutors, who spared none they could seize. Worshipful conclaves were called together at irregular intervals in some lonely glen, under some beetling crag, or at some isolated cavern reeking with the sweat and slime of ages. The oppression made new converts, and the number of the Presbyterians increased rather than diminished, until at last the hunted Covenanters resorted to arms. Rallying from far and wide they made a desperate stand at Pentland Hills. Amid the dismal highlands that environ Edinburgh the forlorn fugitives met in battle the trained soldiery of England led by the ferocious Daziel. The outcome was inevitable. After raging all day the battle ended in the night, and the sun rose the following morning upon the saddest spectacle that even Scotland had ever witnessed. If the battle of Pentland Hills was to be taken as an omen, then surely the fate of the Scottish church had been sealed in blood.

On a beautiful Sabbath morning in June, 1679, was fought under the frowning brow of Loudon Hill the battle of Drumclog, a repetition in its results of that by Pentland Hills. The cruelty of the conquerors passes belief. Clergymen, who had no share in the strife, were hung in chains; women, whose greatest crime had been to weep over the dreadful death of loved ones, were thrown into dungeons filled with vermin and horrors that fail of description. Innocent children, if not put to death, were sent into slavery in faraway lands. The same authority I have already quoted from says: "In the deepest and wildest recesses of their native land the more resolute and enthusiastic of the Covenanters kept untarnished the purity of the Scottish faith. On the dank morass, where the peat water was their only drink; in dark and misty glens, overhung by forests that skirted lofty mountains; in rifts of earth hidden deep amidst the bogs; in caverns covered by brushwood and wet with unwholesome distillations from the rock might be seen groups of wild and stalwart men, with grizzly beards, eyes gleaming with strange light, and countenances often glowing amidst their suffering with a holy joy. . . . Each man carried a sword and a little clasped Bible. And these were the remnant of those who had gathered in joy on the banks of the Clyde, or collected in joyous throngs under the broad shelter of Loudon Hill."

The records of these brave leaders of religious trials and triumph more worthy of the magic touch of the Wizard's* pen than the heroes he pictured in such vivid language read like the wonder fables of old, while they treat of real life. Prominent among the martyrs to the holy cause was John Welch, a descendant of John Knox, already mentioned. This eloquent preacher was highly educated, and he abandoned a wealthy church that he might minister to the fugitive followers of his faith. A large reward was offered for his head, and he was hunted by men and bloodhounds, but for twenty years he managed to elude his enemies, who never seemed to sleep. During the trying years of his wandering pastorates the voice of this meek yet eloquent "rebel" never ceased to echo amidst his native hills, while no enemy was so artful as to catch him napping. Wherever he went vast numbers of eager followers sprang as if by magic into his presence, listening to his burning messages. Were it whispered that John Welch was near, churches were deserted and the dim aisles of the forest were filled with his audience. Always armed, and never daring to count upon his safety from those who were eager to get the five hundred pounds set upon his life, one day he was at Pentland Hills sharing the perils of a losing fight, escaping by a three days' ride in the saddle without food or sleep, on another he held his great audience enthralled with his eloquence on the flooring of the frozen Tweed, with a block of ice for his pulpit. Anon he was celebrating communion at the long table spread in the green meadows of his native heath, with more than three thousand of his people with him. This was in 1678, and in less than two years, broken in health and worn out with his wonderful endeavors, but full of hope for the future, he crossed by stealth the Scottish border and fled from his native land, never to return except as his body was brought back by loving disciples and given rest beside the home he had forsaken that he might help sustain his people in their years of darkness.

A sterner type of the dissenter was Donald Cargill; if more uncompromising than his colleague not a whit less forceful in his arguments, nor lacking in courage or daring. He detested the backslider, and openly declared him more despicable than the open enemy. Wherever he went great numbers thronged

*Scott.

to listen to him, becoming his converts or gaining new faith from his bold declarations. One day, as he stood before a multitude in one of the valleys of western Scotland, his voice suddenly failed him. Stricken dumb, the strong man wept his first tears, believing that henceforth he must look in silence upon his suffering people. His enemies asserted that it was a retribution for rebellious utterances. If so, it quickly passed, for a few days later, when he arose as he had done hundreds of times to address his audiences, speech suddenly returned, as unexpectedly as it had left him, and his voice was clearer and more impressive than before. In sooth, he seemed to have greater strength and power to win over to the cause the faltering and intimidated ones that came from far and near to listen to his inspired messages. But constantly haunted by his enemies, he was continually defying death and running the gantlet of snares and ambuscades laid for him. Preaching, baptizing, and marrying, yesterday at Nithsdale and Galloway, today at Bothwell, he was wounded, surrounded and seized by the prelatical forces. Again a wonderful versatility of escape enabled him to elude his foes once more, and he continued to invoke the judgment of heaven upon the false Stuarts and prophesy the fall of Monmouth and his allies. This could not go on always, and finally the master of prayer and dispenser of unbounded charity was captured and borne in triumph to the cross at Edinburgh. Defiant to the last, he went to his fate with a prayer for his friends upon his lips and words of startling denunciation for those who had wrought so bitterly against his country.

A close companion and worthy ally of this brave prophet, priest and revolutionist was Richard Cameron, and all that has been said of Cargill can be applied with greater emphasis to him, who boldly denied any allegiance to Charles II., who dared to denounce the Duke of York as anti-Christ; who dared to foretell the coming freedom of his people from the thralldom of such false rulers, never sparing those nearer home who had betrayed their most sacred trust. Cameron was the founder of a religious sect that has outlived his stormy days. He was in the midst of one of his fiery sermons in his open church on Aird Moss when the bullet of a cowardly marksman shot him down like a hunted deer, and his mutilated body was tossed aside as an image of worthless clay.

The story of Cameron's untimely fate heralded abroad, one of his companions and most ardent admirers, Alexander Pleden, came to kneel upon the sod sanctified with his blood. Uplifting his hands to Heaven, Pleden uttered those sincere words dear to every Scot after over two hundred years:

"O to be wi' Richie!"

His grave on Aird Moss is marked with a plain headstone, but it does not require any memorial to keep fresh in the minds of his followers the memory of the generous-hearted Richard Cameron. Hundreds of others just as brave and self-sacrificing as these mentioned, among them Henderson, the first to rally them at Glasgow, Pleden, exhorting to his disciples in his willow-covered cavern-church, the beautiful Renfrew, last of the brave Covenanters to fall a sacrifice to the religious principles of their heroic lives, might be cited, but it is not necessary. Their names appear almost to a man in the "Vital Records of Londonderry, N. H.," though the majority had found their way hither through the emigration to the north of Ireland in the midst of the oppression at home.

In the meantime those Scotch Presbyterians who had returned—1612 to 1620—from western Scotland to the north of Ireland, the very country their ancestors had deserted more than thirty generations before, had not been idle nor left in peace. The same power which had attempted to crush them had overrun and depopulated the land here. They had been encouraged to come here by King James I. in the hope that their presence would help him quell the turbulent spirit that had caused him so much trouble in Ireland. The ancient town of Derry was rebuilt from the ruins left by the warlike forces that had overrun the country in the conquest of James. To the name of this olden monastery was added that of London, the capital of England, and from that day the city has been known as Londonderry, singularly enough a mingling in name of the memory of those races so long at variance. It became a stronghold of Protestantism, and when the wheel of religious fortune had turned again in England, it was an object to attract the attention of James II. The inhabitants bidding defiance to the papal power, a siege was laid to the city on

April 18, 1689, and maintained for 105 days of horror and suffering. Seven thousand men were inside the garrison at the beginning, but this number was reduced to three thousand before the end. The besieged were compelled to eat their horses and dogs, and were on their last ration of tallow and salted hides when relieved.

This part of the story has been told in the histories of Londonderry, so I am passing over it hastily. William of Orange had come to the rescue of the Protestants in the British Isles, and the shadow of oppression no longer overhung the homes of the Presbyterians. In Scotland, at least, the smile of peace and prosperity settled over brown moor and bracken-matted glen, in home and church, and in place of warlike training, her people turned to brighter ways, established schools, literature and pursuits that have won lasting renown.

While the ban upon their church had been lifted, still absolute freedom was denied the people in the north of Ireland, and finally some of them resolved to try their fortunes in New England. Accordingly an agent was sent to investigate the situation, and his report was so favorable that a goodly number came over in the summer of 1718, the leading spirit of the party being Rev. James MacGregor. Landing at Boston August 4, 1718, before another spring a grant of country twelve miles square was obtained of New Hampshire, and the foremost of the little colony reached Nutfield, the original name for this township, in April, 1719. Upon the morning of April 11, O. S., 1719, the little band of pilgrims met under the spreading branches of a majestic oak standing on the east shore of Beaver Pond. Immediately Parson McGregor returned thanks to the Great Benefactor for having brought them safely over sea that they might plant a new home here in the wilderness. He exhorted his followers to be faithful to the trust reposed in them, taking for the text of his first sermon Isaiah xxxii, second verse: "And a man shall be as a hiding place from the wind, and a covert from the tempest; as the shadow of a great rock in a weary land." Certainly a most fitting thought, and under the ancient rooftree in the heart of the wilderness was founded the Presbyterian church in New England. I know of no grander scene in the history of this country.

Without wishing to engage in the controversy that has arisen over the name commonly given these people, I would remind the seeker after the facts that the original inhabitants of Ireland were of the Celtic race. Then, after five hundred years, or such a matter, the Milesians or Scots appeared upon the scene. An enlightened people, they naturally assumed supremacy over the others, gave their titles to the country, and intermingling, more or less, with the Celts, affirmed the family names. In 626 certain ones of this uneasy population crossed over the North Channel into Ancient Caledonia to overpower and absorb the Picts on the highlands and the Saxons on the lowlands, just as they had the Celts in Ireland. Then the country became known as Scot's Land or Scotland. In time they changed their religion, but the voice of Patrick Hamilton did not reach Ireland. Eventually some of the descendants of those immigrants to Caledonia went over into Ireland, the land of their remote ancestors, the Scots and Celts. But it is well to remember that in that long interval the Scots had mingled more freely with Pict and Saxon than ever with Celt, and that over thirty generations of this mixed product had appeared and vanished during a period long enough to have obliterated many racial characteristics; aye, to have created a new race in the crucible of destiny.

G. WALDO BROWNE.

RECORDS OF BIRTHS

From the Earliest Record to the End of 1910

Abbott, Charles W., b. May 10, 1863, and Emma H. Perkins. Son: Harold V., Apr. 21, 1888. (See Perkins.)

Joseph G. and Phylena A. Noyes. Son: James N., Feb. 26, 1907.

Nehemiah and Anna. Children: Joseph, Apr. 24, 1789; Lydia, Sept. 7, 1790; Dolly Varnum, Feb. 9, 1793; Jonathan, Oct. 22, 1795; Betsey, Feb. 3, 1801; Jonas, Mar. 4, 1804.

Adams, Charles and Mary. Son, Dec. 22, 1852.

David and Janet. Children: Jane, James, Mary M., Robert W., William, David B., John B., Jonathan, and a ch. who d. in infancy.

David and Martha. Children: Patty, Nov. 24, 1781; Robert, Nov. 13, 1783.

David and Mary. Children: Samuel, Apr. 20, 1779; Mary, Mar. 29, 1781; David, Nov. 4, 1782; John Woodman, Aug. 22, 1785; Hannah, Aug. 20, 1788; Betsey, Dec. 12, 1792; Sally, Feb. 20, 1795.

Edmund and Betsey. Dau.: Susan P., Apr. 20, 1810.

Frank and Alma E. Whidden. Dau.: Rowena.

Gilman I. and Ruby A. Elliott. Children: Wesley, July 2, 1872; Roy B., 1879.

James and Anne. Children: John, Oct. 17, 1793; Benjamin, Oct. 13, 1795; David, Oct. 19, 1797; Hannah, May 16, 1799; Edmund, Feb. 4, 1802; Polly, July 12, 1805; Sarah, July 13, 1808.

James and Lois A. Son, Oct. 15, 1855.

James and Sarah. Dau.: Elisabeth, Feb. 5, 1744-5.

Jonathan and Sarah. Children: Jean Smith, Sept. 12, 1759; Jonathan, May 20, 1762; William, July 5, 1764; James, May 21, 1766; Mary Todd, Aug. 15, 1772.

Jonathan and Sarah Smith. Children: Jane, d. unm.; Jonathan, remained upon homestead; William, m. Margaret Duncan; James, m. Judith Rolfe; Mary, m. William Eayres, removed to Rutland, Vt.; Susannah, d. unm.

Adams, John and Betsey. Children: James, Dec. 26, 1817; Charles, Aug. 13, 1819; Horace, June 3, 1821; Eliza, Aug. 31, 1823.

John and Betsey. Children: Sarah, Jan. 23, 1790; Robert, June 20, 1791; Mary, Dec. 31, 1792; Betsey, Nov. 19, 1795; John, Apr. 5, 1798.

John and Betsey. Children: Nathan, July 22, 1825; Clarrisa, July 28, 1828; Otis, June 9, 1830.

Nathan and Elisabeth Jane. Children: Lucelia, Dec. 26, 1845; Rovena I., Feb. 10, 1850; George, Jan. 2, 1852; Frank, Nov. 2, 1853; Charles, Mar. 13, 1860; Gertrude, Jan. 19, 1870.

Nathan and Jane. Son: Charles, Mar. 13, 1860.

Samuel and Sarah. Children: Caroline, Aug. 25, 1819; Louisa, Feb. 17, 1822.

William, Feb. 6, 1755, son of James. Children: Infant ch., lived but few hours; Mary, m. Elder John Holmes in 1881; James, Nov. 7, 1785, graduate of Dartmouth College in 1813.

William, son of Jonathan, and Margaret Duncan. Children: Mary, Jane, and Sarah.

William H. and Margaret. Dau., Apr. 9, 1853.

William and Margaret. Children: Polly McGregor, Aug. 5, 1801; Jane Duncan, Jan. 6, 1804; Samuel Smith, Sept. 12, 1805.

Addison, William and Eleanor W. (McAllister), wid. of David. Dau.: Eleanor.

Aiken, Daniel and Mary. Son, Sept. 19, 1861.

Daniel C. and Louisa M. Son: Walter M., Feb. 8, 1876.

Edward and Betsey. Children: Sarah Ann, Feb. 17, 1810; Jonathan, Jan. 3, 1812; Hiram, Mar. 10, 1814; James, Feb. 9, 1817; Daniel, Sept. 24, 1819; Andrew S., Dec. 11, 1824.

Edward and Martha. Children: Jonathan, Mar. 18, 1759; Daniel, Jan. 8, 1761; Jennet, Dec. 11, 1763; William, Nov. 1, 1767; Mary, Mar. 31, 1770.

Francis and Lavina. Dau.: Amanda L. (Chase), Apr. 13, 1882.

George and Amanda. Children: Dau., Aug. 20, 1855; George F., May 18, 1858; son, May 4, 1860; son, Mar. 7, 1871.

George F. and Addie J. Dau.: Georgia F., Apr. 30, 1880.

James and Elizabeth. Children: Saley, Oct. 8, 1769; Mary, July 26, 1771; James, Sept. 26, 1773; John, Jan. 8, 1775.

James and Joan. Children: Elisabeth, Aug. 31, 1726; James, June 1, 1731.

Aiken, John and Elizabeth. Children: James, Oct. 6, 1762; Jean, Jan. 28, 1767; Daniel, Apr. 4, 1769; Edward, May 26, 1771; Agnes, Jan. 21, 1774.

Nathaniel and Margaret. Children: Edward, Sept. 2, 1727; son, Nov. 18, 1728; Jeline, Nov. 1, 1730; Nathaniel, May 31, 1732; Creistian, May 10, 1733; Jean, June 16, 1736; James, Oct. 4, 1738; Ninien, Mar. 3, 1740–41.

Samuel H. and Hannah J. Children: Charles Philip Sheridan, Nov. 16, 1870; son, Oct. 16, 1871.

Samuel H. and Mary C. Children: Samuel B., Nov. 2, 1882; son, Feb. 14, 1885.

Samuel H. and Mary Casey. Son: July 23, 1888.

William and Jenat. Children: Agnes, Sept. 17, 1726; Edward, Aug. 10, 1728; Mary, Aug. 21, 1730; Jonathan, Oct. 22, 1732; Martha, Apr. 8, 1734; William, July 2, 1737.

Aldrich, Charles E. and Laura Ella Moar. Son: Frederick Charles, July 27, 1882. (See Moar.)

Alexander, Alphonso and Nellie F. Children: Twin sons, Dec. 17, 1878.

Charles H. (23 yrs.) and Jennie D. Young (22 yrs.). Children: Dau., Sept. 22, 1893; son, Sept. 18, 1895; son, Oct. 7, 1897; dau., Mar. 1, 1900; son, Mar. 19, 1902; son, Sept. 17, 1903; Myrtie, Jan. 18, 1906; dau., Jan. 21, 1907; son, Jan. 23, 1910.

George and Mary. Children: William, May 10, 1816; Jonathan H., June 2, 1821.

James and Janet. Children: John, Dec. 21, 1760; Ann, Feb. 18, 1763; James, Dec. 21, 1764; Elisabeth, Jan. 28, 1767; Joseph, Apr. 30, 1769.

James and Mary. Children: Agnis, Sept. 15, 1722; Joseph, June 30, 1727.

Jonathan and Sarah. Children: Caroline, July 9, 1805; Ann, Feb. 5, 1807; Joseph, Oct. 14, 1808; Hannah J., Oct. 4, 1810; James, Aug. 12, 1812; Harriet, Dec. 11, 1814; Alanson, Jan. 14, 1817.

John and Elisabeth. Children: Elisabeth, Oct. 28, 1764; Robert, Aug. 31, 1767.

Randle and Jenat. Children: Robert, Nov. 14, 1720; Mary, Mar. 5, 1721-2; Isabel, Feb. 16, 1723-4; David, Apr. 4, 1728; John, Apr. 22, 1730.

Robert and Mary. Children: Jean, Oct. 18, 1747; Janet, Sept. 15, 1749; Mary, Aug. 27, 1751; John, June 9, 1753; Hugh, May 14, 1756.

William and Eleanor. Children: Sally, Mar. 15, 1793; Robert, Apr. 2, 1795; John, Dec. 6, 1799; James, Apr. 19, 1802; William, Oct. 1, 1804.

Alexander, William and Eunice. Children: Eunice, Mar. 26, 1772; Hannah, Jan. 16, 1774; Sarah, Mar. 9, 1776; Mary, Sept. 29, 1777; William, Apr. 27, 1779.

Aleson, Samuel and Janat. Children: Samuel, Apr. 2, 1749; Janat, July 13, 1751; Andrew, Feb. 26, 1754; Margaret, Mar. 31, 1756.

Allan, Milo and Julia A. Varel. Son: Arthur F. (See Parshley record.)

Allen, Samuel C. and Mary. Dau.: Martha H., Apr. 28, 1798.

Alley, Moses and Hannah Smithurst, 1st wife. Dau.: Alice Philips, Jan. 10, 1824, at Lynn, Mass.

Allison, Samuel and Catherine. Children: Martha, Mar. 31, 1721; Samuel, Oct. 8, 1722; Rebecca, Apr. 15, 1724.

Anderson, Charles W. and Evelina. Dau.: Dorothy E., June 25, 1900.

Edmond G. and Mabel. Children: Charles E., Nov. 8, 1891; Mary E., June 15, 1899.

(Elder) David, b. Apr. 21, 1816, and Persis (Tenney), b. Oct. 4, 1823; m. Oct. 13, 1842. Children: Helen F., July 14, 1843; Eliza G., Oct. 27, 1844; George V., Nov. 2, 1846; Persis, Sept. 15, 1849; Mary J. S., Jan. 26, 1852.

Francis D. and Jane (Davidson). Children: Charles L., Oct. 31, 1833; William Henry, Jan. 12, 1836.

George Edward, b. June 14, 1833, and Sarah A. (Lane), b. Sept., 1838, 1st wife. Children: George L., Dec. 31, 1860; Clara A., May 2, 1862; Emma J., May 29, 1865; Martin E., Jan. 24, 1867.

George V. and Mary J. S. Kelley; m. Apr. 27, 1867. Children: Edmund G., Mar. 29, 1868; Charles W., Apr. 29, 1869.

Georgietta W. and Wilbur E. Barrett, m. Dec. 12, 1894. Children: George W., May 6, 1896; Helen F., Aug. 3, 1898. (See Barrett.)

Helen F. and Wesley B. Knight; m. Apr. 7, 1862. Dau.: Georgietta W., Nov. 13, 1864. (See Knight.)

Hughey and Jean. Children: William, Feb. 16, 1798; John Nesmith, Mar. 16, 1800; Elisabeth Nesmith, Feb. 9, 1800 (?).

James, Oct. 6, 1783.

James and Margaret. Children: Thomas, May 28, 1720; David, Mar. 19, 1723–4; dau., Apr., 1726; son, Sept. 3, 1728.

John and Eliza. Dau.: Almira J., July 12, 1831.

John and Jane. Children: Robert, Apr. 1, 1706; James, Jan. 28, 1709–10; John, Apr. 20, 1722; Ann, Apr. 20, 1722.

Anderson, John and Lucy. Children: Dau., Aug. 22, 1852; dau., May 3, 1854; son, Dec. 21, 1855.
John W. and Edna J. Son: William H., Aug. 22, 1878.
Jonathan and Mary. Children: Thomas, Sept. 9, 1722; William, Sept. 9, 1725; Mary, Sept. 11, 1725.
Rev. Rufus, b. Mar. 5, 1765, son of James and Nancy (Woodburn); m. Hannah Parsons, Sept. 8, 1795. Children: Rufus, Isaac, and James.
Robert and ———. Son: James, 1749.
Robert and Sally. Children: Nancy, Sept. 26, 1804; Robert, Aug. 3, 1806; John, Feb. 26, 1808; Lettice, June 5, 1810; James, May 28, 1812; William, Jan. 7, 1815.
Rufus, b. 1816, and Martha A. (Richards), b. 1828.
Thomas and Jane. Son: William, Aug. 21, 1756.
William and Agnes. Children: Elisabeth, Dec. 10, 1784; John, Oct. 11, 1788.
William and Agnes. Children: Hughy, July 4, 1770; Robert, July 12, 1772; Maryam, Aug. 16, 1774; James, Jan. 10, 1777; William, Sept. 16, 1779; Lettice, June 8, 1782. Nancy (Campbell), Aug. 7, 1789.
William and Polly. Dau.: Maryam N., Mar. 17, 1809.
William Henry and Mary A. Hines, b. Aug. 19, 1840. Dau.: Frances W., Dec. 20, 1868.

Annis, Benjamin F. and Catharine. Children: Dau., Apr. 30, 1853; dau., Mar. 5, 1855.
Charles and Mary W. Dau., Feb. 14, 1856.
Charles U. and Sarah. Children: Roy R., Apr. 30, 1893; Helen L., Mar. 10, 1904.
Daniel G. and Mina A. Son: John Samuel, Sept. 24, 1871.
Daniel M. and Mary. Children: Dau., Mar. 1, 1860; dau., July 24, 1861.
David L. and Susan Grace Griffin, b. Dec. 26, 1841; m. Nov. 13, 1858. Children: Nina, m. ——— Johnson of Boston, Mass.; dau., Ova, died young.
Fred E. and Carabel. Children: Hazel L., Feb. 13, 1894; Helen M., June 16, 1898.
George W., b. Nov. 19, 1835, son of Joseph and Sarah (Blodgett); m. Elvira French, b. Nov. 27, 1836. Children: Willette, Apr. 21, 1860; Lora H., Dec. 4, 1861; Angie J., Sept. 11, 1863; Addie M., Sept. 11, 1863; George Walter, Jan. 25, 1866; Edgar C., Apr. 8, 1868; Elmer E., Aug. 29, 1870; Eliza M., Jan. 27, 1873; Edith M., Jan. 19, 1875; Lillian E., Mar. 22, 1877; George W., Jr., July 23, 1879; Ernest H., Sept. 11, 1881.
Ira Dan and Fannie Thorp. Children: Nina, Feb. 3, 1895; Eva May, Apr. 7, 1902.

Annis, Isaac and Hannah. Children: Sally, Oct. 4, 1787; John, Oct. 13, 1790; Jerry, Aug. 6, 1793; Jesse, Aug. 6, 1793; James, June 11, 1796; Joseph, May 20, 1799; Lydia, May 1, 1802; Moses, Sept. 4, 1804.

James and ——— Leach. Children: Martha, Sept. 25, 1824; Mary Etta, 1826; David L., Mar. 4, 1830; Esthermate B., June 13, 1833.

Jesse and Mildred. Children: Roxanna, Dec. 27, 1822; twin sons, Feb. 15, 1825; Isaac B., Jan. 31, 1826; Charles D., July 19, 1828; Samuel W., Feb. 20, 1831; Sarah Ann, Apr. 15, 1833; James Monroe, May 31, 1836; Daniel Morrill, May 31, 1836; Clarrisa L., Oct. 29, 1838; Mary Ann, July 11, 1840; Isaac H. H., Aug. 5, 1844.

John and Delilah. Children: Olive, Dec. 3, 1821; Adeline, Feb. 19, 1823; William, Sept. 11, 1824; Sampson, Jan. 27, 1826; Martha, Apr. 5, 1827; Matthew P., Aug. 5, 1828; Joel C., June 16, 1833; Delia, Mar. 17, 1835; Mariam, Sept. 7, 1837; Daniel G., Jan. 25, 1839; Eliza Jane, Apr. 29, 1843.

John, 2d, and Martha. Son, Sept. 11, 1853.

Martha m., Sept., 1845, Amos Webster of Nashua, N. H., b. Oct. 4, 1824, at Bolton, Vt. Children: Laura B., Sept. 20, 1863; Cleon L., Sept. 10, 1865. (See Webster.)

Parker and Sarah. Children: Edward Parker, Sept., 1851; Willie Elmore, 1857.

Parker B. and Roxanna. Dau., Feb. 28, 1881.

Roswell and Ella Jane McClary. Son: Earle M., Dec. 16, 1886. (See McClary.)

Roswell and Luella A. Son: Cleon C., Sept. 21, 1876.

Sampson and Nancy D. Children: Winslow M., Jan. 26, 1855; Harry O.; Ira Dan, Nov. 20, 1861.

Samuel W., son of Jesse and Mildred, b. Feb. 20, 1831, and Mehitable (Page), b. Jan., 1830. Children: Eva, Apr. 11, 1863; Charles U., Oct. 2, 1865; Fred E., July 20, 1868.

William and Betsey Mullins. Children: Rosilla, June 24, 1848; Roswell, Oct. 29, 1849; Augusta M., May 7, 1860.

Archambault, Joseph and Abbie. Dau.: Ida, Feb. 7, 1883.

Archibald, John and Ann. Son: Robert, Jan. 30, 1726–7.

John and Margaret. Children: Robert, May 15, 1722; Elenor, June 5, 1724; Elisabeth, Jan. 20, 1726–27; John, Jan. 25, 1729–30; James, Jan. 25, 1731–2.

Jonathan and Agnes. Son: Arthur, May 28, 17—.

Armes, Rev. Arza and Blanche. Son: Henry Lyman, Oct. 7, 1890.

Armstrong, George F. and Adeline Greeley. Son: Maurice G., Sept. 6, 1889.

Austin, Joshua, b. Oct. 17, 1800, and Betsey Barker, b. Jan. 23, 1802; m. Jan. 14, 1824. Children: Mary, July 28, 1824; Alice J., Feb. 7, 1828; Abigail C., Apr. 20, 1830.

Perley E., b. May 19, 1862, in Me., and Milly Higgins, b. Apr. 28, 1868, in Providence; m. in Manchester, July 25, 1894. Son: William Stewart, Oct. 8, 1896.

Averill, Foster and Rebekah. Children: John, July 24, 1822; Jeremiah Mason, Apr. 21, 1826.

Avery, Charles L. and Louisa Annis. Children: Dau., Jan. 10, 1894; son, Dec. 14, 1896.

Foster and Rebekah Robinson. Children: John, Jeremiah Mason, Dorcas, Ephraim, Sarah P., Eda Ann, and Harry.

Frank E. and Florence E. Putnam. Children: Ch., Aug. 10, 1891; son, Nov. 16, 1900; son, May 4, 1902.

Jeremiah Mason and Julia A. Upton. Children: Ida F., 1856; Paulina M.; Mark A.

John and Melinda E. Hartford. Children: Henry F., 1849; Rev. George S., 1854; Charles L., 1861.

Mason and Julia M. Dau., Mar. 21, 1874.

Peter and Frances Smith. Child, Oct. 3, 1891.

Wilbur and Martha Elisabeth (Young). Dau.: Dorothy May, Apr. 16, 1909, Derry, N. H.

Bacon, Albert J. and Carrie Louisa Moar. Children: Edna L., Apr. 10, 1881; Albert Reed, Apr. 22, 1884. (See Moar.)

Albert R. and Amy P. Fiske. Son: Albert F., June 18, 1908.

Bagley, Capt. Jonathan R., b. Mar. 16, 1820.

Bailey, Addie Gusta and Charles H. Rice. Dau.: Vera Belle, Dec. 22, 1909.

Charles R., b. Mar. 2, 1851, and Augusta G. Hunkins, b. Sept. 16, 1857; m. Aug. 8, 1878. Children: Edwin James, Oct. 31, 1879, at Manchester; Fred Charles, Apr. 26, 1881, at Manchester; Addie Gusta, Apr. 15, 1883, at Manchester; Anna May, Dec. 30, 1884, at Londonderry; Asa Bell, Nov. 10, 1886; Berta Effie, Jan. 31, 1889; Emma Adelaide Sweetzer, June 12, 1891; Grace Hunkins, Aug. 26, 1893; Ruth Pike, Mar. 17, 1895; Elva Guyneth, June 21, 1897; Earl Ransom, Sept. 28, 1899.

Walter E. and Mary McDonough. Children: Alberta Louise, Apr. 14, 1899; Walter Herman, July 31, 1900; Samuel McDonough, Dec. 5, 1902.

Baker, Ezra N. and Clara L. Maker. Children: Doris Louise, Apr. 7, 1909; Donald Ezra, Apr. 7, 1909.

James H. and Helena Tootell. Dau.: Lucy Mildred, July 13, 1898.

Ball, George M. and Ida M. McCoy. Dau.: Mary Elisabeth, June 6, 1895.

Ballou, Alexander and Susan. Dau., Nov. 2, 1852.

Alexander McGregor, b. Feb. 18, 1835, at Londonderry.

Nathaniel and Eda Ann Avery. Three children. (See Avery.)

Bancroft, Caleb H. and Sarah. Children: Son, Oct. 4, 1852; son, Oct. 1, 1854.

David E., b. Mar. 24, 1824.

Fred L. and Ida M. Fitzgerald. Children: Son, Nov. 25, 1906; dau., July 21, 1909.

John E. and Annie G. Children: Jennie E., June 6, 1873; Anna G., Feb. 8, 1875; son, Mar. 15, 1879.

John M. and Mary J. Dau.: Clara M., June 28, 1872.

Bannon, Patrick and Bridgett. Children: Ellen T., July 4, 1858; son, Nov. 5, 1860.

Barker, David C. and Eliza Jane. Children: Clara Jane, Nov. 9, 1847; Mary Ann, June 26, 1851; Sarah Etta, Nov. 24, 1853; John Charles, June 14, 1856; Affa, June 27, 1860; Effie, June 27, 1860.

John Charles and Nellie (Richardson), b. Jan. 22, 1861. Children: Herbert Arthur, June 22, 1880; Amy Florence, Dec. 1, 1883; David Charles, Aug. 11, 1885; Eva Mildred, July 23, 1887; Ralph William, Mar. 27, 1890.

Samuel C. and Hannah. Children: Angeline, Aug. 13, 1838; Charles O., Mar. 17, 1836; Rhoda Ann, Aug. 16, 1842; David W., Dec. 28, 1844.

Silas, b. Dec. 11, 1769, son of Ebenezer and Hannah, m. Abigail Clark, b. Mar. 28, 1782. Children: Betsey, Sat., Jan. 23, 1802; Silas, Tues., Feb. 14, 1804; Abigail, Tues., Oct. 16, 1806; Benjamin, Fri., Sept. 2, 1808; Ebenezer, Wednes., Sept. 19, 1810; Samuel, Thurs., Oct. 15, 1812; Asa, Fri., Feb. 3, 1815; Hannah, Sun., Dec. 28, 1817; David, Mon., Dec. 13, 1819; John W., Mon., Jan. 28, 1822; Lydia, Tues., Dec. 7, 1824.

Silas (Spring Silas), b. Tues., Feb. 14, 1804, and Hannah (Bodwell), b. Oct. 3, 1810. Children: William S., Dec. 19, 1831; Eliza Jane, Oct. 10, 1841; Mary, June, 1848; David, Mar. 11, 1851.

Timothy and Abiah. Children: Asa, Apr. 16, 1792; Mehitable G., July 2, 1793; Nancy, Feb. 14, 1800; Sarah, Aug. 21, 1802; Lucy, Jan. 13, 1805; Eliza, Mar. 16, 1807; Daniel K., Mar. 7, 1809; Sophia, Mar. 5, 1811; Mary Ann, Apr. 12, 1813; Charles O., May 20, 1815; James K., July 9, 1817; Clarasina, Oct. 6, 1820.

Barnat, James and Ruth. Children: Moses, Dec. 21, 1782; Ruthy Prentice, Sept. 27, 1784; Ephraim Clark, July 28, 1786; Robert, Oct. 2, 1788; William Davidson, Dec. 3, 1791.

John and Ann. Children: Sarah, Nov. 29, 1761; Ann, May 29, 1762.

John and Joan. Children: Rebecca, Oct. 18, 1722; Sara, Sept. 18, 1724; William, Feb. 15, 1726–7; Frances, Feb. 3, 1728–9; John, June 7, 1731; Fanna, Feb. 24, 1732–3; Robert, Jan. 5, 1734–5.

Moses and Joan. Children: Mary, Apr. 7, 1732; Rebecca, Apr. 25, 1734; Margrat, Jan. 27, 1736; William, Sept. 29, 1738; John, June 12, 1744; Jannet, Dec. 12, 1746; Robert, Sept. 15, 1749; Sara, Dec. 19, 1754; Margrat, Apr. 23, 1741.

Robert and Elisabeth. Children: George, Oct. 11, 1765; John, Oct. 6, 1767; Serra, Aug. 31, 1769.

Barnes, Thompson and Elisabeth. Son: Oct. 14, 1860.

Barnett, Jonathan and Ruth. Children: John, July 6, 1795; Amos Merrill, Mar. 15, 1797; Robert, Nov. 8, 1798; William Davidson, Sept. 8, 1800; James, Mar. 25, 1802; Gilman, Feb. 11, 1804; Jonathan, Aug. 7, 1807; David, Nov. 9, 1810.

Jonathan and ———. Dau.: Maria, Oct. 18, 1813.

Moses and Mary. Son: William D., Jan. 1, 1802.

Barr, Samuel and Mary. Children: John, Oct. 31, 1742; Jane, Jan. 4, 1744; Margrat, Apr. 30, 1747.

Barrett, James and Emeline. Dau., Feb. 18, 1863.

Wilbur E. and Georgietta W. Knight. Children: Dau., Aug. 3, 1898; George Wilbur, May 6, 1896. (See Anderson.)

Bartlett, Ebenezer and Mary. Dau.: Almina, Nov. 11, 1808.

Bartley, Robert, M. D., b. June 13, 1759. (Physician in Londonderry, 1792.)

Battles, George F. and ———. Son, Jan. 15, 1869.

Bean, Abram and Augusta W. Blodgett. Child, July 12, 1891.

Frank P. and Rilla F. Wilson. Son: Norman Wilson, May 16, 1903.

G. H. and Rosie L. (Titcomb). Children: George G., Charles T., Harold H. (See Titcomb.)

Bebo, Ezra and Sophia. Son, Apr. 14, 1855.

Beede, George W. and Annis S. Moody. Children: Dau., Jan. 21, 1901; son, Nov. 28, 1901; son, Dec. 19, 1903; Florence Grace, Feb. 18, 1905; Helen Beatrice, Feb. 6, 1907; George E. S., Jan. 28, 1908.

Julius N., b. 1837.

Beede, William W. and Esther M. Son: Ralph Clifford, Feb. 16, 1899.

Bell, Hon. John and Persis Thom. (See Thom records.)
John, son of John and Elisabeth, b. Aug. 15, 1730; m., Dec. 21, 1758, Mary Ann Gilmore, b. 1737. Children: Samuel, Sept. 28, 1723; Mary, Jan. 25, 1727–8; Elisabeth, Dec. 28, 1725; John, Aug. 15, 1730.
John and Mary Ann. Children: Susana, Feb. 26, 1761; Elisabeth, Feb. 10, 1763; John, July 20, 1765; James, Oct. 10, 1767; Samuel, Feb. 9, 1770; Jean, May 3, 1772; Mary Ann, Jan. 30, 1775; Jonathan, Dec. 2, 1778.

Belmore, Paul and Philomon Vellen. Son, June 14, 1889.

Benson, Andrew J., b. Jan. 9, 1833, and Ruth J. (Page), b. Aug. 9, 1835; m. Jan. 1, 1851. Children: Charles O., Nov. 18, 1851; Frank A., Apr. 7, 1853; Ella F., July 11, 1854; Frank A., Aug. 13, 1858; Ida M., Apr. 6, 1860; George W., Jan. 1, 1862; Willie H., Mar. 19, 1864; Oscar P., June 24, 1866; George W., Feb. 28, 1868; Fred G., Mar. 12, 1870; Alice J., Jan. 29, 1872; Harry L., Oct. 20, 1875.
Frank A. and May B. Wilson. Children: Maniford, Apr. 1881; Howard, Mar. 12, 1888; Eva May, Feb. 26, 1892; Clifford, Dec., 1899.
George T. and Ida N. Steele. Son: Aug. 5, 1910.

Bergeron, George I. and Harriet F. Christie. Son: Richard I., Sept. 6, 1907.
Joseph P. and Lizzie Archambault. Children: James Oscar, July 5, 1891; Joseph F., Mar. 12, 1893; son, Dec. 16, 1895; Ernest Arthur, Nov. 16, 1902.

Berry, Frank and Abbie A. Gilcreast. Children: Doris E., May, 1907; William E., Dec., 1909.
Joseph and ———. Dau., June 1, 1868.
Joseph A. and Mary J. Sampson. Son: Albert P., Aug. 9, 1875.

Blair, James and Isabella. Children: David, Apr. 23, 1729; Alexander, Feb. 21, 1730–1.
John and Jean. Children: William, Sept. 26, 1726; dau., Jan. 15, 1727–8; Elisabeth, Oct. 7, 1731; William, Mar. 5, 1734–5; David, Dec. 13, 1735; Margaret, Sept., 1738.
Jonathan and Jean. Son: Robert, Feb. 4, 1741–2.

Blake, William J. and E. A. ———. Son, July 19, 1856.

Blanchard, James E. and Annie E. Sillivan. Dau., Apr. 19, 1898.

Blear, John and Jennet. Son: David, Oct. 18, 1737.

Blenns, Walter L., b. Feb. 9, 1848.

Blodgett, Joshua, b. Apr. 6, 1779, and Sarah Vickery. Children: Mary Vickery, June 15, 1804; Isaac, May 26, 1807; Zilpha M., May 10, 1810; Elisabeth Vickery, Apr. 10, 1813; Augusta Watts, July 21, 1818.

Joshua and Bethiah Read. Children: Ruth M. E., Sept. 18, 1844; Augusta W., Apr. 24, 1847; Celestia A., Nov. 11, 1849; Isaac J., Apr. 4, 1854; Izietta B., Aug. 12, 1857.

Blood, Charles L. and Frances M. (Smith). Children: John L., 1868; Alice C., June 15, 1870; Charles L., 1875; Charles Warren, July 19, 1876; Arthur Vernon, Sept. 21, 1880.

Wilbur L. and Bernice N. Thompson. Children: Harland Burton, May 9, 1893; dau., July 3, 1895; son, June 23, 1898.

Boice, James and Mary. Children: Samuel, Oct. 11, 1751; Rose, Sept. 22, 1753.

Boles, George and Annie. Son: Arthur James, Sept. 1, 1900.

William and Katherine Ferron. Dau.: Mildred Rosa, Oct. 14, 1910.

William and Katherine McVigor. Son: William, Feb. 26, 1910.

William A. and Marion B. Nugent. Dau.: Irvilla May, Sept. 28, 1902.

Bolles, Lewis and Eliza. Children: Charles, Apr. 19, 1854; Carrie W., Dec. 7, 1843.

Bollis, Alvin and Alice Carpenter. Dau., Aug. 22, 1898.

Bonnenfant, Pierre and Delphine Blanchet. Son, Dec. 23, 1897; dau., Feb. 3, 1900.

Bowker, James F. and Ella. Son, Mar. 1, 1862.

Bowles, Martin M., b. at Lisbon, N. H., Nov. 29, 1840; m. Mary E. (Noyes) Norcross, Dec. 19, 1869. (See Norcross rec.)

Boyce, Capt. Benjamin, b. Dec. 25, 1791, and Sally White. Children: Ephraim W., Sept. 5, 1820; George W., Dec. 7, 1821; Stephen M., Oct. 10, 1823; Nathan C., Aug. 12, 1825; Jeremiah Mason, July 9, 1827; Freeman C., July 18, 1829; Horatio Nelson, Sept. 28, 1833.

Charles F. and Sarah F. Wheeler. Dau.: Elsie Louise, Sept. 20, 1890.

Elbridge A., b. Dec. 19, 1860, Londonderry, N. H., and Sarah E. Fay, b. Feb. 7, 1870, Spencer, Mass. Children: Son, Oct. 12, 1860; dau., Feb. 1, 1893; John A., Nov. 24, 1895, Newburyport, Mass.; William W., May 2, 1897, Derry, N. H.; Margaret A., Mar. 15, 1900, Derry, N. H.; Elbridge A., Jr., Apr. 20, 1903, Derry, N. H.; George S., Jan. 8, 1907, Londonderry, N. H.; Walter Edward, May 8, 1910, Londonderry, N. H.

Boyce, Ephraim W. and Annis. Children: May Frances, July 31, 1851; Cora, b. in California, Oct. 5, 1853.

Frank A. and ———. Dau.: Edith F., 1883.

Giles Ladd and Clara M. Goodwin. Children: Myra F., Mar. 18, 1872; Annie R., Dec. 9, 1874.

Hazen G. Children: David, Sept. 4, 1827; Jacob, Oct. 11, 1830; Mary, 1835.

Hugh, b. July 5, 1773, and Susanna (Garvin), b. Oct. 12, 1778. Children: James, Oct. 26, 1798; Hazen G., Oct. 8, 1800; Samuel, Nov. 9, 1802; David, Apr. 22, 1805; Daniel, Feb. 28, 1808; Jacob, Sept. 10, 1810; Carlos Alonzo, May 7, 1813; Hugh, Aug. 25, 1815.

Margaret, Sept. 8, 1753; Mary, Oct. 13, 1755; James, Apr. 6, 1758; Jennet, May 23, 1760; Lydia, Apr. 18, 1762; Samuel, Sept. 14, 1764; Sarah, May 27, 1767; Joseph, June 5, 1769; Robert, July 5, 1771; Hugh and William, twins, July 5, 1773; Jennet, June 3, 1776.

Nelson and Sarah J. Melvin. Children: Son, Apr. 29, 1852; Horace C., Apr. 19, 1853; Frank A., Aug. 23, 1855; Orietta, Aug. 31, 1856; Charles F., May 18, 1859; Ella F., Feb. 2, 1866.

Newell, son of Samuel, and Cylinda Flanders. Children: Edgar A., Sept. 25, 1862; Sam N., Dec. 25, 1876.

Samuel and Susan P. Dickey. Children: Hannah Jane, Mar. 8, 1831; Lorinda Newell, Apr. 25, 1835; Susanna, 1838 (?); Charles.

William (called Lafayette), b. Jan. 6, 1807, and Wealthy Fling. Children: Giles Ladd, Sept. 21, 1835; Maria B., Dec. 4, 1836; Charles Tyler, Mar. 17, 1841; Edwin H., Dec. 22, 1844; Alphonso, Mar. 8, 1848; Mason V., Nov. 8, 1849; Daniel F., Sept. 5, 1852; George C., Jan. 13, 1855.

William M., b. Sept. 12, 1809, and Hannah M. Whidden. Children: Angeline W., Nov. 26, 1842; Betsey M., Nov. 29, 1848; Belinda J., Apr. 28, 1850; Deroy M., Dec. 27, 1851; George H., Dec. 29, 1854; Sewall W., Nov. 21, 1853; Clarence A., Nov. 10, 1856; Jennete, June 27, 1862.

Willis Prescott, b. Aug. 1, 1864, at Londonderry, son of George W. and Martha (Annis), and Ida E. Reed, b. Mar. 31, 1862, at Derry. Children: Stephen Moore, June 11, 1885; Edgar Reed, Feb. 16, 1889; Clyde George, Apr. 6, 1894; Helen Rebessa, Aug. 30, 1896; Anita Catherine, Dec. 1, 1900. Children all born in California.

Boyd, ——— and Minnie L. Gilmore, b. Mar. 23, 1864. Children: Marion, 1888; Dorothy, 1890. (See Richardson records.)

Boyd, Abby E. and Frank G. Crowell; m. Jan. 2, 1878. Children: Mary E., Nov. 21, 1878; Clarence M., Feb. 2, 1881.

Calvin and Charlotte W. Shepard; m. Dec. 24, 1844. Children: Lucy M., Oct. 11, 1846; William W., Mar. 26, 1848; Frank F., May 15, 1850; Florence E., Aug. 25, 1853.

Daniel M. and Hattie P. Mullins; m. May 7, 1884. Dau., Nov. 16, 1886.

Emma D. and Fred A. Young; m. Nov. 26, 1885. Children: Maurice, Sept. 1, 1889; Arthur B., May 22, 1891; Mason J., Feb. 9, 1894.

Mason and Mary H. Dodge; m. Jan. 2, 1851. Children: Martha J., Feb. 25, 1852; Abby E., Nov. 20, 1854; Maria W., Aug. 30, 1856; Daniel M., Apr. 23, 1858; Emma D., May 3, 1863; George H., Feb. 3, 1865; Mary, May 25, 1874.

William, b. 1756; m., Jan. 30, 1816, Martha Dickey, b. Aug. 11, 1780. Children: Calvin, Mar. 15, 1818; Maria, Aug. 19, 1819; Mason, Aug. 28, 1821.

William and Annois. Children: William, Oct. 6, 1782; Latuc, Sept. 26, 1784; Robert, May 15, 1787; James, May 4, 1792; Maria McKeen, Apr. 17, 1797.

Boyes, Robert and Jenat. Children: Samuel, Jan. 20, 1723-4; William, Apr. 20, 1726.

Robert and Persis. Children: Nelson, Mar. 5, 1823; Elisabeth Jane, Mar. 12, 1824; Reuben, Nov. 30, 1825; William, Jan. 15, 1827; Jacob, Jan. 15, 1827; Clarissa M., Oct. 20, 1829; Walter, Aug. 20, 1831; Adeline A., Apr. 26, 1833; Esther W., Jan. 13, 1835; Mary Ann, Oct. 17, 1836; Suel W., Aug. 29, 1838; Robert M., June 8, 1842.

Rufus and Susan. Children: Dau., Mar. 21, 1854; son, Nov. 7, 1855.

William M. and Hannah. Son, Nov. 21, 1853.

Boys, Robert and Sarah. Children: Janet, Sept. 11, 1744; Robert, Dec. 31, 1746; Alexander, Nov. 23, 1758.

Brainard, Timothy G. and Harriet P. Children: Harriet P., Sept. 9, 1842; Julia Dana, Nov. 24, 1843; Henry H., Jan. 31, 1845; Martha Cilley, Nov. 12, 1846; Hannah H., Sept. 22, 1848; Henry Green, May 23, 1852.

Bresnan, William and Anne. Son, July 29, 1885.

William and Ellen. Dau., Apr. 3, 1884.

Brewster, Isaac and Jean. Children: David, Sept. 2, 1753; Martha, Mar. 9, 1755; Elisabeth, Mar. 6, 1757; James, Oct. 31, 1758; Mary, Dec. 10, 1760; Isaac, June 11, 1763; Susanna, July 8, 1765; Rachel, Oct. 14, 1767; John, June 23, 1770; Jean, Apr. 14, 1774.

Brickett, Charles F. and Emily Spinney, b. May 29, 1819. Children: Charles Henry, Aug. 8, 1846, res. California; George W., Dec. 31, 1848; Frank H., Feb. 18, 1850, res. Concord, N. H.

Charles H. and Maggie. Children: Emilie, Oct. 31, 1872; Charlotte, Sept. 22, 1874; Birdie, Nov. 10, 1876; Henrietta, Feb. 22, 1879; Charles F., May 28, 1883. All born and live in California.

Frank Herbert and Mary A. Pervere, b. Jan. 27, 1855; m. Sept. 8, 1872. Children: Mabel H., Mar. 21, 1875; Addie E., Apr. 13, 1882; Emma E., Mar. 6, 1889; Lizzie A., Apr. 30, 1893; Florence M., Aug. 16, 1895.

Henry W. and Annah H., b. Nov. 3, 1831. Children: Edwd. Clarence, Ellen Louise, Little Alice.

James and Anna Wheeler. Children: Hannah, Dec. 14, 1786; Jonathan, May 31, 1789; James, July 7, 1791; Nathaniel, May 17, 1793; Ralph, Feb. 15, 1795; Ann, June 18, 1797; Delia, July 31, 1799; Esther, Dec. 5, 1801; Mary, Sept. 14, 1803; James, May 4, 1806; Richard Kimball, July 18, 1808; Louisa, Mar. 8, 1811; Moody Hills, Oct. 10, 1813.

Jonathan, b. June 19, 1789, and Lydia (Kent), b. May 24, 1790. Children: Alice, Nov. 25, 1810; James Kent, July 31, 1812; Harriet Newell, Dec. 17, 1815; Delia, Aug. 21, 1820; Charles F., Feb. 28, 1825; Henry W., Aug. 11, 1828; Herbert K., Jan. 30, 1830; Elisabeth Poor, Jan. 1, 1833.

Brooks, Addison and Martha Morrison. Son, Dec. 23, 1852.

Edward Q. F. and Margaret Oliver. Dau.: Lillian Ardelle, Aug. 24, 1910. Res. Sunapee, N. H.

Edward W., b. Sept. 24, 1836, son of James W. and Rebecca, and Anna M. Buck, b. May 7, 1835, New Bedford, Mass. Children: Ardelle, Aug. 8, 1863, Woburn, Mass.; James L., July 12, 1867, Woburn, Mass.; Charles E., Dec. 28, 1868, Reading, Mass.; John W., June 21, 1872, Washington, N. H.; Edward Q. F., Feb. 5, 1877, Washington, N. H.

James L. and Myra F. Boyes. Children: Clara A., Aug. 12, 1894; John E., June 28, 1896; Harold W., Feb. 18, 1901; Helen M., Aug. 22, 1903; Natalie Inez, Aug. 27, 1904.

Brown, Alberto C. and Persis T. A. Children: Walter C., Feb. 21, 1874; Bertha L., Dec. 12, 1880; Chester A., May 13, 1884.

Arthur E. and Merilda York. Children: Bernard, Nov. 23, 1904; Bertha, May 1, 1906.

Irving J. and Nellie E. Son, Feb. 28, 1888.

Lawrence and Elisabeth. Son: William, Nov. 17, 1790.

Louis F. and Sarah Noble. Children: Son, May 29, 1889; ch., May 18, 1891; dau., Dec. 11, 1893; dau., Jan. 19, 1896.

Brown, Nathaniel H. and Clara Jane, wid. of Alfred A. Corning; m. in 1873. Children: Hattie L., 1877; Louis E., 1880. (See Rowell.)

Bunker, Joshua O. and Helen M. Fellows. Son: Eli Joshua, May 5, 1896.

Burbank, Frank A. and Bertha M. Towne. Children: John Chase, Apr. 4, 1905; Willis Patton, May 6, 1907; son, Feb. 26, 1909.

John H. and Jane C. Dau., Mar. 18, 1853.

Burgess, Jeffery, b. May 24, 1822, in Nova Scotia.

Burke, Henry and Hattie. Dau., May 21, 1867.

Burns, Benajah, son of George and Mary Baird, m. Sarah Carlton in Pelham, N. H. Parent of 8 sons and 3 daus.

Daniel, b. Jan. 28, 1788, in Dracut, Mass., son of Benajah and Sarah Carlton, m. Rachel Hunt, b. June 19, 1794, in Warner, N. H. They had 3 sons and 3 daus.

Daniel Hardy, b. Mar. 20, 1831, Warner, N. H., son of Daniel and Rachel Hunt, m., Nov. 21, 1850, at Londonderry, Lydia C. March, b. May 24, 1833, at Londonderry, N. H. Dau.: Ardell Cornelia, Sept. 9, 1851. M. 2d wife, Eliza A. S. Goss, Jan. 24, 1854, at Londonderry, N. H. She was b. Sept. 25, 1832. Children: Ella Josephine, Aug. 2, 1855; Frank Eugene, Dec. 7, 1857.

Ella Josephine m., Feb. 27, 1909, O. William Ellery, b. Aug. 11, 1863, New Braintree, Mass.

Frank Eugene m., Sept. 6, 1883, Jennie Gerry, b. July 18, 1864.

George, b. in Scotland, m. Mary Baird and settled in Dracut, Mass. He was the parent of eight daus. and one son.

Burroughs, Alfred descended from George Burroughs of Salem, Mass. He settled in Hudson, N. H., and m. Mary Melvin. Children: William, Rhoda, and Polly.

Alfred, b. Oct. 11, 1815, Hudson, N. H., settled in Londonderry about 1840; m. Mariah Corning. Children: Alfred D., in Londonderry, N. H.; John H., in Londonderry, N. H.; Lydia M., in Londonderry, N. H.; Mary E., in Bow, N. H.; Melinda J., in Bow, N. H.; Sarah E., in Bow, N. H.; Edwin P., in Bow, N. H.; Frank E., in Bow, N. H.

John Hamilton, 2d son of Alfred and Mariah, b. in Londonderry, removed in boyhood to Bow, N. H.; m. Helen M. Baker of Dunbarton. Children: Sherman E,. lawyer in Manchester; Evelyn B. of Dayton, Ohio; J. Russell, civil engineer on B. & M. R. R.; Martha Grace, in N. H. State Library.

Burroughs, William and Rachel Searles. Children: Josiah, Lydia, James, Alfred, and Melinda.

Butterworth, William, b. in England, came to America in 1839; to Londonderry in 1875. Born March 9, 1830.

William A. and Edith Belle Lowd. Children: Frank Alfred, July 4, 1894; Clayton Andrew, May 27, 1897.

Buttrick, Isaac and Mary E. Dau.: Sarah M., June 24, 1880.

Calderwood, James and Margaret. Son: Robert, Feb. 22, 1726–7.

Caldwell, Henry J. and Abbie F. Dau.: Mary N., Nov. 5, 1878.

James and Lotus. Son: Samuel, Sept. 12, 1725.

Jefferson, b. Nov. 11, 1803, son of James and Jane, m. Nancy Upton, 1st wife, b. Mar. 21, 1810; m. Nancy ———, 2d wife, b. Nov. 6, 1811. Children: Hattie N., Dec. 5, 1831; Harry J., Dec. 28, 1847.

Joseph, b. Nov., 1771, and Mary, wife, b. Sept., 1773.

Thomas and Mary. Children: Jean, Oct. 26, 1725; son, Jan. 18, 1728–9; William, Sept. 26, 17—.

Call, George M. and Allettie V. Simpson. Children: Son, June 22, 1899; son, Nov. 5, 1900; dau., Apr. 20, 1902; dau., June 14, 1904.

Campbell, Alexander and Jane. Son: Alexander, Feb. 28, 1776.

Dea. Samuel, b. Sept. 1, 1819, son of Robert and Anna Carr. Children: Cassius S., Nov. 19, 1845; Francena E., 1848; Alphonso F., Nov. 30, 1855; Harlan E., Oct. 31, 1860.

Dr. William J., b. 1820, son of David and Lydia K., m. for 1st wife Sarah Cutter; for 2d wife, Charlotte A. M. Philbrick, b. Jan. 31, 1830, dau. of Nathan Philbrick and Esther Mudgett. Children of latter wife: Eugene L., July 26, 1850; Luella A., May 7, 1852; William A., Mar. 18, 1855; Winnifred J., Feb. 20, 1866; Pliny M., Apr. 23, 1869.

Eugene L. and Martha G. Children: Maude E., May 31, 1874; Blanche C., Mar. 23, 1876; Luella Agnes, May 26, 1888.

James E. and Evelyn Prescott. Children: Son, Sept. 26, 1897; son, July 7, 1901.

John and Elisabeth. Children: William, May 23, 1782; Robert Moor, July 3, 1784.

John E. and Mary J. Son, Dec. 26, 1870.

John G. and Mary. Children: Twin sons, May 11, 1872.

Matthew M. and Mary J. Children: Percy A., Jan. 30, 1880; Roy Hills, June 14, 1883.

Campbell, Pliny M. and Emma B. Abbott. Son, Sept. 2, 1903; son, Abbott R., Oct. 28, 1905.

Robert and Deborah. Son: James, Jan. 8, 1744.

Cargill, David and Mary. Children: John, Mar. 22, 1723; James, Oct. 24, 1725; John, Oct. 8, 1727-8; David, July 5, 17—.

Carlton, William B., b. Aug. 3, 1826, and Betsey Ann Webster; m. at Lowell, Mass., July 3, 1860. Children: George Washington, July 31, 1862; Mary Elisabeth, Feb. 19, 1867; Frances Virginia, Feb. 13, 1865. (See Webster.)

Carney, William J. and Mary Wynne. Son: William, June 15, 1899.

Champaigne, Oliver and Delia. Dau., May 31, 1868.

Chappman, George W. and Marion E. (Watts.) Children: 3 daus. and 1 son. Res. in Manchester. (See Watts records.)

Charbonneau, George H. and Mary R. Mercir. Dau.: Alice A., Dec. 20, 1903.

Charland, William A. and Ada Welcome. Children: Ch., Nov. 10, 1895; son, Aug. 9, 1909.

Chase, Edmond and Lavina. Children: Dau., June 26, 1855; William Frances, Aug. 24, 1857.

Elijah G., b. Sept. 29, 1858, and Laura Esther Corning, b. Aug. 21, 1867. Children: Ethel Mary, May 19, 1890; Guy Wetherbee, Dec. 7, 1891; Curtis Corning, Dec. 27, 1893; Carl Eddrie, Jan. 4, 1902.

Elijah, b. Mar. 22, 1819, and Phebe Maria Hale, b. July 20, 1822. Adopted son: Elijah Clinton, Feb. 22, 1845.

Esther m. Edwin Follansbee.

Francis M. and Lavina. Children: Alvin Jones, May 30, 1817; George Farrer, Sept. 3, 1820; Sarah McAllister, Dec. 15, 1823.

Fremont and Mary. Son, Mar. 26, 1882.

Harry E. and Clara B. Weaver. Son: Harry G., Sept. 18, 1896.

Isaac and Elisabeth. Children: Ephraim, Apr. 13, 1844; Clarry, May 1, 1845.

Jacob S. and Hattie F. Stevens. Dau., May 31, 1907.

Jacob and Molly. Dau.: Polly, Apr., 1792.

James J. and Eliza H. Son, Feb. 12, 1883.

John and Polly. Dau.: Mary Nancy, Dec. 13, 1815.

John M., b. June 9, 1826, son of Simon and Huldah, and Hannah F. Clark, b. Apr. 30, 1833. Children: Emery M., July 7, 1853; Fremont, 1856; Elijah G., Sept. 29, 1858; Addie Annah, Nov. 15, 1861; Cora M., Feb. 13, 1867; Eugene, 1871; Fidelia A.; George, Feb. 3, 1875.

Chase, Nathan P., b. June 13, 1812, and Mary J. Whidden, b. Sept. 1, 1820; m. Aug. 9, 1843. No children.

Nathaniel, b. Aug. 5, 1790, and Lydia, b. May 7, 1783. Children: Ann, Jan. 8, 1821; Esther, Feb. 18, 1816.

Simon, b. June 27, 1791, and Huldah, b. Oct. 20, 1791. Children: Mary Ann, Oct. 16, 1814; Elijah Gardian, Mar. 22, 1819; Huldah, Oct. 14, 1822; Simon, Mar. 22, 1824; John Morrison, June 9, 1826; Amasa K., Apr. 8, 1833; Trueworthy D., Sept. 11, 1828.

Trueworthy D. and Addie Ella Flood. Son: Cecil, Dec. 23, 1896.

Trueworthy Dudley, b. Sept. 11, 1828, and Nancy M. Pettingill, b. July 6, 1832. Children: Alnora Maria, May 11, 1854; Clara Ella, May 12, 1855; Julia Myra, Dec. 9, 1856; Ida Cora, Dec .13, 1858; Trueworthy Dudley, Jr., Sept. 16, 1860; Frank Emery, Nov. 21, 1862; John Henry, May 19, 1864; ch., Dec. 30, 1866; ch., Jan. 3, 1868.

Cheney, Stephen Danforth and ———. Son: Stephen, May 23, 1819.

Choat, Aaron and Eunice. Children: Jonathan, July 31, 1783; Aaron, Dec. 28, 1786; Amelia, Dec. 20, 1788; Isaac Perkins, Dec. 9, 1790; James, July 20, 1792; Jeremiah, Apr. 7, 1794; Eliza, Apr. 21, 1797.

William and Sukey. Children: Sukey, Aug. 21, 1786; John, May 13, 1788; Sally, Apr. 11, 1790; Lydia, Apr. 7, 1792; Nabby, Mar. 21, 1793; David, Mar. 30, 1796; George, June 23, 1797; Mary, Oct. 6, 1798; Nathan, June 30, 1801.

Caroline, dau. of ———, b. Apr. 8, 1825.

Chrispeen, George W. and Hannah. Son, Aug. 11, 1852.

Christie, Jesse and Mary. Dau.: Christey, Jan. 1, 1728–9.

John W. and Emma J. Finnigan. Children: Dau., May 22, 1888; Arthur Edward, Oct. 15, 1897; Irene, June 23, 1900; dau., July 27, 1902; Robert Lee, July 12, 1904; dau., Aug. 27, 1906.

Clark, Edward C. and Hannah. Dau., Feb. 8, 1854.

Everett W. and Josephine Baker. Son, Feb. 19, 1910.

James, b. Aug. 17, 1791, and Martha Hamilton, b. Feb. 15, 1801. Children: Sarah Ann; John; George A., Apr. 12, 1831; Mary E., Dec. 18, 1833; James, Dec. 25, 1834; Martha L., Feb. 5, 1836; William M., Aug. 5, 1837; Robert, Nov. 13, 1839; Ellen M., Apr. 13, 1845; Thomas; Charles H.; Barnard.

James and Elisabeth. Children: John, Mar. 31, 1723; Samuel, Apr. 12, 1726; George, Apr. 15, 1728; Elliner, Apr. 20, 1730; Matthew, June 30, 1732.

Clark, John and Sarah. Children: Eliza, Oct. 21, 1804; Mary Jane, Dec. 13, 1806; Sarah C., Aug. 28, 1809; Nancy M., Sept. 12, 1811; Sophia, June 16, 1813.

Joseph S. and Rose. Son: Alfred S., Jan. 24, 1881.

Matthew and Elisabeth. Children: Margaret, Mar. 15, 1722–3; Jean, June 1, 1729; George, July, 1725.

Matthew and Hannah. Children: Hannah, Mar. 23, 1792; Mary, Nov. 30, 1793; Betsey, Sept. 11, 1795.

Matthew and Nancy. Children: John, Feb. 23, 1784; Jennet Dickey, May 14, 1785; Margaret, Oct. 24, 1787; Betsey, Oct. 24, 1788; James Linsey, May 15, 1790; Polley, Jan. 30, 1792.

Ninian, b. Oct. 7, 1770, and Sally Warner, b. July 13, 1781; m. in 1803.

Reed P., b. July 6, 1807, and Elisabeth Perkins, b. Mar. 2, 1808. Children: Joseph R., Nov. 2, 1838; Sarah Allina, Oct. 21, 1840; Marianna Perkins, June 19, 1842; William, July 22, 1844; Sarah Elisabeth, Jan. 5, 1847; Alice W. (McIntire), Mar. 22, 1852.

Robert and Elisabeth. Children: Robert, Nov. 14, 1764; Elisabeth, Mar. 25, 1766.

Robert and Letus. Son: William, Jan. 18, 1734–5.

Samuel and Mary. Children: James, Feb. 21, 1758; Margaret, Oct. 3, 1759; John, Dec. 3, 1761; Samuel, Jan. 20, 1764; George, Mar. 15, 1766; Robert, May 20, 1768; Matthew, May 21, 1770.

Samuel and Sally. Children: Hannah P., July 2, 1810; Phinehas, Sept. 9, 1812.

William and Alice. Children: Reed Paige, Aug. 19, 1878; Ralph Warner, Nov. 27, 1882.

William and Julia Myra Chase, b. Oct. 19, 1851. Children: Frederick W., Jan. 11, 1875; Alvina Nora, July 12, 1876.

Clendenin, Archibald and Merrian. Children: Robert, Mar. 20, 1720; Archibald, Oct. 21, 1722; Rebecca, Oct. 21, 1722.

Clendinin, Andrew and Jane. Son: William, May 27, 1752.

Andrew and Jenat. Children: Merrian, Jan. 13, 1729; David, Oct. 16, 1731; Rebecca, June 21, 1733; Martha, June 10, 1735; Archibald, May 20, 1737; Andrew, June 1, 1739; Janet, May 16, 1741.

Robert and Mary. Children: John, Dec. 5, 1749; Hannah, April 17, 1751; James, Nov. 5, 1754.

William and Anna. Dau.: Mary, June 15, 1740.

William and Hanna. Son: Robert, June 23, 1745.

Clifford, Moses and Esther. Children: Philander, Aug. 2, 1813; Letotes, Aug. 11, 1815.

Clinding, William and Nellie. Children: Archibald, Mar. 5, 1785; Martha, Oct. 22, 1786; Sarah, Feb. 22, 1789; Samuel Moor, Aug. 22, 1791; Polly, Dec. 3, 1793; Sophia, Nov. 4, 1795; Andrew, Jan. 19, 1798.

Clough. Two Clough bros., names not given, m. Hannah J. Boyce successively. Son of one union: Harry S., July 12, 1851 or 56. (See Boyce record.)

Sarah J., b. 1813; m. Isaac Kimball, Jr.

Coburn, Daniel, b. 1654; m. Sarah Blood.

Edward, b. 1618; m. Hannah ———.

Elder Daniel G., b. Dec. 31, 1799, and Roxanna Blodgett, b. Apr. 26, 1803. Dau.: Orra A. R., Jan. 7, 1828.

Frank and Luella A. Campbell. Children: Frank C., Nov. 23, 1907; William Everett, Jan. 1, 1909; Paul Wayne, May 9, 1910.

George Milton and Anna F. Baker. Dau.: Mary Florence, Jan. 19, 1909.

Isaac, b. July 23, 1812.

Isaac and Eliza. Children: L. Herbert, Apr. 6, 1837; Georgietta, Mar. 2, 1839; Washington Irving, Jan. 4, 1842; David, Apr. 28, 1845.

Jacob, b. 1696; m. Johanna Varnum.

Jacob, b. 1729; m. Lydia Hall.

Cochran, Andrew and Mary. Children: Jenat, Jan. 13, 1725–6; son, Apr. 4, 1729; Ann, May 30, 1733; Mary, Nov. 20, 1735.

Isaac Wallace, b. Oct. 13, 1821, and Lucy (Woolner) Tilley, b. Mar. 15, 1846. Children: Fred Bartlett, Mar. 20, 1874; May Bell, Oct. 4, 1877. Son by a former marriage, Charles L. Tilley, Oct. 21, 1867.

James and Janet. Children: Joseph, Aug. 17, 1739; William, Dec. 28, 1740; James, Feb. 29, 1743–4; Mary, Jan. 22, 1745–6.

John and Elisabeth. Son: James, Dec. 15, 1754.

John and Mary. Children: Cristen, June 2, 1760; Elisabeth, Oct. 17, 1765; Barnett, Feb. 27, 1768; Jannat, June 10, 1771.

Ninian and Agnes. Son: Jonathan, May 3, 1733.

Ninian and Elisabeth. Dau.: Margaret, May 28, 1731.

Peter and Jean. Children: John, Oct. 31, 1726; Sally, Apr. 30, 1728; Peter, Mar. 12, 1730–31; Robert, Mar. 9, 1733; George, Mar. 24, 1737.

Robert and Abigail. Children: Robert, Apr. 29, 1734; William, Jan. 9, 1735–6.

Robert and Christine. Children: John (?), Oct. 31, 1726; Robert, July 24, 1730.

Cochran, Samuel and Agnes. Children: Margaret, June 28, 1768; Maryann, Nov. 26, 1769; John, June 12, 1771; Isaac, May 9, 1773; Elisabeth, Mar. 6, 1775; Andrew McClary, Nov. 22, 1776; William, Sept. 29, 1778; Agnes, June 2, 1780; Susanna, May 12, 1782; Sarah, Apr. 11, 1784.

Coffin, Clark and Eunice. Son, Mar. 15, 1862.
David W. and Anna. Son, Apr. 2, 1863.
Jonathan and Eunice. Dau., Jan. 29, 1854.

Cogswell, Annie G. (Bampas), b. Mar. 16, 1876, Scottstown, Quebec.
Daniel M., b. Aug. 24, 1808, and Eliza A. (Hall), b. Apr. 9, 1832. Children: William H., Oct. 29, 1866; Charles E., Oct. 18, 1868; John J., Dec. 25, 1871.
Ebenezer, b. May 29, 1802, and Sarah (Philbric), b. July 13, 1808. Children: Albert P., Oct. 2, 1826; Washington, May 22, 1832; Moses F., July 27, 1839.
Frank Nesmith, son of Washington, b. Aug. 17, 1856.
Frank and Annie. Dau.: Arvilla N., Oct. 28, 1904.
Joseph and Abigail. Children: Abigail, Apr. 4, 1797; Mary C., Dec. 16, 1798; Elisabeth, Sept. 23, 1800; Thomas, Apr. 6, 1802; Moses and Aaron, Apr. 6, 1802; Ebenezer, Feb. 23, 1804; William, Oct. 23, 1806; Edward, Oct. 17, 1807.
William H. and Anna C. Brooks, b. 1880. Dau.: Ruth Anna, Feb. 16, 1902.

Conant, Nathaniel and Rhody. Children: Henry, Dec. 17, 1797; Sally McAllister, Mar. 20, 1800; Nathaniel, Apr. 11, 1802; William H., Dec. 29, 1808; Samuel M., May 29, 1810; John, 1823.
William and Rachel W. Garvin, b. Apr. 11, 1813. Children: Annie E., Mar. 22, 1837; Antoinette H., Dec. 6, 1838; Lyman A., May 1, 1840; Charles E., Nov. 25, 1843; Julia M., Nov. 3, 1845; Sarah A., Aug. 24, 1848; Clara F., Sept. 17, 1850; Selwyn S., Apr. 5, 1852; Grace E., Oct. 29, 1854.

Conn, ——— and Ruby. Son, July 10, 1859

Connell, Edward and ———. Son: Francis, Jan. 26, 1909.

Corbin, Charles and Anna C. Dau.: Mabel.

Corey, John N. and Chloe Jane. Dau., July 6, 1888.

Corliss, Harry C. and Marian B. Nugent. Children: Elsie Violet, June 5, 1906; dau., Apr. 10, 1908; Eugenia A., Apr. 4, 1909.
John F. and Elsie M. Loveland. Children: Dau., Jan. 31, 1891; dau., Mar. 12, 1898; dau., Apr. 18, 1900.

Corning, Alexander M., b. Apr. 26, 1833, son of Nathaniel and Mary, and Roxanna (Bryant), b. Sept. 5, 1830. Children: Almira Newell, Nov. 7, 1855; Anna Jane, Oct. 27, 1857; Alice M., July 9, 1859; Jennie S., Nov. 15, 1861.

Corning, Fred P. and Nellie A. Crowell. Children: Carrol Theron, May 25, 1898; Elbert Newman, Mar. 24, 1903.

Freeman, b. Apr. 8, 1803 (son of Nathan), m. Esther (White), 1st wife, b. Oct. 17, 1805; m. 2d wife, Laura A. (Blaisdell), b. July 5, 1816. Children of 1st wife: Elias Randall, July 12, 1830; George W., June 25, 1832; John Anderson, June 26, 1834; Hannah B., Aug. 5, 1836; Charles Freeman, June 28, 1838; Sarah Elisabeth, Sept. 23, 1840. Children of 2d wife: Esther Ann, July 15, 1847; Mary Ellen, Oct. 1, 1848; Esther Frances, Oct. 23, 1850.

John Anderson, m. Celinda P. Parker, Dec., 1861. Dau.: Georgie, Feb. 26, 1866. (See Parker records.)

John, b. Aug. 22, 1757, and Sally (Crowell), b. Dec. 13, 1773. Children: Seth E., Susan and Murial, and nine others.

John and Sally. Children: Judith, Nov. 20, 1790; John, Jan. 17, 1792; Peter, Apr. 11, 1794; Judith, Mar. 28, 1796; Polly, June 30, 1798; Samuel, May 10, 1801; Hiram, Sept. 10, 1803; Sally, Dec. 1, 1805; Louisa, Nov. 11, 1808.

John and Lydia Richardson. Son: Gilman, Nov. 2, 1815.

Joseph Franklin, b. Oct. 24, 1847, and Lucy A. H. (Crosby), b. June 30, 1850; m. May 23, 1868. Children: Henrietta Josephine, Dec. 4, 1869; Joseph Alfred, Apr. 25, 1871; Peter Winslow Franklin, Dec. 14, 1872; Lucy Annie Moda, June 21, 1874; Emma Florence, Jan. 14, 1877; Alice Girtrude, June 8, 1879; Ada Estor, Aug. 11, 1881; Hellen Frances, June 13, 1884; Mabel Frances, Apr. 19, 1886.

Ensign Nathan and Hannah. Children: Sarah, Dec. 15, 1798; Miriam, Jan. 22, 1800; Freeman, Apr. 8, 1802; Hannah, Dec. 29, 1804; Nathan, Mar. 14, 1808; Warren, Sept. 30, 1809; Betsey, May 10, 1812; Nelson, Mar. 4, 1816; William, June 25, 1818.

Nathaniel, b. July 17, 1804, and Mary McMurphy, b. Apr. 4, 1808. Children: Nathaniel, Jr., Feb. 9, 1839; George W., Aug. 21, 1843.

Peter, b. Apr. 1, 1794, and Lydia Read, b. Oct. 28, 1806. Son: Sylvester R., Nov. 5, 1833.

Samuel and Mary. Children: John C., Aug. 17, 1794; Polly, May 25, 1797; Samuel, Nov. 16, 1798; Rachel, Oct. 25, 1801; Nathaniel, July 17, 1804.

Sylvester and Sarah J. Currier, b. Aug. 12, 1844. Children: Fred Peter, Oct. 16, 1867; Sam A., June 16, 1869; Grace L., June 14, 1873; Nettie J., Feb. 1, 1875; Susie M., Nov. 4, 1877; Orin B., Aug. 22, 1881; Blanche L., July 7, 1883.

William P., b. Dec. 11, 1836, and Hannah, b. Aug. 5, 1836. Children: Mary Esther, Aug. 21, 1861; Laura Freeman, Aug. 21, 1867.

Corthell, Albin and Abbie Adella Goodwin. Son: Myron Goodwin, Mar. 29, 1895.

Levi H. and Jane C. Children: Son, Oct. 4, 1871; Everett G., May 25, 1874; Alden Levi, June 7, 1877.

Cote, Ferdinand and Albena Robillard. Son: Ernest David, Dec. 14, 1910.

Courreur, Charles E., b. June 21, 1850, and Mary Ann Emerson. Dau.: Hester, m. George A. Hall, Manchester, N. H. (See Emerson records.)

Cowan, Patrick and Jennet. Children: Elisabeth, Jan. 12, 1733–4; Mary, Jan. 9, 1735–6.

Cox, Rev. Joseph, b. Dec. 30, 1840, Canning, Kings Co., Nova Scotia; removed to N. H. in 1867.

Craig, John and Annas. Children: Martha, July 27, 1760; John, Sept. 10, 1762; Mary, Jan. 27, 1765; Joseph, Nov. 27, 1767; Anne, Dec. 17, 1771; Jean, Dec. 23, 1774.

Jonathan and Mary. Son: John, May 3, 1732.

Craige, Alexander and Grizel. Children: Samuel, Apr. 25, 1733; John, Sept. 17, 1736.

Cressey, William and Abbie F. Gilcreast, 1st hus.; res. Derry, N. H. Children: Carle E., Oct., 1877; Clarence W., Oct. 1881. (See Gilcreast.)

Crimminge, Joseph and Mary. Dau., May 15, 1884.

Cristey, Jesee and Mary. Children: Dau., Jan. 1, 1728–9; George, Oct. 1, 1731.

Thomas and Sarra. Children: Joan, July 30, 1752; Mary, Aug. 12, 1754.

Crocker, John and ——. Children: Sarah Choat, Aug. 17, 1797; Elisabeth, Aug. 11, 1800; Lydia, Aug. 26, 1802.

John and Margaret. Children: John, Aug. 2, 1804; Lydia, Nov. 25, 1808.

Crombee, John and Rebecca. Children: Moses, Oct. 31, 1764; Jean, Mar. 2, 1771; Mary, Apr. 22, 1773; John, Apr. 15, 1776.

Crombie, Moses and Sophia. Son: Robert Moore, Apr. 23, 1825.

Crooker, Japhat and Lidy. Children: Peter Patterson, Sept. 5, 1797; Samuel, June 24, 1799.

Melzer and Migall. Children: Migall, Dec. 7, 1796; Melzer, Mar. 15, 1800.

Cross, Addison and Hattie J. Son, Mar. 9, 1886.

Addison and Myra. Dau., Sept. 8, 1884.

Arthur H. and Lelia M. Fiske. Children: Son, May 14, 1899; son, May 20, 1903.

Charles D. and Flora F. Son, Sept. 27, 1887.

Cross, Levi and Fannie Goodwin. Sons: Levi E., Aug. 1831.
William G. and Clara. Children: Hiram N., Mar. 3, 1876; John E., Dec. 17, 1879.
William G. and Clarrine Colburn. Children: Dau., June 6, 1890; dau., July 12, 1891.

Crowell, Charles A. and Mary L. Schwartz. Children: Milton Frederic, Nov. 8, 1895; Henry Plummer, Aug. 11, 1897.
Daniel and Eliza. Son, Sept. 8, 1853.
David and ———. Children: David, Aug. 7, 1782; Jesee, Sept. 14, 1784; Samuel, Nov. 17, 1786; Polly, Apr. 19, 1790; Betsey, Aug. 29, 1792; Peter, Mar. 14, 1795; Isaac, Oct. 21, 1797.
David and Hannah. Dau.: Cena, Feb. 12, 1800.
David and Martha McNeil. Children: Ora, Clara, Susan, Frank, and Albert; no dates.
Frank S. and Abbie E. Boyd. Children: Mary Eliza, Nov. 21, 1878; Clarence Mason, Feb. 2, 1881.
Henry, b. June 22, 1828, son of Samuel and Sarah (Smithers), and Judith Plummer, dau. of Dr. Plummer, Auburn, N. H. Children: Frank S., Dec. 8, 1854; Plummer H., Nov. 21, 1858; Charles Albert, June 27, 1868.
John M. and Sarah Grant. Children: Mary Harriet and Frank Grant. Res. in Kansas.
Peter, b. Mar. 14, 1795, son of David, and Ora Martin. Son: David, Nov. 21, 1818.
Peter and Harriet (Hardy), 2d wife, b. 1798. Children: Elisabeth, Nov. 5, 1821; John M., Oct. 2, 1823; Daniel Thurston, Feb. 11, 1826; Amasa A., July 6, 1828; James, Aug. 14, 1830; Sarah A., Jan. 29, 1833; Martha S., Sept. 27, 1836.
Samuel, Jr., b. Nov. 4, 1813, and Hannah Eastman, b. Mar. 2, 1817. Children: Sarah Elisabeth, Dec. 4, 1842; William Henry, Dec. 11, 1844; Hannah Elisabeth, May 1, 1853; Sarah Eastman, Nov. 1, 1858.
Stephen and Eliza. Son, Mar. 13, 1863.
William Harrison and Josie A. Son: Henry W., Mar. 28, 1873.
William H. and Almira. Children: Nellie Imogene, Nov. 12, 1867; Mary Eastman, Nov. 13, 1869; Myron, Nov. 2, 1874.

Crowningshield, George and Mary Platts, b. in Salem, Mass. (See Platts.)
——— and Sophia Platts. (See Platts records.)

Crumsey, John and Jean. Children: Hugh, Oct. 16, 1722; James, Mar. 1, 1723–4; William, Mar. 1, 1723–4; son, Mar. 15, 1725–6; Elisabeth, Mar. 28, 1728; Jenat, Mar. 15, 1729–30; Agnes, Jan. 11, 1731–2.

Cummings, Isaac and Mary. Son, Mar. 13, 1839.

Cunningham, Cornelius and Mary Dobbin. Children: Francis, Aug. 7, 1901; Stephen Henry, June 19, 1904.

Currier, Joshua P. and Esther J. Son, Nov. 10, 1852.

Cushman, William and ——. Dau., May 12, 1871.

Cutler, Herbert W. and Esthermate B. (Annis). Son: Charles H., Oct. 17, 1866.

Daley, Daniel J., son of John, b. Aug. 1, 1873.

James P. and Catherine Healy. Children: John H., Oct. 29, 1894; Mary C., Jan. 8, 1896; James Joseph, Sept. 26, 1898.

John, b. in Ireland, Feb., 1839.

Daly, Matthew and Bridgett. Son, July 8, 1861.

Dana, Jonathan and ——. Son: George W., Nov. 8, 1839.

Danforth, Eliphalet and Sally. Children: Eliza, Dec. 2, 1808; William Choate, Feb. 22, 1815.

William and Lucy. Children: Lucy, Oct. 16, 1781; Simon, Dec. 2, 1783; Patty, Apr. 26, 1785; Orpah, Jan. 2, 1789; Nabby Prime, Mar. 25, 1791.

Davenport, Eddie H. and Harriet J. Nevins. Son: Nevins, June 20, 1909.

Davidson, Robert and Ellen Parker. Dau.: Mattie R. Dell, Aug. 30, 1895.

*Rev. William and Frances. Children: Wilton, Feb. 21, 1743; John, June 13, 1745; Ann, Apr. 30, 1747; Hamilton, June 29, 1749; Frances, Apr. 14, 1756.

Davis, Dr. ——, of Webster, Mass., m. Bertha Rowell, 1st wife; m. Emma Dow, 2d wife; no children. (See Rowell.)

Francis and ——. Children: Daniel, Oct. 13, 1817; Benjamin, Apr. 25, 1819; Alfred, Apr. 24, 1821; Harriet, Sept. 18, 1822.

Joseph, uncle of Mrs. Charles F. Boyce, b. Feb. 23, 1821.

Oscar H. and Hattie E. Cooley. Dau.: Ruth Hazel, Aug. 11, 1895.

Davison, Lee W., b. in 1873 in Nova Scotia, and Delia A. (Paige), b. 1873 in Weare, N. H.; m. Aug. 1, 1892. Children: Viola G. July 4, 1893; Olive F., July 11, 1896; Velda B., Sept. 27, 1897; Wylie L., Nov. 7, 1898; Harold, Feb. 18, 1900; Wilfred, Apr. 1, 1901; Beatrice M., Apr. 19, 1902; Mildred, Jan. 4, 1904; Ralph, Aug. 25, 1905; Nelson, Dec. 24, 1906; Ruby, Oct. 12, 1908.

* Rev. William ordained over East Parish in 1740.

Day, Benjamin and Frances Vinton. Son: Elder Joseph L., Jan. 9, 1831.

Denver, John, m. Abigail Sampson, b. Feb. 5, 1806. (See Sampson.)

Derrasiers, Edmond and Lula Theiss. Children: Hilda Bertha, Jan. 20, 1904; Lawrence E., June 22, 1906; Norman R., May 18, 1908; Edna M., Dec. 17, 1909.

De Varney, David W. and Almira Beauregard. Children: Lillian Helen, Sept. 10, 1901; Eva, Aug. 8, 1903; dau., June 18, 1906.

Dickey, Adam, b. Apr. 17, 1740, and Jane Nahor. Children: Mary, Sept. 15, 1766; Samuel, Aug. 9, 1768; Jane, Aug. 23, 1773; James, June 13, 1777; William, June 22, 1779.

David and Isabel. Children: Adam, Dec. 25, 1724; Bart, May 1, 1728; John, Mar. 6, 1726; David, May 19, 1730; Jenit, July 10, 1744.

David and Mary (Davis). Son: George W., July 21, 1834.

David T., b. June 20, 1860.

David Woodburn, b. Dec. 16, and Sarah Ann (Campbell), b. Oct. 9, 1815. Children: Margaret Ann, Jan. 26, 1838; Harrison Tyler, Feb. 6, 1841; Horace Greeley, May 3, 1843; Robert Campbell, Aug. 26, 1845; Frank Augustus, Mar. 3, 1849; Myron Parsons, Feb. 19, 1852.

Elias and Rosanna. Children: William, James, and Elias at Londonderry, N. H.; Elisabeth, at Boston, Mass.

George L. and Florence E. Richardson. Children: William L., Dec. 11, 1907; George Robert, Dec. 30, 1909.

George W. and Sarah Ann. Children: George Arthur, Oct. 30, 1857; Nellie Sarah, July 7, 1860; Etta Grey, Oct. 26, 1862.

Isaac S., b. Nov. 1, 1819, and Margaret J. Pettingill, b. Sept. 9, 1817. Children: Irvin Thornton, Nov. 21, 1843; Henry Clay, Mar. 28, 1845; Phineas Warren, June 17, 1850; Winfield Scott, July 10, 1852.

Elder John of Pres. church and 1st wife, Caroline P. (Cogswell), b. Aug. 26, 1830, Boscawen, N. H.; no children.

Elder John and 2d wife, Susan Ellen (Hill), b. June 15, 1828, at Claremont, N. H.; no children.

John, b. Oct. 6, 1778, son of Robert, and Margaret (Woodburn), b. May 8, 1780. Children: Robert, Mar. 28, 1807; Hannah, Jan. 18, 1809; David Woodburn, Dec. 16, 1810; Margaret, May 7, 1813; Susanna, May 19, 1815; John, Feb. 13, 1824.

Dickey, John and Rhoda. Children: John Pinkerton, Aug. 21, 1796; James Varnum, Sept. 11, 1797; Phinehas Whiting, Dec. 26, 1798; Hannah, Aug. 4, 1800; Janet, Dec. 3, 1801; son, Mar. 4, 1803; William G., Aug. 8, 1804; Gilman, Mar. 8, 1806; Matthew W., Dec. 5, 1807.

Joseph, b. Oct. 15, 1823 (son of Joseph and Fanny D., b. June 7, 1783), and Elisabeth White. Children: Fannie Montgomery, Dec. 13, 1859; Sarah Kendall, Dec. 13, 1859.

Joseph and Fanny. Children: Rebecca, Dec. 19, 1813; Montgomery, Nov. 19, 1815; Mary, Mar. 19, 1818; Frances, Oct. 8, 1819; Margarett, Nov. 26, 1821.

Lyman A., b. Oct. 20, 1840, and Emma A. (Libbee). Children: Nelson H., Sept. 9, 1868; William G., Nov. 24, 1870; Carrie May, Aug. 16, 1873.

Lyman A. and Lana S. (George), 2d wife, b. Nov. 5, 1843. Son: George L., Sept. 7, 1881.

Nelson H. and Clara B. Carr. Dau.: Winona Clara, Sept. 17, 1903.

Robert, b. Nov. 4, 1786, and Jenny Morrison, b. May 2, 1792. Children: Robert Morrison, Mar. 1, 1822; Zoe Ann, June 3, 1824.

Robert, b. Feb. 10, 1748, son of Samuel, and Hannah Woodburn, b. 1753. Children: Samuel, May 25, 1777; John, Oct. 25, 1778; Martha, Aug. 11, 1780; Mary, Mar. 20, 1782; Joseph, May 5, 1784; Robert, Nov. 4, 1786; Susannah, Jan. 4, 1789; Jannat, Dec. 4, 1790; David Woodburn, Dec. 26, 1794; Adam, Oct. 21, 1796; Roxanna, Aug. 19, 1799.

Samuel and Sophia. Children: Samuel W., July 12, 1810; Elisabeth, July 28, 1812; Mary Jane, Sept. 3, 1814; Sarah, Mar. 11, 1820; Benjamin F., May 16, 1822.

Samuel and Martha. Children: Sarah B., 1733; Elisabeth, May 29, 1733; Joseph, Nov. 26, 1737; Adam, Apr. 17, 1740; Jannet, Apr. 17, 1742; Nansey, June 2, 1744; Mary, Sept. 9, 1746; Robert, Feb. 10, 1748; Martha, Mar. 17, 1750.

Samuel and Nancy. Children: Isaiah, Oct. 4, 1807; Hannah J., Dec. 25, 1805; John M., Oct. 10, 1808; Robert, Dec. 2, 1810.

Samuel, b. May 25, 1777, son of Robert, and Nancy Humphrey, b. Dec. 7, 1779. Children: Isaiah, Oct. 4, 1807; Hannah Jane, Dec. 23, 1805; Robert, Dec. 17, 1809; Nancy Humphrey, Nov. 6, 1811; Martha Boyd, May 15, 1813; Samuel Ficher, June 11, 1820; Daniel Dana, July 17, 1823; Fannie M., Oct. 1, 1826.

Zoe Ann. Dau.: Clara Dilla, Aug. 13, 1843; Ransom Flanders, one-half bro., Oct. 7, 1849.

Dickman, Thomas and Polly. Dau.: Bartrieth, Oct. 12, 1772.

Dill, James W. and Clara L. Dickey. Children: Leona, Mar. 24, 1898; James William, Nov. 30, 1899; DeWitt Clinton, Nov. 30, 1899; Rebecca Ann, Mar. 17, 1902.

Dinsmoor, James and Mary. Children: David, Sept. 14, 1772; Robert, June 6, 1774; James, Mar. 11, 1776; Samuel, Mar. 1, 1778; Agnes, June 23, 1782; John, July 7, 1784; Mary, Mar. 13, 1786; William, Sept. 23, 1789.

Dinsmore, Robert and Margaret. Son: William, May 10, 1731.

Doage, James and Jannet. Dau.: Sarah, Nov. 13, 1769.

Doak, James and Jenat. Children: Marget, Apr. 16, 1771; Martha, May 12, 1773; Fanny, July 3, 1775; Bettey, Mar. 8, 1781; James, June 12, 1783; John, June 30, 1785; Nancy, Sept. 13, 1788.

Dodge, John and Hannah. Son: John, June 30, 1812.

Malachi F. and Hannah P. Children: James Everett, Mar. 2, 1854; Frank Ellsworth, Sept. 23, 1862.

Parker and Marey. Children: Edner, Nov. 27, 1771; Martha, Jan. 22, 1774; Mary, Feb. 12, 1776; Sarah, Mar. 6, 1778; Alice, June 1, 1780; Abigall, Jan. 16, 1783; Elisabeth, June 25, 1785; Joseph, Sept. 23, 1789; Ledia, Nov. 18, 1790.

Samuel and Agness. Children: Sarah, Feb. 1, 1772; John, July 21, 1774; Samuel, Apr. 30, 1777.

Samuel and Anar. Children: Susana, Aug. 4, 1762; Davidlow, Dec. 14, 1765; Joshua, Feb. 27, 1767.

Doherty, Charles P. and Nellie A. Robie. Dau., May 29, 1897.

James T. and Cevie C. Towne. Dau.: Celia Ann, May 1, 1890.

Doiron, Moses and Caroline Peters. Children: Arthur, Feb. 4, 1909; Francis Theodore, Jan. 22, 1910.

Doland, John, b. June 22, 1803.

Dooley, Frank J. and Lydia M. Children: Son, July 4, 1876; Bertha Jane, July 4, 1876; ch., Apr. 19, 1881.

James, b. Oct. 11, 1831, in Ireland, and Martha J. Goodwin, b. Oct. 26, 1839. Children: Frank J., Oct. 8, 1852; Clara A., Mar. 19, 1860; Ella J., Jan. 11, 1862; Ida A., Sept. 3, 1864; George N., Jan. 1, 1871; Martha L., Feb. 28, 1874; Charles James, Dec. 8, 1883.

Dougan, Alexander and Annie Bennett. Dau., Apr. 1, 1907.

Douragh, Charles and Sarah. Son: Thomas, Oct. 7, 1740.

Dow, John, b. May 1, 1850.

Drucher, Walter A. and Edith A. Children: Lottie A., Sept. 8, 1883; Lora A., Sept. 8, 1883.

Dubeau, Joseph T., b. Apr. 18, 1858, St. Croix, Ca., and Lulu E. (Pike), b. June 24, 1875, Marshfield, Vt.; 2d wife, m. in 1898. Children: Wilma E., Oct. 4, 1892, by 1st wife; Joseph D., May 6, 1899, by 2d wife.

Dufraine, Herman Nigilde and ——— L. Girard. Children: Herman Nigilde, Apr. 16, 1902; Celeste P., Feb. 25, 1908.

Duglass, John and Mary. Children: James, Mar. 25, 1738; John, Mar. 25, 1740; Mary, Aug. 23, 1742.

Duncan, George and Mary. Children: Elisabeth, June 9, 1755; Rachell, July 9, 1759; Ester, Sept. 25, 1762; Rosanna, Dec. 28, 1764; George, June 21, 1767; Mary, Jan. 23, 1769; Sarah Todd, Nov. 12, 1771.

John and Jane. Children: Hannah, Apr. 26, 1798; Mary, May 9, 1800.

Dunlap, James and Sarah. Son: James, Mar. 5, 1732.

Dunton, George S., b. Feb. 12, 1852, and Ella, b. Feb. 20, 1855. Children: Harvey H., May 23, 1881; Bertha B., July 17, 1885.

Durant, George W. and Georgianna. Dau., Apr. 3, 1885.

Durham, Jonathan and Mary. Children: David, Dec. 30, 1740; Jonathan, Dec. 30, 1740.

Dustin, ——— and Ida M. Mullins. Dau.: Edith L.; m. Seth W. Wright, Manchester, N. H. (See Mullins.)

Dwinal (Dwinnel), John and Elisabeth. Children: Sally, July 30, 1777; Polly, Mar. 26, 1779; John, Sept. 24, 1782; Patty, May 24, 1785; Hannah, June 23, 1788.

Eaton, Joseph, son of Joseph, b. Feb. 27, 1839, and Rhoda A. (Weed), b. July 6, 1832. Son: William J., Dec. 27, 1866.

William J. and Gertie Speare. Dau.: Vivian Gertrude, Apr. 27, 1891.

Eayrs or **Eayres,** James and Jenat. Son: William, Apr. 5, 1765.

Edeson, William and Elenor. Dau.: Elenor, May 29, 1754.

Edwards, Charles E. and Mary E. Quarmby. Dau.: Helen Delicia, Apr. 26, 1903.

Ela, David W. and Martha E. Children: Anna Belle, Feb. 25, 1884; Edward Chester, Dec. 25, 1888; Dollie Mildred, Mar. 4, 1895.

Edward, b. Mar., 1780, and Mary Dickey, b. Mar. 20, 1782. Children: Samuel D., Jan. 29, 1816; Mary, Aug. 16, 1819.

Edward and Hannah. Children: Nanne, May 10, 1774; Sarah, Apr. 5, 1777; Edward, Feb. 26, 1780.

Ela, Edward and Sarah Page. Son: Edward P., Jan. 6, 1812.
Edward P. and Isabel (Gregg), b. July, 1816. Children: Samuel G., Sept. 17, 1845; George E., Nov. 13, 1847; David Willis, May 3, 1849; John A., Oct. 27, 1857.
George E. and M. Elisabeth Low. Children: George Ed- May Hartford, b. July 12, 1872, Londonderry, N. H.
Isabel (Gregg), b. July, 1816.

Ellis, Everett Burley, b. Oct. 20, 1864, Brentwood, N. H., and Mary Estella (Fitts), b. Sept. 17, 1866, Dunbarton, N. H. Children: Annie May, May 6, 1888, Dunbarton, N. H.; Myron Peasley, May 23, 1890, Londonderry, N. H.; ch., Jan. 1, 1892; Evelyn Belle, Apr. 23, 1893; John Oscar, Aug. 18, 1895; Ralph Everett, July 8, 1897; Laura Hattie, Aug. 23, 1899; Olive Estella, Apr. 11, 1902; Viola Perkins, Dec. 12, 1904; Bernard Sheridan, Sept. 22, 1906; Clifton Fitts, July 2, 1907.
George Ellsworth, b. Oct. 11, 1868, Bow, N. H., and Annie May (Hartford), b. July 12, 1872, Londonderry, N. H. Children: Ethel May, Feb. 25, 1894; Emma Hartford, June 7, 1876; Howard Ellsworth, Mar. 31, 1898; Florence Eleanor, Feb. 3, 1901.
Orrion P. and Mary E. Woodbury. Son: Clarence Woodbury, May 15, 1893.

Emerson, Mary Ann, and Charles E. Courreur. Dau.: Hester, m. George A. Hall, Manchester, N. H.
Susan D., and Thomas B. Platts. Children: Frank G. and Charles Wesley.
William P. and Mary A. Children: Sarah H., Nov. 18, 1853; dau., Nov. 18, 1854.
William P., b. 1807, and Jane (McDuffee), 1st wife, m. at Auburn, N. H. Children: Charles, b. at Auburn, N. H., has children; Stephen DeKata, b. in Auburn, N. H., has children; Susan D. m. Thomas Platts, 1st hus., and Charles Clement, 2d hus., res. Manchester, N. H.; Frank, b. in Londonderry.
William P. m., 2d wife, Mary Ann Manter, July 8, 1848. Eight children: Isabel, b. 1849, m. George Wells, had two sons; Mary Ann, b. June 28, 1850, m. Charles E. Courreur, one dau.; William P., Jr., m. in Maine, one son; Sarah H., b. 1853, m. Frank Proctor, one son; John P. m. twice, no children; Adeline m. George Webster, one son; Ida m. Oscar Griffin of Derry, N. H., no children; Clara m. Charles White of Amherst, N. H., no children.

Emery, Harry A. and Lydia E. Son, June 3, 1870.
John and Susanna. Children: Lydeah, Aug. 19, 1784; John, July 15, 1788.

Emery, John R. and Esther W. Children: Nelson White, May, 1853; ——, Oct. 9, 1862; Mary Elisabeth, 1860. (See White record.)

Sarah M., b. May 15, 1823.

Estey, Daniel, b. Apr. 8, 1808, and Rebecca (Hawkins), b. Apr. 23, 1807. Children: Daniel Milton, Dec. 21, 1835; George Franklin, Aug. 5, 1837; Horace Peabody, Mar. 2, 1839; Harriet Emeline, Apr. 21, 1840; John Crowell, Feb. 23, 1842; Charles Enos, May 27, 1843; Stephen Augustus, Nov. 1, 1844; Hannah Jane, July 12, 1846.

George and ——. Children: Georgia Annah, Jan. 5, 1862; Ida Frances, July 3, 1866.

Horace and Nancy. Dau.: Mary Eliza, Mar. 12, 1861.

Stephen and Lizzie. Son: Arthur Henry, Sept. 2, 1889.

Evans, Arthur L. and Anna Mabel (Wing), b. June 25, 1875. Children: Ruth Augusta, Mar. 14, 1897; Paul Blodgett, Mar. 13, 1900; Read Gage, July 14, 1902; Warren Arthur, Oct. 21, 1904; Katheryn Bertha, Nov. 28, 1906; Kenneth, Jan. 9, 1909.

Oliver Dodge, b. Jan. 14, 1845, and Augusta W. (Blodgett), b. Apr. 24, 1847. Children: Arthur Loren, May 4, 1872; Myron Isaac, Sept. 8, 1874; Bertha Augusta, Jan. 19, 1881.

Myron Isaac, b. Sept. 8, 1874, and Margaret Drysdale, b. Dec. 7, 1875. Children: Oliver Drysdale, Dec. 10, 1898; Sheridan Blodgett, Apr. 15, 1900; Russell Myron, Dec. 13, 1901; Reginald Lewis, Nov. 30, 1903.

Eyres, William and Jean. Son, Sept. 14, 1729.

Farley, Augustus L., b. Apr. 25, 1833, and ——. Dau., Sept. 17, 1859.

Feagan, Charles and Mary. Children: Dau., July 27, 1860; son, May 7, 1862.

Fellows, Almus W. and Georgia Lemere. Children: George Warren, Feb. 8, 1899; Edith Ruth, Aug. 13, 1900.

Augustus B. and Anna B. Wiley. Children: Relph Edward, Sept. 24, 1893; Berttie May, Sept. 9, 1880.

Fenton, Lander and Rosa B. Elkins. Child, Oct. 18, 1892.

Moody W. and Mary R. Lafonte. Dau.: Bertha Alice, Dec. 10, 1904.

Fisher, Ebenezer and Polly. Children: Abigail Ellis, Oct. 17, 1798; Amelia, Dec. 22, 1799; Samuel, Dec. 1, 1801; Ellis, Dec. 2, 1803; Maria, Dec. 8, 1808.

John and Betsey. Children: Lucy Chickering, Sept. 4, 1799; Betsey Dean, Apr. 15, 1801; Nathaniel Dean, Mar. 15, 1804; John, May 13, 1806; Samuel, May 8, 1808; Phinehas, Dec. 6, 1810; James P., Jan. 1, 1813; Caleb Ellis, May 13, 1815; Mary, May 4, 1817.

Fisher, Samuel and Sarah. Children: Mary, May 6, 1757; Samuel, Aug. 26, 1758; Margaret, Apr. 18, 1760; William, Dec. 1, 1762; Abenezer, Apr. 9, 1764; Martha, Jan. 14, 1766; John, Jan. 9, 1769.

Fisk, William F. and Estella A. Cleveland. Dau.: Ida Merrill, Sept. 23, 1899.

Fitts, Currier and Sally. Son: George, June 23, 1800.

Jesse L. and Lila Prime. Children: George Lewis, Aug. 19, 1904; ch., Nov. 17, 1905.

Fitzgerald, George and Martha. Children: Alice, Nov. 24, 1880; dau., Dec. 24, 1882.

George m. Martha E. Watts, Derry, N. H. Four daus. and one son. (See Watts.)

Flanders, Charles Jaqueth, b. 1819, Hebron, N. H.

Frank B. and Sarah A. (Livengood). Children: Clara E., May 12, 1884; Nute Boyce, Mar. 17, 1887; Esther, Feb. 9, 1893; Paul B., May 22, 1899.

Mark B. and Etta P. (Hurlburt). Dau.: Etta W.

Reuben W. and Priscilla. Son: Mark B., Jan. 14, 1863.

Samuel B. and Emily. Children: Cylinda or Salinda C., Mar. 26, 1837; Reuben W., Feb. 14, 1839; Simeon D., Jan. 25, 1841; Hannah F., June 9, 1844; Emily Josephine, Mar. 19, 1847; Clara L. M., Oct. 13, 1849; Frank B., July 25, 1855.

Samuel B., b. Sept. 7, 1811, Dunbarton, N. H., and Emily (Colby), b. Dec. 2, 1813.

Zoe Ann. Children: Clara Dilla, Aug. 13, 1843; Ransom B., Oct. 7, 1849.

Fling, Charles H. and Jennie W. (Flannigan). Children: May, Apr. 30, 1892; Clifton, Mar. 7, 1894.

Daniel W. and Asenath (Patten), 1st wife, b. Nov. 24, 1818. Children: John P., Mar. 22, 1848; Ida Gertrude, July 18, 1855.

John W., b. July 14, 1824, and Mary A. (Goodwin), b. Feb. 16, 1837. Children: Fannie M., July 4, 1858; Martha E., June 19, 1861; Minnie M., Oct. 14, 1864; Charles H., Jan. 14, 1867; son, Mar. 17, 1869; Emma E., Dec. 19, 1870.

William M., b. 1785, and Susanna, b. 1787. Children: Edmond, 1808; Daniel W., 1811; Rachel, 1812; Wealthy, Sept. 26, 1814; William M., 1820; Charles W., Jan. 8, 1820; Rufus, 1823; John W., July 14, 1824.

Flood, Addie Ella, wife of Trueworthy D. Chase, Jr., b. Feb. 5, 1866.

Floyd, Carl and Gertrude E. Simpson. Children: Mary Eliza, Dec. 16, 1907; Elwin Stanley, Feb. 4, 1910, 4th ch.

James K. and Hattie (Crowell). Son, Feb. 3, 1872.

Follansbee, Edwin and Esther H. Children: Charles E., Mar. 18, 1846; Estella A., May 17, 1856; Mary A., Dec. 6, 1858.

John, Jr., and Mary A. Child, Sept. 18, 1852.

Foster, Alfred and Pauline Hausell. Dau.: Pauline R., Oct. 7, 1906.

Obediah R. and Harriet E. Children: Harriet M., Feb. 26, 1844; Charles F., June 20, 1845; Herbert A., Dec. 5, 1848; Emma A., Jan. 23, 1856.

Phinehas and Huldah C. Sampson, b. July 30, 1871. (See Sampson.)

William and Phebe. Children: Phebe Barker, Nov. 24, 1806; Israel, Nov. 26, 1809.

Foye, E. Elmer. m. Lura B. Wilson, Sept. 21, 1893. Dau.: Dorothy C., Mar. 29, 1900. (See Wilson.)

Franklin, ——— and Maria. Dau.: Myra Louise, Dec. 19, 1892.

Friend, George E. and Ina V. Fletcher. Dau.: Vera, Dec. 31, 1900.

Furber, Edward, b. 1849, and Eliza Sprague, b. 1848; m. Feb., 1876; came to Londonderry from Maine in 1878. Children: Mayola F., Aug. 18, 1877, in Me.; dau., Feb. 6, 1879; Mattie Bertha, Jan. 21, 1881; Ida Bell, July 20, 1883; Edwina E., Oct. 3, 1887.

Frank O. and ———. Children: Charles F., Apr. 16, 1879; Lilly May, June 15, 1881; Harry Olwin, Feb. 8, 1886.

John S., b. Oct. 14, 1819, and Laura J. (Wallace), b. Oct. 20, 1621. Children: John W., Aug. 6, 1846; Laura Jane, Oct. 7, 1847; Lewis Irving, Oct. 5, 1848; Oscar E., June 11, 1851; Frank Olwin, Aug. 26, 1852; Elbridge Wallace, Mar. 30, 1863.

Lewis I. and ———. Children: George Elbridge, Apr. 11, 1884; Frank Lewis, Apr. 11, 1884; Edgar Lewis, Mar. 17, 1886.

Oscar E. and ———. Children: Edith, June 21, 1884; Mabelle, Feb. 1, 1889.

Gage, Billy and Nancy. Children: William Washington, Dec. 30, 1818; Leander, Oct. 2, 1820; Abigail, June 20, 1822; Aaron H., Nov. 13, 1824.

Billy R. and Rebekah. Son: Charles, Mar. 5, 1815.

John and Martha T. Children: Dau., Jan. 17, 1855; Nancy J., June 9, 1861; Annie, Sept. 29, 1856.

Richard and Jane. Children: William, Feb. 12, 1803; Eliza Kimball, June 10, 1805; Tenney Kimball, Feb. 29, 1808; Almira, June 10, 1810.

Gage, W. W. and Carrie (Raymond). Children: Guy Elliott, Feb. 27, 1907; dau., Aug. 6, 1908; dau., Nov. 2, 1909.

W. W. and Hattie E. (Roach). Children: Ch., Mar. 3, 1892; ch., Mar. 14, 1894. (Both stillborn.)

William H., b. Feb. 4, 1846; m. Lucelia E. Adams, Dec. 13, 1871; no children. (See Adams.)

Galbien, Richard and E. Giouet. Son, Mar. 12, 1907.

Galvin, Catherine, b. Apr. 10, 1888.

Jeremiah L., June 10, 1884.

Gardner, Charles H. and Carrie D. Son, Oct. 17, 1887.

Elisabeth S. m. Walter Libby Blenns Oct. 12, 1881. He was b. Feb. 9, 1848. Res. Manchester, N. H. No children.

Lorenzo and Susan. Children: Dau., Dec. 9, 1860; son, June 16, 1863; son, Sept. 11, 1867.

Stephen and Mary P. Children: Charles N., Jan. 30, 1849; Elisabeth, Oct. 24, 1852.

Stephen and Mary P. Smith, Aug. 31, 1845. (See Smith rec.)

Garvin or **Garven,** Arthur O. and Hattie G. Children: Olwin; Frank B., July 1, 1883.

Augustus F. and Susan F. Poor. Dau.: Georgietta, Sept., 1868.

Benjamin F. and Nancy. Children: Augustus F., Feb. 24, 1842; Eldora, Apr. 19, 1843; Norman C., Aug. 12, 1846; Elwyn W., Apr. 6, 1857; Capt. George S., Mar. 18, 1845; Clarence N., Jan. 7, 1854; Arthur O., Feb. 11, 1862.

Clarence N. and Abbie D. Wilson; m. Feb., 1872. Children: Fred Elwyn, July 5, 1873; Lilla Belle, Nov. 29, 1876; Chester Arthur, May 3, 1886.

Fred E. and Emma Provencher. Children: Dau., May 11, 1895; son, June 22, 1896; Beatrice Nancy, Aug. 7, 1900.

Capt. George S. and Laura J. Furber. Son: George Olwin. Sept. 27, 1880.

Georgietta and William Proctor. Dau.: Mabel.

Jacob, b. 1770, and Margaret Watts, b. 1772. Children: Tamar, Feb. 24, 1793; Betsey, Mar. 18, 1795; Mary, Dec. 2, 1796; Thirsey, Feb. 9, 1799; Perses, May 19, 1801; Tamar, Sept. 22, 1803; Clarisa, Feb. 10, 1806; Hasen, Apr. 3, 1808; Nelson, Apr. 17, 1810; Zora or Lora, Oct. 3, 1812; Rachel, Apr. 11, 1815; Benjamin F., Feb. 16, 1820.

Gayne, George F. and Beatrice Ashford. Children: George Francis, Sept. 6, 1908; Ernest James, Aug. 20, 1909.

Gembell, William and Elisabeth. Dau.: Betty, Mar. 1, 1734–5.

George, George W., b. Nov., 1817.

Gibson, John Calvin, b. July 8, 1831, and Sarah Jane White, b. Apr. 10, 1842. Children: Grace Harriet, May 13, 1869; Paul, June 9, 1870; John Cardinal, Nov. 3, 1873; Robert Guy, Apr. 14, 1875; Anna Florence, Apr. 20, 1877; Alice Helen, June 24, 1879; Hiram Cutler, Oct. 14, 1882.

Gilchrist, George, b. July 14, 1822.

Gilcreast, David and Sarah. Children: David, Apr. 14, 1807; James M., Oct. 24, 1813; Sarah, Sept. 5, 1816; John, July 13, 1819; Samuel, Nov. 7, 1822.

David, Jr., and Sally. Children: Sarah Jane, Mar. 12, 1832; Mary Adeline, Nov. 4, 1833; Frederick Augustus, Mar. 13, 1835; Ann Eliza, Oct. 7, 1842; Nancy A., Apr. 29, 1848.

Fred A. and Mary. Dau., June 2, 1872.

James Madison and Eveline Peabody. Children: Eugene M., June 22, 1848; Ella Eliza, Aug. 12, 1850; John P., Sept. 21, 1852; Clara J., Sept. 23, 1854; Abbie F., Aug. 27, 1856; Georgie A., Nov. 28, 1858; Lafarest J., June, 1860.

John and Miranda (Peabody), b. Mar. 19, 1827. Dau., Apr. 11, 1868.

John P. and Emma Cressey. Children: Ernest E., Oct., 1886; Abbie A., 1888; Ralph H., 1892.

John R. and Anna L. Children: Dau., Nov. 2, 1883; son, Oct. 8, 1885; dau., Nov. 26, 1886; son, Dec. 29, 1888.

Samuel and Nancy Proctor, b. Apr. 5, 1818. Children: Ella A., Jan. 3, 1850; Elwin A., Jan. 3, 1850; Emma Florence, Dec. 6, 1853.

Giles, Benjamin and Jenny. Children: John, Feb. 18, 1799; Sophia, Oct. 3, 1800.

John and Mary. Children: Hannah, Feb. 12, 1777; Nathaneal, Apr. 22, 1780.

Gill, Andrew and Mary. Children: Son, Sept. 8, 1853; son, Dec. 26, 1855.

Gilman, Henry F. and Lydia. Dau.: Helen, Feb. 17, 1845.

Gillmore, Jonathan and Elisabeth. Children: James, Jan. 28, 1758; Genet, Nov. 11, 1759; David, Aug. 10, 1761; Elisabeth, Oct. 8, 1763; Robert, Mar. 3, 1765; Ann, Feb. 11, 1767; Mary Ann, May 28, 1769; William, Apr. 8, 1771.

Gilmor, Robert and Elisabeth. Children: John, May 3, 1737; Rodger, July 31, 1739; Mirem, Sept. 27, 1742; Jamima, Feb. 3, 1744; Robert, July 4, 1749; William, Nov. 22, 1751.

Gilmore, James and Jean. Children: Joan, Dec. 27, 1721; Margaret, Apr. 24, 1724; John, Aug. 26, 1726; Jonathan, Mar. 11, 1728–9; Elisabeth, Mar. 12, 1730–31.

Gilmore, Robert and Ann. Children: James, Sept. 20, 1731; Elisabeth, May 1, 1733.

William and Elisabeth. Children: William, Oct. 1, 1721; son, Aug. 10, 1728; Robert, May 23, 1724; Jean, July 23, 1726; Mary, Jan. 8, 1730–31.

Giouet, Fred and Catharine. Son: William R., June 24, 1908.

Girard, Dominick and Victoria Baudien. Son: Herman Walter, Aug. 9, 1903.

Napoleon and Cora Saiver. Son: Leo Thedo, Apr. 6, 1903.

Glidden, J. A. R. and Caroline E. Whidden. Children: Abbie A., 1853; William D., 1854; A. Eugene, 1858; Martha; James, 1863.

Goff or **Goffe,** John and ———. Children: John, Ma.r 16, 1700–1; Hannah, Feb. 4, 1705–6; Sarah, Aug. 19, 1709; Mary, Apr. 12, 1711.

John and Hanna. Children: Hanna, Jan. 16, 1723–4; Esther, Feb. 15, 1725–6; son, Feb. 17, 1727–8; Marrey, June 12, 1730.

John Henry and Ina Ada Goule. Son: John Wesley, Nov. 21, 1909.

Gooden, Charles and Alma. Son, Apr. 22, 1870.

——— and Clara M. Dau., Feb. 27, 1863.

Daniel and Abigail. Children: Ira Fremont, Oct. 13, 1856; John H. S., Sept. 21, 1859; Abbie A., Nov. 27, 1861.

David and Mary. Children: Eliza Jones, May 21, 1831; Sarah Hale, Apr. 11, 1833; Harriet, Oct. 12, 1835; Ann Maria, Sept. 28, 1836; David Tenney, July 21, 1838; Mary, Dec. 4, 1839; Charles, Sept. 24, 1842.

George N. and Susan B. Children: Elbridge N., Mar. 22, 1874; Agnes S., Mar. 20, 1877; Martha, 1878.

Joseph S. and Fannie S. Children: Son, June 22, 1877; Clarence W., June 10, 1878; Bertha Mabel, Dec. 8, 1880.

Goodhue, Ralph H., b. in Clinton, Me., on Dec. 26, 1845, and Juline F. Miner, b. July 26, 1847, at Canaan, N. H. Children: Fred Miner, May 17, 1871; son, July 17, 1873; Elsie Christine, Dec. 20, 1874; Ralph Worthen, May 20, 1876; Amy Helen, Dec. 28, 1878.

Goodwin, Daniel W. and Sarah A. Dau.: Sarah Agnes, Mar. 23, 1888.

David T. and Arabella L. Son, Oct. 26, 1876.

Joseph S. and Maria L. Palmer. Children: Alice May, Feb. 7, 1889; Loretta Frances, May 10, 1894; stillborn dau., May 10, 1894.

Joshua and Rebecca. Children: Joshua, Jr., Nov. 13, 1801; David, Aug. 22, 1803.

Goodwin, Joshua and Elisabeth. Children: Josiah, Nov. 28, 1807; Rev. Daniel, Jan. 25, 1809; Rebecca, Nov. 25, 1810.

Joshua, Jr., b. Nov. 13, 1801, and Polly Mary Jones, b. Jan. 13, 1804. Children: Rebecca J., Dec. 24, 1832; Amos J., Mar. 6, 1835; Mary Ann, Feb. 16, 1837; Martha Jane, Oct. 26, 1839; Clara Melvina, Sept. 18, 1842; George Newman, Jan. 31, 1848.

Josiah and Esther. Children: Daniel, Sept. 9, 1832; Henry, Mar. 30, 1835; John, May 23, 1838; Esther M., Feb. 3, 1841; Joseph Stone, Aug. 31, 1846.

Henry and Mary Ann Moar. Son: Arthur Worthington, Dec. 5, 1865. (See Moar.)

Gordon, Charles H. and Caroline. Child: Stillborn son, Jan. 9, 1883.

Irving D. and Anna M. Payne. Son: Everett P., Mar. 29, 1896.

Gould, Solon S., b. Dec. 22, 1826, and Lucy M. Boyd, b. Oct. 11, 1846. Son: Norman Willis, Nov. 23, 1875 (?).

Graham, Joseph H. and Mary J. Ransom. Dau., Mar. 24, 1894.

Joseph H. and Mary G. Hansel. Children: Viola Gertrude, Jan. 5, 1903; Robert V., Apr. 5, 1908.

Levi C. and Dorcas Avery. (See Avery record.)

Graves, Samuel and Sara. Children: Sara, Dec. 17, 1709; Samuel, Apr. 16, 1711; James, Apr. 22, 1714; Anna, July 26, 1716; Ebenezer, July 2, 172–; Lydia, July 9, 1724.

Samuel and Martha. Children: Martha, July 16, 1726; Mary, July 21, 1729.

Greeley, Alfred and Mary. Children: Dau., July 20, 1855; son, Oct. 3, 1860.

Alfred D., b. 1816, and Lucy Senter, b. 1820 (1st wife). Children: George A., 1842; Lucy M., 1845; Francis O., 1847.

Alfred D. and Ann Dart, b. 1822 (2nd wife). Children: Horace H., 1851; Ella J., 1852; Sarah A., 1854; Mary E., 1855; John W., 1857; Charles E., 1860; George E., 1863; Frank L., 1867; Flora P., 1869.

George W., b. Oct. 3, 1830, at Amherst, N. H., and Alice Phillips (Alley), b. Jan. 10, 1824, at Lynn, Mass. Children: Hannah Jane, May 31, 1847; Sarah Arvilla, Apr. 28, 1850, in Derry, N. H.; Charles Sylvester, Nov. 27, 1852, in Derry, N. H.; Herbert Alley, Dec. 16, 1854; Franklin Perkans, Oct. 21, 1860, Acworth, N. H.

Greeley, Charles E. and Phebe A. Church, b. 1869. Children: George A., 1888; Perley R., Sept. 27, 1889; Lettie M., Feb. 18, 1891; Eva B., May 3, 1893; Blanche M., Apr. 30, 1894; Hazel C., Aug. 6, 1899; Rose L., June 11, 1904; Lena H., July 28, 1906; Ethel G., 1908.

Charles S. and Hattie A. Allen, b. Jan. 8, 1859. Children: Howard Franklin, July 19, 1881; Arvilla May, Oct. 2, 1883; Katherine, Aug. 10, 1888; Edith Allen, Oct. 30, 1892; George Woodburn, Dec. 10, 1901.

Elbridge G., b. June 15, 1816, and Julia A. Blood, b. Apr. 19, 1816. Children: Martha A., Feb. 26, 1843; Adeline, May 5, 1848; Emeline B., Nov. 9, 1854.

Horace, b. Feb. 3, 1811, Amherst, N. H. (Eminent journalist.)

Dea. John W., son of Dustin and Sarah Woodburn, b. Mar. 25, 1819, and ——— Dodge, b. July 31, 1822. Son: Eugene O., Mar. 19, 1852.

John W. and Carrie J. Osborne. Children: Dau., Oct. 6, 1889; dau., July 23, 1892; Arthur Harry, Apr. 25, 1896.

John J. and Effie R. Duffy. Dau.: Jennie, July 10, 1910.

Greenough, George A. and Fannie A. Richardson. Dau.: Hattie Clare, June 3, 1880. (See Richardson.)

Gregg, David A. and Martha H. Children: Joseph A., Jan. 27, 1819; Martha H., Dec. 14, 1821; James B., May 5, 1824; Frances P., May 11, 1826.

James and Margaret. Dau.: Lydia, Nov. 3, 1798.

Prof. Jarvis, son of Dea. James, b. Sept., 1808, and Alice Webster, 1836, niece of Daniel Webster.

John and Agnes. Children: John, May 7, 1728; William, Oct. 23, 1730; Elisabeth, Nov. 27, 1732; Joseph, Dec. 10, 1741; Benjamin, Dec. 10, 1743.

John and Nancy. Children: James, Dec. 9, 1725; Hugh, Dec. 9, 1725.

John and Mary. Children: Jenny, Aug. 12, 1799; Sylvester, Jan. 14, 1801; Stephen, Nov. 10, 1803; Mary, May 26, 1806; Paulina, May 9, 1809.

Joseph and Lucy. Dau.: Lucy, Mar. 24, 1821.

Joseph and Mary. Children: Sally Malvina, May 3, 1806; Charles, Sept. 6, 1809; Susanna, June 15, 1812; Joseph Sept. 30, 1814; Catharine, May 7, 1818.

Joseph and Susannah. Children: Anna, Dec. 22, 1765 Margaret, Nov. 28, 1767; Susannah, Nov. 19, 1770; Elisabeth, Mar. 3, 1773; John, July 2, 1775; Nathaniel, July 16, 1777; Joseph, July 22, 1779; David A., Mar. 12, 1788

Samuel and Mary. Son: James, Feb. 1, 1732-3.

Gregg, William and Jenat. Children: James, June 15, 1726; dau., Mar. 1, 1727–8; Jenat, Nov. 3, 1760.
William, son of Capt. John, b. Oct. 3, 1730.

Griffin, Daniel and ———. Son, Apr. 11, 1871.
Daniel and Ella M. Dau.: Ella May, June 1, 1879.
Daniel and Martha. Dau.: Ada B., May 10, 1881.
Estes J. and Laura W. Parshley. Son: Clarence E., Feb. 19, 1908.
Fidelia, b. Dec. 17, 1840.
Frank and Margaret Drea. Children: Ann, Jan. 28, 1893; Ellen, Dec. 8, 1896; Francis, Jan. 31, 1898; Charles, July 9, 1899; Treasa, Oct. 7, 1900; son, Jan. 4, 1902; stillborn son, Oct. 21, 1903; dau., Apr. 4, 1906.
Frederick and Elenor. Son, Sept. 16, 1861.
John and Abigail. Dau., Feb. 22, 1853.
Moses and Elizabeth M. Children: Jonathan, Mar. 17, 1800; George F., Jan. 6, 1802; Moses, July 5, 1803.
Rufus, b. Feb. 25, 1831, and Harriet D. Major, b. Feb. 13, 1826.
Thomas and Polly. Children: Louisa, Nov. 4, 1804; Hannah H., June 22, 1806.

Gutterson, Eli S., b. July 19, 1818.

Hadley, Rodney and Lydia. Son: Harry A., Nov. 2, 1871.

Hale, Etta M., wife of Samuel C., b. Dec. 6, 1851.

Hall, Charles F. and Elvira S. Son, May 31, 1873.
George A., b. July 24, 1869, and Hester C. Cousens, b. Dec. 11, 1871. Children: Olive Marion, May 26, 1895; Ralph Edwin, Dec. 8, 1896; John Parker, May 27, 1898; Charles Henry, Dec. 16, 1902; George Leon, Dec. 26, 1904; Mary Elisabeth, Feb. 11, 1907; Grace Mildred, June 14, 1909.
Henry R. and Ella M. Watts, 1st wife, b. Jan. 23, 1856. Dau.: Elsie L., Feb. 18, 1887.
Robert, son of Samuel, b. in Manchester in 1853.
Robert, son of Samuel, b. Mar. 11, 1819.
Robert and Nancy Wheeler. Children: Robert S., Apr. 7, 1848; Henry R., July 6, 1853.
Robert S. and Mary F. C. March, b. Aug. 17, 1846. Children: Mary A., Sept. 30, 1873, in Iowa; Henry A., May 31, 1878, in Iowa.

Hamblett, Samuel B. and Annie M. Powell. Children: Bertha Margaret, Sept. 2, 1904; Bernice Annie, Aug. 11, 1905.

Hamlet, Augustus F. and Mary C. Children: Son, June 4, 1855; son, Nov. 28, 1861.
Howard and Lovina. Dau., May 10, 1870.

Handy, Frank and Mary F. Son: Frank M., Feb. 19, 1882.

Hardy, Aaron P., b. Oct. 8, 1815, and Delia W. Brickett. Children: George H., May 24, 1851; Harriet E., Jan. 17, 1854; John P., Sept. 13, 1855; Frank Aaron, Nov. 10, 1865.

Benjamin, b. July 2, 1802, and Clarrissa Parker, b. 1810. Children: Benjamin, Jr., Mar. 14, 1834; dau.; John, 1837; Lorenzo, May 29, 1841; Sylvester, 1843; Clarrissa, 1845.

Daniel, Aug. 25, 1769, and Sarah, b. May 1, 1777. Dau.: Harriet, 1798.

David and Sally. Dau.: Eliser, Jan. 8, 1803.

Frank, son of ———, and Clarrissa Hardy, b. 1887.

Frank A. and Fannie Ardelle Pike, b. 1872. Children: Aaron Parker, Nov. 5, 1895; dau., June 19, 1900; Frances Adams, Oct. 7, 1910.

George A., b. Jan. 1, 1843, and Etta J. Moar, b. May 20, 1848. Children: Charles A., Sept. 3, 1870; Freeman, Nov. 16, 1872; Fred M., July 11, 1875.

George H. and Ida J. Kendall, b. July, 1858. Children: Son, Nov. 25, 1884; Ethel H., Nov. 16, 1885.

John P. and Mattie E. Wiley, b. Mar. 9, 1859. Dau.: Inez Eva, Mar. 26, 1879.

William G., b. 1816, and Mary Whittier. Children: Mary A.; William D., 1849; John G., 1853.

Haron, John and Johanna. Son: William, Apr. 9, 1753.

Harrise, Edward and Abigail. Dau.: Betty, Feb. 1, 1779.

Harriman, Sarah, b. May 30, 1777.

Hart, John D. and Abbie A. Children: Dau. and son, no dates.

John W. and Mattie S. Hastings. Children: Willis Clay, Mar. 23, 1893; son, Nov. 12, 1894; Lyle Evans, Aug. 10, 1896.

Hartford, Frank S. and Gertrude I. Dau.: Beatrice Marion, May 29, 1905.

James Truman, b. Nov. 29, 1852, at Smithfields, Me., and Eleanor M. Smith, b. Dec. 29, 1853, at Londonderry. Children: Amra M., July 12, 1872; Lizzie, July 5, 1874; Ella, Mar. 29, 1877; Frank S., Apr. 9, 1882.

Walter F. and Mabel E. Richardson. Son: Theodore B., Oct. 24, 1910.

Hartop, Arthur and Annie E. Boles. Children: William Lionel, July 25, 1898; Arthur Daniel, Aug. 11, 1900; Frederick Winston, Apr. 22, 1904; Annie E., Sept. 1, 1906.

Ira White and Florence Hartop. Dau.: Ida Willena, Feb. 24, 1910.

Harvell, Lieut. Joseph, b. Feb. 16, 1788, and Mary L. Underwood, b. July 3, 1797. Children: Joseph, Jr., Jan. 7, 1818; Elisabeth Underwood, Nov. 18, 1821.

Harvell, Joseph, Jr., and Sarah H. Menter, b. Oct. 26, 1818. Children: Sarah J., Jan. 9, 1843; James Erving, July 8, 1845; Julia F., May 26, 1851; George Parker, Jan. 4, 1854; Marcia, April 30, 1847.

Harvey, Gilman, b. 1803, and Nancy, b. 1804. Children: John, 1824; Jonas, 1826; Gilman, 1828; Nancy; Sarah; Maria J., 1835; Warren, 1837; Cynthia; Eliza J., 1842; Josephine M.; Josiah A., 1847.

John, b. Dec. 14, 1787, and Rebecca Emerson, b. Nov. 11, 1790. Children: Sarah A., Nov. 28, 1813; Esther J., Dec. 9, 1815; Rebecca C., Jan. 2, 1822; Ephraim W., Dec. 12, 1824; John P., July 22, 1826; Rejina M., Mar. 7, 1829; Rachel M., Sept. 2, 1831; Jerome B., Feb. 8, 1834.

Jonas, b. July 11, 1777; Sally, 1st wife, b. 1781; Rachel, 2d wife, b. 1783; Rachel, 3d wife, b. Mar. 13, 1787.

Jonas, Jr., b. Jan. 1, 1809, and Sophronia, b. May 10, 1811.

Jonathan, b. 1795, and Susan, b. 1795. Son: Manas, 1833.

Rebekah, b. Jan. 2, 1822.

Sarah Ann, b. 1844.

Warren, b. 1837, and Josephine S. Dustin, 1st wife, b. 1846; Mary E. Cheever, 2d wife, b. 1856.

Warren and Mary. Dau.: Gracie A., 1866.

Haselton, David C. and Lillie Bell. Son, Feb. 21, 1882.

Hawkins, Harry Franklin and Bertha McAllister. Children: Harold Franklin, June 9, 1910; Dorothy Elisabeth, Aug. 1, 1911.

Hayes, Rev. Amasa A., b. Jan., 1798, in Granby, Conn.; ordained over West Parish, Londonderry, June 25, 1827.

Daniel W. and Sarah McGregor. Dau.: Hattie L., July 14, 1873.

Healey, Albert L. and Hattie F. Dau., Feb. 20, 1887.

Hebert, Joseph J. and Mary E. Bailey. Dau.: Licille Esther, July 9, 1910.

Hemphill, Nathaniel and Isabella. Children: Robert, May 24, 1731; Isabella, Apr. 4, 1733; Hanna, May 1, 1735; Nathaniel, May 12, 1737.

Herbert, Thomas W. and Hattie. Dau., Mar. 22, 1869.

Herrick, Nehemiah and Sarah. Children: Mary, May 17, 1808; James D., Apr. 20, 1810; Jonathan S., Apr. 20, 1810.

Hicks, Henry, son of Robert and Ann Loyd, b. Sept. 7, 1807, Norfolk, Eng., and Susanna O. Greve, b. Jan. 3, 1816, in England. Children: Israel F., Feb. 22, 1839, at Derby, Vt.; Elisabeth B., Nov. 5, 1842, at Derby, Vt.; Harris L., May 25, 1857, at Derby, Vt.

Israel F. and Eliza A. Upton. Son, Oct. 23, 1893.

Hill, Daniel C. and Violetta. Dau.: Lizzie Annie, Sept. 26, 1880.

James and Nabby. Children: Lucinda, Jan. 22, 1803; Moses, Nov. 5, 1705.

Robert M. and Zylpha J. Son, Jan. 31, 1886.

Hills, Gilbert, b. May 20, 1811, sheriff of Hillsborough Co., N. H., and Sarah J., b. 1820.

Hinckley, Owen, b. Oct. 3, 1832, at Monmouth, Me., and Carrie M. Simpson b. Oct. 14, 1846, New Castle.

Hobbs, Joseph and Mary. Children: Fanny, Dec. 17, 1799; Mary, Dec. 17, 1801.

Hogg, John and Mary. Children: Mary, July 15, 1743; Frances, Oct. 9, 1747; John, Sept. 25, 1753; Robert, July 10, 1756.

Thomas and Agnes. Children: John, Apr. 22, 1732; Joseph, Feb. 16, 1733–4.

William and Elisabeth. Children: John, Mar. 11, 1724–5; Thomas, July 23, 1726; ———, July 29, 1728; Alexander, June 17, 1732.

Holden, Charles A. and Mary E. Dau.: Flora M., June 24, 1873.

William G. and Eliza D. Dau.: Lucy E., Aug. 25, 1871.

Holmes, Abraham and Martha. Dau.: Mary, June 13, 1723.

John and Grizell. Children: Sarah, May 1, 1735; Margaret, Oct. 21, 1736; Abraham, May 18, 1738; Aeurs, June 15, 1740; Robert, Sept. 28, 1742; Mary, Nov. 4, 1744; Thomas, Dec. 9, 1746; Mereon, May 8, 1749; Martha, Nov. 14, 1752.

John and Sarah. Children: James, Apr. 14, 1811; Thomas, Mar. 16, 1813; Ann Davidson, Feb. 22, 1815.

Matthew and Betsey. Children: Matthew H., July 30, 1824; Lidia Ann, Jan. 14, 1826; Almira J., Sept. 11, 1827; Elisabeth F., July 10, 1829; Margarette P., Apr. 4, 1831; Mary Adams, Oct. 10, 1833.

Moses N. and Harriet A. Coffin. Children: William House, Apr. 16, 1860; Edwin Clarence, Aug. 3, 1862; Josephine Frances, Aug. 8, 1865; Walter Noyes, June 29, 1867; Milton Wilcox, Dec. 24, 1868; David Coffin, July 11, 1870; Lucy Jane, Nov. 10, 1872; Charles Franklin, Sept. 2, 1878.

M. Henry, b. July 30, 1824, and Hannah T. (Rowe), b. Aug. 3, 1825. Children: Etta M., Apr. 25, 1861; Addie M., Aug. 28, 1862; Joseph Matthew, Mar. 17, 1865; Gertrude, May 26, 1867; Katie L., Oct. 13, 1868.

Robert and Elisabeth Anderson. Son: Charles M., Apr. 10, 1820.

Holmes, Thomas and Margaret. Children: Sarah, Dec. 18, 1776; John, Dec. 19, 1779; Grizel, June 18, 1782; Peter, Oct. 10, 1783; Robert, Apr. 7, 1785; Margaret, Feb. 12, 1787; Thomas, Dec. 18, 1788; Abram, Oct. 13, 1791; James, Mar. 26, 1793; Matthew, Oct. 2, 1795; William Morrison, May 24, 1797; Jane Fullerton, Apr. 3, 1799.

Thomas M. and Georgia M. Spaulding, 1st wife, b. Dec. 25, 1844. Children: Charles H., Sept. 30, 1867; Arthur T., Oct. 15, 1869.

William A. and Frances. Dau., Aug. 15, 1854.

William and Mary. Children: John, Dec. 1, 1730; Robert, Aug. 16, 1734; Margaret, Oct. 18, 1736; Elisabeth, Jan. 5, 1739.

William M. and Judith N. Children: Moses Noyes, Mar. 24, 1834; Harriet S., Jan. 2, 1837; Lucy J., Jan. 18, 1839; William Frank, Jan. 1, 1841; Thomas M., Aug. 1, 1842; Judith F., Mar. 23, 1844.

Hopkins, James and Mary. Children: John, July 18, 1747; James, May 31, 1749; Robert, Nov. 1, 1750.

Jonathan and Elisabeth. Son: John, Mar. 18, 1730–31.

Horner, Thomas and Margaret. Dau.: Elisabeth, Jan. 2, 1726–7.

House, Rev. William and Fannie (Savage). Son: James S., Aug. 14, 1860.

Houston or **Hewston,** Samuel and Mary. Children: David, Dec. 27, 1719; John, Apr. 4, 1722; Agnas, Aug. 24, 172–; William, May 18, 1732; Joseph, Jan. 3, 1733–4; Robert, Feb. 24, 1737; Alexander, Nov. 26, 1738.

Hovey, Charlotte. Dau., Jan. 29, 1861.

John and Abigail (Dustin). Son: Albert G., July 11, 1824.

Howe, J. Madison and Alice M. Cross. Dau., Nov. 6, 1887.

Hoyt, Luke and Susan. Dau., Apr. 28, 1854.

Hubbard, Eugene A. and Mary A. Dau.: Flora Vina, Feb. 21, 1879.

Humphrey, James and Jean. Children: Nancy, Dec. 7, 1779; Hannah, Jan. 10, 1782; Samuel Fisher, Apr. 28, 1784; John, June 12, 1786; Jenny, May 20, 1788; Jonathan, July 19, 1790; Sally, Dec. 1, 1792; Jean, Jan 22. 1795.

Jonathan and Amelia. Children: Samuel F., May 8, 1822; Daniel, Sept. 4, 1823; Mary Elisabeth; Hannah Low; James Ebenezer; Lucy Almira, Sept. 11, 1831; John Calvin; Sarah Jane; George Ellis; Frank A.

William and Mary. Dau.: Mary, Feb. 1, 1729.

Huntee, Currier and Fanny. Dau.: Susan F., Nov. 5, 1851.
William C. and Lovilla E., b. May 2, 1842. Children: James E., Mar. 3, 1871; Charles M.

Huntress, Edward and Ella. Son: Joseph E., June 5, 1881.

Hurd, Charles, b. May 28, 1791, and Rachel Lovejoy, b. Apr. 16, 1797. Children: George, July 14, 1823; Charles, Jr., Jan. 5, 1822 (?); Henry L., Nov. 6, 1834.
Elmer E. and Effie Estella Loud. Dau.: Nancy Jane Woodburn, Apr. 27, 1903.
George and Nancy J. Woodburn, b. Mar. 13, 1834. Children: Florence, Apr. 10, 1851; Henry L., Aug. 7, 1852; Horace P., June 25, 1855; Walter, July 5, 1858; Elmer E., Mar. 18, 1861; George A., July 10, 1863; Nancy M., Nov. 26, 1869; Laura H., Jan. 19, 1873.

Irving, John H. and Mary Y. Kimball. Dau.: Mea or Mae, June 21, 1898.

Jackson, George E. and Mary E. Call. Children: Dau., Aug. 27, 1901; Howard D., Jan. 23, 1908.

Jaques, Horace E. and Eva N. Townsend. Son: Henry William, May 27, 1897.

Jeannotte, Alfred M. and Sophia A. Son: Albert Anthony, Sept. 1, 1884.

Jenkins, Martha C., b. Sept. 17, 1817.
Thomas and Evelyn Duclos. Son: Everett Leon, Feb. 4, 1910. (4th ch.)

Jewett, Jonathan and Hannah. Children: Moses, Feb. 2, 1793; Hannah, Sept. 3, 1795; Samuel Haite, Aug. 20, 1797.

Johnson, Frank and Mary E. Son: Vernice Frank, Dec. 3, 1880.
Herbert W. and E. Miriam Pratt. Dau., Dec. 18, 1908.
Nathan and Betsey. Children: Hannah, Jan. 12, 1802; Robinson, Mar. 12, 1804; Nathan, Sept. 23, 1806; John, Dec. 5, 1808.

Johnston, Alden and Georgie A. Gilcreast. Son: Eugene, Nov., 1880. (See Gilcreast.)
Alexander and Elisabeth W. Dau.: Elisabeth Jane, Sept. 13, 1851.

Joins, Jesse and Hannah. Children: Polly, Jan. 14, 1786; Benjamin Kidder, Dec. 31, 1788; Lois Reed, Feb. 26, 1791; Polley Caster, Aug. 24, 1793; Levina, Nov. 6, 1796; Hannah, Apr. 21, 1800.

Jones or **Joans,** Amos, b. Feb. 22, 1773, and Rebecca Dimond, b. Feb. 26, 1775. Children: Anna, Jan. 26, 1799; Ephraim, Mar. 12, 1800; Amos, Dec. 16, 1801; Polly, Jan. 13, 1804; Hannah, July 25, 1805; Rebecca, Oct. 28, 1806; Newman, Mar. 19, 1809; Fanny, Aug. 13, 1811; Eliza, Oct. 9, 1813; Harriet, Dec. 17, 1815; Lorinda, Oct. 5, 1818.

Josiah and Lovey. Children: David McGregore, Apr. 10, 1787; Pattey Caster, Apr. 30, 1791.

Josiah and Rebecca. Children: Chadwallader Ford, Feb. 7, 1775; Hannah, Apr. 27, 1783.

Josiah, Jr., and Jenney. Children: Jenney Alexander, Feb. 11, 1800; Josiah, Nov. 28, 1801.

Josiah, Jr., and Sarah. Children: Josiah, June 28, 1779; Sally Annis, Mar. 30, 1785; Mary Treysy (?), Mar. 26, 1789; Jesse, Dec. 20, 1790.

Keddy, James W. and Vera Weagle. Dau., Dec. 22, 1910.

Kelsey or **Kalso** or **Kelsea,** Alexander and Ann. Children: Margaret, Jan. 17, 1737–8; Jonathan, Jan. 30, 1739; William, Jan. 30, 1739.

Arthur S. and Elisabeth A. Sweatt. Children: Andrew, May 4, 1876; Sadie, 1878; Rosie M., Jan. 13, 1879; Perley E., Aug. 18, 1880; Sauria D., Sept., 1882.

William and Elisabeth. Children: John, Feb. 8, 1733–4; Margaret, Mar. 13, 1735–6.

Kembal or **Kimball,** John and Azubah. Children: Jonathan, Jan. 26, 1806; Samuel Nowell, Aug. 25, 1808.

Kenady or **Kennedy,** Robert and Miriam. Son: Hugh, Oct. 16, 1722.

Kendall, Everett C., b. Aug. 19, 1824, at Merrimack, N. H., and Harriet Goss, b. June 8, 1827. Children: Emma R.; Ida J., July, 1858.

Hamilton A. and Mary A. Son, Sept. 29, 1881.

Stephen and Easter. Children: John C., Aug. 15, 1801; Metepher, Mar. 5, 1803; Esther, Jan. 8, 1805; Betsey, Dec. 11, 1806; James, Jan. 3, 1809.

Kennedy, James and Mary. Dau., Feb. 24, 1861.

Kidd, Alexander and E. Hercrark. Son: Alexander, Sept. 8, 1723.

Kidder, A. H. and Emeline. Dau., Mar. 3, 1872.

Benjamin and Sareh. Children: ———, June 24, 1728; Mary, Aug. 9, 1730.

Frank E. and Abbie A. Children: Son, Aug. 26, 1881; Nora F., July 29, 1883.

Kimball, Frederick E. and Flora M. Hamblett. Children: Frederick Edward, Oct. 7, 1898; Hazel May, Nov. 23, 1903; George Irving, Nov. 15, 1905.

Isaac and Judah. Children: Isaac, Jr., Apr. 10, 1821; Abel, July 4, 1825; Judah Maria, Aug. 26, 1828; Mary Jane, Feb. 7, 1831.

Isaac, Jr., and Sarah. Son: Nahum C., Feb. 23, 1851.

Isaac, Jr., and Rebecca. Children: George W., Feb. 17, 1853; Milton J., Apr. 1, 1854; Charles G., June 3, 1855; Sarah Jane, Sept. 1, 1856; Daniel W., Apr. 10, 1858.

John and Phebe. Son: John, May 7, 1792.

Richard H. and Ida L. Dailey. Son: Wilfred, Sept. 14, 1896.

King, John H. and ——— Blair. Son: Oliver Judson, Feb. 2, 1910.

Knight, Wesley B. and Helen F. Anderson. Dau.: Georgietta W., Nov. 13, 1864. (See Anderson.)

Knowlton, Charles and Addie S. Young. Dau., Nov. 4, 1899.

La Belle, Joseph N. and Edith E. Smart. Son: Joseph, May 25, 1904.

Lafaud, William E. and Nellie Parker. Son: William E., Aug. 2, 1907.

Lang, George E. and Sarah Mertie Smith. Son: Norton Ballou, Oct. 12, 1908. (See John Smith.)

Larkin, John F. and Mary E. Horan. Dau.: Alice, Dec. 17, 1905.

Larrien, John and Jennie Harris. Dau.: Gertrude, Aug. 9, 1902.

Lassley, Lasslie, Lesley or **Lislie,** Alexander and Lucy. Children: Hannah, May 23, 1781; Lucy, May 11, 1783; Daniel, Aug. 10, 1785; Susannah, Sept. 12, 1787; John Warrant, Aug. 12, 1789.

James and Mary. Children: Janat, June 15, 1718; Sarah, July 14, 1720; Barber, Apr. 8, 1722; Daniel, Jan. 28, 1723–4; James, Mar. 12, 1732–3.

Lawson, ——— and Ann. Dau., Mar. 8, 1868.

Leach, David Rollins, b. Aug. 8, 1806.

Le Branch, William and Josie Gallant. Children: Hattie C., Sept., 1865; Benney, May, 1867; Samuel, 1869; Amy White, Sept., 1879; dau., Oct. 27, 1904.

Lewis, Guy A. and Josephine Pettingill. Children: Lillian Frances, Aug. 16, 1900; Edna Mae, Apr. 28, 1902, at Methuen, Mass.; Elsie Elvira, Oct. 5, 1905, at Pelham, N. H.

Lewis, Phillips F., b. at Charlestown, Mass.; came to Londonderry in 1898.

Lezott, George W. and Elisabeth. Dau., Sept. 3, 1899.

Libby, Richard, Feb. 17, 1823.

Lincoln, Anna P., b. Oct. 16, 1869.

Silas E. and Emma E. Dau.: Gertrude Florence, Apr. 18, 1889.

Linehan, Daniel, b. in Ireland, and Mary Ann (Connor), b. May 6, 1865, at Manchester, N. H. Children: Timothy, June 22, 1893, in Manchester, N. H.; Daniel, July 18, 1895, in Londonderry, N. H.; Catherine, June 28, 1897, in Londonderry, N. H.; Johanna, July 10, 1899, in Londonderry, N. H. Two died in infancy.

Lines, Harriet West, b. in Eng., Nov. 27, 1831; mother of Harriet W. Lewis.

Kattie Josephine, b. in Eng., niece of Harriet West Lewis.

Linton, John E., b. 1828, and Mary. Dau., Dec. 27, 1852.

Long, James and Ellen O'Brien. Dau., Dec. 17, 1898.

Lord, William Loren, b. May 1, 1826, and Claradilla. Son: George Chandler, Aug. 30, 1864.

Loveland, Hollis P. and Ida M. Son: Frank W., Sept. 30, 1878.

Low, Elias and Sarah. Children: Sarah, Mar. 31, 1790; David, Feb. 26, 1792; Betsey, Sept. 8, 1796; Mary, Sept. 17, 1798; Peggy, Oct. 12, 1800; William, Mar. 30, 1804.

Lowd, Andrew J. and Ardell. Son, May 26, 1870.

Frank and Clara J. Dau., Dec. 12, 1870.

Sedley A. and Julia. Children: ——, June 4, 1871; Mabel, Apr. 9, 1872; Edith B., July 20, 1875; Jennie A., Aug. 1, 1877; Sedley H., Aug. 31, 1879; Effie E., Aug. 31, 1879; William H., Apr. 30, 1886.

William B., b. at Portsmouth, N. H., Sept., 1817, and Martha Grant, b. Jan. 17, 1820. Children: Sedley, Apr. 21, 1841; Lydia M., Aug., 1842; Andrew G.; Arabella, Apr. 1847; Susan F., Aug. 15, 1849; Annie M., 1851; Sarah F., 1853; Charles E., Jan. 1, 1859.

Lund, John and Bridgett T. Connelly. Dau., May 26, 1899.

John and Mary Etta. Dau., Oct. 29, 1870.

Robert J., b. Apr. 7, 1837, in England.

William and Harriet. Son, July 9, 1868.

Lyons, William and Martha. Children: Margaret, Dec. 25, 1782; James, June 27, 1784; Mary, June 18, 1786; Thomas, Sept. 25, 1788; Betsey, June 25, 1791; Patty, —— 13, 1797.

MacCallister, David and Allennor. Son: Alexander, Jan. 15, 1737–8.

MacClury, Charles and Esther. Children: Robert, Aug. 18, 1726; George, May 18, 1728; Mary, June 5, 1730; John, Sept. 8, 1734.

MacCollum, Alexander and Jenat. Children: John, Mar. 23, 1729–30; Alexander, Mar. 22, 1731–2; Archibald, Sept., 1737; Thomas, Jan. 16, 1739.

MacConachy, John and Mary. Dau.: Jenat, Mar. 26, 1731.

MacGregore, Andrew and Elisabeth. Children: Jean, Oct. 22, 1775; Lettice, May 6, 1777; Elisabeth, Nov. 10, 1778; John, Aug. 7, 1780; Sibella, Mar. 19, 1782; Robert, Feb. 16, 1784; Andrew, Jan. 19, 1786; Daniel, Dec. 14, 1788.

Andrew W. and Frances A. Preston. Children: Wallace Preston, Nov. 7, 1863; Anne Belle, Sept. 16, 1867; John Preston, July 22, 1872.

Rev. David,* b. in Ireland, Nov. 6, 1710, and Mary Boyd, b. 1723. Son, Robert.†

Mack, Andrew and Elizabeth. Children: Jean, Oct. 22, 1775; Lettice, May 6, 1777; Elisabeth, Nov. 10, 1778; John, Aug. 7, 1780; Sibella, Mar. 19, 1782; Robert, Feb. 16, 1784; Andrew, Jan. 19, 1786; Daniel, Dec. 14, 1788.

Andrew W. and Frances A. Children: Wallace Preston, Nov. 7, 1863; Ann-Belle, Sept. 16, 1867; John Preston, July 22, 1872.

Edward Henry, son of Ethel J., b. Dec. 12, 1910.

John and Libby. Children: Jannet, Mar. 6, 1732–3; Martha, May 16, 1735; John, Aug. 31, 1736.

Jonathan and Feba. Son: Robert, May 9, 1739.

Robert and Ann. Children: Robert Clark, Dec. 31, 1818; Andrew W., Sept. 13, 1820.

Wallace P. and Harriet L. Pillsbury. Children: Lillian W., Mar. 6, 1893; Lavinia P., Sept. 11, 1894; Andrew R., Jan. 18, 1896; Wallace Preston, Nov. 5, 1900.

William and Susanna. Children: Martha, Feb. 10, 1744–5; Agnas, Apr. 5, 1746; John, Jan. 7, 1748–9; Robert, Apr. 4, 1752.

Mackay, James W., b. Mar. 22, 1825, and Abbie M. Thompson, b. Jan. 25, 1824. Children: Willie Weston, Jan. 5, 1854; Mary Abbie, Mar. 10, 1856; Arthur E., Sept. 27, 1861; Hattie E., July 16, 1866.

*First minister over West Parish.

†Robert married Elizabeth Reid, daughter of Gen. George Reid of Revolutionary fame. He built, in 1792, the first bridge to span the Merrimack, the original McGregor bridge.

MacLaughlin, Jonathan and Mary. Son: James, July 5, 1731.

MacMurphy, James and Mary. Children: Jean, Aug. 8, 1765; Alexander, Mar. 21, 1768; Janet, Apr. 25, 1770; Pegey, Nov. 25, 1772; Mary, Apr. 4, 1775.

MacNeal, Alexander and Jean. Children: Mary, May 30, 1729; Elisabeth, Aug. 4, 1731; Jenat, Sept. 7, 1733.

Madden, John and ——. Son, Mar. 30, 1881.

Joseph M. and Elisabeth M. McLynn. Son, June 22, 1901.

Magoon, John Quincy, b. at E. Patton, Canada, Mar. 9, 1855, and Cora B. Brown, b. at Manchester, N. H., Mar. 29, 1858. Children: Charles Manfred, Mar. 10, 1885; Hattie G., July 31, 1887; Susan P., Sept. 14, 1889.

Manifold, John and Susannah. Son, John, Nov. 17, 1797.

Manter, Charles P. and Mary A. Lawrence. Dau.: Georgie B., May 7, 1871.

Corydon L. and Emma A. Potter, b. Aug. 13, 1859. Children: Frank Harvey, Apr. 11, 1887; Jerauld A., Dec. 30, 1889; Fred Sandford, July 23, 1893; Ralph Monroe, Mar. 24, 1895.

Daniel and Sarah A. Son, Nov. 7, 1854.

David and Mary A. Dau., Mar. 2, 1859.

David and Philena. Dau., Sept. 13, 1852.

David, son of Jabez, and ——. Two sons and one dau.; dau. m. Charles Rigbery.

George,* b. Oct. 16, 1767, and Nancy Richmond. Children: David and Alden.

George and Polly or Mary Senter, 2d wife. Children: Col. Francis, Dec. 2, 1797; Capt. Samuel, Mar. 28, 1799; Mary m. Samuel Whittier of Hooksett, N. H., no children; Parvel Cathruff lived unm.

Col. Francis and Harriet Crowninshield (1st wife). Children: George D., surgeon of N. H. 3d Regt. Vol., Aug. 22, 1824; Harriet M., Oct. 28, 1829; Mary Florence, May 6, 1837.

Col. Francis and Elisabeth Ann Smith (2d wife); no children.

George Francis, dentist, and Lucinda Adelaide Wilbur, b. June 29, 1847. Son: George W., Dec. 17, 1872, Wellfleet, Mass.

George W. and Alice Mount, b. June 8, 1879. Children: Hellen Adelaide, Apr. 10, 1899; Louisa A., July 13, 1900; Luis Everett, Sept. 7, 1903.

*George Manter's sons, Alden and David, and his first wife, Nancy, all died early, in Plymouth, Mass., about 1795; he settled then in south part of Londonderry. In 1808 bought the McDuffie mills and the Hunter mills, located on the Little Cohas brook in northern part of Londonderry. Buried at Stowell cemetery, Manchester.

Manter, Dr. George W. and Almira Richardson, b. May 13, 1826. Children: George Francis, dentist, Apr. 5, 1847; Mary Olena, Oct. 27, 1854; Croydon L., May 16, 1857.

Grafton, b. 1770, Plymouth, Mass., and Lydia Leach. Children: James; Phineas, Mar. 28, 1794, m. Mary Bancroft Feb. 24, 1820; Jabez.

Jabez and Eliza Holt. Children: Maryett, b. in Litchfield, N. H.; Josiah, b. in Litchfield, N. H.; Hattie, b. in Litchfield, N. H.; David, b. in Litchfield, N. H.; Lydia, b. in Litchfield, N. H.; Philena, b. in Litchfield, N. H.; Mary Ann, Apr. 26, 1835; Philena, May, 1836.

James and Mehitable Dwinnell. Dau.

Josiah and Almira Greeley. Children: Adelbert, Allen.

Phinehas and Mary Bancroft. Children: Phileno, Sept. 1, 1821; Mary A., Apr. 1, 1824; Mehitable, Apr. 18, 1825; Jane, Mar. 10, 1827; Daniel, May 3, 1829; Serena, Oct. 5, 1831; Allen, Apr. 4, 1834; James, Dec. 3, 1837; Charles P., Aug. 31, 1838; Lorilla, May 2, 1842.

Captain Samuel and Isabel Reed. Children: Mary Ann, Jan. 19, 1824; Samuel, Jr., Nov. 21, 1825; David, July 19, 1828; James, July 19, 1828; Isabel, July 19, 1828; Clarissa, Aug. 8, 1841.

March, Henry C. and Mary A. Son, Nov. 17, 1851.

Marden, George and ———. Dau., Jan. 3, 1856.

Maring, Joseph H. and Rebecca. Children: Dau., Oct. 2, 1871; Delia H., Jan. 31, 1875; William S. Pillsbury, Sept. 1, 1877.

Marsh, Samuel and Mary Ann. Children: Sarah, Oct. 17, 1773; Ephraim, Sept. 7, 1775; Erabella, July 24, 1777; Samuel, Nov. 2, 1779.

Samuel and Lettuce. Dau.: Mary Ann, July 2, 1810.

Winfield S. and Lizzie B. Children: Dau., Apr. 14, 1887; Una Belle, June 2, 1888.

Marshall, Benjamin and Sarah. Son, Sept. 2, 1852.

Benjamin and ———. Dau., Aug. 20, 1859.

Philip and Matilda Robinson. Children: Elanson P., April 24, 1832; John N., 1834.

Robert and Patience. Son: John D. K., Sept. 16, 1837.

Marten, William and Hannah. Children: Marey, Nov. 30, 1742; James, Jan. 7, 1744–5; Nathaniel, May 9, 1747.

Martin, Cyrus A., b. Jan. 13, 1867, and Effie M. Gilcreast, b. Nov. 21, 1865. Children: Arthur Ellsworth, Dec. 12, 1889; Harriet Major, Oct. 22, 1896; James Henry, Dec. 19, 1897; Julia, Oct. 20, 1900; Theodore Roosevelt, Jan. 5, 1903; Ralph Augustus, Sept. 18, 1904; Mary Alice, July 18, 1906; Edwin Blanchard, Nov. 22, 1907.

Martin, Henry A. and Mary A. Dau.: Elisabeth Esther, May 24, 1889.

William H. and Mary. Children: Dau., Feb. 3, 1853; dau., Feb. 23, 1854.

William H. and ———. Ch., June 6, 1854.

Matthews, Hiram C., b. Jan. 17, 1817.

Maxfield, Clarence E. and Ethel M. Plummer. Dau.: Mina Annis, Dec. 5, 1909.

Daniel A., b. Oct. 19, 1863, and Hattie S. Gould, Oct. 20, 1872. Children: Andrew Clark, Mar. 13, 1892; Albert Dan, Oct. 14, 1894; Ella Arvilla, May 22, 1897; Clyde Gould, May 11, 1901; son, May 24, 1904; Leslie Ernest, July 22, 1905.

George F., b. Nov. 10, 1856, and Sarah E. Burroughs, b. Sept. 27, 1857. Children: Frank C., June 26, 1883; George H., July 2, 1885; C. Elwin, Jan. 30, 1888; Roy Burroughs, Sept. 3, 1894.

McAfee, Charles A. and Susie E. Children: Dau., Apr. 18, 1884; son, May 14, 1887.

McAllister, Angus, b. in Ireland, and Margaret Boyle, b. in Ireland.* Children: William, David, John, and five daughters. Of these children, William m. Jeanette Cameron and had children: John, David, William, Peter, Hugh, Thomas, Andrew, and one dau.; David, son of Angus, m. Eleanor Wilson, and had children: Alexander, b. Jan. 15, 1737–8, John, Archibald, George, Jeanette, and Margaret. Archibald, son of David and Eleanor, had children: David, Lydia, and Margaret Clark. Upon his death in 1778, wid. m. —— Arbuckle, and moved to Vermont. Of the daus. of Angus and Margaret, Mary Ann, the oldest, m. David Morrison; her sisters m. Thomas Knox, James White and John White. (See marriages.)

Benjamin and Caroline Savory, b. Mar. 14, 1821. Children: Thomas Savory, July 10, 1847; George, Aug. 4, 1850; Charles, Nov. 10, 1852.

Bertha Hayes and Harold Franklin Hawkins. Children: Harold Franklin, June 9, 1910; Dorothy Elizabeth, Aug. 1, 1911; Ruth McAllister, Jan. 2,0 1913.

Charles and Mary Graves. Children: Thomas Savory, May 5, 1886; Linda Graves, Feb. 13, 1890; Donald, May 21, 1895; Paul, Jan. 7, 1898; Ruth, Apr. 20, 1900.

George Isaac and Mattie M. Hayes, b. Sept. 14, 1857. Children: Bertha Hayes, Sept. 27, 1887; Harold Cleveland, Mar. 28, 1893.

*Settled in Leominster, Mass., 1718; in Londonderry, N. H., 1731.

McAllister, Isaac and Sarah Harriman, b. Feb. 16, 1778. Children: Isaac, Jr., Oct. 13, 1815; Jonathan, Mar. 12, 1817; Benjamin, Mar. 25, 1819; Sarah, Jan. 20, 1821.

John and Jane Caldwell. Children: Henderson, Benjamin, Andrew.

John and Mrs. Rebekah Henderson White. Children: Sarah, Isaac, Jan. 19, 1776, Benjamin, John.

Jonathan and Caroline Choate, b. Apr. 8, 1823. Son: George Isaac, Dec. 11, 1853.

McClary, Charles F. and ———. Son in state of Washington. M. 2d wife in Manchester; no children.

Ella Jane, and Roswell Annis. Son: Earle M., Dec. 16, 1886. (See Annis.)

John and Jane H. Runell (1st wife), b. 1827. Children: Charles F., June 30, 1850; Ella Jane, May 17, 1859.

Thomas, b. Apr. 7, 1790, and Eleanor Watts, b. May 13, 1795. Children: Thomas, Nov. 17, 1814; Hugh, May 11, 1816; Eliza, Aug. 20, 1818; Charles, Jan. 4, 1821; David, Mar. 18, 1823; John, June 6, 1825; Jane, Sept. 25, 1827.

McCorday, Robert and Agness. Children: Margaret, Dec. 23, 1743; John, Apr. 17, 1745.

McCoy, Judith R., b. 1828.

McCurdy, James and Elisabeth. Children: Jenat, Jan. 23, 1728–9; Mary, Apr. 17, 1732.

McDonald, Edgar F., b. Oct. 14, 1870, and Annie R. Boyce, b. Dec. 9, 1875. Children: Clayton Abner, Sept. 15, 1895; Lilla Frances, Feb. 22, 1897; Hazel May, Sept. 5, 1898; Ralph, Sept. 3, 1900; Edgar Francis, July 22, 1902; Bernice Marion, June 19, 1905; son, May 17, 1908.

Joseph R. and Mary P. Son: Stewart P., Sept. 8, 1901.

McDuffe, Daniel and Ruth. Children: Hugh, Mar. 25, 1721; John, Sept. 14, 1723.

McDuffee, Daniel and Margaret. Children: John, June 16, 1766; Jennett, Feb. 1, 1768; Ruth, Nov. 5, 1769; Samuel, Sept. 27, 1773; James, Aug. 21, 1775; Mary, Aug. 21, 1777; Margaret, Mar. 20, 1779; Daniel, Mar. 7, 1781; Agnes, Feb. 28, 1783; Sarah, Mar. 1, 1786.

McEntosh, Alexander and Elisabeth. Son: Alexander, Aug. 18, 1738.

Archibald and Elisabeth. Children: Jonathan, Nov. 13, 1740; Elisabeth, Nov. 1, 1742.

McGenness, Patrick and Bridgett. Children: Son, Feb. 1, 1853; son, Sept. 16, 1855.

McGrath, Theron and Grace Fisk. Dau., June 12, 1896.

McGregor, Alexander, b. Nov. 6, 1809, and Sarah Wise, b. June 8, 1813. Children: Sarah, 1839, Boston, Mass.; Alexander, Jr., Nov. 5, 1841; Rosa A., Sept. 7, 1846.

Alexander, Jr., m. a widow of Spartansburg, S. C. Six children: Helen, died ———; Mattie, Lilly, Alexander, Viola, and Charlie. He died in Trough, S. C., July 27, 1911.

David, b. Jan. 12, 1817, and Marietta (Nesmith), b. May 8, 1820. Children: George F., Jan. 9, 1841; Charles, Dec. 13, 1842; Mary Delia, Nov. 14, 1844; Francena N., June 21, 1848; Harriett L., June 26, 1850; David Brewster, Apr. 2, 1852; Etta R., Mar. 20, 1854; Emma N., Aug. 16, 1856; Carrie E., Nov. 25, 1858; William R., June 19, 1861; Frank M., Sept. 1, 1864.

David Brewster and Florence Hurd. Children: George H., June 18, 1876; William Guy, Sept. 27, 1877; Annie Maria, Nov. 5, 1879, in Derry; Carrie E., May 28, 1882; Rachel Lovejoy, Dec. 17, 1883, in Derry; Eva Florence, Jan. 18, 1885, in Derry; Walter Brewster, July 26, 1888, in Derry.

Frank M. and Alice Waugh, b. Dec. 3, 1868. Children: Donald Roy, Apr. 20, 1888; Carl F., Mar. 23, 1894; Edith, Dec. 4, 1896; Lillian M., Oct. 5, 1900; Dorothy K., Aug. 19, 1909. All live in Derry, N. H.

Fred Davis and Mary Corrinne Bennett. Children: Bennett, Apr. 10, 1893; Allan Barker, Nov. 3, 1894; Barbara Frances, May 15, 1902; George Edwards, Apr. 15, 1907; Fred Davis, Jr., Apr. 15, 1907. All live in Haverhill, Mass.

Frank P. and Lucia Sanderson. Children: Frank S., Ruth.

George F. and Rhoda A. Barker. Children: Fred Davis, Sept. 24, 1866; Sam Alby, Aug. 29, 1872.

Henry F. and Elisabeth Stevens. No children.

Isaac B. and Adella Coats. Dau.: Grace.

James L. and Mary A. Haselton. Dau.: May Belle, Nov. 8, 1886.

Lewis Aiken, b. Aug. 12, 1812, and Augusta W. (Blodgett), b. July 21, 1818. Children: James L., Isaac B., Frank P., Henry F., and Belle D.

Rosa A. and Frank Lincoln. Dau.: Anna P., Oct. 16, 1869.

William R. and Augusta May Annis, 1st wife. Dau.: Gracie, Dec. 14, 1887.

William R. and Martha L. Watts, 2d wife. Children: Herbert, Oct. 17, 1893; Blake Nesmith, Sept. 6, 1894; Mary Augusta, Jan. 20, 1896; Chester Annis, July 30, 1900; Gladys Rose, July 3, 1904. All born in Derry.

McGregore, Alexander and Mary Pinkerton. Son: John P., adopted by Major Pinkerton. (See Pinkerton.)

McGregore, Rev. David,* born in Ireland, Nov. 6, 1710.
James and Rosanna. Children: Nancy, Oct. 10, 1804; Isabella, Nov. 7, 1806; Alexander, Nov. 6, 1809.

McIntosh, William G. and Harriet E. W. Nugent. Son, Aug. 3, 1902.

McKeen, Daniel and Betsey. Children: Eliza, Oct. 1, 1817; Daniel, Oct. 9, 1819.

Daniel and Jenny. Children: Daniel, Jan. 16, 1791; John, Dec. 5, 1792; Mary, Oct. 7, 1794; Anne, July 27, 1796; James, Feb. 22, 1798; Levi, May 18, 1804; Jane, May 18, 1806.

James and Annas. Dau.: Martha, Dec. 14, 1723.

James and Annis. Dau.: Margaret, Mar. 30, 1726.

James and Elisabeth. Children: David, June 1, 1749; Mary, Sept. 7, 1751.

James and Hunis.† Dau.: Jean, Dec. 28, 1721.

James, Jr., b. Sept. 9, 1719; 2d birth in Londonderry, N. H.

John and Mary. Children: James, June 15, 1739; Jannat, Oct. 4, 1741; John, Feb. 4, 1746–7; Robert, Aug. 12, 1749; William, Jan. 20, 1751–2.

John, b. in Ireland, Apr. 13, 1715.

Rev. Joseph, D. D., son of John, b. Oct. 15, 1757, Londonderry.

Robert and Elisabeth. Children: Jean, Jan. 29, 1723–4; Robert, Aug. 4, 1726.

Samuel and Agnes. Children: John, Feb. 20, 1725–6; James, Apr. 3, 1728; Isabella, July 12, 172–.

McMurphy, Alexander and Jenat. Children: Jean, Oct. 27, 1726; Alexander, Apr. 1, 1728; Daniel, July 8, 1731; James, July 26, 1733.

Alexander and Lydia. Dau.: Jane, Apr. 1, 1788.

Archibald and Elisabeth. Children: James, Feb. 7, 1726–7; John, July 1, 1732.

John,‡ b. 1682, in Ireland; Mary, his wife, b. 1683.

John and Elisabeth. Son: James, Feb. 6, 1779.

*Mr. McGregore was the first minister of the west parish. His son Robert married Elizabeth, daughter of Gen. George Reid of Revolutionary fame, and settled in Goffstown. He built the first bridge across the Merrimack river, where the McGregor bridge now stands. Not many considered this a feasible project, and among others who were incredulous was Gen. John Stark, who declared: "You may succeed, Robert, but when the first passenger crosses over I shall be ready to die." The doughty old warrior, as a matter of fact, lived twenty years after the completion of the bridge, and crossed it many times.

†Probably this and Annas and Annis were different ways of spelling the same name.

‡John McMurphy died at Portsmouth, N. H., Sept. 21, 1755. He was Esquire, Justice of the Quorum, and was buried at Londonderry, N. H.

McMurphy, John and Mary. Children: Jean, Aug. 7, 1711; Isabell, July 15, 1713; Cristine, June 12, 1715; Alexander, July 16, 1717; John, Jan. 5, 1720-1; Robert, Jan. 30, 1723-4; Judith, Sept. 3, 1728; Elisabeth, Sept. 3, 1728.

Robert and Jane. Children: John, Feb. 12, 1748-9; James, Sept. 19, 1750; Robert, Feb. 1, 1752; Mary, Nov. 8, 1754; William, May 8, 1756; Matthew, Sept. 27, 1758; Alexander, Oct. 30, 1759.

Robert, Jr., and Jane. Children: Hugh, Dec. 5, 1781; Moley Tolford, Aug. 3, 1783; William, Aug. 8, 1785; Jane, Oct. 8, 1789.

McNeal, John and Christine. Children: Margaret, Nov. 12, 1721; Daniel, Nov. 17, 1723; Merian, Feb. 11, 1725-6; James, Feb. 26, 1731-2.

McNeill, Robert and Jenet. Children: Elisabeth, Jan. 23, 1758; Martha, Jan. 3, 1763; Agness, July 3, 1765; Jenet, July 3, 1765; Mary, Sept. 28, 1767; William, Apr. 18, 1770; Ann, Sept. 1, 1772.

McQuesten, Daniel M. and Mary E. Crowell. Children: James Crowell, Jan. 18, 1894; Imogene, June 15, 1896; Ruth Caroline, Jan. 21, 1898.

George B., b. Feb. 12, 1821, at Litchfield, and Lydia Manter, 1st wife. Children all d. young. Lucy J. Drew, 3d wife, b. 1830.

Melvin, Gilman and Jane. Children: Gilman P., Aug. 15, 1837; Alfred C., Aug. 25, 1841; Joseph M., Sept. 28, 1844; Malinda, Aug. 15, 1848.

Prescott and Rachel. Children: Abram S., Mar. 16, 1829; Sarah Jane, Mar. 22, 1832.

Reuben and Giza McN. Children: William Prescott, Apr. 21, 1837; Wealthy Ann, May 1, 1839; Martha Jane, May 22, 1841; Reuben Gustine, July 25, 1843.

Merrill, Carrol A., b. Mar. 8, 1863, Hardwick, Vt., and Fannie (Gray), b. May 8, 1865. Children: Bertha B., Jan. 19, 1887; James J., July 28, 1888; Ella Eva, Apr. 3, 1890; Millard M., Oct. 6, 1891; Harry H., Mar. 17, 1893.

John, b. July 21, 1820, and Paulina L. Hovey, b. Jan. 12, 1825. Children: John Edward, July 31, 1842; Eunice Emeline, Nov. 4, 1843; Richard, Sept. 16, 1846; Calvin, Nov. 23, 1851; Ellen Frances, Mar. 19, 1854; Ida, June 21, 1870.

Oliver and Emma N. Smith. Children: Walter Smith, Sept. 17, 1896; Clinton Everett, Sept. 16, 1902; Etta Maria, Jan. 17, 1907.

William Parker, b. Aug. 22, 1831, and Maria Boyce. Children: Shirley, Sept. 22, 1862; Oliver, Dec. 26, 1867.

Messer, Amos H. and Clara Flanders. Dau.: Sarah J., May 13, 1874.

Chandler and Angeline. Son: Joseph A., July 12, 1858.

William Freeman, b. Sept. 14, in Haverhill, Mass., and Lucy H. Noyes, b. Mar. 7, 1859, in Londonderry. Children: Edith Barstow, Nov. 18, 1890; Bessie Isabel, Sept. 12, 1896.

Miller, Archibald and Martha. Children: Robert, May 13, 1738; John, Nov. 26, 1744; Martha, Nov. 18, 1747.

Emmeline, b. in 1823.

George W., b. May 1, 1850, at Acton, Me., and Nettie E. (Brown), b. Oct. 26, 1848. Children: Arthur G., Sept., ———; Alice E., June 1, 1869; Lillian M., Feb. 18, 1886.

James and Mary. Children: James, Feb. 9, 1758; David, Oct. 9, 1760; Robert, June 11, 1762; Hannah, Mar. 20, 1764; Jannet, Jan. 30, 1767.

Samuel and Mary. Children: Agnes, June 24, 1728; Mathew, June 24, 1831.

Mills, Albert R. Bacon and Amy P. Fiske. Son: Albert F., June 18, 1908.

Ernest L. and Alice E. Hamlett. Son: Lyndon Earle, Aug. 25, 1892.

John, b. June 1, 1836, in Dunbarton, N. H.

Gust P., son of John, b. Apr. 9, 1862, at Londonderry, and Sarah J. Miles, b. Apr. 2, 1869, South Hampton, N. H. Children: Oscar H., July 19, 1890, at Londonderry, N. H.; Gusty T., Dec. 6, 1894, Sandown, N. H.

Moar, Aretta Josephine and George A. Hardy. Children: Charles Albert, Sept. 3, 1870; Freeman H., Nov. 16, 1872; Fred Monroe, July 1, 1875.

Carrie Louisa and Albert J. Bacon. Children: Edna L., Apr. 10, 1881; Albert Read, Apr. 22, 1884.

Edna L. Bacon and Kenneth W. C. Torrey. Dau.: Murial J., May 23, 1908.

Harriet Louisa and Charles E. Perkins. Dau.: Harriet Louisa, July 29, 1862.

Joshua A., b. Nov. 10, 1814, at Peterborough, N. H., and Louisa Witherspoon. Children: Mary Ann, Jan. 7, 1839; Harriet Lavina, Sept. 11, 1841; Maria Jane, Apr. 13, 1846; Aretta Josephine, May 17, 1848; Laura Ella, Apr. 8, 1851; Carrie Louisa, Nov. 18, 1856; Hattie Eliza, July 9, 1863.

Laura Ella and Charles E. Aldrich. Son: Frederick Charles, July 27, 1882.

Mary Ann and Henry Goodwin. Son: Arthur Worthington, Dec. 5, 1865.

Moar, Susan E. Lindon and Charles Albert Hardy. Children: George M., Feb. 22, 1902; Pertia E., July 19, 1905; Charles Richard, Sept. 25, 1909.

William and Martha. Children: James, Oct. 2, 1757; John, Sept. 28, 1759; William, Aug. 16, 1761; Henry, Aug. 26, 1763; Hannah, Nov. 30, 1767; Hugh, May 7, 1770; Jannet, June 7, 1772; Andrew, June 12, 1778; Daniel, May 17, 1780.

Molden, ——— and Catherine. Dau., Nov. 18, 1854.

Montgomery, Hugh and Joan. Children: Elisabeth, Mar. 20, 1720–1; Mary, June 13, 1723; Hugh, July 29, 1726.

William and Mary. Dau.: Jane W., May 27, 1814.

Moody, Edward P. and Antoinnette. Children: Dau., Dec. 3, 1859; son, Mar. 14, 1862.

Frederick E. and Eva F. McGregor. Children: Frederick E., Apr. 25, 1908; David Samuel, Oct. 31, 1909; Mary Delia, Dec. 29, 1910.

Gamet W. and Lillian B. Kinnear. Son, Sept. 28, 1910.

Jameson and Martha. Children: James, Aug. 9, 1755; Jannet, Mar. 28, 1757; Eleanor, Dec. 28, 1759.

Jeremiah Bean, b. Nov. 8, 1824, and Dolly McDonald, b. May 12, 1829. Children: Ann Elisabeth, July 31, 1849; Samuel Elisha, May 22, 1851; Sally A., May 9, 1853; Mary Frances, Aug. 26, 1856; Levi Jay, Aug. 31, 1858; Frederick H., Nov. 21, 1863; Mary Susan, Feb. 9, 1865.

Samuel E., b. May 22, 1851, and Mary E. Palmer, b. June 23, 1856. Children: Martha E., Sept. 7, 1874; Charles Edward, Oct. 23, 1875; Samuel E., Sept. 5, 1878; Frederick E., Dec. 12, 1880; Annie S., Nov. 25, 1883.

Samuel Eugene, b. Sept. 5, 1878, and Mary F. McKean. Children: Dau., Aug. 1, 1903; Royce Douglas, Aug. 21, 1904; Gysta Clare, Aug. 15, 1905; Jessie E., Aug. 9, 1906; Marjorie K., Aug. 7, 1908; Warren Eugene, Nov. 15, 1910.

Volney H., b. Mar. 26, 1859, and Nancy J. Gage. One son. (See Gage.)

Moore, John and Jean. Children: Samuel, Jan. 30, 1727–8; Robert, May 22, 172–; Agnus, July 19, 1729; William, Sept. 26, 1731.

John and Mareyan. Children: William, Sept. 27, 1758; Andrew, Jan. 12, 1761; John, June 2, 1763; Abraham, Sept. 8, 1768; James, Aug. 3, 1770; Samuel, July 17, 1772; Maor, Sept. 27, 1774.

Jonathan and Mary. Children: Agnus, July 19, 1729; William, Sept. 26, 1731.

Joshua A. and Lovina. Dau., July 9, 1863.

Moore, William R. and Blanche Campbell. Children: Eugene W., Dec. 23, 1895; Ira Campbell, June 24, 1899; dau., Sept. 1, 1902; Lloyd Elbert, Sept. 5, 1904; Hugh Russell, Nov. 25, 1906; Bernice Luella, May 28, 1909.

Morell, Inion and ——. Dau.: Hanna, Sept. 12, 1768.

Moreson, Halbert and Mary. Dau.: Martha, June 13, 1750.
James and Martha. Children: Peggy, July 26, 1783; Rebecca, Feb. 7, 1787; James, Mar. 17, 1789; Thomas, Apr. 4, 1792; John, Aug. 29, 1794.
John and Elisabeth. Children: Ann, Nov. 1, 1747; John, Jan. 21, 1750; James, Oct. 2, 1751; Samuel, Sept. 11, 1754.
John and Elisabeth. Children: David, Aug. 29, 1750; Samuel, Mar. 5, 1752; John, Sept. 27, 1755; James, May 9, 1757; Elisabeth, Jan. 2, 1766.
John and Margaret. Children: Jonathan,* Sept. 8, 1719; Jennat, Apr. 6, 1722; Elisabeth, June 11, 1723–4; Janet, Feb. 13, 1728; John, Sept. 20, 1726; Hanna, Apr. 10, 1730; Moses, June 7, 1732.

Morison, Robert and Elizabeth. Son: William, Nov. 30, 1722.
Samuel and Margaret. Children: Samuel, Mar. 13, 1726–7; Abraham, May 29, 1731.
Samuel and Mary. Children: Shusanna, Sept. 17, 1731; Samuel, July 23, 1734; Mary, Oct. 6, 1736.
Samuel and Martha. Dau.: Martha, Oct. 25, 1723.
Thomas and Mary. Son: Jonathan, July 8, 1740.
William and Jane. Children: Jane, Sept. 4, 1758; Marey, Jan. 27, 1761.
Rev. William and Jean. Children: William Fullerton, Nov. 6, 1785; Jenny, Nov. 6, 1785; Daniel, June 24, 1787; James, Mar. 21, 1789; Sally, Mar. 21, 1789.

Morow, James and Mary. Children: Margaret, Sept. 10, 1740; David, Nov. 2, 1742; William, Oct. 2, 1744; James, July 16, 1747; Robert, Aug. 16, 1754; Mary, Aug. 3, 1756.

Morrell, Simeon and Sarah. Children: Maley, Sept. 18, 1771; Lidal, Apr. 21, 1774.

Morris, George R. and Jennie L. Dau.: Grace, Feb. 15, 1877.

Morrison, Abraham and Mary. Children: Hamilton, Feb. 17, 1770; Nathaniel, Feb. 15, 1773; Joseph, Feb. 9, 1775; Elisabeth, Feb. 9, 1777; John H., June 4, 1779; Mary, Apr. 25, 1783; Jonathan, June 4, 1785; George, Aug. 25, 1788.
James and Janat. Children: John, Aug. 16, 1722; Thomas, May 15, 1724; ——, Sept. 24, 1728; ——, Nov. 22, 1782; James, July 29, 1788.

*First birth in Londonderry, N. H.

Morrison, James G. and Phebe A. Children: Mary Adelaide, May 6, 1856; Robert Giles, Aug. 16, 1857; Eliza Frances, June 27, 1859; Charles Albert, Nov. 21, 1862.

John, b. Aug. 29, 1794, and Sally Coburn, b. Sept. 5, 1805. Children: Franklin G., June 13, 1833; James, May 13, 1835; Dorcas Cutter, Nov. 23, 1836; Elisabeth, May 23, 1838; Harlan Page, June 6, 1840; Belinda Co, Sept. 3, 1841; Emeline, Mar. 18, 1844.

Mark and Sarah Bean. Children: Son, Jan. 3, 1854; son, Oct. 3, 1855; dau., Jan. 22, 1859; dau., Sept. 29, 1861; Josie K., Aug. 19, 1872.

Royal G. and Ella F. Dau.: Abbie Almyra, Jan. 29, 1881.

Thomas, b. Apr. 4, 1782, and Sareh Giles, b. 1794. Children: Martha M., m. Addison Brooks; Mark, m. Sarah Bean; James G., m. Phebe A. Robinson, d. in army; Margaret, 1832; Charles H., m. Abbie Floyd, d. in Civil War.

Rev. William, b. 1748.

William O. and Nettie E. Corbett. Children: Dau., Jan. 15, 1893; Lulu Mary, Oct. 17, 1897.

Morse, Andrew J., b. 1832, and Mary Adeline (Gilcreast), b. Nov. 4, 1833. Children: Dau., June 4, 1853; dau., Sept. 10, 1854.

George E. and Lucinda A. Children: Eliza M., Mar. 15, 1882; dau., Feb. 28, 1885.

John and Mary. Son, July 4, 1855.

John F. and Elisabeth A. Son: Alfred H., June 30, 1878.

Stephen and Rebecca. Children: Fanny, July 28, 1841; Nancy, Jan. 12, 1843; Almira, June 24, 1844.

Mullins, Arthur and Margaret. Son: James, Feb. 7, 1747–8.

Benjamin and Agness. Children: James, May 23, 1764; Elisabeth, Sept. 10, 1765.

Charles W. and Katie Feely. Children: Son, June 3, 1894; Mary Catherine, May 20, 1896.

Cleon E. and Lena M. Smith. Children: Harriet N. L., Nov. 26, 1907; Lee Huse, Apr. 13, 1909.

Cyrus, b. Sept. 15, 1801, and Lydia, b. 1807. Children: Lucien H., Aug. 25, 1834; Arvilla Colby, Aug. 18, 1836; Luzetah, 1841.

Eugene N.* and Emeline Greeley. Children: Roy, Oct. 9, 1884; Ida Louise, Jan. 26, 1887; Emogine, May, 1888.

Frank A. and Clara Belle Corning, b. July 31, 1868. Children: Eva Marion, Dec. 13, 1892; Adeline Bell, Nov. 11, 1894.

*Eugene N. became a physician in Baldwinville, Mass.

Mullins, George Mayo* and Mary A. Kane. Children: Simon M., 1891; Ida Lucelia, 1894; Louise, 1900.

Ida M., dau. of Simon and Harriet Cheney, m. —— Dustin. Dau.: Edith L.

Israel, Nov. 18, 1792, and Mary Garvin, b. Dec. 2, 1796. Children: Robert, Mar. 23, 1820; T. Jane, Mar. 20, 1822; Simon, Feb. 24, 1824; Betsey, Mar. 23, 1826; Clara, Oct. 17, 1828; Hason, Mar. 20, 1831; Amanda R., Nov. 27, 1833; Augusta B., Mar. 21, 1840.

Simon, b. Feb. 24, 1824, and Harriet (Cheney), b. Dec. 13, 1827. Children: Ida M., Jan. 7, 1848; Eugene N., Jan. 28, 1851; Louise Ella, Apr. 12, 1852; Hattie Pauline, Oct. 15, 1858; George Mayo, Feb. 4, 1865.

Nason, John Wesley, b. Kennebunkport, Me., Mar. 12, 1834.

Nesmith, James and Elisabeth. Children: Arthur, Apr. 3, 1721; Jean, Aug. 12, 1723; Mary, Jan. 24, 1725–6; ——, Feb. 7, 1727–8; Elisabeth, Jan. 8, 1729–30; Benjamin, Sept. 14, 1734; Thomas, Mar. 26, 1732.

James and Marey. Children: James, Nov. 29, 1744; Margaret, Feb. 7, 1747–8; Eliza, Mar. 9, 1749; Jean, Sept. 12, 1751.

James and Mary. Children: Eliza C., June 17, 1816; Margaret, May 2, 1818; Maryette, May 8, 1820; Samuel C., Aug. 13, 1822; Sarah F., Feb. 18, 1825; Nathaniel S., Apr. 28, 1827; Jane M., June 18, 1831.

John, b. Oct. 10, 1840.

John and Isabela. Children: James, Feb. 6, 1758; Arthur, Feb. 23, 1760; Elisabeth, Apr. 19, 1762; Mary, Apr. 8, 1764; John, Nov. 26, 1762 (1766 (?)); Ebenezer, Mar. 27, 1769; Jane, July 14, 1772; Thomas, Oct. 7, 1774.

John and Lucy. Son: Hugh Martin, Sept. 20, 1786.

John and Lydia. Children: Albert S., June 28, 1818; Charles E., July 29, 1821.

John and Sukey. Children: John P., Nov. 16, 1797; Isabella A., Nov. 16, 1799; Sukey H., Sept. 21, 1801; Samuel W., Aug. 21, 1803; James P., Sept. 29, 1805; Mary, Apr. 10, 1808; Thomas, July 24, 1811; Elisabeth, Sept. 22, 1813.

Jonathan Young, b. July 6, 1827, and Adeline A. Boyce, b. Apr. 26, 1833. Children: Oreal, 1859; Frank A., Sept. 27, 1866.

Lucien H. and Louise E. Mullins. Son: Cleon E., Oct. 30, 1883.

Martha Ann, Nov. 16, 1835.

Robert and Jane. Children: Thomas, Sept. 16, 1691; James, Sept. 3, 1793; Betsey, July 18, 1795; Cyrus, Sept. 15, 1801; Martha, Jan. 15, 1804.

*George Mayo was a teacher and lawyer and settled in Denver, Col.

Nesmith, Capt. Thomas, b. Jan., 1791, and Nancy B., b. 1725. Son: Jonathan Young, July 6, 1827.

Nevins, Dea. James, b. 1798, and Mary Plummer, b. 1809. Children: John, 1831; Harriet, June 27, 1833; James E., 1838; William P., May 23, 1841; Henry A., 1843; Sarah E., 1846.

William P. and Julia D. Shipley, b. Nov. 5, 1846. Children: Mabel Fannie Montgomery, June 21, 1872; Charles Henry, Feb. 6, 1876; Harriet Julia, Apr. 29, 1878; ch., Aug. 29, 1888; William Shipley, Mar. 1, 1890.

Newman, Clarence and Etta M. Young. Son d. at 11. (See Young.)

Nichols, Jacob and Hannah. Children: Samuel, May 28, 1794; Moody Morse, Nov. 1, 1796; Stephen Chase, Feb. 26, 1799; Holt, Feb. 2, 1802; James, Jan. 6, 1804; Eliza Choat, July 12, 1805.

Jacob and Hannah. Son: George, Jan. 12, 1856.

James and Fannie. Son, July 6, 1863.

James, b. 1751.

James, b. 1764.

James, b. 1733, and Dinah Woodburn, 1st wife; and Hannah Caldwell, 2d wife, b. 1742. Children of James and Dinah: David, 1761, m. Nancy Newman; Anna, 1763, never married; James, Mar. 31, 1766, m. Nancy Fowler; William. lost at sea; Thomas, 1771; Woodburn, m. Annie Nichols, lost at sea.

James and Hannah. Children: Alexander, Apr. 26, 1774, m. Pinder N. Pendleton; Samuel, Dec. 3, 1775, m. Mary Cunningham; Hannah, Aug. 22, 1777, m. Isaac Carver; Dinah, Nov. 17, 1779, m. Benjamin Young; Nancy, 1780, m. James Berry; Mary, Apr. 22, 1783, m. John Park; Margaret, Dec. 10, 1784, m. Samuel Park.

James and Nancy Fowler. Children: William, b. Mar. 1, 1798, and Sally Lancaster, 1st wife; Sarah Baker, 2d wife.

Samuel and Mary Cunningham. Children: Samuel, Aug. 5, 1800, m. Sarah Sleeper; William, Mar. 26, 1802, m. Nancy Nichols.

William, son of James and Margaret, and Ann Cochran, b. 1700. Children: Alexander, 1727; Margaret, 1733, m. James Kincaid.

William,* b. 1754, and Abigail, b. 1762. Children: Margaret, 1781; Abigail, 1786; Benjamin R., Susan, Amos, Borden, dau., Moses, James, Aaron.

Nicholson, Enoch E. and Lydia. Dau., Jan. 20, 1853.

*Moved his family to Ossipee, N. H., about 1801.

Noble, Fred R. and Nettie J. Crosby. Dau.: Grace Crosby, Jan. 4, 1901.

Noireux, William H. and Pheabe Dessaubrier. Son: Walter George, Oct. 26, 1902.

Norcross, Frank E. and Fronia Aiken, b. Aug. 20, 1855. Children: Frederic E., May 27, 1883; Viva A., 1889 (?), m. George V. Eddy.

Joshua L., b. 1828, at Lincoln, Maine, and Mary Elisabeth Noyes, b. Aug. 21, 1836. Children: George N., 1857; Frank E., June 6, 1859; Mary, Mar. 19, 1861.

Mary E. (Noyes), and Martin M. Bowles, b. Nov. 29, 1840. No ch.

Noyes, Andrew J. and Hattie. Son: Harry A., July 20, 1882.

Benning, b. June 2, 1805, at Bow, N. H., and Mary Barstow Warren, b. Oct. 15, 1815. Children: Mary Elisabeth, Aug. 21, 1836, Blue Hill, Me.; Joseph T., Mar. 24, 1839; Charlestown, Mass.; Andrew Warren, July 29, 1841, Blue Hill, Me.; Sylvester C., Dec. 27, 1843, East Boston, Mass.; Charles H., Sept. 15, 1846, East Boston, Mass.; Abbie J., Dec. 17, 1847, East Boston, Mass.; George B., Apr. 23, 1850; Clara J., Dec. 25, 1852; Martha C., Feb. 9, 1854; James M., Sept. 19, 1855; Ella L., June 21, 1857; Lucy H., Mar. 7, 1859.

Benning and Emilie L. Boone. Son: Muriel C., May 4, 1905.

Carlos W. and Clara J. Richardson. Son: Warren Walter, Apr. 19, 1860. (See Richardson.)

Charles W. and Clara. Son, Apr. 19, 1860.

James M. and Amanda P. Austin, b. Jan. 15, 1854. Children: Fred E., Nov. 9, 1873; Charles W., Jan. 15, 1877; Walter E., June 19, 1879; Benning, Nov. 28, 1881; Bertha M., Dec. 30, 1883; Herbert M., May 15, 1886; Eva F., Mar. 28, 1888; Phylena A., Apr. 17, 1890; Albert C., Nov. 28, 1892; Millard E., June 20, 1894; Harold R., Apr. 5, 1897; Myron E., Sept. 24, 1898.

Walter E. and Nellie A. Quint. Children: Gertrude May, Feb. 20, 1902; Clifford Robert, May 22, 1905.

Nugent, Thomas P. and Antoinette. Children: M. B., Aug. 3, 1883; Harriet H., Dec. 3, 1884.

O'Leary, Jeremiah T. and Sarah Lacy. Son: Richard, Mar 25, 1904.

Oliver, Frank M. and Louisa H. Son, June 30, 1882.

Olsen, Albert D. A. and Grace M. Theiss. Son: Kenneth Clifton, July 9, 1910.

Olzendam, G. A., Jr., and Edith B. Dutton. Son: Alvin Paul Nov. 16, 1908.

Ouellette, Theophile and Annie Arnold. Son: Charles Victor, July 18, 1904.

Orill, Anthony and ———. Dau., July 18, 1854.
William H. and Laura E. Dau.: Leona E., Nov. 14, 1881.

Otto, Edward C. and Eva Wadge. Son: Edward, May 28, 1901.

Oughterson, James and Ann. Dau.: Agness, July 30, 1770.

Pace, Fred and Augusta Young. Children: Son, May 11, 1899; Annie May, Mar. 22, 1904.

Page, Andrew H. and Effie Marshall. Children: Dorothy L. Pearl, May 29, 1904; Alfred H., July 2, 1906.
Charles and Henrietta. Dau., Apr. 14, 1855.
Charles P. and Mehitable. Dau., Oct. 5, 1852.
Horace and Lucy A. Son, May 7, 1877.
Joel, b. Oct. 23, 1808, and Rachel Fling, b. July 24, 1812. Children: Randal, Aug. 12, 1835; Armenia, Oct. 15, 1837; Darius, Dec. 8, 1839; Charles E., Feb., 1842; Sarah R., Mar. 23, 1844; Eldusta M., July 17, 1846; Olin W., Nov. 19, 1848; Orren L., May 18, 1851.
Joseph and Rhoda. Children: Stephen, July 6, 1810; Joseph, Sept. 13, 1812; Eliza Ann, June 3, 1814; Almira, Mar. 25, 1816; Hannah, Mar. 27, 1818; James, June 9, 1820; Rebecca, Mar. 1, 1822; Nancy, Dec. 11, 1823; Joseph, Dec. 10, 1825; Lydia, May 15, 1828; John, Mar. 11, 1830; Samuel N., Jan. 11, 1832; Ruth, Aug. 9, 1834.
Mehitable, Jan., 1830.
Orlando and Susan Clark. Children: Son, Apr. 20, 1853; son, June 22, 1855.

Palmer, John and ———. Children: John, Apr. 3, 1789; Moses H., Jan. 28, 1792; Nathaniel, May 10, 1794; Stephen, Nov. 17, 1796; Samuel, Feb. 20, 1800; Thomas J., Dec. 21, 1802; Sally, May 26, 1805; Moody Morse, Feb. 20, 1810.
Moses and Polly. Children: Rebecca C., Oct. 8, 1820; Elisabeth H., Feb. 24, 1822; Charles Harriman, Aug. 17, 1824.

Paquette, George A. and Mary Boulanger. Son: Joseph W. W., June 18, 1909.

Parie, Joseph A. and Octive C. Webster. Children: Dau., Feb. 21, 1905; Oscar A., July 11, 1906.

Parker, Celinda P. and John Anderson Corning. Dau.: Georgie, Feb. 26, 1866.
Edward and Mary R. Kindall, b. June 6, 1809. Children: Mary K., Dec. 2, 1833; Celinda Perham, Dec. 26, 1835; Horatio Nelson, Oct. 2, 1837; Eliza A., Sept. 3, 1839; Harriet J., Jan. 28, 1842; Almira Alden, Dec. 5, 1843; John, June 21, 1846; Charles Edward, May 14, 1849.

Parker, Rev. Edward Lutwyche,* b. in Litchfield, N. H., July 28, 1785. He was the son of Dr. Jonathan Parker, who died in Sept., 1791, the parent of ten children. Rev. Edward m. Mehitable Kimball, 1811. They had two sons and two daughters.

Elder John, b. July 28, 1783, and Polly Peabody, b. 1787. Son: Edward, Sept. 6, 1806.

John and Eldora M. Dodge, b. Dec. 17, 1847, Litchfield, N. H. Children: Eliza K., Apr. 24, 1868; Gerry Flint, July 21, 1879; Frank Laten, Mar. 16, 1887.

Mary K. and Francis R. Bruce, b. 1832. No children.

William and Elisabeth. Children: Ann, May 18, 1771; Alexander, Oct. 29, 1772; Sibbella, Dec. 23, 1773; Henery, Feb. 18, 1775.

Parshley, Arthur F. and Lauria D. Hobbs. Children: Marguerite, July 1, 1891, in Newport, N. H.; David H., July 26, 1893, in Newport, N. H.; Le Roy, Apr. 20, 1901, in Haverhill, Mass.; Keneth M., Oct. 7, 1903.

Enoch, b. June 26, 1842, in Greenland, N. H., and Julia A. Varel, b. Mar. 22, 1851, in Meredith, Ill. Children: Ida A., Aug. 1, 1870, in Derry, N. H.; Warren S., Apr. 23, 1872, in Derry, N. H.; Frank D., Sept. 28, 1873; Edward A., Aug. 25, 1875; Mary V., June 2, 1877; Enoch H., Aug. 9, 1879; Laura W., Aug. 30, 1881; Cora L., Oct. 14, 1883; Edna F., July 6, 1885; John H., Nov. 12, 1887; Russell V., Mar. 2, 1891.

John H. and Elisabeth E. Parker. Son: Edward D., Mar. 27, 1907.

Milo Allen and Julia A. Varel. Son: Arthur F., Apr. 13, 1867.

Russell V. and Maude A. Webster. Dau.: Doris E., Oct. 4, 1909.

Patnaud, Theophile and Celina Godet. Son, Aug. 22, 1897.

Patten, J. William and Georgia A. Powers. Dau., Oct. 4, 1907.

Patterson, David and Sarah Betton. Children: James Betton, Sept., 1781; William, July 28, 1784; John, May 27, 1788; Betsey, Feb. 9, 1793; James, Mar. 8, 1790; Nancy, July 23, 1795; Sally, Aug. 6, 1799; Mary Boyd, June 6, 1801.

John and Jean. Son: Petter, Jan. 9, 1778.

John D. and Hannah. Children: William Wallace, Sept 29, 1847; Hannah Elisabeth, Jan. 19, 1850.

Peter, b. 1716, and Grisey, b. 1722. Children: Robert, 1744 Thomas, Oct. 23, 1746; John, 1750; Rachel (McNeill) 1752; Margaret (Holmes), 1755; Sarah (Melandy), 1758 Grisey (Burns), 1761; Elisabeth (Burns), 1765.

*Mr. Parker was the author of a History of Londonderry, which he left i manuscript, to be completed and published by his son, Edward Parker, in 1851.

Patterson, Peter and Mary. Children: Robert W., Nov. 3, 1815; Elisabeth J., Sept. 11, 1817; Mary, Apr. 24, 1820; Susan B., Sept. 25, 1821.

Robert and Esther. Children: James, July 5, 1810; Alfred S., Jan. 3, 1812.

Thomas and Elisabeth Wallace. Children: Grisey, Mar. 26, 1776; James, Nov. 21, 1777; Peter, Nov. 14, 1779; Robert, Apr. 24, 1781; Mary, Apr. 1, 1783; Margaret (Taylor), Oct. 10, 1784; Thomas, Aug. 11, 1786; William, June 4, 1789; Elisabeth, June 10, 1791; David, Feb. 11, 1793; Jane (Frank), Aug. 30, 1795; Hannah (Duncan), Apr. 26, 1798; George Washington, Nov. 11, 1799.

Thomas and Elizabeth. Children: Grizel, Mar. 26, 1776; James, Nov. 21, 1777; Peter, Nov. 14, 1779; Robert, Apr. 24, 1781; Marey, Apr. 1, 1783; Margret, Oct. 10, 1784; Thomas, Aug. 11, 1786; William, June 4, 1789; Elisabeth, June 10, 1791; Jinney, Aug. 30, 1795; George Washington, Nov. 11, 1799.

Thomas and Hannah. Children: Jane D., Mar. 19, 1819; John D., Apr. 13, 1821; Elisabeth W., Mar. 6, 1823; Thomas, Jan. 30, 1825; Hannah D., Apr. 10, 1827; George W., Aug. 3, 1833; Mary Caroline, Nov. 13, 1835.

Pattingale, Phinehas and Elisabeth. Children: Asa, Dec. 5, 1783; Rachel, Feb. 21, 1785; James, Aug. 26, 1787; Warren, May 1, 1790.

Pay, Frank B. and Sarah J. Flanders. Dau.: Mary, Oct. 2, 1906.

Payne, Charles H. and Anna. Children: Edward, 1876; Esther, 1880, Derry; dau.

George E. and Mary C. Children: Ethel Maude, May 8, 1877; Harry N., Jan. 30, 1884; Roland, Mar. 8, 1892.

John P. and Anna. Children: Bertha, June 16, 1877; Frank; Nellie; Mabell; dau.

Mary C. Corning, wife of George E. Payne, b. Feb. 25, 1851.

Nelson and Abbie. Dau.: Josephine Maude, Apr. 15, 1879.

Samuel N., b. Apr. 1, 1822, and Nancy D. Page, b. Dec. 11, 1824. Children: Nelson S., Apr. 12, 1847; Charles Herbertson, 1849; Algeron, Oct., 1850; George E., Sept. 2, 1851; John P., Sept. 6, 1854; Frank, Aug. 16, 1856; Wesley W., Oct. 18, 1858; Anna M., Jan. 9, 1861; Julia M., Jan. 18, 1864.

Wesley W. and Mabel L. Son: Charles Wesley, Jan. 19, 1891.

Peabody, Asa and Anne. Son: John Gould, Dec. 26, 1791.

Peabody, Elbridge W., b. June 3, 1833, at Milan, N. H., and Mary A. Combs (Perham), b. June 25, 1840. Children: Elwin C., July 17, 1860; Augustus W., July 19, 1805; Eugene P., June 17, 1869, at Shelburne, N. H.; Cyrus O., Nov. 1, 1881.

Elwin C. and Minnie M. Fling. Children: Mildred Angeline, Oct. 20, 1896; Bertrand E., Oct. 12, 1905.

Fred L. and Retta M. Robie. Children: Eula M., Grace, and Vivian.

Henrietta and Joseph Roach. Children: Harriet E., Jan. 29, 1874; Fred L., Aug. 13, 1877; Mary E., Aug. 22, 1880.

Jonathan Warren and Mary Tenney, m. Apr. 16, 1846. Children: Henrietta, May 13, 1848; Elbridge A., Dec. 17, 1854.

Orriville A., b. 1825, and Maria (White), 1st wife, b. Mar. 20, 1823. Children: Ida, Nov. 3, 1851; Willie W., Feb. 19, 1855; James N., Oct. 18, 1859; son, Feb. 28, 1862.

———. Children: Eliza, July 22, 1819; Jonathan Warren, July 21, 1821; Eveline, Sept. 29, 1823; Orriville A., 1825; Augustus; Elbridge W., June 3, 1833.

Pereau or **Perault,** Adolph and Josephine M. Largess. Son: George Henry, Sept. 23, 1891; Georgianna, Nov. 23, 1892.

Perkins, Charles E. and Harriet L. Moar. Dau.: Harriet Louisa, July 29, 1862.

David Flanders and Jennie S. Corning, b. Nov. 15, 1861. Children: Alice Bertha, Mar. 19, 1885; Marion, May 9, 1894.

Deacon James, b. Jan. 2, 1780, and Sally Smith, b. Feb. 12, 1790. Children: Elisabeth, Mar. 2, 1808; Sally, Feb. 28, 1810; Joseph, Nov. 8, 1811, killed in Mexican war; James, Aug. 13, 1814; William O., July 31, 1816, m. Sarah A. Bartlett.

Joseph, b. Sept. 3, 1752, in Ipswich, Mass., and Mary Foster, b. Mar. 13, 1752. Son: Deacon James, Jan. 2, 1780.

Philemon Smith and Mary Poland, b. 1759. Dau.: Sally Smith Perkins.

Washington and Jane Youngman, b. Feb. 21, 1828, in Wilmot, N. H. Children: Mary E., Nov. 15, 1853; Lucy Watts, May 23, 1856; David Flanders, Nov. 3, 1858; Emma H., Aug. 27, 1864.

William H. and Susan. Son, Aug. 10, 1853.

———. Children: Washington, Sept. 20, 1821; Franklin, July 24, 1823; Sarah, Oct. 11, 1825.

Perrett, William and Mary Collins. Children: Virginia Hortense, Mar. 13, 1897; Collins Arthur, May 24, 1899; Theophile, Mar. 12, 1901.

Perron, Louis and ———. Son, May 11, 1881.
Louis and Mary Brock. Son: Eustis Raymond, July 31, 1896.

Perry, Antoine, b. Feb. 26, 1850, Redford, N. Y., and Emma Barrett, b. Nov. 13, 1859, Syracuse, N. Y. Son: Bernard N., Aug. 12, 1891. All came to Londonderry, 1893.

Peterson, Peeter and Grisell. Children: Robert, Dec. 6, 1746; Thomas, Oct. 23, 1748; John, Jan. 21, 1751; Rachell, Dec. 4, 1753; Margarett, Nov. 5, 1755.
Samuel and Elisabeth. Children: Grisell, Apr. 8, 1745; William, Mar. 29, 1747; Ann, Feb. 3, 1754.

Pettingill, David and Eliza. Son, Aug. 27, 1861.
George C. and Eva A. Simpson. Children: Virginia Laretta, Dec. 28, 1906; Richard Henry, Jan. 30, 1909; Elvira Irene, Dec. 1, 1910.
George M. and Sarah A. Shehan. Children: Warren M., Feb. 23, 1894; Gladys, Oct. 9, 1902.
James B. and Ada Bartlett. Children: Edith May, Mar. 28, 1885; George Herbert, Dec. 23, 1886; Grace Lillian, Mar. 22, 1890; Frank Gordon, June 4, 1895; Bessie Hazel, Feb. 8, 1897.
James and Eliza Adams. Children: George, Dec. 10, 1849; Annie, Feb. 27, 1852; James B., May 10, 1858; Herbert, May 10, 1860.
Nathaniel, b. Nov. 8, 1814, and Elvira (Hobbs) Libby, b. Dec. 15, 1823, at Salisbury, N. H. Son: Richard Libby, Aug. 14, 1856.
Richard Libby and Philimon Rousseau, b. Nov. 27, 1855. Children: George C., Sept. 15, 1875; Josephine, Jan. 7, 1881; Henry H., Sept. 1, 1884.
Warren Martin, b. Feb. 23, 1838, and Angeline M. Barker, b. Aug. 13, 1838. Children: Addie J., Sept. 25, 1862; Cynthia A., Jan. 23, 1864; Edgar P., Nov. 3, 1865; Hannah B., Aug. 13, 1869, Candia, N. H.; George M., Apr. 14, 1871; James F., Sept. 11, 1872, Candia, N. H.; Laura M., June 29, 1876, Auburn, N. H.
William and ———. Children: Jane, Jan. 16, 1810; David, Sept. 9, 1812.
William and ———. Children: Nathaniel, Nov. 8, 1814; James, Dec. 25, 1817.
William, son of Phinehas, b. Dec. 8, 1771, in Methuen, Mass., and Margaret Watts, 1st wife, b. 1779. Children: Betsey, Nov. 28, 1801; Rachel, Jan. 21, 1804; William, Sept. 11, 1806; Hugh, Dec. 15, 1808.

Pettengill, William, Jr., and Eliza. Son, August 12, 1853.

Pickering, Ebenezer and Harriet. Children: ———, Apr. 15, 1855; Orrin A., Jan. 30, 1858.

Oliver and Mary O. Son, Nov. 15, 1855.

Pierce, Joseph W. and Emma L. Davis. Children: Dau., July 12, 1888; son, June 11, 1890.

Pike, Alfred and Mary Steele. Dau.: Helen Gertrude, Feb. 23, 1904.

Pillsbury, Ambrose B. and Florence M. Aiken. Dau., Aug. 25, 1910.

Charles George and Alice E. Miller. Children: Helen Iona, Mar. 8, 1895; Vera Dix, May 25, 1897; Grace Lillian, July 6, 1909.

Charles H. L. and Fannie A. Tyson; removed to Denver, Colo. Children: Viola, William Ira, Martha L., and Francis.

Charles S., b. Apr. 14, 1828, at Webster, N. H., and Mary C. Clough of Warner, N. H., b. Dec. 24, 1863. Children: Charles George, Feb. 15, 1865; Adams Dix, Mar. 23, 1868; John Arthur, Aug. 26, 1872.

Josiah H. and Alnora F. Pervier. Son, Jan. 31, 1854.

Leonard H. and Evelyn Sanborn. Children: Fred S., Ambrose Burnside, Edwin, William S., and Grace L. No dates. All reside in Derry, N. H.

Rosecrans W. and Annie E. Watts. Children: Maria, Sept 18, 1886; Horace Watts, Sept. 5, 1891; Dorothy, Jan. 8, 1896.

Rev. Steven, son of Micajah, b. Oct. 30, 1781, who came to Londonderry in 1839, and Lavinia Hobart, b. Nov. 1, 1795. Children: Mary B., Jan. 5, 1817; Lavinia H., Nov. 8, 1818; Josiah H., Aug. 15, 1821; Stephen, Jan. 25, 1824; Edwin, Mar. 26, 1826; Ann Judson, July 1, 1828; A. Judson, June 11, 1830; William S., Mar. 16, 1833, Sutton, N. H.; Leonard Hobart, Dec. 25, 1835.

Ulysses G. and Edith (Davis). Children: Marian, Aug. 30, 1897; William S., Apr. 12, 1899.

William S. and Martha S. Children: Annie Sarah, Mar. 16, 1860; John Thurston, Feb. 6, 1862; Rosecrans W., Sept. 18, 1863; Charles H. L., Mar. 16, 1866; Stephen P., July, 1859; Harriet L., Oct. 27, 1870; Arthur A., Dec. 13, 1872; Martha E., Mar. 29, 1874; Ulysses G., Nov. 24, 1876.

Pinkerton, Deacon James, brother of Major John, and Elisabeth Nesmith. Children: Isabella and James, died in infancy; Betsey; Jane; Mary B.; Clarissa.

Pinkerton, Deacon James and 2d wife, Sarah Wallace, dau. of Samuel Wallace. Children: Rebecca W. m. Perkins A. Hodge; Frances C.; David H.

John,* known as Elder or Major, b. in Ireland, 1720, and Rachel Duncan, 1st wife, b. May 11, 1745. Children: Mary, May 8, 1768; Naomi, Jan. 13, 1770; Elisabeth, Sept. 1, 1771; John, Oct. 12, 1777; Esther.

John came from North Ireland to Londonderry, 1724; settled in West Parish and died in 1780, leaving nine children: David, b. in Ireland; John, "The Benefactor," b. in Ireland; Samuel, James, Mary, Elisabeth, Rachel, Jane, and Matthew; last seven all b. in Londonderry.

John Morrison,† b. Feb. 6, 1818.

Mary and Alexander McGregor. Son: John P., adopted by Major Pinkerton.

Major Pinkerton and 2d wife, Polly Tufts. No children.

Matthew and ———. Children: John, James, David, settled in Boscawen, N. H.

Theron R. and Harriet M. B. White. Children: Frank R., Aug., 1860; Emma F., Oct., 1861; Carrie, Aug., 1863; Blake A., July, 1865; Ella, Aug., 1867; Theron, June, 1872.

Platts, Eliza, b. May 11, 1800. Son: Thomas B.

George W., b. 1828, and Mary (Manter), b. Londonderry. Children: Ida Florence, Mar. 7, 1856; George Henry, May 9, 1854; Charles Fremont, Feb. 23, 1859; George Manter, 1864; Frederick Allen, Oct. 31, 1866; Nathaniel Tucker, Jan. 11, 1872; Harold James, 1876.

James, b. 1755, in Rowley, was a Revolutionary soldier, and Mary Warner, b. Nov., 1755. Children: Mary, 1780; Susan, June 14, 1782; Nancy, Mar. 14, 1785; Sarah, Sept. 10, 1789; Mehitable, Feb. 22, 1790; Abigail, Jan. 11, 1792; James, May 6, 1794; Wesley,‡ July, 1797; Eliza, May 11, 1800; Sophia (Crowningshield) (Johnson); Mary (Crowningshield), m. George Crowningshield, b. Salem, Mass.

James Monroe, b. Dec. 2, 1824, came to Londonderry in 1844, and Harriet (Manter), b. Oct. 28, 1829. Children: Ella Frances, July 28, 1854; Clarence M., June 26, 1856; Hattie S., Nov. 6, 1858; Francis Manter, May 1, 1860; Egbert, May 21, 1863; Mamie Edith, Jan. 9, 1867; Florence Ethel, Oct. 18, 1871.

*Major John at his death left $90,000 to the East Parish and a like sum to the West Parish in Londonderry, also $13,000 to found the "Pinkerton Academy," in Derry, N. H.

†John Morrison Pinkerton was a noted counselor-at-law in Boston, and at his death gave $200,000 to Pinkerton Academy, Derry, N. H.

‡Wesley Platts, m. and resided in New York; later in Jackson, Mich.; had seven children: a son, Robert S., served in the Confederate army, Virginia.

Platts, Samuel and Jonathan, b. in Eng.; came to Rowley, Mass., 1640.

Thomas B. and Susan D. Emerson. Children: Frank G. and Charles Wesley. (See Emerson.)

Platt, William, b. Nov. 11, 1859, in Liverpool, Eng., and Emily Crowell, b. Jan. 14, 1861. Children: Emily Rose, Mar. 5, 1884, Liverpool, Eng.; Gilbert, Dec. 25, 1885, Liverpool, Eng.; Earle Percy, Apr. 5, 1888, Londonderry, N. H.; Ethel May, May 12, 1891, Windham, N. H.; Lillie F., Oct. 2, 1894, Londonderry, N. H.

Plummer, Abel came from Rowley to Londonderry in 1775. Sons: Nathan, served in Revolutionary war; Davis, served in Revolutionary war; Capt. Abel.

Capt. Abel and Elisabeth Hale. Children: Persis, Arley, Abigail, Eliza, Warren, Abel, Hale.

Abel and Mary Anderson. Children: Mary, Nancy, John Anderson, William, Susan, Elmira, and Sarah.

Albert C., b. Sept. 24, 1851.

George Nathan and Eliza M. Annis. Children: Charlotte May, July 24, 1899; Robert Nathan, Sept. 12, 1900; Hazel Marian, Mar. 12, 1902.

Granville Flanders, b. Sept. 11, 1844, and Kate E. Hughes, b. July 23, 1847. No children.

Capt. John Anderson, b. Aug. 5, 1814, and Eliza P. Coffin, b. 1815. Children: Mary N., m. Joseph Vickery, Norwalk, Ohio; Elmira E., m. Rev. Henry B. Copp; Emma A., m. Capt. J. F. Hobbs, Lake City, Ia.; Laura A., m. Charles M. Noyes, Nashua, N. H.

Nathan, b. Nov. 15, 1809, and Charlotte Towns (Boyd), b. Dec. 1, 1815. Children: Robert Kittredge, Dec. 18, 1847; George Nathan, Nov. 28, 1849.

Robert Kittredge and Laura S. Benson. Children: George Kittredge, Mar. 17, 1903; Gertrude Martha, Jan. 29, 1906.

William, b. Sept. 4, 1860, in Inverness, P. Q., and Sarah Wilson (McCharg), b. Apr. 28, 1870, in Leeds. Children: Ethel Maude, Feb. 8, 1888; Stanley Weston, June 30, 1891; Mabel Alice, Jan. 22, 1892.

William and Sybil Ann. Son, Feb. 16, 1856.

Poff, William J. and Caroline A. Children: Sylvester William, Jan. 30, 1877; Cara Bell, Sept. 17, 1878.

Pond, George W. and Lucy A. Mariam. Dau., Oct. 10, 1889.

William J. and Anna J. Son: William Fales, Nov. 10, 1861.

Poor, Perry and Caroline M. Chipman. Dau., May 8, 1853.

Porter, Edward A. and Eliza D. Rollins. Son: Charles Edward, Dec. 30, 1890.

Potter, Albert and Alma J. Son: Franklin Louis, Mar. 16, 1881.

Prentice,* Hon. John, b. 1748, and 1st wife, Ruth Lemon, had six children; 2d wife, Tabitha Sargent, six children.

Preston, William and Ellen. Dau.: Ida, Aug. 1, 1882.

Proctor, Frank and Sarah H. Emerson. One son. (See Emerson record.)

Henry Sherman, b. 1866, Dunstable, Mass., and Lizzie R. Webster, b. Dec. 2, 1864. Children: Pearl C., Oct. 24, 1886; Royal S., Apr. 7, 1889; Iva B., Jan. 18, 1891; Ruby G., Sept. 13, 1892; H. Earle, Jan. 4, 1894; Muriel A., July 29, 1899. All came to Londonderry in 1901.

Iva B. and Morley E. Hollingshead, June 14, 1909.

Jacob and Lucy. Children: Jacob, Sept. 22, 1776; Humphra, Oct. 8, 1777; Edward, Oct. 8, 1779; Thomas, July 11, 1781; Lucy, Aug. 8, 1783; Joseph, Aug. 26, 1785; Silas, Sept. 21, 1787; Asa, July 18, 1790.

Lester A. and Emma G. Townsend. Dau.: Marian G., June 12, 1906.

Pearl C. and Seth G. Wing, b. June 28, 1881. Children: Hazel E., Dec. 20, 1905; Marjorie I., Feb. 12, 1908.

Royal S. and Edith F. Boyce, b. 1884. Children: Gladys G., July 27, 1907; Beatrice A., Aug. 20, 1909.

William and Georgietta Garvin. One dau., Mabel. (See Garvin.)

Purdy, Jeremiah D. and Ellen F. Dau., May 16, 1884.

Purno, Nicholas and Mary A. Dau., July 5, 1854.

Putnam, Elbert O. and Maude Campbell. Dau.: Martha Ethell, Sept. 19, 1894.

Ramsey, Hugh and Ann. Children: John, Aug. 14, 1717; Mary, June 5, 1719; James, Mar. 16, 1721; Hugh, Jan. 15, 1724; Mathew, May 29, 1726; Margaret, July 9, 1729.

Rankin, William and Mary. Dau.: Jane, Oct. 20, 1756.

Ratte, Harry and Josephine Pellen. Children: Mary Eva, June 18, 1901; son, Aug. 19, 1903; George H., Feb. 23, 1906; Joseph Albert, Apr. 12, 1908.

Rattray, James W. and Mary. Son, Oct. 2, 1851.

Ray, Charles W., b. Aug. 1, 1877, at Auburn, N. H., and Isabella S. Fitts, b. Sept. 11, 1874, at Dunbarton, N. H. Children: Lewis Clark, May 13, 1897; Gladys Eva, June 11, 1903; Carolyn E., Jan. 29, 1906.

John Edward, b. Oct. 3, 1873, Auburn, N. H., and Annie M. (Stone), b. Nov. 11, 1874. Children: James Harold, Oct. 31, 1895; Mildred Elisabeth, Feb. 17, 1897; George Clifton, Nov. 12, 1899.

*He was Representative thirteen years; Speaker 1794-5 and from 1798 to 1803.

Raymond, John H. and Clara. Son: John, Mar. 27, 1874.

Read, Bethiah, b. Dec. 20, 1818.

Redfield, Charles and Betsey. Children: Mary Ann, May 1, 1815; Charles, Jan. 15, 1817; Sarah E., Jan. 2, 1820; Jane, Dec. 2, 1825.

Reed, Jonathan and Sarah. Dau.: Elisabeth, June 10, 1776.

Reid, Elizabeth and Robert McGregor, son of Rev. David McGregor.

Gen. George and Mary Woodburn.* Children: Betty, May 5, 1766; James, Dec. 10, 1767; Mary Boyd, Oct. 11, 1769; John, Oct. 23, 1771; George,† Jan. 29, 1774.

James and Mary. Children: Matthew, Apr. 2, 1728; Thomas, May 3, 1730; Gen. George, 1733.

Phineas Aiken, b. Aug. 8, 1854, at Litchfield, N. H., and Addie Annah Chase, b. Nov. 15, 1861. Children: Pearl Agnes, July 20, 1887; Mercia Burnham, July 28, 1890; Harold Morrison, Oct. 1, 1891; Walter Phineas, Oct. 1, 1891; Lillian May, Sept. 17, 1901.

Walter, b. May 31, 1842, and Phila S. Gage (changed by law to Young), b. Dec. 7, 1839. No children.

Renken, Alexander and Mary. Dau.: Agness, Aug. 5, 1729.

Reynolds, Daniel and Hannah. Children: Stephen, Jan. 10, 1768; Sally, Oct. 22, 1769; Daniel, Oct. 7, 1771; Hamelton, July 5, 1773; Polly Spofford, July 5, 1773; Hannah, Mar. 16, 1776; Joseph Spofford, Oct. 20, 1779; Thomas Kemball, Oct. 20, 1781; Esther Sergent, Jan. 18, 1783; Betsey, Mar. 30, 1785.

Rice, Charles H. and Addie J. Bailey. Dau.: Vera Belle, Dec. 22, 1907.

Richards, Frank C. and Emma M. Lafond. Son: Frank A., Dec. 29, 1907.

(Richardson family, as compiled by C. R. Richardson and others.)

Richardson, Ammi George, b. Aug. 26, 1857, son of Stephen C. and Regina (Harvey) Richardson, and Nettie E. Smith, b. May 1, 1884. Three children. (For names see Smith record.)

*Mary (Woodburn) Reid is the one of whom Gen. Stark once remarked, "If there is a woman in New Hampshire fit to be *Governor* 'tis Molly Reid."

†George Reid graduated at Dartmouth College in 1797. Practised law in Maine; married Mary Bosland in 1809; Harriet Davidson in 1835.

Richardson, Caleb, of Methuen, and Tryphena Bodwell, dau. of Capt. Daniel Bodwell, and Eliza Parker. Children: Mary, Jan. 8, 1736; Parker, Mar. 7, 1738; Caleb, Sept. 26, 1741, killed at Ticonderoga; Tryphena, Jan. 13, 1743; Abigail, Sept. 8, 1746; Samuel,* Feb. 22, 1749; John,* Sept. 1, 1751; Abigail, Feb. 25, 1754; William,† Oct. 21, 1756; Eliphalet, July 6, 1759.

Clara J. and Charles W. Noyes. Son: Warren Walter, Apr. 19, 1860. (See Noyes family.)

Fannie A. and George A. Greenough, Oct. 8, 1874. Dau.: Hattie Clare, June 3, 1880.

Hattie Clare and Mr. Smith. Dau.: Dorothy A., Jan. 28, 1900.

Joseph and Margaret Browne,‡ b. 1635. Children: Mary, Apr. 16, 1682; William, Mar. 22, 1684; Joseph, Dec. 31, 1686; Elizabeth, Feb. 28, 1689; Daniel, Apr. 4, 1692; Sarah, June 19, 1694; Thomas, Feb. 15, 1697; Caleb, June 9, 1704.

Mary L. and Charles H. Gilmore. Children: Minnie L., Mar. 23, 1864; Charles W., Dec. 29, 1866; Addison K., Feb. 13, 1874.

Minnie L. Gilmore and Mr. Boyd. Children: Marion, 1888; Dorothy, 1890.

Myron and Augusta R. Nutt, half sister to Commodore Nutt, b. Aug. 1, 1866. Children: Myron Harold, Mar. 4, 1895; Sarah Augusta, Jan. 15, 1897.

Nellie M. and John R. McKean, b. Mar. 23, 1862. Children: Andrew W., Mar. 15, 1884; Mary F. R., Mar. 31, 1885; Clara H., Sept. 29, 1888; J. M. Roy, Sept. 17, 1890; Clyde D., Mar. 13, 1893; Barbara A., July 16, 1895; Beatrice H., Nov. 12, 1897; Mildred F., May 20, 1900.

Samuel and Mary Grace Fox, b. Aug. 4, 1858. Children: Bernice May, Apr. 20, 1883; Persis Annie, Aug. 29, 1888.

Warren Richardson family, collected by Mrs. Nellie M. (Richardson) McKean of Londonderry, N. H.

Warren, b. Jan. 3, 1814, at Westford, Mass., and 1st wife, Clarissa Dix. Son: Warren, Feb. 13, 1837.

Warren and 2d wife, Mary Jane Wilson, b. Jan. 27, 1817. Children: Clara J., Aug. 15, 1842; Mary L., Aug. 6, 1846; John W., Dec. 17, 1850; Fannie A., June 12, 1854; Nellie M., Aug. 26, 1859.

*Samuel and John were drafted in the Revolutionary war.

†William was a drummer in Revolutionary war.

‡Margaret Browne was the daughter of Peter Godfrey and Mary Browne, who was the daughter of Thomas Browne, "weaver," who came to this country in 1635. According to the "History of Newbury and Savage's Genealogy" she *was the first white child born in Newbury.*

Richardson, Warren, 2d, and Mary A. Kabis, Cheyenne, Wyoming. Children: Victoria A. D., res. Cheyenne, Wyo.; Warren, res. Cheyenne, Wyo.; Clarence B., res. Mexico; Emile, res. Cheyenne, Wyo.; Laura V. D., res. Missouri; Mary Valeria, res. Cheyenne, Wyo.

William of Newbury and Elizabeth Wiseman. Children: Joseph, May 18, 1655; Benjamin, Mar. 13, 1657; Elizabeth, Mar. 14, 1658.

William and Lydia Messer, b. 1767. Children: Caleb, Jan. 3, 1786; Lydia, Dec. 14, 1792; William M., Feb. 12, 1795; Sophia S., Apr. 7, 1797; Nathaniel W., Mar. 12, 1799; Thomas J., June 14, 1801; Elizabeth P., July 25, 1803; Samuel R., July 19, 1807; Mary H., Aug. 29, 1809.

William Messer and Betsey Pettengill, b. Nov. 28, 1801. Children: William Pettengill, July 26, 1821; Margaret, Feb. 5, 1823; Eliza Jane, Sept. 7, 1827; Mary Ann, Nov. 15, 1837; Samuel, Mar. 30, 1845.

William Pettengill and Sarah Hale Goodwin, b. Aug. 11, 1833. Children: Harry, July 14, 1857; William, Feb. 26, 1860; Myron, Mar. 21, 1864; Sarah, Apr. 10, 1866.

William of Newbury, b. in Eng. about 1620.*

William, M. D., and Esther F. Whidden, b. Jan. 1, 1858. Children: Florence E., Mar. 28, 1886; Sarah B., Jan. 27, 1888; Mabel E., Nov. 21, 1890, Westford, Conn.; William Percy, Nov. 17, 1894; Lester Earl, Sept. 23, 1897; two daughters died in infancy.

Ridell, Robert and Mary. Children: Susanna, May 11, 1750; Gann, Feb. 22, 1753.

Ripley, Joseph and Matilda Sampson, b. Dec. 23, 1807. Children: George H., Martin C., Susan M.

Martin and Sarah A. Dau.: Minnie, Aug. 5, 1867.

Rivers, Joseph F. and Honora M. Tucker. Children: Honora Melvina, Mar. 18, 1899; Merrimack Guy, Apr. 10, 1901.

Roach, Fred S. and Retta M. Robie. Children: Dau., May 11, 1898; Elwin, May 27, 1899; Grace Muriel, Dec. 28, 1900.

Joseph and Henrietta Peabody, b. 1849. Children: Hattie E., Jan. 29, 1874; Frederic L., Aug. 13, 1877; Mary Etta, Aug. 22, 1880.

Robie, Alonzo and ———. Son, May 7, 1868.

Edward and Mary (Prescott). Son: Samuel Prescott, Sept. 30, 1831.

Frank E. and Minnie Josephine Marden, m. Mar. 11, 1893, Apopka, Florida. Children: Fannie Latica, Feb. 21, 1896; Edison Frank, Nov. 2, 1898; Harrison Alexander, Mar. 8, 1904.

*The descendants of Parker Richardson possess the coat-of-arms.

Robie, Frank L. and Jennie. Son: Larazine F., June 15, 1872.

James and Rebecca (Chase) Rowell, b. May 13, 1837. Children: Nellie Adaline, Oct. 4, 1857, Derry, N. H.; Perley Samuel, May 28, 1862; Frank Everett, Nov. 13, 1864; George William, May 1, 1879.

Perley S. and Mabel Eva Buttrick. Son: Myron Perley, Sept. 19, 1900.

Robinson, Charles H. and Alice E. Richards. Children: Ch., July 20, 1892; dau., July 30, 1894.

Horace and Betsey. Children: Son, Mar. 24, 1853; son, Apr. 29, 1855; Clarrissa, Aug. 3, 1858.

John and Agness. Children: George, July 29, 1774; Samuel, Mar. 21, 1779.

John and Jean. Son: Samuel, July 15, 1776.

William E. and Sarah. Children: Son, Sept. 2, 1855; son, Dec. 19, 1868.

Roby, Joseph and Mary L. Son, May 7, 1854.

Rodgers, Fred T. and Alice E. Bailey. Son, June 15, 1890.

James and Joan. Children: Martha, May 3, 1723; Thomas, July 7, 172–; William, Feb. 27, 1726–7; ——, Jan. 25, 1729; James, Feb. 22, 1731–2.

James and Lidah. Son: Hugh, Nov. 10, 1752.

Rogers, Edmund and Mary. Children: Maria S., Nov. 8, 1814; Charles S., Sept. 27, 1816.

James and Margaret. Children: David, Nov. 7, 1762; James, Nov. 22, 1764.

Justin and Rosa St. Pierre. Son: Justin Earl, Jan. 23, 1906.

Justin C. and Flora M. Dau.: Nellie May, May 25, 1894.

Thomas and Mary. Children: Louisa, Oct. 11, 1808; Mary, June 20, 1811; Elisabeth, Nov. 12, 1813; William A., Jan. 12, 1816.

Wallace and Mary McCuepin. Dau.: Flora May, Nov. 10, 1904.

William and Abigell. Children: Abigell, Nov. 25, 1763; Jean, Mar. 21, 1766; Eduth, July 21, 1768; Hanna, Jan. 11, 1771.

Rollins, George H. and Idelia Daniels. Son: Carlos D., Sept. 7, 1900.

Ross, Napoleon and Cora Houle. Children: Napoleon E., Aug. 9, 1909; Herbert Edward, Aug. 19, 1910.

Roullier, Napoleon and Eva Hall. Dau.: Mary B. A., Apr. 7, 1905.

Rouse, William M. and Hattie L. Brown. (See Rowell record.)

Rowe, William B. and Hellen M. Spencer. Son, Mar. 13, 1903.

Rowell, Irving J. and Sarah Crosby, 1st wife, Pepperell, Mass. Dau.: Bertha, m. Dr. Davis, Webster, Mass. 2d wife, Emma Dow. No children.

John, son of Job Rowell and Abigail Pollard, b. Apr. 4, 1809, at Manchester, N. H., and Jane P. Spinney, b. Mar. 16, 1814. Children: Clara Jane, Apr. 17, 1846; Irving John, Nov. 23, 1850; Laura Z., Feb. 12, 1854.

Joseph M., b. Apr. 11, 1807, sheriff at Manchester, N. H., and Janett (Hall), b. Sept. 7, 1809. Children: Mary Jane, May 10, 1834; Abby Lowell, Oct. 31, 1836, res. Manchester, N. H.; Ellen Balou, Sept. 21, 1839; Joseph Elwyn, Aug. 4, 1842.

Russell, John and Angie Page. Three children: Charles, Clarence, and Arthur.

Warren and Lizzie J. Dau.: Ethmer I., Oct. 12, 1878.

Rush, James and Bertha Camron. Son: George Henry, Nov. 26, 1893.

Ryan, James and Alice. Son, Feb. 1, 1856.

Sampson family as compiled by Turner Sampson of Londonderry, N. H., 1910.

Sampson, Anna D. and Levi R. Starrett. Children: Sara A. Starrett, Apr. 11, 1880, Andover, Mass.; Arthur R., June 2, 1884.

Branch,* b. Nov. 20, 1769, in Duxbury, Mass., and Polly (Crocker), b. Mar. 26, 1772, Pembroke, Mass. Children: Polly or Mary, Jan. 2, 1800, at Londonderry; Agnes, July 30, 1802; Branch, Mar. 2, 1804, in Londonderry; Abigail, Feb. 5, 1806; Matilda, Dec. 23, 1807; Huldah C., July 30, 1811; Turner, Dec. 1, 1814; Lydia A., May 9, 1819.

Polly m. John Clark; Branch m., Apr. 11, 1833, Alice K. Simonds, b .Apr. 5, 1816; Abigail m. John Denver; Matilda m. Joseph Ripley; Huldah C. m. Phineas Foster; Turner m. for 1st wife Eliza Holly, for 2d, Sybal Taylor, 1861; Lydia m. Albert V. Stevens at Londonderry, Nov., 1838; he was born Apr. 8, 1808, Belfast, Me.

*N. B. John Carver came over in the May Flower with his wife Katherine in 1620. They had a daughter who married a Turner. This Turner had a daughter who married the Great-grandfather "Sampson." This daughter's brother took up a settlement in Maine which was called the town of "Turner." This Great-grandfather had one son, called Branch Sampson. Branch Sampson had two sons, Branch and Turner, and six daughters, viz.: Mary or Polly, Agnes, Abigail, Matilda, Huldah and Lydia.

Sampson, Branch and Alice K. Children: John, Apr. 3, 1836; m. Elizabeth F. Sanborn, Nov. 28, 1867; she was b. May 16, 1847. Edward, Feb. 1, 1839; m. Hannah W. Colby, July 26, 1864, in Phila., Pa., b. Nov. 13, 1840; m. 2d wife, Jennie U. Mudgett, b. July 15, 1840, Aug. 11, 1866; m. 3d wife, Carrie A. Lord, b. July 18, 1842, Apr. 16, 1890. Lucy A., Aug. 8, 1841. Mary J., Aug. 21, 1844; m. Joseph A. Berry, Oct. 6, 1872; he was b. Oct. 14, 1830, in Middleton, Mass. Turner, Feb. 18, 1847, in Londonderry; m. Mary C. Wilkins, May 22, 1894; she was b. June 19, 1858, in Dorchester, Mass. Anna D., Feb. 28, 1851; m. Levi R. Starrett, May 27, 1879; he was b. June 14, 1851, in New Boston, N. H.

Edward and Hannah W. Colby. Dau.: Flora E., Apr. 22, 1865.

Edward and Jennie U. Mudget. Son: George E., Mar. 29, 1871, at Lynn, Mass.; m. Esther E. C. Peterson, Aug. 15, 1901; she was b. July 22, 1882, in Sweden.

Frank E. and Nellie G. Hilgore. Children: Donald H., Mar. 31, 1904; Richard E., Jan. 17, 1906; Helen, Sept. 16, 1909. All b. in Concord, N. H.

George E. and Jennie U. Mudgett. Children: Edward O., May 25, 1902, Lynn, Mass.; Evelyn A., Apr. 18, 1905, Lynn, Mass.

Huldah C. and Phineas Foster. Children: Charles, George, Horace B., Laura E. All b. at North Andover, Mass.

John and Abigail Sampson of Denver. Children: Richard, John; both b. in Maine.

John and Elizabeth F. Sanborn. Children: Frank E., Dec. 7, 1868, m. Millie G. Hilgore, Dec. 25, 1893, b. July 11, 1869, in Norway, Mass.; Ida E., Nov. 11, 1870.

John and Polly. Children: Nancy Clark, b. in Londonderry, m. John J. Grant; Henry, b. in Londonderry.

Lydia A. and Albert V. Stevens. Children: Lydia Stevens, Aug. 25, 1839, m. Charles Haines; George A., Mar. 9, 1842; Henrietta S., b. in Haverhill, Mass., m. Joseph A. Maddox; Harriet, Oct. 8, 1850, at Haverhill, Mass.; Sarah A. Stevens, Dec. 24, 1855, at Dover, N. H.

Mary J. and Albert P. Berry. Children: Albert R. Berry, Mar. 18, 1902, No. Andover, Mass.; Raymond F., Apr. 17, 1905, No. Andover, Mass.

Mary J. and Joseph A. Berry. Son: Albert P. Berry, Aug. 9, 1875; m., June 16, 1897, Sarah S. Rea, b. Aug. 19, 1874, North Andover, Mass.

Sampson, Matilda and Joseph Ripley. Children: Eliza A. Ripley, b. in Londonderry, m. William C. Greeley; George H., b. in Londonderry, m. Mrs. Harn; Martin C., b. in Londonderry, m. Mrs. Sarah Ann (Annis) Manter, 1867, Londonderry; Susan M., b. in Londonderry, 1st hus. Royal T. Snell, 2d hus. Zachariah K. Whittemore.

Turner and Eliza Holly. Son: Henry, b. at Andover, Mass.

Turner and May C. Wilkins. Dau.: Alice M., Jan. 27, 1896.

Turner and Sybal A. Taylor. Son: Henry T., b. at Lawrence, Kan.

Sanborn, Cyrus and Jane. Dau., Oct. 5, 1861.

Cyrus and Lavinia. Son, Nov. 3, 1862.

Josiah, son of John and Betsey, b. Apr. 13, 1822, Chester, N. H., and Martha A. Dolan, b. Aug. 15, 1833, at Derry, N. H.; removed to Londonderry, Mar. 4, 1864. Children: Eliza B., July 10, 1864; Willie S., May 16, 1875.

Justin, b. Jan. 9, 1847, in Sandown, N. H., and Sarah L. (Hazelton), b. May 16, 1852, in Chester, N. H.; came to Londonderry in 1893. No children.

Orrin N., b. 1867, and Nellie E. Bowers, b. 1865; both b. in Sanbornton, N. H. Children: Ernest Will, Apr. 16, 1898; Nathaniel Orrin, June 15, 1901; both b. in Londonderry, N. H.

Willie S. and Lillian Avery, b. Mar. 21, 1874. Son: Harold A., July 30, 1904.

Savage, Eugene A. and Alice V. Son, Sept. 7, 1881.

Frank A. and Mildred D. Children: Willie Amasa, Oct. 22, 1881; Lottie E., Dec. 10, 1883.

Savory, Jonathan and Abigail Coffin, b. Jan. 4, 1814. No children.

Thomas and Grizel (Grissey Holmes (?)). Children: Elisabeth, May 9, 1810; Jonathan, May 7, 1812; Caroline, Mar. 14, 1821.

Sawyer, Priscilla, b. in 1843.

Royal G. and Annie. Children: Annie Bell, Jan. 25, 1877; Thomas J., Aug., 1831, Gorham, Me.

Schindler, Richard F. and A. A. Schwarzenberg. Son: Walter R., May 28, 1907.

Schwartz, Frederick L., b. 1827, and Cordelia, b. 1837. Children: Louis B., May, 1855; Nellie, Feb. 1, 1858; Mary L., Apr. 1, 1870.

Seavey, Emira Coburn, wife of John March, b. Oct. 30, 1815, in Dracut, Mass.

Senter, Benjamin L. and Abigail. Son, Sept. 10, 1852.

John and Jean. Children: Samuel, Jan. 31, 1720–1; Joseph, Mar., 1724; Jean, Oct. 8, 1725–6.

Severance, Harvey, b. May 4, 1860, and Ortensia M. Smith. Son: William Bernard, Aug. 10, 1882.

Shackett, Ruth, b. Sept. 2, 1902.

Shattuck, Andrew J. and Mary E. Children: Alice J., May 31, 1873; Amy Irene, Apr. 23, 1875.

George W. and Hattie E. Merrill. Son, Nov. 13, 1893.

Shedd, Julia A., b. Jan. 25, 1841.

Shipley, Daniel T. and Ellen A. Son: Wilber Abbott, Aug. 16, 1862.

John, b. Apr. 10, 1809, and Rebecca (Dickey), b. Dec. 19, 1813. Children: Joseph Lucian, Mar. 31, 1836; Mary Frances, Oct. 30, 1838; Julia Dickey, Nov. 5, 1846.

Short, George and Rose A. Jerome. Children: Son, June 29, 1885; Henry G., Aug. 3, 1887; Forest A., Sept. 12, 1888.

Shute, Benjamin and Lucy. Children: Sarah, Nov. 8, 1803; George, Aug. 19, 1807; Juliann, Sept. 26, 1809; Almira, Mar. 12, 1812.

Benjamin and Rebecca. Children: Rebecca, Feb. 12, 1788; Mary, Aug. 11, 1789; Samuel, May 17, 1793; Michael, Jan. 20, 1795; William B., Sept. 9, 1796; Daniel, July 17, 1798.

Michael and Olive. Son: James A., Jan. 4, 1819.

Sides, Albert H., b. Jan. 13, 1850, and Elisabeth A. (Colby), b. Oct. 30, 1856. Son: Percival C., May 1, 1889.

Simpson, William H. and Abby M. Dau., May 21, 1855.

Skogland, Alexander and Inez V. Bean. Son, July 19, 1909.

Slate, Lyman and Abby B. Son, Aug. 23, 1855.

Sleeper, Josiah, b. Apr. 2, 1798, at Chester, N. H., and Hannah Jane (Dickey), b. Dec. 23, 1805. Dau.: Elisabeth Patterson, Mar. 16, 1834.

Smiley, John B., b. 1864, in Maine, and Mary (Burke), b. 1867, in Manchester, N. H. Son: James Ernest, Oct. 23, 1901.

Smith, Alexander, b. July 24, 1793, and Sarah Melvin, b. July 10, 1797, dau. of Reuben and Sarah Marshall. Children: Reuben Alonzo, Mar. 8, 1823; Sarah Ann, Sept. 14, 1825; Daniel Dinsmore, June 14, 1827; Clarisa Melvin, Feb. 22, 1830; Mary Jane, June 5, 1832; Charles Sidney, May 1, 1834; Walter Alexander, Nov. 5, 1840.

Charles E. and Mary McCann. Son: Edward Lafayette, Oct. 13, 1891.

Charles and Esther L. Steele. Dau.: Irene Delia, Aug. 31, 1899.

Smith, Daniel Dinsmore and Sarah Ann Ballou, b. Mar. 11, 1833. Children: Ortensia Mazota, May 26, 1856; Nettie Esdell, June 10, 1858; Minnie Defransa, Nov. 17, 1860; Annie Theressa, Nov. 15, 1865; Clarabel A., Mar. 15, 1868 (see Fred E. Annis); Sarah Myrtle, June 2, 1872; Alexander Daniel, Nov. 11, 1875; Melvin Dinsmore, Mar. 27, 1877.

Elias and Agnes. Dau.: Hannah Berker, Apr. 4, 1795.

Elisha, b. Jan. 20, 1801, son of David and Polly (Page), who came to Londonderry Mar. 25, 1799, and Rachel Sanborn, b. Feb. 10, 1810. Children: Nathan S., June 20, 1831; Sherburn Dana, Apr. 4, 1834; Henry Clay, July 13, 1844.

Fred W. and Harriet F. Son, Aug. 5, 1901.

Henry Clay and Susan D. Hazelton, b. July 27, 1847, at Chester, N. H. Children: Alice B., Feb. 12, 1878; Nelson E., May 14, 1880; Grace R., June 21, 1882; Ella Nancy, Mar. 3, 1885; Fred H., Jan. 24, 1887.

James and Jean. Children: William, Feb. 9, 1715; Rebecca, Apr. 19, 1718; Samuel, Mar. 29, 1720; James, May 12, 1723.

John and Iliza (Fish) Lang. Son: George E. Lang, May 3, 1869. (Father took the surname of mother.)

Kirk Leigh, b. May 19, 1857, at Wilmot, N. H., and Nellie A. (Annis), b. Mar. 1, 1860, at Londonderry. Children: Leigh, Nov. 10, 1885, Contoocook, N. H.; Laura Mae, Sept. 10, 1889, Webster, N. H.; Ada Julia, Mar. 27, 1893, Londonderry, N. H.; Mildred Grace, Dec. 28, 1894, Londonderry, N. H.

Louis and Margaret Bresnon. Son: Harold O., Oct. 17, 1908.

Melvin Dinsmore and Edith May Fisher, b. July 3, 1877, So. Hadley, Mass., dau. of Joshua and Sarah (Jones) Fisher. Children: Halsey, May 13, 1901; Myrtle Edith, Mar. 21, 1903.

Nathaniel, b. Sept. 9, 1792, Tewksbury, Mass., and Elisabeth M. (Selden), b. Jan. 6, 1797. Children: Elisabeth A., Sept. 2, 1816; Mary P., Nov. 2, 1819, res. Manchester, N. H.; Harriet E., 1822; Robert Selden, Apr. 9, 1828; Ellen J., Feb. 16, 1832; Cornelia H., Feb. 3, 1835, res. Nashua, N. H.

Nelson E. and Frances V. Whittle. Children: Grace R., Sept. 9, 1906; Ernest Wilbur, July 10, 1910.

Nettie Esdell and Ammi George Richardson, b. Aug. 26, 1857, son of Stephen C. and Regina (Harvey) Richardson. Children: Ammi Carlton, Apr. 16, 1885; Nettie Vivian, Jan. 24, 1897; Ella Elwyn, Aug. 4, 1899. Family resides in Haverhill, Mass.

Smith, Reuben A. and Laura Jones, b. May 24, 1825. Children: Stasy, Alonzo, and Etta Laura.

——— and Hattie Clare Greenough. Dau.: Dorothy A., Jan. 28, 1900.

Robert Selden and Hannah L. Colburn, b. Nov. 5, 1830. Children: Eleanor M., Dec. 29, 1853 (see J. T. Hartford); George P., Mar. 7, 1858, res. Genesee, Ill.

Robert and Sarah. Children: Kettie, Mar. 2, 1767; Joseph, Aug. 29, 1768; Mary, Aug. 26, 1770; Bettie, Mar. 9, 1772.

Samuel, b. in Hudson, N. H., Dec. 16, 1763, son of John and Betsey McNiel, and Agnes Grimes, b. July 9, 1767. Children: Hannah, John, Alexander, James, Abraham, Hugh, Samuel, Olive, Fanny, Ann.

Sherburn Dana and Nancy Hodgeman, b. Mar. 28, 1838. Children: Mary Etta, May 18, 1866; Emma N., Sept. 17, 1867.

Timothy A. and Mary. Son, June 2, 1861.

William H. and Abigail M. Dau., Dec. 2, 1852.

Solford, William and Isabella. Dau.: Elisabeth, Feb. 13, 1736.

Spalding, Jacob F., Rev. and M. D., b. July 11, 1842, and Delia (Annis), b. Mar. 17, 1835, Londonderry, N. H. Children: Ephraim, Sept. 27, 1866; Albert, Nov. 29, 1867; Elisabeth, June 20, 1870; Hattie L., Apr. 14, 1874; all of Hudson, N. H.; Alice, Sept. 17, 1876, Londonderry, N. H.; Charles, Apr. 24, 1879.

Spear, James and Augusta E. Dau., July 6, 1875.

Spinney, John D., son of Alexander and Zillah M., b. Dec. 7, 1816, and Zillah M. (Taylor), b. 1816. Children: Georgia F., June 28, 1844; Julia M., Dec. 31, 1846; Eugene Laroy, Nov. 19, 1849; Ellen A., May 17, 1852; Emma K., Sept. 6, 1856.

Stacy, Fred E. and Jennie M. Gilcreast. Dau., Apr. 1, 1887.

Stark, Alden D., b. Oct. 30, 1878, Lyme, N. H., and Harriet N. Runnals, b. Feb. 3, 1879, Norwich, Vt. Children: Thalma M., Dec. 2, 1900; Marjorie Maud, Dec. 31, 1901; Dories J. V., Feb. 14, 1903; Norman G., Oct. 26, 1904; Mabel B., Dec. 10, 1906; Frank Alden, June 19, 1909.

Archibald and Nellie. Children: Ann, June 20, ———; William, Apr., 172–.

Gen. John, b. Aug. 28, 1728, son of Archibald and Eleanor Nichols.

Stearns, Lyman M., b. Mar. 4, 1858, Lynn, Mass., and Alnora M. Chase, b. May 11, 1854. No children.

Stell, David and Janet. Son: Thomas, March 5, 1754.

Stephenson, Charles E. and Clara M. Child, 1882.

Stevens, Francis and Joanna. Dau., May 19, 1854.
Horace E., b. Feb. 24, 1837, Manchester, N. H., and Betsey Ann Ambrose, b. June 6, 1838. Children: Clarence A., Nov. 11, 1872, Manchester, N. H.; Florence A., Oct. 24, 1876.
Susanna, Jan. 28, 1824.
William F. and Emma P. Dau.: Lucy S., Feb. 26, 1882.

Stewart, Charles and Mary. Children: Elisabeth, Jan. 11, 1728–9; Mary, May 5, 1730; Margaret, Oct. 4, 1731; William, Feb. 12, 1732–3.
John and Jean. Son: John, June 29, 1737.

Stiell, Thomas and Martha. Children: Thomas, Dec. 25, 172–; James, Mar. 28, 172–; David, Jan. 30, 1726–7.

Stiles, Lewis and Sarah P. Avery. One dau. (See Avery.)

Stoddley, Arthur and Mary L. London. Son: Joseph H., Jan. 18, 1907.

Stokes, Harrie D. and Annie L. Smith. Children: Clifton H., May 30, 1900; Orrin Parker; Jennie Harriet, Dec. 18, 1908.
Moses D., b. June 12, 1806, Manchester, N. H., and Irene (French), b. Apr. 14, 1807. Children: Henry P., Dec. 18, 1830; Gilman M., May 10, 1835; Irene A., June 7, 1839; John F., Nov. 1, 1841; Orrin B., Feb. 20, 1847.
Orrin B. and Jennie P. Durrah, b. Dec. 24, 1849. Children: Fred L., Sept. 28, 1870; Harrie D., Oct. 26, 1878; Orrin Parker, Apr. 26, 1886.

Stone, James G., b. May 20, 1844, Stark, N. H., and 2d wife, Elisabeth B. Hicks, b. Nov. 5, 1842. Dau.: Annie M., Nov. 11, 1874.

St. Onge, John G. and Josephine Cason. Son, Jan. 31, 1904.

Strong, Fred H. and Emma H. Dau., Feb. 2, 1885.

Stuart, John and Jean. Son: John, June 29, 1737.

Sweatt, Abby, b. 1807, Salisbury, N. H.
Joseph A., b. Feb. 2, 1835, and Sarah J. Thompson, 1st wife, b. Sept. 6, 1838. Children: James M., Jan. 31, 1856; Elisabeth A., Dec. 15, 1859.
Joseph A. and Mary L. Galencia, 3d wife. Children: Millie, Aug. 7, 1905; Lizzie, Aug. 7, 1905.
Moses, b. 1803, Salisbury, N. H.

Tabor, Joseph and Alma J. Son, July 3, 1872.

Tagart, John and Mary. Children: Merrian, Apr. 25, 1723; Agnus, June 7, 1731; Margaret, Aug. 22, 1733; Jennat, Oct. 16, 1735.
Neall and Roas. Son, July 23, 1739.

Taggart, Rev. Irad, b. Jan. 22, 1828, and Lucina Peck, b. May 25, 1828.
Rev. Samuel, son of James, b. 1750.
Thomas and Jean. Children: Margrat, Oct. 7, 1763; James, Apr. 25, 1765; John, Feb. 28, 1769; Robert, Dec. 30, 1770; Samuel, June 18, 1773; Thomas, Sept. 26, 1776.

Talford, William and Isabella. Dau.: Elisabeth, Mar. 13, 1736.

Taylor, Abraham and Betsey McKenney. Dau.: Helen M. (McKenney), b. Nov., 1836, Londonderry, N. H.
James Calvin, b. Jan. 12, 1858, and Elizabeth Patterson Sleeper, b. Nov. 17, 1818.
James and Persis. Children: Samuel Harvey, Oct. 3, 1807; Nathaniel Milton, Sept. 30, 1809; Almira, Oct. 12, 1811; Caroline Persis, Aug. 11, 1813; Harriet, Oct. 21, 1815; James Calvin, Nov. 17, 1818; Sarah Jane, May 18, 1821; Mary E.; Emma. "Parker's History."
John and Rachel. Son, Nov. 15, 1867.
Mathew and Jennat. Children: John, Sept. 22, 1721; Illine, Jan. 19, 1723-4; Agnes, Mar. 6, 1725-6; Mathew, Oct. 30, 1727; Jenat, June 10, 1731; William, Mar. 23, 1732-3; David, Aug. 10, 1735; Adam, Aug. 15, 1737; Martha, Aug. 15, 1739.
Samuel and Eunice. Children: Sally, Sept. 17, 1775; Jenney, Sept. 6, 1778; Samuel Fisher, Nov. 26, 1780; Henry, Nov. 19, 1782; James, Oct. 19, 1784; Polly, Oct. 11, 1789; triplets, all died young.
Samuel and Sarah. Son: Matthew, Oct. 22, 1771.
Samuel F. and Margaret. Children: Mary Jane, Dec. 26, 1810; Henry G., May 21, 1812.

Tenney, Albert and Mary Ann Young, b. Apr. 7, 1823. Children: Martha M., May 4, 1843; Albert W., Mar. 16, 1846; Esther Jane, July 21, 1851.
Asa, b. Jan. 2, 1758, and Molly, b. 1754. Son: David, 1790.
Charles A. and Lizzie J. Head, b. at Hooksett, N. H., 1st wife. Children: Dau., Aug. 19, 1887; Angie R., Nov. 1, 1889.
Charles and Eliza Coffin Peabody, b. July 22, 1819. Children: Arley P., Apr. 15, 1844; Ardelle A., Feb. 8, 1847; Charles A., May 24, 1851; George C., July 9, 1856.

Tenney, David and Persis Plummer, b. Feb. 1, 1797. Children: Eliza, Dec. 9, 1817; Albert, Dec. 9, 1819; Charles, Nov. 13, 1821; Persis, Oct. 4, 1823; David, Oct. 17, 1825; Mary, Oct. 6, 1827; Martha, Oct. 28, 1829; Arly P., Dec. 30, 1831; Warren P., Jan. 30, 1834; Lydia C., Sept. 29, 1836.

George G. and Nancy E. Rowell, b. Oct. 16, 1865, 1st wife. Son: Frank Leland, Nov. 12, 1884.

Tewksbury, Charles S., b. 1869, and Mamie A. Fleming, b. 1870. Children: Eva M., Sept. 25, 1890; son, Sept. 25, 1893; son, Sept. 25, 1893; son, Nov. 20, 1896; son, Aug. 21, 1898; Berth Gladys, Mar. 1, 1901; dau., Mar. 13, 1903; dau., Nov. 22, 1905; Walter L., Aug., 1897.

Sumner, b. Nov. 25, 1841, and Dora M., b. May 10, 1840.

Thayer, Albert T. and Nellie Spears. Son, Feb. 28, 1896.

Bernice and Susanna Boyce. Children: Minnie, Haverline, Cassius.

Thibeault, Wilfred and Helarine. Dau., Dec. 30, 1885.

Thom, Dr. Isaac,* b. Mar. 1, 1746, in Windham, N. H., son of William and Elisabeth Wiar, and Persis Sargent. Of eleven children two d. in infancy; nine reached adult age: Christopher S., William S., Persis, Susan, Isaac, James, Nathaniel, Eliza, and George.

Thomas, Frank L. and Mabel V. Chick. Son: Clifton Durrell, Oct. 24, 1905.

Joseph D., b. Nov. 2, 1825, in Lincoln, Maine, and Judith D. Emmons, b. Oct. 26, 1828.

Thompson, James and Peggy. Son: Jonathan Gregg, Aug. 12, 1792.

James and Martha. Children: Whitfield Gilmore, Sept. 13, 1795; Robert, Oct. 16, 1797; Margaret, Jan. 6, 1799.

James and Margaret. Dau.: Sally Boyse, Mar. 3, 1800.

John and Martha. Children: Margaret, June 22, 1772; John, Jan. 8, 1774; Jane Roggers, Apr. 4, 1779; Samuel, Aug. 24, 1781; Martha, Nov. 23, 1783; Mary, Mar. 28, 1785; Hannah, Apr. 6, 1787; Andrew, July 11, 1789.

Thomson, John and Sarah. Dau.: Ester, May 15, 1755.

Robert and Mary. Children: Jeremiah Smith, Oct. 17, 1767; John, June 28, 1770.

Robert and Margaret. Children: William, June 3, 1778; Thomas, Dec. 9, 1772; Sarah, Jan. 31, 1775.

Samuel and Sarah. Son: James, Feb. 14, 1767.

Rev. Thomas and ———. Son: Alexander, Aug. 3, 1738.

*Dr. Thom practiced medicine in Londonderry 13 yrs. He was the first postmaster in town.

Thomson, William and Hanna. Children: David, Nov. 15, 1723; Sarah, Nov. 17, 1723; James, Jan. 19, 1725–6.

Thornton, Hon. Matthew, b. in Ireland, 1714.

Patrick, b. in Ireland, 1858, and Mary Kelley, b. in Ireland, 1862. Children: Francis, 4th ch., June 1, 1900, Londonderry, N. H.; dau., Apr. 25, 1903, Londonderry, N. H.

Tilley, ——— and Lucy Woolner, 1st marriage. Son: Charles H., Oct. 21, 1867.

Titcomb, Charles K. and Laura E. Nichols, b. Jan. 28, 1858, in Nashua, N. H. Children: Rosie L., Jan. 6, 1876; Martha E., Mar. 6, 1878; Annie B., Jan. 11, 1880; Ida S., Sept. 29, 1888.

Simeon, b. May 4, 1814, in Pelham, N. H., and Sally H. (Webster), b. Aug. 25, 1814, in Pelham, N. H.; came to Londonderry in 1842. Children: Albert O., July 27, 1846; Charles K., Apr. 9, 1850; Frank F., Nov. 12, 1853; Nellie J., May 13, 1855.

Todd, Andrew and Beatrix. Children: James, Aug. 1, 172–; Samuel, June 3, 1726; dau., July 31, 1728; Alexander, Jan. 2, 1730–31; Rachel, Apr. 14, 1733; John, Apr. 18, 1735; Jean, Mar. 9, 1736–7; Andrew, Jan. 11, 1738–9.

Samuel and Hannah. Son: John, Apr. 3, 1757.

Solomon and Elisabeth. Children: Henery, Apr. 8, 1775; John, Feb. 15, 1777.

Torrey, Kenneth W. C. and Edna L. Bacon. Dau.: Murial J., May 23, 1908.

Towle, Harris, b. Jan. 28, 1856, at Norway, Me., and Claradilla (Dickey), b. Aug. 13, 1843, at Londonderry, N. H.; res. in Cuba.

Towns, John C. and Amy M. Children: Clara Amy, Oct. 7, 1875; John Albert, May 11, 1881.

John C. and Amy P. Son: Arthur J. C., Feb. 14, 1870.

Oscar and Antoinetta. Son, Oct. 16, 1861.

Silas and Phebe A. Children: Harry S., May 20, 1871; dau., Sept. 1, 1875.

True, Levi and Etta. Dau., June 15, 1861.

Tucker, Charles H. and Anna Barney. Children: Dau., Mar. 29, 1897; Charles William, Mar. 23, 1841.

James and Sally Tucker. Dau.: Mary A., Oct. 25, 1826.

Turgette, Carl and Kate Mahon. Son: Frederick William, Apr. 6, 1900.

Tuttle, Effie J., b. Sept. 8, 1871.

Twiss, George W. and Laura B. Towns. Dau.: Beatrice Corinne, Apr. 22, 1897.

J. and F. Dau., Oct. 22, 1859.

Varel, ——— and Julia A. Son: Arthur F., April 13, 1867.

Varrell, Luther and Isabel G. Son, Mar. 5, 1887.

Vezina, Napoleon and Malvina Preva. Children: Dau., Mar. 22, 1903; Lena M., Aug. 7, 1906; Omer Lincoln, Jan. 13, 1910.

Vickery, Sarah, b. Feb. 11, 1780.

Walch, William Benjamin, b. Jan. 5, 1869, at Londonderry, N. H., and Lucy A. (Corning), b. June 21, 1874, Danvers, Mass. Children: Ethel M., June 16, 1892, Londonderry; Franklin Edward, Oct. 19, 1893; Eva Muriel, Feb. 14, 1896; William Benjamin, Jan. 12, 1897; Gladys Alberta, Aug. 10, 1910.

Waldo, Almon and Mary Etta Annis. Two children. (See Annis rec.)

Walker, Alexander and Martha. Children: Robert, Aug. 11, 1722; Andrew, Mar. 5, 1719; Martha, Aug. 20, 1724.

From Patterson monument, Glenwood cemetery:

Wallace, James, b. 1712, and Mary (Wilson), b. 1710. Children: Thomas, 1745; Robert, 1749; Elisabeth (Patterson), Nov. 14, 1755; William, 1760; James, 1762.

James and Mary. Children: Elisabeth, Dec. 18, 1743; Thomas, Nov. 28, 1744; Robert, Sept. 3, 1749; Ann, Oct. 19, 1750; Janey, Oct. 13, 1753; Elisabeth, Oct. 14, 1755; William, Jan. 17, 1760; James, May 6, 1762.

John and Annas. Children: James, July 17, 1722; Rebecca, Feb. 16, 1723; William, Feb. 5, 1725; John, Apr. 12, 1727; Jenat, Jan. 28, 1733; Ann, June 16, 1736; Samuel, Jan. 23, 1738-9; Sarah, Nov. 8, 1741.

John and Jenet. Children: James, Mar. 27, 1731; George, Jan. 24, 1745.

John (brother of Joseph) came to Londonderry about 1726; m. Janet Steele. Children: Jane, m. David Jennings; Mary, m. Samuel Millet; Elisabeth, m. Solomon Todd; Margaret, m. Samuel Gregg; Janet, m. Hugh McCutchins; Ann, m. Samuel Cherry. "Parker's History."

Jonathan and Agnes. Children: William B., Feb. 5, 1725; Jonathan, Apr. 12, 1728; Thomas, Aug. 10, 1730.

Joseph,* b. in Ireland.

Thomas and Jean. Children: Jennat, Dec. 11, 1733; James, Nov. 11, 1735; Joseph, Oct. 11, 1737; William, Nov. 26, 1739; Margaret, Dec., 1741; Ann, Nov. 24, 1743; John, Dec. 15, 1744.

Thomas and Lettice. Son: James,† Nov. 15, 1782.

*Joseph came from Ireland to Londonderry about 1726, with a son, William, about five yrs. old; other children were b. of whom little is known.

†First child baptized by Rev. William Morrison, Feb. 16, 1783.

Wallace, William and Hanna. Children: John, June 13, 1757; William, Dec. 26, 1758; Katren, Dec. 6, 1760; James, Mar. 31, 1763; Hanna, Jan. 26, 1765; Mathew, Nov. 1, 1770.

William P. and Addie W. Children: Dau., June 9, 1862; George W., Apr. 3, 1872; Gracie May, Nov. 13, 1880.

Walsh, David and Kate. Son: Frank Heber Newton, Dec. 6, 1877.

Washburn, Lorenzo and Elisabeth. Dau., Sept. 8, 1863.

Watts, Peggy, June 16, 1772. Jinny, Mar. 28, 1782. Daniel, Apr. 15, 1785. Susanna, Dec. 2, 1787. John, July 11, 1791. Rachel, Aug. 23, 1798. (From Watts, Mullins and Garvin family records.)

Caleb M. and Martha J. Flanders, b. 1826, 1st wife. Children: Hattie M., 1850; Frank M., Sept. 1, 1852; infant, ———; Ella M., Jan. 23, 1856 (see Henry R. Hall).

Caleb M. and Anna C. Palmer, b. Oct. 17, 1832, 2d wife. Children: George Alvah, July 2, 1861; Willie E., Jan. 4, 1863; Ernest M., Aug., 1865; Walter J., 1867; Nathan P., 1869; infant, 1872; Clarence O., Apr. 7, 1874; Edson W., 1875; Hermon L., Jan. 24, 1878.

Charles H. and Mariam P. Annis, b. Sept. 7, 1837. Children: Delia May, June 11, 1863; Nellie M., May 13, 1866; Martha L., July 4, 1870; Olive A., July 16, 1873; Leo Parker, Sept. 18, 1875; Maude M., July 15, 1878; Addie W., Dec. 7, 1880.

Charles H., 2d, b. Sept. 1, 1861, son of Freeman C. and Mary E. Wheeler, and Mabel Andrews, b. Feb. 17, 1870. Children: Henry P., Aug. 4, 1888; infant, Nov. 14, 1889; Arthur E., July 22, 1891.

Clarence O. and Marion R. Cook. Children: Esther Marion, Aug. 5, 1904; Hazel Eva, Feb. 6, 1907.

Edson W. and Jennie A. Lowd. Children: Ainslee Earl, May 13, 1900; Winfield M., Oct. 26, 1908.

Ernest M. and Georgie Corning. Children: Ralph Leslie, Jan. 18, 1889; Celinda Palmer, July 5, 1892; John Parker, June 11, 1894; Perley Anderson, July 7, 1895; Everett Ernest, Dec. 13, 1909.

Freeman C., b. Sept. 7, 1822, and Elisabeth J. (Wheeler), b. July 24, 1832. Children: Mariam E., Aug. 27, 1852; James F., July 25, 1854; George N., Jan. 14, 1857; Martha E., Apr. 12, 1859; Charles H., Sept. 1, 1861; Lilla Jones, June 6, 1865.

George Alvah and Martha E. Fling, b. June 19, 1861. Children: Clayton E., Mar. 27, 1889; Norman F., June 8, 1891.

Hermon L. and Alice J. Fitts, b. Aug. 6, 1876, in Dunbarton, N. H. Five children, all d. young.

Watts, Horace Perkins, b. Nov. 12, 1819, son of Daniel, and Maria (Boyd), b. Aug. 19, 1819. Children: Martha Boyd, Feb. 27, 1843; Daniel Mason, Aug. 26, 1845; May Alice, Dec. 28, 1858; Annie Eliza, Aug. 7, 1860.

James, b. June 24, 1759, and Deborah (Corning), b. Mar. 21, 1768. Children: Joshua, July 16, 1790; Mary, Dec. 29, 1792; James, Oct. 6, 1794; Susannah, Nov. 30, 1796; Moses, Nov. 7, 1798; Deborah, July 8, 1800; Hugh, Aug. 3, 1802; Martha, Apr. 25, 1804; John, June 28, 1806; Peggy, May 30, 1808; Esther, Oct. 3, 1810; Margaret, Sept. 10, 1816.

Joshua C., b. July 21, 1790, and Martha (Goodwin), b. June 6, 1799. Children: Caleb M., Apr. 8, 1824; Martha M., June 6, 1831; Esther Jane, Feb. 17, 1834, m. Walter Boyce, no children; Margaret, Dec. 19, 1836; Charles H., July 19, 1840.

Walter J. and Evelyn M. Wheeler. Children: Neil Edson, June 7, 1891; dau., July 25, 1895.

Waugh, Robert, b. July 23, 1826, at Keat's Hill, Maine, and Eliza Williams, b. Nov. 18, 1835.

Wear, Robert and Martha. Dau.: Elisabeth, Nov. 4, 1723.

Webster, Amos and Martha M. Annis. Children: Laura V., Sept. 20, 1863; Cleon L., Sept. 10, 1865.

Amos C., b. Feb. 10, 1813, Manchester, N. H., and Elisabeth K. Whittaker, 2d wife, b. Feb. 22, 1820. Children: Hattie L., June 19, 1859; Sidney A., Aug. 2, 1861.

Betsey Ann and William B. Carlton, b. Aug. 3, 1826. Children: George Washington, July 31, 1862; Mary Elisabeth, Feb. 19, 1867; Frances Virginia, Feb. 13, 1865.

Caleb and Elna J. Thurson, Danvers, Mass. Son: Daniel A.

Charles Warren, b. July 1, 1857.

Ebenezer and Betsey. Children: Roxanna, June 3, 1787; Betsey, June 4, 1788; Asa, Oct. 3, 1790; Nancy, Oct. 1, 1792; Sally, Dec. 14, 1794; Rebecca, Jan. 7, 1797; Mary, Jan. 21, 1799; Catherine, Apr. 8, 1801; William Gage, Aug. 20, 1803; Daniel K., Nov. 9, 1805; Hariet, Feb. 10, 1808; Benjamin, Oct. 20, 1810.

James and Mehitable. Children: Mehitable F., Nov. 2, 1843; James M., Jan. 24, 1846.

Jonathan and Mary A. Dau., May 7, 1852.

Jonathan and Mary Ann Everton. Children: William Wallace, Dec. 5, 1833; Caleb, Feb. 24, 1839; Betsey Ann, Apr. 23, 1841; David, June 29, 1843; Martha, Mar. 17, 1845; Hannah C., May 7, 1852.

Nathaniel and Maria. Dau., July 25, 1854.

Webster, Sidney A. and Mary Etta Smith. Children: Marion Louise, Feb. 5, 1896; Oscar Dana, Dec. 15, 1897; Jessie Imogene, Dec. 26, 1898.

William Wallace and Caroline Chase, b. Sept. 1, 1836. Dau.: Etta Leora, Feb. 2, 1859, Marlboro, Mass.

Weeden, David R. and Myra R. Bickford. Dau.: Cora Florence, June 21, 1901.

Welcome, William G. and Mary L. Clouthier. Son: William, Feb. 3, 1907.

Wells, Alonzo and Regina. Dau., Dec. 21, 1861.

John K. and Zulian Cole. Son: George, June 9, 1891.

West, Harriet, b. at Northampton, Eng., May 29, 1856.

Westgate, Elzi R. and Ida M. Wilcox. Dau., Dec. 9, 1900.

Wetherbee, Capt. Hezekiah, b. May 18, 1786, and Grace Baker, b. Sept. 9, 1786. Children: Susan A., Jan. 9, 1825; John H., Sept. 16, 1827; William B., Sept., 1829.

William B., b. Sept., 1829, and Sarah E. Corning, b. Sept. 23, 1840.

Wheeler, John F. and Etta M. Swimington. Children: Joseph J., Apr. 3, 1906; Wilfred L., June 30, 1907.

Joshua F. and Mary E. Corning, b. Oct. 1, 1848. Children: Evelyn M., July 14, 1867; Sarah F., Oct. 16, 1869; Charles H., Apr. 23, 1873; Elmer F., Mar. 17, 1891.

Lucinda R., b. Apr. 12, 1817.

Nancy E., Mar. 30, 1819.

Tilly H., b. Jan. 31, 1809, and Rebecca Goodwin, 1st wife, Nov. 25, 1810. Children: Elisabeth J., July 24, 1832; Persis Emily, Feb. 8, 1834; Hannah Jane, Feb. 6, 1836; David Gooden, Jan. 22, 1838; Joshua Franklin, Dec. 15, 1839; Charles H., Apr. 16, 1842; James Sumner, Apr. 18, 1845; Nancy Ann, May 18, 1847; Daniel Goodwin, May 26, 1850.

Tilly H. and Ann Lincoln, 2d wife, b. May 7, 1818. Children: Albert M., Jan. 14, 1859; William L., Feb. 23, 1862; Jason S., Apr. 24, 1860.

Whidden, Abigail and Benjamin Senter. Children: James, Winfield Scott.

Asabel G. and Angie M. Children: Son, Apr. 2, 1871; Edgar Asabel, June 2, 1878; Charles Leroy, Aug. 3, 1880.

Harrison and Mary J. Children: Son, July 6, 1872; William, July 31, 1881.

Henry H. and Susan. Dau., May 30, 1871.

Henry O. and Sylvia Wood. Children: Lillie, Oct. 4, 1861; Carrie, 1868; Hattie, 1872; Helen, 1875.

Whidden, John P. and Alice J. Austin. Children: Charles F., Oct. 3, 1848; Alice M., Jan. 9, 1851; Elbridge A., May 14, 1853; Alma E., Aug. 23, 1855; Ellen M., Nov. 27, 1857; James Warren, June 18, 1859.

Joshua, b. July 13, 1824, and Adeline Boyce. Children: Ch., Sept. 27, 1849; William Henry, Oct. 18, 1850; Rufus Monroe, Oct. 21, 1851; Mary Frances, Dec. 13, 1852; Martha Ellen, Sept. 9, 1854; John Alberto, Jan. 1, 1856; Esther Francies, Jan. 1, 1857; Walter, Mar. 26, 1858; Mary Josephine, May 21, 1860; Baby Adeline, Nov. 27, 1861.

Michael, b. Nov. 10, 1796, and Hannah Morrill, b. Oct. 2, 1801. Children: Mary Jane, Sept. 1, 1820; Hannah M., Sept. 22, 1822; John P., 1825; Joshua, 1824; Abigail, 1828; Elbridge, 1830; Caroline, 1833; George M., 1834; Sarah B., 1836; Henry O., 1838.

Samuel and Mary. Son: John, Oct. 18, 1815.

William H. and Nellie A. Kendall. Son: William Kendall, July 2, 1903.

Whitcomb, Harriet C., wife of H. B. Corliss, b. Dec. 17, 1826.

White, Henry Harrison and Sarah A. Moore, b. Oct. 22, 1839. Children: Lilla Belle, Dec. 16, 1865; Bessie Carrol, Nov. 6, 1878.

Isaac K. and Elisabeth. Son: Edgar William, Feb. 1, 1854.

John, b. July 16, 1787, son of Ephraim and Esther (Moore), and Susanna (Dickey), dau. of Robert; res. Litchfield, N. H. Children: Clarrissa, Jan. 10, 1818; Mary, Feb. 5, 1821; Susan, Apr. 24, 1825; John, Aug. 13, 1827.

Reuben, b. 1795, and Rachel Corning, b. 1801. Children: Samuel C., June 12, 1825; Maria, Jan. 5, 1827; Esther, Feb. 12, 1829; Harriet M. B., May 3, 1831; Nelson, Dec. 17, 1833, remained unm.; Emily Colby, Oct. 31, 1835; Eliza Ann, Jan. 1, 1837; Henry Harrison, June 19, 1840; Ruel Baldwin, Aug. 1, 1842, remained unm.
Sally, b. May 17, 1788.

Samuel C. and Caroline G. Woodbury. Dau.: Manella, 1854.

Whitford, George C. and Katherine Haverstock. Son: George Clarence, Feb. 10, 1910, 3d ch.

Whitney, Leonard M. and Lottie A. Currier. Son: Norman Morrison, July 7, 1900.

Robert M. and Cora. Dau.: Maud May, Feb. 21, 1882.

Whittemore, Amy Edna and Charles W. Killam. Children: Muriel Esther, Horace Goodwin, Roger Wilson, and Mary Whittemore.

Whittemore, Rev. Elias J. and Clara Bartley of Reading, Mass. Children: Jennie Mabel and Arthur Henry.

Harry Ernest and Ethel E. Graham. Children: Ruth Caroline, Philip Graham, Paul Goodwin, and Esther Elisabeth.

Henry J. and Esther M. Goodwin. Children: Mary Estella, Mar. 20, 1863; Lewis Goodwin; Willis Parry; Amy Edna, May 17, 1871; Harry Ernest.

Rev. Joshua Lewis, b. Mar. 1, 1810, Canton, Mass., son of Joshua and Eunice Morse, and Amy Lanton (Parry), b. in Rehoboth, Mass., 1815. Children: Three died in infancy; Henry J., Oct. 23, 1838, Dighton, Mass.; Elias J., 1843, Middleboro, Mass.

Rev. Joshua L. and 2d wife, Mary E. Dimond, Claremont, N. H. No children. Settled in Londonderry in 1857.

Zachariah and Susan M. Sampson (Snell). (See Whittemore rec.)

Whittier, Ebenezer and Emily. Children: Emily Louisa, Dec. 5, 1830; Clarrissa Maria, Aug. 4, 1832.

Ebenezer and Emily. Children: Jackson Vanbuna, Mar. 15, 1835; Sarah Eliza, Mar. 7, 1838; May Frances, Oct. 17, 1840; George Newton, Feb. 27, 1844; Horatio Belknap, Mar. 3, 1845.

Ebenezer and Lucy S. Son: Charles Franklin, Oct. 10, 1842.

Joshua and Abigail. Children: John, Nov. 8, 1795; Ebenezer F., Jan. 26, ——; Samuel F., July 19, 1798; Isaac, May 25, 1800; William, Sept. 20, 1802; Martha, Jan. 15, 1804; Maria, Aug. 3, 1807; David, Dec. 11, 1810.

Whittle, John W. and Emily J. (Flanders). Children: Ernest W., June 29, 1868; Carrie J., Nov. 27, 1869; Emily C., Mar. 15, 1877; Frances V., Apr. 17, 1882.

Whorf, Benjamin, b. Feb. 22, 1783, and Shuah, b. June 6, 1787. Son: Benjamin F., May 5, 1828.

Benjamin F. and Juliette A. B. (Page), b. Apr. 12, 1833. Dau.: Hattie M., Nov. 21, 1865.

Wiley, Charles and Saloma Jones. Children: Carrie A., Aug. 16, 1877; Lucy L., Mar. 16, 1886.

Ephraim A., b. Dec. 20, 1817, Lynnfield, Mass., and Nancy A. Blood, b. Sept. 7, 1823. Children: Charles, Dec. 6, 1842; Lucy E., Jan. 27, 1845; Sarah E., Jan. 27, 1845; Mary E., May 11, 1847; George B., May 25, 1850; Martha M. E., Mar. 9, 1859; Mary A., Jan. 16, 1866.

George B. and Ella A. Gilcreast, Aug. 12, 1850. Son: Alverton, Apr. 9, 1872.

Wilkie, Joseph and Mabel L. Brown. Dau., Aug. 13, 1897.

Wilkins family as compiled by Mrs. Elisabeth Wilkins Young:

Wilkins, Archibald M. and Ellen E. Hartwell of Bedford, Mass. Son: William Green, Nov. 15, 1876.

Daniel, b. Feb. 3, 1795, and Elisabeth (Russell), b. May 15, 1806, 1st wife, in Worcester, N. Y. Children: Elijah Russell, May 20, 1822; Daniel Orramel, Mar. 14, 1825; son, Mar. 4, 1827; dau., Mar. 4, 1828; William Wesley, June 19, 1829; son, July 9, 1833; son, no record; son, no record.

Daniel and Mary McMurphy (Thompson), 2d wife, b. June 24, 1814. Children: Elisabeth, Aug. 20, 1836; Archibald McMurphy, Nov. 4, 1838, Derry, N. H.

Daniel and Sarah Hartwell, 3d wife, b. Mar. 8, 1820, Ashburnham, Mass. Children: Daniel, no date; Daniel, Jr., Mar. 13, 1845, Fitchburg, Mass.; Walter Scott, Oct. 22, 1846, Methuen, Mass.; Edwin Oscar, Oct. 18, 1851; Norman Stanley, Nov. 10, 1854; Sarah Isabel, Wilougsby Hartwell and Victor d. in infancy.

Daniel, Jr., and Susan Brown, b. at Boston, Mass. Children: Eva May, 1872; Gertrude; Daniel, m. Nellie Goodrich, res. Portland, Conn.; Fred.

Elijah R. and Harriet N. (Davis), b. at Martin's Ferry, Hooksett, N. H. Children: Hattie M., Mar. 28, 1847; Betsey Jane, ———; Wesley Jerome, Apr. 12, 1852, Concord, N. H.; Minnie, July 28, 1854, Chesterfield, N. H.

Fred and Eva Young. Children: Fred Guy, Stanley Howard, and Edgar.

Herbert Emerson and Lillian Lamprey, b. at Laconia, N. H. Son: Malcolm, b. at Bellows Falls, Vt.

Hiram and Maryette Manter. Children: Isabella and Irving.

Walter Scott and Elnora Lucy Rousa of New York state. Son: Harry Eugene, Nov. 4, 1888.

Wesley Jerome, son of Elijah R., and Alice Perley, b. Aug. 25, 1850, at Lebanon, N. H. Children: Herbert Emerson, May 26, 1874, Keene, N. H.; Benson Perley, Feb. 8, 1876, Keene, N. H.

Wesley Jerome and 2d wife, Annie Lincoln, b. Oct. 8, 1871.

William Green m. Elisabeth M. McLane (?), Sept. 25, 1898.

William Wesley and Persis Laurinda Morse, b. July 9, 1829, at Manchester, N. H. Children: Charles Wesley, Mar. 25, 1855, Manchester, N. H.; Mary Eva, May 7, 1859, Henniker, N. H.; Annie Elisabeth, Aug. 23, 1865, Bedford, N. H.

Benson Perley and Martha Fiefield of Methuen, Mass. Dau.: Doris.

Willard, Nathaniel and Hattie Manter. Sons: Daniel, Clarence.

Willey, Benjamin F. and Sarah A. Dau.: Edith E., July 28, 1868.

Jacob N., b. Feb., 1804, and Rachel T., b. May 18, 1822. Children: Etta M., Dec. 6, 1850; son, Aug. 28, 1852; Henry J., Sept. 30, 1854; son, July 12, 1859.

Mark W. and Ellen J. Son, May, 1884.

Williams, Lester E. and Ellen Bassett. Son, Nov. 13, 1900.

Samuel and Elisabeth. Children: Jean, June 7, 1758; Margaret, Dec. 30, 1760; Samuel, Feb. 4, 1764; Elisabeth, Apr. 2, 1766; Maryann, Feb. 8, 1768; Rachel, Apr. 8, 1774.

Willson, Thomas and Sarah. Children: Margaret, Jan. 22, 1761; Grisell, Nov. 11, 1762; Martha, Sept. 2, 1764; Elisabeth, Aug. 16, 1766; Joan, Sept. 25, 1768; James, July 13, 1771; John, May 21, 1777; Saley, Apr. 1, 1780.

Wilson, George W. and Mary J. Nelson, b. Nov. 25, 1846, Sutton, N. H. Children: Son, Dec. 7, 1868; Lura B., Mar. 2, 1870.

Hugh and Ann. Children: Hugh, Apr. 7, 1744; Samuel, Apr. 14, 1746; Mary, Oct. 11, 1748.

Hugh and Margaret. Children: Ann, Mar. 20, 1724–5; Robert, July 8, 1731; Margaret, July 8, 1733.

James and Eleanor. Children: Robert, June 26, 1759; Martha, Jan. 31, 1761; James, Mar. 15, 1763; Jennet, Apr. 1, 1765; David, Dec. 11, 1768; Agness, June 1, 1771; Eleanor, Nov. 1, 1775; Samuel, Mar. 17, 1779; Betsey, Oct. 19, 1781.

James and Jenat. Children: Agnes (?), Aug. 7, 1728; George, Dec. 2, 1729; James, Jan. 4, 1730–31; Alexander, May 5, 1731; Robert, Apr. 25, 1733; James, May 13, 1733 (?); Alexander, May 15, 1735 (?).

James,* son of James (son of James), b. Mar. 15, 1763.

John Pinkerton and Adeline Annis, b. Feb. 19, 1823. Children: Robert Henry, Mar. 10, 1845; Rebecca P., Dec. 31, 1846; George W., Sept. 10, 1848; Thomas H., Jan. 10, 1851; John Eddy, Apr. 25, 1853; Abby Delia, Dec. 28, 1855; May Belinda, Nov. 29, 1858; Lilla J., 1861; David Brewster, Aug. 31, 1865.

Joseph and Rebecca. Dau.: Mary, Sept. 25, 1738.

Robert and Margaret. Children: Thomas, Sept. 11, 1785; Eleanor, May 23, 1787; James, Feb. 9, 1789; Robert, Feb. 9, 1789; David, Feb. 13, 1791; Sarah, July 21, 1793; Ebenezer, Dec. 12, 1795; John Adams, Feb. 6, 1799; Boyd, June 29, 1801; Samuel, Sept. 3, 1802; Peggy, May 19, 1805.

*He made the first pair of terrestrial and celestial globes ever made in America.

Wilson, Robert Henry and Eldora J. Garvin. Children: Frank P., Apr. 6, 1866; Eva Dora, Sept. 23, 1869; Harry E., Apr. 4, 1871.

Thomas and Grizall. Children: Grizall, Oct. 17, 1722; Thomas, Aug. 14, 1725; James, Sept. 1, 1735.

Thomas, b. 1776, and Rebecca (Pinkerton), 1st wife, b. 1786. Son: John Pinkerton, Jan. 23, 1818.

William and Betty. Son: Adam, Dec. 22, 1724.

William and Elisabeth. Children: Margaret, June 9, 1726; Samuel (?), July 31, 1728.

Wilsone, Benjamin and Margaret. Children: Rebecca, Apr. 22, 1728; John, Apr. 6, 1730.

Wing, Edward L. and Alice F. Colby. Dau.: Gertrude Irene, Feb. 12, 1909.

Seth G. and Pearl C. Proctor. Dau.: Margerie Eva, Feb. 12, 1910, 2d child.

Wood, Solomon and Ellen Kelley. Dau.: Elisabeth A., Nov. 26, 1907.

William N. and Nellie Ellsworth. Son: Shirley E., Jan. 7, 1906.

Woodburn, David and Margaret. Son: James, Sept. 6, 1774.

John and Ada. Dau., Oct. 10, 1854.

John and Mary. Children: Ann, June 5, 1726; dau., Jan. 15, 1727–8; Margaret, Dec. 20, 1729; Sarah, Dec. 23, 1731; Mary, Apr. 7, 1734–5; David, Aug. 4, 1745.

John and R. Dau., Jan. 26, 1860.

Woodbury, Benjamin F. and Louisa Sargent. Children: John Albert; dau.

Charles Edgar, b. Feb. 13, 1864, son of Benjamin F., and Eva J. Wheeler. Children: Walter Edgar, May 7, 1886; Benjamin Leroy, June 15, 1887; Harland Sumner, Sept. 10, 1888; Norris Elwin, Jan. 19, 1891; Luke Augustus, Mar. 25, 1893; Ruth, Mar. 13, 1895; William Elliott, Sept. 23, 1896; Arthur Joseph, Mar. 25, 1898; Ida May, May 5, 1899; Margaret Elisabeth, Aug. 31, 1903; John Clayton, Mar. 3, 1909.

Eben and Hannah Smith. Children: Eben, Samuel, William, Abram, Martha, and Hannah.

Samuel, 2d son of Eben, b. Sept. 28, 1812, and Louisa J. Baker, b. Nov. 4, 1816. Children: Martha J., Sept. 24, 1838; James G., June 14, 1840; Benjamin F., Mar. 24, 1842; Samuel Leroy, Feb. 15, 1845; Alma J., Mar. 27, 1847; Charles W., May 15, 1849; Abram A., Aug. 21, 1851; John G., Feb. 22, 1854; Willie E., Jan. 21, 1856.

Samuel and Louisa. Grandson: Edgar C., Feb. 13, 1864.

Woodbury, Samuel, son of —— and Hannah (Barker), b. Feb. 11, 1838.

Samuel and Harriet. Children: Alma Jane, June 9, 1860; Annah Augusta, Dec. 22, 1862; Frank Antoine, Sept. 27, 1866.

Woods, Ensign C., b. Jan. 29, 1831, and Alice H. (Fellows), b. Mar. 16, 1841. Dau.: Mattie M., Sept. 22, 1866.

Worcester, Charles and Ida M. Dau., Aug. 20, 1883.

Wychoff, Joseph A., 4th N. H. Vols., b. June 5, 1830, and Elisabeth, b. Jan. 18, 1824. Children: Julia E., July 20, 1853; Maroia, Dec. 18, 1861.

Young, Ephraim, b. 1814, and Martha (Plummer), b. Feb. 10, 1805. Children: Nathan P., 1843; Ephraim J., Oct., 1847.

Ernest Garvin and Grace Wilson. Son: Earl.

Frank S. and Lena O. Son, July 23, 1885.

Frederic Augustus and Emma D. Boyd. Children: Maurice, Sept. 1, 1889; Arthur Boyd, May 22, 1891; Mason James, Feb. 9, 1894.

Greenleaf and Rachel Harvey, b. Sept. 2, 1831. Children: Etta M., May 26, 1858; Ernest Garvin, Oct., 1861.

Henry J. and Sarah. Dau., July 17, 1870.

Israel, b. in Manchester, N. H., and Esther Stevens. Children: Charles Edward, Nov. 25, 1821; Mary Ann, Apr. 25, 1823; Jonathan, June 3, 1825; John Henry; Hastings, Feb. 26, 1828; James Franklin, Nov. 15, 1831; Daniel Hamblett, May 10, 1833; Taylor Southwick; Sarah Elisabeth.

Israel and Mary. Dau.: Marietta, Dec. 17, 1858.

James Franklin and Elisabeth Wilkins, b. Aug. 20, 1836. Children: Annie Caroline, June 26, 1854; Charles Franklin, Sept. 22, 1856; Wesley James, Feb. 3, 1859; Frederic Augustus, Sept. 10, 1861; William David, Mar. 27, 1864; Mary Esther, Sept. 17, 1867; John Herbert, May 3, 1870; Walter Stevens, Sept. 29, 1878.

Johnnie L. and Luella E. Badger. Dau.: Ethel Maud, July 15, 1889.

Jonathan, b. Apr. 9, 1803, Manchester, N. H., and Charlotte M. Boyce, b. May 21, 1803. Children: Greenleaf, Nov. 15, 1829, at Manchester, N. H.; Mary Jane, Mar. 5, 1832.

Jonathan, 2d, and Margaret. Children: Son, Aug. 29, 1852; dau., Feb. 7, 1854.

Wesley James and Lilla A. Booth. Children: Edwin Henry, July 4, 1878; Charles Wesley, Feb. 16, 1880; Herbert Wilkins, Oct. 16, 1881; Martha Elisabeth, May 5, 1883; Harry Arthur, Jan. 30, 1885; Hattie May, May 16, 1886; Ernest Franklin, June 21, 1888; Carrie Isabel, Oct. 10, 1889.

Young, William David and Maria Louisa Parmenton. Children: Marjorie, Feb. 25, 1895; Archie Wilkins, Aug. 12, 1896; Isabel Helen, Nov. 21, 1897; Olive Elisabeth, Sept. 10, 1899; Marion Sarah, June 5, 1902; David William, Nov. 12, 1903; Kenneth Henry, Oct. 22, 1904. Children b. and reside in Manchester, N. H.

MARRIAGE INTENTIONS

From the Earliest Record to the End of 1910

Abbott, Chas. W. and Emma H. Perkins, Feb. 2, 1888.
Ellen F. and Daniel T. Shipley, Jan. 10, 1861.
Emma B. and Pliny M. Campbell, June 2, 1902.
Etta M. and Nathan A. Pollard, Sept. 10, 1860.
Josiah and Betsey Allison, Nov. 14, 1808.
Lydia and Thomas Bartlett, Nov. 26, 1810.
Adams, Betsey and Chas. Redfield, Mar., 1814.
Charles and Mattie M. Woods, Oct. 21, 1885.
Edmund and Betsey Kembal, Sept. 18, 1809.
Edmund, Jr., and Elisabeth Karr, Dec. 20, 1808.
Edmund and Jane Marsh, 1828–9.
Elisabeth L. and Daniel Stevens, Mar., 1817.
Frank and Alma E. Whidden, June 8, 1875.
Hannah and John McGaw, Dec. 4, 1810.
Hannah and Stephen Johnston, Mar., 1817.
John and Elisabeth Corning, Mar., 1818.
John Marsh and Polly Jackson, Oct. 30, 1810.
Mary and John Holmes, 1821–22.
Moses and Susanna Johnston, Mar., 1817.
Otis and Frances S. Webster, Nov. 24, 1862.
Patty and Amos Kendall, Nov. 14, 1808.
Parker and Miss Bond, 1812.
Robert and Sally Jackson, Jan. 4, 1810.
Robert, Jr., and Jane Campbell, 1826–7.
Samuel, 3d, and Sarah Fitz, Mar., 1817.
Samuel, 3d, and Harriet Norton, 1826–7.
Sarah and David Steel, 1821–22.
Wesley and Mabel F. M. Nevins, June 17, 1908.
Aiken, Andrew J. and Mary A. Carroll, Oct. 19, 1903.
Ann and Abner Campbell, Mar., 1814.
Fronia L. and Frank E. Norcross, Sept. 10, 1880.
Geo. F. and Addie Jane Pettengill, Oct. 27, 1879.
John and Eliza Pinkerton, Apr. 26, 1807.
Joshua and Jane Pinkerton, Mar., 1816.
Nathaniel and Mary Giles, Mar., 1817.
Polly and Benj. Griffin, 1818.
Samuel and Sally Coffin, Mar. 13, 1815.
Samuel H. and Hannah J. Estey, Aug. 5, 1868.

Alexander, Alphonso and Nellie F. Merrill, Nov. 26, 1873.
Amy Mabel and Wm. G. Dickey, July 10, 1905.
Chas. H. and Della M. Miller, Oct. 22, 1888.
Chas. H. and Jennie D. Young, May 24, 1890.
David and Nabby Smith, May 2, 1808.
George and Mary Holmes, Mar. 13, 1815.
Nathaniel C. and Ellen J. Roach, June 14, 1866.
Sally and Thomas Cheney, Mar. 7, 1812.
William and Dorothy Bailey, 1819–20.
William and Sally Brown, Mar., 1816.

Allen, Achsah J. and Will Smith, Jan. 29, 1890.
Anna and Asa Proctor, 1818.
Charlotte and Humphrey Proctor, Feb. 24, 1806.
George E. and Maria Naylor, Mar. 23, 1876.
Harriet A. and Chas. S. Greeley, Dec. 23, 1879.
Nancy and Laomi Searles, Sept. 8, 1860.

Allison, Betsey and Josiah Abbott, Nov. 14, 1808.

Anderson, Almira and Dr. John Haynes, July 3, 1871.
Anna B. and Dea. Matthew Holmes, Sept. 9, 1856.
Benjamin and Lydia Jackson, Mar., 1814.
Betsey and James M. Towns, Mar. 13, 1815.
Betsey and John Stinson, Mar., 1817.
Charles W. and Evalena W. French, June 2, 1898.
Edmond G. and Martha M. Sawyer, Dec. 11, 1890.
Elisabeth and Moses Dustin, Mar., 1818.
Elisabeth and Robert Holmes, Mar 11, 1811.
George E. and Sarah J. Harvell, Apr. 19, 1869.
Helen F. and Wesley B. Knight, Apr. 7, 1862.
James and Nancy Anderson, Mar., 1814.
James and Nancy Campbell, Mar. 13, 1815.
Jane and David Woodburn, Mar., 1816.
Jane and Robert Holmes, Nov. 14, 1809.
Martha and Samuel Davidson, Mar. 13, 1815.
Mary and Abel Plummer, Mar. 7, 1808.
Mary W. and Wm. Montgomery, Mar., 1814.
Nancy and Billy R. Gage, Mar., 1818.
Nancy and David Sargent, Sept. 16, 1809.
Nancy and James Anderson, Mar., 1814.
Robert and Jane Wilson, 1819–20.
Robert, 3d, and Anna B. Davidson, 1820–21.
Sally and John Campbell, Mar., 1814.
Sarah and John Holmes, Mar. 28, 1808.
William and Mary Bell, Mar. 21, 1808.
William and Nancy Williams, 1812.
William and Susan Choate, Mar., 1817.

Andrews, Mabel A. and Chas. H. Watts, 2d, Mar. 22, 1886.

Annis, Benj. F. and Catherine M. Robinson, Dce. 24, 1859.
Charles U. and Sarah Richardson, Oct. 21, 1888.
Daniel G. and Mina A. Gilcreast, June 17, 1868.
Daniel G. and Fannie M. Fling, Nov. 24, 1886.
Daniel M. and Mary J. Page, June 2, 1859.
Delia and Jacob F. Spalding, Apr. 6, 1864.
Edgar C. and Mary C. Durant, Feb. 5, 1892.
Fred E. and Caddie A. Smith, Oct. 16, 1889.
Henry H. and Rosilla Annis, Nov. 1, 1871.
James and Polly Leach, 1824–5.
Joel C. and Cornelia H. Smith, Dec. 23, 1856.
John and Delidah Coburn, 1819–20.
Joseph and Sarah Blodgett, 1822–23.
Lora H. and Chas. R. Avery, Nov., 1891.
Mariam P. and Chas. H. Watts, Jan. 1, 1861.
Parker B. and Roxanna Whidden, Nov. 17, 1858.
Rosilla and Henry H. Annis, Nov. 1, 1871.
Roswell and Luella A. Campbell, Dec. 8, 1874.
Roswell and E. Jennie McClary, Aug. 12, 1884.
Sally and Elisha Dwinell, 1824–5.

Arwain, James and Martha Wilson, 1821–22.

Atwood, Rebecca and David Hobbs, Nov. 26, 1810.
Thomas and Susanah Holmes, July 10, 1809.

Averill, Foster and Rebecca Robinson, 1821–22.

Avery, Charles R. and Lora H. Annis, Nov., 1891.
Climela and William Whidden, 1826–7.
Ida S. and Wilbur E. Barrett, July 6, 1885.

Ayer, Hezekiah and Polly Little, 1818.

Bachelder, Ellen G. and Mark W. Willey, Nov. 24, 1883.

Bacheldor, Sarah and Humphrey Holt, Mar., 1818.

Bacheller, Phebe A. (Mrs.) and Samuel Woodbury, Nov. 1, 1898.

Badger, Luella E. and Johnnie L. Young, June 27, 1889.

Bailey, Dorothy and William Alexander, 1819–20.
Elisabeth P. and Wm. C. Bancroft, Mar. 1, 1866.
Jacob and Ann Rogers, 1819–20.
Joseph and Lydia Towns, Oct. 3, 1808.
Mary Esther, 21, and Jos. Jeffery Herbert, 26, June 7, 1909.
Prudence and Joseph Shute, 1812.

Baker, Carabel A. and Henry Plummer Crowell, Dec. 24, 1879.
Ezra Norwell and Clara Louise Maker, Oct. 21, 1907.
Josephine Augusta, 22, and Everett Newton Clark, 30, May 27, 1909.

Bancroft, Betsa and Edward Putnam, Mar. 12, 1869.
Fred Lewis and Ida May Fitzgerald, Sept. 24, 1906.
Mary and Phineas Manter, 1821–22.
Savory and Betsey Cheney, 1822–23.
Warren and Mary Conant, 1826–7.
William C. and Elisabeth P. Bailey, Mar. 1, 1866.

Barker, Angeline and Chas. R. Barker, Apr. 1, 1861.
Angeline M. and Warren M. Pettengill, Apr. 9, 1859.
Carrie F. and Albert H. Dix, Oct. 7, 1867.
Chas. R. and Angeline Barker, Apr. 1, 1861.
Elisabeth and James Williams, Aug. 18, 1870.
Elisha and Charlotte Emery, 1819–20.
Eliza J. and David Pettengill, Nov., 1859.
John Chas. and Nellie Richardson, June 27, 1879.
Lucy and John Dismore, 1827–8.
Martha and James Holmes, 1823.
Mary and John Wilson, Mar. 13, 1815.
Mary and Joshua W. Norris, 1824–5.
Mehitable G. and Robert Call, 1822–23.
Ralph W., 20, and Elsa A. Mertsch, 20, July 9, 1910.
Rhoda and William Harris, 1820–21.
Rhoda A. and Geo. F. McGregor, May 2, 1865.
Sally and Jos. H. Brown, 1821–22.
Sarah and John Moulton, 1824–5.
Sophia and Dudley Hardy, 1821–22.
Susie A. and Geo. N. Goodwin, Sept. 28, 1872.

Barnes, Annie M. and Gayton H. Russell, Dec. 3, 1898.

Barnet, Ephraim and Charlotte Proctor, 1812.

Barnett, David and Grisey Patterson, Mar., 1814.
Mary and Nathaniel Johnston, Mar. 10, 1807.
Moses and Mary Clark, Mar. 7, 1812.
Robert and Sarah N. Brown, 1821–22.
Susannah and James Melvin, Jan. 26, 1807.

Barrett, Abel and Sarah Davis, 1820–21.
James E. and Emeline G. Hamlet, Jan. 12, 1860.
Violetta and Daniel C. Hill, Oct. 28, 1880.
Wilbur E. and Ida S. Avery (1st wife), July 6, 1885.
Wilbur E. and Sarah Muncaster (3d wife), Jan. 1, 1907.

Barron, Alice V. and Eugene A. Savage, Nov. 22, 1880.
Lillian S. and Harry C. Vincent, Apr. 26, 1879.

Bartlett, Ada E. and Dr. James B. Pettengill, Sept. 20, 1881.
F. Henry and Etta M. Proctor, Jan. 10, 1893.
Thomas and Lydia Abbott, Nov. 26, 1810.

Bartley, Nancy and John Jackson, Mar., 1817.

Bassan, Mary and Nathaniel Smith, Mar., 1816.

Batchelor, Daniel K. and Clarrina French, Jan. 15, 1880.
Beals, Flora E. and George F. Hamblett, Sept. 19, 1878.
Bean, Benjamin F. and Abbie Wheeler, Dec. 4, 1869.
Eliza and Geo. A. Hill, Sept. 8, 1858.
Beard, David and Sarah Dwinell Plumer, 1819–20.
Beede, George W. and Annie S. Moody, Apr. 23, 1900.
Bell, Mary and William Anderson, Mar. 21, 1808.
Bennett, Emma J. and Frank A. Jenks, June 15, 1886.
Benson, Andrew J. and Mrs. Eliza Rowell, Nov. 17, 1884.
Ella F. and John H. Connor, Nov. 28, 1876.
Bergeron, George and Harriet F. Christie, May 19, 1906.
Berry, Samuel and Sarah Gregg, Mar. 7, 1812.
Black, Hannah and Samuel Dunkley, 1819–20.
Jane and Joseph Dodge, May 16, 1809.
Mary and Thomas Bruce, Mar., 1817.
Blackburn, Alfred Ernest and Almeda Rebecca Cox, June 20, 1905.
Blaisdell, Betsey and John Leach, 1821–22.
Blodgett, Augusta W. and Oliver D. Evans, Apr. 18, 1866.
Sarah and Joseph Annis, 1822–23.
Blood, Chas. L. and Frances M. Smith, Dec. 31, 1861.
Boles, Annie E. and Leroy S. Hartshorn, Oct. 21, 1902.
Florence J. and Osmond E. E. Corthell, Sept. 19, 1901.
Bolles, Caroline W. and John Goodwin, Mar. 17, 1863.
Bond, Daniel and Betsey Nichols, Mar., 1818.
Horace and Sarah Burrill, 1822–23.
Gilbert, Jr., and Sarah Silver, 1822–23.
Miss ——— and Parker Adams, 1812.
Thomas J. and Ann C. Brown, 1826–7.
Booth, Lillia A. and Wesley I. Young, Dec. 7, 1877.
Boss, Edgar H. and Alice M. Whidden, June 20, 1872.
Bowker, James A. and Ella Maria Colby, Mar. 17, 1862.
Boyce, Annie R. and Edgar F. McDonald, Apr. 19, 1894.
Chas. F. and Sarah F. Wheeler, Oct. 9, 1888.
Chas. F. and Mrs. Nellie A. Whidden, June 14, 1908.
Edith F. and Royal S. Proctor, July 30, 1906.
Esther W. and Alonzo F. Clark, Apr. 22, 1859.
Horace C. and Adella Brooks, Oct. 13, 1889.
May E. and Ransom Flanders, Apr. 30, 1877.
Myra F. and James L. Brooks, July 14, 1891.
Orietta J. and Elbridge A. Whidden, Nov. 11, 1876.
Sam N. and Estella Goud, Dec. 26, 1903.
Samuel and Julia Conant, May 30, 1881. (Never married.)

Boyce, Sewall W. and Eliza J. Davis, Nov. 30, 1882.
Walter and Esther Jane Watts, Dec. 16, 1861.

Boyd, Abby E. and Frank S. Crowell, Jan. 1, 1878.
Betsey and John Cogswell, 1824–5.
Daniel M. and Hattie P. Mullins, May 6, 1884.
Emma D. and Fred A. Young, Nov. 24, 1885.
Lettuce and Samuel Marsh, May 16, 1809.
Mary and Nathaniel Warner, Mar., 1814.
Polly and Amos Shipley, Dec. 13, 1802.
Robert and Mary Ann Towns, 1812.
Robert and Betsey Choate, Mar., 1814.
William and Ruth C. Gardner, Sept. 19, 1808.
William and Margaret Holmes, Jan. 30, 1809.
William and Martha Dickey, Mar., 1816.
William and Lucy Hovey, 1818.

Boyes, Allice and Ebenezer Hansor, Mar. 13, 1815.
Esther and Sewall Worster, 1824–5.
Hazen G. and Elsa Squars, 1827.
James and Martha Ramsey, Aug. 14, 1809.
John and Martha Stewart, Nov. 14, 1809.
Margaret and Amos Carlton, 1818.
Nathaniel and Martha Watts, 1828–9.
Peggy and William Whidden, Mar., 1818.
Robert and Elisabeth McMurphy, June 15, 1804.
Robert and Jane Moar, 1826–7.
Samuel and Sally Crowell, 1828–9.
Sarah and John Gross, 1824–5.
Sophey and William Cheney, Apr. 1, 1811.

Boys, Benj. and Sally White, 1819–20.
John and Vina Boys, 1812.
Nancy and Thomas Nesmith, 1820–21.
Nina and John Boys, 1812.
Robt., Jr., and Prescilla Garvin, 1822–23.
Susan and John C. Poor, 1822–23.

Brackett, Sarah E. and William Major, Dec. 19, 1861.

Bradley, Jeremiah and Jane Holmes, Mar. 31, 1810.

Bragdon, Cyrena and Edward B. Buxton, Feb. 1, 1875.

Bragg, Capt. John and Mary Kenney, 1824–5.

Braley, Lemuel P. and Angeline McKenney, Mar. 25, 1869.

Breed, Joseph and Tryphena Bruce, 1819–20.
Josiah and Jane Gregg, 1819–20.

Brewster, David and Margaret Wilson, July 10, 1809.
David and Mary McMurphy, Mar., 1818.
Rebecca and John Humphrey, Mar. 13, 1815.

Brickett, Emily and Orriville A. Peabody, Dec. 16, 1873.

Brooks, Adelle and Horace C. Boyce, Oct. 13, 1889.
Anna C. and William H. Colby, June 13, 1897.
Edw. Q. F. and Margaret Olliver, June 1, 1908.
James L. and Myra F. Boyce, July 14, 1891.

Brown, Amnio and Elisabeth Wilson, 1819–20.
Ann C. and Thomas J. Bond, 1826–7.
Arthur E. and Marilla Jones, Sept. 14, 1901.
David and Sally Senter, Mar., 1816.
Ebenezer and Rosanna McDuffee, Mar., 1817.
Ebenezer, Jr., and Mary Melvin, 1822–23.
Eunice and Joseph Proctor, Dec. 20, 1808.
James and Anna G. Warner, Mar., 1817.
Jennie and Allen S. Manter, Aug. 6, 1885.
Joseph H. and Sally Barker, 1821–22.
Kate M., 20, and Alfred F. Manter, 24, Oct. 23, 1910.
Mary and Jacob Couch, Mar. 13, 1815.
Prissilla and Joshua Marsh, 1819–20.
Robert A. and Amanda R. Mullins, Apr. 7, 1890.
Sally and Wm. Alexander, Mar., 1816.
Sarah N. and Robert Barnett, 1821–22.
William and Hattie F. Burrill, Oct. 29, 1888.

Bruce, Franklin W. and Abigail Mitchel, Mar. 13, 1815.
Nancy and Ezra Roads, Sept. 16, 1809.
Sally and David Worthen, Mar., 1814.
Susan and David Gile, Jan. 8, 1810.
Thomas and Mary Black, Mar., 1817.
Tryphena and Joseph Breed, 1819–20.

Buckingham, Jos. and Rebecca Nichols, Mar., 1814.

Burbank, Abraham and Mrs. Sarah C. Hazeltine, Aug. 26, 1853.

Burlard, Irene A. and George Whittondon, Mar. 27, 1887.

Burnham, Abigail Maria and Jonathan Ireland, 1822–23.
Eliza and John Doland, 1824–5.

Burrill, Hattie F. and William Brown, Oct. 29, 1888.
Sarah and Horace Bond, 1822–23.

Butterworth, Wm. A. and Edith Belle Lowd, May 11, 1893.

Buttrick, Carrie A. and Arthur A. White, Nov. 21, 1906.
Cyrus O. and Eliza J. Dismore, Apr. 23, 1863.
Mabel E. and Perley S. Robie, Jan. 17, 1894.
Nathan and Catherine Witherspoon, 1822–23.

Buxton, Edward B. and Cyrena Bragdon, Feb. 1, 1875.

Caldwell, Alexander and Lois Reed Jones, 1812.
Ebenezer and Anna McMurphy, Mar., 1818.
Ephraim and Margaret Jewett, Mar., 1816.
Janet and John McAllister, Oct. 6, 1806.

Caldwell, Jefferson and Nancy H. Dickey, Dec. 8, 1864.
Henry J. and Abbie F. Greeley, Nov. 1, 1875.
Thomas and Lettice Gregg, Dec. 30, 1807.
Rachel and Benjamin Proctor, Oct. 12, 1807.
Rebecca and David M. C. Thompson, Jan. 23, 1809.

Calef, Joseph and Margaret McKinsey, July 8, 1807.

Call, Mary L. and George E. Jackson, Feb. 3, 1892.
Robert and Mehitabal G. Barker, 1822–23.

Campbell, Abner and Ann Aiken, Mar., 1814.
Anna and John Ela, Lt., 1823.
Betsey and Thomas Carleton, Mar., 1818.
Blanche C. and Wm. Runell Moore, Dec. 29, 1894.
Daniel, Jr., and Nancy Gile, 1822–23.
Eugene L. and Martha T. Goss, Sept. 30, 1873.
Harriet B. and Harvey S. Gould, Aug. 12, 1862.
Jane and Robert Adams, Jr., 1826–7.
John and Sally Anderson, Mar., 1814.
Luella A. and Roswell Annis, Dec. 8, 1874.
Mary and Jabish Towns, 1812.
Maude E. and Elbert O. Putnam, Apr. 16, 1892.
Nancy and James Anderson, Mar. 13, 1815.
Pliny M. and Emma B. Abbott, June 2, 1902.
Sally and Lyman Cheney, 1826–7.

Carleton, Farnum H. and Olive Proctor, Mar., 1818.
John and Raches Morrell, Mar., 1818.
Moses and Ruth Watters, Mar., 1814.
Thomas and Betsey Campbell, Mar., 1818.
William and Sally Kemball, Mar., 1816.
William B. and Betsey Ann Webster, July 2, 1860.

Carlton, Amos and Margaret Boyes, 1818.
Bethiah and James Palmer, Jr., 1821–22.
Daniel and Mary Morse, Mar. 24, 1809.
Jeremiah and Sally Carlton, 1820–21.
Ruth and James Palmer, Jan. 26, 1807.
Sally and Jeremiah Carlton, 1820–21.

Carpenter, Rena H. and Joseph L. Galvin, Dec. 19, 1906.

Carr, Clara B. and Nelson H. Dickey, Mar. 24, 1896.
Joseph and Ruth Corning, 1820–21.
Moses and Almira Murry, 1822–23.

Carroll, Mary A. and Andrew J. Aiken, Oct. 19, 1903.

Caskin, Isaac and Mary Eaton, Dec. 13, 1807.

Caverly, Lizzie and George E. Ela, Nov. 26, 1885.

Chadwick, Sally and William B. Shute, Mar., 1818.

Chandler, William and Rebekah Cobb, Mar., 1817.

Chase, Abigail and Joseph Eaton, 1820–21.
Addie A. and Phineas A. Reid, Jan. 9, 1886.
Cora M. and Geo. A. Waugh, May 10, 1888.
Daniel and Hannah E. Chase, Mar., 1814.
Daniel and Ednar Eaton, 1819–20.
Elijah G. and Lottie F. Corning, Jan. 5, 1889.
Elisabeth and Jabez Towns, 1828–9.
Elisabeth M. and Frank J. Johnson, Feb. 18, 1880.
Emily A. and Joseph R. Clark, Aug. 26, 1862.
Francis M. and Lovinia Jones, Mar., 1817.
Fred E. and Allettie M. Young, May 31, 1887.
Hannah E. and Daniel Chase, Mar., 1814.
Harry E. and Clara B. Weaver, May 13, 1896.
Henry and Betsey B. Warner, 1820–21.
Henry and Mariam Page, 1826–7.
James I. and Eliza H. Page, Sept. 28, 1873.
James I., 59, and Mrs. Mary J. Chase, 86, Jan. 14, 1907.
James I., 61, and Mrs. Marcia M. Senter, 67, July 5, 1909.
Joanna and Andrew Robinson, 1826–7.
John and Polly C. Jones, Mar., 1816.
John M. and Mrs. Susan Page, July 22, 1896.
Lucy and Lewis Warren, July 11, 1890.
Margaret and Stephen Emery, Mar., 1818.
Mary J. (Mrs.), 86, and James I. Chase, 59, Jan. 14, 1907.
Mary and James Young, Mar. 13, 1815.
Nancy and Hughy Gault, 1812.
Nathaniel and Lydia Mott, Aug. 20, 1810.
Samuel Morral and Polly Morral, Sept. 16, 1809.
Shuah and Benj. Whorf, Mar., 1817.
Sophronia C. and Augustus L. Farley, Feb. 25, 1857.
Thomas and Mary Plummer, Mar. 14, 1809.
Thomas and Mary Giles, 1821–22.

Cheever, Elisabeth and William Cox, 1821–22.
Osgood and Jane Martin, Mar., 1817.

Cheney, Betsey and Savory Bancroft, 1822–23.
David and Mahala Cobb, Mar., 1816.
David F. and Sarah E. Page, Nov. 17, 1886.
Joshua and Hannah Kelsey, Mar. 13, 1815.
Lyman and Sally Campbell, 1826–7.
Rebecca and James French, Mar., 1816.
Seth and Eliza P. Danforth, Mar. 13, 1815.
Thomas and Sally Alexander, Mar. 7, 1812.
William and Sophey Boyes, Apr. 1, 1811.

Chesley, Samuel and Hannah B. Waters, 1821–22.

Chesly, Joseph and Polly Ranken, Mar., 1816.

Chick, Mabel Vincent and Frank Lewis Thomas, Nov. 14, 1904.

Childs, Mary L. and Willie E. Watts, Oct. 5, 1885.

Choate, Betsey and Robert Boyd, Mar., 1814.
Humphrey and Betsey Law, 1820–21.
James and Abigaile Cogswell, Mar., 1818.
Jonathan and Anne C. Welch, July 3, 1810.
Nehemiah and Sally Cogswell, Mar. 13, 1815.
Sally and Benjamin Haseltine, Mar., 1817.
Susan and William Anderson, Mar., 1817.
William and Mary B. Pinkerton, Mar., 1816.

Chrispeen, Geo. W. and Betsey T. Putnam, May 11, 1875.
Jennie S. and Levi H. Corthell, Sept. 22, 1869.

Christie, Harriet F. and George Bergeron, May 19, 1906.

Christy, Sarah and Robert McMurphy, Feb. 14, 1811.

Claggett, Edward G. and Sally Clark, 1820–21.

Clark, Alice and John Moar, Jr., 1821–22.
Alonzo F. and Esther W. Boyce, Apr. 22, 1859.
Ann and Robert Mack, Mar., 1814.
Catherine Edna, 27, and Samuel A. Gratto, 30, June 16, 1909.
Clarrissa H. and Oren Kimball, Nov., 1859.
Ernest Newton, 30, and Josephine Augusta Baker, 22, May 27, 1909.
Flora F. and Chas. D. Cross, Sept. 24, 1886.
George A. and Lizzie P. Towns, Nov. 6, 1861.
Grissel and James Woodburn, Mar. 13, 1809.
Jane and Nathaniel Hemphilı, Mar., 1818.
John and Mary Taylor, 1819–20.
John and Mary Cross, 1826–7.
Joseph R. and Emily A. Chase, Aug. 26, 1862.
Joshua and Eliza Spollett, Mar., 1817.
Lucinda and David T. Ingalls, 1826–7.
Margaret and Jonathan Merrill, 1822–23.
Marrianna P. and Wm. H. Seaman, Aug. 27, 1873.
Mary and Moses Barnett, Mar. 7, 1812.
Mary and Asahel P. Ripley, 1826–27.
Michal and Irene Collins, 1822–23.
Sally and Thomas Follansbee, Mar., 1816.
Sally and Edward G. Claggett, 1820–21.
William and Alice W. McIntire, Aug. 17, 1876.

Clay, Walter and Sarah Danforth, Jan. 20, 1807.

Clements, Carrie E. and Geo. E. Currier, June 16, 1888.

Clindining, Polly and David Steel, Mar. 13, 1810.

Cobb, Betsey and Chandler Spofford, Mar. 7, 1812.
Rebekah and Wm. Chandler, Mar., 1817.

Cobb, Susan and Benj. McMurphy, Mar. 13, 1815.
Mahela and David Cheney, Mar., 1816.

Coburn, Delilah and John Annis, 1819–20.
Gideon and Mary McFarland, Jan. 26, 1807.
Isaac and Sally McGrath, May 2, 1808.
Joseph and Eliza Plumer, 1826–7.
Reuben and Abia A. Conant, Jan. 28, 1811.

Cochran, Frances B. and Caleb Redfield, Mar., 1818.
James and Mary Martin, Mar., 1817.
John and Rebeccah Waterman, 1826–7.
Isaac W. and Lucy Tilley, Feb. 7, 1874.
William and Betsey Wilson, June 9, 1807.

Coffin, Betsey and Samuel Wallace, Mar. 7, 1810.
Eliza and Maus Perkins, 1824–5.
Harriet A. and M. Noyes Holmes, Jan. 20, 1857.
Sally and Samuel Aiken, Mar. 13, 1815.

Cogswell, Abigail and James Choate, Mar., 1818.
John C. and Eliza W. Kimball, 1821–22.
John and Betsey Boyd, 1824–5.
Joseph and Mehitable Howe, Mar., 1818.
Nathaniel and Lucy Perkins, 1826–7.
Sally and Nehemiah Choate, Mar. 13, 1815.

Colby, Ella Maria and James A. Bowker, Mar. 17, 1862.
Emerson and Mary Greeley, Mar., 1818.
Emma J. and Chas. G. Kimball, Oct. 13, 1880.
F. Alice, 23, and Edward L. Wing, July 9, 1908.
Isaac and Hannah Jones, 1826–7.
William H. and Anna C. Brooks, June 13, 1897.

Collens, Lydia and John Craige, Mar., 1816.

Collins, Irena and Michal Clark, 1822–23.

Conant, Abia A. and Reuben Coburn, Jan. 28, 1811.
Henry and Mary S. Hovey, May 10, 1856.
Julia M. and Samuel Boyce, May 30, 1881. (Never married.)
Julia M. and William Packer, June 18, 1884.
Mary and Phillip Garat (?), 1823.
Mary and Warren Bancroft, 1826–7.
Nathaniel and Susan Senter, Mar., 1818.
Sally and Isaac Crowell, 1819–20.

Connor, John H. and Ella F. Benson, Nov. 28, 1876.

Cook, Marion R. and Clarence O. Watts, Sept. 14, 1903.
Olive S., 31, and John H. S. Goodwin, 50, May 17, 1910.

Corbett, Mattie E. and William O. Morrison, Dec. 19, 1891.

Corey, Emma F. and Silas E. Lincoln, Sept. 26, 1888.

Corliss, Harry C. and Marion Bly Nugent, Apr. 27, 1904.

Corning, Abel P. and Susan Wells, Mar. 13, 1815.
Benj. and Mary Flint, 1812.
Carrie M. and George E. Payne, Aug. 24, 1876.
Clara Belle and Frank A. Nesmith, Dec. 21, 1889.
Elisabeth and John Adams, Mar., 1818.
Ernest E. and H. Josephine Corning, July 10, 1890.
Fred P. and Nellie I. Crowell, Mar. 31, 1897.
Georgie and Ernest M. Watts, Dec. 17, 1887.
H. Josephine and Ernest E. Corning, July 10, 1890.
Hannah and Morrison Jackson, 1828–9.
Jennie S. and David F. Perkins, Feb. 12, 1884.
John and Lydia Richardson, Mar., 1816.
John C. and Elisabeth Nesmith, Mar., 1817.
Judith and Asa Perly, Mar., 1818.
Lottie F. and Elijah G. Chase, Jan. 5, 1889.
Lucy A. and Wm. Benj. Walch, Mar. 16, 1892.
Martha and Joseph Leach, Mar., 1816.
Mary E. (Mrs.) and David McGregor, Dec. 13, 1886.
Miriam and James Watts, Jr., 1819–20.
Nathaniel and Judith Giles, 1827–8.
Polly and James Nesmith, Mar., 1816.
Polly and James Currier, 1818.
Rachel and Ruben White, 1824–5.
Regina V. and Alonzo R. Wells, Apr. 30, 1861.
Ruth and Joseph Carr, 1820–21.
Sylvester R. and Sarah J. Currier, Feb. 22, 1866.

Corthell, Albin and Abbie Adella Goodwin, Dec. 26, 1892.
Levi H. and Jennie S. Crispeen, Sept. 22, 1869.
Osmond E. E. and Florence J. Boles, Sept. 19, 1901.

Couch, Jacob and Mary Brown, Mar. 13, 1815.

Cousens, Hester C. and George A. Hall, June 26, 1894.

Cowdrey, Joseph S. and Jennie E. Fogg, June 24, 1876.

Cox, Almeda Rebecca and Alfred E. Blackburn, June 20, 1905.
James, 3d, and Ann Eliza Rogers, 1822–23.
William and Elisabeth Cheever, 1821–22.

Craig, Whitfield and Nabby Richardson, 1820–21.

Craige, John and Lydia Collens, Mar., 1816.

Cram, Perry and Mary A. Sculley, Jan. 30, 1860.

Creasy, Joseph and Miss Betsey Eastman, Sept. 7, 1807. (West Parish records.)

Crocker, Hannah and Dr. Geo. Farrar, 1822–23.
Margaret and Williard Holbrook, 1819–20.
Mary and John Proctor, 1826–27.

Crosby, Abigal and Robert Doak, Nov. 3, 1810.

Cross, Alice M. and J. Madison Howe, Apr. 12, 1887.
Arthur H. and Lelia M. Fiske, Oct. 18, 1895.
Chas. D. and Flora F. Clark, Sept. 24, 1886.
Hiram N., 34, and Ernestine E. Nugent, 36, May 24, 1909.
Mary and John Clark, 1826–7.

Crowell, Asenath and Ira Leach, 1818.
Charles A. and Mary L. Schwartz, Dec. 22, 1889.
Eliza and Stephen Danforth, Mar. 7, 1812.
Frank S. and Abby E. Boyd, Jan. 1, 1878.
H. Plummer and Carabel A. Baker, Dec. 24, 1879.
Hannah and John March, 1828–9.
Harriet E. and James Floyd, June 3, 1865.
Isaac and Sally Conant, 1819–20.
Lizzie H. and Stephen A. Estey, Aug. 11, 1886.
Martha S. and Wm. S. Pillsbury, Apr. 7, 1856.
Mary and George McAllister, Feb. 14, 1811.
Mary E. and Daniel M. McQuesten, Oct. 5, 1892.
Nellie I. and Fred P. Corning, Mar. 31, 1897.
Peter and Orra Martin, Mar., 1818.
Peter and Harriet Hardy, 1820–21.
Rose J. (Mrs.) and Chas. A. Tenney, Apr. 6, 1895.
Sally and Samuel Boyes, 1828–9.
Wm. H. and Almira A. Parker, Sept. 19, 1866.

Crowningshield, Harriet and Francis Manter, 1819–20.
Sophia and James Platts, 1823.

Cunningham, John C. and Ann S. Prentis, 1826–7.

Currier, George E. and Carrie E. Clements, June 16, 1888.
James and Polly Corning, 1818.
Sarah J. and Sylvester R. Corning, Feb. 21, 1866,

Cutler, Hiram and Lucinda Miller, Dec. 30, 1875.

Cutter, Antoinette De Grave and Alfred Brook Knight, Sept. 11, 1865.

Dailey, Lillian J. and Sedley H. Lowd, Mar. 18, 1898.

Daley, James P. and Katie Haley, June 24, 1890.

Danforth, Barker and Mary Laland, Mar., 1817.
Eliza P. and Seth Cheney, Mar. 13, 1815.
Jennie and Frank Walch, Aug. 5, 1868.
Lucy and Daniel Warner, Dec. 30, 1807.
Orpah and Oliver Lund, Mar., 1816.
Sarah and Walter Clay, Jan. 20, 1807.
Stephen and Eliza Crowell, Mar. 7, 1812.

Daniels, Clovis J., 24, and Kate Lines, 19, May 11, 1910.

Darrah, John and Easter Holt, Sept. 17, 1810.
Samuel and Betsey Palmer, 1824–5.
Sophia and James Senter, Mar., 1817.

Davenport, E. Horace and Harriet Julia Nevins, June 25, 1906.

Davidson, Abigal and Samuel Hardy, Mar. 12, 1810.
Anna B. and Robt. Anderson, 3d, 1820–21.
Samuel and Martha Anderson, Mar. 13, 1815.
Sarah D. and John Morrison, 1824–25.

Davis, Edith H. and Ulysses G. Pillsbury, Nov. 19, 1896.
Elisabeth and Isaac Smith, 1824–25.
Eliza J. and Sewall W. Boyce, Nov. 30, 1882.
Francis and Betsey Stephens, Mar., 1818.
Hannah and Matthew McDuffee, 1818.
Henriette and Harvelin Thayer, Oct. 9, 1877.
John F. and Harriet Griffin, Sept. 25, 1861.
Nancy and Samuel K. Nickels, 1820–21.
Ruthy and John Greenough, 1821–22.
Sarah and Abel Barrett, 1820–21.
William and Mary Sargent, 1819–20.

Davison, Viola G., 16, and Osborne L. West, 27, Sept. 25, 1909.

Day, Elisabeth K. and Woodburn Nichols, 1821–22.
Ella Louisa, 19, and Frank C. Maxfield, 26, June 17, 1910.
Joseph and Lucretia Worthen, 1826–7.
Leonard L. and Sally Nichols, Mar., 1816.
Little and Margaret Reid, Mar., 1817.
Little and Margaret Morrison, 1821–22.

Dearborn, Syrnne and Amos Jenness, 1812.

Demeritt, Frank J. and Isabel D. McGregor, Sept. 25, 1883.

Densmore, Anna and John P. Payne, July 1, 1876.

Derborn, Jonathan and Jane Stinson, May 7, 1810.

Dickey, Clara D. and Wm. L. Lord, Dec. 11, 1863.
Geo. L. and Florence E. Richardson, Mar. 27, 1906.
Jane and Samuel Gregg, 1812.
John and Margaret Woodburn, Mar. 2, 1805.
Joseph and Frances Montgomery, Mar. 7, 1812.
Lyman A. and Henrietta Neal, Apr. 22, 1908.
Martha and William Boyd, Mar., 1816.
Mary and Edward Ela, Mar. 13, 1815.
Mary J. and Albert Tenney, May 19, 1875.
Nancy H. and Jefferson Caldwell, Dec. 8, 1864.
Nelson H. and Clara B. Carr, Mar. 24, 1896.
Robert and Jenney Morrison, 1821–22.
Samuel and Nancy Humphrey, Feb. 11, 1805.
Susan and John White, Mar., 1818.
William G. and Amy M. Alexander, July 10, 1905.

Dinsmoore, John and Mary Rogers, Apr. 17, 1809.

Dismoor, Frances and Samuel C. Pope, Dec. 15, 1806.

Dismore, Abraham and Hannah Nichols, Feb. 13, 1809.
Eliza J. and Cyrus O. Buttrick, Apr. 23, 1863.
John and Lucy Barker, 1827–8.
Sarah and Ensign Nichols, 1819–20.

Dissmore, Chas. O. and Mary J. Fiefield, May 5, 1865.
Eliza and David Jackson, 1828–9.

Dix, Albert H. and Carrie F. Barker, Oct. 7, 1867.
Timothy and Betsey Dwinell, 1820–21.

Doak, Robert and Abigal Crosby, Nov. 3, 1810.

Dodge, Elisabeth and Joseph Whitiker, 1824–5.
Joseph and Jane Black, May 16, 1809.
Lydia and Hughey Mills, 1812.
Mary and Samuel Jackson, Mar., 1816.
Mary and Kent Merrill, 1818.
Mehitable and Belcher Mentor, Jan. 21, 1811.
Stillman and Sally Highlands, Mar., 1817.

Doherty, Chas. P. and Nellie A. Robie, Dec. 22, 1894.
Cilvilla C. and Wm. A. Osborn, Jan. 1, 1897.
James T. and Syvella C. Towne, June 17, 1889.

Doland, John and Eliza Burnham, 1824–5.

Dooley, Geo. N. and Ella W. Hadley, Jan. 14, 1907.

Dore, Sophia and Samuel Spolett, 1821–22.

Dow, John C. and Laura Z. Rowell, June 30, 1875.
Isabella J. and Clinton J. Farley, Apr. 3, 1864.

Drake, Doty and Joseph Jenness, July 17, 1809.

Dudley, Emma H. and Wm. H. Ramsey, Nov. 29, 1888.

Dufee, Mary and James Wilson, 1819–20.

Duffield, Grace, 27, and Geo. Olwing Garvin, 28, Sept. 26, 1908.

Duncan, Hannah and Thomas Patterson, 1818.
Mary and John Jackson, 1822–23.

Dunkley, Samuel and Hannah Black, 1819–20.

Durant, Geo. W. and Anne F. Kimball, Oct. 15, 1867.
Mary C. and Edgar C. Annis, Feb. 5, 1892.

Dustin, Abigail and John Hovey, 1820–21.
Edith Louise and Ralph W. Wright, June 3, 1906.
Moses and Elisabeth Anderson, Mar., 1818.
Ruth and Francis Smily, 1822–23.

Dwinell, Betsey and Timothy Dix, 1820–21.
Elijah and Rebecca Russell, May 21, 1804.
Elijah and Emilia Eastman, Mar. 7, 1812.

Dwinell, Elisha and Sally Annis, 1824–5.
Lois and Joseph Holt, Mar., 1818.
Lois and Joseph Holt, 1826–7.

Dwinells, Benj. J. and Mary Ann Woodburn, 1821–22.
Mehitable and James Menter, Mar., 1818.

Eastman, Betsey (Miss) and Joseph Creasy, Sept. 7, 1807. (West Parish records.)
Dustimony and John Greeley, May 16, 1809.
Emilia and Elijah Dwinell, Mar. 7, 1812.
Mary and John Follansbee, Mar., 1816.
Sally and George Moar, 1822–23.

Eaton, Ednar and Daniel Chase, 1819–20.
Joseph and Abigail Chase, 1820–21.
Joseph and Rhoda A. Weed, Nov. 29, 1865.
Mary and Isaac Caskin, Dec. 13, 1807.
Wm. J. and Mabel G. Spear, May 17, 1890.

Ela, Clark and Mary Waterman, 1822–23.
David W. and Sarah A. Robie, Mar. 24, 1879.
David W. and Martha E. Lovejoy, Feb. 6, 1883.
Edward and Sally Page, Nov. 26, 1810.
Edward and Mary Dickey, Mar. 13, 1815.
George E. and Lizzie Caverly, Nov. 26, 1885.
George E. and Mary E. N. Low, Aug. 31, 1904.
Lt. John and Anna Campbell, 1823.
Louisa and Richard Kent, Aug. 20, 1810.
Sally and Stephen Reynolds, Jan. 21, 1811.
William and Polly Moar, 1812.

Ellis, George E. and Annie M. Hartford, May 1, 1893.

Emerson, Adda F. and Geo. C. Webster, Aug. 30, 1878.
Jessey O. and Anna J. Owen, Mar. 20, 1860.
Joseph and Betsey Simonds, Mar. 7, 1812.
Louisa and Wm. Humphrey, Mar., 1816.
Samuel and Nancy Wilson, 1826–7.
Susan D. and Thomas B. Platts, May 12, 1856.

Emery, Charlotte and Elisha Barker, 1819–20.
Jacob and Betsey March, 1819–20.
Rebecca and Joseph Nichols, Mar., 1814.
Rhodia and Benjamin Wilson, 1827.
Stephen and Margaret Chase, Mar., 1818.

Estey, Hannah J. and Samuel H. Aiken, Aug. 5, 1868.
Hannah J. and Reuben K. Pratt, Oct. 30, 1891.
Harriet E. and Samuel Woodbury, Dec. 1, 1858.
Horace P. and Nancy G. Reed, Nov. 22, 1859.
Stephen A. and Mary A. Remington, Nov. 28, 1877.
Stephen A. and Lizzie H. Crowell, Aug. 11, 1886.

Evans, Ellen M. and Walter D. Reed, Sept. 30, 1871.
Emma F. and Chas. H. Fellows, Aug. 13, 1884.
Oliver D. and Augusta W. Blodgett, Apr. 18, 1866.

Farley, Augustus L. and Sophronia C. Chase, Feb. 25, 1857.
Clinton J. and Isabella J. Dow, Apr. 3, 1864.

Farmer, Thomas M. and Hannah Marshall, 1823.

Farnham, John and Olive Hibard, 1812.
Sarah F. and Zacheus Patterson, 1823.

Farnum, Ezra Marsh and Susan Richey, Mar., 1818.
Nathaniel and Elisabeth Knight, 1821–22.

Farrar, Dr. George and Sarah Prentice, July 10, 1809.
Dr. George and Hannah Crocker, 1822–23.

Fellows, Alice H. and Ensign C. Woods, Aug. 23, 1861.
Chas. H. and Emma F. Evans, Aug. 13, 1884.

Ferrin, Elisabeth and Alexander Jack, 1826–7.

Fiefield, Martha W. and William Smith, 1821–22.
Mary J. and Chas. O. Dissmore, May 5, 1865.

Fields, Charles and Eliza Freeman, 1821–22.

Fisher, Amelia and Jonathan Humphrey, 1821–22.
Ebenezer and Jane Orr, Mar., 1816.
Thomas and Mary Rollins, May 7, 1800.

Fisk, Eleanor W. and Arlbey Nason, 1826–7.

Fiske, Lelia M. and Arthur H. Cross, Oct. 18, 1895.

Fitts, Alice J. and Herman L. Watts, Dec. 22, 1897.

Fitz, Hannah and Ebenezer Stickney, Feb. 27, 1809.
Sarah and Samuel Adams, 3d, Mar., 1817.

Fitze, Betsey and Matthew Holmes, 1823.

Fitzgerald, Ida May and Fred Lewis Bancroft, Sept. 24, 1906.

Flanders, Martha and John Major, May 16, 1809.
Mrs. May E. and Chas. J. Hobbs, Oct. 11, 1905.
Ransom and May E. Boyce, Apr. 30, 1877.
Reuben W. and Precilla W. Sawyer, Mar. 11, 1861.

Flanigan, Jennie W. and Chas. H. Fling, June 23, 1891.

Fling, Chas. H. and Jennie W. Flanigan, June 23, 1891.
Fannie M. and Daniel G. Annis, Nov. 24, 1886.
John W. and Mary A. Goodwin, Nov. 30, 1857.
Martha E. and Geo. Alvah Watts, Oct. 15, 1883.
Minnie M. and Elwin C. Peabody, Oct. 14, 1885.

Flint, Martha and Wm. G. Hardy, Apr. 11, 1861.
Mary and Benjamin Corning, 1812.

Floyd, Abby A. and Chas. H. Morrison, July 19, 1858.
James and Harriet E. Crowell, June 3, 1865.
John S. and Sarah F. Lowd, May 25, 1879.
W. Claud and Ada B. Wells, Mar. 20, 1888.

Fogg, Jennie E. and Joseph S. Cowdrey, June 24, 1876.

Follansbee, John and Mary Eastman, Mar., 1816.
Thomas and Sally Clark, Mar., 1816.

Foster, Betsey A. and Silas Proctor, Mar. 13, 1815.
William and Phebe Holt, Mar. 23, 1805.

Fowler, Hannah and Winthrop Rollins, Sept. 26, 1808.

Franch, Mary and Samuel Whidden, Nov. 14, 1809.

Francis, Edward, 40, and Mrs. Frances H. Kimball, 53, Oct. 26, 1908.

Freeman, Eliza and Charles Fields, 1821–22.
Leonard A. and Emma K. Spinney, Nov. 16, 1878.

French, Clarrissa and Daniel K. Batchelor, Jan. 15, 1880.
Dorothy and Varnum Perry, 1820–21.
Evalena W. and Chas. W. Anderson, June 2, 1898.
James and Rebecca Cheney, Mar., 1816.
William and Olive Merrill, Apr. 13, 1808.

Furber, Frank O. and Mary A. Mackay, May 29, 1877.
Mattie B. and George P. Harvell, Apr. 18, 1900.

Gage, Billy R. and Nancy Anderson, Mar., 1818.
Sarah and Henry March, 1819–20.
Wm. W. and Hattie E. Roach, Apr. 15, 1890.

Galencia, May Louise and Joseph A. Sweatt, Sept. 24, 1903.

Galvin, Joseph L. and Rena H. Carpenter, Dec. 19, 1906.

Garat, Philip (?) and Mary Conant, 1823.

Garden, Wells and Sally Holt, 1812.

Gardner, Charles I. and Mary J. Whittier, May 24, 1856.
Isabella and Eli Truman (both colored people), Mar., 1818.
Ruth C. and William Boyd, Sept. 19, 1808.
Susie L. and Frank O. Jameson, Mar. 20, 1894.

Garland, Amelia A. and Martin L. Moore, Apr. 3, 1861.
Mary and John Remington, Aug. 4, 1856.

Garvin, Fred E. and Emma Provencher, July 21, 1894.
Geo. O., 28, and Grace Duffield, 27, Sept. 26, 1908.
Prescilla and Robt. Boys, Jr., 1823.

Gault, Hughey and Nancy Chase, 1812.

Gaut, Lovey and Samuel Shute, 1824–5.

Gibson, Grace H. and Edward P. Pressey, June 24, 1897.
Nancy and Alexander Nichols, Mar. 13, 1815.
Robert and Nancy Nichols, Mar. 7, 1810.

Giddings, Ann E. and Abel Hildrith, 1820–21.
Hannah and Nathaniel W. Pilsbury, 1824–25.

Gilcreast, Effie M. and Cyrus A. Martin, June 17, 1889.
Ella A. and Chas. O. Huse, Mar. 31, 1879.
Ella E. and Geo. B. Wiley, June 28, 1871.
Emma Florence and Eugene O. Greeley, Sept. 28, 1876.
Frederick A. and Mary Nevins, Aug. 23, 1865.
Frank L. and Anna J. Sloane, Feb. 3, 1873.
Mina A. and Daniel G. Annis, June 17, 1868.
Rebeckah and John King, 1828–9.
Sarah J. and George E. Upton, Nov. 22, 1856.

Gile, David and Susan Bruce, Jan. 8, 1810.

Giles, Hannah and John Gregg, Mar., 1817.
Judith and Nathaniel Corning, 1827–8.
Mary and Nathaniel Aiken, Mar., 1817.
Mary and Thomas Moar, 1819–20.
Mary and Thomas Chase, 1821–22.
Nancy and Daniel Campbell, Jr., 1822–23.

Gilford, Jonathan and Abigal Merrel, July 12, 1810.

Gilmore, Chas. H. and Mary L. Richardson, Nov. 19, 1862.

Given, Charlotte and Jonathan Nichols, Oct. 15, 1804.

Goings, Katie L. and Horace P. Hurd, July 3, 1880.

Goodwin, Abbie Adella and Albin Corthell, Dec. 26, 1892.
Daniel W. and Sarah A. Moody, May 10, 1873.
Daniel W. and Mrs. Ida F. Russell, Jan. 25, 1892.
Eliza J. and Geo. W. Skinner, Feb. 7, 1856.
Esther M. and Henry J. Whittemore, Apr. 21, 1862.
Frances E. and James A. Nichols, May 17, 1862.
George N. and Susie A. Barker, Sept. 28, 1872.
Henry and Mary A. Moar, May 16, 1860.
Ira F. and Ida L. Searles, Nov. 26, 1878.
John and Caroline W. Bolles, Mar. 17, 1863.
John H. S. and Nellie D. Schwartz, Nov. 24, 1896.
John H. S., 50, and Olive S. Cook, 31, May 17, 1910.
Joseph S. and Fanny S. Smith, Nov. 26, 1868.
Joseph S. and Maria L. Palmer, Oct. 22, 1886.
Sarah J. and Charles Smith, Mar. 9, 1869.
Martha and Joshua C. Watts, 1821–22.
Mary Ann and John W. Fling, Nov. 30, 1857.

Goss, Allen and Jane McMurphy, May 28, 1810.
Martha T. and Eugene L. Campbell, Sept., 1873.
Mary and Joseph Page, Apr. 24, 1862.

Goud, Estella and Sam N. Boyce, Dec. 26, 1903.

Gould, Harvey S. and Harriet B. Campbell, Aug. 12, 1862.

Graham, Joseph H. and Mary G. Harvell, July 12, 1901.

Gratto, Samuel Alex., 30, and Catherine Edna Clark, 27, June 16, 1909.

Graves, Mary A. and Charles McAllister, July 17, 1885.

Grealey, Moody and Ellis Marsh, Mar., 1814.

Greeley, Abbie F. and Henry J. Caldwell, Nov. 1, 1875.
Arvilla May and Harold E. Hacker, May 31, 1908.
Chas. S. and Hattie A. Allen, Dec. 23, 1879.
Dustin and Sarah Woodburn, Mar., 1816.
Emma B. and Eugene N. Mullins, M. D., Nov. 28, 1883.
Eugene O. and Emma F. Gilcreast, Sept. 28, 1876.
Flora P. and Herbert G. Tomlinson, July 13, 1887.
Gilbert and Lucy Sawyer, Dec. 18, 1810.
Irving H. and Mary H. Roach, Feb. 9, 1885.
John and Dustimony Eastman, May 16, 1809.
John and Polly Nichols, 1828–9.
John W. and Carrie Osborn, June 6, 1887.
Laura Maude and Francis H. Poff, Oct. 5, 1879.
Mary and Emerson Colby, Mar., 1818.
Sally and Clark Simonds, 1828–9.
Zaccheus and Mary Woodburn, July 26, 1807.

Greenough, George A. and Fanny A. Richardson, Oct. 7, 1874.
John and Ruthy Davis, 1821–22.

Gregg, Jane and Josiah Breed, 1819–20.
John and Hannah Giles, Mar., 1817.
John and Mary Shipley, 1828–9.
Joseph and Lucy Warner, 1819–20.
Lettice and Thomas Caldwell, Dec. 30, 1807.
Mary and Thomas B. Shipley, 1828–9.
Nancy and John Wilson, 1818.
Samuel and Jane Dickey, 1812.
Sarah and Samuel Berry, Mar. 7, 1812.

Griffin, Benjamin and Polly Aiken, 1818.
Clarrissa H. and Elbridge Wyman, 1828–9.
Harriet and John F. Davis, Sept. 25, 1861.
James S. and Hannah H. Ritchey, Mar. 7, 1812.
Mary and Samuel Straw, Mar., 1817.

Grimes, William and Polly Jones, Mar. 2, 1805.

Gross, John and Sarah Boyes, 1824–5.

Gutterson, Lucinda R. and Robert Hall, Sept. 20, 1869.

Hacker, Harold E. and Arvilla May Greeley, May 31, 1908.

Hadley, Ella W. and Geo. N. Doolye, Jan. 14, 1907.

Haggerty, Dennis and Josie Lyons, Feb. 1, 1893.

Haigh, Sarah and Chas. F. Morrison, Dec. 22, 1888.

Hale, Leonard and Betsey Miltemore, Mar., 1818.

Haley, Katie and James P. Daley, June 24, 1890.

Hall, Daniel L. and Fanny E. Temple, Apr. 8, 1874.
George A. and Hester C. Cousens, June 26, 1894.
Henry R. and Letta J. McQuesten, Sept. 16, 1895.
Josiah and Martha Reid, 1826–7.
Robert and Lucinda R. Gutterson, Sept. 20, 1869.
Robt. S. and Mary F. C. March, June 27, 1872.
Timothy and Eliza McGregor, 1821–22.
Waty and Benjamin Pitsley, Oct. 15, 1810.

Ham, Joanna R. and Clarence O. Watts, Dec. 22, 1897.

Hamblett, Geo. F. and Flora E. Beals, Sept. 19, 1878.
Samuel B. and Annie M. Powell, Nov. 25, 1902.
Sarah and George Rolfe, Dec. 15, 1856.

Hamlet, Emeline G. and James E. Barrett, Jan. 12, 1860.

Hamlett, Almira and Wm. P. Lund, Apr. 1, 1867.

Hansor, Ebenezer and Allice Boyes, Mar. 13, 1815.

Hardy, Dudley and Sophia Barker, 1821–22.
Frank A. and Fannie A. Pike, June 12, 1893.
George A. and Etta J. Moar, Aug., 1867.
George H. and Ida J. Kendall, Jan. 5, 1883.
Harriet and Peter Crowell, 1820–21.
John and Eunice Peterson, Sept. 23, 1879.
John P. and Martha M. E. Wiley, June 11, 1878.
Lorenzo and Mary C. Howe, Dec. 30, 1863.
Samuel and Abigal Davidson, Mar. 12, 1810.
William and Nabby Hillton, Apr. 7, 1809.
Wm. G. and Martha Flint, Apr. 11, 1861.

Harriman, Sally and Isaac W. McAllister, Mar., 1814.

Harris, Hattie R. and John H. Smith, Apr. 17, 1871.
William and Rhoda Barker, 1820–21.

Hartford, Annie M. and Geo. E. Ellis, May 1, 1893.
Frank S. and Gertrude J. Hartford, Jan. 30, 1903.
Gertrude I. and Frank S. Hartford, Jan. 30, 1903.
James T. and Elenor M. Smith, Feb. 16, 1872.

Hartshorn, Leroy S. and Annie E. Boles, Oct. 21, 1902.

Harvell, George P. and Mattie B. Furber, Apr. 18, 1900.
Mary G. and Joseph H. Graham, July 12, 1901.
Sarah Jane and Geo. Edw. Anderson, Apr. 19, 1869.

Harvey, John and Betsey White, Mar., 1814.

Haseltine, Benj. and Sally Choate, Mar., 1817.

Haskell, Charles and Lucy Warner, May 2, 1806.
Thomas and Hannah Warner, Mar., 1818.

Haynes, Dr. John and Almira J. Anderson, July 3, 1871.

Hazeltine, James and Betsey McMurthy, Mar., 1816.
Sarah C. and Abraham Burbank, Aug. 26, 1853.

Hazelton, Susie D. and Henry C. Smith, Apr. 21, 1877.
Head, John and Mary H. Messer, 1820–21.
Healey, Elbirh L. and Hattie F. Ladd, Jan. 23, 1886.
Heath, Nathaniel and Sally Pattin, Mar. 13, 1815.
Reuben and Mary Mills, Mar., 1816.
Hemphill, Nathaniel and Jane Clark, Mar., 1818.
Persis and James Taylor, June 9, 1807.
Herbert, Joseph Jeffery, 26, and Mary Esther Bailey, 21, June 7, 1909.
Heselton, Mary A. and James L. McGregor, Dec. 1, 1884.
Hibard, Olive and John Farnham, 1812.
Highland, Anna and David McCleary, Mar., 1814.
Highlands, Sally and Stillman Dodge, Mar., 1817.
Hildrith, Abel and Ann E. Giddings, 1820–21.
Hill, Clarence A. and Emma D. Sprague, Mar. 11, 1881.
Daniel C. and Violetta Barrett, Oct. 28, 1880.
George A. and Eliza Bean, Sept. 8, 1858.
Hills, Nancy and Samuel F. Whittier, 1827–8.
Hillton, Nabby and William Hardy, Apr. 7, 1809.
Hinckley, Owen and Carrie M. Simpson, July 3, 1868.
Hobbs, Chas. J. and Mrs. May E. Flanders, Oct. 11, 1905.
David and Rebecca Atwood, Nov. 26, 1810.
David and Lydia Jack, Mar. 13, 1815.
Isaac F. and Emma A. Plummer, Nov. 30, 1868.
Mary and Phinehas Nichols, 1823.
Prescilla and James M. Pettengill, Sept. 11, 1858.
Hodge, Perkins A. and Margaret Morrison, 1827–8.
Hodgman, Nancy J. and Shurburn D. Smith, May 10, 1860.
Holbrook, Williard and Margaret Crocker, 1819–20.
Holmes, Grissey and Thomas Savory, Nov. 14, 1809.
James and Martha Barker, 1823.
Jane and Robt. M. Holmes, Mar. 7, 1808.
Jane and Jeremiah Bradley, Mar. 31, 1810.
John and Sarah Anderson, Mar. 28, 1808.
John and Mary Adams, 1820–21.
Jonathan and Eliza Thompson, 1812.
M. Henry and Hannah T. Rowe, May 17, 1860.
Margaret and William Boyd, Jan. 30, 1809.
Mary and George Alexander, Mar. 13, 1815.
Matthew and Betsey Fitze, 1823.
Matthew and Anna B. Anderson, Sept. 9, 1856.
Moses Noyes and Harriet A. Coffin, Jan. 20, 1857.
Robert and Jane Anderson, Nov. 14, 1809.

Holmes, Robert and Elisabeth Anderson, Mar. 11, 1811.
Robert M. and Jane Holmes, Mar. 7, 1808.
Susannah and Thomas Atwood, July 10, 1809.
Wm. Franklin and Martha B. Watts, May 31, 1864.

Holt, Easter and John Darrah, Sept. 17, 1810.
Eliza and Jabez Manter, Mar., 1817.
Humphrey and Sarah Bachalder, Mar., 1818.
Joseph and Lois Dwinall, Mar., 1818.
Joseph and Lois Dwinel, 1826–7.
Mary and Isaac Morse, Jan. 30, 1809.
Phebe and William Holt, Mar. 23, 1805.
Sally and Wells Garden, 1812.
William and Phebe Holt, Mar. 23, 1805.

Hopkins, Isabella and John Reid, Mar., 1817.

House, Rev. William and Fanny Savage, May 30, 1859.

Hovey, John and Elenor White, Sept. 3, 1810.
John and Abigail Dustin, 1820–21.
Lucy and William Boyd, 1818.
Mary S. and Henry Conant, May 10, 1856.

Howard, Jane and Levi White, 1821–22.

Howe, James Madison and Alice M. Cross, Apr. 12, 1887.
Mary E. and Lorenzo Hardy, Dec. 30, 1863.
Mehitable and Joseph Cogswell, Mar., 1818.

Hughes, Kate E. and Granville F. Plummer, Nov. 24, 1874.

Hughs, Hannah and James Patterson, May 11, 1809.

Humphrey, Benj. F. and Margaret Paul, 1821–22.
Hannah and Eleazer Low, Mar., 1817.
Jane and John Warner, 1820–21.
John and Rebecca Brewster, Mar. 13, 1815.
Jonathan and Amelia Fisher, 1821–22.
Nancy and Samuel Dickey, Feb. 11, 1805.
William and Louisa Emerson, Mar., 1816.
William and Margaret Nichols, Mar., 1818.

Hunt, Daniel and Polly Page, Mar., 1818.
Frederick H. and Martha A. B. March, Feb. 16, 1867.

Huntee, James and Cynthia G. Keyes, Nov. 17, 1876.
Wm. C. and Loville E. Manter, Oct. 16, 1867.

Hurd, Florence and David B. McGregor, Jan. 20, 1875.
Horace P. and Katie L. Goings, July 3, 1880.

Huse, Chas. O. and Ella A. Gilcreast, Mar. 31, 1879.

Hutchinson, Amos and Rachel Ripley, Mar. 13, 1815.

Ingalls, David T. and Lucinda Clark, 1826–7.

Ingerson, Rhoda and Samuel Shute, 1821–22.

Ireland, Jonathan and Abigail Maria Burnham, 1822–23.

Jack, Alexander and Elisabeth Ferrin, 1826–7.
Lydia and David Hobbs, Mar. 13, 1815.
Polly and James McMurphy, Oct. 21, 1807.

Jackman, Eliza and John Warner, Jr., 1822–23.

Jackson, Adelaide F. and Wm. T. Kelley, Nov. 29, 1893.
David and Eliza Dissmore, 1828–9.
George E. and Sarah A. Randall, Feb. 3, 1891.
George E. and Mary L. Call, Feb. 3, 1892.
John and Nancy Bartley, Mar., 1817.
John and Mary Duncan, 1822–23.
Joseph and Betsey White, Mar., 1816.
Lydia and Benjamin Anderson, Mar., 1814.
Morrison and Hannah Corning, 1828–9.
Polly and John Marsh Adams, Oct. 30, 1810.
Sally and Robert Adams, Jan. 4, 1810.
Samuel and Mary Dodge, Mar., 1816.

Jameson, Frank O. and Susie L. Gardner, Mar. 20, 1894.
Mary and Wm. McQuesten, 1819–20.
Nancy and Daniel Taylor, 1823.

Jaquith, Mary A. and Edward K. Whittemore, Dec. 13, 1862.
Thomas and Maunda Tarbox, 1827–8.

Jeffers, Robert and Martha Patton, Mar., 1818.

Jenkins, B. Jarreldign and Frank W. Stevens, Nov. 9, 1877.

Jenks, Frank A. and Emma J. Bennett, June 15, 1886.

Jenness, Amos and Syrnne Dearborn, 1812.
Joseph and Doty Drake, July 17, 1809.

Jewett, Abigail and Thomas Wilson, 1828–9.
Elisabeth and Robert Stocker, 1822–23.
Margaret and Ephraim Caldwell, Mar., 1816.
Sally and Ebenezer Kimball, July 10, 1809.

Johnson, Alice Nana and Willis D. Northrop, Sept. 16, 1907.
Dolly I. and Daniel P. McQuesten, 1818.
Ebenezer and Lucinda Sears, 1826–7.
Frank J. and Elisabeth M. Chase, Feb. 18, 1880.
Louissa and William Kimball, 1824–5.
Mary and Warren Wyman, Oct. 12, 1883.
Samuel and Nancy Warner, Mar. 7, 1812.
Susanah and Robert Ramsey, Jan. 23, 1809.

Johnston, Nathaniel and Mary Barnett, Mar. 10, 1807.
Stephen and Hannah Adams, Mar., 1817.
Susanna and Moses Adams, Mar., 1817.

Jones, Benj. R. and Betsey Powell, June 18, 1810.
Ellen E. and James F. Watts, Feb. 8, 1878.

Jones, Hannah and Isaac Colby, 1826–7.
Joseph and Elisabeth McDuffee, 1828–9.
Lois Reed and Alexander Caldwell, 1812.
Lovinia and Francis M. Chase, Mar., 1817.
Merilla and Arthur E. Brown, Sept. 14, 1901.
Nehemiah and Ruth Mirick, Aug. 28, 1860.
Polly and William Grimes, Mar. 2, 1805.
Polly C. and John Chase, Mar., 1816.
Sally and Leo Walker, Nov. 15, 1804.

Karr, Elisabeth and Edmund Adams, Jr., Dec. 20, 1808.

Keddy, William, 30, and Vera L. Weagle, 19, Aug. 14, 1909.

Kelley, William T. and Adelaide F. Jackson, Nov. 29, 1893.

Kelso, Alexander and Elisabeth T. Kent, Dec. 21, 1807.

Kelsy, Hannah and Joshua Cheney, Mar. 13, 1815.

Kemball, Betsey and Edmund Adams, Sept. 18, 1809.
Sally and William Carleton, Mar., 1816.

Kendall, Amos and Patty Adams, Nov. 14, 1808.
Ida J. and George H. Hardy, Jan. 5, 1883.

Kenney, Mary and John Bragg, 1824–5.

Kent, Elisabeth T. and Alexander Kelso, Dec. 21, 1807.
Richard and Louisa Ela, Aug. 20, 1810.

Keyes, Cynthia G. and James Huntee, Nov. 17, 1876.

Kimball, Anne F. and George W. Durant, Oct. 15, 1867.
Benjamin and Molly C. Smith, 1826–7.
Betsey and Jonathan Savory, 1821–22.
Charles G. and Emma J. Colby, Oct. 13, 1880.
Ebenezer and Sally Jewett, July 10, 1809.
Eliza W. and John C. Cogswell, 1821–22.
Frances H., 53, and Edward Francis, 40, Oct. 26, 1908.
George W. and Frances H. Young, Apr. 13, 1877.
Mary J. and Rufus L. Veazey, Sept. 8, 1856.
Mehitable and Rev. Edw. L. Parker, Mar. 7, 1812.
Oren and Clarrissa H. Clark, Nov., 1859.
Samuel and Margaret Stinson, 1812.
Samuel and Eliza Stinson, 1824–5.
William and Louissa Johnson, 1824–5.

King, John and Rebeckah Gilcreast, 1828–9.

Knight, Alfred Brook and Antoinette DeGrave Cutter, Sept. 11, 1865.
Elisabeth and Nathaniel Farnum, 1821–22.
Hattie A. and Walter A. Smith, Nov., 1867.
Samuel and Annas McAllister, Oct. 3, 1808.
Wesley B. and Helen F. Anderson, Apr. 7, 1862.

Knights, Caleb G .and Triphosa Putnam, 1821–22.

Ladd, Hattie F. and Elbirh L. Healey, Jan. 23, 1886.
Laland, Mary and Barker Danforth, Mar., 1817.
Lary, George and Annie Peabody, Sept. 30, 1903.
Lawrence, Mary A. and Chas. P. Manter, Apr. 1, 1867.
Laws, Sidney E. and Susie F. Merritt, Apr. 17, 1899.
Leach, Ira and Asenath Crowell, 1818.
John and Betsey Blaisdell, 1821–22.
Joseph and Martha Corning, Mar., 1816.
Olive and Ephraim Stevens, 1820–21.
Polly and James Annis, 1824–5.
Sally and Abel Senter, 1818.
Lebrun, Laura E. and Wm. H. Orrill, Mar. 27, 1880.
Lee, George W. and Rosie M. Wyatt, July 25, 1905.
Lewis, E. J. Lucinda and Joshua Whidden, Nov. 12, 1862.
Guy A. and Josephine Pettengill, Oct. 9, 1899.
Lines, Kate, 19, and Clovis J. Daniels, 24, May 11, 1910.
Lincoln, Silas E. and Emma F. Corey, Sept. 26, 1888.
Little, Jacob and Polly Nourse, Mar., 1817.
Polly and Hezekiah Ayer, 1818.
Robert E. and Clarrissa Pinkerton, 1827.
Littlefield, Wm. H. and Martha M. Taylor, Nov. 21, 1885.
Lord, Mrs. Clara D. and Harris Towle, Nov. 8, 1887.
Harry F. and Estella F. Wells, Mar. 21, 1893.
Wm. L. and Clara D. Dickey, Dec. 11, 1863.
Lovejoy, Martha E. and David W. Ela, Feb. 6, 1883.
Lovell, George A. and Fannie B. McCutcheon, Sept. 28, 1891.
Low, Betsey and Humphrey Choate, 1820–21.
Eleazer and Hannah Humphrey, Mar., 1817.
Mary Elisabeth N. and George E. Ela, Aug. 31, 1904.
Lowd, Edith Belle and Wm. A. Butterworth, May 11, 1893.
Jennie A. and Edson W. Watts, Nov. 29, 1897.
Sarah F. and John S. Floyd, May 25, 1879.
Sedley H. and Lillian J. Dailey, Mar. 15, 1898.
Lowell, Nellie J. and John Orral, July 1, 1876.
Lund, Oliver and Orpah Danforth, Mar., 1816.
Wm. P. and Almira Hamlett, Apr. 1, 1867.
Lurvey, Cora M., 20, and Fred H. Smith, 22, Sept. 13, 1909.
Lyons, Josie and Dennis Haggerty, Feb. 1, 1893.
Mack, Andrew W. and Frances A. Preston, Mar. 18, 1861.
Elisabeth and David Stiles, Aug. 26, 1808.
Robert and Ann Clark, Mar., 1814.
Wallace P. and Harriett L. Pillsbury, Feb. 16, 1892.

Mackay, Mary Abby and Frank O. Furber, May 29, 1877.

Madden, Joseph M. and Elisabeth M. McLinn, Oct. 20, 1898.

Magee, Addie M. and Chas. F. Whidden, Jan. 31, 1885.

Major, John and Martha Flanders, May 16, 1809.
William and Sarah E. Brackett, Dec. 19, 1861.

Maker, Clara Louise and Ezra Norwell Baker, Oct. 21, 1907.

Malden, William and Mary Tuttle, 1818.

Manter, Alfred F., 24, and Kate M. Brown, 20, Oct. 3, 1910.
Allen S. and Jennie Brown, Aug. 6, 1885.
Chas. P. and Mary A. Lawrence, Apr. 1, 1867.
Francis and Harriet Crowningshield, 1819–20.
Francis and Elisabeth Smith, Sept. 10, 1860.
George and Poley Senter, Sept. 2, 1795.
Jabez and Eliza Holt, Mar., 1817.
Loville E. and Wm. C. Huntee, Oct. 16, 1867.
Phinehas and Mary Bancroft, 1821–22.
Samuel and Isabella Reid, 1823.

March, Betsey and Jacob Emery, 1819–20.
Henry and Sarah Gage, 1819–20.
John and Hannah Crowell, 1828–9.
Lydia and John R. Merrill, 1828–9.
Martha A. B. and Frederick H. Hunt, Feb. 16, 1867.
Mary F. C. and Robert S. Hall, June 27, 1872.

Marr, Oliver and Abbie M. Scott, Apr. 18, 1882.

Marsh, Ellis and Moody Grealey, Mar., 1814.
Enoch S. and Martha Whittier, 1824–5.
Jane and Edmund Adams, 1828–9.
Joshua and Prissilla Brown, 1819–20.
Rebecca P. and Aaron Senter, 1819–20.
Samuel and Lettuce Boyd, May 16, 1809.

Marshall, Ann and Tilley H. Wheeler, Dec. 30, 1856.
Celia and Ichabod C. Smith, Dec. 20, 1886.
Emily J. and David F. Robinson, Jan. 24, 1867.
Hannah and Thomas M. Farmer, 1823.
Jemima and John Robinson, June 22, 1805.
Mary E. and Chas. A. Nodding, Mar. 12, 1869.
Williard and Clarrissa S. Tarbox, 1824–5.

Martin, Cyrus A. and Effie M. Gilcreast, June 17, 1889.
Jane and Osgood Cheever, Mar., 1817.
Mary and James Cochran, Mar., 1817.
Orra and Peter Crowell, Mar., 1818.

Mathews, Wm. D. and Mary S. Prentice, Mar., 1817.

Maxfield, Clarence Elwin, 21, and Ethel M. Plummer, 21, June 1, 1909.

Maxfield, Frank C., 26, and Ella Louisa Day, 19, June 17, 1910.
McAllister, Annas and Samuel Knight, Oct. 3, 1808.
Charles and Mary A. Graves, July 17, 1885.
George and Mary Crowell, Feb. 14, 1811.
Isaac W. and Sally Harriman, Mar., 1814.
John and Janet Caldwell, Oct. 6, 1806.
McClary, Eleanor Jennie and Roswell Annis, Aug. 12, 1884.
John and Mrs. Martha A. Sanborn, Mar. 6, 1884.
Thomas and Eloner Watts, 1812.
McCleary, David and Anna Highland, Mar., 1814.
McCormick, Betsey and David Murray, 1826–7.
McCutcheon, Fannie B. and George A. Lovell, Sept. 28, 1891.
McDonald, Edgar F. and Annie R. Boyce, Apr. 19, 1894.
Joseph R. and Mary V. Parshley, Aug. 15, 1900.
McDuffee, Elisabeth and Joseph Jones, 1828–9.
Martha and Dudley C. Swain, 1826–7.
Mary and Hugh McMurphy, 1826–7.
Matthew and Hannah Davis, 1818.
Rosanna and Ebenezer Brown, Mar., 1817.
McFarland, Mary and Gideon Coburn, Jan. 26, 1807.
McGaw, John and Hannah Adams, Dec. 4, 1810.
Robert and Sarah Morrison, Mar. 7, 1812.
McGrath, Sally and Isaac Coburn, May 2, 1808.
McGregor, D. Brewster and Florence Hurd, Jan. 20, 1875.
David and Mrs. Mary E. Corning, Dec. 13, 1886.
Eliza and Timothy Hall, 1821–22.
Florence E. and Frederick E. Moody, Sept. 10, 1906.
Frank M. and Alice A. Waugh, July 6, 1887.
Geo. F. and Rhoda A. Barker, May 2, 1865.
Isabel D. and Frank J. Demeritt, Sept. 25, 1883.
James A. and Myra H. Nelson, July 21, 1871.
James L. and Mary A. Heselton, Dec. 1, 1884.
McGregore, David and Abigail Curtis Thornton, 1824–5.
Mary and Thomas D. Rogers, Oct. 16, 1807.
Rosanna and Dearborn Whittier, 1826–7.
McGurrill, Agnes and Chas. J. Templeton, June 16, 1884.
McIntire, Alice W. and William Clark, Aug. 17, 1876.
McKean, Daniel and Lucy Nesmith, 1812.
John R. and Nellie M. Richardson, Sept. 7, 1883.
Mary Frances and Samuel G. Moody, Jan. 16, 1903.
McKeen, Daniel and Betsey Ordway, Mar., 1816.
John and Peggy Taylor, 1818.
Mary and James Wilson, 1820–21.
McKenney, Angeline and Lemuel P. Braley, Mar. 25, 1869.

McKinsey, Margaret and Joseph Calef, July 8, 1807.
McLinn, Elisabeth M. and Joseph M. Madden, Oct. 20, 1898.
McMurphy, Anna and Ebenezer Caldwell, Mar., 1818.
Benjamin and Susan Cobb, Mar. 13, 1815.
Betsey and James Hazeltine, Mar., 1816.
Ebenezer and Martha Stinson, 1818.
Elisabeth and Robert Boyes, June 15, 1804.
Elisabeth and William McNeal, Apr. 10, 1807.
Hugh and Mary McDuffee, 1826–7.
James and Polly Jack, Oct. 21, 1807.
Jane and Allen Goss, May 28, 1810.
Mary and David Brewster, Mar., 1818.
Robert and Sarah Christy, Feb. 14, 1811.
Robert and Mary Ann Pressey, 1819–20.
Sally and William Moar, 1819–20.
McNeal, James and Rose Taylor, Apr. 8, 1811.
William and Elisabeth McMurphy, Apr. 10, 1807.
McNeil, Abraham and Mary Patterson, Jan. 26, 1807.
McQuesten, Daniel M. and Mary E. Crowell, Oct. 5, 1892.
Letta J. and Henry R. Hall, Sept. 16, 1895.
McQuestion, Sally G. and Eliphilit Richards, Mar., 1816.
McQueston, Daniel P. and Dolly I. Johnson, 1818.
William and Mary Jameson, 1819–20.
Melvin, Dioclesian and Fannie Smith, 1824–5.
Elisabeth and Levi Trask, 1827–8.
Florence and Abraham Smith, 1826–7.
James and Susanah Barnet, Jan. 26, 1807.
Mary and Ebenezer Brown, Jr., 1822–23.
Mehitable and John Woodburn, 1819–20.
Sarah and Alexander Smith, 1821–22.
Mentor, Belcher and Mehitable Dodge, Jan. 21, 1811.
James and Mehitable Dwinalls, Mar., 1818.
Merrel, Abigal and Jonathan Gilford, July 12, 1810.
Merrill, David and Hannah Merrill, Sept. 16, 1809.
Hannah and David Merrill, Sept. 16, 1809.
Hattie E. and Geo. W. Shattuck, June 13, 1893.
John R. and Lydia March, 1828–9.
Jonathan and Margaret Clark, 1822–23.
Kent and Mary Dodge, 1818.
Nellie F. and Alphonso Alexander, Nov. 26, 1873.
Olive and William French, Apr. 13, 1808.
Oliver and Emma N. Smith, Apr. 17, 1893.
Samuel and Mary Nichols, Mar. 7, 1810.
Stephen and Elisabeth Santer, July 10, 1809.
Merritt, Susie F. and Sidney E. Laws, Apr. 17, 1899.

Mertsch, Elsa A., 20, and Ralph W. Barker, 20, July 9, 1910.

Messer, Mary H. and John Head, 1820–21.

Miller, Adams and Annie Robinson, Nov. 28, 1805.
Alice E. and Chas. Geo. Pillsbury, June, 1894.
Della M. and Chas. H. Alexander, Oct. 22, 1888.
Lucinda and Hiram Cutler, Dec. 30, 1875.

Mills, Hughy and Lydia Dodge, 1812.
Lydia and Henry J. Willey, Aug. 26, 1876.
May and Reuben Heath, Mar., 1816.

Miltimore, Betsey and Leonard Hale, Mar., 1818.

Mirick, Ruth and Nehemiah Jones, Aug. 28, 1860.

Mitchell, Abigail and Franklin W. Bruce, Mar. 13, 1815.

Moar, Etta I. and George A. Hardy, Aug., 1867.
George and Sally Eastman, 1822–23.
Harriet L. and Chas. E. Perkins, Oct. 7, 1861.
Hugh and Eliza Ors, Mar. 13, 1814.
Jane and Robert Boyes, 1826–7.
John, Jr., and Alice Clark, 1821–22.
Joseph and Sophia Richardson, 1824–5.
Martha and George N. Warner, 1822–23.
Mary A. and Henry Goodwin, May 16, 1860.
Peter and Loisa Proctor, 1812.
Polly and William Ela, 1812.
Thomas and Mary Giles, 1819–20.
William and Sally McMurphy, 1819–20.

Montgomery, Frances and Joseph Dickey, Mar. 7, 1812.
Wm. and Mary W. Anderson, Mar., 1814.

Moody, Annie S. and Geo. W. Beede, Apr. 23, 1900.
Chas. Edward and Nettie E. Rouse, Mar. 20, 1899.
Frederick E. and Florence E. McGregor, Sept. 10, 1906.
Samuel G. and Mary Frances McKean, Jan. 16, 1903.
Sarah A. and Daniel W. Goodwin, May 10, 1873.

Moore, Martin L. and Amelia A. Garland, Apr. 3, 1861.
Sarah A. and Henry H. White, Nov. 6, 1860.
Walter H. and Martha M. Scollay, Oct. 12, 1876.
Wm. Russell and Blanche C. Campbell, Dec. 29, 1894.

Morral, Polly and Samuel M. Chase, Sept. 16, 1809.

Morrell, Raches and John Carleton, Mar., 1818.

Morrison, Betsey and James Wilson, Mar. 7, 1812.
Chas. F. and Sarah Haigh, Dec. 22, 1888.
Charles H. and Abby A. Floyd, July 19, 1858.
James and Betsey Warner, Mar., 1814.
Jane and Robt. M. Wallace, Dec. 11, 1810.
Jenney and Robert Dickey, 1821–22.

Morrison, John, Jr., and Sarah D. Davidson, 1824–25.
Joseph and Jane Paul, Sept. 24, 1810.
Margaret and Little Day, 1821–22.
Margaret and Perkins A. Hodge, 1827–8.
Mark M. and Susie A. Swallow, Nov. 14, 1885.
Phebe A. (Mrs.) and Silas T. Towns, Mar. 24, 1864.
Robert G. and Nellie E. Woodbury, Mar. 12, 1881.
Sally and John Morrison, Feb. 27, 1809.
Sarah and Robert McGaw, Mar. 7, 1812.
William O. and Mattie E. Corbett, Dec. 19, 1891.
John and Sally Morrison, Feb. 27, 1809.

Morse, Amos, Jr., and Abigail Rogers, 1819–20.
Euretta J. and Abram A. Woodbury, May 26, 1874.
Isaac and Mary Holt, Jan. 30, 1809.
Mary and Daniel Carlton, Mar. 24, 1809.
Moody, 2d, and Susan Spaulding, 1826–7.

Mott, Lydia and Nathaniel Chase, Aug. 20, 1810.

Moulton, John and Sarah Barker, 1824–5.

Mullins, Amanda R. and Robt. A. Brown, Apr. 7, 1890.
Eugene N. and Emma B. Greeley, Nov. 28, 1883.
Hattie P. and Daniel M. Boyd, May 6, 1884.

Muncaster, Sarah and Wilbur E. Barrett, Jan. 1, 1907.

Murray, David and Betsey McCormick, 1826–7.

Murry, Almira and Moses Carr, 1822–23.

Nason, Arlbey and Eleanor W. Fisk, 1826–7.

Naylor, Maria and George E. Allen, Mar. 23, 1876.

Neal, Henrietta and Lyman A. Dickey, Apr. 22, 1908.

Nelson, Mira H. and James L. McGregor, July 21, 1871.

Nesmith, Cleon E. and Lena Mae Smith, Oct. 25, 1905.
Elisabeth and John C. Corning, Mar., 1817.
Frank A. and Clara Belle Corning, Dec. 21, 1889.
James and Polly Corning, Mar., 1816.
James and Sarah P. Rolfe, Nov. 24, 1862.
John and Lydia Sargent, Mar., 1817.
Lucy and Daniel McKean, 1812.
Thomas and Nancy Boys, 1820–21.

Nevins, Harriet Julia and E. Horace Davenport, June 25, 1906.
Mabel F. M. and Wesley Adams, June 17, 1908.
Mary and Frederick A. Gilcreast, Aug. 23, 1865.
Wm. P. and Julia D. Shipley, Sept. 12, 1871.

Nicholes, Betsey and Daniel Bond, Mar., 1818.
James and Sally Senter, Mar., 1818.
Margaret and Wm. Humphrey, Mar., 1818.

Nicholis, Ruben and Asenath Senter, 1812.

Nichols, Archie B. and May C. Osborne, May 28, 1894.
Ensign and Sarah Dismore, 1819–20.
Francis R., 19, and Ada J. Smith, 17, Oct. 11, 1910.
Hannah C. and Frederick Spullet, 1819–20.
Isaac L. and Eliza Smith, 1828–9.
James A. and Frances E. Goodwin, May 17, 1862.
Jonathan and Charlotte Given, Oct. 15, 1804.
Phinehas and Mary Hobbs, 1823.
Sally and Leonard L. Day, Mar., 1816.
Samuel and Sally Towns, Mar. 13, 1815.
Woodburn and Elisabeth K. Day, 1821–22.

Nickals, Jacob and Martha Woodbury, Mar. 8, 1809.
Joseph and Rebecca Emery, Mar., 1814.
Mary and Samuel Merrill, Mar. 7, 1810.
Nancy and Robert Gibson, Mar. 7, 1810.
Polly and John Greeley, 1828–9.
Rebecca and Joseph Buckingham, Mar., 1814.

Nickels, Olive and William Townes, Apr. 8, 1804.

Nickols, Alexander and Nancy Gibson, Mar. 13, 1815.
Hannah and Abraham Dismore, Feb. 13, 1809.
Jacob and Hannah Pierce, 1818.
Polly and John Greeley, 1828–9.
Samuel K. and Nancy Davis, 1820–21.
Stephen and Eliza Town, 1819–20.

Nodding, Chas. A. and Mary E. Marshall, Mar. 12, 1869.

Norcross, Frank E. and Fronia L. Aiken, Sept. 10, 1880.

Norris, Joshua W. and Mary Barker, 1824–5.

Northrop, Willis Dickerman and Alice Nana Johnson, Sept. 16, 1907.

Norton, Harriet and Samuel Adams, 1826–7.
Sally and Ebenezer Wilson, 1824–5.

Nourse, Polly and Jacob Little, Mar., 1817.

Noyes, Joseph T. and Mary A. Richardson, Dec. 11, 1871.
Walter E. and Nellie Allen Quint, Apr. 15, 1899.

Nugent, Ernestine Eliza, 36, and Hiram N. Cross, 34, May 24, 1909.
Marian Bly and Harry C. Corliss, Apr. 27, 1904.

Nutt, Augusta R. and Myron Richardson, Nov. 28, 1889.

Olliver, Margaret and Edw. Q. F. Brooks, June 1, 1908.

Olsen, Albert D. A., 35, and Grace Margaret Theiss, 27, June 19, 1909.

Ordway, Betsey and Daniel McKeen, Mar., 1816.

Orr, Jane and Ebenezer Fisher, Mar., 1816.
Susan and John Warner, Mar., 1814.

Orrall, John and Nellie J. Lowell, July 1, 1876.

Orrill, Wm. H. and Laura E. Lebrun, Mar. 27, 1880.

Ors, Eliza and Hugh Moar, Mar. 13, 1814.

Osborn, Carrie and John W. Greeley, June 6, 1887.
Wm. A. and Cilvilla C. Doherty, Jan. 1, 1897.

Osborne, May C. and Archie B. Nichols, May 28, 1894.

Owen, Anna J. and Jessey O. Emerson, Mar. 20, 1860.

Pace, Fred W. and Augusta Young, Feb. 24, 1897.

Page, Deborah and Paul Page, 1823.
Eliza H. and James I. Chase, Sept. 28, 1873.
Hannah and James Pinkerton, Jr., Oct. 17, 1808.
Joseph and Mary Goss, Apr. 24, 1862.
Juliaette A. B. and Benj. F. Whorf, Sept. 26, 1859.
Mariam and Henry Chase, 1826–7.
Mary J. and Daniel M. Annis, June 2, 1859.
Paul and Deborah Page, 1823.
Polly and Daniel Hunt, Mar., 1818.
Ruth and Samuel Page, Mar., 1816.
Sally and Edward Ela, Nov. 26, 1810.
Samuel and Elisabeth Webster, Jan. 5, 1810.
Samuel and Ruth Page, Mar., 1816.
Sarah E. and David F. Cheney, Nov. 17, 1886.
Susan (Mrs.) and John M. Chase, July 22, 1896.

Palmer, Betsey and Samuel Darrah, 1824–5.
Hannah and James Steele, Mar., 1814.
James and Ruth Carlton, Jan. 26, 1807.
James, Jr., and Bithiah Carlton, 1821–22.
John and Sarah Rogers, 1824–5.
Maria L. and Joseph S. Goodwin, Oct. 22, 1886.
Washington and Margaret Steele, Mar., 1814.

Parker, Almira A. and Wm. H. Crowell, Sept. 19, 1866.
Rev. Edward L. and Mehiteble Kimball, Mar. 7, 1812.

Parmerton, Maria L. and Wm. D. Young, May 5, 1894.

Parshley, Mary V. and Joseph R. McDonald, Aug. 15, 1900.

Patee, Ludenna and Benjamin Thompson, 1827.

Pattan, Martha and Robert Jeffers, Mar., 1818.

Patterson, Grisey and David Barnett, Mar., 1814.
James and Hannah Hughs, May 11, 1809.
Margaret and Samuel F. Taylor, Mar. 7, 1810.
Mary and Abraham McNeil, Jan. 26, 1807.
Peter and Mary Wallace, Mar. 13, 1815.
Thomas and Hannah Duncan, 1818.
Zacheus and Sarah F. Farnham, 1823.

Pattin, Sally and Nathaniel Heath, Mar. 13, 1815.

Paul, Jane and Joseph Morrison, Sept. 24, 1810.
Margaret and Benj. F. Humphrey, 1821–22.
Nancy and Moses Wingate, Mar., 1814.

Payne, George E. and Carrie M. Corning, Aug. 24, 1876.
John P. and Anna Densmore, July 1, 1876.
Nelson S. and Abbie J. Walch, Aug. 18, 1877.

Peabody, Annie and George Lary, Sept. 30, 1903.
Elbridge W. and Mary A. Perham, May 16, 1859.
Elwin C. and Minnie M. Fling, Oct. 14, 1885.
Henrietta L. and Joseph S. Roach, Jan. 2, 1871.
Orriville A. and Mrs. Emily Brickett, Dec. 16, 1873.

Pecker, William and Julia M. Conant, June 18, 1884.

Perham, Mary A. and Elbridge W. Peabody, May 16, 1859.

Perkins, Chas. E. and Harriet L. Moar, Oct. 7, 1861.
David F. and Jennie S. Corning, Feb. 12, 1884.
Emma H. and Chas. W. Abbott, Feb. 2, 1888.
Lucy and Nathaniel Cogswell, 1826–7.
Maus and Eliza Coffin, 1824–5.

Perley, Asa and Judith Corning, Mar., 1818.

Perry, Varnum and Dorothy French, 1820–21.

Peterson, Eunice and John Hardy, Sept. 23, 1879.

Pettengal, Warren and Jane Watts, Dec. 10, 1810.

Pettengill, Addie Jane and Geo. F. Aiken, Oct. 27, 1879.
Betsey and Wm. M. Richardson, 1820–21.
David and Eliza J. Barker, Nov., 1859.
Emeline (Mrs.) and John P. Young, Dec. 23, 1868.
George C. and Eva A. Simpson, June 16, 1906.
James B., Dr., and Ada E. Bartlett, Sept. 20, 1881.
James M. and Prescilla C. Hobbs, Nov. 11, 1858.
Josephine and Guy A. Lewis, Oct. 9, 1899.
Rachel and Nathaniel Watts, Nov. 20, 1810.
W. Martin and Angeline M. Barker, Apr. 9, 1859.

Philbrook, Lidia and Ruben Senter, Sept. 26, 1808.

Pierce, Adeline and Israel Talbot, 1824–5.
Hannah and Jacob Nickols, 1818.

Pike, Fannie A. and Frank A. Hardy, June 12, 1893.

Pillsbury, Charles G. and Alice E. Miller, June, 1894.
Harriet L. and Wallace P. Mack, Feb. 16, 1892.
Maria, 24, and Harold Scott Taylor, 27, Sept. 14, 1910.
Rosecrans W. and Annie E. Watts, Dec. 8, 1885.
Ulysses G. and Edith H. Davis, Nov. 19, 1896.
Wm. S. and Martha S. Crowell, Apr. 7, 1856.

Pilsbury, Nathaniel W. and Hannah Giddings, 1824–5.

Pinkerton, Clarrissa and Robert E. Little, 1827.
Eliza and John Aiken, Apr. 26, 1807.
James and Sally Wallace, May 16, 1809.
James, Jr., and Hannah Page, Oct. 17, 1808.
Jane and Joshua Aiken, Mar., 1816.
Mary Ann and Robert S. Rogers, 1826–7.
Mary B. and William Choate, Mar., 1816.
Rebecca and Thomas Wilson, Jan. 26, 1807.

Pitsley, Benjamin and Waty Hall, Oct. 15, 1810.

Platt, Emily, 25, and Delphus O. Tuttle, 28, Dec. 22, 1909.

Platts, James and Sophia Crowningshield, 1823.
Nancy and Josiah Walker, Sept. 22, 1806.
Sally and Ruben Walker, Oct. 23, 1809.
Thomas B. and Susan D. Emerson, May 12, 1856.

Plumer, Granville F. and Kate E. Hughes, Nov. 24, 1874.
Persis and David Tenny, Mar., 1817.
Sarah Dwinell and David Beard, 1819–20.

Plummer, Abel and Mary Anderson, Mar. 7, 1808.
Eliza and Joseph Coburn, 1826–7.
Emma A. and Isaac F. Hobbs, Nov. 30, 1868.
Ethel M., 21, and Clarence E. Maxfield, 21, June 1, 1909.
Mary and Thomas Chase, Mar. 14, 1809.

Poff, Francis H. and Laura Maude Greeley, Oct. 5, 1879.

Pollard, Nathan A. and Etta M. Abbott, Sept. 10, 1860.

Poor, John C. and Susan Boys, 1822–23.

Pope, Samuel C. and Frances Dismoor, Dec. 15, 1806.

Potter, Albert and Elma J. Woodbury, July 26, 1879.

Powel, Betsey and Benj. R. Jones, June 18, 1810.

Powell, Annie M. and Samuel B. Hamblett, Nov. 25, 1902.

Prasser, William and Naomi Taylor, Mar., 1816.

Pratt, Reuben K. and Hannah J. Estey, Oct. 30, 1891.

Prentice, Mary S. and Wm. D. Mathews, Mar., 1817.
Sarah and Dr. Geo. Farrar, July 10, 1809.
Susan and William Redfield, Mar., 1816.

Prentis, Ann S. and John C. Cunningham, 1826–7.

Pressey, Edward P. and Grace H. Gibson, June 24, 1897.
Mary Ann and Robert McMurphy, 1819–20.

Preston, Frances A. and Andrew W. Mack, Mar. 18, 1861.

Proctor, Asa and Anna Allen, 1818.
Benjamin and Rachel Caldwell, Oct. 12, 1807.
Charlotte and Ephrim Barnet, 1812.
Etta M. and F. Henry Bartlett, Jan. 10, 1893.
Humphrey and Charlotte Allen, Feb. 24, 1806

Proctor, Jane Elisabeth and Joseph Richardson, Jan. 10, 1873.
John and Mary Crocker, 1826–7.
Joseph and Eunice Brown, Dec. 20, 1808.
Loisa and Peter Moar, 1812.
Olive and Farnum H. Carleton, Mar., 1818.
Pearl G. and Seth G. Wing, Apr. 5, 1904.
Royal S. and Edith F. Boyce, July 30, 1906.
Silas and Betsey Abbott Foster, Mar. 13, 1815.

Provencher, Emma and Fred E. Garvin, July 21, 1894.

Putnam, Betsey T. and Geo. W. Chrispeen, May 11, 1875.
Edward and Betsa Bancroft, Mar. 12, 1869.
Elbert O. and Maude E. Campbell, Apr. 16, 1892.
Triphosa and Caleb G. Knights, 1821–22.

Quint, Nellie Allen and Walter E. Noyes, Apr. 15, 1899.

Ramsey, Martha and James Boyes, Aug. 14, 1809.
Robert and Susannah Johnson, Jan. 23, 1809.
William H. and Emma H. Dudley, Nov. 29, 1888.

Randall, Sarah A. and Geo. E. Jackson, Feb. 3, 1891.

Ranken, Polly and Joseph Chesly, Mar., 1816.

Ray, John Edw. and Anna M. Stone, July 2, 1894.

Redfield, Caleb and Frances C. Cochran, Mar., 1818.
Charles and Betsey Adams, Mar., 1814.
William and Susan Prentice, Mar., 1816.

Reed, Maryann and Alexander Wilson, Feb. 27, 1809.
Nancy G. and Horace P. Estey, Nov. 22, 1859.
Walter D. and Ellen M. Evans, Sept. 30, 1871.

Reid, Isabella and Samuel Manter, 1823.
John and Isabella Hopkins, Mar., 1817.
Margaret and Little Day, Mar., 1817.
Martha and Josiah Hall, 1826–7.
Phineas A. and Addie A. Chase, Jan. 9, 1886.

Remington, John and Mary Garland, Aug. 4, 1856.
Mary A. and Stephen A. Estey, Nov. 28, 1877.

Remix, Lydia and John P. Wilson, 1824–25.

Reynolds, Stephen and Sally Ela, Jan. 21, 1811.

Richards, Eliphilet and Sally G. McQuestion, Mar., 1816.

Richardson, Fanny A. and Geo. A. Greenough, Oct. 7, 1874.
Florence E. and Geo. L. Dickey, Mar. 27, 1906.
Isaac and Jane P. Sadmen, Mar. 7, 1810.
Joseph and Jane Elisabeth Proctor, Jan. 10, 1873.
Lydia and John Corning, Mar., 1816.
Mary Ann and Joseph T. Noyes, Dec. 11, 1871.
Mary L. and Chas. H. Gilmore, Nov. 19, 1862.
Myron and Augusta R. Nutt, Nov. 28, 1889.

Richardson, Nabby and Whitefield Craig, 1820–21.
Nellie and John C. Barker, June 27, 1879.
Nellie M. and John R. McKean, Sept. 7, 1883.
Sarah and Chas. N. Annis, Oct. 21, 1888.
Sophia and Joseph Moar, 1824–5.
Wm. M. and Betsey Pettengill, 1820–21.
Wm. Dr. and Esther F. Whidden, Aug. 23, 1884.
Zachariah and Sally Smith, Mar. 13, 1815.

Richey, Susan and Ezra M. Farnum, Mar., 1818.

Ripley, Asahel P. and Mary Clark, 1826–7.
Joseph, Jr., and Matilda Sampson, 1827.
Rachel and Amos Hutchinson, Mar. 13, 1815.
Susan M. and Zachariah K. H. Whittemore, Apr. 1, 1867.

Ritchey, Hannah H. and James S. Griffin, Mar. 7, 1812.

Roach, Ellen J. and Nathaniel C. Alexander, June 14, 1866.
Fred L. and Retta M. Robie (Mrs.), July 12, 1897.
Hattie E. and W. W. Gage, Apr. 15, 1890.
Hattie E. and Nathan P. Watts, June 9, 1906.
Joseph S. and Henrietta L. Peabody, Jan. 2, 1871.
Mary E. and James S. Webster, Jan. 17, 1903.
Mary H. and Irving H. Greeley, Feb. 9, 1885.

Roads, Ezra and Nancy Bruce, Sept. 16, 1809.

Roberts, Nellie and Thomas Valentine, May 19, 1897.

Robie, Nellie A. and Charles P. Doherty, Dec. 22, 1894.
Perley S. and Mabel E. Buttrick, Jan. 17, 1894.
Retta M. (Mrs.) and Fred L. Roach, July 12, 1897.
Sarah A. and David W. Ela, Mar. 24, 1879.

Robinson, Andrew and Joanna Chase, 1826–7.
Annie and Adams Miller, Nov. 28, 1805.
Rebecca and Foster Averill, 1821–22.
David F. and Emily J. Marshall, Jan. 24, 1867.
John and Jemima Marshall, June 22, 1805.
John and Sarah J. Rolfe, Aug. 27, 1856.
Catherine M. and Benj. F. Annis, Dec. 24, 1859.
Sarah and Caleb G. Wiley, Mar. 12, 1869.

Rogers, Abigail and Amos Morse, Jr., 1819–20.
Ann and Jacob Bailey, 1819–20.
Ann Eliza and James Cox, 3d, 1822–23.
Edmund and Mary Smith, Mar., 1814.
Hanah and Joseph Taylor, Dec. 20, 1806.
Mary and John Dinsmoore, Apr. 7, 1809.
Mary and Jacob Sargent, Mar., 1814.
Robert S. and Mary Ann Pinkerton, 1826–7.
Sarah and John Palmer, 1824–5.
Thomas D. and Mary McGregore, Oct. 16, 1807.

Rolf, Stephen and Ann Wilson, Mar., 1816.

Rolfe, George and Sarah Hamblett, Dec. 15, 1856.
Sarah J. and John Robinson, Aug. 27, 1856.
Sarah P. and James Nesmith, Nov. 24, 1862.

Rollins, Mary and Thomas Fisher, May 7, 1800.
Winthrop and Hannah Fowler, Sept. 26, 1808.

Rouse, Nettie E. and Chas. Edw. Moody, Mar. 20, 1899.

Rowe, Hannah T. and M. Henry Holmes, May 17, 1860.

Rowell, Mrs. Eliza and Andrew J. Benson, Nov. 17, 1884.
Laura Z. and John C. Dow, June 30, 1875.
Nancy E. and Geo. G. Tenney, Nov. 21, 1883.

Russell, Gayton H. and Annie M. Barnes, Dec. 3, 1898.
Ida F. (Mrs.) and Daniel W. Goodwin, Jan. 25, 1892.
Rebecca and Elijah Dwinell, May 21, 1804.

Ryan, Jennie Marion and Fred Bruce Wentworth, Mar. 23, 1894.

Sadmen, Jane P. and Isaac Richardson, Mar. 7, 1810.

Sampson, Anna D. and Levi R. Starrett, May 26, 1879.
John and Lizzie F. Sanborn, Nov. 25, 1867.
Matilda and Joseph Ripley, Jr., 1827.
Turner and May C. Wilkins, May 19, 1894.

Sanborn, Lizzie F. and John Sampson, Nov. 25, 1867.
Martha A. (Mrs.) and John McClary, Mar. 6, 1884.

Santer, Elisabeth and Stephen Merrill, July 10, 1809.

Sargent, David and Nancy Anderson, Sept. 16, 1809.
David and Rebecca Shute, 1821–22.
Jacob and Mary Rogers, Mar., 1814.
Lydia and John Nesmith, Mar., 1817.
Mary and William Davis, 1819–20.

Savage, Eugene A. and Alice V. Barron, Nov. 22, 1880.
Fanny and Rev. William House, May 30, 1859.

Savory, Jonathan and Betsey Kimball, 1821–22.
Thomas and Grissey Holmes, Nov. 14, 1809.

Sawyer, Lucy and Gilbert Greeley, Dec. 18, 1810.
Mattie M. and Edmund G. Anderson, Dec. 11, 1890.
Precilla W. and Reuben W. Flanders, Mar. 11, 1861.

Schwartz, Mary L. and Chas. A. Crowell, Dec. 22, 1889.
Nellie D. and John H. S. Goodwin, Nov. 24, 1896.

Scollay, Martha M. and Walter H. Moore, Oct. 12, 1876.
William and Roxanna Senter, June 22, 1881.

Scott, Abbie M. and Oliver Marr, Apr. 18, 1882.

Sculley, Mary A. and Perry Cram, Jan. 30, 1860.

Scully, Maria C. and Chas. O. Taylor, Aug. 12, 1868.

Seaman, Wm. H. and Marianna P. Clark, Aug. 27, 1873.

Searles, Ida L. and Ira F. Goodwin, Nov. 26, 1878.
Laomi and Nancy Allen, Sept. 8, 1860.

Sears, John A. and Sarah L. Simonds, June 28, 1864.
Lucinda and Ebenezer Johnson, 1826–7.

Senter, Aaron and Rebecca P. Marsh, 1819–20.
Abel and Sally Leach, 1818.
Asenath and Ruben Nicholis, 1812.
James and Sophia Darrah, Mar., 1817.
Marcia M., 67, and James I. Chase, 61, July 5, 1909.
Poley and George Manter, Sept. 2, 1795.
Roxanna and Wm. Scollay, June 22, 1881.
Ruben and Lydia Philbrook, Sept. 26, 1808.
Sally and David Brown, Mar., 1816.
Sally and James Nicholes, Mar., 1818.
Susan and Nathaniel Conant, Mar., 1818.

Shattuck, Geo. W. and Hattie E. Merrill, June 13, 1893.

Shipley, Amos and Polly Boyd, Dec. 13, 1802.
Daniel T. and Ellen F. Abbott, Jan. 10, 1861.
Julia D. and Wm. P. Nevins, Sept. 12, 1871.
Mary and John Gregg, 1828–9.
Thomas B. and Mary Gregg, 1828–9.

Shute, Joseph and Prudence Bailey, 1812.
Rebecca and David Sargent, 1821–22.
Samuel and Rhoda Ingerson, 1821–22.
Samuel and Lovey Gaut, 1824–5.
Wm. B. and Sally Chadwick, Mar., 1818.

Silver, Sarah and Gilbert Bond, Jr., 1822–23

Simonds, Betsey and Joseph Emerson, May 7, 1812.
Clark and Sally Greeley, 1828–9.
Sarah L. and John A. Sears ,June 28, 1864.

Simpson, Carrie M. and Owen Hinckley, July 3, 1868.
Ella S. and Albert O. Titcomb, June 5, 1866.
Eva A. and Geo. C. Pettengill, June 16, 1906.

Skinner, Geo. W. and Eliza J. Goodwin, Feb. 7, 1857.

Sleeper, Elisabeth P. and James C. Taylor, Jan. 12, 1858.

Sloane, Anna J. and Frank L. Gilcreast, Feb. 3, 1873.

Smily, Francis and Ruth Dustin, 1822–23.

Smith, Abraham and Florence Melvin, 1826–7.
Ada J., 17, and Francis R. Nichols, 19, Oct. 11, 1910.
Alexander and Sarah Melvin, 1821–22.
Caddie A. and Fred E. Annis, Oct. 16, 1889.
Charles and Sarah J. Goodwin, Mar. 9, 1869.
Cornelia H. and Joel C. Annis, Dec. 23, 1856.

Smith, David and Susan Warner, Mar. 13, 1815.
Elisabeth and Francis Manter, Sept. 10, 1860.
Eliza and Isaac L. Nichols, 1828–9.
Eleanor and James T. Hartford, Feb. 16, 1872.
Emma N. and Oliver Merrill, Apr. 17, 1893.
Fannie and Dioclesian Melvin, 1824–25.
Fanny S. and Joseph S. Goodwin, Nov. 26, 1868.
Frances M. and Chas. L. Blood, Dce. 31, 1861.
Fred H., 22, and Cora M. Lurvey, 20, Sept. 13, 1909.
George P. and Sarah M. Wilson, Sept. 16, 1881.
Hannah and Benjamin Woodbury, Aug. 13, 1810.
Henry C. and Susie D. Hazelton, Apr. 21, 1877.
Ichabod C. and Celia Marshall, Dec. 20, 1886.
Isaac and Elisabeth Davis, 1824–25.
James and Mary D. Warner, 1821–22.
John and Anna Woodbury, Mar. 7, 1812.
John H. and Hattie R. Harris, Apr. 17, 1871.
Lena Mae and Cleon E. Nesmith, Oct. 25, 1905.
Mary and Edmund Rogers, Mar., 1814.
Mary Etta and Sidney A. Webster, Dec. 28, 1889.
Molly C. and Benjamin Kimball, 1826–7.
Naby and David Alexander, May 2, 1808.
Nathaniel and Mary Bazzan, Mar., 1816.
Nelson E. and Frances Veloria Whittle, Aug. 24, 1904.
Sally and Zachariah Richardson, Mar. 13, 1815.
Sherburn D. and Nancy J. Hodgman, Mar. 10, 1860.
Walter A. and Hattie A. Knight, Nov., 1867.
Will and Achsah J. Allen, Jan. 29, 1890.
William and Martha W. Fiefield, 1821–22.

Spalding, Jacob F. and Delia Annis, Apr. 6, 1864.

Spaulding, Susan and Moody Morse, 2d, 1826–7.

Spear, Mabel G. and William J. Eaton, May 17, 1890.

Spinney, Emma K. and Rev. Leonard A. Freeman, Nov. 16, 1878.

Spofford, Chandler and Betsey Cobb, Mar. 7, 1812.

Spolett, Samuel and Sophia Dore, 1821–22.

Spollett, Eliza and Joshua Clark, Mar., 1817.

Sprague, Emma D. and Clarence A. Hill, Mar. 11, 1881.

Spullet, Frederick and Hannah C. Nichols, 1819–20.

Squars, Elsa and Hazen G. Boyes, 1827.

Starrett, Levi B. and Anna D. Sampson, May 26, 1879.

Steel, David and Polly Clindining, Mar. 13, 1810.
David and Sarah Adams, 1821–22.

Steele, James and Hannah Palmer, Mar., 1814.
Margaret and Washington Palmer, Mar., 1814.

Stephen, Betsey and Francis Davis, Mar., 1818.
Geo. H. and Martha J. Stephen, Mar. 5, 1859.
Martha J. and Geo. H. Stephen, Mar. 5, 1859.

Stevens, Daniel and Elisabeth L. Adams, Mar., 1817.
Ephraim and Olive Leach, 1820–21.
Frank W. and Jarreldign B. Jenkins, Nov. 9, 1877.
Henry T., 50, and Stupeley J. G. White, 58, June 30, 1910.

Stewart, Martha and John Boyes, Nov. 14, 1809.

Stickney, Ebenezer and Hannah Fitz, Feb. 27, 1809.

Stiles, David and Elisabeth Mack, Aug. 26, 1808.

Stimpson, Harriet and Moody B. Towns, 1828–9.

Stinson, Eliza and Samuel Kimball, 1824–5.
John and Betsey Anderson, Mar., 1817.
Jane and Jonathan Dearborn, May 7, 1810.
Margaret and Samuel Kimball, 1812.
Martha and Ebenezer McMurphy, 1818.

Stocker, Robert and Elisabeth Jewett, 1822–23.

Stone, Abigail and John Warner, Jan. 4, 1810.
Anna M. and John E. Ray, July 2, 1894.

Straw, Samuel and Mary Griffin, Mar., 1817.

Swain, Dudley C. and Martha McDuffee, 1826–7.

Swallow, Susie A. and Mark M. Morrison, Nov. 14, 1885.

Sweatt, Joseph A. and May L. Galencia, Sept. 24, 1903.

Swett, Frank and Sarah J. Whittemore, Aug. 1, 1859.

Talbot, Israel and Adeline Pierce, 1824–5.

Tarbox, Mannda and Thomas Jaquith, 1827–8.
S. Clarrissa and Williard Marshall, 1824–5.

Tarleton, Stilman and Martha Warner, 1821–22.

Taylor, Charles O. and Maria C. Scully, Aug. 12, 1868.
Daniel and Nancy Jameson, 1823.
Harold Scott, 27, and Maria Pillsbury, 24, Sept. 14, 1910.
James and Persis Hemphill, June 9, 1807.
James C. and Elisabeth P. Sleeper, Jan. 12, 1858.
Joseph and Hannah Rogers, Dec. 20, 1806.
Martha M. and Wm. H. Littlefield, Nov. 21, 1885.
Mary and John Clark, 1819–20.
Naomi and William Prasser, Mar., 1816.
Peggy and John McKeen, 1818.
Rose and James McNeal, Apr. 8, 1811.
Sally and Nathaniel Warner, Mar., 1818.
Samuel F. and Margaret Patterson, Mar. 7, 1810.

Temple, Fanny E. and Daniel L. Hall, Apr. 8, 1874.

Templeton, Chas. J. and Agnes McGurrill, June 16, 1884.

Tenney, Albert and Mary J. Dickey, May 19, 1875.
Chas. A. and Mrs. Rose J. Crowell, Apr. 6, 1895.
David and Persis Plumer, Mar., 1817.
Geo. G. and Nancy E. Rowell, Nov. 21, 1883.
May Bell (Mrs.) and Willie E. Woodbury, 54, Mar. 16, 1910.

Thayer, Harvelin and Henrietta Davis, Oct. 9, 1877.

Theiss, Grace Margaret, 27, and Albert D. A. Olsen, 35, June 19, 1909.

Thom, Eliza and Alinson Tucker, Feb. 13, 1809.

Thomas, Frank Lewis and Mabel Vincent Chick, Nov. 14, 1904.

Thompson, Benjamin and Ludenna Patee, 1827.
David M. C. and Rebecca Caldwell, Jan. 23, 1809.
Eliza and Jonathan Holmes, 1812.
William and Jane Wilson, May 25, 1807.

Thornton, Abigail C. and David McGregore, 1824–5.

Tilly, Lucy and Isaac W. Cochran, Feb. 7, 1874.

Titcomb, Albert O. and Ella S. Simpson, June 5, 1866.

Tomlinson, Herbert G. and Flora P. Greeley, July 13, 1887.

Towle, Harris and Mrs. Clara D. Lord, Nov. 8, 1887.

Town, Eliza and Stephen Nickols, 1819–20.

Towne, Moses E. and Flora L. Weston, June 9, 1900.
Syvella C. and James T. Doherty, June 17, 1889.

Towns, Jabish and Mary Campbell, 1812.
Jabez and Elisabeth Chase, 1828–9.
James M. and Betsey Anderson, Mar. 13, 1815.
Laura D. and George W. Twiss, July 14, 1893.
Lydia and Joseph Bailey, Oct. 3, 1808.
Lizzie P. and George A. Clark, Nov. 6, 1860.
Mary Ann and Robert Boyd, 1812.
Moody B. and Harriet Stimpson, 1828–9.
Sally and Samuel Nichols, Mar. 13, 1815.
Silas T. and Mrs. Phebe A. Morrison, Mar. 24, 1864.
William and Olive Nickels, Apr. 8, 1804.

Trask, Levi and Elisabeth Melvin, 1827–8.

Truman, Eli and Isabella Gardner (both colored), Mar., 1818.

Tucker, Alanson and Eliza Thom, Feb. 13, 1809.

Tuttle, Delphus O., 28, and Emily Platt, 25, Dec. 22, 1909.
Mary and William Malden, 1818.

Twiss, George W. and Laura D. Towns, July 14, 1893.

Upton, George E. and Sarah J. Gilcreast, Nov. 22, 1856.

Valentine, Thomas and Nellie Roberts, May 19, 1897.

Veazey, Rufus L. and Mary J. Kimball, Sept. 8, 1856.

Vincent, Harry C. and Lillian S. Barron, Apr. 26, 1879.

Walch, Abbie J. and Nelson S. Payne, Aug. 18, 1877.
Frank and Jennie Danforth, Aug. 5, 1868.
Wm. Benj. and Lucy A. Corning, Mar. 16, 1892.

Walker, Josiah and Nancy Platts, Apr. 22, 1806.
Leo and Sally Jones, Nov. 15, 1804.
Ruben and Sally Platts, Oct. 23, 1809.

Wallace, Ann and Robert Wilson, Mar., 1818.
Mary and Peter Patterson, Mar. 13, 1815.
Robert M. and Jane Morrison, Dec. 11, 1810.
Sally and James Pinkerton, May 16, 1809.
Samuel and Betsey Coffin, Mar. 7, 1810.
William P. and H. Addie Whittemore, Apr. 17, 1861.

Warner, Anna G. and James Brown, Mar., 1817.
Betsey and James Morrison, March, 1814.
Betsey and Leonard Wilson, 1820–21.
Betsey B. and Henry Chase, 1820–21.
Daniel and Lucy Danforth, Dec. 30, 1807.
George N. and Martha Moar, 1822–23.
Hannah and Thomas Haskell, Mar., 1818.
John and Abigail Stone, Jan. 4, 1810.
John and Susan Orr, Mar., 1814.
John and Jane Humphrey, 1820–21.
John, Jr., and Eliza Jackman, 1822–23.
Lucy and Charles Haskell, Mar. 2, 1806.
Lucy and Joseph Gregg, 1819–20.
Martha and Stilman Tarleton, 1821–22.
Mary D. and James Smith, 1821–22.
Nancy and Samuel Johnson, Mar. 7, 1812.
Nathaniel and Mary Boyd, Mar., 1814.
Nathaniel and Sally Taylor, Mar., 1818.
Susan and David Smith, Mar. 13, 1815.

Warren, Lewis and Lucy Chase, July 11, 1890.

Waterman, Mary and Clark Ela, 1822–23.
Rebecca and John Cochran, 1826–7.

Waters, Hannah B. and Samuel Chesley, 1821–22.

Watters, Ruth and Moses Carleton, Mar., 1814.

Watts, Annie E. and Rosecrans W. Pillsbury, Dec. 8, 1885.
Chas. H. and Mariam P. Annis, Jan. 1, 1861.
Chas. H., 2d, and Mabel A. Andrews, Mar. 22, 1886.
Clarence O. and Joanna R. Ham, Dec. 22, 1897.
Clarence O. and Marion R. Cöok, Sept. 14, 1903.
Edson W. and Jennie A. Lowd, Nov. 29, 1897.
Elaner and Thomas McClary, 1812.
Ernest M. and Georgie Corning, Dec. 17, 1887.
Esther Jane and Walter Boyce, Dec. 16, 1861.

Watts, Geo. Alvah and Martha E. Fling, Oct. 15, 1883.
Herman L. and Alice J. Fitts, Dec. 22, 1897.
Hugh and Syntha Whidden, 1827.
Jane and Warren Pettengal, Dec. 10, 1810.
James, Jr., and Miriam Corning, 1819–20.
James F. and Ellen E. Jones, Feb. 8, 1878.
Joshua C. and Martha Goodwin, 1821–22.
Martha and Nathaniel Boyes, 1828–9.
Martha B. and Wm. Franklin Holmes, May 31, 1864.
Nathan P. and Harriet E. Roach, June 9, 1906.
Nathaniel and Rachel Pettengill, Nov. 20, 1810.
Willie E. and Mary L. Childs, Oct. 5, 1885.
Walter J. and Evelyn M. Wheeler, Oct. 16, 1889.

Waugh, Alice A. and Frank M. McGregor, July 6, 1887.
George A. and Cora M. Chase, May 10, 1888.

Weagle, Vera L., 19, and William Keddy, 30, Aug. 14, 1909.

Weaver, Clara B. and Harry E. Chase, May 13, 1896.

Webster, Betsey Ann and Wm. B. Carleton, July 2, 1860.
Elisabeth and Samuel Page, Jan. 5, 1810.
Frances S. and Otis Adams, Nov. 24, 1862.
George C. and Adda F. Emerson, Aug. 30, 1878.
James S. and Mary E. Roach, Jan. 17, 1903.
Jessee and Betsey Wilson, 1822–23.
Sidney A. and Mary Etta Smith, Dec. 23, 1889.

Weed, Rhoda A. and Joseph Eaton, Nov. 29, 1865.

Welch, Anne C. and Jonathan Choate, July 3. 1810.

Wells, Ada B. and W. Claud Floyd, Mar. 20, 1888.
Alonzo R. and Regina V. Corning, Apr. 30, 1861.
Estella F. and Harry F. Lord, Mar. 21, 1893.
Susan and Abel P. Corning, Mar. 13, 1815.

Wentworth, Fred Bruce and Jennie Marion Ryan, Mar. 23, 1894.

West, Osborne L., 27, and Viola G. Davison, 16, Sept. 25, 1909.

Weston, Amos and Betsey Wilson, Mar. 13, 1815.
Flora L. and Moses E. Towne, June 9, 1900.

Wheeler, Abbie and Benjamin F. Bean, Dec. 4, 1869.
Evelyn M. and Walter J. Watts, Oct. 16, 1889.
Sarah F. and Charles F. Boyce, Oct. 9, 1888.
Tilly H. and Ann Marshall (?), Dec. 30, 1856.

Whidden, Alice M. and Edgar H. Boss, June 20, 1872.
Alma E. and Frank Adams, June 8, 1875.
Chas. F. and Addie M. Magee, Jan. 31, 1885.
Elbridge A. and Orietta J. Boyce, Nov. 11, 1876.
Esther F. and Dr. Wm. Richardson, Aug. 23, 1884.
Joshua and E. J. Lucinda Lewis, Nov. 12, 1862.

Whidden, Nellie A. (Mrs.) and Chas. F. Boyce, June 14, 1908.
Roxanna and Parker B. Annis, Nov. 17, 1858.
Samuel and Mary Franch, Nov. 14, 1809.
Syntha and Hugh Watts, 1827.
William and Climela Avery, 1826-7.
William and Peggy Boyes, Mar., 1818.

White, Arthur A. and Carrie A. Buttrick, Nov. 21, 1906.
Betsey and John Hovey, Mar., 1814.
Betsey and Joseph Jackson, Mar., 1816.
Elenor and John Hovey, Sept. 3, 1810.
Henry H. and Sarah A. Moore, Nov. 6, 1860.
John and Susan Dickey, Mar., 1818.
Joseph L. and Mary P. Whitefield, 1826-7.
Levi and Jane Howard, 1821-22.
Ruben and Rachel Corning, 1824-5.
Sally and Benjamin Boys, 1819-20.
Stuckley J. G., 58, and Henry T. Stevens, 50, June 30, 1910.

Whitefield, Mary P. and Joseph L. White, 1826-7.

Whitiker, Joseph and Elisabeth Dodge, 1824-5.

Whittemore, Edward K. and Mary A. Jaquith, Dec. 13, 1862.
H. Addie and Wm. P. Wallace, Apr. 17, 1861.
Henry J. and Esther M. Goodwin, Apr. 21, 1862.
Sarah J. and Frank Swett, Aug. 1, 1859.
Zachariah K. H. and Susan M. Ripley, Apr. 1, 1867.

Whittier, Dearborn and Roxanna McGregore, 1826-7.
Martha and Enoch S. Marsh, 1824-5.
Mary Jane and Chas. I. Gardner, May 24, 1856.
Samuel F. and Nancy Hills, 1827-8.

Whittle, Frances V. and Nelson E. Smith, Aug. 24, 1904.

Whittondon, George and Irene A. Burlard, Mar. 27, 1887.

Whorf, Benjamin and Shuah Chase, Mar., 1817.
Benjamin F. and Juliaette A. B. Page, Sept. 26, 1859.

Wiley, Caleb G. and Sarah Robinson, Mar. 12, 1869.
George B. and Ella E. Gilcreast, June 28, 1871.
Martha M. E. and John P. Hardy, June 11, 1878.

Wilkins, May C. and Turner Sampson, May 19, 1894.

Willey, Henry J. and Lydia Mills, Aug. 26, 1876.
Mark W. and Ellen G. Bachelder, Nov. 24, 1883.

Williams, James and Elisabeth Barker, Aug. 18, 1870.
Nancy and William Anderson, 1812.

Wilson, Alexander and Mary Ann Reed, Feb. 27, 1809.
Ann and Stephen Rolf, Mar., 1816.
Benjamin and Rhodia Emery, 1827.
Betsey and Amos Weston, Mar. 13, 1815.

Wilson, Betsey and Jessee Webster, 1822–23.
Betsey and William Cochran, June 9, 1807.
Ebenezer and Sally Norton, 1824–25.
Elisabeth and Amnio Brown, 1819–20.
James and Betsey Morrison, Mar. 7, 1812.
James and Mary Duffee, 1819–20.
James and Mary McKeen, 1820–21.
Jane and Robert Anderson,1819–20.
Jane and William Thompson, May 25, 1807.
John and Mary Barker, Mar. 13, 1815.
John and Nancy Gregg, 1818.
John P. and Lydia Remix, 1824–25.
Leonard and Betsey Warner, 1820–21.
Margrat and David Brewster, July 10, 1809.
Martha and James Arwain, 1821–22.
Nancy and Samuel Emerson, 1826–7.
Robert and Ann Wallace, Mar., 1818.
Sarah M. and George P. Smith, Sept. 16, 1881.
Thomas and Abigail Jewett, 2d wife, 1828–9.
Thomas and Rebecca Pinkerton, Jan. 26, 1807.

Wing, Edward L. and F. Alice Colby, July 9, 1908.
Seth G. and Pearl G. Proctor, Apr. 5, 1904.

Wingate, Moses and Nancy Paul, Mar., 1814.

Witherspoon, Catherine and Nathan Butrick, 1822–23.

Woodburn, David and Jane Anderson, Mar., 1816
James and Grissel Clark, May 13, 1809.
John and Mehitable Melvin, 1819–20.
Margret and John Dickey, Mar. 2, 1805.
Mary and Zaccheus Greeley, July 26, 1807.
Mary Ann and Benj. J. Dwinells, 1821–22.
Sarah and Dustin Greeley, Mar., 1816.

Woodbury, Abram A. and Euretta J. Morse, May 26, 1874.
Anna and John Smth, Mar. 7, 1812.
Benjamin and Hannah Smith, Aug. 13, 1810.
Elma J. and Albert Potter, July 26, 1879.
Etta M. and Geo. H. Young, Nov. 23, 1893.
Martha and Jacob Nickals, May 8, 1809.
Nellie E. and Robt. G. Morrison, Mar. 12, 1881.
Samuel and Harriet E. Estey, Dec. 1, 1858.
Samuel and Pheba A. Bacheller (Mrs.), Nov. 1, 1898.
Willie E., 54, and Mrs. May Bell Tenney, Mar. 16, 1910.

Woods, Ensign C. and Alice H. Fellows, Aug. 23, 1861.
Mattie M. and Charles Adams, Oct. 21, 1885.

Worster, Sewall and Esther Boyes, 1824–5.

Worthen, David and Sally Bruce, Mar., 1814.
Lucretia and Joseph Day, 1826–7.

Wright, Ralph W. and Edith L. Dustin, June 3, 1906.

Wyatt, Rosie M. and Geo. W. Lee, July 25, 1905.

Wyman, Elbridge and Clarrina H. Griffin, 1828–9.
Warren and Mary Johnson, Oct. 12, 1883.

Young, Allettie M. and Fred E. Chase, May 31, 1887.
Augusta and Fred W. Pace, Feb. 24, 1897.
Chas. Edward and Margaret A. Young (Mrs.), Aug. 7, 1895.
Frances H. and George W. Kimball, Apr. 13, 1877.
Fred A. and Emma D. Boyd, Nov. 24, 1885.
George H. and Etta M. Woodbury, Nov. 23, 1893.
James and Mary Chase, Mar. 13, 1815.
Jennie D. and Chas. H. Alexander, May 24, 1890.
John P. and Mrs. Emeline Pettengill, Dec. 23, 1868.
Johnnie L. and Luella E. Badger, June 27, 1889.
Margaret Ann (Mrs.) and Chas. Edw. Young, Aug. 7, 1895.
Wesley J. and Lillia A. Booth, Dec. 7, 1877.
William D. and Maria L. Parmerton, May 5, 1894.

RECORDS OF MARRIAGES

From the Earliest Record to the End of 1910

Abbott, Emma B., 34, and Pliny M. Campbell, 32, June 11, 1902. Res. at Derry, N. H.
Etta M. and Nathan A. Pollard, Sept. 11, 1860.
Charles B. and Susie F. Lowd, June 13, 1868.
Lydia and Thomas Bartlett, Jan. 1, 1811.
Mercy and Ebenezer Bartlett, Feb., 1807.
Samuel W. and Clarrissa Clagget, Nov. 25, 1834.

Abernathey, Mary and David Cargill, June 21, 1722, by the Rev. Mr. McGregor.

Adams, Abby, ———.
Betsey and Charles Redfield, Dec. 16, 1813.
Charles and Mary Hall, spring season, 1843. Golden wedding 1893.
Charles and Mattie M. Woods, Oct. 22, 1885.
David and Janet or Jenny Wilson, Mar. 27, 1800.
Edmond and Betsey Kimball, Sept. 26, 1809.
Edmond and Elisabeth Karr, Dec. 29, 1808.
Eliza and James Pettengill, Dec. 26, 1848.
Frank and Alma E. Whidden, June 9, 1875.
Horace and Lucy A. Anderson (2nd wife), Dec. 20, 1860.
Horace and Margaret Richardson (1st wife), ———.
James and Judith Rolfe, ———.
Jane and Ammi Buck, Mar. 15, 1836.
John and Ann Morrison, Oct. 31, 1799.
John and Betsey Cochran, Feb. 26, 1789.
John M. and Polly Jackson, Nov. 6, 1810.
Rev. John R. and Mary Ann McGregor, 1832.
Jonathan and Sarah Smith, ———.
Martha and Amos Kendall, Dec. 15, 1808.
Mary and Elder John Holmes, 1821.
Mary and William Ayers, ———.
Nathan and Elisabeth Jane Boyce, Nov. 20, 1845.
Patience and James Moar, Feb. 4, 1796.
Polly and Ebenezer Johnson, Feb. 19, 1801.
Robert and Sally Jackson, Dec. 7, 1809.
Samuel and Elisabeth Woodman, Dec. 4, 1799.

Adams, Samuel and Eliza Prentice, Sept. 21, 1801.
Wesley, 35, and Mabel F. M. Nevins, 35, June 21, 1908.
William and Janet Taylor, Feb. 6, 1779.
William and Margaret Duncan, ——.
William and Peggy Duncan, Mar. 14, 1799.

Aiken, Andrew J., 42, and Mary A. Carroll, 45, Oct. 19, 1903.
Betsey and Phillip Stephens, Nov. 11, 1802.
Elisabeth and David H. Pettingill, ——.
George and Susan W. Corning (1st wife), Dec. 1, 1838.
George and —— Weston (2nd wife), ——.
George and Esther Dow (3d wife), Aug. 20, 1849.
George and Amanda L. Chase (4th wife), Jan. 1, 1852.
George F., 26, and Addie Pettingill, 17, Oct. 29, 1879.
Georgia F., 20, and George Tasker, Sept. 1, 1900. Res. Haverhill, Mass.
James and Elizabeth Pinkerton, ——.
James and Jean Cochran, Oct. 26, 1725, by the Rev. Mr. McGregor.
John and Betsy Pinkerton, ——.
Joseph and Eliza Gregg, May 24, 1801.
Joshua and Jane Pinkerton, July 28, 1815.
Nathaniel and Margaret Cochran, Dec. 1, 1726, by the Rev. Mr. McGregor.
Samuel, 4th, and Sally Coffin, May 26, 1814.
Samuel and Hannah J. Estey, Aug. 16, 1868.
Thomas and Jane Gregg, Sept. 30, 1802.
William and Jenat Wilson, Dec. 23, 1725, by the Rev. Mr. McGregor.

Aldrich, Charles E. and Ella J. Moar, Nov. 10, 1880.
Lyman and Abigail J. Batchelder, Feb. 19, 1850.

Alexander, Alphonso and Ellen F. Merrill, Nov., 1873.
Amy Mabel, 28, and William G. Dickey, 34, July 11, 1905. Res. Derry, N. H.
Betsey and George Barnett, Dec. 31, 1799.
Betsey and Hugh Alexander, Mar. 3, 1801.
Betsey and John McConihue, Mar. 1, 1804.
Charles H., 23, and Jennie D. Young, 22, May 26, 1890.
Charles J. and Mary A. Humphrey, Apr. 3, 1877.
David and Nabby Smith, May 12, 1808.
Hugh and Betsey Alexander, Mar. 3, 1801.
John and Sally Estey, Nov. 27, 1827. Golden wedding 1877.
John and Sarah A. Rowell, July 27, 1854.
John and Sarah Ann Brown, Nov. 2, 1855.
Jonathan and Sarah Davidson, Mar. 17, 1803.
Moses and Nancy, Feb. 21, 1805.

Alexander, Rebecca and —— McColm, Feb. 23, 1797.
Sally and Thomas Cheney, Dec. 31, 1811.

Allan, Milo and Julia A. Varel, July 1, 1866. (Later divorced.)

Allen, Achsah J., 40, and Will Smith, 35, Jan. 29, 1890.
Charlotte and Humphrey Proctor, Mar. 6, 1806.
George E. and Maria Noglar, Mar. 23, 1876.
Hattie A. and Charles S. Greeley, Dec. 24, 1879.
Nancy G. and Loami Searles, Sept. 8, 1860.

Alley, Alice P. and George W. Greeley, Apr. 16, 1846.
Moses and Hannah Smithurst (1st wife), Mar., 1823.
Moses and Jane D. Boyce (2nd wife), ——.

Ambrose, Betsey Ann and Horace E. Stevens, Feb. 17, 1869, Manchester, N. H.
Greenleaf and Sally R. Sawyer, 1843, Manchester, N. H.

Anderson, Alexander and Patty McGilvery, Nov., 1804.
Almira J. and John Haynes (soldier and doctor), July 3, 1871.
Anna B. and Elder Matthew Holmes, Sept. 11, 1856.
Benjamin and Lydia Jackson, Mar. 13, 1813.
Charles W., 29, and Evalena W. French, 29, June 4, 1898.
David and Elisabeth Anderson, Feb. 24, 1867.
Elder David and Persis Tenney, Oct. 13, 1842. Golden wedding 1892.
Edmond G., 22, and Martha M. Sawyer, 21, Dec. 11, 1890.
Elisabeth and David Anderson, Feb. 4, 1867.
Elisabeth and Moses Dustin, Jr., Dec. 25, 1817.
Eliza and Robert Holmes, June 4, 1811.
George E. and Sarah J. Harvell, Apr. 22, 1869.
George V., and Mary J. S. Kelley, Apr. 27, 1867.
Helen F. and Wesley B. Knight, Apr. 7, 1862.
Hughey and Jane Nesmith, Mar. 2, 1796.
James and Nancy Anderson, Dec. 28, 1813.
Jane and David Woodbury, Jan. 23, 1816.
Jane and Robert Holmes, Nov. 8, 1809.
Jean and James Taggart, Jr., Nov. 15, 1733, by the Rev. Thomas Thompson of Londonderry.
Jenny and Alexander McCollom, Feb. 7., 1802.
Jenny and James Moar, Apr. 1, 1823.
Jessee and —— Morrison (Dea. Morrison's dau.), Feb. 14, 1805.
John N. and Eliza K. Gage, Nov. 26, 1829.
John and Elisabeth Corning, May 22, 1834.
Lucy A. and Horace Adams, Dec. 20, 1860.
Mary and James Dinsmoor, Dec. 3, 1772.
Mary and James Wason, Feb. 14, 1804.

Anderson, Mary and Robert Dinsmore, Dec. 31, 1801.
Mary and William Anderson, June 11, 1789.
Mary Ann Nancy and Robert Dickey, Apr. 30, 1837.
Mary J. and James C. Steele, May 23, 1848.
Mary Jane S. and Matthew M. Campbell, Nov. 30, 1876. Res. Litchfield, N. H.
Nancy and David Sargeant, Sept. 16, 1809.
Nancy and James Anderson, Dec. 28, 1813.
Nancy and John Armstrong, Apr. 23, 1803.
Nancy and Simeon Danforth, Mar. 10, 1807.
Persis and Alberto C. Brown, May 20, 1873. Res. Mass.
Polly and Abel Plummer, Mar., 1808.
Polly and David Robinson, Dec. 12, 1798.
Robert and Agnes Craige, 1748.
Rev. Rufus and Hannah Parsons, Sept. 8, 1795.
Rufus and Martha A. Richards, May 8, 1848.
Samuel, 2nd, and Jane Campbell, Jan. 26, 1823.
Sally and William Gregg, Feb., 1802.
Sarah and John Campbell, Feb. 7, 1814.
Thomas and Jane Craige, 1755.
William and Betsey Clark, Feb. 24, 1801.
William and Mary Anderson, July 11, 1789.
William and Mary Bell, Apr. 5, 1808.
William Henry and Mary Hines, Oct. 1, 1868.

Andrews, Hannah and William Holt, Feb. 16, 1804.
Mabel A. and Charles H. Watts, 2nd, Mar. 23, 1886.
William A. and Williette Annis, Dec. 23, 1884.

Annaise (?), James and Martha Wilson, Mar. 14, 1822.

Annis, Adeline and John P. Wilson, Apr. 18, 1844.
Augusta May and William R. McGregor, Jan. 25, 1882.
Benjamin F. and Catherine McKinley, Feb. 27, 1851.
Benjamin F. and Catherine M. Robinson, Dec. 25, 1859.
Charles D. and Mary S. Vickery, May 22, 1855.
Charles U., 23, and Sarah Richardson, 22, Oct. 16, 1888.
Daniel G. and Fannie M. Fling, Dec. 1, 1886.
Daniel G. and Mina A. Gilcreast, June 18, 1868.
Daniel M. and Mary J. Page, June 4, 1859.
David L. and Susan Grace Griffin, Nov. 13, 1858.
Delia and Jacob F. Spalding, Apr. 7, 1864.
Earle M. and Hattie Belle Heath, June 14, 1911. Res. Manchester, N. H.
Edgar C., 23, and Mary C. Durant, 17, Feb. 22, 1892.
Eliza Jane and Frank W. Davis, Nov. 29, 1871.
Eliza Maud, 25, and George N. Plummer, 49, May 17, 1898.
Eva and Samuel Corning, June 17, 1886.
Fred E., 21, and Caddie A. Smith, 20, Oct. 17, 1889.

Annis, George W. and Elvira E. French, June 29, 1859.
Hannah J. and Daniel P. Flanders, Nov. 25, 1847.
Henry H. andRosilla Annis, Dec. 5, 1871.
Ira Dan and Fannie M. Thorp, Feb. 20, 1894. Res. Croton, Ohio.
James and ——— Leach (1st wife), ———.
James and Elisabeth Dix (2nd wife), Mar. 6, 1837.
Jesse and Mildred Blodgett, Dec. 25, 1821.
Joel C. and Cornelia H. Smith, Dec. 25, 1856.
John and Betsey Coburn, Nov. 2, 1854 (2nd wife).
John and Delilah Coburn, Feb. 17, 1820 (1st wife).
Lillian E. and Frederic H. Quimby, June 2, 1906. Res. Derry, N. H.
Lora H. and Charles L. Avery, Nov. 10, 1891.
Lucy F. and William Flanders, Apr. 30, 1850.
Lydia and Benjamin Blodgett, Dec. 11, 1823.
Mariam P. and Charles H. Watts, Jan. 1, 1861.
Martha C. and George W. Boyce, Oct. 3, 1849.
Martha J. and Amos Webster, Sept. 29, 1846.
Matthew Parker and Sarah M. Morse, Sept. 26, 1850.
Olive and Ephraim P. Bailey, Aug. 23, 1848.
Rosilla and Henry H. Annis, Dec. 5, 1871.
Roswell and Ella Jenny McClary, Sept. 14, 1884.
Roswell and Luella A. Campbell, Dec. 10, 1874.
Roxanna B. and George F. Chase, Mar. 8, 1843.
Sampson and Nancy M. Dickey, Oct. 18, 1849.
Samuel W. and Mehitable Page, Jan. 1, 1856.
Sarah Ann and Daniel Manter, ———.
William and Betsey Mullins, Dec. 5, 1846.
Williette and William A. Andrews, Dec. 23, 1884.

Archer, Elisabeth and Nehemiah Richardson, Oct., 1867.

Archibald, Robert and Peggy Martin, Dec. 31, 1801.

Armstrong, Alma A. and Martha E. Titcomb, June 14, 1908. Res. Windham.
Deborah E. and Joseph S. Clark, Dec. 9, 1846.
George F. and Adeline Greeley, Nov. 20, 1884. Res. Windham, N. H.
James and Jenny Armstrong, Dec. 28, 1803.
Jenny and James Armstrong, Dec. 28, 1803.
John and Nancy Anderson, Apr. 23, 1803.
Nancy E. and Elder John A. Moore, Nov. 25, 1854.

Arnot, Galen and Sally Chandler, Nov. 21, 1802.

Atwood, Albert L. and Lydia C. Barker, Jan. 1, 1845.
Austin L. M. and Zenora Emery, ———.
Isaac and Betsey Chandler, Dec. 27, 1798.

Austin, Frye and Abigail Barker, Sept. 15, 1825.
Joshua and Betsey Barker, Feb. 12, 1824.

Austins, Abby C. and Daniel Goodwin, Oct. 19, 1853.
Alice J. and John P. Whidden, Nov. 11, 1847.
Amanda P. and James M. Noyes, July 4, 1872.
Mark J. and Jennie A. Thompson, Dec. 10, 1868.
Mary and Leonard Page, Feb. 7, 1846.
Perley E. and Millie Higgins, July 25, 1894, Manchester, N. H. Res. Londonderry, N. H.

Avery, Alice Lillian and Willie S. Sanborn, Apr. 12, 1899.
Charles L. and Lora H. Annis, Nov. 10, 1891.
Ida F. and Wilbur E. Barrett, July 7, 1885.
Jeremiah M. and Julia A. Upton, Oct. 16, 1854.
Sarah P. and Lewis Stiles, Aug. 3, 1856.

Ayers, Ayres, Eyres, Eayres, Eayers, Ayer, Benjamin Francis and Helen M. Stott, July 3, 1873.
Benjamin Francis and Mrs. Abbie Frances Cressey (Gilcreast), Oct. 13, 1888.
Christopher and Jean Galt, Mar., 1724–5, by Rev. Mr. McGregor, minister of Londonderry, N. H.
Elisabeth and James McCurdy, Mar. 22, 1727, by the Rev. Mr. McGregor of Londonderry, N. H.
Mary and Charles Stewart, Nov. 15, 1727, by Rev. Mr. McGregor.
William and Jenat Callwell, June 21, 1727, by the Rev. Mr. McGregor.
William and Mary Adams, ———.

Babb, Miss Mary E. and Warren Corning, ———. Res. Manchester, N. H.

Babcock, Rev. E. G. and Eliza Hibbard, May 31, 1830.

Bachelder, Ellen G. and Mark W. Willey, Nov. 29, 1883.
Mary Bell and George G. Tenney, ———. (2nd wife.)
Phebe A., 38, and Samuel Woodbury, 60, Nov. 7, 1898. (2nd wife.)
William and Minnie Thayer, ———.

Bacon, Albert Reed and Amy P. Fiske, June 18, 1907.
Albert J. and Carrie L. Moar, Sept. 10, 1879.
Edna Louise and Kenneth W. C. Torrey, Mar. 12, 1907.
Mary and John Chase, ———.

Badger, Luella, 26, and Johnnie Young, 23, June 27, 1889.

Bailey, Addie Augusta and Charles H. Rice, ———.
Charles R. and Augusta G. Hunkins, Aug. 8, 1878. Res. Manchester, N. H.
Elisabeth P. and William C. Bancroft, Mar. 1, 1866.

Bailey, Ephraim P. and Olive Annis, Aug. 23, 1848.
Jacob and Anne Rogers, Nov. 20, 1819.
Joseph and Lydia Towns, Dec. 9, 1808.
Julia Ann and Jason Carr, Dec. 21, 1845.
Lillian A. and Charles W. Noyes, 24, Nov. 21, 1901.
Lydia T. and Jonathan Cate, Jan. 21, 1837.
Mary E., 21, and Joseph J. Hebert, 26, June 15, 1909.
Sarah and Rev. Stephen Pillsbury, Jr., ———.

Baker, Ezra Norwell, 26, and Clara Louise Maker, 25, Nov. 6, 1907.
Grace and Hezekiah Wetherbee, ———.
Helen M. and John Hamilton Burroughs, ———, Dunbarton, N. H.
Josephine Augusta, 22, and Newton Everett Clark, 30, May 29, 1909.
Louisa J. and Samuel Woodbury, July 12, 1837.

Ballard, David L. and Submit Tarbox, Nov. 15, 1808.

Ballou, Edward and Isabella McGregor, Nov. 13, 1823.
Sarah A. and Daniel D. Smith, Oct. 25, 1855. Golden wedding 1905.

Bampas, Annie G. and Frank N. Colby, Oct. 21, 1903.

Bancroft, Alzina Carolyn and George Thompson Eams, in Wilmington, Mass., Jan., 1902.
Betsey and Edward Putnam, Mar. 12, 1869.
Caleb H. and Sarah Whittaker, Apr. 21, 1851.
Ebenezer, Tyngsboro, Mass., and Alzina Carolyn Nichols. Children: Minnie Ardella, Jan. 3, 1873; Lila May, Nov. 27, 1877; Luther Eben, Jan. 1, 1881.
Eliza J. and Daniel D. Crowell, Apr. 26, 1849.
Elisabeth and Joseph A. Wychoff, Jan. 23, 1853.
Fred Lewis, 24, and Ida May Fitzgerald, 20, Sept. 24, 1906.
Martha R. and John N. Rice, May 9, 1846.
Mary and Phineas Manter, Feb. 24, 1820.
Savory and Betsey Cheney, Dec. 12, 1822.
Susan E. and Lorenzo Gardner, Nov. 22, 1855.
William C. and Elisabeth P. Bailey, Mar. 1, 1866.
William C. and Myra F. Robinson, Sept. 15, 1876.

Baras (?), Lucy and Jacob Putnam, Apr. 27, 1803.

Barker, Abigail and Frye Austin, Sept. 15, 1825.
Abigail J. and Thomas Bullock, Aug. 26, 1868.
Angeline M. and Warren M. Pettengill, Apr. 13, 1859.
Asa and Matilda Jennings, Aug. 30, 1836.
Benjamin and Clarrissa Corning, Mar. 30, 1830.
Betsey and Franklin Page, Apr. 18, 1839.
Betsey and Joshua Austin, Jan. 14, 1824.

Barker, Clara Jane and Benjamin L. Frasuer, Dec. 21, 1892. Res. Salisbury, N. H.
David C. and Eliza J. Richardson, Sept. 29, 1845.
David P. and ——— Bullock. Res. Manchester, N. H.
Ebenezer and Rhoda Jennings, May 1, 1834.
Elisabeth B. and James Williams, 1870.
Eliza Jane and David Pettengill, Nov. 15, 1859. Res. Manchester, N. H.
Hannah and Eben Woodbury, Nov. 27, 1834.
James A. and Ella M. Colby, Mar. 17, 1862.
John Charles and Elisabeth W. Doe, Mar. 24, 1903.
John Charles and Nellie Richardson, July 3, 1879.
John W. and Sarah Jane Moor, Feb. 2, 1846.
Lydia C. and Albert L. Atwood, Jan. 1, 1845.
Martha and James Holmes, Feb. 27, 1823.
Mary A. and Charles D. Fall, Apr. 7, 1874.
Mehitable G. and Robert Call, May 12, 1822.
Melana and George F. Manter (dentist), Mar. 16, 1868. Res. Manchester, N. H.
Pearl and Charles Herbert Holmes, 39, Apr. 24, 1906. Out West.
Polly and Andrew Robertson, July 1, 1802.
Polly and Benjamin Corning, Sept. 17, 1807.
Ralph W., 20, and Elsa A. Mertsch, 20, July 29, 1910.
Rhoda A. and George F. McGregor, May 3, 1865. Silver wedding 1890.
Silas and Hannah Bodwell, May 10, 1831.
Sophia and Gilman Farley, Apr. 29, 1832.
Samuel C. and Hannah D. Page, July 10, 1834. Golden wedding 1884.
Susie A. and George N. Goodwin, Oct. 1, 1872.
Capt. William S. and Lucinda M. Hackett, Dec. 26, 1857.

Barnar (?), Mary and Nathaniel Smith, Feb. 21, 1816.

Barnard, Annis and John Walis, May 17, 1721, by the Rev. Mr. McGregor. (See also Wallace record.)

Barnes, Annie M., 36, and Gayton H. Russell, 37, Dec. 3, 1898.
Emily and David Pettengill, Dec. 24, 1835, Litchfield, N. H.
Emily and John P. Young, Dec. 14, 1868.

Barnet, Ann and John Karr, Mar. 10, 1805.
Annis and John Walis, May 18, 1721. First marriage in Londonderry.
Betsey and William Dinsmore, Apr. 9, 1807.
David and Grisey Patterson, Feb. 20, 1814.
Ephraim and Charlotte Proctor, Mar., 1813.
George and Betsey Alexander, Dec. 31, 1799.

Barnet, James and Ruth Lamriel, Dec. 17, 1781.
John and Jenny McCollum, Feb. 13, 1799.
John and Joan Seaforth, Nov. 2, 1721, by Rev. Mr. McGregor.
Mary and Nathan Johnson, May 17, 1807.
Robert and Betsey Varnum, Dec. 15, 1801.

Barnett, John, ———.
Sarah and Thomas Cristy, Dec. 5, 1749.

Barret, James E. and Emeline G. Hamlet, Jan. 12, 1860.
Joel and Lidia Towns, July 14, 1804.
Susannah and James Melvin, Feb. 4, 1807.
Timothy and Hannah Hert (?), May 5, 1803.

Barrett, Amanda and Christopher T. Boyce, June 22, 1848.
Violetta and Daniel C. Hill, Oct. 28, 1880.
Wilbur E. and Georgie Knights, Dec. 12, 1894.
Wilbur E. and Ida F. Avery, July 7, 1885.
Wilbur E., 49, and Sarah Muncaster, 36, Jan. 22, 1907.

Barron, Lillian S. and Harry C. Vincent, May 7, 1879.

Barrows (?), Dolly and John Phillips, Mar. 10, 1805.

Bartevell, Robinson and Hannah Dickey, Mar. 26, 1833.

Bartlett, Ada E. and James B. Pettengill, Sept. 22, 1881.
Ebenezer and Mercy Abbott, Feb., 1807.
F. Henry, 30, and Etta M. Proctor, 26, Jan. 11, 1893.
Joseph and Jane P. Nahor, Mar. 30, 1832.
Thomas and Lidia Abbott, Jan. 1, 1811.

Bartwell, Robinson and Susannah Dickey, Jan. 28, 1841.

Basset, Jane and Charles Wintworth, Oct. 11, 1802.
Rhoda and Joseph Colby, Mar. 7, 1797.
Susannah and James Melvin, Feb. 4, 1807.

Batchelder, Abigail J. and Lyman Aldrich, Feb. 19, 1850.
Daniel H. and Pricilla H. Coffin, Jan. 15, 1852.
Mary A. and Charles M. Holmes, Nov. 25, 1848.
Sarah and Humphrey Holt, Sept. 11, 1817.
Sarah H. and Leverett S. Pelton, Sept. 25, 1845.

Batchelor, Daniel K. and Clarrissa French, Jan. 16, 1880.

Beals, Flora E. and George F. Hamblett, Sept. 19, 1878.

Bean, Benjamin F. and Abbie Wheeler, Dec. 5, 1869.
Eliza and George A. Hill, Sept. 18, 1858.
Florence and George N. Watts, July 4, 1885.
George H. and Rosie L. Titcomb, Dec. 25, 1895. Res. Derry, N. H.
Louisa A. and Anderson Holman, Dec. 2, 1855.

Beede, George W., 22, and Annie S. Moody, 18, Apr. 25, 1900.

Bell, John and Mary Ann Gilmore, Dec. 21, 1758.
John, Hon., and Persis Thom.
Dr. Luther V. and Frances Pinkerton, Sept. 2, 1834.
Mary and William Anderson, Apr. 5, 1808.

Bennett, Emma J. and Frank A. Jencks, June 16, 1886.
Mary Corinne and Fred D. McGregor, June 17, 1891. Res. Haverhill, Mass.

Benson, Andrew J. and Ruth J. Page, Jan. 1, 1851.
Andrew J. and Mrs. Eliza Rowell, Nov. 20, 1884.
Ella F. and John H. Connor, Nov. 30, 1876.
Laura L., 19, and Robert K. Plummer, 55, 1902.

Bergeron, George, 22, and Hattie F. Christie, 22, May 21, 1906.

Berry, Hermon and Mary B. Twiss, Mar. 15, 1848.
John W. and Ednah S. Putnam, July 2, 1864.
Joseph A. and Mary Jane Sampson, Oct. 6, 1872.
Mary and George Way, Mar. 24, 1867.

Besse, Edward H. and Rosetta H. Frost, Oct. 2, 1861.

Betton, Elisabeth and Abner Campbell, Mar., 1805.

Bickford, William G. and Mary Jane Holmes, Aug. 18, 1836.

Bixby, Miss ——— and Simeon Chase, Dec. 20, 1807.

Black, Hannah and Samuel Dunkley, Mar. 7, 1820.

Blackburn, Alfred E., 29, and Almeda' Rebecca Cox, 25, June 21, 1905.

Blair, Blaire, Hannah and William Thompson, Feb. 21, 1722, by Rev. Mr. McGregor.

Blaisdell, Laura A. and Freeman Corning, Oct. 11, 1846.

Blenus, Walter L. and Lizzie S. Gardner, Oct. 12, 1881. Res. Manchester, N. H.

Blodgett, Augusta W. and Oliver Dodge Evans, Apr. 18, 1866.
Augusta Watts and Lewis Aiken McGregor, Nov. 30, 1843.
Benjamin and Lydia Annis, Dec. 11, 1823.
Fanny and Joseph W. Tuttle, Nov. 6, 1831.
Isaac and Bethiah Reed, May 4, 1843.
Joshua and Sarah Vickery, Sept. 29, 1803.
Mildred and Jesse Annis, Dec. 25, 1821.
Roxanna and Daniel Gage Coburn, Apr. 5, 1827.

Blood, Arthur V. and Nellie Kirkwood, Mar. 22, 1907.
Charles A. and R. Ida Moulton, Dec. 12, 1875. Both of Manchester, N. H.
Charles L. and Frances M. Smith, Jan. 1, 1862.
George W. and Adeline M. Moor, May 17, 1849.
Julia Ann and Elbridge G. Greeley, Apr. 16, 1842.
Nancy A. and Ephraim A. Wiley, Sept. 16, 1841. Golden wedding 1891.

Blood, Oliver F. and Jane P. Hill, Feb. 8, 1842.

Bodwell, Christopher H. and Almira T. Cate, July 7, 1846.
Hannah and Silas Barker, May 10, 1831.
Jennie M. and William H. Woodman, July 18, 1880.

Boles, Annie E., 17, and Leroy S. Hartshorn, 23, Oct. 24, 1902.
Florence J., 18, and Osmond E. Corthell, 29, Sept. 25, 1901.
Mary and John Smith, May 15, 1829.

Bolles, Carrie W. and John Goodwin, May 17, 1863.

Bolser, George A. and Hattie M. Wilkins, ——. Res. Middleton, N. S.

Bond, Martha and Samuel Graves, Jan. 29, 1724-5, by Rev. Mr. Brown, Haverhill.

Boone, Emiley L. and Bennie Noyes, 19, Sept. 1, 1900.

Boors (?), John and Martha Steward, Nov. 2, 1809.

Booth, Lilla A. and Wesley J. Young, Dec. 8, 1877. Res. Derry, N. H.

Boss, Edgar H. and Alice M. Whidden, June 20, 1872.

Boverington, Eliphalet and Susannah Nicholes, Dec. 3, 1801.

Bowles, Martin M. and Mary E. (Noyes) Norcross, Dec. 19, 1869.

Boyce, Adeline and Joshua Whidden, about 1848.
Adeline A. and Jonathan Y. Nesmith, Nov. 25, 1852.
Almira and William B. Hovey, Nov. 4, 1841.
Angeline M. and Andrew J. McKenny, Apr. 10, 1862.
Annie R., 19, and Edgar F. McDonald, 23, Apr. 28, 1894.
Capt. Benjamin and Sally White, Dec. 30, 1819.
Charles F., 29, and Sarah F. Wheeler, 19, Oct. 16, 1888.
Charles F., 49, and Nellie A. Whidden, 47, June 17, 1908.
Charlotte and Jonathan Young, 3d, Oct. 30, 1828.
Christopher T. and Amanda Barrett, June 22, 1848.
Edith F., 23, and Royal S. Proctor, 18, Aug. 9, 1906.
Elbridge A. and Sarah E. Fay, Jan. 7, 1890, at Derry.
Elisabeth Jane and Nathan Adams, Nov. 20, 1845.
Ella F. and William F. Marsh, Oct. 7, 1891. Res. Hudson, N. H.
Esther W. and Alonzo F. Clark, Apr. 23, 1859.
Frank A. and Annie F. Conant, Aug. 27, 1881.
George W. and Martha C. Annis, Oct. 3, 1849.
Giles Ladd and Clara M. Goodwin, Apr. 1, 1871.
Hannah and Nathaniel Corning, 1797.
Hannah Jane and first and second Clough Bros. All lived and died in the West.
Hannah Jane and —— Turner (3d hus.).
Haverline and Carrie Delaney.

Boyce, Horace C., 36, and Addelle Brooks, 26, Oct. 14, 1889.
Hugh and Susanna Garvin, Nov., 1797.
James and Molley Giles, Apr. 8, 1784.
Jane D. (2d wife) and Moses Alley, ———.
Jenny and Josiah Jones, Oct. 19, 1799.
Maria and William Parker Merrill, about 1860. Res. Manchester, N. H.
Mary and Archibald Wear, Apr. 7, 1723-4 (?).
Mary and Frank Mussey, ———, in Maine.
Mary and Rev. John Morse, Feb. 2, 1837.
Mary and Robert Miller, Nov. 17, 1808.
May E. and Ransom Flanders, May 22, 1877.
Minnie and William Bachelder.
Myra F., 19, and James L. Brooks, 24, July 14, 1891.
Nelson and Sarah J. Melvin, Apr. 11, 1850.
Newell and Cylinda Flanders, Mar. 31, 1859.
Orietta J. and Elbridge A. Whidden, Nov. 11, 1876.
Robert and Betsey McMurphy, June, 1804.
Robert and Perses Garvin, Jan., 1823.
Salley and James Nutt, Feb. 24, 1791.
Sam N. 27, and Estella Goud, 20, Dec. 27, 1903.
Samuel and Mary Boyce, Feb. 20, 1773.
Sewall W. and Eliza J. Davis (Annis), Nov. 30, 1882.
Sophia and William Cheney, Aug. 3, 1811.
Stephen Moore and Susie Waters, Apr. 10, 1907. Res. California.
Susan and Elijah L. Watts, Apr. 19, 1859.
Susan and Joseph Steele, July, 1804.
Susanna and Burnice Thayer, ———.
Walter and Esther Watts, Dec. 19, 1861.
William and Wealthy Fling, Dec. 9, 1833.
William M. and Hannah M. Boyce, Apr. 1, 1847.
William Matthew and Hannah M. Whidden, Apr. 1, 1847.
Willis Prescott and Ida E. Reed, June 23, 1884. Res. Cal.

Boyd, Abby E. and Frank S. Crowell, Jan. 2, 1878.
Abigail and Henry March, July 4, 1839.
Calvin and Charlotte W. Shepard, Dec. 24, 1844.
Daniel M. and Hattie P. Mullins, May 7, 1884.
Emma D. and Fred A. Young, Nov. 26, 1885.
George Henry and Ella Alma Grimes, June 15, 1892.
Lettice and Samuel Marsh, Aug. 30, 1809.
Lucy Maria and Solon Southerd Gould, Feb. 5, 1874.
Maria and Horace P. Watts, Mar. 24, 1842.
Mary and John Woodburn, Jan. 2, 1725, by the Rev. Mr. McGregor.
Mary and Nathaniel Warner, Dec. 30, 1813.

Boyd, Mason and Mary H. Dodge, Jan. 2, 1851.
Patty and Amos Shipley, Dec. 23, 1802.
Robert and Polly Towns, Dec. 24, 1812.
Robert W. and Emeline T. Spalding, May 24, 1855.
William and Margaret Holmes, Feb. 21, 1809.
William and Martha Dickey, Jan. 30, 1816.

Boynton, Edward P. and Emeline Morrison, Apr. 7, 1868. Res. Cambridge, Mass.
Frank Morrison and Eleanor Patton Chew Grafton, June 29, 1909. Res. Newton, Mass.
Mrs. Lucy Jane and Rev. Daniel Goodwin, ———, Pepperell, Mass.
Martha and Rev. Daniel Goodwin, Aug. 24, 1846, Pepperell, Mass.

Bradford, Thomas S. and Emily Merrill, Nov. 16, 1843. Res. Derry, N. H.

Bradley, Jeremiah and Jane Holmes, Apr. 19, 1810.

Brady, L. P. and Angeline M. (Boyce) McKenney, 1869.

Brainerd, Rev. Timothy G. and Harriet Poor Cilley, 1841.

Breed, Joseph and Tryphena Bruce, Apr. 7, 1819.
Josiah and Jane Gregg, Nov. 14, 1819.

Bresnon, John Bernard, 23, and Eva Lupien, 23, Nov. 26, 1910.

Brewster, David and Margaret Wilson, July 12, 1809.
Mary and John Duncan, Nov. 5, 1835.

Brickett, Addie E. (dau. of Frank H. and Mary A. Pervere) and Alonzo H. Huntoon, May 23, 1904. Res. Bedford, N. H.
Birdie* and Nelson Mager.
Charles Franklin and Emily Spinney, Sept. 16, 1844.
Charles Henry and Maggie ———, 1871. Res. California.
Charlotte* and Harry Lawrence.
Delia W. and Aaron P. Hardy, May 5, 1842.
Emilie* and Augustus Jorick, 1892.
Mrs. Emily and Orriville A. Peabody, Dec. 17, 1873.
Frank Herbert and Mary A. Pervere, Sept. 8, 1872. Res. Bedford, N. H.
Henrietta* and Allen Pinyan.
Mabel H. (dau. of Frank H. and Mary A. Pervere) and Herbert A. Mack, Sept. 12, 1895. Res. Manchester, N. H.

Broadhead, Arthur B. and Nellie Louise Perkins, Feb. 29, 1903.

Brooks, Adelle, 26, and Horace C. Boyce, 36, Oct. 14, 1889.
Anna C., 17, and William H. Colby, 30, June 17, 1897. Res. Washington, N. H.

*Daughters of Charles Henry and Maggie Brickett. The husbands of these four sisters all died in California prior to 1909.

Brooks, Edward Q. F., 31 and Margaret Oliver, 24, June 3, 1908.
Edward W. and Anna M. Buck, at Reading, Mass., July 1, 1862.
James L., 24, and Myra F. Boyce, 19, July 14, 1891.
Sarah R. and Daniel W. Kimball, Nov. 28, 1883.

Brothers, Catherine and David R. Howe, Mar. 4, 1852.

Brown, Alberto C. and Persis T. Anderson, May 20, 1873.
Ammi and Elisabeth Wilkins, Dec. 2, 1819.
Ann Groves and Joseph C. Moore, 1823. (Spinner Joe.)
Arthur E., 27, and Marilla Jones, 27, Sept. 14, 1901.
Cora B. and John Quincy Magoon, Feb. 10, 1881.
David and Sally Senter, Dec. 7, 1815.
Ebenezer, Jr., and Mary Melvin, Sept. 3, 1822.
Frank V. and Hattie L. Spalding, Jan. 15, 1902. Res. Salisbury, Mass.
Jennie and Allen S. Manter, Aug. 6, 1885.
John S. and Phebe C. Hayes, Nov. 1, 1832.
Katie M., 20, and Alfred F. Manter, 24, Oct. 5, 1910.
Mary and Thomas Caldwell, Nov. 26, 1723, by Rev. Mr. McGregor.
Minnie A. and Lyman A. Conant, June 18, 1865.
Nathaniel H., Capt., and Mrs. Clara Corning (Rowell), 1873.
Nellie and Charles Spalding, Apr. 8, 1903. Res. Salisbury, Mass.
Nettie E. and George W. Miller, June 5, 1876.
Priscilla and Joshua Marsh, Dec. 24, 1819.
Robert A., 58, and Amanda R. Mullins, 55, Apr. 8, 1890.
Sarah Ann and John Alexander, Nov. 2, 1855.
William, 26, and Hattie F. Burrill, 32, Dec. 28, 1888.

Bruce, Nancy and David Worthen, Sept., 1813.
Nancy and Ezra Rhodes, Jr., Aug. 24, 1809.
Susan and David Gile, Mar. 20, 1810.
Tryphena and Joseph Breed, Apr. 7, 1819.

Bryant, Roxana and Alexander M. Corning, Feb. 9, 1854.

Buck, Ammi and Jane Adams, Mar. 15, 1836.
Anna M. and Edward W. Brooks, July 1, 1862.

Buckham, Eliza J. and Henry H. Parker, Feb. 22, 1872.

Buckingham, Joseph and Rebecca Nichols, Jan. 6, 1814.

Bullock, Miss ——— and David P. Barker, ———. Res. Manchester, N. H.
Thomas and Abigail J. Barker, Aug. 26, 1863.

Bunker, Ethel M. and Edward A. Parshley, May 27, 1907. Res Derry, N. H.

Bunton, Robert H. and Mary M. Pettengill, Apr. 12, 1853.
Burbank, Abraham and Prescilla Savory (1st wife), Feb. 4, 1807.
Abraham and Sarah C. Hasaltine (2nd wife), Aug. 31, 1858.
Harriet and David Coffin, Apr. 13, 1837.
John H. and Miss Clare, May, 1848.
Burgess, Jeffery and Mrs. Mary E. McGregor, ———.
Burlard, Irene A., 35, and George Whittondon, 65, Mar. 27, 1887.
Burnett, Emma J. and Frank A. Jenks, June 16, 1886.
Noah and Dorothy Hall, Sept. 4, 1823.
Perry C. and Nancy A. Gilcreast, June 10, 1873.
Burnham, Myra and William McKay, Nov. 19, 1902.
Burns, Daniel D. H., b. Mar. 20, 1831, and Lydia C. March. Dau., Ardella Cornelia, Sept. 9, 1851.
Ella Josephine and Ovlia William Ellery, Feb. 27, 1909, at Littleton, N. H.
Timothy and Eliza J. Langley, Mar. 11, 1867.
Burrill, Hattie F., 32, and William Brown, 26, Dec. 28, 1888.
Burroughs, Alfred and Mariah Corning, Dec. 31, 1840.
Alfred and Mary Melvin, ———. Res. Hudson, N. H.
John Hamilton and Helen M. Baker, ———. Res. Dunbarton, N. H.
Sarah E. and George F. Maxfield, Oct. 25, 1881, Bow, N. H.
William and Rachel Scarles, ———. Res. Hudson, N. H.
Butterfield, Dolly and Isaac Kent, Dec. 26, 1810.
John and Sarah Smith, Dec. 19, 1849.
Butterworth, William and Mary A. Way, Unity, N. H., Nov. 30, 1854. Golden wedding 1904, at Merrimack, N. H.
William A., 22, and Edith Belle Lowd, 18, Mar. 17, 1893.
Buttrick, Carrie A., 30, and Arthur R. White, 29, Nov. 21, 1906.
Cyrus O. and Eliza J. Dismore, Apr. 23, 1863.
Eva Mabel, 22, and Perley S. Robie, 31, Jan. 31, 1894.
Nathan and Catherine Witherspoon, Apr. 4, 1822.
Buxton, Rev. Edward and Louisa F. Pillsbury, Dec. 29, 1871.
Caldwell, Alexander and Loies Jones, Mar. 21, 1813.
Hannah and James Nichols (2nd wife), ———.
Henry J. and Abbie F. Greeley, Nov. 3, 1875.
Janet and William Eyers, Jr., June 21, 1727.
Jefferson and Nancy H. Dickey, Dec. 8, 1864.
Jefferson and Nancy Upton, ———.
Matty and Samuel Thompson, Dec., 1797.

Caldwell, Peggy and David Thompson, Jan., 1809.
Thomas and Lettuce Gregg, Dec. 30, 1807.
Thomas and Mary Browne, Nov. 26, 1723, by Rev. Mr. McGregor of Londonderry, N. H.
William and Hannah Giles, Feb. 1, 1816.

Call, Mary L., 20, and George E. Jackson, 28, Feb. 3, 1892.
Robert and Mehitable Gage Barker, Mar. 12, 1822.

Calwell, James and Lettus Murdock, Oct. 23, 1724, by the Rev. Mr. Adams of Newington, N. H.

Cammet (?), Polly and Edward Richardson, Oct. 26, 1797.

Campbell, Abner and Elisabeth Betton, Mar., 1805.
Alexander and Jane Carr, Apr. 18, 1775.
Amy and John Ela, Apr. 1, 1823.
Blanche C., 18, and William Russell Moore, 25, Jan. 1, 1895.
David and Nancy Giles, Jan. 21, 1823.
Eleanor and Joseph Scoby, Aug. 20, 1798.
Eugene L. and Martha Goss, Oct. 2, 1873.
Harriet and Asa Cummings, Dec. 17, 1834.
Harriet B. and Harvey S. Gould, Aug. 12, 1862.
Isabel and William Houston, Feb. 11, 1799.
Jane and Samuel Anderson, 2nd, Jan. 26, 1823.
John and Sarah Anderson, Feb. 7, 1814.
Luella A. and Roswell Annis, Dec. 10, 1874.
Luella Agnes, 18, and Frank Milton Coburn, Feb. 11, 1907.
Mary and Benjamin March, Dec. 31, 1801.
Matthew M. and Mary Jane S. Anderson, Nov. 30, 1876.
Maude E., 18, and Elbert O. Putnam, 21, Apr. 27, 1892.
Percy Anderson and Ada W. Mosher, Aug. 14, 1907.
Pliny M., 32, and Emma B. Abbott, 34, June 11, 1902. Res. Derry, N. H.
Sally and Lyman Cheney, Sept. 7, 1826.
Dea. Samuel and Lydia E. Crowell, Sept. 19, 1844. Res. Windham, N. H.
Sara Ann and David Woodburn Dickey, Oct. 9, 1815.
Dr. William J. and Charlotte A. M. Philbrick (2nd wife), Nov. 15, 1849.
Dr. William J. and Sarah E. Cutter (1st wife), ———.
William A. and Izetta G. Smith, June 8, 1887.

Caney, John L. and Mary March, Jan. 1, 1842.

Cargil, David and Mary Abernathy, June 21, 1722, by the Rev. Mr. McGregor.

Carleton, Hitty and John Ewins, Feb. 19, 1795.
James M. and Salley Corning, Sept. 11, 1834.
Moses and Ruth Watters, July, 1813.
William B. and Betsey Ann Webster, July 2, 1860.

Carpenter, Lena H., 18, and Joseph L. Galvin, 22, Dec. 19, 1906.

Carr, Clara B., 28, and Nelson H. Dickey, 29, Mar. 25, 1896.
David and ——.
Jane and Alexander Campbell, Apr. 18, 1775.
Jason and Julia Ann Bailey, Dec. 21, 1845.

Carroll, David and Lucretia Peabody, Feb. 14, 1804.
Herbert and Annie Elisabeth Wilkins, ——. Res. Concord, N. H.
Mary A., 45, and Andrew J. Aiken, 42, Oct. 19, 1903.

Cate, Almira T. and Christopher H. Bodwell, July 7, 1846.
Jonathan and Lydia T. Bailey, Jan. 21, 1837.
Mary and Reed C. March, Oct. 6, 1844.

Caverly, Hannah and William Davison, Aug. 4, 1803.
Lizzie and George E. Ela, Nov. 26, 1885.

Chamberlain, Susanna and David Young, Sept., 1797.

Chandler, Betsey and Isaac Atwood, Dec. 27, 1798.
Sally and Galen Arnot, Nov. 21, 1802.
Seth Carle and Mary Jane Chever, Sept. 28, 1837.

Chase, Addie A. and Phineas A. Reid, Jan. 14, 1886.
Alnora Maria and Lyman M. Stearns, June 5, 1878.
Anna and Charles Pelham, Jan. 1, 1850.
Clara Ella and Elijah Clinton Chase, Oct. 12, 1881.
Cora M., 20, and George A. Waugh, 24, June 6, 1888.
Daniel and Hannah Chase, ——.
Ebenezer and Sally Chase, Dec. 26, 1805.
Elijah Clinton and Clara Ella Chase, Oct. 12, 1881.
Elijah G. and Laura Esther Corning, Jan. 9, 1889.
Elisabeth M. and Frank J. Johnson, Feb. 21, 1880.
Emily A. and Joseph R. Clark, Aug. 27, 1862. Res. Derry, N. H.
Esther H. and Edwin Follansbee, Jan. 11, 1844.
Fred E., 21, and Allettie M. Young, 15, May 31, 1887.
George F. and Roxanna B. Annis, Mar. 8, 1843.
Hannah and John Weston, ——.
Harry E., 18, and Clara B. Weaver, 15, May 14, 1896.
Ida Cora and Charles Warren Webster, July 1, 1884.
Isaac and Elisabeth Pettengill, Mar. 20, 1843.
Jacob and Molly Hardy, ——.
Jacob and Rhoda Sargent, ——.
James Irving and Eliza H. Page, Sept. 28, 1873.
James Irving, 59, and Mary J. Chase, 86, Jan. 15, 1907.
James Irving, 61, and Marcia M. Senter, 67, July 7, 1909.
John and Mary Bacon, ——.
John Morrison and Hannah F. Clark, about 1851.

Chase, John Morrison, 70, and Susan (Clark) Page, 70, Jan. 23, 1897.
Jonas and Eunice Hardy, ———.
Julia Myra and William Clark, Mar. 2, 1874.
Lottie, Mrs., and Samuel E. Moody, Dec. 8, 1893 (2nd wife).
Lucy, 38, and Lewis Warren, 49, July 12, 1890.
Margaret and Addison Knight, Oct. 3, 1844.
Mary Ann and Charles R. Clark, Nov. 25, 1841.
Mary J., 86, and James I. Chase, 59, Jan. 15, 1907.
Nancy and Hugh Gault, Dec. 3, 1812.
Nathan P. and Mary Jane Whidden, Aug. 9, 1843.
Peaslee and Hannah King, May 14, 1838.
Polly and James Young, ———.
Robert R. and Elisabeth Harvell, Dec. 22, 1842.
Sally and Ebenezer Chase, Dec. 26, 1805.
Samuel and Betsey McCoy, ———.
Sarah and George Woods, Dec. 28, 1830.
Sarah M. and Rufus E. Drew, Mar. 3, 1842.
Simeon and Miss ——— Bixby, Dec. 20, 1807.
Thomas and Mary Plummer and Polly Giles.
Trueworthy D. and Nancy Maria Pettengill, May 19, 1853.
Trueworthy D., Jr., and Addie Ella Flood, June 12, 1895.
——— and John H. Burbank, May, 1848.

Cheney, Barnet H. and Hannah Hurd, Aug. 31, 1846.
Betsey and Savory Bancroft, Dec. 12, 1822.
David and Mahala Cobb, Feb. 22, 1816.
David F. and Sarah E. Page, Nov. 17, 1886.
Eliza and Elisha Taylor, Mar. 29, 1808.
Harriet and Simon Mullins, Dec. 23, 1847.
John E. and Sarah Kimball, June 25, 1848.
Joseph A. and Henrietta Flanders, Apr. 23, 1848.
Lyman and Sally Campbell, Sept. 7, 1826.
Mary and Horace Greeley (journalist), Mar. 18, 1837.
Sally and John Major, Jan. 20 or 28, 1802.
Thomas M. and Sally Alexander, Dec. 31, 1811.
William and Sophey Boyes, Aug. 3, 1811.

Chesley, Betsey and Samuel Veasey, Nov. 23, 1809.

Cheswell, Joshua B. and Elisabeth H. Plummer, Sept. 8, 1823.

Chever, Mary Jane and Seth Carle Chandler, Sept. 28, 1837.

Chick, Mabel V., 21, and Frank L. Thomas, 20, Nov. 16, 1904.

Chickering, Jacob and Sarah J. McMurphy, Nov. 26, 1835.

Childs, Israel and Margaret McDuffee, Apr. 8, 1832.
Mary L. and Willie E. Watts, Oct. 7, 1885.

Chipman, Caroline and Perry Poor, May 13, 1852.

Choate, Caroline and Jonathan McAllister, Nov. 11, 1852.
William and Mary B. Pinkerton, Dec. 27, 1815.

Chrispeen, George W. and Hannah Woodbury, Apr. 12, 1842.
George W. and Mrs. Betsey T. Putnam, May 13, 1875.
Jennie S. and Levi H. Corthell, Sept. 22, 1869.
Ruby and George Connor, Dec. 27, 1831.

Christie, Hattie F., 22, and George J. Bergeron, 22, May 21, 1906.

Christy, Catherine and John Moor, Mar. 9, 1797.

Church, Phebe A. and Charles E. Greeley, 1887.

Cilley, Harriet Poor and Rev. Timothy G. Brainerd, 1841.

Clagget, Clarissa and Samuel W. Abbott, Nov. 25, 1834.
Elisabeth and Daniel Moor, Dec. 31, 1833.
Littitia M. and Noah Johnson, Nov. 10, 1840.
Priscilla and George T. Wheeler, Nov. 10, 1840.

Clark, Aaron S. and Sarah M. Clark, Nov. 24, 1853.
Agnes and Samuel McKeen, Aug. 15, 1723.
Alice and John Moor, Jr., Apr. 4, 1822.
Alonzo F. and Esther W. Boyce, Apr. 23, 1859.
Anne and Robert Mack, Dec. 28, 1813.
Betsey and William Anderson, Feb. 24, 1801.
Catherine E., 27, and Samuel A. Gratto, 30, June 16, 1909.
Charles A. M. and Mary C. Noyes, July 3, 1879. (1st wife.)
Charles A. M. and Carrie Hazelton, Apr. 2, 1910. (2nd wife.)
Col. Charles R. and Mary Ann Chase, Nov. 25, 1841.
Eleanor and Moses Sargeant, Jan. 31, 1805.
Emri W. and Sarah J. Robie (Kimball), Dec.12, 1907. Res. Nashua, N. H.
Everett Newton, 30, and Josephine Augusta Baker, 22, May 29, 1909.
Flora F. and Charles D. Cross, Sept. 25, 1886.
George A. and Lizzie P. Towns, Nov. 8, 1860.
Hannah F. and John Morrison Chase, about 1851.
James and Elisabeth Willson, May 22, 1722, by Rev. Mr. McGregor.
James and Sally Downs, Oct. 19, 1799.
John and Sarah Taylor, Mar. 4, 1802.
John and Mary Taylor, Oct. 5, 1819.
Joseph R. and Emily A. Chase, Aug. 27, 1862. Res. Derry, N. H.
Joseph S. and Deborah E. Armstrong, Dec. 9, 1846.
Margarett and David Woodman, Feb. 16, 1773.
Margaret and Jonathan Merrill, July 2, 1822.
Marrianna P. and William H. Seaman, Aug. 27, 1873.
Mary and Levi Neal, May 26, 1796.

Clark, Mary and Robert Clark, Feb. 7, 1779.
Mary and Samuel McKeen, Apr. 25, 1799.
Mary E. and Augustus F. Hamlet, July 4, 1853.
Mary E. and David D. Richardson, Oct. 4, 1871.
Mathew and Elizebath Lindsey, Apr. 15, 1722, by Rev. Mr. McGregor.
Robert and Mary Clark, Feb. 7, 1799.
Reed P. and Elisabeth Perkins, Apr. 2, 1835.
Robert and Mary Cochran, Nov. 23, 1797.
Sally and Thomas Follansbee, Sept. 24, 1815.
Samuel and Emily J. Pettengill, Feb. 25, 1858. Golden wedding 1908.
Sarah M. and Aaron S. Clark, Nov. 24, 1853.
Susan and Orlando Page, ———.
Susan Page, 70, and John M. Chase, 70, Jan. 23, 1897.
William and Alice M. McIntire, Aug. 23, 1876.
William and Julia Myra Chase, Mar. 2, 1874.

Clay, Lyman H. and Mary Ann Martin, Dec. 25, 1844.
Walter and Sarah Danforth, Jan. 20, 1807.

Clements, Carrie E., 22, and George E. Currier, 25, June 16, 1888.

Clendenin, John H. and Betsey Humphrey, May 18, 1802.
Polly and David Steele, Jr., Mar. 29, 1810.

Clifford, Isaac P. and Carrie A. Woodburn, Nov. 10, 1858.

Clough, Mary C. and Charles S. Pillsbury, Dec. 24, 1863, in Warner, N. H.
Olive A. and David H. Young, Mar. 20, 1856. Res. Manchester, N. H.

Clyde, Ann and John Marshall, Dec. 27, 1798.
John and Hitty Sargent, Feb. 7, 1805.
Joseph, 3d, and Mehitable Griffin, Feb. 8, 1803.

Cobb, Betsey and Chandler Spofford, May 21, 1812.
Mahala and Daniel Cheney, Feb. 22, 1816.

Coburn, Betsey (2nd wife) and John Annis, Nov. 2, 1854.
Daniel Gage, Elder, and Roxanna Blodgett, Apr. 5, 1827.
Delilah (1st wife) and John Annis, Feb. 17, 1820.
Frank Milton and Luella Agnes Campbell, Feb. 11, 1907.
Gideon and Mary McFarlin, Feb. 4, 1807.
Isaac and Sally McGrath, Sept. 8, 1808.
Isaac, Jr., and Eliza Nesmith, Dec. 29, 1836.
Joel and Harriet Flanders, June 5, 1845.
Reuben and Abiah Adams Conant, Feb. 28, 1811.
Sally and John Morrison, Mar. 31, 1831.

Cochran, Andrew and Mary Rowan, Nov. 15, 1723, by Rev. Mr. McGregor.

Cochran, Ann and William Nickels, Oct. 20, 724, by Rev. Mr. Tapine of Newbury.
Betsey and John Adams, Feb. 26, 1789.
Christiane and Robert Cochran, Feb. 9, 1724–5, by Rev. Mr. McGregor.
Daniel and Polly Moor, May 17, 1798.
Elisabeth and Samuel Wilson, Dec. 29, 1801.
Isaac Wallace and Lucy (Woolner) Tilley, Jan. 13, 1873.
Jean and James Aiken, Oct. 26, 1725, by the Rev. Mr. McGregor.
Jean and John Moore, Apr. 2, 1723, by the Rev. Mr. McGregor.
John and Anna Wilson, Feb. 14, 1799.
John and Mary Machard, June 18, 1731, by Rev. Mr. Brown, Haverhill.
John and Sally Heath, Dec., 1806.
Margaret and Hugh Wilson, Feb. 6, 1723–4, by Rev. Mr. McGregor.
Margaret and Jessee Hall, Oct. 8, 1832.
Margaret and Nathaniel Aiken, Dec. 1, 1726, by Rev. Mr. McGregor.
Mary and Robert Clark, Nov. 23, 1797.
Mary Ann and Hugh Wilson, Dec., 1805.
Peggy and Samuel Cochran, Mar. 21, 1797.
Peter and Joan Wilson, Feb. 7, 1723–4.
Robert and Christiane Cochran, Feb. 9, 1724–5, by Rev. Mr. McGregor.
Samuel and Peggy Cochran, Mar. 21, 1797.
William and Elizabeth MacKertney, Nov. 26, 1730.

Coffin, Abigail and Jonathan Savory, Mar., 1836.
Betsey and Samuel Walace, May 3, 1810.
David and Harriet Burbank, Apr. 13, 1837.
Harriet A. and Moses Noyes Holmes, Jan. 22, 1857. Went West.
Priscilla H. and Dr. Daniel H. Batchelder, Jan. 15, 1852.
Sally and Samuel Aiken, 4th, May 26, 1814.
Sybil Ann and William Plummer, 2nd, Apr. 29, 1847.

Cogswell, Caroline P. and Elder John Dickey, July 3, 1851.

Colbath or **Calbreath**, Jean and William Nutt, May 29, 1723, by Rev. Mr. Symms of Bradford.

Colburn, Ann Maria and William B. Wellman, May 3, 1880.
Clarrissa and William G. Cross, 1785, in Hudson, N. H.
Edward S. and Addie J. Pettengill, 43, 1905. Res. Newton, Mass.
Hannah L. and Robert S. Smith, Oct. 27, 1850.

Colby, Albert P. and Charlotte M. Emerson, Nov. 2, 1847.
Daniel M. and Eliza A. Hall, June 5, 1865.
Daniel M. and Sarah Hall, May 4, 1848.
Doratha and Robert Taylor, Nov. 25, 1802.
Ebenezer and Sarah Philbrick, July 13, 1825.
Ella M. and James A. Barker, Mar. 17, 1862.
Emily and Samuel B. Flanders, Feb. 4, 1836.
Emerson and Mary Greeley, Aug. 28, 1817.
Emma J. and Charles G. Kimball, Oct. 14, 1880.
F. Alice, 23, and Edward L. Wing, 24, July 11, 1908.
Frank N. and Annie G. Bampas, Oct. 21, 1903.
Hannah W. and Edward Sampson, July 26, 1864.
Joseph and Rhoda Barret, Mar. 7, 1797.
Levi and Rachel Sargent, Nov. 16, 1797.
Lizzie A. and Albert H. Sides, Jan. 13, 1887. Res. Portsmouth, N. H.
Mary and Perley Wallace, Apr. 10, 1838.
Moses F. and Sarah Lane Robinson, June 3, 1874.
Moses F. and Viola C. Smith, Dec. 27, 1908.
Washington and Arvilla Nesmith, Nov. 1, 1855.
William H., 30, and Anna C. Brooks, 17, June 17, 1897. Res. Washington, N. H.
William W. and Sarah Freste (?), Feb. 24, 1824.

Colwell, Matty and Samuel Thompson, Dec., 1797.

Combs, Mary A. (Perham) and Elbridge W. Peabody, May 19, 1859.

Conant, Abiah Adams and Reuben Coburn, Feb. 28, 1811.
Annie and L. Foster Morse, May 2, 1861.
Annie F. and Frank A. Boyce, Aug. 27, 1881.
Antoinette H. and Edward P. Moore, Nov. 11, 1854.
Charles E. and Georgie F. Spinney, Oct. 21, 1866.
Clara F. and Thomas Stephenson, July, 1878.
Henry and Mary F. Hovey, June 11, 1856.
Julia M. and William Pecker, June 18, 1884.
Lyman A. and Minnie A. Brown, June 18, 1865.
Nathaniel and Rhody March, Aug. 17, 1798.
Sarah and Isaac Crowell, Dec. 2, 1819.
Sarah A. and Benjamin L. Willey, July 5, 1865.
Selwyn S. and Sarah Valler, Jan., 1878.
Sibil and Simon Howard, July 24, 1840.
William H. and Rachel Watts Garvin, June 29, 1835.

Conner, George and Ruby Chrispeen, Dec. 27, 1831.
John H. and Ella F. Benson, Nov. 30, 1876.
Nathan and Betsey Dana, Apr. 11, 1839.

Cook, Marion R., 26, and Clarence O. Watts, 29, Sept. 16, 1903. (2nd wife.)

Cook, Olive S., 31, and John H. S. Goodwin, 50, May 18, 1910. (2nd wife.)

Cooms, Mary Ann and Rev. Elbridge G. Perham, Nov. 13, 1854.

Corbett, Mattie E., 22, and William O. Morrison, 22, Dec. 19, 1891.

Corcoran, Elsie and Ephraim Spalding, Dec. 14, 1896.

Corey, Emma F., 17, and Silas E. Lincoln, 28, Sept. 26, 1888.

Corliss, Alonzo and Sarah A. Greeley, Mar. 26, 1874.
Harry C., 20, and Marian B. Nugent, 20, Apr. 27, 1904.

Corning, Alexander M. and Roxana Bryant, Feb. 9, 1854.
Alfred A. and Clara J. Rowell, about 1865.
Benjamin and Polly Barker, Sept. 17, 1807.
Carrie and George E. Payne, Aug. 24, 1876.
Clara Belle, 21, and Frank A. Nesmith, 23, Dec. 22, 1889.
Clarrissa and Benjamin Barker, Mar. 30, 1830.
Daniel and Anny McKnight, Nov. 8, 1798.
Daniel L. and Mary Ann Manter, July 3, 1861.
Elisabeth and John Anderson, May 22, 1834.
Ernest E., 20, and H. Josephine Corning, 20, July 13, 1890.
Fred P., 29, and Nellie Imogene Crowell, 29, Mar. 31, 1897.
Freeman and Esther White, Dec. 29, 1829.
Freeman and Laura Ann Blaisdell, Oct. 11, 1846.
Georgie, 22, and Ernest M. Watts, 22, Dec. 21, 1887.
Gilman and Lucinda D. Dow, Dec. 28, 1828.
H. Josephine, 20, and Ernest E. Corning, 20, July 13, 1890.
Hannah B. and William P. Corning, Aug. 19, 1860.
Harriet M. and Manas Harvey, Sept. 1, 1853.
Jennie S. and David F. Perkins, Feb. 13, 1884.
John Anderson and Celinda P. Parker, Dec., 1861.
John C. and Elisabeth Nesmith, June 12, 1817.
Judith and Asa Perley, June 4, 1817.
Laura E., 21, and Elijah G. Chase, 30, Jan. 9, 1889.
Louisa and Nelson Hemphill, Nov. 12, 1840.
Lucy A., 18, and William B. Walsh, 22, May 16, 1892.
Mariah and Alfred Burroughs, Dec. 31, 1840.
Martha and Joseph Leach, Dec. 25, 1815.
Mary E. and Joshua F. Wheeler, Oct. 9, 1863.
Mary E. and Warren Corning, ——. (1st husband.)
Miriam and James Watts, Jr., Feb. 17, 1820.
Mrs. Mary E. and David McGregor, Dec. 14, 1886. (2nd husband.)
Mrs. Mary E. McGregor and Jeffery Burgess, ——. (3d husband.)
Nathan, 3d, and Susan Corning, Nov. 17, 1836.

Corning, Nathaniel and Hannah Boys, 1797.
Peter and Lydia Read, Oct. 22, 1829.
Polly and James Nesmith, Feb. 1, 1816.
Sally and James M. Carlton, Sept. 11, 1834.
Samuel and Eva Annis, June 17, 1886.
Sarah and James Simmons, July 23, 1837.
Sarah Elisabeth and William B. Wetherbee, May 3, 1862.
Susan and Nathan Corning, 3d, Nov. 17, 1836.
Susan W. and George Aiken, Dec. 1, 1838.
Sylvester R. and Sarah J. Currier, Feb. 22, 1866.
Warren and Miss Mary E. Babb, ———. Res. Manchester, N. H.
William P. and Hannah B. Corning, Aug. 19, 1860.

Corthell, Albin, 49, and Abbie Adella Goodwin, 31, Dec. 28, 1892.
Levi H. and Jennie S. Chrispeen, Sept. 22, 1869.
Osmond E. E., 29, and Florence J. Boles, 18, Sept. 25, 1901.

Corwin, Caroline Laura and Harvey Perley Hood, 1850, at Tunbridge, Vt. Res. Derry, N. H.

Cousens, Hester C., 22, and George A. Hall, 24, July 4, 1894.

Cowdrey, Joseph S. and Jennie E. Fogg, June 27, 1876.

Cox, Almeda Rebecca, 25, and Alfred E. Blackburn, 29, June 21, 1905.

Craige, Agnes and Robert Anderson, 1748.
David and Sarah Currier, June 23, 1785.
Jennie and David McAllister, Oct. 20, 1797.
Jean and Thomas Anderson, 1755.

Crawford, Jennie and Archibald Cunningham, June 13, 1799.

Cresey, Joseph and Betsey Eastman, Sept., 1807.
Mary and Joseph Hobbs, June 13, 1799.

Cressey, Abbie Frances (Gilcreast) and Benjamin Francis Ayer, Oct. 13, 1888.

Cristy, Thomas and Sarah Bennett, Dec. 5, 1749.

Crocker, Margaret and Williard Holbrook, June 22, 1819.
Polly and Branch Sampson, Dec. 25, 1798.

Crombie or **Crumey,** John and Jean Rankin, Nov. 17, 1721, by the Rev. Mr. McGregor.

Crosby, Sarah and Irving J. Rowell (1st wife). Res. Pepperell, Mass.

Cross, Alice M. and James M. Howe, 29, Apr. 13, 1887.
Amos and Betsey Thompson, July 1, 1802.
Arthur H., 22, and Lelia M. Fiske, 22, Oct. 23, 1895.
Charles D. and Flora F. Clark, Sept. 25, 1886.

Cross, Hiram N. 34, and Ernestine E. Nugent, 36, June 14, 1909.
Huldah P. and Joseph Kidder, Mar. 21, 1813.
Nancy H. and George W. Farley, Feb. 17, 1848.
William G. and Clarrissa Colburn, 1875, in Hudson, N. H.

Crowell, Charles A., 21, and Mary L. Schwartz, 19, Dec. 24, 1889.
Daniel D. and Eliza J. Bancroft, Apr. 26, 1849.
David and Betsey Towns, Nov. 17, 1803.
David and Martha Jane McNeil, Mar. 18, 1841.
Elisabeth E. and Charles Spear, June 30, 1841.
Emily and William Platt, Mar. 25, 1883.
Frank S. and Abbie E. Boyd, Jan. 2, 1878.
Hattie E. and James K. Floyd, June 8, 1865.
Henry and Judith C. Plummer, Oct. 3, 1850.
Henry C. and Margaret Watts, Oct. 10, 1838.
Isaac and Sarah Conant, Dec. 2, 1819.
John M. and Sarah Grant, May, 1866.
Lizzie H. and Stephen A. Estey, Aug. 11, 1886.
Lydia E. and Dea. Samuel Campbell, Sept. 19, 1844. Res. Windham, N. H.
Martha S. and William S. Pillsbury, Apr. 15, 1856. Golden wedding 1906.
Mary E., 22, and Daniel McQuesten, 25, Oct. 5, 1892.
Nellie Imogene, 29, and Fred Peter Corning, 29, Mar. 31, 1897.
Peter and Harriet Hardy, Feb. 1, 1821.
Peter and Orra Martin, Dec. 23, 1817.
Rose J., 43, and Charles A. Tenney, 43, Apr. 7, 1895.
Sarah and John E. Quimby, Oct. 6, 1880.
Sarah and Justin Spear, Oct. 15, 1834.
Sarah A. and William S. Pillsbury, May 8, 1854.
Thomas W. and Ruth E. Tenney, June 11, 1906. Res. Derry, N. H.
William H. and Almira A. Parker, Sept. 12, 1866.

Crowningshield, Harriet and Francis Manter, Feb. 28, 1820.
Sophia and James Platts, Mar. 11, 1823.

Crumey (see Crombie).

Cummings, Asa and Harriet Campbell, Dec. 17, 1834.
Ephraim and Rhoda Senter, Oct. 27, 1803.

Cunningham, Archibald and Jennie Crawford, June 13, 1799.
Marian and Elijah Dwinell, Apr., 1797.
Mary and Samuel Nickels, Oct. 24, 1799.

Currier, George E., 25, and Carrie E. Clements, 22, June 16, 1888.
Joshua P. and Esther Jane Harvey, Feb. 14, 1839.

Currier, Polly and Michael Dollahuntee, Sept. 22, 1801.
Sarah and David Craige, June 23, 1785.
Sarah J. and Sylvester R. Corning, Feb. 22, 1866.

Cutler, Hiram and Lucinda Miller, Jan. 1, 1876.

Cutter, Antoinette De Grace and Alfred B. Knight, Sept. 12, 1865.

Dailey, Lillian J., 22, and Sedley H. Lowd, 19, Mar. 15, 1898.

Dana, Betsey and Nathan Conner, Apr. 11, 1839.
Jonathan and ——— Corning (1st wife), ———.
Jonathan and Abbie R. Reed (Hazen), 1880 (2nd wife).

Danforth, Eliphalet and Sally Hovey, Oct. 8, 1808.
Eliza and James M. H. Dow, Jan. 22, 1834.
Jennie and Frank Walch, July 5, 1868.
Lucy and Daniel Warner, Dec. 30, 1807.
Sarah and Walter Clay, Jan. 20, 1807.
Simon and Nancy Anderson, Mar. 10, 1807.
William and Lucy Pollard, Oct. 10, 1779.
William and Sarah Smith, May 9, 1802.

Darrah, John and Easter Holt, Sept. 25, 1810.
Mary and Thomas Killicut, Sept. 3, 1822.

Dart, Ann and Alfred D. Greeley, 1850.

Davenport, Eddie H., 36, and Harriet Julia Nevins, 28, June 27, 1906.

Davidson, Margaret and Sampson Marsh, Apr. 23, 1812.
Sarah and Jonathan Alexander, Mar. 17, 1803.
William and Hannah Caverly, Aug. 4, 1803.

Davis, Christopher C. and Betsey C. Towns, Dec. 21, 1843.
Daniel and Sally Robinson, Feb. 7, 1805.
Edith H., 18, and Ulysses G. Pillsbury, 20, Nov. 25, 1896.
Eliza J. and Sewall W. Boyce, Nov. 30, 1882.
Eunice and Reuben Sargent, July 13, 1813.
Frank W. and Eliza J. Annis, Nov. 29, 1871.
Harriet N. and Rev. Elijah R. Wilkins, June 19, 1845, at Derry, N. H.
John F. and Harriet Griffin, Sept. 25, 1861.
Louisa J. and Samuel Woodbury, July 12, 1837.

Davison, Viola G., 16, and Osborn L. West, 27, Sept. 25, 1909.

Day, Ella L., 19, and Frank C. Maxfield, 26, June 22, 1910.
John S. and Sarah G. Towns, May 11, 1837.
Elder Joseph L. and Laura Gould, ———, Hampden, Me.
Elder Joseph L. and Mrs. Susan A. Gove Angell, ———.

Deane, Polly and Ebenezer Fisher, Aug. 20, 1797.

Dearborn, Ella and Edward O. Dodge, Nov. 2, 1871.

Delaney, Carrie and Haverlin Thayer, ———, at Derry, N. H.
Demeritt, Frank J. and Isabel D. McGregor, Sept. 26, 1883.
Densmore, Anna M. and John P. Payne, July 2, 1876.
Mary and Frank W. Parkhurst, July 7, 1881.
Dickerman, Willis, 37, and Alice Nana Johnson, 25, Sept. 5, 1907.
Dickey, Adam and Jane Nahor, Dec. 26, 1765.
Claradilla and Harris Towle, Nov. 8, 1887.
Claradilla and William L. Lord, Dec. 11, 1863.
David and Isabell McGlaughlan, Feb. 1, 1724, by Rev. Mr. McGregor.
David and Jenett Gregg, Feb. 21, 1833.
David Woodburn and Sarah Ann Campbell, Oct. 9, 1815.
Elias and Rosanna McDonald (sometimes McDaniel), Feb. 7, 1743.
George L., 24, and Florence E. Richardson, 20, May 28, 1906.
George W. and Mrs. Sarah A. Dickey, Mar. 17, 1857, in Derry, N. H.
Hannah and Robinson Bartewell, Nov. 26, 1833.
Isaac S. and Margaret J. Pettengill, Dec. 20, 1842.
Isaac S. and Mary J. McQuesten, Oct. 19, 1893, at Manchester, N. H.
Jane and Josiah Sleeper, Apr. 4, 1833.
Jane and Samuel Gregg, Dec. 29, 1812.
Elder John and Caroline Parker Cogswell, July 3, 1851.
Elder John and Susan Ellen Hill, June 10, 1891. Res. Leominster, Mass.
John and Peggy (or Margaret) Woodburn, Apr. 2, 1805.
John and Rhoda Varnum, Nov. 12, 1795.
Joseph, Jr., and Elisabeth White, Apr. 20, 1854.
Joseph and Fanny D. Montgomery, Apr. 7, 1813. Golden wedding 1863.
Lyman A. and Emma A. Libbie, July, 1864.
Lyman A. and Mrs. Harrietta Neal, Apr. 22, 1908.
Lyman A. and Lana S. George, Dec., 1879.
Margaret and Franklin Perham, Jan. 24, 1837.
Martha and William Boyd, Jan. 30, 1816.
Mary and Edward Ela, Mar. 15, 1815.
Mary J. and Albert Tenney, May 20, 1875.
Nancy H. and Jefferson Caldwell, Dec. 8, 1864.
Nancy M. and Sampson Annis, Oct. 18, 1849.
Nelson H., 29, and Clara B. Carr, 28, Mar. 25, 1896. Res. in Derry N. H.
Phineas W. and Ella J. Moore, June 6, 1877. Res. Manchester, N. H.

Dickey, Rebecca and John Shipley, Feb. 25, 1834.
Robert and Hannah Woodburn, June 10, 1776.
Robert and Jenney Morrison, May 24, 1821.
Robert and Mary Ann Nancy Anderson, Apr. 30, 1837.
Mrs. Sarah A. and George W. Dickey, Mar. 17, 1857. Res. Derry, N. H.
Samuel and Martha Taylor, 1732.
Samuel and Nancy Humphrey, Feb. 26, 1805.
Susan and John White, Mar. 25, 1817.
Susannah and Robinson Bartwell, Jan. 28, 1841.
William G., 34, and Amy Mabel Alexander, 28, July 11, 1905. Res. Derry, N. H.
William M. and Ester Perham, Feb. 15, 1798.
Zoe Ann and Charles Jaqueth Flanders, Mar. 15, 1848.

Dillingham, E. V. and Sarah G. Wallace, Nov. 23, 1871.

Dimond, Rebecca and Amos Jones, Mar. 1, 1798.

Dinsmore, Fanny and Samuel Pope, Dec., 1806.
James and Mary Anderson, Dec. 3, 1772.
Mary and Joseph Parker, Feb. 25, 1797.
Robert and Mary Anderson, Dec. 31, 1801.
Samuel and Maria Boyd Reid, June 19, 1798.
William and Betsey Barnett, Apr. 9, 1807.

Dismore, Abraham and Hannah Nichols, Feb. 23, 1809.
Eliza and David Jackson, July 1, 1828.
Eliza J. and Cyrus O. Buttrick, Apr. 23, 1863.
Sarah and Ensign Nichols, July 8, 1819.

Dix, Elisabeth and James Annis, Mar. 6, 1837.

Doak, Betsey and John Orne, Feb. 13, 1803.

Dodge, Abby R. and Roger M. Rollins, Oct. 31, 1848.
Caleb and Thersy Garvin, Nov., 1815.
Edward O. and Ella Dearborn, Nov. 2, 1871.
Lydia and Alexander McMurphy, Dec. 28, 1786.
Mary A. and Elder John W. Greeley, May 2, 1844.
Mary H. and Mason Boyd, Jan. 2, 1851.
Mehitable and Belcher Manter, Jan. 24, 1811.
Parker and Marey Little, Jan. 4, 1770.

Doe, Elisabeth Walker and John Charles Barker, Mar. 24, 1903.

Doherty, Charles P., 23, and Nellie A. Robie, 19, Dec. 25, 1894.
Civilla C., 26, and William A. Osborne, 25, Jan. 2, 1897.
James T., 24, and Syvella C. Towne, 18, June 18, 1889.

Dolan, Martha A. and Josiah Sanborn, Apr. 29, 1863.
Martha A. (Sanborn) and John McClary, Mar. 9, 1884.

Dollahuntee, Michael and Polly Currier, Sept. 22, 1801.

Donahue, Hannah and Thomas Sargent, Apr. 11, 1805.

Dooley, George N., 36, and Ella W. Hadley, 24, Jan. 17, 1907.
James and Martha J. Goodwin, July 10, 1855.

Dow, Emma (2nd wife) and Irving J. Rowell. Res. Pepperell, Mass.
Esther and George Aiken, Aug. 20, 1849.
Isabella J. and Clinton J. Farley, Apr. 3, 1864.
Jacob and Esther Smith, June 14, 1838.
James M. H. and Eliza H. Danforth, Jan. 22, 1834.
John Clark and Laura Z. Rowell, July 1, 1875.
Lucinda D. and Gilman Corning, Dec. 28, 1828.
Samuel and Mary Watts, Dec. 28, 1823.
Zillah and Alexander Spinney, Dec., 1806.

Downer, Annie M. and Alexander Melrose, Oct. 23, 1889. Goffe's Falls, N. H.

Downs, Sally and James Clark, Oct. 19, 1799.

Drake, Emma R. and James Warren Whidden, Dec. 19, 1883. Res. Haverhill, Mass.

Drew, Lucy J. and George B. McQuesten (3d wife).
Rufus E. and Sarah M. Chase, Mar. 3, 1842.
Sarah and Joseph D. Vickery, July 3, 1845.

Drysdale, Margaret and Myron Isaac Evans, June 11, 1898.

Dudley, Emma H., 28, and William H. Ramsey, 40, Nov. 29, 1888.

Duffield, Grace, 27, and George Olwin Garvin, 28, Sept. 25, 1908.

Duncan, Hannah and David Kar, Mar., 1801.
Hannah and Thomas Patterson, Apr. 30, 1818.
John and Mary Brewster, Nov. 5, 1835.
Margaret and William Adams, ———.
Mary and John Jackson, Oct. 8, 1822.
Peggy and William Adams, Mar. 14, 1799.
Rachel and Major John Pinkerton, ——— (1st wife).
William and Elisabeth Patterson, Nov. 17, 1842.
William and Mary McMurphy, Nov. 19, 1801.
William and Naomi McMurphy, Apr. 21, 1836.

Dunkley, Samuel and Hannah Black, Mar. 7, 1820.

Dunton, George S. and Ella M. French, May 19, 1880, at Georgia, Vt.

Durant, George W. and Anna F. Kimball, Dec. 31, 1867.
Mary C., 17, and Edgar C. Annis, 23, Feb. 22, 1892.

Durrah, Mary and Thomas Killicut, Sept. 3, 1822.

Dustin, Abigail and John Hovey, 1820–21.
Betsey and Stephen Poor, Nov. 24, 1795.
Edith Louise, 26, and Ralph W. Wright, 25, June 11, 1906.
Hannah and Moses Dustin, Sept. 24, 1801.
Moses and Hannah Dustin, Sept. 24, 1801.
Moses, Jr., and Elisabeth Anderson, Dec. 25, 1817.
Ruth and Francis Smiley, June 6, 1822.
Ruth and Simeon Dustin, July 4, 1819.
Sarah and John C. Rowell, May 26, 1853.
Simeon and Ruth Dustin, July 4, 1819.

Dwinell, Elijah and Emelia Eastman, Feb. 13, 1811.
Elijah and Marion Cunningham, Apr., 1797.
Eunice and Moses Towns, Nov. 17, 1797.
John and Debby Plummer, Nov. 25, 1806.
Mehitable and James Manter, July 1, 1817.
Mehitable and Samuel Lovejoy, Nov. 18, 1822.
Polly and Henry March, Dec., 1799.

Eastman, Betsey and Joseph Cresey, Sept., 1807.
Dustimony and John Greeley, June 16, 1809.
Emelia and Elijah Dwinell, Feb. 13, 1811.

Eaton, George E. and Etta L. Farley, Nov. 17, 1880.
Hannah and John D. Patterson, Sept. 24, 1846.
Joseph and Rhoda A. Weed, Nov. 29, 1865.
William J., 23, and Mabel G. Spear, 18, May 20, 1890.

Eaves, Teresa J. and Henry J. Holt, July 12, 1880.

Eayers (see Ayers).

Edwards, William H. and Maria A. Slate, July 4, 1855.

Ela, David Willis and Martha E. Lovejoy, Feb. 7, 1883.
Edward and Mary Dickey, Mar. 15, 1815.
Edward and Sally Page, Dec. 27, 1810.
Edward P. and Isabel Gregg, Nov. 30, 1843.
George E. and Lizzie Caverly, Nov. 25, 1885.
George E. and Mary E. N. Low, Sept. 1, 1904.
John and Amy Campbell, Apr. 1, 1823.
Louisa and Richard Kent, Sept. 11, 1810.

Elder, Margaret and Benjamin Wilsone, June 4, 1725, by Rev. Mr. McGregor.

Elkins, John and Sally Nickels, Sept., 1798.

Ellery, Ovlia, William, and Ella Josephine Burns, Feb. 27, 1909, at Littleton, N. H.

Elliot, George and Adeline Shatell, Nov. 30, 1854.

Ellis, Eunice B. and A. A. Hanaford, Nov. 28, 1867.
George E., 24, and Annie M. Hartford, 20, May 1, 1893.
Ossian P. and Mary E. Woodbury, Oct. 14, 1891.

Emerson, Charlotte M. and Albert P. Colby, Nov. 2, 1847.
Edna and Edward Young, Dec. 10, 1828.
Jesse O. C. and Anna J. Owen, Mar. 7, 1860.
Jonathan and Mary McGregor, June 1, 1848.
Susan D. and Thomas B. Platts, May 12, 1856.
William P. and Jane McDuffee (1st wife), Auburn, N. H.
William P. and Mary Ann Manter (2nd wife), July 8, 1848.

Emery, Frank E. and Emma D. Seaward, Dec. 22, 1878.
Jacob and Betsey March, Mar. 9, 1820.
John R. and Esther White, June 3, 1852.
Rebecca and Joseph Nickels, Nov. 12, 1813.
Thomas W. and Sarah Vickery, 1874.
Zenora and Austin A. M. Atwood, ———.

Emmons, Judith and Joseph D. Thomas, Mar. 14, 1848, in Maine.

Estey, Daniel and Rebecca Hawkins, May 18, 1835.
Eliza and Charles E. Thorne, Oct. 7, 1880.
Harriet E. (1st wife) and Samuel Woodbury, Dec. 3, 1858.
Hannah J. and Samuel Aiken, Aug. 6, 1868.
John Crowell and Hattie L. Evans, Nov. 28, 1867. Res. California.
Mrs. Hannah J. (Woodbury), 45, and Reuben K. Pratt, 46, Oct. 30, 1891.
Sally and John Alexander, Nov. 27, 1827. Golden wedding 1877.
Stephen A. and Lizzie H. Crowell, Aug. 11, 1886.
Stephen A. and Mary A. Remington, Nov. 29, 1877.

Evans, Arthur Loren and Anna Mabel Wing, Oct. 26, 1893.
Ella M. and Walter D. Reed, Oct. 1, 1871.
Emma F. and Charles H. Fellows, Aug. 23, 1884.
Hattie L. and John Crowell Estey, Nov. 28, 1867. Res. Oakland, Cal.
Oliver D. and Augusta W. Blodgett, Apr. 18, 1866.
Marietta and Henry C. Fellows, July 4, 1871.
Myron Isaac and Margaret Drysdale, June 11, 1898.

Everton, James and Anne Harriman, Nov., 1806.
Martha and Asa B. Stratton, Nov. 29, 1842.
Mary Ann and Jonathan Webster, Oct. 25, 1831.

Ewins, John and Hitty Carleton, Feb. 19, 1795.

Eyers (see Ayers).

Fall, Charles D. and Mary A. Barker, Apr. 7, 1874.

Farley, Clinton J. and Isabella J. Dow, Apr. 3, 1864.
Etta L. and George E. Eaton, Nov. 17, 1880.
George W. and Nancy H. Cross, Feb. 17, 1848.
Gilman and Sophia Barker, Apr. 29, 1832.
Mary and William A. Flint, Dec. 22, 1835.

Favor, Frank W. and Emily J. Whittle, Dec. 24, 1884.

Farnum, John and Ollive Hibbard, Apr. 15, 1813.

Farwell, Darius A. and Susan Plumer, Dec. 14, 1848.

Fellows, Alice H. and Ensign Woods, 1861.
Charles H. and Emma F. Evans, Aug. 23, 1884.
Henry C. and Marietta Evans, July 4, 1871.

Field, Sarah C. and Capt. George S. Garvin, Dec. 22, 1897 (2nd wife).

Fisher, Ebenezer and Polly Deane, Aug. 20, 1797.
Nathaniel Deane and Almira Gage, Aug. 3, 1835.
Thomas and Mary Rollins, Nov. 2, 1810.

Fisk, Mark and Eleanor Wilson, Apr. 2, 1801.
Dea. Moses and Abigail Platts (2nd wife), Oct. 10, 1839.
Dea. Moses and Susan Platts (1st wife). Res. Fort Covington, N. Y.
Sarah and John Hutchins, Feb. 11, 1800.

Fiske, Amy P. and Albert Reed Bacon, June 18, 1907.
Lelia M., 22, and Arthur H. Cross, 22, Oct. 23, 1895.
Lulu Christine and George Forrest Kimball, Nov. 13, 1898. Res. Manchester, N. H.

Fitts, Alice J., 21, and Herman L. Watts, 20, Dec. 25, 1897.

Fitz, Hannah and Ebenezer Stickney, Mar. 2, 1809.
Nabby and James Miltmore, Oct. 22, 1799.

Fitzgerald, Ida May, 20, and Fred Lewis Bancroft, 24, Sept. 24, 1906.

Flanders, Charles J. and Myra Sanborn, Oct. 12, 1862.
Charles Jaqueth and Zoe Ann Dickey, Mar. 15, 1848.
Charles S. and Miss Emma Twiss, 1870.
Clara L. M. and Amos H. Messer, Oct. 28, 1868.
Cylinda and Newell Boyce, Mar. 31, 1859.
Daniel P. and Hannah J. Annis, Nov. 25, 1847.
Emily Josephine and Frank W. Favor, Dec. 24, 1884.
Emily Josephine and John Wesley Whittle, Jan. 1, 1864. Res. Malden, Mass.
Frank B. and Sarah A. Livengood, Oct. 19, 1881.
Harriet and Joel Coburn, June 5, 1845.
Henrietta and Joseph A. Cheney, Apr. 23, 1848.
Mrs. Lucy B. and Daniel Watts, Feb. 6, 1855.
Mark B. and Etta P. Hurlburt, Aug. 1, 1891, in Boston, Mass. Res. Manchester, N. H.
Martha J. and Caleb M. Watts, about 1848 (1st wife).
May E., 47, and Charles J. Hobbs, 49, Oct. 12, 1905.
Ransom and May E. Boyce, May 22, 1877.
Reuben W. and Josephine M. Harvey, Jan. 1, 1871. Res. Manchester, N. H.

Flanders, Reuben W. and Priscilla W. Sawyer, Mar. 13, 1862.
Samuel B. and Emily Colby, Feb. 4, 1836, in Bow, N. H. Res. in Londonderry, N. H.
William and Lucy F. Annis, Apr. 30, 1850.

Flannigan, Jennie, 22, and Charles H. Fling, 24, June 24, 1891.

Fletcher, Edna E. and Frederick Hill, Oct. 27, 1880.
Irena and Lyman A. Hamblett, Mar. 25, 1861.

Fling, Charles H. and Jennie Flannigan, June 24, 1891.
Daniel W. and Asenath Patten, Dec. 25, 1844. Res. Manchester, N. H.
Fannie M. and Daniel G. Annis, Dec. 1, 1886.
John P. and Nellie Moore, May 5, 1884, at Kansas, Mo. Res. Auburn, N. H.
John W. and Mary Ann Goodwin, Jan. 2, 1857.
John W. and Miss Colby, ——— (1st wife).
Martha E. and George A. Watts, Oct. 18, 1883.
Minnie M. and Elwin C. Peabody, Oct. 14, 1885.
Rachel and Joel Page, Nov. 19, 1833.
Wealthy and William Boyce, Dec. 9, 1833.

Flint, Martha and William G. Hardy, May 21, 1861.
William A. and Mary Farley, Dec. 22, 1835.

Flood, Addie Ella and Trueworthy D. Chase, Jr., June 12, 1895.

Floyd, James K. and Hattie E. Crowell, June 8, 1865.
W. Claud, 22, and Ada B. Wells, 16, Mar. 24, 1888.

Fogg, Jennie E. and Joseph S. Cowdrey, June 27, 1876.

Follansbee, Edwin and Esther H. Chase, Jan. 11, 1844.
Thomas and Sally Clark, Sept. 24, 1815.
Walter B. and Hannah C. Webster, Jan., 1874, at West Newbury, Mass.

Forsaith, Catherine R. and Amos H. McGregor, June 1, 1848.

Fortness, Elisabeth and Benjamin Griffin, Dec. 7, 1842.

Foss, Angeline and Abraham Mitchell, Mar. 23, 1867.

Foster, Charles W. and Mary Delia McGregor, Oct. 21, 1890.
Obediah R. and Harriet E. Smith, 1843.
Phineas and Huldah Sampson, Nov. 21, 1833.
Waldo and Fannie J. Holmes, Sept. 11, 1872.

Fowler, Nancy and James Nichols, about 1788.

Fox, Mary Grace and Samuel Richardson, Dec. 25, 1880. Res. Auburn, N. H.

Foye, E. Elmer and Lulu B. Wilson, Sept. 21, 1893. Res. Everett, Mass.

Francis, Edward, 40, and Frances H. Kimball, 53, Oct. 26, 1908.

Frasner, Ben L. and Clara Jane Barker, Dec. 21, 1892. Res. Salisbury, N. H.

Freeman, Leonard A. and Emma K. Spinney, Nov. 19, 1878.
Moses H. and Jane L. Lewis, Apr. 13, 1843.

French, Clarrissa and David K. Batcheler, Jan. 16, 1880.
Ella M. and George S. Dunton, May 19, 1880, in Georgia, Vt. Res. Londonderry, N. H.
Elvira E. and George W. Annis, June 29, 1859.
Evalena W., 29, and Charles W. Anderson, 29, June 4, 1898.
Irene and Moses D. Stokes, Feb. 11, 1830.
William and Olive Merrill, June 23, 1808.

Frete, Sally and Nathaniel Giles, June, 1804.

Freste (?), Sarah and William W. Colby, Feb. 24, 1824.

Frost, Charles R. and Sarah E. Russell, Apr. 6, 1849. Golden wedding 1899.
Rosetta and Edward H. Besse, Oct. 2, 1861.
Sarah E. and William G. Hunt, Jan. 24, 1858.

Frothingham, Newell and Elisabeth Spalding, Apr. 18, 1889, in Salisbury, Mass.

Fullerton, Ethel (Dooley), adopted dau., and Edgar B. Harrington, Sept. 29, 1903. Res. Manchester, N. H.

Furber, Edward and Eliza Sprague, Feb., 1876, in Maine. Res. Londonderry.
Frank Olwin and Mary Abbie Mackay, May 30, 1877. Res. Saco, Me.
John S. and Laura J. Wallace, June 11, 1845.
Laura Jane and Capt. George S. Garvin, Oct. 26, 1877.
Lewis Irving and Clara J. Marshall, Oct. 26, 1881. In the West.
Mattie B. and George P. Harvell, Apr. 25, 1900. (No children.)
Oscar E. and Lizzie Murray, Nov. 30, 1882. Boston, Mass.

Gage, Aaron H. and Hannah L. Humphrey, Mar. 20, 1849.
Almira and Nathaniel Deane Fisher, Aug. 3, 1835.
Eliza K. and John N. Anderson, Nov. 26, 1829.
John A. and Martha Tenney, May 6, 1851.
Nancy J. and Volney H. Moody, Sept. 3, 1885.
William H. and Lucelia Adams, Dec. 13, 1871.
William W. and Sarah W. Griffin, Aug. 27, 1846.
William Washington, 25, and Hattie E. Roach, 17, Apr. 16, 1890.

Galencia, May Louise, 30, and Joseph A. Sweatt, 65, Sept. 24, 1903.

Galt, Jean and Christopher Eyers, Mar., 1724-5, by Rev. Mr. McGregor, minister of Londonderry, N. H.

Galvin, Joseph I., 22, and Lena H. Carpenter, 18, Dec. 19, 1906.
Miss —— and Nathan P. Watts (1st wife), ——.

Gamble, Samuel and Mary Ann Wilson, Dec. 20, 1836.
Thomas and Hannah Gooden, Dec. 3, 1829.

Gardner, Elisabeth S. and Walter L. Blenus, Oct. 12, 1881. Res. Manchester, N. H.
Lorenzo and Susan E. Bancroft, Nov. 22, 1855.
Stephen and Mary P. Smith, Aug. 31, 1845.
Susie L., 16, and Frank O. Jameson, 19, Mar. 21, 1894.

Gardt, Chauncey H. and Lucy L. Willey, June 10, 1908. Res. Galisburg, N. Y.

Garland, Mary and John Remington, Aug. 4, 1856.

Gateswere, Gideon and Mary E. Greeley, 1878.

Garvin, Augustus F. and Susan F. Poor, July 5, 1863, in Goffstown, N. H. Res. Revere, Mass.
Benjamin Franklin and Nancy M. Spinney, Jan. 20, 1841.
Betsey and Israel Merrill, Dec., 1810.
Capt George S. and Laura Jane Furber, Oct. 26, 1877.
Capt. George S. and Sarah C. Field, Dec. 22, 1897.
Clarence N. and Abbie D. Wilson, Feb., 1872, Derry, N. H.
Clarrissa and John Peabody, Apr. 3, 1830.
Eldora J. and Robert Henry Wilson, Apr., 1865.
Fred Elwyn, 21, and Emma Provencher, 16, July 28, 1894. Res. Derry, N. H.
George Olwin, 28, and Grace Duffield, 27, Sept. 25, 1908.
Georgietta and William Proctor. Res. Revere, Mass.
Jacob and Margaret Watts, Dec., 1792.
Mary and Israel Mullins, Apr. 25, 1819.
Moses and Jenney Watts, Dec. 26, 1799.
Perses and Robert Boyce, Jan., 1823.
Rachel and William Conant, June, 1834.
Rachel Watts and William H. Conant, June 29, 1835.
Susanna and Hugh Boyce, Nov., 1797.
Thersy and Caleb Dodge, Nov., 1815.

Gault, Hugh and Nancy Chase, Dec. 3, 1812.

Gauser, Margaret and Harold James Platts, 1907. Res. Almeda, Cal.

George, Lana S. and Lyman A. Dickey, Dec., 1879.

Gibson, Anna Florence and George N. Holcomb, June 11, 1905. Res. Amherst, Mass.
Grace Harriet, 28, and Edward P. Pressey, 28, June 25, 1897.
Hiram Cutler and ——, Nov. 27, 1908. Res. Greenfield, Mass.
John Calvin and Sarah Jane White, Aug. 5, 1868.

Gibson, Nabby and John Woodbury, Oct. 13, 1797.
Sarah A. and Alexander McMurphy, Apr. 25, 1844. Res. Derry, N. H.

Gilchrist, Daniel and Polly Senter, Nov. 9, 1801.

Gilcreast, Ann E. and Alonzo J. Gregg, July 1, 1863.
Effie M., 23, and Cyrus A. Martin, 22, June 19, 1889.
Ella A. and Charles O. Huse, Apr. 2, 1879.
Ella Eliza and George B. Wiley, June 29, 1871.
Emma Florence and Eugene O. Greeley, Sept. 30, 1876.
Frank L. and Anna J. Sloane, Feb. 3, 1873.
Frederick A. and Mary Nevins, Aug. 24, 1865.
James M. and Eliza H. Tenney, Nov. 12, 1840.
James M. and Eviline Peabody, Sept. 9, 1847.
John and Marinda Peabody, Nov. 15, 1849.
Mina A. and Daniel G. Annis, June 18, 1868.
Nancy A. and Perry C. Burnham, June 10, 1873.
Samuel and Nancy Proctor, Nov. 27, 1845. Golden wedding 1895.
Sarah D. and Charles Edward Young, Apr. 13, 1848.
Sarah J. and George E. Upton, Nov. 27, 1856.

Gile, David and Susan Bruce, Mar. 20, 1810.
Nancy E. and Charles E. Jones, Mar. 9, 1872.

Giles, Benjamin and Jenney McCoy, Feb. 8, 1798.
Hannah and William Caldwell, Feb. 1, 1816.
James and Ann G. Smith, Dec. 17, 1835.
Molley and James Boyce, Apr. 8, 1784.
Nancy and David Campbell, Jan. 21, 1823.
Nathaniel and Sally Frete, June, 1804.
Polly and Thomas Chase.
Sally and Thomas Morrison, Dec. 15, 1824.

Gillingham, Mary M. and Thomas A. Rowell, May 4, 1862.

Gilmore, Charles H. and Mary I. Richardson, Nov. 27, 1862, or Nov. 26, 1861.
Henry F. and Lydia D. Page, Sept. 18, 1844.
Mary Ann* and John Bell, Dec. 21, 1758.

Given, Grizzel and ——— Holms, Aug. 1, 1734, by Rev. Mr. Thomson.

Goffe, Hannah and Edward Linkfield, Sept. 9, 1723, by Rev. Mr. McGregor.
John and Hannah Gregs, Oct. 16, 1722, by Rev. Mr. Walter of Roxbury.

Goings, Katie L. and Horace P. Hurd, July 5, 1880.

*A lady of much personal beauty, great prudence and good sense.

Goodhue, Ralph H. and Juline F. Miner, Sept. 8, 1869, in Manchester, N. H. Res. 10 yrs. in Londonderry.

Gooding (see Goodwin).

Goodspeed, Naaman and Luella Isabel Rolfe, July 4, 1872.

Goodwin, Gooden, Gooding, Abbie Adella, 31, and Albin Corthell, 49, Dec. 28, 1892.
Clara M. and Giles Ladd Boyce, Apr. 1, 1871.
Daniel and Abby C. Austin, Oct. 19, 1853.
Daniel W., 41, and Ida F. Russell (Estey), 25, Jan. 25, 1892.
Daniel W. and Sarah A. Moody, May 11, 1873.
David and Mary Hibbard, Sept. 1, 1829.
Dea. Joshua and Betsey Jones, Jan. 1, 1807.
Dea. Joshua and Mrs. Ann Melvin (3d wife).
Dea. Joshua and Rebecca Jones, Dec. 11, 1800.
Eliza J. and George W. Skinner, Feb. 11, 1857.
Elmer D. and Ella L. Sargent, ——, in Searsport, Me. Res. Manchester, N. H.
Enoch and Sally Wheeler, Oct. 8, 1808.
Esther M. and Henry J. Whittemore, Aug. 21, 1862.
George N. and Susie A. Barker, Oct. 1, 1872.
Hannah and Thomas Gamball, Dec. 3, 1829.
Henry and Mary A. Moar, May 17, 1860.
Ira F. and Ida L. Searles, May 28, 1878. Res. Worcester, Mass.
John and Carrie W. Bolles, May 17, 1863.
John H. S., 37, and Nellie D. Schwartz, 38, Nov. 25, 1896.
John H. S., 50, and Olive S. Cook, 31, May 18, 1910.
Joshua and Mary Jones, Dec. 25, 1823.
Josiah and Esther Jones, Nov. 24, 1831.
Joseph S. and Frances S. Smith (1st wife), Nov. 6, 1868.
Joseph S. and Maria L. Palmer (2d wife), Oct. 31, 1886.
Martha J. and James Dooley, July 10, 1855.
Mary A. and John W. Fling, Jan. 2, 1857.
Rebecca and Tilley H. Wheeler, Sept. 13, 1831.
Rev. Daniel and Julia A. Shute, Feb. 12, 1839, in Derry, N. H.
Rev. Daniel and Martha Boynton, Aug. 24, 1846, in Pepperell.
Rev. Daniel and Mrs. Lucy Jane Boynton, Pepperell.
Sarah H. and William P. Richardson, Dec. 10, 1855.

Gordon, Irving D. and Anna M. Payne, Nov. 28, 1894. Res. Derry, N. H.
Wells and Sally Holt, Mar. 13, 1812.

Goss, Allen and Jane McMurphy, May 30, 1810.
Martha and Eugene L. Campbell, Oct. 2, 1873.
Mary E. and Joseph Page, Apr. 24, 1862.

Goud, Estella, 20, and Sam N. Boyce, 27, Dec. 27, 1903.

Gould, Harvey S. and Harriet B. Campbell, Aug. 12, 1862.
Hattie S., 19, and Dan A. Maxfield, 26, Dec. 3, 1891, at Wolcot, Vt. Res. Londonderry, N. H.
Solon Southard and Lucy M. Boyd, Feb. 5, 1874.

Gove, Villa May and Arthur T. Holmes, 37, May 23, 1906. Res. Derry, N. H.

Grafton, Eleanor Patton Chew and Frank Morrison Boynton, June 29, 1909, in Virginia. Res. Newton, Mass.

Graham, Joseph H., 29, and May G. Harvell, 19, Aug. 29, 1901.
Samuel Schot and Naby Robinson, July 10, 1798.

Grant, John H. and Annie M. Smith, Aug. 1, 1880.
John J. and Nancy Sampson.
Sarah and John M. Crowell, May —, 1866.

Gratto, Samuel A., 30, and Catherine E. Clark, 27, June 16, 1909.

Graves, Mary A. and Charles McAllister, July 21, 1885.
Samuel and Martha Bond, Jan. 29, 1724-5, by Rev. Mr. Brown of Haverhill.

Greeley, Abbie F. and George H. Upton, July 29, 1869.
Abbie F. and Henry J. Caldwell, Nov. 3, 1875.
Adeline and George F. Armstrong, Nov. 20, 1884. Res. Windham, N. H.
Alfred D. and Ann Dart, ——, 1850.
Alfred D. and Lucy Senter, ——, 1841.
Almira and Josiah Manter, Nov. 2, 1841.
Arvilla May, 24, and Harold Eastman Hacker, 24, June 16, 1908.
Charles E. and Phebe A. Church, ——, 1887.
Charles S. and Hattie A. Allen, Dec. 24, 1879, Troy, N. H. Res. Londonderry, N. H.
Elbridge G. and Julia Ann Blood, Apr. 16, 1842.
Elder John W. and Mary A. Dodge, May 2, 1844.
Emeline B. and Eugene N. Mullins, Nov. 29, 1883.
Eugene O. and Emma F. Gilcreast, Sept. 30, 1876.
Flora and Herbert Tomlinson, ——, 1887.
George W. and Alice P. Alley, Apr. 16, 1846.
Hannah Jane and Rev. J. H. Hillman, Apr. 5, 1869, in Acworth, N. H.
Horace (Journalist) and Mary Cheney, Mar. 18, 1837.
Howard Franklin and Charlotte Hemmesch, Nov. 26, 1907. Res. Cold Spring, Minn.

Greeley, Irving H. and Mary H. Roach, Feb. 12, 1885.
James M. and Mary E. (Downing) Mower, Apr. 30, 1873. Res. Derry, N. H.
John and Dustimony Eastman, June 16, 1809.
John W., 27, and Carrie Osburn, 15, June 12, 1887.
Laura Maude and Francis H. Poff, Jr., Oct. 5, 1879.
Lydia and John King, July 20, 1848.
Lydia S. and Hugh H. Ripley, Sept. 9, 1834.
Mary and Emerson Colby, Aug. 28, 1817.
Mary E. and Gideon Gateswere, ———, 1878.
Onslow L. and Gertrude E. Parker, July 4, 1872.
Sarah A. and Alonzo Corliss, Mar. 26, 1874.
Zaccheus and Mary Woodburn, ———, 1807. (Parents of Horace Greeley.)

Green, Grace and Arthur G. Miller, Dec. 25, 1908.

Greenough, Hattie Clare and ——— Smith.
Betsey and David Muffet, Sept. 7, 1797.
Ebenezer and Anna Hughs, Jan. 26, 1797.
Eliza and Joseph Aiken, May 24, 1801.
Hannah and John Goffe (see Gregs).
Isabel and Edward P. Ela, Nov. 30, 1843.
Jane and Josiah Breed, Nov. 14, 1819.
Jane and Thomas Aiken, Sept. 30, 1802.
Janette and David Dickey, Feb. 21, 1833.
John and Mary Knowlton, Nov. 15, 1798.
John and Mary Shipley, July 3, 1828.
John and ——— Rankin, Mar. 11, 1724–5, by Rev. Mr. McGregor.
Joseph and Lucy Warner, Jan. —, 1820.
Joseph and Mary Reid, Feb. 26, 1805.
Lamitt (?) Laurett and Nathan Parker, Jr., Feb. 15, 1870.
Lettice and Thomas Caldwell, Dec. 30, 1807.
Prof. Jarvis and Alice Webster,* ———, 1836.
Samuel and Jane Dickey, Dec. 29, 1812.
Walter F. and Ellen A. Spinney, May —, 1874.
William and Jenat Renkine, Mar. 11, 1724–5, by Rev. Mr. McGregor.
William and Sally Anderson, Feb. —, 1802.

Gregs, Hannah and John Goffe, Oct. 16, 1722, by Rev. Mr. Walter of Roxbury.

Griffin, Benjamin and Elisabeth Fortness, Dec. 7, 1842.
Daniel and Eldora Nichols, Nov. 24, 1867.
Harriet and John F. Davis, Sept. 25, 1861.
James Sevey and Hannah H. Ritchie, Oct. 10, 1811.

*Niece of Daniel Webster.

Griffin, Jonathan and Eliza Page, Nov. 26, 1807.
Mehitable and Joseph Clyde, Feb. 8, 1803.
Sarah W. and William W. Gage, Aug. 27, 1846.
Susan Grace and David L. Annis, Nov. 13, 1858.
Susanna and David Pinkerton, Feb. 14, 1800.
Thomas and Patty Hemphill, Feb. 4, 1804.

Grimes, Ella Alma and George H. Boyd, June 15, 1892.

Gross, Gilman and Mary Moor, Nov. 13, 1828.

Hacker, Harold E., 24, and Arvilla May Greeley, 24, June 16, 1908.

Hackett, Lucinda M. and Capt. William S. Barker, Dec. 26, 1857.

Hadley, Ella W., 24, and George N. Dooley, 36, Jan. 17, 1907.

Haggerty, Dennis, 48, and Josie Lyons, 40, Feb. 1, 1893.

Haigh, Sarah, 32, and Charles F. Morrison, 30, Dec. 22, 1888.

Hall, Dorothea and Noah Burnham, Sept. 4, 1823.
Edward and Rebecca C. Harvey, Jan. 1, 1846.
Eliza A. and Daniel M. Colby, June 5, 1865.
George A,, 24, and Hester C. Cousens, 22, July 4, 1894.
Henry R. and Ella M. Watts, Oct. 19, 1884 (1st wife).
Henry R., 42, and Letta K. McQuesten, 28, Sept. 18, 1895 (2nd wife).
Jane and John P. Young, Mar. 6, 1834.
Jessee and Margaret Cochran, Oct. 8, 1832.
Leroy and Alma Jane Woodbury.
Mary and Charles Adams (Spring), 1843. Golden wedding, 1893.
Mary Ann and Eltan R. Smilie, Sept. 3, 1844.
Mary C. and Charles Warner, Nov. 6, 1841.
Rachel J. and Frank L. Robie, Sept. 17, 1871.
Robert and Lucinda R. Wheeler (Gutterson), Sept. 20, 1869, at Manchester, N. H. Res. Londonderry, N. H.
Robert and Nancy E. Wheeler, July 4, 1842, at Amherst, N. H. Res. in Londonderry, N. H.
Robert S. and Mary F. C. March, June 27, 1872.
Sally and John Lennon, Nov. 17, 1803.
Sarah and Daniel M. Colby, May 4, 1848.
Silence Conn and Abraham Morrison, Feb. 19, 1710. (L. A. Morrison Hist.)

Hallet, Solomon and Harriet Smith, Mar. 13, 1845.

Ham, Joanna R., 19, and Clarence O. Watts, 23, Dec. 25, 1897 (1st wife).

Hamblett, Almira and William Lund, Apr. 2, 1867.
Amos and Sarah Steele, Apr. 2, 1807.

Hamblett, Dustin and Almira Hovey, Sept. 22, 1853.
George F. and Flora E. Beals, Sept. 19, 1878.
Harriet E. and John A. Robinson, Dec. 12, 1852.
Lyman A. and Irena Fletcher, Mar. 25, 1861.
Sarah and George Rolfe, Dec. 15, 1856.
Thomas and Judith Leach, Nov. 26, 1807.

Hamlet, Augustus F. and Mary E. Clark, July 4, 1853.
Charles A. and Kitty Daisy Hamlet, Oct. 4, 1880.
Emeline G. and James E. Barrett, Jan. 12, 1860.
Kitty Daisy and Charles A. Hamlet, Oct. 4, 1880.

Hanley, Catherine and John Stanton, Mar. 15, 1853.

Hannaford, A. A. and Eunice B. Ellis, Nov. 28, 1867.

Hapgood, Joseph and Almira J. Holmes, Aug. 11, 1847.

Hardy, Aaron P. and Delia W. Brickett, May 5, 1842.
Charles Albert and Susan E. Linden, May 24, 1898.
Eunice and Jonas Chase.
Frank A., 27, and Fanny A. Pike, 20, June 14, 1893.
Freeman Henry and Maxime J. Rapp, June 21, 1904.
George A. and Etta J. Moar, Aug. 13, 1867.
George H. and Ida J. Kendall, Jan. 9, 1883.
Harriet and Peter Crowell, Feb. 1, 1821 (2nd wife).
John and Eunice Peterson, Sept. 23, 1879.
John P. and Martha M. E. Wiley, June 12, 1878.
Lorenzo and Ellen Frances More, Mar. 10, 1894.
Lorenzo and Mary C. Howe, Dec. 31, 1863.
Molly and Jacob Chase.
William and Nabby Hillton, June 7, 1809.
William G. and Mary Whittier, Feb. 12, 1846 (1st wife).
William G. and Martha Flint, May 21, 1861 (2nd wife).

Harlow, Lizzie M. and George McAllister, May —, 1896.

Harriman, Anne and James Everton, Nov. —, 1806.
Sally and Isaac McAllister, Feb. 7, 1814.

Harrington, Edgar B. and Ethel (Dooley) Fullerton, adopted dau., Sept. 9, 1903.

Harris, Elbridge and Jennie E. Howe, Mar. 5, 1863.
Hattie R. and John H. Smith, Apr. 20, 1871.

Hartford, Annie M., 20, and George E. Ellis, 24, May 1, 1893.
Frank S., 21, and Gertrude Hartford, Jan. 31, 1903.
Gertrude and Frank S. Hartford, 21, Jan. 31, 1903.
James T. and Eleanor M. Smith, Feb. 16, 1872.

Hartshorn, John and Lovey Jones, Sept. 7, 1797.
Leroy S., 23, and Annie E. Boles, 17, Oct. 24, 1902.
Mrs. Mary A. (2nd wife) and David H. Young, ——, 18—.

Hartwell, Sarah and Daniel Wilkins (3d wife).

Harvell, Elisabeth and Robert R. Chase, Dec. 22, 1842.
George P. and Mattie B. Furber, Apr. 25, 1900.
Joseph, Jr., and Emeline Miller, Nov. 1, 1869.
Joseph, Jr., and Sarah H. Manter, Oct. 24, 1839.
Lieut. Joseph and Mary L. Underwood, Mar. 29, 1817.
May G., 19, and Joseph H. Graham, 29, Aug. 29, 1901.
Sarah Jane and George E. Anderson, Apr. 22, 1869.

Harvey, Cynthia and ——— Severance.
Ephraim W. and Susanna Stevens, Sept. 13, 1857.
Esther Jane and Joshua P. Currier, Feb. 14, 1839.
Josephine M. and Reuben W. Flanders, Jan. 1, 1871.
Manas and Harriet M. Corning, Sept. 1, 1853.
Mrs. Harriet M. and Joseph T. Noyes (1st wife).
Nancy and ——— Crockett.
Rebecca C. and Edward Hall, Jan. 1, 1846.
Sarah and ——— Wells.

Haseltine, Elisabeth L. and George Lawson, July 21, 1855.
Sarah C. and Abraham Burbank, Aug. 31, 1858.

Haskell, Charles and Lucy Warner, Mar. 13, 1806.

Hawkins, Harry Franklin and Bertha Hayes McAllister, Aug. 25, 1909. Res. Manchester, N. H.
Rebecca and Daniel Estey, May 18, 1835.

Hay, Washington L. and Cynthia Moare, Nov. 9, 1848.

Hayes, Daniel W. and Sarah McGregor, Aug. 19, 1869.
Hattie L. and J. T. Rainey, Dec. 14, 1892.
Nettie M. and George Isaac McAllister, Dec. 22, 1886. Res. Manchester, N. H.
Phebe C. and John S. Brown, Nov. 1, 1832.
Rachel E. and Thomas P. Major, Sept. 24, 1845. Res. Derry, N. H.

Haynes, Dr. John and Mary M. (1st wife).
Dr. John and Almira J. Anderson (2nd wife), July 3, 1871.

Hayward, Francis and Margaret L. Whittemore, May 2, 1854.

Hazelton, Carrie and Charles A. M. Clark, Apr. 2, 1910.
Mary A. and James L. McGregor, Dec. 3, 1884.
Susan D. and Henry C. Smith, Apr. 24, 1877.

Head, Lizzie J. and Charles A. Tenney, at Hookset, N. H. (1st wife).

Heath, Dorcas and Thomas Hogg, Nov. 25, 1806.
Sally and John Cochran, Dec. —, 1806.

Hebert, Joseph J., 26, and Mary E. Bailey, 21, June 15, 1909.

Hemmesch, Charlotte and Howard F. Greeley, Nov. 26, 1907, Cold Spring, Minn.

Hemphill, Nelson and Louisa Corning, Nov. 12, 1840.
Patty and Thomas Griffin, Feb. 4, 1804.

Hert (?), Hannah and Timothy Barrett, May 5, 1803.

Hewett, Mary C. and Henry L. Hurd, Nov. 23, 1881.

Hibbard, Eliza and Rev. E. G. Babcock, May 31, 1830.
Harriet and Amos C. Webster, Dec. 30, 1845.
Joshua and Hannah Tenney, Oct. 12, 1802.
Mary and David Goodwin, Sept. 1, 1829.
Olive and John Farnum, Apr. 15, 1813.

Hicks, Elisabeth B. and James G. Stone, June 21, 1871.

Higgins, Millie and Perley E. Austin, July 25, 1894, Manchester, N. H. Res. Londonderry, N. H.

Highlands, Anna and David McClary, Feb. 27, 1814.

Hill, Clarence A. and Emma D. Sprague, Mar. 14, 1881.
Daniel C. and Violetta Barrett, Oct. 28, 1880.
Frederick and Edna E. Fletcher, Oct. 27, 1880.
George A. and Eliza Bean, Sept. 18, 1858.
James and Naby March, Dec. —, 1797.
Jane P. and Oliver F. Blood, Feb. 8, 1842.
Oliver and Margaret McKinley, Nov. 17, 1796.
Susan Ellen and Elder John Dickey, June 10, 1891, Leominster, Mass.

Hillman, Rev. J. H. and Hannah Jane Greeley, Apr. 5, 1869, Acworth, N. H.

Hills, Jean and Moses Hills, Apr. 10, 1791.
Moses and Jean Hills, Apr. 10, 1791.

Hilton, Nabby and William Hardy, June 7, 1809.

Hinckley, Owen and Carrie M. Simpson, July 15, 1868. Res. 40 yrs. in Londonderry.

Hines, Mary and William Henry Alexander, Oct. 1, 1868.

Hobart, Lovinia and Rev. Stephen Pillsbury, Mar. 3, 1816.

Hobbs, Capt. J. S. and Emma A. Plummer.
Charles J., 49, and May E. Flanders, 47, Oct. 12, 1905.
Elvira and Richard Libby, June 2, 1848. Salisbury, N. H.
Elvira (Libbey) M. and Nathaniel Pettingill, Apr. 22, 1855.
Joseph and Mary Cressey, June 13, 1799.
Mrs. Clara A and Lorenzo D. Smith, Oct. 3, 1906. Res. Acton, Maine.
Precilla and James M. Pettengill, Nov. 11, 1858.

Hodgman, Nancy J. and Sherburn D. Smith, May 1, 1860.

Hodge, Perkins A. and Frances C. Pinkerton.

Hogg, Thomas and Dorcas Heath, Nov. 25, 1806.
William and Hannah Towns, Feb 7, 1806.

Holbrook, Walter Scott and Martha Langford, 1867. Res. Haverhill, Mass.
Willard and Margaret Crocker, June 22, 1819.

Holcomb, George N. and Florence A. Gibson, June 11, 1905. Res. Amherst, Mass.

Hollingshead, Morley E., 21, and Iva B. Proctor, 19, June 14, 1909.

Holman, Anderson and Louisa A. Bean, Dec. 2, 1855.

Holmes, Almira J. and Joseph Hapgood, Aug. 11, 1847.
Arthur T., 37, and Villa May Gove, May 23, 1906. Res. Derry, N. H.
Caroline and William Murdock, May 28, 1849.
Charles Herbert, 39, and Pearl Barker, Apr. 24, 1906. Out West.
Charles M. and Mary A. Batchelder, Nov. 25, 1848.
Elder John and Mary Adams, ———, 1821.
Elisabeth and William Thompson, Nov. 10, 1808.
Fanny J. and Waldo Foster, Sept. 11, 1872.
Grizzy and Thomas Savory, Nov. 10, 1809.
Harriet S. and Edward H. Spalding, Dec. 6, 1861.
James and Martha Barker, Feb. 27, 1823.
James and Susannah Webster, July 3, 1832.
Jane and Jeremiah Bradley, Apr. 19, 1810.
Jane and Robert Holmes, Mar., 1808.
Margaret and William Boyd, Feb. 21, 1809.
Martha and William Moar, Feb. 11, 1800.
Mary Jane and William G. Bickford, Aug. 18, 1836.
Matthew and Anna B. Anderson, Sept. 11, 1856.
Moses Noyes and Harriet A. Coffin, Jan. 22, 1857. Went West.
Robert and Jane Anderson, Nov. 8, 1809.
Robert and Eliza Anderson, June 4, 1811.
Robert and Jane Holmes, Mar., 1808.
Sarah and Amos Page, Nov. 15, 1805.
Thomas M. and Georgia M. Spalding, Nov. 7, 1866.
Thomas M. and Julia A. Shedd, Feb. 28, 1877. Oakham, Mass.
William A. and Frances A. Thompson, Nov. 10, 1853.
William A. and Lizzie M. Nichols, Feb. 17, 1871.
William Frank and Martha B. Watts, May 31, 1864.

Holms, Abram(?) & Girzall Given, Aug. 1, 1734, by Rev. Mr. Thomson.

Holt, Eliza and Jabez Manter, Mar. 22, 1817.
Esther and John Darrah, Sept. 25, 1810.
Henry J. and Teresa J. Eaves, July 12, 1880.
Humphrey and Sarah Bachelder, Sept. 11, 1817.
John and Rachel Sawyer, Mar. 25, 1819.
Sally and Wells Gordon, Mar. 13, 1812.
William and Hannah Andrews, Feb. 16, 1804.

Holton, Addie and John L. Willey, Dec. 31, 1866.

Hood, Harvey Perley and Caroline Laura Corwin, ———, 1850, Tunbridge, Vt. Res. Derry, N. H.

Hooper, Walter C. and Ida S. Titcomb, Oct. 28, 1906. Res. Henniker, N. H.

Hopkins, Eleanor and James Wilson, June 1, 1758.

House, Rev. William* and Frances Savage, ———, 1858.

Houston, William and Isable Campbell, Feb. 11, 1799.

Hovey, Almira and Dustin Hamblett, Sept. 22, 1853.
John and Eleanor White (1st wife), Sept. 25, 1810.
John and Betsey White (2nd wife), Dec. 30, 1813.
John and Abigail Dustin (3d wife), ———, 1820–21.
Mary F. and Henry Conant, June 11, 1856.
Pauline L. and John Merrill, Mar. 15, 1842.
Sally and Eliphalet Danforth, Oct. 8, 1808.
Sarah H. and Nicholas Lawrence, Mar. 29, 1866.
William B. and Almira Boyes, Nov. 4, 1841.

Howard, John and Sally Senter, June 21, 1841.
Simon and Sybil Conant, July 24, 1840.

Howe, Daniel R. and Catharine Brothers, Mar. 4, 1852.
Henry and Mary Jane Howe, Aug. 16, 1846.
James M., 29, and Alice M. Cross, 19, Apr. 13, 1887.
Jennie E. and Elbridge Harris, Mar. 5, 1863.
John and Hannah Robertson, June 19, 1810.
Mary C. and Lorenzo Hardy, Dec. 31, 1863.
Mary Jane and Henry Howe, Aug. 16, 1846.

Hoyt, Margaret W. and Ebenezer K. Marden, Dec. 11, 1845.

Hughes, Anna and Ebenezer Gregg, Jan. 26, 1797.
Kate E. and Granville F. Plummer, Nov. 26, 1874.
Sally and James Willson, Sept. 28, 1797.

Hughs, Polly and Joseph Proctor, Mar. 4, 1802.

Humphrey, Betsey and John H. Clendenin, May 18, 1802.
Hannah L. and Aaron H. Gage, Mar. 20, 1849.
Nancy and Samuel Dickey, Feb. 26, 1805.

Hunkins, Augusta G. and Charles R. Bailey, Aug. 8, 1878, at Manchester, N. H. Res. Londonderry, N. H.

*Pastor Pres. Church from 1857 to 1873.

Hunt, Frederick H. and Martha A. B. March, Feb. 17, 1867.
William G. and Sarah E. Frost, Jan. 24, 1858.

Huntee, Currier and Fanny Vickery, July 12, 1849.
Currier and Sally Melvin, Jan. 1, 1839.
Nellie E. and Walter J. Thurston, Oct. 12, 1871.
William C. and Lovilla E. Manter, Oct. 22, 1867.

Huntoon, Alonzo H. and Addie E. Brickett, May 23, 1904. Res. Bedford, N. H.

Hurd, Charles, Jr., and Nancy Maria.
Elmer E. and Cora Jones, Jan. 2, 1886.
Florence and David B. McGregor, Jan 21, 1875.
George A. and Eva Williams, Dec. 24, 1907.
George and Nancy J. Woodburn, Feb. 28, 1850.
Hannah and Barnet H. Cheney, Aug. 31, 1846.
Henry L. and Mary C. Hewett, Nov. 23, 1881.
Horace P. and Katie L. Goings, July 5, 1880.
Rachel and Horace B. Putnam, Nov. 24, 1853.

Hurlburt, Etta P. and Mark B. Flanders, Aug. 1, 1891, in Boston, Mass. Res. in Manchester, N. H.

Huse, Charles O. and Ella A. Gilcreast, Apr. 2, 1879.
Isaac and Joanna Rowell, July 1, 1802.
John B. and Eunice White, Jan. 20, 1830.

Hutchins, John and Sarah Fisk, Feb. 11, 1800.

Ingalls, John and Ellen J. Smith, ——, 1847. Res. in the West.

Jackson, Adelaide F., 30, and William T. Kelley, 31, Nov. 30, 1893.
Alice and Hamilton A. Kendall, Oct. 10, 1876.
Betsey and Asa Philips, Feb. 11, 1800.
David and Eliza Dinsmore, July 1, 1828.
George E., 28, and Mary L. Call, 20, Feb. 3, 1892.
John and Mary Duncan, Oct. 8, 1822.
Joseph and Betsey White, Mar. 30, 1815.
Lydia and Benjamin Anderson, Mar. 13, 1813.
Polly and John M. Adams, Nov. 6, 1810.
Sally and Robert Adams, Dec. 7, 1809.

James, Mary L. and Jessee G. McMurphy, Apr. 27, 1870.

Jameson, Frank O., 19, Susie L. Gardner, 16, Mar. 21, 1894.

Jaquith, Mary A. and Edward K. Whittemore, Dec. 24, 1862.

Jenkins, Austin H. and Bertha M. Noyes, 19, July 19, 1902.

Jenks, Frank A. and Emma J. Burnett, June 16, 1886.

Jennings, Matilda and Asa Barker, Aug. 30, 1836.
Rhoda and Ebenezer Barker, May 1, 1834.

Jewett, Abigail and Thomas Wilson (2nd wife).
Sally and Ebenezer Kimball, June 23, 1809.

Johnson, Alice Nana, 25, and Willis Dickerman, 37, Sept. 5, 1907.
Ebenezer and Polly Adams, Feb. 10, 1801.
Frank J. and Elisabeth M. Chase, Feb. 21, 1880.
George D. and T. Jane Mullins, Nov. 8, 1846.
Jonah and Sophia (Crowningshield) Platts, in New York.
John A. M. and Hannah Watts, Sept. 10, 1835.
Mary and Warren Wyman, Oct. 12, 1883.
Nathan and Mary Barnett,, May 17, 1807.
Noah and Littitia M. Clagget, Nov. 10, 1840.

Johnston, Alexander and Elisabeth W. Patterson, May 4, 1848.

Jones, Amos and Rebecca Dimond, Mar. 1, 1798.
Betsey and Joshua Gooding, Jan. 1, 1807.
Caleb and Eliza T. Woods, Dec. 18, 1834.
Charles E. and Nancy E. Gile, Mar. 9, 1872.
Cora and Elmer E. Hurd, Jan. 2, 1886.
Esther and Josiah Goodwin, Nov. 24, 1831.
Josiah and Jennie Boys, Oct. 19, 1799.
Loies and Alexander Caldwell, May 21, 1813.
Lovey and John Hartshorn, Sept. 7, 1797.
Mary and Joshua Goodwin, Dec. 25, 1823.
Merilla, 27, and Arthur E. Brown, 27, Sept. 14, 1901.
Nehemiah and Ruth Myrick, Aug. 29, 1860.
Rebecca and Joshua Goodwin, Dec. 11, 1800.
Sally and Laomi Walker, Nov. 20, 1804.
Saloma and Charles Wiley, Oct. 25, 1875. Res. Haverhill, Mass.

Judd, George R. and Lavina E. Richardson, Dec. 26, 1845.

Karr, Agnes and Thomas Nickels, Aug. 31, 1797.
David and Hannah Duncan, Mar., 1801.
Elisabeth and Edmond Adams, Dec. 29, 1808.
John and Ann Barnett, Mar. 10, 1805.

Keddy, William, 30, and Vera L. Weagle, 19, Aug. 15, 1909.

Kelley, Edward and Pauline Otterson, Aug. 11, 1860.
Mary J. S. and George V. Anderson, Apr. 27, 1867.
William T., 31, and Adelaide F. Jackson, 30, Nov. 30, 1893.

Kelsey, Arthur S. and Elizabeth A. Sweatt, Apr. 19, 1875, at Salisbury.
Adam (?) and Ann Macmaster, Dec. 27, ——, by Rev. Thomas Thompson.

Kelsey, Adam (?) and Elisabeth Killerist (Gilchrist), Feb. 8, 1733-4, by Rev. Mr. Mathew Clark of Londonderry, N. H.

Kenady, Kennedy, Mary and John MacConahy, May 20, 1730, by Rev. Mathew Clark.

Kendall, Amos and Martha Adams, Dec. 15, 1808.
Hamilton A. and Alice Jackson, Oct. 10, 1876.
Ida J. and George H. Hardy, Jan. 9, 1883.
Jonathan and Hannah Pike, May 25, 1843.

Kendrick, Julia and John Edward Merrill, Nov., 1863.

Kennedy (see Kenady).

Kennerson, Mary O. and Daniel Oliver Pickering, July 21, 1854.

Kent, Isaac and Dolly Butterfield, Dec. 26, 1810.
Richard and Loisa Ela, Sept. 11, 1810.

Kidder, Joseph and Huldah P. Cross, Mar. 21, 1813.
Joseph and Sarah B. Smith, June 20, 1850. Golden wedding 1900. Res. in Manchester, N. H.

Killam, Charles W. and Amy E. Whittemore.

Killerist, Elisabeth and Adam (?) Kelsey, Feb. 8, 1733-4, by Rev. Mr. Mathew Clark of Londonderry, N. H.

Killicutt, Thomas and Mary Durrah, Sept. 3, 1822.

Kimball, Anna F. and George W. Durant, Dec. 31, 1867.
Betsey and Edmond Adams, Sept. 26, 1809.
Charles G. and Emma J. Colby, Oct. 14, 1880.
Daniel W. and Sarah R. Brooks, Nov. 28, 1883.
Ebenezer and Sally Jewett, June 23, 1809.
Frances H., 53, and Edward Francis, 40, Oct. 26, 1908.
George Forrest and Lulu Christine Fiske, Nov. 13, 1898. Res. Manchester, N. H.
George W. and Frances H. Young, Apr. 17, 1877.
Isaac and Sarah J. Clough (1st wife).
Isaac and Rebecca J. Goodwin (2nd wife).
Mehitable and Rev. Edward L. Parker,* 1811.
Sarah and John E. Cheney, June 25, 1848.

Kincaid, James and Margaret Nichols, about 1753.

King, Hannah and Peaslee Chase, May 14, 1838.
John and Lydia Greeley, July 20, 1848.

Kirkwood, Nellie and Arthur V. Blood, Mar. 22, 1907.

Knight, Addison and Margaret Chase, Oct. 3, 1844.
Alfred B. and Antonietta De Grace Cutter, Sept. 12, 1865.
Anna Sarah and Joseph Lucian Shipley, Aug. 25, 1863, at Atkinson, N. H.
Georgietta W. and Wilbur E. Barrett, Dec. 12, 1894.

*Pastor of East Church 40 yrs.

Knight, Samuel and Ann McAllister, Oct. 18, 1808.
Wesley B. and Helen F. Anderson, Apr. 7, 1862.

Knowlton, Mary and John Gregg, Nov. 15, 1798.

Knox, Thomas and ——— McAllister, ———, ———.

Lamsiel, Ruth and James Barnet, Dec. 17, 1781.

Landers, Anabelle F. and Lester C. Paige, July 31, 1907. Res. Manchester, N. H.
Rebecca and Charles Tarbox, Sept. 5, 1806.

Lang, George Edgar (Smith) and Sarah Myrtie Smith, at Haverhill, Mass., May 2, 1906.

Langford, Martha and Walter Scott Holbrook, ——, 1867. Res. Haverhill, Mass.

Langley, Eliza J. and Timothy Burns, Mar. 11, 1867.

Lary, George, 60, and Annie Peabody, 43, Oct. 1, 1903.

Lasley (see Leslie record).

Lawrence, Mary A. and Charles P. Manter, ———, ———.
Nicholas and Sarah H. Hovey, Mar. 29, 1866.—

Laws, Sidney E., 26, and Susie F. Merritt, 26, Apr. 18, 1899.

Lawson, George and Elisabeth A. Haselton, July 21, 1855.
George F. and Parmelia Morse, Mar. 29, 1838.

Leach, Elijah and Martha Nesmith, Mar. 27, 1834.
Hannah and Moses Watts, June 12, 1823.
Joseph and Martha Corning, Dec. 25, 1815.
Judith and Thomas Hamblett, Nov. 26, 1807.
Lydia and Grafton Manter, about 1790.

Leavitt, Samuel D. and Emily C. White, Aug. 7, 1860.

Lee, George W., 39, and Rosie M. Wyatt, 22, July 25, 1905.

Lennon, John and Sally Hall, Nov. 17, 1803.

Leslie, Lasley, Charles C. and Eliza B. Webster, Dec. 16, 1886.
James and Mary McMurphy, Apr. 4, 1723, by Rev. Mr. McGregor.

Lewis, Ei Lucinda and Joshua Whidden, Nov. 13, 1862.
Guy A., 20, and Josephine Pettengill, 18, Oct. 9, 1899.
Jane L. and Moses Freeman, Apr. 13, 1843.
Phillips F. and Harriet West, Sept. 7, 1875, at Charlestown, Mass. Res. Londonderry, N. H.

Libbie, Emma A. and Lyman A. Dickey, July —, 1864.

Libby, Elvira (Hobbs) and Nathaniel Pettingill, Apr. 22, 1855. Res. Londonderry, N. H.
Richard and Elvira Hobbs, Jan. 2, 1848, in Salisbury, N. H.

Lincoln, Ann and Tilley H. Wheeler, ———, 1856 (2nd wife).

Lincoln, Anna P. and D. L. Batchelder, Dec. 17, 1888.
Silas E., 28, and Emma E. Corey, 17, Sept. 26, 1888.

Linden, Susan E. and Charles Albert Hardy, May 24, 1898.

Lindsay, Jenat and John Wallace, Nov. 28, 1729, by Rev. Mr. Mathew Clark.

Lindsey, Elisabeth and Mathew Clark, Apr. 15, 1722, by Rev. Mr. McGregor.

Linkfield, Edward and Hanna Goffe, Sept. 9, 1723, by Rev. Mr. McGregor.

Little, Jonathan and Phebe Poor, Dec. 29, 1803.
Mary and Parker Dodge, Jan. 4, 1770.
Robert E. and Clarissa Pinkerton, ———, ———.

Littlefield, William H. and Martha M. Taylor, Nov. 26, 1885.

Livengood, Sarah A. and Frank B. Flanders, Oct. 19, 1881.

Lord, Carrie A. and Edward Sampson, Apr. 16, 1890.
Clara Dilla (Dickey), 43, and Harris Towle, 37, Nov. 8, 1887.
Harry F., 18, and Estella F. Wells, 17, Mar. 21, 1893.
William L. and Clara D. Dickey, Dec. 11, 1863.

Lovejoy, Martha E. and David W. Ela, Feb. 6, 1883.
Samuel and Mehitable Dwinnell, Nov. 18, 1822.

Lovell, George A., 38, and Fannie B. McCutcheon, 21, Sept. 28, 1891.

Low, Mary E. N., 35, and George E. Ela, 56, Sept. 1, 1904 (2nd wife).

Lowd, Andrew T. and Ardelle A. Tenney, ———, 1867.
Edith Belle, 18, and William A. Butterworth, 22, Mar. 17, 1893.
Jennie A., 20, and Edson W. Watts, 22, Dec. 1, 1897.
Sedley H., 19, and Lillian J. Dailey, 22, Mar. 15, 1898.
Susie F. and Charles B. Abbott, June 13, 1868.

Lund, James W. and Margaret Ann Spaine, Aug. 4, 1909.
William and Almira Hamblett, Apr. 2, 1867.

Lupien, Eva, 23, and John Bernard Bresnon, 23, Nov. 26, 1910.

Lurvey, Bertha M. and Scott B. Stewart, Dec. 23, 1908. Res. in Maine.
Cora M., 20, and Fred H. Smith, 22, Sept. 15, 1909.

Lyons, Josie, 40, and Dennis Haggerty, 48, Feb. 1, 1893.

MacConahy (see McConihue).

MacCurdy (see McCurdy).

Machard (see McHard).

Mack, Andrew W. and Frances A. Preston, Mar. 20, 1861.
Betsey and David Stiles, Sept. 29, 1808.
Herbert A. and Mabel H. Brickett, Sept. 12, 1895. Res. Manchester, N. H.
Robert and Anne Clark, Dec. 28, 1813.
Robert C. and Jane D. Patterson, Mar. 6, 1856.
Wallace P., 28, and Harriet L. Pillsbury, 21, Feb. 24, 1892.

Mackay, Abbie Mary and Frank O. Furber, May 30, 1877. Res. Saco, Me.

MacKertney (see McKertney).

Macmaster (see McMaster).

Macmurphy, MacMurphy (see McMurphy).

Magee, Addie M. and Charles F. Whidden, Jan. 31, 1885.

Magoon, John Quincy and Cora B. Brown, Feb. 10, 1881, in Manchester, N. H. Res. Londonderry, N. H.

Major, John and Sally Cheney, Jan. 20 or 28 (?), 1802.
Thomas P. and Harriet (Nevins) McGregor, ——, 1884. Res. Derry, N. H.
Thomas P. and Rachel E. Hayes, Sept. 24, 1845. Res. Derry, N. H.

Maker, Clara Louise, 24, and Ezra Norwell Baker, 26, Nov. 6, 1907.

Manning, Edward A. and Hannah L. Merrill, Nov. 27, 1834.

Mansur, Harriet N. and Ebenezer Pickering, Jan. 4, 1846.

Manter, Alfred F., 24, and Katie M. Brown, 20, Oct. 5, 1910.
Allen S. and Jennie Brown, Aug. 6, 1885.
Belcher and Mehitable Dodge, Jan. 24, 1811.
Capt. Samuel and Isabel Reed, about ——, 1822.
Charles P. and Mary A. Lawrence, ——.
Clarrissa and Frank Walsh, ——.
Col. Francis and Harriet Crowningshield (1st wife), Feb. 28, 1820.
Col. Francis and Elisabeth Ann Smith (2nd wife), Sept. 13, 1860.
Corydon L. and Emma A. Potter, Nov. 24, 1880, Providence, R. I. Rem. to Londonderry, 1888.
Daniel and Sarah Ann (Annis), —— (1st hus.).
David (one of triplets) and Philena Manter (dau. of Jabez) ——.
Dr. George Francis and Melana A. Barker, Mar. 16, 1868 (1st wife).
Dr. George Francis and Lucinda Adelaide Wilbur, May 16, 1871 (2nd wife). Res. Manchester, N. H.

Manter, Dr. George W. and Almira Richardson, June 17, 1849, Auburn, N. H.
Emma (dau. of Philena) and Frank Moody, ———.
George and Nancy Richmond (1st wife), in Plymouth, Mass., ———.
George and Polly Senter (2nd wife), Sept. 17, 1795. Res. Londonderry, N. H.
George W. and Alice Mount, June 8, 1898. Res. Manchester, N. H.
Grafton and Lydia Leach, about ———, 1790.
Harriet S. and James M. Platts, Oct. 9, 1849.
Jabez and Eliza Holt, Mar. 22, 1817.
James and Mehitable Dwinell, July 1, 1817.
Jerusha M. C. H. and Hiram Wilkins, Dec. 29, 1835.
Josiah and Almira Greeley, Nov. 2, 1841.
Lovilla E. and William C. Huntee, Oct. 22, 1867.
Lydia (dau. of Jabez) and George B. McQuesten, ———.
Mary and Samuel Whittier, ———. Res. Hooksett, N. H.
Mary Ann and William P. Emerson, July 8, 1848.
Mary Ann (dau. of Jabez) and Daniel L. Corning, July 3, 1861, Manchester, N. H., by Rev. M. Tileston.
Mary Florence and George W. Platts, Oct. 20, 1853.
Mehitable and Charles P. Page, July 4, 1845.
Menora (dau. of Philena) and Alphonse Rayner, ———. Res. Goffstown, N. H.
Philena and David Manter (1st hus.), ———.
Philena and ——— Bancroft (2nd hus.), ———.
Phineas and Mary Bancroft, Feb. 24, 1820.
Sarah Ann (Annis) and Martin C. Ripley, ———, 1867 (2nd hus.).
Sarah H. and Joseph Harvell, Oct. 24, 1839.

March, Abigail C. and William Hardy Smith, Feb. 26, 1852.
Benjamin and Mary Campbell, Dec. 31, 1801.
Benjamin and Rhoda Proctor, Feb. 5, 1835.
Betsey and Jacob Emery, Mar. 9, 1820.
Hannah and Charles Stimpson, Oct. 2, 1823.
Henry and Abigail Boyd, July 4, 1839.
Henry and Polly Dwinell, Dec., 1799.
John, 2d, and Eunice Colburn Seavey, June 23, 1857, in Pelham.
John D. and Cynthia Sargent, Nov. 10, 1831.
Lydia and John R. Merrill, Sept. 11, 1828.
Maria B. and Jeremiah B. Webb, Oct. 2, 1834.
Martha A. B. and Frederick H. Hunt, Feb. 17, 1867.
Mary and John L. Caney, Jan. 1, 1842.
Mary F. C. and Robert S. Hall, Jan. 27, 1872.

March, Nabby and James Hill, Dec., 1797.
Reed C. and Mary Cate, Oct. 6, 1844.
Reed C. and Mary Whittemore, Dec. 11, 1834.
Rhoda and Nathaniel Conant, Aug. 17, 1798.
Sophia and Stephen Wright, May, 1833.

Marden, Ebenezer K., and Margaret W. Hoyt, Dec. 1, 1845.
Minnie Josephine and Frank E. Robie, Mar. 11, 1893, Apopka, Fla. Res. Londonderry, N. H.

Marsh, Joshua and Priscilla Brown, Dec. 24, 1819.
Sampson and Margaret Davidson, Apr. 23, 1812.
Samuel and Lettice Boyd, Aug. 30, 1809.

Marshall, Celia and Ichabod C. Smith, Dec. 21, 1886.
Clara J. and Lewis J. Furber, Oct. 26, 1881. In the West.
Emily J. and David F. Robinson, Jan. 24, 1867.
John and Anna Clyde, Dec. 27, 1798.
Matilda and Moody B. Towns, Dec. 28, 1853.
William and Ann Judson Pillsbury, ———.

Martin, Cyrus A., 22, and Effie M. Gilcreast, 23, June 19, 1889.
Forist and Mary McMurphy, Dec. 5, 1805.
Mary Ann and Lyman H. Clay, Dec. 25, 1844.
Orra and Peter Crowell, Dec. 23, 1817 (1st wife).
Peggy and Robert Archibald, Dec. 31, 1801.
Warren and Jane Pettengil, Dec. 20, 1832.

Maxfield, Clarence Elwin, 21, and Ethel M. Plummer, 21, June 9, 1909.
Dan A., 26, and Hattie S. Gould, 19, Dec. 3, 1891, Wolcott, Vt. Res. Londonderry, N. H.
Frank C., 26, and Ella L. Day, 19, June 22, 1910, Gloucester, Mass. Res. Londonderry, N. H.
George F. and Sarah E. Burroughs, Oct. 25, 1881, Bow, N. H. Res. Londonderry, N. H.

Mayo, Joseph and Augusta B. Mullins, Sept. 16, 1862.

McAllister (sometimes written Maccallister), Annie and Samuel Knight, Oct. 18, 1808.
Benjamin and Caroline Savory, May 7, 1846.
Charles and Mary Graves, July 21, 1885.
David and Jenny Craig, Oct. 20, 1797.
George and Lizzie M. Harlow, May, 1896. Res. Boston, Mass.
George,* son of David and Eleanor, m. in succession, Sarah Gargill, Sarah Henderson and Edna Emerson.

*George McAllister lived on farm owned by William Plummer; owned 1909 by Sidney A. Webster. Sold his farm in 1834 and lived with his daughter in Nashua. Died in 1840, aged 94 years.

McAllister, George Isaac and Mattie M. Hayes, Dec. 22, 1886. Res. Manchester, N. H.
Isaac and Sarah Harriman, Feb. 7, 1814.
Isaac, s. of John and Rebekah, b. Jan. 19, 1776, and Sarah Harriman, ——, 1814.
Jannette, dau. of David and Eleanor Wilson, m. Michael Archer of Henniker, N. H.
Jonathan and Caroline Choate, Nov. 11, 1852.
John and Rebeckah (Henderson) White, ——, 1770. Res. Bedford, N. H.
John, s. of David and Eleanor Wilson, m. 1770, Mrs. Rebekah (Henderson) White of Bedford, N. H.
Margaret and Alexander McCoy, ——.
Margaret, dau. of David and Eleanor Wilson, m. Alexander McCoy of Goffstown, N. H.
Mary and Hugh Taggart, June 17, 1728, by Rev. James McGregor.
Peggy and William McAllister, Jan. 18, 1797.
William and Peggy McAllister, Jan. 18, 1797.

McCharg, Sarah Wilson and William Plummer, Apr. 6, 1886, Leeds, P. Q. Res. in Londonderry 7 yrs.

McClary, David and Nancy J. Jeffers. No children.
Ella Jennie and Roswell Annis, Sept. 14, 1884 (2nd wife).
John and Jane H. Russell (1st wife), Dec. 25, 1848.
John and Judith R. McCoy (2nd wife), ——. No children.
John and Martha A. (Dolan) Sanborn (3d wife), Mar. 9, 1884.
Thomas and Eleanor Watts, Mar. 25, 1813.

McClearey, David and Anna Highlands, Feb. 27, 1814.

McCollom, Alexander and Jenney Anderson, Feb. 7, 1802.
Jenny and John Barnet, Feb. 13, 1799.
—— and Rebecca Alexander, Feb. 23, 1797.

McConihue, Elener and John Richey, June 21, 1722, by Rev. Mr. McGregor.
John and Betsey Alexander, Mar. 1, 1804.
John and Mary Kenady, May 20, 1730, by Rev. Mr. Mathew Clark.

McCoy, Alexander and Margaret McAllister, ——.
Betsey and Samuel Chase, ——.
Jenny and Benjamin Gile, Feb. 8, 1798.
Judith R. (2nd wife) and John McClary, ——.

McCurdy, James and Elisabeth Eyres, Mar. 22, 1727, by Rev. Mr. McGregor.

McCutcheon, Fannie B., 21, and George A. Lovell, 38, Sept. 28, 1891.

McCutchins, Hugh and Janet Wallace, ———.

McDole, John W. and Emma E. Parkhurst, Dec. 25, 1880.

McDonald, McDaniel, Edgar F., 23, and Annie R. Boyce, 19, Apr. 28, 1894.
Joseph R., 27, and Mary V. Parshley, 23, Aug. 22, 1900.
Polly B. and Jeremiah B. Moody, Aug. 6, 1848.
Rosanna and Elias Dickey, Feb. 7, 1743.

McDuffee, Anne and Mr. ——— Osgood, Jan. 4, 1802.
Jane and William P. Emerson, ——— (1st wife), Auburn, N. H.
Margaret and Israel Childs, Apr. 8, 1832.

McFarland, Mary and Gidion Coburn, Feb. 4, 1807.
Polly and John Morrill, May, 1798.

McGaw, Robert and Sarah Morrison, June 8, 1811.

McGilvery, Polly and Alexander Anderson, Nov., 1804.

McGlaughlin, Isabell and David Dickey, Feb. 27, 1724, by Rev. Mr. McGregor.

McGrath, Edward and Hannah Morrill, Mar. 14, 1799.
John Bush and Sally Taylor, Mar. 28, 1799.
Sally and Isaac Coburn, Sept. 8, 1808.

McGregor, MacGregore, Alexander and Polly Pinkerton, Feb. 28, 1797.
Amos H. and Catherine R. Forsaith, June 1, 1848.
Charles and Jennie H. McMurphy, Nov. 25, 1908. Res. Derry, N. H.
D. Brewster and Florence Hurd, Jan. 21, 1875.
David and Marietta Nesmith, Sept. 28, 1840.
David and Mrs. Mary E. Corning (2nd wife), Dec. 14, 1886.
Florence E., 20, and Frederic E. Moody, 26, Sept. 23, 1906.
Frank M., 23, and Alice E. Waugh, 20, July 14, 1887. Res. Derry, N. H.
Fred Davis and Mary Corrinne Bennett, June 17, 1891. Res. Haverhill, Mass.
George F. and Rhoda A. Barker, May 3, 1865. Silver wedding 1890.
Harriet (Nevins) (2nd wife) and Thomas P. Major (2nd hus.), ———, 1884. Res. Derry, N. H.
Isabella and Edward Ballou, Nov. 13, 1823.
Isabel D. and Frank J. Demeritt, Sept. 26, 1883.
James L. and Mary A. Hazelton, Dec. 3, 1884.
Lewis Aiken and Augusta Watts Blodgett, Nov. 30, 1843.

McGregor, Mary and Jonathan Emerson, June 1, 1848.
Mary Ann and Rev. John R. Adams, ———, 1832.
Mary Delia and Charles W. Foster, Oct. 21, 1890. Res. Nashua, N. H.
Rosa A. and Frank Lincoln, June 17, 1868.
Sam Alby and Alice Maude White, June 19, 1901. Res. Haverhill, Mass.
Sarah McGregor and Daniel W. Hayes, Aug. 19, 1869.
William K. and Harriet Nevins, Apr. 20, 1854.
William R. and Augusta May Annis (1st wife), Jan. 25, 1882.
William R. and Martha L. Watts (2nd wife), in Derry, N. H. Res. 1909 in Haverhill, Mass.

McHard, Mary and John Cochran, June 18, 1731, by Rev. Mr. Brown of Haverhill.

McIntire, Alice M. and William Clark, Aug. 23, 1876.

McKay, William and Myra Burnham, Nov. 19, 1902. Res. Farmdale Farm, Londonderry, N. H.

McKean, McKeen, John and Judith Wilson, Mar. 30, 1819.
John R. and Nellie M. Richardson, Sept. 19, 1883.
Mary F. and Samuel Eugene Moody, ———.
Samuel and Agnes Clark, Aug. 15, 1723.
Samuel and Mary Clark, Apr. 25, 1799.

McKenney, Andrew J. and Angeline M. Boyce, Apr. 10, 1862.
Angeline M. (Boyce) and L. P. Brady, ———, 1869.

McKertney, Elisabeth and William Cochran, Nov. 26, 1730.

McKinley, Catherine and Benjamin F. Annis, Feb. 27, 1851.
Margaret and Oliver Hill, Nov. 17, 1796.

McKnight, Anna and Daniel Corning, Nov. 8, 1798.

McMaster, Ann and ——— Kelsey, Dec. 27, ——.

McMurphy, Alexander and Lydia Dodge, Dec. 28, 1786.
Alexander and Sarah A. Gibson, Apr. 25, 1844. Res. Derry, N. H.
Betsey and Robert Boys, June, 1804.
Isabela and ——— Tallford, Mar. 11, ——, by Rev. Thomas Thomson.
Isabella and John Thompson, Dec., 1805.
James and Sarah Reed, Apr. 12, 1842.
Jane and Allen Goss, May 30, 1810.
Jean and John Tallford, Jan. 8, 1733-4, by Rev. Mr. Clark, minister of Kingstown.
Jennie H. and Charles McGregor, Nov. 25, 1908. Res. Derry, N. H

McMurphy, Jesse G. and and Mary L. James, Apr. 27, 1870.
Martha and David Reed, Sept. 7, 1797.
Mary and Forist Martin, Dec. 5, 1805.
Mary and James Lasley, Apr. 4, 1723, by Rev. Mr. McGregor.
Mary and William Duncan, Nov. 19, 1801.
Naomi and William Duncan, Apr. 21, 1836.
Robert and Jane Shirley, Mar. 10, 1747.
Robert, Junr., and Jane Rankin, Dec. 28, 1780.
Sarah and William Moar, Dec. 2, 1819.
Sarah J. and Jacob Chickering, Nov. 26, 1835.

McNeil, McNeill, MacNeal, Abram and Mary Patterson,
Alexander and Jean Rankine, Jan. 10, 1726–7, by Rev. Mr. McGregor.
Martha Jane and David Crowell, Mar. 18, 1841.

McQuesten, Daniel M., 25, and Mary E. Crowell, 22, Oct. 5, 1892. Res. Manchester, N. H.
George B. and Lydia Manter, —— (1st wife).
George B. and Lucy J. (Drew) Cross, —— (3d wife).
Letta K., 28, and Henry R. Hall, 42, Sept. 18, 1895.
Mary J. and Isaac S. Dickey, Oct. 19, 1893.
Sally G. and Eliphalet Richards, Jan. 25, 1816.
William and Lydia J. Read, Nov. 4, 1868.

McVier, Samuell and Agnes Clark, Aug. 5, 1723, by Rev. Mr. Perum of Lister.

Melrose, Alexander and Annie M. Downer, Oct. 23, 1889.

Melvin, James and Susannah Barret, Feb. 4, 1807.
Mary and Ebenezer Brown, Sept. 3, 1822.
Mary and Alfred Burroughs, ——. Res. Hudson, N. H.
Mehitable and John Woodburn, Feb. 23, 1820.
Mrs. Ann and Joshua Goodwin, —— (3d wife).
Sally and Currier Huntee, Jan. 1, 1839.
Sarah J. and Nelson Boyce, Apr. 11, 1850.

Merrill, Ellen F. and Alphonso Alexander, Nov., 1873.
Emily and Thomas S. Bradford, Nov. 16, 1843. Res. Derry.
George E. and Lottie D. Sanders, Nov. 8, 1868.
Hannah and Edward A. Manning, Nov. 27, 1834.
Hattie E., 20, and George W. Shattuck, 25, June 14, 1893.
Israel and Betsey Garvin, Dec., 1810.
John and Pauline L. Hovey, Mar. 15, 1842.
John Edward and Julia Kendrick, Nov., 1863.
John R. and Lydia March, Sept. 11, 1828.
Jonathan and Margaret Clark, July 2, 1822.
Laura A. and Eugene L. Spinney, Jan. 1, 1879.

Merrill, Nathaniel L. and Sophia Plummer, Sept. 20, 1836.
Oliver, 25, and Emma N. Smith, 25, Apr. 19, 1893.
Samuel and Mary Nichols, Feb. 8, 1810.
Stephen and Elisabeth Senter, June 16, 1809.
William Parker and Maria Boyce, about 1860. Res. Manchester, N. H.

Merrit, Merritt, Olive and William French, June 23, 1808.
Susie F., 26, and Sidney E. Laws, 26, Apr. 18, 1899.

Mertsch, Elsa A., 20, and Ralph W. Barker, 20, July 29, 1910.

Messer, Amos H. and Clara L. M. Flanders, Oct. 28, 1868.
Lydia and William Richardson, about 1874.
Sarah Josephine and Frank B. Pay, Oct. 12, 1904. Minn.
William F. and Lucy H. Noyes, Mar. 24, 1888.
William T. and Anna Pierce, ——, 1873.

Miles, Sarah J. and Gust P. Mills, Sept. 27, 1887.

Miller, Adams and Ann Robertson, Nov. 28, 1805.
Alice E., 25, and Charles George Pillsbury, 29, June 20, 1894.
Arthur G. and Grace Green, Dec. 25, 1908.
Carrie A. and Frank W. Parkhurst, July 7, 1881.
Emeline and Joseph Harvell, Nov. 1, 1869.
George W. and Nettie E. Brown, June 5, 1876.
Hannah and David Morrison, Dec. 23, 1802.
Lucinda and Hiram Cutler, Jan. 1, 1876.
Robert and Mary Boys, Nov. 17, 1808.

Mills, Gust P. and Sarah J. Miles, Sept. 27, 1887.

Miltemore, Daniel and Nancy Rankin(?), Nov. 1, 1798.
James and Nabby Fitts, Oct. 22, 1799.

Miner, Juline F. and Ralph H. Goodhue, Sept. 8, 1869. Res. Londonderry, N. H. 10 yrs. 1870's.

Mitchell, Abraham and Angeline Foss, Mar. 23, 1867.
Everett B. and Cynthia A. Pettingill, 23, May 31, 1887.
Mehitable and Jethniel Morse, Mar. 2, 1797.

Moar, Adeline M. and George W. Blood, May 17, 1849.
Asetta Josephine and George A. Hardy, Aug. 13, 1867.
Carrie Louise and Albert J. Bacon, Sept. 10, 1879.
Daniel and Elisabeth Clagget, Dec. 31, 1833.
Harriet L. and Charles E. Perkins, Oct. 8, 1861.
James and Jane Morrison, June 19, 1807.
James and Jenny Anderson, Apr. 1, 1823.
James and Patience Adams, Feb. 4, 1796.
John and Catherine Christy, Mar. 9, 1797.
John, Jr., and Alice Clark, Apr. 4, 1822.
Joshua A. and Lovina Witherspoon, Aug. 6, 1837.

Moar, Julia M. and James D. Page, Feb. 25, 1845.
Laura Ella and Charles E. Aldrich, Nov. 10, 1880.
Manuel and Sarah Jane Plumer, Apr. 23, 1850.
Mary and Gilman Gross, Nov. 13, 1828.
Mary Ann and Henry Goodwin, May 17, 1860.
Maria Jane and William W. Packer, Apr. 12, 1882.
Peter and Jenney Reid, Dec. 23, 1802.
Polly and Daniel Cochran, May 17, 1798.
Sarah Jane and John W. Barker, Feb. 2, 1846.
Soloman and Nabby Senter, Mar. 7, 1799.
William and Martha Holmes, Feb. 11, 1800.
William and Sarah McMurphy, Dec. 2, 1819.

Montgomery, Fanny and Joseph Dickey, Capt., Apr. 7, 1813. Golden wedding 1863.

Moody, Annie S., 18, and George W. Beede, 22, Apr. 25, 1900.
Annie S., 18, and George W. Beede, 22, Apr. 25, 1900.
Charles Edward, 23, and Nettie A. Rouse, 21, Mar. 21, 1899.
Frank and Emma Manter, ——.
Frederic E., 26, and Florence E. McGregor, 20, Sept. 23, 1906.
Jeremiah Bean and Dolly B. McDonald, Aug. 6, 1848.
Joseph and Lucinda H. Sargent, Dec. 1, 1853.
Samuel Elisha and Mary E. Palmer, Dec. 14, 1872 (1st wife).
Samuel Elisha and Mrs. Lottie Chase, Dec. 8, 1893 (2nd wife).
Samuel Eugene and Mary F. McKean, ——.
Sarah A. and Daniel W. Goodwin, May 11, 1873.
Volney H. and Nancy J. Gage, Sept. 3, 1885.

Moore, Beatrix and Andrew Todd, Dec. 18, 1722, by Rev. Mr. McGregor.
Cynthia and Washington L. Hay, Nov. 9, 1848.
Edward P. and Antonette H. Conant, Nov. 11, 1854.
Elder John A. and Nancy E. Armstrong, Nov. 25, 1854. Pres. Ch., Londonderry, N. H.
Ella J. and Phineas W. Dickey, June 6, 1877. Res. Manchester, N. H.
John and Jean Cochran, Apr. 2, 1723, by Rev. Mr. McGregor.
Joseph C. and Ann Groves Brown, 1823. (Spinner Joe.)
Nellie and John P. Fling, May 5, 1884. Res. Auburn, N. H.
Sarah A. and Henry H. White, Nov. 29, 1860, Goffe's Falls, N. H. Res. Londonderry, N. H.
Walter H. and Martha M. Scollay, Oct. 18, 1876.

Moore, William Russell, 25, and Blanche C. Campbell, 18, Jan. 1, 1895.

Morey, Luella F. and Daniel A. Ware, ——, 1874.

Morrill, Hannah and Edward McGrath, Mar. 14, 1799.
Hannah and Micheal Whidden, ——, 1810.
John and Polly McFarland, May, 1798.

Morrison, Abraham and Silence Hall of Gifford, Conn., Feb. 19, 1710. L. A. Morrison Hist.
Ann and John Adams, Oct. 31, 1799.
Charles F., 30, and Sarah Haigh, 32, Dec. 22, 1888.
David and Hannah Miller, Dec. 23, 1802.
David and Peggy Nesmith, Feb. 6, 1806.
Deacon's dau. and Jesse Anderson, Feb. 14, 1805.
Emeline and Edward Payson Boynton, Apr. 7, 1868. Res. Cambridge, Mass.
James and Betsey Warner, Nov., 1813.
James G. and Phebe Robinson, May 1, 1855.
Jane and James Moar, June 19, 1807.
Jane and Robert M. Wallace, Dec. 27, 1810.
Jenney and Robert Dickey, May 24, 1821.
John and Jenney Paul, May 28, 1801.
John and Polly Paul, Sept. 22, 1801.
John and Sally Coburn, Mar. 31, 1831.
John and Sally Morrison, Mar. 9, 1809.
Joseph and Mary Ann Reid, Oct. 18, 1803.
Mark M. and Susie A. Swallow, Nov. 18, 1885.
Mary and Matthew A. Paul, Nov. 15, 1804.
Mrs. Phebe A. and Silas P. Towns, Mar. 24, 1864.
Robert G. and Nellie E. Woodbury, Mar. 17, 1881.
Sally and John Morrison, Mar. 9, 1809.
Sarah and Robert McGaw, June 8, 1811.
Susan M. and Nathan P. Webster, May 17, 1860.
Thomas and Sally Giles, Dec. 15, 1824.
William O., 22, and Mattie E. Corbett, 22, Dec. 19, 1891.

Morse, Amos, Jr., and Abigail Rogers, Apr. 20, 1819.
Euretta J. and Abram A. Woodbury, May 27, 1874.
Jethniel and Mehitable Mitchell, Mar. 2, 1797.
L. Foster and Annie Conant, May 2, 1861.
Parmelia and George F. Lawson, Mar. 29, 1838.
Persis L. and Dr. William Wesley Wilkins, Aug. 5, 1852. Res. Manchester, N. H.
Rev. John and Mary Boyes, Feb. 2, 1837.
Sarah A. and Darwin F. Robie, ——, 1872.
Sarah M. and Matthew Parker Annis, Sept. 26, 1850.

Mosher, Ada W. and Percy A. Campbell, Aug. 14, 1907.

Moulton, James N. and Julia M. Spinney, Sept., 1868.
Lucinda and Nathaniel Webster, Dec. 12, 1839.
R. Ida and Charles A. Blood, Dec. 12, 1875. Both of Manchester, N. H.

Mount, Alice and George W. Manter, June 8, 1898. Res. Manchester, N. H.

Mower, Mary E. (Downing) and James M. Greeley, Apr. 30, 1873. Res. Derry, N. H.

Mudgett, Jennie U. and Edward Sampson, Aug. 11, 1866.

Muffet, David and Betsey Gregg, Sept. 7, 1797.

Mullen, Thomas Joseph and Margaret Agatha Owens, Oct. 15, 1895.

Mullins, Amanda R., 55, and Robert A. Brown, 58, Apr. 8, 1890.
Augusta B. and Joseph Mayo, Sept. 16, 1862.
Betsey and William Annis, Dec. 5, 1846.
Clara and Oliver B. Norton, Sept. 18, 185(?).
Eugene N. and Emeline B. Greeley, Nov. 29, 1883.
Hattie P. and Daniel M. Boyd, May 7, 1884.
Israel and Mary Garvin, Apr. 25, 1819.
Louise E. and Lucien H. Nesmith, May 23, 1877.
Simon and Harriet Cheney, Dec. 23, 1847.
T. Jane and George D. Johnson, Nov. 8, 1846.

Muncaster, Sarah, 36, and Wilbur E. Barrett, 49, Jan. 22, 1907.

Murdoch, Lettus and James Caldwell, Oct. 23, 1724, by Rev. Mr. Adams of Newington.

Murdock, William and Caroline Holmes, May 28, 1849.

Murray, Lizzie and Oscar E. Furber, Nov. 30, 1882. Res. Boston, Mass.

Mussey, Frank and Mary Boyce, ——. Res. Maine.

Myrick, Ruth and Nehemiah Jones, Aug. 29, 1860.

Nahor, Jane and Adam Dickey, Dec. 26, 1765.
Jane P. and Joseph Bartlett, Mar. 30, 1832.

Neal, Betsey and Benjamin Robinson, June 14, 1819.
Henrietta, 42, and Lyman A. Dickey, 67, Apr. 22, 1908.
Levi and Mary Clark, May 26, 1796.
Moses L. and Patty Prentice, Feb. 22, 1796.

Nelson, Mary J. and George W. Wilson, Apr. 29, 1867, Sutton, N. H. Res. 1910, Boston, Mass.

Nesmith, Arvilla and Washington Colby, Nov. 1, 1855.
Cleon E., 22, and Lena Mae Smith, 16, Oct. 25, 1905.
Elisabeth and John C. Corning, June 12, 1817.
Eliza and Isaac Coburn, Jr., Dec. 29, 1836.

Nesmith, Frank A., 23, and Clara Belle Corning, 21, Dec. 22, 1889.
James and Polly Corning, Feb. 1, 1816.
Jonathan Y. and Adeline A. Boyce, Nov. 25, 1852.
Jane and Hughey Anderson, Mar. 2, 1796.
Lucien Huse and Louise E. Mullins, May 23, 1877.
Margaret M. and Thomas Parker, Oct. 19, 1837.
Marietta and David McGregor, Sept. 28, 1840.
Martha and Elijah Leach, Mar. 27, 1834.
Peggy and David Morrison, Feb. 6, 1806.

Nevins, Harriet and William K. McGregor, Apr. 20, 1854.
Harriet Julia, 28, and Eddie H. Davenport, 36, June 27, 1906.
Mabel F. M., 35, and Wesley Adams, 35, June 21, 1908.
Mary and Frederick A. Gilcreast, Aug. 24, 1865.
William P. and Julia D. Shipley, Sept. 14, 1871.

Newman, Nancy and David Nichols.

Nichols, Abraham and Hannah Nichols, Feb. 23, 1809.
Archie B., 22, and Mary C. Osborn, 27, May 30, 1894.
David and Nancy Newman.
Eldora and Daniel Griffin, Nov. 24, 1867.
Ensign and Sarah Dismore, July 8, 1819.
Francis R., 19, and Ada J. Smith, 17, Oct. 12, 1910.
Hannah and Abraham Nichols, Feb. 23, 1809.
Hannah C. and Frederick Spullet, Jan., 1820.
James and Dinah Woodburn (1st wife), about 1755.
James and Hannah Caldwell, ——— (2nd wife).
James and Nancy Fowler, about 1788.
James and Sarah Senter, May 6, 1817.
Joseph and Rebecca Emery, Nov. 12, 1813.
Laura E. and Charles K. Titcomb, Mar. 19, 1874.
Lizzie M. and William A. Holmes, Feb. 17, 1871.
Margaret and James Kincaid, about 1753.
Mary and Samuel Merrill, Feb. 8, 1810.
Rebecca and Joseph Buckingham, Jan. 6, 1814.
Sally and John Elkins, Sept., 1798.
Samuel and Mary Cunningham, Oct. 24, 1799.
Stephen and Eliza Towns, June 22, 1819.
Susannah and Eliphalet Boverington, Dec. 3, 1801.
Thomas and Agnes Karr, Aug. 31, 1797.
William and Ann Cochran, Oct. 20, 1724.
William Anderson and Sarah Kelley March, Dec. 25, 1851.

Noglar, Maria and George E. Allen, Mar. 23, 1876.

Norcross, Joshua L. and Mary Elisabeth Noyes, Feb. 18, 1857.

Norcross, Mary E. (Noyes) and Martin M. Bowles, Dec. 19, 1869.
Vira A. and George V.

Norton, Oliver B. and Clara Mullins, Sept. 18, 185(?).

Noyes, Bennie, 19, and Emily L. Boone, Sept. 1, 1900.
Benning and Mary Barstow Warren, Aug. 2, 1835.
Bertha M., 19, and Austin H. Jenkins, July 19, 1902.
Charles W., 24, and Lillian A. Bailey, Nov. 21, 1901.
Clara J. and Almon Richardson, Dec. 25, 1876.
James M. and Amanda P. Austin, July 4, 1872.
Joseph T. and Harriet Corning Harvey (1st wife), ——.
Joseph T. and Mary A. Richardson (2nd wife), Dec. 12, 1871.
Lucy H. and William Freeman Messer, Mar. 24, 1888.
Martha C. and Charles A. M. Clark, July 3, 1879.
Mary Elisabeth and Joshua L. Norcross (1st hus.), Feb. 18, 1857.
Mary Elisabeth and Martin M. Bowles (2nd hus.), Dec. 19, 1869.
Phylena, 16, and Joseph G. Abbott, Sept. 1, 1906.
Walter E., 20, and Nellie A. Quint, Apr. 19, 1899.

Nugent, Ernestine E., 36, and Hiram N. Cross, June 14, 1909.
Marian B., 20, and Harry C. Corliss, Apr. 27, 1904.

Nurse, David and Sally Pike, Apr. 10, 1803.

Nute, Harriet Esther and Walter Stevens Young, June 25, 1910. Res. Worcester, Mass.

Nutt, Augusta R., 23, and Myron Richardson, 25, Nov. 30, 1889.
James and Sally Boyce, Feb. 24, 1791.
William and Joan Colbath, May 29, 1723, by Rev. Mr. Symms of Bradford.

Nutting, Romanzo L. and Martha Woodbury, Mar. 19, 1885.

Oliver, Margaret, 24, and Edw. Q. F. Brooks, 31, June 3, 1908.

Olsen, Albert D. A., 35, and Grace M. Theiss, 27, June 16, 1909.

Orne, John and Betsey Doak, Feb. 13, 1803.

Orr, Lucy and Benjamin Shute, Feb. 10, 1803.
Susan and John Warner, Oct., 1813.

Osborn, Carrie, 15, and John W. Greeley, 2nd, 27, June 12, 1887.
Mary C., 27, and Archie B. Nichols, 22, May 30, 1894.
William A., 25, and Civilla C. Doherty, 26, Jan. 2, 1897.

Osgood, ——— and Anne McDuffee, Jan. 4, 1802.

Otterson, Pauline and Edward Kelley, Aug. 11, 1860.

Otis, Mary Jane and Henry F. Straw, Dec. 18, 1845.

Owen, Anna J. and Jesse O. Emerson, Mar. 7, 1860.

Owens, Margaret Agatha and Thomas Joseph Mullen, Oct. 15, 1895.

Pace, Fred W., 24, and Augusta Young, 20, Feb. 24, 1897.

Packer, William W. and Maria Jane Moar, Apr. 12, 1882.

Page, Almira and Edmund B. Sargent, Sept. 8, 1835.
Amos and Sarah Holmes, Nov. 15, 1805.
Charles P. and Mehitable Manter, July 4, 1845.
Eliza and Jonathan Griffin, Nov. 26, 1807.
Eliza H. and James J. Chase, Sept. 28, 1873.
Franklin and Betsey Barker, Apr. 18, 1839.
Hannah and James Pinkerton, Dec. 1, 1808.
Hannah and William Steele, Dec. 26, 1811.
Hannah D. and Samuel C. Barker, July 10, 1834. Golden wedding 1884.
James D. and Julia M. Moore, Feb. 25, 1845.
Joel and Rachel Fling, Nov. 19, 1833.
Jonathan and Agnes Wallace, May 26, 1797.
Joseph and Mary E. Goss, Apr. 24, 1862.
Leonard and Mary Austin, Feb. 7, 1846.
Lydia D. and Henry F. Gilmore, Sept. 18, 1844.
Mary J. and Daniel M. Annis, June 4, 1859.
Mehitable and Samuel W. Annis, June 1, 1856.
Nancy D. and Samuel N. Payne, May 1, 1845.
Ruth J. and Andrew J. Benson, Jan. 1, 1851.
Sally and Edward Ela, Dec. 26, 1810.
Samuel and Betsey Webster, Dec. 27, 1809.
Sarah E. and David F. Cheney, Nov. 17, 1886.
Susan (Clark), 7–, and J. Morrison Chase, 70, Jan. 23, 1897.

Paige, Alice E. and Nelson W. Paige, Oct. 9, 1890.
Lester C. and Annabelle F. Landers, July 31, 1907. Res. Manchester, N. H.
Nelson W. and Alice E. Paige, Oct. 9, 1890. Res. Manchester, N. H.

Palmer, Anna C. and Caleb M. Watts, about 1859 (2nd wife).
Hannah and James Steele, Nov. 12, 1813.
Maria L. and Joseph S. Goodwin, Oct. 31, 1886.
Mary E. and Samuel E. Moody, Dec. 14, 1872.

Parker, Almira A. and William H. Crowell, Sept. 12, 1866.
Celinda P. and John A. Corning, Dec., 1861.

Parker, Eliza A. and Andrew J. Kike, Nov. 17, 1861. Res. Litchfield, N. H.
Rev. Edward L. and Mehitable Kimball, ——, 1811. Pastor East Church 40 years.
Gertrude E. and Onslow L. Greeley, July 4, 1872.
Henry H. and Eliza J. Buckham, Feb. 22, 1872.
Lafayette W. and Hamrand Wyman, Dec. 7, 1845.
Nathan, Jr., and Lauraett Gregg, Feb. 15, 1870.
Thomas and Margaret M. Nesmith, Oct. 19, 1837.

Parkhurst, Emma E. and John W. McDole, Dec. 25, 1880.
Frank W. and Carrie A. Miller, July 7, 1881.

Parks, Joseph and Mary Dinsmore, Feb. 25, 1797.

Parmerton, Maria Louisa and William D. Young, May 10, 1894. Res. Manchester, N. H.

Parshley, Edward A. and Ethel M. Bunker, May 27, 1907. Res. Derry, N. H.
Enoch and Mrs. Julia A. Varel, Oct. 5, 1869, in Ottawa, N. Y. Res. Londonderry, N. H.
Mary V., 23, and Joseph R. McDonald, 27, Aug. 22, 1900.
Russell V. and Maude A. Webster, June 16, 1909. Res. Derry, N. H.

Parsons, Hannah and Rev. Rufus Anderson, Sept. 8, 1795.

Patten, Asenath and Daniel W. Fling, Dec. 25, 1844. Res. Manchester, N. H.
Jane and Hugh Smith, Dec. 15, 1795.

Patterson, Elisabeth and William Duncan, Nov. 17, 1842.
Elisabeth W. and Alexander Johnston, May 4, 1848.
Grizzy and David Barnett, Feb. 20, 1814.
Jane D. and Robert C. Mack, Mar. 6, 1856.
John D. and Hannah Eaton, Sept. 24, 1846.
Margaret and Samuel F. Taylor, Mar. 22, 1810.
Mary and Abram McNeal, Feb. 2, 1807.
Peter and Mary Wallace, Nov. 8, 1814.
Thomas and Elisabeth Wallace, June 1, 1775.
Thomas and Hannah Duncan, Apr. 30, 1818.

Paul, Jenny and John Morrison, May 28, 1801.
Martha and Adam Taylor, Feb. 1, 1798.
Matthew A. and Mary Morrison, Nov. 15, 1804.
Nancy and Moses Wingate, Mar. 3, 1814.
Polly and John Morrison, Sept. 22, 1801.
Samuel and Mary Thompson, Dec. 30, 1804.

Pay, Frank B. and Sarah Josephine Messer, Oct. 12, 1904. Res. Minn.

Payne, Anna M. and Irving D. Gordon, Nov. 28, 1894. Res. Derry, N. H.

Payne, Charles Herbertson and Anna M. Johnson, Oct. 18, 1874.
Charles Herbertson and ——— Pressey, ———.
George E. and Carrie Corning, Aug. 24, 1876.
John P. and Anna M. Densmore, July 2, 1876.
Nelson S. and Abbie J. Walsh, Aug. 19, 1877.
Samuel N. and Nancy D. Page, May 1, 1845.
Wesley W. and Maroia Wychoff, Dec. 25, 1885.
Wesley W. and Mabel L. Sefton, Oct. 23, 1889 (2nd wife).

Peabody, Annie 43, and George Lary, 60, Oct. 1, 1903.
Asa A. and Lydia Cutter Tenney, Apr. 6, 1853.
Elbridge W. and Mary A. Combs (Perham), May 19, 1859, in Derry, N. H. Res. Londonderry, N. H.
Elisabeth and Charles Tenney, Apr. 6, 1843.
Elwin C. and Minnie M. Fling, Oct. 14, 1885.
Eviline and James M. Gilcreast, Sept. 9, 1847.
Henrietta L. and Joseph Roach, ———, 1870.
Jonathan Warren and Mary Tenney, Apr. 16, 1846.
John and Clarrissa Garvin, Apr. 3, 1830.
Lucretia and David Carroll, Feb. 14, 1804.
Marinda and John Gilcreast, Nov. 15, 1849.
Orriville A. and Maria White, ———, 1850.
Orriville A. and Mrs. Emily Brickett, Dec. 17, 1873.

Peck, Lucina and Rev. Irad Taggart, Jan. 22, 1851. Golden wedding 1901.

Pecker, William and Julia M. Conant, June 18, 1884.

Pelham, Charles and Anna Chase, Jan. 1, 1850.

Pelton, Leverett S. and Sarah H. Batchelder, Sept. 25, 1845.

Perham, Esther and William McClintock Dickey, Feb. 15, 1798.
Franklin and Margaret Dickey, Jan. 24, 1837.
John and Eliza C. Prentiss, Apr. 23, 1870.
Mary and Jonathan Young, Dec. 25, 1794. Res. Manchester, N. H.
Rev. Elbridge G. and Mary Ann Coames, Nov. 13, 1854.

Perkins, Charles E. and Harriet L. Moar, Oct. 8, 1861.
David F. and Jennie S. Corning, Feb. 13, 1884.
Dea. James and Sally Smith, Nov. 20, 1806.
Elisabeth and Reed P. Clark, Apr. 2, 1835.
Nellie Louise and Arthur B. Broadhead, Feb. 29, 1908.
Washington and Jane Youngman, July 2, 1850.

Perley, Asa and Judith Corning, June 4, 1817.
Charles W. and Nellie Margaret Morey, Jan. 4, 1868.

Perley, Charles W. and Mary E. Williston, Dec. 25, 1874.
Charles W. and Rosilla F. (Rines) (Currier), Dec. 31, 1879. Res. Hopkinton, N. H.

Perry, Richard and Betsey Rand, Oct. 12, 1841.

Pervere, Mary A. and Frank H. Brickett, Sept. 8, 1872. Res. Bedford, N. H.

Pervier, Almira F. and Josiah H. Pillsbury.

Peterson, Esther E. C. and George E. Sampson, Aug. 15, 1901.
Eunice and John Hardy, Sept. 23, 1879.

Pettengill, Addie J., 17, and George F. Aiken, 26, Oct. 29, 1879.
Addie J., 43, and Edward S. Colburn, June 27, 1905. Res. Newton, Mass.
Betsey and William M. Richardson, Dec. 28, 1820.
Cynthia A., 23, and Everett B. Mitchell, May 31, 1887.
David and Eliza J. Barker, Nov. 15, 1859.
David and Emily Barnes, Dec. 24, 1835.
Elisabeth and Isaac Chase, Mar. 20, 1843.
Emeline Mrs. and John P. Young, Dec. 24, 1868.
Emily J. and Samuel Clark, Feb. 25, 1858. Golden wedding 1908.
George C., 30, and Eva A. Simpson, 21, June 17, 1906.
George M., 22, and Sarah A. Shehan, July 4, 1893. Res. Haverhill, Mass.
James and Eliza Adams, Dec. 26, 1848.
James B., M. D., and Ada E. Bartlett, Sept. 22, 1881.
James M. and Priscilla C. Hobbs, Nov. 11, 1858.
Jane and Oliver McArthur, about 1865.
Jane and Warren Martin, Dec. 20, 1832.
Josephine, 18, and Guy A. Lewis, 20, Oct. 19, 1899. Res. Pelham, N. H.
Margaret J. and Isaac S. Dickey, Dec. 20, 1842.
Mary M. and Robert H. Bunton, Apr. 12, 1853.
Nancy Maria and Trueworthy D. Chase, May 19, 1853.
Nathaniel and Mrs. Elvira Libby, nee Hobbs, Apr. 22, 1855. at Merrimack, N. H. Res. Londonderry, N. H.
Rachel and Nathaniel Watts, Nov. 22, 1810.
Richard L. and Philimon Rousseau, Dec. 15, 1874, at Lowell, Mass. Res. Londonderry.
Warren and Jane Watts, Dec. 11, 1810.
Warren Martin and Angeline M. Barker, Apr. 13, 1859.
William and Peggy Watts, Aug. 10, 1798.

Philbrick, Charlotte A. M. and Dr. William J. Campbell, Nov. 15, 1849 (2nd wife).
Sarah and Ebenezer Colby, July 13, 1825.

Phillips, Asa and Betsey Jackson, Feb. 11, 1800.
John and Dolly Barrow (?), Mar. 10, 1805.
Joseph L. and Salome Ripley, Aug. 14, 1837.

Pickering, Daniel O. and Mary O. Kennerson, July 21, 1854.
Ebenezer and Harriet A. Mansur, Jan. 4, 1846.

Pierce, Anna and William T. Messer, ——, 1873.
Stephen and Sarah Platts, ———. Res. New Ipswich, N. H.

Pike, Andrew J. and Eliza A. Parker, Nov. 17, 1861. Res. Litchfield, N. H.
Fanny A., 20, and Frank A. Hardy, 27, June 14, 1893.
Hannah and Jonathan Kendall, May 25, 1843.
Sally and David Nurse, Apr. 10, 1803.

Pillsbury, Ann Judson and William Marshall, ———.
Charles George, 29, and Alice E. Miller, 25, June 20, 1894.
Charles L. and Fannie A. Tyson, ———. Res. Denver, Col.
Charles S. and Mary C. Clough, Dec. 24, 1863, in Warner, N. H. Res. Londonderry.
Edith (Davis) and George P. Wallace, Apr. 24, 1907. Res. Manchester, N. H.
Edwin and Mary Ann Reed, ———.
Harriet L., 21, and Wallace P. Mack, 28, Feb. 24, 1892.
Josiah H. and Alnora F. Pervier, ———.
Leonard Hobart and Evelyn Sanborn, ———. Res. Derry, N. H.
Louisa F. and Rev. Edward Buxton, Dec. 29, 1871.
Maria, 24, and Harold Scott Taylor, 27, Sept. 14, 1910. Res. Manchester, N. H.
Rosecrans W. and Annie E. Watts, Dec. 10, 1885.
Sally and Thomas Raynolds, Oct., 1804.
Stephen, Rev., and Lovinia Hobart, Mar. 3, 1816.
Stephen, Jr., and Sarah Bailey, ———, at Andover, N. H.
Ulysses Grant, 20, and Edith H. Davis, 18, Nov. 25, 1896.
William S., Col., and Sarah A. Crowell, May 8, 1854.
William S., Col., and Martha S. Crowell, Apr. 15, 1856. Golden wedding 1906.

Pinkerton, Anna and Samuel Warren, Dec. 27, 1798.
Clarissa and Robert E. Little, ———.
David and Susanna Griffin, Feb. 14, 1800.
Frances C. and Dr. Luther V. Bell, Sept. 2, 1834.
Major John and Rachel Duncan, ——— (1st wife).
Major John and Polly Tufts, Dec. 18, 1801 (2nd wife).
James and Hannah Page, Dec. 1, 1808.
James and Sally Wallace, May 15, 1809.
Jane and Joshua Aiken, July 28, 1815.
Mary B. and William Choate, Dec. 27, 1815.
Polly and Alexander McGregore, Feb. 28, 1799.

Pinkerton, Rebecca and Thomas Wilson, Feb. 4, 1807.
Rebecca W. and Perkins A. Hodge, ——.

Pitcher, Theron R. and Harriet M. B. White, Oct. 16, 1854. Res. Canton, Mass.

Platt, Emily R., 25, and Delphus O. Tuttle, 29, Dec. 25, 1909.
William and Emily Crowell, Mar. 23, 1883.

Platts, Abigail (2nd wife) and Dea. Moses Fisk, Oct. 10, 1839.
George W. and Mary F. Manter, Oct. 20, 1853.
Harold James and Margaret Gauser, ——, 1907. Res. Alameda, Cal.
James and Sophia Crowningshield, Mar. 11, 1823. Res. Brasher, N. Y.
James M. and Harriet Manter, Oct. 9, 1849.
Nancy and Josiah Walker, Nov. 4, 1806.
Nathaniel T. and Bertha Young, ——, 1908. Res. Manchester, N. H.
Sarah and Reuben Walker, Oct. 26, 1809. Res. Bedford, N. H.
Sarah and Stephen Pierce, ——. Res. New Ipswich, N. H.
Sophia (Crowningshield) and Jonah Johnson, in New York (2nd hus.).
Susan (1st wife) and Dea. Moses Fisk, ——. Res. East Covington, N. Y.
Thomas B. and Susan D. Emerson, May 12, 1856.

Plumer, Abel and Polly Anderson, Mar., 1808.
Abel and Sophia Sargent, Feb. 4, 1834.
Betsey and Jonathan Shute, June, 1806.
Debby and John Dwinell, Nov. 25, 1806.
Elisabeth H. and Joshua B. Cheswell, Sept. 8, 1823.
Emma A. and Capt. J. F. Hobbs, ——, 1868.
Granville F. and Kate E. Hughes, Nov. 26, 1874.
Mary and Stephen Poor, Sept. 1, 1801.
Mary and Thomas Chase, ——.
Sarah Jane and Manuel Moar, Apr. 23, 1850.
Sophia and Nehemiah L. Merrill, Sept. 20, 1836.
Susan and Darius A. Farwell, Dec. 14, 1848.
William, 2nd, and Sybil Ann Coffin, Apr. 29, 1847.

Plummer, Ethel Maude, 21, and Clarence E. Maxfield, 21, June 9, 1909.
George Nathan, 49, and Eliza Maude Annis, 25, May 17, 1898.
Judith C. and Elder Henry Crowell, Oct. 3, 1850.
Nathan and Charlotte Towns (Boyd), ——, 1846.
Robert Kittredge, 55, and Laura Levica Benson, 19, ——, 1902.

Plummer, William and Sarah Wilson McCharg, Apr. 6, 1886, in Leeds, P. Q. Rem. to Londonderry, 1903.

Poff, Francis H., Jr., and Laura Maude Greeley, Oct. 5, 1879.

Pollard, Lucy and William Danforth, Oct. 10, 1779.
Nathan A. and Etta M. Abbott, Sept. 11, 1860.
Susan and John Taylor, Feb. 14, 1822.

Poor, Perry and Caroline Chipman, May 13, 1852.
Phebe and Jonathan Little, Dec. 29, 1803.
Stephen and Betsey Duster, Nov. 24, 1795.
Stephen and Mary Plumer, Sept. 1, 1801.
Susan E. and Augustus F. Garvin, July 5, 1863. Res. Revere, Mass.

Pope, Samuel and Fanny Dismore, Dec., 1806.

Porter, Billy and Lettice Wallace, June 8, 1797.

Potter, Albert and Alma J. Woodbury, July 26, 1879.
Emma A. and Corydon L. Manter, Nov. 24, 1880, in Providence, R. I. Res. Manchester, N. H.
Nabby and Samuel Stinson, Aug. 1, 1799.

Pratt, Reuben K., 46, and Hannah J. Estey, 45, Oct. 30, 1891.

Prentice, Eliza and Samuel Adams, Sept. 21, 1801.
Patty and Moses L. Neal, Feb. 22, 1796.

Prentiss, Eliza C. and John Perham, Apr. 23, 1870.

Pressey, Edward P., 28, and Grace H. Gibson, 28, June 25, 1897.

Preston, Frances A. and Andrew W. Mack, Mar. 20, 1861.

Proctor, Charlotte and Ephraim Barnet, Mar., 1813.
Etta M., 26, and F. Henry Bartlett, 30, Jan. 11, 1893.
Herman and Sarah Whittemore, Nov. 28, 1833.
Humphrey and Charlotte Allen, Mar. 6, 1806.
Iva B., 19, and Morley E. Hollingshead, 21, June 14, 1909. Res. Derry, N. H.
Joseph and Polly Hughs, Mar. 4, 1802.
John and Lucy Proctor, Jan. 20, 1803.
Lucy and John Proctor, Jan. 20, 1803.
Mrs. ——— and Joseph Richardson, ———, 1873, of Manchester, N. H.
Nancy and Samuel Gilcreast, Nov. 27, 1845. Golden wedding 1895.
Pearl C., 18, and Seth G. Wing, 22, Apr. 5, 1904.
Rhoda and Benjamin F. March, Feb. 5, 1835.
Royal S., 18, and Edith F. Boyce, 23, Aug. 9, 1906.
William and Georgietta Garvin, ———. Res. Revere, Mass.

Provencher, Emma, 16, and Fred E. Garvin, 21, July 28, 1894. Res. Derry, N. H.

Putnam, Ednah S. and John W. Berry, July 2, 1864.
Edward and Betsey Bancroft, Mar. 12, 1869.
Elbert O., 21, and Maude E. Campbell, 18, Apr. 27, 1892. Res. Litchfield, N. H.
Horace B. and Rachel Hurd, Nov. 24, 1853.
Jacob and Lucy Baras(?), Apr. 27, 1803.
Mrs. Betsey T. and George W. Chrispeen, May 13, 1875.

Quimby, Frederic H. and Lillian E. Annis, June 2, 1906. Res. Derry, N. H.
John E. and Sarah Crowell, Oct. 6, 1880.

Quint, Nellie A., 19, and Walter E. Noyes, 20, Apr. 19, 1899.

Rainey, Joseph T. and Hattie L. Hayes, Dec. 14, 1892.

Ramsey, William H., 40, and Emma H. Dudley, 28, Nov. 29, 1888.

Rand, Betsey and Richard Perry, Oct. 12, 1841.

Rankin, Jane and Robert McMurphey, Jr., Dec. 28, 1780.
Jean and John Crombie, Nov. 17, 1721, by Rev. Mr. McGregor.
Joan and Alexander McNeal, Jan. 10, 1726–7.
Nancy(?) and Daniel Miltemore, Nov. 1, 1798.

Rankine, Jenat and William Gregg, Mar. 11, 1724–5, by Rev. Mr. McGregor.
——— and John Gregg, Mar. 11, 1724/5, by Rev. Mr. McGregor.

Rapp, Maxime J. and Freeman H. Hardy, June 21, 1904.

Ray, John Edw., 20, and Anna M. Stone, 19, July 3, 1894.

Rayner, Alphonso and Menora Manter, ———. Res. Goffstown, N. H.

Raynolds, Thomas and Sally Pillsbury, Oct., 1804.

Read, Lydia J. and William McQuestion, Nov. 4, 1868.

Redfield, Charles and Betsey Adams, Dec. 16, 1813.

Reed, Abby R. (Hazen) and Jonathan Dana, ———, 1880.
Bethiah and Isaac Blodgett, May 4, 1843.
David and Martha McMurphy, Sept. 7, 1797.
George W. and Mary M. Smith, Nov. 27, 1842.
Ida E. and Willis Prescott Boyce, June 23, 1884. Res. California.
Isabel and Capt. Samuel Manter, about 1822.
Mary Ann and Edwin Pillsbury (son of Rev. Stephen, Sen.), ———.
Sarah and James McMurphy, Apr. 12, 1842.
Walter D. and Ella M. Evans, Oct. 1, 1871.

Reid, Anne and Alexander Wilson, Mar., 1809.
Gen. George and Mary Woodburn, Apr. 16, 1765.
Jenny and Peter Moar, Dec. 23, 1802.
Maria Boyd and Samuel Dinsmore, June 19, 1798.
Mary and Joseph Gregg, Feb. 26, 1805.
Mary Ann and Joseph Morrison, Oct. 18, 1803.
Phineas A. and Addie A. Chase, Jan. 14, 1886.
Walter and Philomelia S. Young, ———, 1869.

Remington, John and Mary Garland, Aug. 4, 1856.
Mary A. and Stephen A. Estey, Nov. 29, 1877.

Reside (?), Betsey and Robert Taggart, Feb. 7, 1800.

Rhodes, Ezra, Jr., and Nancy Bruce, Aug. 24, 1809.
Reuben and Hannah Steele, Feb., 1807.

Rice, Charles H. and Addie Gusta Bailey, ———.
John N. and Martha R. Bancroft, May 9, 1846.

Richards, Eliphalet and Sally G. McQuesten, Jan. 25, 1816.
Martha A. and Rufus Anderson, May 8, 1848.

Richardson, Almira and Dr. George W. Manter, June 17, 1849. Res. Auburn. N. H.
Almon C. and Clara J. Noyes, Dec. 25, 1876.
David D. and Mary E. Clark, Oct. 4, 1871.
Edward and Polly Cammett (?), Oct. 26, 1797.
Eliza J. and David C. Barker, Sept. 29, 1845.
Florence E., 20, and George L. Dickey, 24, May 28, 1906.
Isaac and Jane P. Sidman, Mar. 24, 1810.
Joseph and Mrs. Proctor, ———, 1873, of Manchester, N. H.
Lavina E. and George R. Judd, Dec. 26, 1845.
Margaret (1st wife) and Horace Adams, ———.
Mary Ann and Joseph T. Noyes, Dec. 12, 1871.
Mary L. and Charles H. Gilmore, Nov. 27, 1862, or Nov. 26, 1861.
Myron, 25, and Augusta R. Nutt, 23, Nov. 30, 1889.
Nehemiah and Elisabeth Archer, Oct., 1867.
Nellie and John Charles Barker, July 3, 1879.
Nellie M. and John R. McKean, Sept. 19, 1883.
Pearson and Betsey Simonds, Dec. 31, 1795.
Samuel and Mary Grace Fox, Dec. 25, 1880. Res. Auburn, N. H.
Sarah, 22, and Charles H. Annis, 23, Oct. 16, 1888.
William Pettengill and Sarah H. Goodwin, Dec. 10, 1855.
William and Elisabeth Wiseman, Aug. 22, 1654, at Newbury, Mass.
William and Lydia Messer, about 1784.
William Messer and Betsey Pettengill, Dec. 28, 1820.
William M. D. and Esther F. Whidden, Aug. 27, 1884.

Richmond, Nancy and George Manter, ——, 17— (1st wife).

Rines, Rosilla F. and Charles W. Perley, Dec. 31, 1879.

Ripley, Hugh H. and Lydia S. Greeley, Sept. 9, 1834.
Martin C. and Mrs. Sarah A. Manter, ——, 1867.
Saloma and Joseph L. Phillips, Aug. 14, 1837.
Susan W. and Zachariah K. H. Whittemore, Apr. 2, 1867.

Ritchie, Hannah H. and James Sevey Griffin, Oct. 10, 1811.
John and Elener McConihue, June 21, 1722, by Rev. Mr. McGregor.

Roach, Fred L., 20, and Retta M. Robie (Morse), 22, July 13, 1897.
Hattie E., 17, and William Washington Gage, 25, Apr. 16, 1890.
Hattie E. (Gage), 32, and Nathan P. Watts, 37, June 12, 1906.
Joseph and Henrietta L. Peabody, ——, 1870.
Mary H. and Irving H. Greeley, Feb. 12, 1885.

Robbins, Elizabeth A. and Rev. Roy Eugene Whittemore.

Roberts, Nellie, 36, and Thomas Valentine, 31, May 19, 1897.

Robertson, Andrew and Polly Barker, July 1, 1802.
Anne and Adams Miller, Nov. 28, 1805.
Rebecca and Elbridge Robie, Dec. 22, 1836.

Robie, Abby and Gilbert Weaver, June 23, 1870.
Darwin F. and Sarah A. Morse, ——, 1872.
Elbridge and Rebecca Robertson, Dec. 22, 1836.
Frank E. and Minnie Josephine Marden, Mar. 11, 1893, Apopka, Fla. Res. Londonderry.
Frank L. and Rachel J. Hall, Sept. 17, 1871.
Nellie A., 19, and Charles P. Doherty, 23, Dec. 25, 1894.
Perley S., 31, and Mabel E. Buttrick, 22, Jan 31, 1894.
Retta M., 22, and Fred L. Roach, 20, July 13, 1897.
Samuel P. and Adeline K. Rowell, Aug. 31, 1856. Golden wedding 1906.
Sarah J. (Kimball) and Emri W. Clark, Dec. 12, 1907. Res. Nashua, N. H.

Robinson, Benjamin and Betsey Neal, June 14, 1819.
Catherine M. and Benjamin F. Annis, Dec. 25, 1859.
Daniel and Rhoda Steel, Mar. 15, 1804.
David and Patty Anderson, Dec. 12, 1798.
David F. and Emily J. Marshall, Jan. 24, 1867.
Hannah and John Howe, June 19, 1810.
John A. and Harriet E. Hamblett, Dec. 12, 1852.
Leonora J. and John E. Woodburn, Nov. 18, 1880.

Robinson, Myra F. and William C. Bancroft, Sept. 15, 1878.
Nabby and Samuel Schot Graham, July 10, 1798.
Noah and Nancy Senter, Mar. 10, 1805.
Phebe and James G. Morrison, May 1, 1855.
Sally and Daniel Davis, Feb. 7, 1805.
Sarah Lane and Moses F. Colby, June 3, 1884.

Rogers, Abigail and Amos Morse, Jr., Apr. 20, 1819.
Anne and Jacob Bailey, Nov. 20, 1819.
Edmund and Mary Smith, Jan., 1814.
Mary and Jacob Sargent, Nov., 1813.
Micajah and Lorahannah Stephens, Sept. 21, 1797.

Rolfe, George and Sarah Hamlett, Dec. 15, 1856.
Judith and James Adams, ———.
Luella Isabel and Naaman Goodspeed, July 4, 1872.
Stephen and Mary Ann Wilson, Dec. 7, 1815.

Rollins, Mary and Thomas Fisher, Nov. 2, 1810.
Rodney M. and Abby R. Dodge, Oct. 31, 1848.

Rouse, Nettie A., 21, and Charles Edw. Moody, 23, Mar. 21, 1899.

Rousseau, Philimon and Richard L. Pettingill, Dec. 15, 1874, Lowell, Mass. Res. Londonderry.

Rowan, Mary and Andrew Cochran, Nov. 15, 1723, by Rev. Mr. McGregor.

Rowell, Adeline K. and Samuel P. Robie, Aug. 31, 1856. Golden wedding 1906.
Clara Jane and Alfred A. Corning (1st hus.), about 1865.
Clara Jane and Capt. Nathaniel H. Brown (2nd hus.), ———, 1873. Res. Derry, N. H.
Irving J. and Sarah Crosby (1st wife), ———. Res. Pepperell.
Irving J. and Emma Dow (2nd wife), ———. Res. Pepperell.
Joanna and Isaac Huse, July 1, 1802.
John and Jane P. Spinney, Dec. 11, 1839.
John C. and Sarah Dustin, May 26, 1853.
Laura Z. and John C. Dow, July 1, 1875.
Laura Z. (Dow) and James Tabor, Apr. 27, 1877. Res. Derry, N. H.
Mrs. Eliza and Andrew J. Benson, Nov. 20, 1884 (2nd wife and 2nd hus.).
Nancy E. and George G. Tenney, Nov. 27, 1883.
Sarah A. and John Alexander, July 27, 1854.
Thomas A. and Mary A. Gillingham, May 4, 1862.

Russell, Elisabeth and Daniel Wilkins (1st wife).
Gayton H., 37, and Annie M. Barnes, 36, Dec. 3, 1898.
Ida F. (Estey), 25, and Daniel W. Goodwin, 41, Jan. 25, 1892. (2nd wife and 2nd hus.)
Jane H. and John McClary, Dec. 25, 1848.
Sarah E. and Charles R. Frost, Apr. 6, 1849. Golden wedding 1899.

Ryan, Jennie M., 22, and Fred B. Wentworth, 26, Mar. 26, 1894.

Sampson, Anna D. and Levi R. Starrett, May 27, 1879.
Branch and Alice K. Simonds, Apr. 11, 1833.
Branch and Polly Crocker, Dec. 25, 1798.
Edward and Hannah W. Colby, July 26, 1864, Philadelphia, Pa. (1st wife).
Edward and Jennie U. Mudgett, Aug. 11, 1866 (2nd wife).
Edward and Carrie A. Lord, Apr. 16, 1890 (3d wife).
George E. and Esther E. C. Peterson, Aug. 15, 1901.
Huldah and Phineas Foster, Nov. 21, 1833.
John and Lizzie F. Sanborn, Nov. 28, 1867.
Lydia A. and Albert V. Stevens, Nov., 1838.
Mary J. and Joseph A. Berry, Oct. 6, 1872.
Turner and Eliza H., ——— (1st wife).
Turner and Sybal A. Taylor, ———, 1861.
Turner, 47, and May C. Wilkins, 36, May 22, 1894.

Sanborn, Evelyn and Leonard Hobart Pillsbury, ———. Res. Derry, N. H.
Josiah and Martha A. Dolan, Apr. 29, 1863.
Lizzie F. and John Sampson, Nov. 28, 1867.
Martha A. and John McClary, Mar. 9, 1884.
Mary J. and Albert D. Shepard, Jan. 12, 1867.
Myra and Charles J. Flanders, Oct. 12, 1862.
Nancy Jane and James G. Stone, ——— (1st wife).
Rachel and Elisha Smith, Nov. 25, 1830, at Sandown, N. H.
Willie S. and Alice Lillian Avery, Apr. 12, 1899. Res. Nashua, N. H.

Sanders, Lottie D. and George E. Merrill, Nov. 8, 1868.
Mamie L. and Benjamin Leroy Woodbury, June 11, 1909, at Nashua, N. H.
Rufus and Lucy A. Smith, Jan .8, 1851.

Sargent, Cynthia and John D. March, Nov. 10, 1831.
David and Nancy Anderson, Sept. 16, 1809.
Edmund B. and Almira Page, Sept. 8, 1835.
Ella L. and Elmer D. Goodwin, 1887, at Searsport, Me. Res. Manchester, N. H.

Sargent, Hitty and John Clyde, Feb. 7, 1805.
Jacob and Mary Rogers, Nov., 1813.
Lucinda H. and Joseph Moody, Dec. 1, 1853.
Moses and Eleanor Clark, Jan. 31, 1805.
Persis and Dr. Isaac Thom, Nov. 17, 1769.
Rachel and Levi Colby, Nov. 16, 1797.
Reuben and Eunice Davis, July 13, 1813.
Rhoda and Jacob Chase, ———.
Sophia and Abel Plummer, Feb. 4, 1834.
Thomas and Hannah Donahue, Apr. 11, 1805.

Saunders, George B. and Reva M. Scollay, Nov. 24, 1870.

Savage, Frances and Rev. William House, ———, 1858. Pastor Pres. Ch. 1857 to 1873.

Savory, Caroline and Benjamin McAllister, May 7, 1846.
Jonathan and Abigail Coffin, Mar., 1836.
Priscilla and Abraham Burbank, Feb. 4, 1807.
Thomas and Gressey Holmes, Nov. 10, 1809.

Sawyer, Martha M., 21, and Edmund G. Anderson, 22, Dec. 11, 1890.
Priscilla W. and Reuben W. Flanders, Mar. 13, 1862.
Rachel and John Holt, Mar. 25, 1819.
Sally R. and Greenleaf Ambrose, 1843, at Manchester, N. H. Res. Londonderry, N. H.
Tryphena and Thomas Senter, Jr., Dec. 12, 1805.

Scarles, Rachel and William Burroughs, ———. Res. Hudson, N. H.

Schwartz, Mary L., 19, and Charles A. Crowell, 21, Dec. 24, 1889.
Nellie D., 38, and John H. S. Goodwin, 37, Nov. 25, 1896.

Scoby, Joseph and Eleanor Campbell, Aug. 20, 1798.

Scollay, Maria C. and Charles Taylor, Aug. 12, 1868.
Reva M. and George B. Saunders, Nov. 24, 1870.
William and Catherine, ——— (1st wife).
William and Roxanna Senter (2nd wife), June 23, 1881.

Seaforth, Joan and John Barnet, Nov. 2, 1721. Second marriage in town.

Seaman, William H. and Marrianna P. Clark, Aug. 27, 1873.

Searles, Ida L. and Ira F. Goodwin, Nov. 28, 1878.
Loami and Nancy G. Allen, Sept. 8, 1860.

Sears, John A. and Sarah L. Simonds, June 28, 1864.

Seavey, Emira Coburn and John March, 2d, June 23, 1857, in Pelham, N. H.

Seaward, Emma D. and Frank E. Emery, Dec. 22, 1878.

Sefton, Mabel F. and Wesley W. Payne, ——, 1889. Res. Derry, N. H.

Seldon, Elisabeth M. and Nathaniel Smith, ——, 1814.

Senter, Elisabeth and Stephen Merrill, June 16, 1809.
Lucy and Alfred D. Greeley, ——, 1841.
Marcia M., 67, and James J. Chase, 61, July 7, 1909.
Nabby and Solomon Moar, Mar. 7, 1799.
Nancy and Noah Robinson, Mar. 10, 1805.
Polly and Daniel Gilcreast, Nov. 9, 1801.
Polly and George Manter, Sept. 17, 1795.
Rhoda and Ephraim Cummings, Oct. 27, 1803.
Roxanna and William Scollay, June 23, 1881.
Sally and David Brown, Dec. 7, 1815.
Sally and John Howard, June 21, 1841.
Sarah and James Nichols, May 6, 1817.
Thomas and Eunice White, Jan., 1802.
Thomas, Jr., and Tryphena Sawyer, Dec. 12, 1805.

Shatell, Adeline and George Elliott, Nov. 30, 1854.

Shattuck, George W., 25, and Hattie E. Merrill, 20, June 14, 1893.

Shedd, Julia A. and Thomas M. Holmes, Feb. 28, 1877. Oakham, Mass.

Shehan, Sarah A. and George M. Pettengill, 22, July 4, 1893. Res. Haverhill, Mass.

Shepard, Albert D. and Mary J. Sanborn, Jan. 12, 1867.
Charlotte W. and Calvin Boyd, Dec. 24, 1844.

Shipley, Amos and Patty Boyd, Dec. 23, 1802.
John and Rebecca Dickey, Feb. 25, 1834.
Joseph Lucian and Anna Sarah Knight, Aug. 25, 1863, at Atkinson, N. H.
Joseph Lucian and Margaret H. Weeks, Oct. 4, 1864, at Colchester, Conn.
Julia D. and William P. Nevins, Sept. 14, 1871.
Mary and John Gregg, July 3, 1828.

Shirley, Jane and Robert McMurphy, Mar. 10, 1747/8.

Shute, Benjamin and Lucy Orr, Feb. 10, 1803.
Jonathan and Betsey Plummer, June, 1806.
Julia A. and Rev. Daniel Goodwin, Feb. 12, 1839. Derry, N. H.
Martha G. and Walter D. Stevens, Nov. 14, 1870.

Sides, Albert H. and Lizzie A. Colby, Jan. 13, 1887. Res. Portsmouth, N. H.

Sidman, Jane P. and Isaac Richardson, Mar. 24, 1810.

Simonds, Alice K. and Branch Sampson, Apr. 11, 1833.
Betsey and Pearson Richardson, Dec. 31, 1795.
James and Sarah Corning, July 23, 1837.
Sarah L. and John A. Sears, June 28, 1864.

Simpson, Carrie M. and Owen Hinckley, July 15, 1868. Res. 40 yrs. in Londonderry.
Ella S. and Albert Titcomb, June 1, 1866.
Eva A., 21, and George C. Pettengill, 30, June 17, 1906.
Flora and Isaac Stewart, June 10, 1802.
Joseph and Jenny Wilson, Sept. 8, 1803.

Skinner, George W. and Eliza J. Goodwin, Feb. 11, 1857.

Slate, Maria A. and William H. Edwards, July 4, 1855.

Sleeper, Elisabeth P. and James C. Taylor, Jan. 12, 1858.
Josiah and Jane Dickey, Apr. 4, 1833.

Sloane, Anna J. and Frank L. Gilcreast, Feb. 3, 1873.

Smilie, Elton R. and Mary Ann Hall, Sept. 3, 1844.
Francis and Ruth Dustan, June 6, 1822.

Smith, Ada J., 17, and Francis R. Nichols, 19, Oct. 12, 1910
Alexander and Sarah Melvin, Feb. 19, 1822.
Ann G. and James Giles, Dec. 17, 1835.
Ann Maria and Calvin M. White, Sept. 11, 1861.
Annie L. and Harrie D. Stokes, May 19, 1898. Res. Derry, N. H.
Annie M. and John H. Grant, Aug. 1, 1880.
Carabel A., 20, and Fred E. Annis, 21, Oct. 17, 1889.
Cornelia H. and Joel C. Annis, Dec. 25, 1856.
Charles Sydney and Elnora Caroline Woodard, Dec. 31, 1868. Lynn, Mass.
Daniel and Margaret Smith, Dec. 18, 1855.
Daniel D. and Sarah A. Ballou, Oct. 25, 1855. Golden wedding 1905.
Eleanor and James Turner Hartford, Feb. 16, 1872.
Elisabeth M. and Col. Francis Manter, Sept. 13, 1860.
Elisha and Rachel Sanborn, Nov. 25, 1830, at Sandown, N. H. Res. Londonderry, N. H.
Ellen J. and John Ingalls, ———, 1847. Res. in the West.
Emma N., 25, and Oliver Merrill, 25, Apr. 19, 1893.
Esther and Jacob Dow, June 14, 1838.
Frances M. and Charles L. Blood, Jan. 1, 1862.
Frances S. and Joseph S. Goodwin, Nov. 26, 1868.
Fred H., 22, and Cora M. Lurvey, 20, Sept. 15, 1909.
George P. and Sarah M. Wilson, Sept. 17, 1881.
Hannah and Benjamin Woodbury, Aug. 1, 1810.
Harriet and Solomon Hallett, Mar. 13, 1845.
Harriet Emeline and Obediah R. Foster, ———, 1843.

Smith, Henry Clay and Susan D. Hazelton, Apr. 24, 1877.
Hugh and Jane Patten, Dec. 15, 1795.
Ichabod C. and Celia Marshall, Dec. 21, 1886.
Izetta G. and William A. Campbell, June 8, 1887.
John and Mary Boles, May 15, 1829.
John H. and Hattie R. Harris, Apr. 10, 1871.
Joseph B. and Martha Smith, Sept. 13, 1836.
Lena Mae, 16, and Cleon E. Nesmith, 22, Oct. 25, 1905.
Lorenzo D. and Mrs. Clara D. Hobbs,* Oct. 3, 1906. Res. Acton, Maine.
Lucy A. and Rufus Sanders, Jan. 8, 1851.
Margaret and Daniel Smith, Dec. 18, 1855.
Martha and Joseph B. Smith, Sept. 13, 1836.
Mary and Edmund Rogers, Jan., 1814.
Mary Etta, 23, and Sidney A. Webster, 28, Dec. 25, 1889.
Mary M. and George W. Reed, Nov. 27, 1842.
Mary P. and Stephen Gardner, Aug. 31, 1845.
Melvin Dinsmore and Edith May Fisher, May 29, 1900. Haverhill, Mass.
Nabby and David Alexander, May 12, 1808.
Nathaniel and Elisabeth M. Selden, ———, 1814.
Nathaniel and Mary Barras(?), Feb. 21, 1816.
Nelson E., 24, and Frances V. Whittle, 22, Sept. 7, 1904.
Nettie Esdell and Ammi George Richardson, May 1, 1884.
Ortensia M. and Harvey Severance, May 4, 1881.
Reuben A. and Laura Jones, Oct. 2, 1848.
Robert Selden and Hannah L. Colburn, Oct. 27, 1850.
Sally and Dea. James Perkins, Nov. 20, 1806.
Samuel and Agnes Grimes, Oct. 18, 1787.
Sarah and Jonathan Adams, ———.
Sarah and John Buterfield, Dec. 19, 1849.
Sarah and William Danforth, May 9, 1802.
Sarah B. and Joseph Kidder, June 20, 1850. Golden wedding 1900. Res. Manchester, N. H.
Sarah Mertie and George E. Lang, May 6, 1906, at Haverhill, Mass.
Sherburn Dana and Nancy Hodgman, May 1, 1860.
Viola C. and Moses F. Colby, Dec. 27, 1908.
Walter Alexander and Harriet Adosa Knight, Nov. 27, 1867. Atkinson, N. H.
Will, 35, and Achsah J. Allen, 40, Jan. 29, 1890.
William Hardy and Abigail C. March, Feb. 26, 1852.

Smithurst, Hannah and Moses Alley, Mar., 1823.

Solford (?), ——— and Isabella McMurphy, Mar. 11, ———.

*Both died about 3 yrs. later, within 24 hours—a double funeral.

Spaine, Margaret Ann and James W. Lund, Aug. 4, 1909.

Spalding, Alice and Max de Rochmont, Sept. 17, 1902. Res. New Rochelle, N. Y.
Charles and Nellie Brown, Apr. 8, 1903. Res. Salisbury, Mass.
Edward H. and Harriet S. Holmes, Dec. 6, 1861.
Elisabeth and Newell Frothingham, Apr. 18, 1889. Res. Salisbury, Mass.
Emeline T. and Robert W. Boyd, May 24, 1855.
Ephraim and Elsie Corcoran, Dec. 14, 1896. Res. in Cambridgeport, Mass.
Georgia M. and Thomas M. Holmes, Nov. 7, 1866.
Hattie L. and Frank V. Brown, Jan. 15, 1902. Res. Salisbury, Mass.
Jacob F. and Delia Annis, Apr. 7, 1864.

Spaulding, Warren E. and Hattie S. Storer, Apr. 26, 1869.

Spear, Charles and Elisabeth E. Crowell, June 30, 1841.
Justin and Sarah Crowell, Oct. 15, 1834.
Mabel G. 18, and William J. Eaton, 23, May 20, 1890.

Spinney, Alexander and Zillah Dow, Dec., 1806.
Ellen A. and Walter F. Gregg, May, 1874.
Emily and Charles Franklin Brickett, Sept. 16, 1844.
Emily (Brickett) and Orriville A. Peabody, Dec. 17, 1873.
Emma K. and Leonard A. Freeman, Nov. 19, 1878.
Eugene L. and Laura A. Merrill, Jan. 1, 1879.
Georgie F. and Charles E. Conant, Oct. 21, 1866.
Jane P. and John Rowell, Dec. 11, 1839.
John D. and Zillah M. Taylor, Dec. 7, 1841.
Julia M. and James N. Moulton, Sept., 1868.
Nancy and Benjamin F. Gervin, Jan. 20, 1841.

Spofford, Chandler and Betsey Cobb, May 21, 1812.

Sprague, Eliza and Edward Furber, Feb., 1876, in Maine. Res. Londonderry.
Emma D. and Clarence A. Hill, Mar. 14, 1881.

Spullet, Frederick and Hannah C. Nichols, Jan., 1820.

Stanton, John and Catherine Hanly, Mar. 15, 1853.

Stark, Alden D. and Harriet N. Runnels, Jan. 3, 1900.

Starrett, Levi R. and Anna D. Sampson, May 27, 1879.

Stearns, Lyman M. and Alnora Maria Chase, June 5, 1878.

Steele, David J. and Polly Clendenin, Mar. 29, 1810.
Hannah and Reuben Rhoades, Feb., 1807.
James and Hannah Palmer, Nov. 12, 1813.
James C. and Mary J. Anderson, May 23, 1848.

Spaine, Joseph and Susan Boys, July, 1804.
Rhoda and Daniel Robinson, Mar. 15, 1804.
Sarah and Amos Hamblett, Apr. 2, 1807.
William and Hannah Page, Dec. 26, 1811.

Stephen, George H. and Martha J. Stephen, Mar. 9, 1859.
Martha J. and George H. Stephen, May 9, 1859.

Stephens, Lorahanna and Micajah Rogers, Sept. 21, 1797.
Phillips and Betsey Aiken, Nov. 11, 1802.

Stephenson, Thomas and Clara F. Conant, July, 1878.

Stevens, Albert V. and Lydia A. Sampson, Nov., 1838.
Esther and Israel Young, Aug., 1818. Res. Manchester, N. H.
Henry T., 50, and Stukley J. G. White, 58, July 3, 1910.
Horace E. and Betsey Ann Ambrose, Feb. 17, 1869. Res. Manchester, N. H.
Susanna and Ephraim W. Harvey, Sept. 13, 1857.
Walter D. and Martha G. Shute, Nov. 14, 1870.

Steward, Charles and Mary Eyres, Nov. 15, 1727, by Rev. Mr. James McGregor.
Martha and John Boors(?), Nov. 2, 1809.

Stewart, Scott B. and Bertha M. Lurvey, Dec. 23, 1908. Res. Maine.

Stickney, Ebenezer and Hannah Fitz, Mar. 2, 1809.

Stiles, David and Betsey Mack, Sept. 29, 1808.
Lewis and Sarah P. Avery, Aug. 3, 1856.

Stilphen, Marguerite and William E. Tabor, Oct. 6, 1909. Res. Derry, N. H.

Stimpson, Charles and Hannah March, Oct. 2, 1823.

Stinson, Samuel and Nabby Potter, Aug. 1, 1799.

Stokes, Harrie D. and Annie L. Smith, May 19, 1898.
Moses D. and Irene French, Feb. 11, 1830.

Stone, Anna M., 19, and John E. Ray, 20, July 3, 1894.
Frank and Delia May Watts, July 17, 1884. Silver wedding 1909. Res. Derry, N. H.
James G. and Nancy Jane Sanborn (1st wife), in 1867.
James G. and Elisabeth B. Hicks, June 21, 1871 (2d wife).

Storer, Hattie S. and Warren E. Spaulding, Apr. 26, 1869.

Stott, Helen M. and Benjamin Francis Ayer, July 3, 1873.

Stratton, Asa B. and Martha Everton, Nov. 29, 1842.

Straw, Henry F. and Mary Jane Otis, Dec. 18, 1845.

Stuart, Isaac and Flora Simpson, June 10, 1802.

Swallow, Susie A. and Mark M. Morrison, Nov. 18, 1885.

Sweatt, Elizabeth A. and Arthur S. Halsey, Apr. 14, 1875, at Salisbury, N. H.
James M. and Maria C. Chase, July 15, 1875. No children.
Joseph A. and Sarah J. Thompson (1st wife), Feb. 15, 1855.
Joseph A. and Mary M. Herbert (2nd wife), Oct. 1, 1884.
Joseph A., 65, and May Louise Galeucia (3d wife), Sept. 24, 1903.

Tabor, James and Laura Z. (Rowell) Dow, Apr. 26, 1877. Res. Derry, N. H.
William E. and Marguerite Stilphen, Oct. 6, 1909. Res. Derry, N. H.

Taggart, Tagart, Hugh and Mary Maccalester, June 17, 1723, by Rev. Mr. James McGregor.
James and Jean Anderson, Nov. 1, 1733, by Rev. Mr. Thomas Thomson of Londonderry.
Jenat and James Wilson, Nov. 10, 1727, by Rev. Mr. McGregor.
Mary and John Woodburn, Jan. 20, 1744.
Rev. Irad and Lucina Peck, Jan. 22, 1851. Golden wedding 1901.
Rev. Samuel and Elizabeth Duncan, ———.
Robert and Betsey Reside(?), Feb. 7, 1800.

Talford, ——— and Jean MacMurphy, Jan. 8, 1733.

Tarbox, Samuel and Rebecca Landers, Sept. 5, 1806.
Submit and David L. Balard, Nov. 15, 1808.

Tasker, George and Georgia F. Aiken, 20, Sept. 1, 1900. Res. Haverhill, Mass.

Taylor, Adam and Martha Paul, Feb. 1, 1798.
Charles and Maria C. Scollay, Aug. 12, 1868.
Elisha and Elisa Chena, Mar. 29, 1808.
Harold Scott, 27, and Maria Pillsbury, 24, Sept. 14, 1910. Res. Manchester, N. H.
James C. and Elisabeth Sleeper, Jan. 2, 1858. Res. Derry, N. H.
Janet and William Adams, Feb. 6, 1779.
John and Susan Pollard, Feb. 14, 1822.
Martha and Samuel Dickey, ———, 1732.
Martha M. and William H. Littlefield, Nov. 26, 1885.
Mary and John Clark, Oct. 5, 1819.
Robert and Dorothy Colby, Nov. 25, 1802.
Sally and John Bush McGrath, Mar. 28, 1799.
Samuel F. and Margaret Patterson, Mar. 22, 1810.
Sarah and John Clark, Mar. 4, 1802.
Sargeant B. and Sophia Whittle, June 10, 1823.
Sybal A. and Turner Sampson, ———, 1861.
Zillah M. and John D. Spinney, Dec. 7, 1841.

Tenney, Albert and Mary Ann Young, Apr. 21, 1842.
Albert and Mary J. Dickey, May 20, 1875. She was a granddaughter of Gen. John Stark.
Ardelle A. and Andrew T. Lowd, ———, 1867.
Charles and Eliza Coffin Peabody, Apr. 6, 1843.
Charles A. and Lizzie J. Head (1st wife), of Hooksett, N. H.
Charles A., 43, and Mrs. Rose J. Crowell (2nd wife), 43, Apr. 7, 1895.
Eliza H. and James M. Gilcreast, Nov. 12, 1840.
George G. and Nancy E. Rowell, Nov. 27, 1883 (1st wife).
George G. and Mary Bell Batchelder, ——— (2nd wife).
Hannah and Joshua Hibbard, Oct. 12, 1802.
Lydia Cutter and Asa Augustus Peabody, Apr. 6, 1853.
Martha and John A. Gage, May 6, 1851.
Mary and Jonathan Warren Peabody, Apr. 16, 1846.
Mrs. May Bell, 43, and Willie E. Woodbury, 54, Mar. 16, 1910.
Persis and Elder David Anderson, Oct. 13, 1842. Golden wedding 1892.
Ruth E. and Thomas W. Crowell, June 11, 1906. Res. Derry, N. H.

Tewksbury, Samuel G., 20, and Nellie M. Watts, 23, Oct. 5, 1889. Res. Derry, N. H.

Thayer, Burnice and Susanna Boyce, dau. of Samuel Boyce and Susan P. Dickey, ———.
Haverline, son of Burnice and Susanna, and Carrie Delaney, ———, at Derry, N. H.
Minnie, dau. of Burnice and Susanna, and William Bachelder, ———.

Theiss, Grace M., 27, and Albert D. A. Olsen, 35, June 16, 1909.

Thom, Eliza and Alanson Tucker, Esq., ———.
Dr. Isaac and Persis Sargent, Nov. 17, 1769.
Persis and Hon. John Bell, ———.

Thomas, Frank L., 20, and Mabel V. Chick, 21, Nov. 16, 1904.
Joseph D. and Judith Emmons, Mar. 14, 1848, in Maine.

Thompson, Thomson, Betsey and Amos Cross, July 1, 1802.
David and Peggy Caldwell, Jan., 1809.
Frances A. and William A. Holmes, Nov. 10, 1853.
Jennie and Mark A. Austin, Dec. 10, 1868.
John and Isabella McMurphy, Dec., 1805.
Mary and Samuel Paul, Dec. 20, 1804.
Mary McMurphy and Daniel Wilkins, May 5, 1836.
Samuel and Mattie Colwell, Dec., 1797.

Thompson, William and Elisabeth Holmes, Nov. 10, 1808.
William and Hannah Blaire, Feb. 21, 1722, by Rev. Mr. McGregor.

Thorne, Charles E. and Eliza Estey, Oct. 7, 1880.

Thorp, Fannie M. and Ira Dan Annis, Feb. 20, 1894. Res. Croton, Ohio.

Thurston, Walter J. and Nellie E. Hunter, Oct. 12, 1871.

Tilley, Lucy (Woolner) and Isaac Wallace Cochran, Jan. 13, 1873.

Titcomb, Albert and Ella S. Simpson, June 1, 1866.
Charles K. and Laura Nichols, Mar. 19, 1874.
Ida S. and Walter C. Hooper, Oct. 28, 1906. Res. Henniker, N. H.
Martha E. and Alma A. Armstrong, June 14, 1908. Res. Windham, N. H.
Rosie L. and George H. Bean, Dec. 25, 1895, in Derry, N. H. Res. Londonderry later.
Simeon C. and Sally H. Webster, ——, 1842, at Pelham, N. H. Rem. to Londonderry 1842.

Todd, Andrew and Beatrix Moore, Dec. 18, 1722, by Rev. Mr. McGregor.

Tomlinson, Herbert and Flora Greeley, ——, 1887.

Torrey, Kenneth W. C. and Edna Louise Bacon, Mar. 12, 1907.

Towle, Harris, 37, and Clara Dilla Lord (Dickey), 43, Nov. 8, 1887. Res. 1905, La Gloria, Cuba.

Towne, Moses E., 25, and Flora L. Weston, 20, June 10, 1900.
Syvella C., 18, and James T. Doherty, 24, June 18, 1889.

Townes, Laura D., 24, and George W. Twiss, 27, July 18, 1893.

Towns, Betsey and David Crowell, Nov. 17, 1803.
Betsey C. and Christopher C. Davis, Dec. 21, 1843.
Charlotte (Boyd) and Nathan Plummer, ——, 1846.
Eliza and Stephen Nichols, June 22, 1819.
Hannah and William Hogg, Feb. 7, 1806.
Lizzie P. and George A. Clark, Nov. 8, 1860.
Lydia and Joel Barret, July 14, 1804.
Lydia and Joseph Bailey, Dec. 9, 1808.
Moody B. and Matilda Marshall, Dec. 28, 1853.
Moses and Eunice Dwinell, Nov. 17, 1797.
Polly and Robert Boyd, Dec. 24, 1812.
Sarah G. and John S. Day, Mar. 11, 1837.
Silas T. and Mrs. Phebe A. Morrison, Mar. 24, 1864.

Tucker, Esquire Alanson and Eliza Thom, ———.

Tuffts, Polly and Major John Pinkerton, Dec. 18, 1801 (2nd wife).

Tuttle, Delphus O., 29, and Emily R. Platt, 25, Dec. 25, 1909.
Joseph W. and Fanny Blodgett, Nov. 6, 1831.

Twiss, Emma and Charles S. Flanders, ———, 1870.
George W., 27, and Laura D. Townes, 24, July 18, 1893.
Mary B. and Hermon Berry, Mar. 15, 1848.

Tylor (or Taylor), Sargent B. and Sophia Whittle, June 10, 1823.

Tyson, Fannie A. and Charles L. Pillsbury, ———. Res. Denver, Col.

Underwood, Mary L. and Lieut. Joseph Harvell, Mar. 29, 1817.

Upton, George E. and Sarah J. Gilcreast, Nov. 27, 1856.
George H. and Abbie F. Greeley, July 29, 1869.
Julia A. and Jeremiah M. Avery, Oct. 16, 1854.

Valentine, Thomas, 31, and Nellie Roberts, 36, May 19, 1897.

Valler, Sarah and Selwyn S. Conant, Jan., 1878.

Varel, Mrs. Julia A. and Enoch Parshley, Oct. 5, 1869, in Ottawa, Ill. Res. Londonderry, N. H.

Varnum, Betsey and Robert Barnett, Dec. 15, 1801.
Rhoda and John Dickey, Nov. 12, 1795.

Veasey, Samuel and Betsey Chesley, Nov. 23, 1809.

Vickery, Fannie and Currier Huntee, July 12, 1849.
Henry M. and Lizzie A. Wheeler, May 8, 1867.
Joseph D. and Sarah Drew, July 3, 1845.
Mary S. and Charles D. Annis, May 22, 1855.
Sarah and Joshua Blodgett, Sept. 29, 1803.
Sarah and Thomas W. Emery, ———, 1874.

Vincent, Harry C. and Lillian S. Barron, May 7, 1879.

Walch, Frank and Jennie Danforth, July 5, 1868.

Walker, Josiah and Nancy Platts, Nov. 4, 1806.
Laomi and Sally Jones, Nov. 20, 1804.
Reuben and Sally Platts, Oct. 26, 1809.

Wallace, Walis, Agnes and Jonathan Page, Mar. 26, 1797.
Elisabeth and Thomas Patterson, June 1, 1775.
George P. and Edith Pillsbury (Davis), Apr. 24, 1907. Res. Manchester, N. H.
James and Mary Wilson,* Dec. 17, 1742.
James and Mary Wallace, Nov. 30, 1749.
Jean and Thomas Wallace, Mar. ——.
Jeanette and Hugh McCutchins, ———.

*This is "Ocean Mary," described in the Introduction.—EDITOR.

Wallace, John and Annis Barnard,* May 18, 1721, by Rev. Mr. McGregor.
John and Jeanette Lindsay, Nov. 28, 1729, by Rev. Mr. Mathew Clark.
Laura J. and John S. Furber, June 11, 1845.
Lettice and Billy Porter, June 8, 1797.
Mary and James Wallace, Nov. 30, 1749.
Mary and Peter Patterson, Nov. 8, 1814.
Perley and Mary Colby, Apr. 10, 1838.
Robert M. and Jane Morrison, Dec. 27, 1810.
Sally and James Pinkerton, May 15, 1809.
Samuel and Betsey Coffin, May 3, 1810.
Sarah G. and E. V. Dillingham, Nov. 23, 1871.
Thomas, Junr., and Jean Wallace, Mar., ——, by Rev. Mathew Clark.
William P. and H. Addie Whittemore, Apr. 18, 1861.

Walsh, Abbie J. and Nelson S. Payne, Aug. 19, 1877.
Frank and Clarrissa Manter, ———.
William Benjamin, 22, and Lucy A. Corning, 18, Mar. 16, 1892.

Ware, Daniel A. and Luella F. Morey, ———, 1874.

Warner, Betsey and James Morrison, Nov., 1813.
Charles and Mary C. Hall, Nov. 6, 1841.
Daniel and Lucy Danforth, Dec. 30, 1807.
John and Widow Webster, May 14, 1801.
John and Susan Orr, Oct., 1813.
Lucy and Charles Haskell, Mar. 13, 1806.
Lucy and Joseph Gregg, Jan., 1820.
Nathaniel and Mary Boyd, Dec. 30, 1813.

Warren, Lewis, 49, and Lucy Chase, 38, July 12, 1890.
Mary Barstow and Benning Noyes, Aug. 2, 1835. Near Boston, Mass.
Samuel and Anne Pinkerton, Dec. 27, 1798.

Wason, James and Mary Anderson, Feb. 14, 1804.

Waters, Ruth and Moses Carleton, July, 1813.
Susie and Stephen M. Boyce, Apr. 10, 1907. Res. California.

Watts, Annie E. and Rosecrans W. Pillsbury, Dec. 10, 1885.
Caleb M. and Martha J. Flanders (1st wife), about ———, 1848.
Caleb M. and Anna C. Palmer (2nd wife), about ———, 1859.
Charles H. and Mariam P. Annis, Jan. 1, 1861.
Charles H., 2nd, and Mabel A. Andrews, Mar. 23, 1886.

*First couple married in town.

Watts, Clarence O., 23, and Joanna R. Ham, 19, Dec. 25, 1897 (1st wife).
Clarence O., 29, and Marion R. Cook, 26, Sept. 16, 1903 (2nd wife).
Daniel and Mrs. Lucy B. Flanders, Feb. 6, 1855.
Dillia May and Frank Stone, July 17, 1884. Silver wedding 1909. Res. Derry, N. H.
Edson W., 22, and Jennie A. Lowd, 20, Dec. 1, 1897.
Eleanor and Thomas McClary, Mar. 25, 1813.
Elijah L. and Susan Boyce, Apr. 19, 1859.
Ella M. (1st wife) and Henry R. Hall, Oct. 19, 1884.
Ernest M., 22, and Georgia Corning, 22, Dec. 21, 1887.
Esther and Walter Boyce, Dec. 19, 1861.
Freeman C. and Elisabeth J. Wheeler, Sept. 9, 1851.
George Alvah and Martha E. Fling, Oct. 18, 1883.
George N. and Florence Bean, July 4, 1885.
Hannah and John A. M. Johnson, Sept. 10, 1835.
Herman L., 20, and Alice J. Fitts, 21, Dec. 25, 1897.
Horace P. and Maria Boyd, Mar. 24, 1842.
James, Jr., and Miriam Corning, Feb. 17, 1820.
Jane and Warren Pettengill, Dec. 11, 1810.
Jenny and Moses Garvin, Dec. 26, 1799.
Margaret and Henry C. Crowell, Oct. 10, 1838.
Margaret and Jacob Garvin, Dec., 1792.
Martha B. and William Frank Holmes, May 31, 1864.
Mary and Samuel Dow, Dec. 28, 1823.
Maude and James Winn, Jan., 1904. Res. Derry, N. H.
Moses and Hannah Leach, June 12, 1823.
Nathan P. and Miss Galvin (1st wife), ———.
Nathan P., 37, and Hattie E. Roach, 32, June 12, 1906.
Nathaniel and Rachel Pettengill, Nov. 22, 1810.
Nellie M., 23, and Samuel G. Tewksbury, 20, Oct. 5, 1889. Res. Derry, N. H.
Peggy and William Pettengill, Aug. 10, 1798.
Willie E. and Mary L. Childs, Oct. 7, 1885.
Walter J., 22, and Evelyn M. Wheeler, 22, Oct. 19, 1889.

Waugh, Alice E., 20, and Frank M. McGregor, 23, July 14, 1887. Res. Derry, N. H.
George A., 24, and Cora M. Chase, 20, June 6, 1888.
Robert and Eliza Williams, Sept. 25, 1855, in Maine. Golden wedding 1905. Res. Derry, N. H.

Way, George and Mary Berry, Mar. 24, 1867.
Mary A. and William Butterworth, Nov. 30, 1854. Golden wedding 1904, at Merrimack, N. H.

Weagle, Vera L., 19, and William Keddy, 30, Aug. 15, 1909.

Wear, Archibald and Mary Boys, Apr. 7, 1724, by Rev. Mr. McGregor.

Weaver, Clara B., 15, and Harry E. Chase, 18, May 14, 1896.
Gilbert and Abbie Robie, June 23, 1870.

Webb, Jeremiah B. and Mariah B. March, Oct. 2, 1834.

Webster, Alice and Prof. Jarvis Gregg, ——, 1836. (Niece of Daniel Webster.)
Amos and Martha J. Annis, Sept. 29, 1846.
Amos C. and Harriet Hibbard, Dec. 30, 1845 (1st wife).
Amos C. and Elisabeth K. Whittaker, —— (2nd wife).
Betsey and Samuel Page, Dec. 27, 1809.
Betsey Ann and William B. Carleton, July 2, 1860, at Lowell, Mass.
Caleb A. and Edna J. Thurston, Sept. 18, 1861, Danvers, Mass.
Charles Warren and Ida Cora Chase, July 1, 1884.
Eliza B. and Charles C. Leslie, Dec. 16, 1880.
Hannah C. and Walter B. Follansbee, Jan., 1874, at West Newbury, Mass.
Jonathan and Mary Ann Everton, Oct. 25, 1831, by Rev. John Adams.
Maude A. and Russell V. Parshley, June 16, 1909. Res. Derry, N. H.
Nathan P. and Susan M. Morrison, May 17, 1860.
Nathaniel and Lucinda Moulton, Dec. 12, 1839.
Sally H. and Simeon C. Titcomb, ——, 1842, in Pelham, N. H. Rem. to Londonderry, 1842.
Sidney A., 28, and Mary Etta Smith, 23, Dec. 25, 1889.
Susanna and James Holmes, July 3, 1832.
Widow and John Warner, May 14, 1801.
William Wallace and Caroline Chase, Sept. 1, 1836.

Weed, Rhoda A. and Joseph Eaton, Nov. 29, 1865.

Weeks, Margaret H. and Joseph Lucian Shipley, Oct. 4, 1864. Colchester, Conn.

Welch, Sylvester S. and Martha Woodbury, June 24, 1861.

Wellman, William B. and Ann Maria Colburn, May 3, 1880.

Wells, Ada B., 16, and W. Claud Floyd, 22, Mar. 24, 1888.
Estella F., 17, and Harry F. Lord, 18, Mar. 21, 1893.

Wentworth, Charles and Jane Barret, Oct. 11, 1802.
Fred Bruce, 26, and Jennie M. Ryan, 22, Mar. 26, 1894.

West, Harriet and Phillips F. Lewis, Sept. 7, 1875, Charlestown, Mass. (No children.)
Osborne L., 27, and Viola G. Davison, 16, Sept. 25, 1909.

Weston, Flora L., 20, and Moses E. Towne, 25, July 10, 1900.
John and Hannah Chase, ——.
—— (2d wife) and George Aiken, ——.

Wetherbee, Hezekiah and Grace Baker, ——. (Parents of William B. Wetherbee.)
William B. and Sarah Elisabeth Corning, May 3, 1862.

Wheeler, Abbie and Benjamin F. Bean, Dec. 5, 1869.
Elisabeth J. and Freeman C. Watts, Sept. 9, 1851.
Eva J. and Charles Edgar Woodbury, May 20, 1885. Res. Nashua, N. H.
Evelyn M., 22, and Walter J. Watts, 22, Oct. 19, 1889.
George T. and Priscilla Clagget, Nov. 10, 1840.
Joshua F. and Mary E. Corning, Oct. 9, 1863.
Lizzie A. and Henry M. Vickery, Mar. 8, 1867.
Lucinda R. and Robert Hall, Sept. 20, 1869.
Nancy E. and Robert Hall, July 4, 1842.
Sally and Enoch Gooden, Oct. 8, 1808.
Sarah F., 19, and Charles F. Boyce, 29, Oct. 16, 1888.
Tilley H. and Rebecca Goodwin, Sept. 13, 1831. (1st wife.)
Tilley H. and Ann Lincon, 1856. (2nd wife.)

Whidden, Alice M. and Edgar H. Boss, June 20, 1872.
Alma E. and Frank Adams, June 9, 1875.
Charles F. and Addie M. Magee, Jan. 31, 1885.
Elbridge A. and Orrietta J. Boyce, Nov. 11, 1876.
Esther F. and Dr. William Richardson, Aug. 27, 1884.
George M. and Mary A. Whidden, Apr. 12, 1860.
Hannah M. and William M. Boyce, Apr. 1, 1847.
James Warren and Emma R. Drake, Dec. 19, 1883. Res. Haverhill, Mass.
John P. and Alice Austin, Nov. 11, 1847. Fortieth anniversary 1887.
Joshua and Adeline Boyce, about 1848. (1st wife.)
Joshua and Ei Lucindy Lewis, Nov. 13, 1862. (2nd wife.)
Mary A. and George M. Whidden, Apr. 12, 1860.
Mary J. and Nathan P. Chase, Aug. 9, 1843. (1st hus.)
Mary J. and James J. Chase, Jan. 15, 1907. (2nd hus.)
Michael and Hannah Morrill, 1818.
Mrs. Nellie A., 47, and Charles F. Boyce, 49, June 17, 1908.

White, Alice Maude and Sam Alby McGregor, June 19, 1901.
Arthur R., 29, and Carrie A. Buttrick, 30, Nov. 21, 1906.
Betsey and John Hovey, Dec. 30, 1813. (2nd wife.)
Betsey and Joseph Jackson, Mar. 30, 1815.
Calvin M. and Ann Maria Smith, Sept. 11, 1861.
Eleanor and John Hovey, Sept. 25, 1810. (1st wife.)
Elisabeth and Joseph Dickey, Jr., Apr. 20, 1854.

White, Emily C. and Samuel D. Leavitt, Aug. 7, 1860. Eastport, Me.
Esther and Freeman Corning, Dec. 31, 1829.
Esther and John R. Emery, June 3, 1852.
Eunice and Thomas Senter, Jan., 1802. (1st hus.)
Eunice and John B. Huse, Jan. 20, 1830 (2nd hus.).
Harriet M. B. and Theron R. Pitcher, Oct. 26, 1854. Res. Canton, Mass.
Henry H. and Sarah A. Moore, Nov. 29, 1860, at Goffe's Falls, N. H. Res. Londonderry, N. H.
John and Susan Dickey, Mar. 25, 1817.
Maria and Orriville A. Peabody, 1850.
Rebeckah (Henderson) and John McAllister, 1770. Res. Bedford, N. H.
Sally and Benjamin Boyce, Dec. 30, 1819.
Samuel C. and Caroline G. Woodbury, Jan. 20, 1853. Res. Lawrence, Mass.
Sarah Jane and John Calvin Gibson, Aug. 5, 1868.
Stuckley J. G., 58, and Henry T. Stevens, 50, July 3, 1910.

Whittaker, Elisbaeth K. (2nd wife) and Amos C. Webster.
Sarah and Caleb H. Bancroft, Apr. 21, 1851.

Whittemore, Amy E. and Charles W. Killam, ——.
Edward K. and Mary A. Jaquith, Dec. 24, 1862.
H. Addie and William P. Wallace, Apr. 18, 1861.
Henry J. and Esther M. Goodwin, Apr. 21, 1862.
Margarett L. and Francis Hayward, May 2, 1854.
Mary and Reid C. March, Dec. 11, 1834.
Roy, Eugene, Rev., and Elizabeth A. Robbins.
Sarah and Herman Proctor, Nov. 28, 1833.
Zachariah K. H. and Susan W. Ripley, Apr. 2, 1867.

Whittier, Mary and William G. Hardy, Feb. 12, 1846. (1st wife.)
Samuel and Mary Manter, ——. Res. Hooksett, N. H.

Whittle, Frances V., 22, and Nelson E. Smith, 24, Sept. 7, 1904.
John Wesley and Emily Josephine Flanders, Jan. 1, 1864. Res. Malden, Mass.
Sophia and Sargeant B. Taylor, June 10, 1823.

Whittondon, George, 65, and Irene A. Burlard, 35, Mar. 27, 1887.

Wilbur, Lucinda Adelaide and George F. Manter, dentist, May 16, 1871. Res. Manchester, N. H.

Wiley, Charles and Saloma Jones, Oct. 25, 1875. Res. Haverhill, Mass.
Ephraim A. and Nancy Blood, Sept. 16, 1841. Golden wedding 1891.
George B. and Ariana M. Hale, Oct. 17, 1889.

Wiley, George B. and Ella E. Gilcreast, June 29, 1871.
Lucy L. and Chauncey H. Gardt, June 10, 1908. Res. Galesburgh, Ill.
Martha M. E. and John P. Hardy, June 12, 1878.

Wilkins, Annie Elisabeth (dau. of Dr. William Wesley) and Herbert Carroll, ——. Res. Concord, N. H.
Daniel and Elisabeth Russell, ——. (1st wife.)
Daniel and Mary McMurphy Thompson, May 5, 1836. (2nd wife.)
Daniel and Sarah Hartwell, ——. (3d wife.)
Elijah R., Rev., and Harriet N. Davis, June 19, 1845, at Derry, N. H.
Elisabeth and Ammi Brown, Dec. 2, 1819.
Elisabeth and James F. Young, Apr. 26, 1853.
Hattie M. (dau. of Rev. Elijah R.) and George A. Bolser, ——. Res. Middleton, N. S.
Hiram and Jerusha M. C. H. Manter, Dec. 29, 1835.
May C., 36, and Turner Sampson, 47, May 22, 1894.
Wesley Jerome (son of Elijah R.) and Alice Perley (1st wife), in Lebanon, N. H.
Wesley Jerome (son of Elijah R.) and Annie Lincoln (2nd wife), in Chesterfield, N. H.
William Wesley, Dr. (son of Daniel) and Persis Lourinda Morse, Aug. 5, 1852, in Lawrence, Mass.

Willey, Benjamin L. and Sarah A. Conant, July 5, 1865.
John L. and Addie Holton, Dec. 31, 1866.
Mark W. and Ellen G. Bachelder, Nov. 29, 1883.

Williams, Eliza and Robert Waugh, Sept. 25, 1855. Golden wedding 1905. Res. Derry, N. H.
Eva and George A. Hurd, Dec. 24, 1907.
James and Elisabeth B. Barker, 1870.

Wilson, Wilsone, Abbie D. and Clarence N. Garvin, Feb., 1872. Res. Derry, N. H.
Alexander and Anne Reed, Mar., 1809.
Anna and John Cochran, Feb. 14, 1799.
Benjamin and Margaret Elder, June 4, 1725, by Rev. Mr. McGregor.
Betty and William Wilson, Feb. 20, 1723-4.
Eleanor and Mark Fisk, Apr. 2, 1801.
Elisabeth and James Clark, May 22, 1722, by Rev. Mr. McGregor.
George W. and Mary J. Nelson, Aug. 29, 1867. Res., 1910, Boston, Mass.
Hugh and Margaret Cochran, Feb. 6, 1723-4, by Rev. Mr. McGregor.
Hugh and Mary Ann Cochran, Dec., 1805.

Wilson, James and Eleanor Hopkins, June 1, 1758.
James and Janet Tagart, Nov. 10, 1727, by Rev. Mr. McGregor.
James and Saley Hughes, Sept. 28, 1797.
Jean and Petter Cochran, Feb. 1, 1724, by Rev. Mr. McGregor.
Jenat and William Aiken, Dec. 23, 1725, by Rev. Mr. McGregor.
Jenny and David Adams, Mar. 27, 1800.
Jenny and Joseph Simpson, Sept. 8, 1803.
John Pinkerton and Adeline Annis, Apr. 18, 1844.
Judith and John McKean, Mar. 30, 1819.
Lulu B. and E. Elmer Foye, Sept. 21, 1893. Res. Everett, Mass.
Margaret and David Brewster, July 12, 1809.
Margaret and Robert Wilson, Nov. 18, 1784.
Martha and James Annaise (?), Mar. 14, 1822.
Mary and James Wallace, Dec. 17, 1742.
Mary Ann and Samuel Gamble, Dec. 20, 1836.
Mary Ann and Stephen Rolfe, Dec. 7, 1815.
Robert Henry and Eldora J. Garvin, Apr., 1865.
Robert and Margaret Wilson, Nov. 18, 1784.
Samuel and Elisabeth Cochran, Dec. 29, 1801.
Sarah M. and George P. Smith, Sept. 17, 1881.
Thomas and Rebecca Pinkerton, Feb. 4, 1807. (1st wife.)
Thomas and Abigail Jewett, ——. (2nd wife.)
William and Betty Wilson, Feb. 20, 1723-4, by Rev. Mr. McGregor.

Wing, Anna Mabel and Arthur Loren Evans, Oct. 26, 1893.
Edward L., 24, and F. Alice Colby, 23, July 11, 1908.
Seth G., 22, and Pearl C. Proctor, 18, Apr. 5, 1904.

Wingate, Moses and Nancy Paul, Mar. 3, 1814.

Winn, James and Maude Watts, Jan., 1904. Res. Derry, N. H.

Wiseman, Elisabeth and William Richardson, Aug. 22, 1654. Res. Newbury, Mass.

Witherspoon, Catherine and Nathan Buttrick, Apr. 4, 1822.
Lovina and Joshua A. Moar, Aug. 6, 1837.

Woodburn, Carrie A. and Isaac P. Clifford, Nov. 10, 1858.
David and Margarett Clark, Feb. 16, 1773.
Dinah and James Nichols, about 1755. (1st wife.)
Hannah and Robert Dickey, June 10, 1776.
John and Mary Boyd, Jan. 2, 1725, by Rev. Mr. McGregor.
John and Mary Taggart, Jan. 20, 1744.
John and Mehitable Melvin, Feb. 23, 1820.
John E. and Leonora J. Robinson, Nov. 18, 1880.
Mary and George Reid, Gen., Apr. 16, 1765.

Woodburn, Mary and Zaccheus Greeley, 1807. Parents of Horace Greeley.
Nancy J. and George Hurd, Feb. 28, 1850.
Peggy and John Dickey, Apr. 2, 1805.

Woodbury, Abram A. and Euretta J. Morse, May 27, 1874.
Alma J. and Albert Potter, July 26, 1879.
Alma Jane and Leroy Hall, ——.
Benjamin and Hannah Smith, Aug. 1, 1810.
Benjamin Leroy and Mamie L. Sanders, June 11, 1909. Res. Nashua, N. H.
Caroline G. and Samuel C. White, Jan. 20, 1853. Res. Lawrence, Mass.
Charles Edgar and Eva J. Wheelet, May 20, 1885. Res. Nashua, N. H.
David and Jane Anderson, Jan. 23, 1816.
Eben and Hannah Barker, Nov. 27, 1834.
Etta M., 30, and George H. Young, 25, Nov. 23, 1893.
Hannah and George W. Chrispeen, Apr. 12, 1842.
John and Naby Gibson, Oct. 13, 1797.
John C. and Mina Litch, Sept. 23, 1875.
Martha and Romanzo L. Nutting, March 19, 1885. (2d mar.)
Martha and Sylvester S. Welch, June 24, 1861.
Mary E. and Ossian P. Ellis, Oct. 14, 1891.
Nellie E. and Robert G. Morrison, Mar. 17, 1881.
Samuel and Louisa J. Baker, July 12, 1837.
Samuel and Harriet E. Estey, Dec. 3, 1858. (1st wife.)
Samuel, 60, and Phebe A. Bacheller, 38, Nov. 7, 1898. (2nd wife.)
Willie Eugene, 54, and Mrs. May Bell Tenney, 43, Mar. 16, 1910.

Woodman, Elisabeth and Samuel Adams, Dec. 4, 1799.
William H. and Jennie M. Bodwell, July 18, 1880.

Woods, Eliza T. and Caleb Jones, Dec. 18, 1834.
Ensign C. and Alice H. Fellows, 1861.
George and Sarah Chase, Dec. 28, 1830.
Mattie M. and Charles Adams, Oct. 22, 1885.

Worthen, David and Nancy Bruce, Sept., 1813.

Wright, Ralph W., 25, and Edith Louise Dustin, 26, June 11, 1906.
Stephen and Sophia March, May, 1833.

Wyatt, Rosie M. and George W. Lee, 39, July 25, 1905.

Wychoff, Joseph A. and Elisabeth Bancroft, Jan. 23, 1853.
Maroia and Wesley W. Payne, Dec. 25, 1885 (1st wife, who died Jan. 25, 1887.)

Wyman, Hannah and Lafayette W. Parker, Dec. 7, 1845.
Warren and Mary Johnson, Oct. 12, 1883.

Yeaton, John W. of Epsom and Rowena I. Adams, June 15, 1882.
Young, Alletie M., 15, and Fred E. Chase, May 31, 1887.
Young, Augusta, 20, and Fred W. Pace, 24, Feb. 24, 1897.
Bertha and Nathaniel T. Platts, 1908. Res. Manchester, N. H.
Charles Edward and Sarah D. Gilcreast, Apr. 13, 1848.
Charles Edward and Mrs. Margaret (Moore) Young, Aug. 4, 1895.
David and Susanna Chamberlain, Sept., 1797.
David Hamblett and Olive A. Clough, Mar. 20, 1856. (1st wife.) Res. Manchester, N. H.
David Hamblett and Mrs. Mary A. Hartshorn, ——. (2d wife.) Res. Manchester, N. H.
Edward and Edna Emerson, Dec. 10, 1828.
Frances H. and George W. Kimball, Apr. 17, 1877.
Frances H., 53, and Edward Francis, 40, Oct. 26, 1908.
Fred A. and Emma D. Boyd, Nov. 26, 1885.
George H., 25, and Etta M. Woodbury, 30, Nov. 23, 1893.
Israel and Esther Stevens, Aug., 1818. Res. Manchester, N. H.
James F. and Elisabeth Wilkins, Apr. 26, 1853.
James and Polly Chase, ——.
Jennie D., 22, and Charles H. Alexander, 23, May 26, 1890.
John P. and Jane Hall, Mar. 6, 1834.
John P. and Mrs. Emeline Pettengill, Dec. 24, 1868.
Johnnie, 23, and Luella Badger, 26, June 27, 1889.
Jonathan and Mary Perham, Dec. 25, 1794. Res. Manchester, N. H.
Jonathan, 3d, and Charlotte Boyes, Oct. 30, 1828.
Mrs. Margaret (Moore) and Charles Edward Young, Aug. 4, 1895.
Mary Ann and Albert Tenney, Apr. 21, 1842.
Phila S. and Walter Reid, 1869.
Walter Stevens and Harriet Esther Nute, June 25, 1910.
Wesley J. and Lilla Booth, Dec. 8, 1877. Res. Derry, N. H.
William D., 30, and Maria Louisa Parmerton, 32, May 10, 1894. Res. Manchester, N. H.
Youngman, Jane and Washington Perkins, July 2, 1850.

RECORDS OF DEATHS

From the Earliest Record to the End of 1910

Abbott, Infant son of Charles H. and Emma A., Mar. 26, 1882.
Joseph C., 4th Reg. N. H. Vol., at Port Royal in 1862.
Nancy Ann, dau. of John Aiken and Margaret Hunt, May 14, 1894, aged 62 yrs., 6 mos., 13 dys.

Ackerman, Jonathan B., Aug. 21, 1826.
Susan D., wife, Apr. 5, 1825.

Adams, Charles, s. of John, Sept. 7, 1885.
Charles, s. of Nathan and Elisabeth J. Boyce, Oct. 26, 1907.
Clarissa, dau. of John and Betsey, July 17, 1830.
George, s. of Nathan and Elisabeth J. Boyce, Aug. 31, 1874, aged 22 yrs., 8 mos.
James, Jr., s. of James and Lois A., Nov. 7, 1867, aged 3 yrs.
James, June 28, 1875, aged about 55 yrs.
James, May 1, 1853, aged 83 yrs.
John, May 20, 1872, aged 78 yrs.
Lois A., wife of James, May 4, 1884.
Margaret, April 8, 1853.
Mary, Sept. 4, 1859.
Melinda, dau. of Ebenezer Emerson and Mary Blake, Sept. 15, 1898.
Nathan, s. of John, June 30, 1897, in Bedford, N. H. Buried in Londonderry.
Otis, s. of John and Elisabeth Corning, Feb. 25, 1903, aged 72 yrs., 8 mos., 16 dys.
Roy B., s. of Israel G. and Ruby A. Elliott, Sept. 28, 1899, aged 20 yrs., 12 dys.
Thompson, Apr. 5, 1871, aged 16 mos.
William, Apr. 28, 1855, aged 36 yrs.

Aiken, Daniel W., s. of Edward and Elisabeth, Dec. 15, 1883, aged 64 yrs.
Charles, s. of Samuel and Hannah Estey, Feb. 12, 1909, aged 36 yrs.
Effie, dau. of George and —— Chase, Nov. 6, 1901, aged 32 yrs., 10 dys.
George, Dec. 7, 1889, aged 74 yrs., 5 mos.
George F., Feb. 8, 1880.

Alexander, Ann, dau. of Jonathan and Sarah, Mar. 22, 1816.
Arthur P., s. of Alphonso and Ellen F., Aug. 7, 1879.
Asa Emery, s. of Charles H. and Jennie M. Young, July 13, 1904, aged 2 yrs., 3 mos., 6 dys.
Ellen, dau. of —— Roach, Nov. 3, 1889, aged 53 yrs., 9 mos., 20 dys.
Harriet A., Nov. 10, 1885.
Harvey, Nov. 22, 1870, at Derry, N. H., aged 23 yrs.
Horace E., Nov. 23, 1904, aged 3 mos., 18 dys.; bu. at Londonderry.
Ida May, Aug. 5, 1908, Derry, N. H., aged 31 yrs., 3 mos.; bu. at Londonderry.
Infant s. of Alphonso and Ellen F., Dec. 19, 1878.
Infant s. of Alphonso and Ellen F., Dec. 20, 1878.
James, s. of Jonathan and Sarah, Oct. 29, 1816.
James D., Aug. 16, 1896, aged 71 yrs., 8 mos., 24 dys., Derry, N. H.; bu. at Londonderry.
John, Mar. 19, 1887, aged 86 yrs., 3 mos., 13 dys.
John, s. of John and Sally Esety, Oct. 20, 1906, aged 74 yrs., 2 mos., 16 dys.
Joseph, s. of John and Sally Estey, Aug. 1, 1897, aged 69 yrs., 6 mos.
Mertie E., dau., of Charles H. and Jennie M. Young, May 12, 1906, aged 3 mos., 25 dys.
Nathaniel C., s. of John and Sally Estey, Jan. 19, 1906, aged 75 yrs., 4 mos., 7 dys.
Richard, s. of John and Sally Estey, May 29, 1893, Pelham, N. H., aged 53 yrs., 9 mos.
Sally, wife, Feb. 7, 1888, aged 78 yrs., 2 mos., 14 dys.
Sarah, Oct. 18, 1907, Goffstown, N. H., aged 73 yrs., 2 mos., 14 dys.; bu. at Londonderry.
Warren, son, Feb. 10, 1888, aged 53 yrs., 7 mos., 6 dys.
William C., Dec. 11, 1907, Lawrence, Mass., aged 85 yrs., 3 mos., 26 dys.; bu. at Londonderry.
William, s. of William and Elener, May 31, 1806.

Allen, William H., s. of Pardon and Hannah, Sept. 30, 1888, aged 60 yrs., 1 mo.

Ambrose, Charlotte P., June 14, 1893, aged 93 yrs., 5 mos.
Greenleaf, Mar. 27, 1891, aged 74 yrs., 8 mos., 14 dys.

Anderson, Ann, Apr. 30, 1724.
Caroline (Mrs.), ——, 1865, aged 47 yrs.
Eliza H., dau. of Richard and Jane Gage, July 29, 1872, aged 67 yrs.
John Nesmith, Esquire, July 3, 1865, aged 65 yrs.
Mary Ann (Miss), Mar. 30, 1870, Derry, N. H., aged 95 yrs.

Anderson, Mary J., w. of George V., Oct. 13, 1897, aged 51 yrs., 10 mos., 2 dys.
William, from Ireland, ——, 1744.

Andrews, Amelia B., dau. of Robert K., Feb. 22, 1893, aged 29 yrs., 2 mos., 18 dys.
Belinda J., dau. of William M. Boyce and Hannah, Mar. 3, 1871, aged 21 yrs.
Mrs., Nov. 21, 1869.

Angier, Nedone E., s. of Reuben, Apr. 9, 1907, aged 43 yrs., 7 mos., 17 dys.

Annis, Adeline, dau. of John and Delilah, Oct. 27, 1903.
Bersey (Coburn), 2d w. of John Annis, Nov. 19, 1894.
Charles D., s. of Jessee and Mildred Blodgett, May 18, 1864. Soldier in Battle, Wilderness.
Cleon C., s. of Roswell and Luella Campbell, Dec. 27, 1876.
Delilah, w. of John, Sept. 29, 1853.
Eliza Jane, dau. of John and Delilah, Feb. 24, 1892.
Fannie M. (Fling), 2d w. of Daniel G., Jan. 16, 1901, aged 42 yrs.
Jessee, s. of Isaac and Hannah, May 31, 1879.
Joel C., s. of John and Delilah, Mar. 8, 1898.
John, s. of Isaac and Hannah, Apr. 22, 1871.
Joseph, s. of Isaac and Hannah, Apr. 1, 1883.
Luella A., w. of Roswell, June 24, 1883.
Olive, dau. of John and Delilah, Sept. 4, 1854.
Mariam P., dau. of John and Delilah, July 2, 1894.
Martha C., dau. of John and Delilah, May 12, 1906, in California.
Matthew Parker, s. of John and Delilah, Apr. 22, 1865.
Mildred, w. of Jessee, Oct. 31, 1855.
Mina A., 1st w. of Daniel G., Feb. 19, 1885, aged 37 yrs.
Sampson, s. of John and Delilah, Oct. 24, 1861.
Sarah M. (Morse), w. of Matthew P. Annis, Jan. 16, 1892, aged 62 yrs., 8 mos., 4 dys.
William, s. of John and Delilah, Mar. 17, 1883.
Willie E., s. of Matthew P. and Sarah Morse, 1879, aged 22 yrs.
Winslow M., s. of Sampson, Oct. 2, 1875, aged 20 yrs.

Ansart, Abel, s. of Louis and —— Wimble, Nov. 10, 1892.

Atwood, Albert, 4th N. H. Vol., killed at Petersburg, July, 1864.

Austin, Betsey (Barker), w. of Joshua, Aug. 29, 1896.
Joshua, May 27, 1861.

Averill, Ephraim (Mrs.), Nov. 22, 1869, aged 86 yrs.

Averill, Foster, 1867, aged 74 yrs.
Henry F., Aug. 28, 1871, aged 22 yrs.

Avery, Charles L., s. of John and Melinda Hartford, Feb. 7, 1897, aged 35 yrs., 7 mos., 12 dys.
Jeremiah M., s. of Foster and Rebecca Robinson, Mar. 6, 1906, aged 80 yrs., 10 mos., 13 dys.
John, son of Foster and Rebecca Robinson, Oct. 10, 1883.
Lilla C., dau. of Charles L. and Laura, May 9, 1906, aged 12 yrs., 3 mos., 20 dys.
Melinda E. (Hartford), Mar. 4, 1897, aged 72 yrs., 1 mo.
Pauline U., June 23, 1886, aged 27 yrs.
———, ch., May 3, 1902.
———, s. of Charles L. and Laura, Dec. 14, 1896.

Bachelder, Charles S., hus., July 22, 1898, aged 40 yrs.
Frank A., s. of Charles S. and Phebe A. Newhall, May 7, 1894, aged 1 yr., 5 mos., 3 dys.
Martha V., dau. of Charles S. and Phebe A. Newhall, June 5, 1891, aged 3 yrs., 9 mos., 21 dys.

Bagley, Jonathan R., July 19, 1900, aged 80 yrs., 5 mos., Derry, N. H.; bu. at Londonderry.
Martha J., Dec. 25, 1891, aged 67 yrs., 11 mos., 14 dys.
Sarah, dau. of Ezekiel and Sarah, Sept. 3, 1867, aged 83 yrs.

Bailey, Arvilla, dau. of F. T. Bailey, Oct. 12, 1872, aged 9 yrs.
Foster T. (Mrs.), dau. of John and Elisabeth Towns, 1878, aged 51 yrs.
Foster T., s. of Joseph and Lidia Towns, Dec. 22, 1903, aged 78 yrs., 7 mos., 15 dys.
Lydia (Towns), w. of James Bailey, Aug. 12, 1872, aged 83 yrs.
Samuel M., s. of Walter E. and Mary McDonough, Dec. 13, 1902, aged 8 dys.
Walter H., s. of Walter E. and Mary A. McDonough, Aug. 18, 1900, aged 19 dys.

Baker, Elisabeth P., June 6, 1875, aged 84 yrs.

Ballou, Edward, July 8, 1851.

Bancroft, Savory, ——, 1864.

Baril, Agnes, dau. of Louizon Rocheleau and Anabella Lapiere, Feb. 26, 1909.

Barker, Abigail, dau. of Silas and Abigail, May 10, 1888.
Abigail, Sept. 4, 1866, aged 84 yrs., 6 mos.
Asa, s. of Silas and Abigail, May 19, 1864; in civil war.
Asa, ———, 1866, aged 74 yrs.
Charles O., s. of Timothy, Jan. 29, 1876, aged 60 yrs., Methuen, Mass.
David C., s. of Silas and Abigail Clark, June 17, 1896, aged 76 yrs., 6 mos., 4 dys.

Barker, David Charles, s. of John C. and Nellie, Nov. 24, 1906, aged 21 yrs.
David W., s. of Samuel C. and Hannah Page, at Philadelphia, Aug. 27, 1900, aged 55 yrs.
D. Kimball, July 31, 1869, aged 60 yrs.
Ebenezer, s. of Silas and Abigail, Jan. 27, 1886.
Elisabeth W., dau. of Samuel and Margaret Cochran, May 26, 1879, aged 74 yrs.
George F., s. of Charles O., drowned at St. Stephen, N. B., Aug. 4, 1891.
Hannah, dau. of Silas and Abigail, Apr. 1, 1868.
Hannah D., w. of Samuel C., Dec. 11, 1894, aged 76 yrs.
John W., s. of Silas and Abigail, July 28, 1864; in civil war.
Lucinda (Hackett), w. of Capt. William S., Sept. 25, 1908, aged 66 yrs.
Nellie (Richardson), w. of John Charles, Feb. 9, 1891, aged 30 yrs.
Samuel C., s. of Silas and Abigail, Aug. 16, 1893, aged 80 yrs., 10 mos.
Silas, July 17, 1836, aged 66 yrs., 7 mos.
Silas, s. of Silas and Abigail, Mar. 10, 1865, aged 60 yrs.
Timothy, Dec. 14, 1858, aged 88 yrs.
William S. (Capt.), s. of Silas and Hannah Bodwell, Feb. 8, 1908, aged 75 yrs.

Barley, Joseph, Feb. 17, 1859, aged 77 yrs.

Barnes, Eliza A. S., dau. of John Goss and Rachel French, Jan. 6, 1895, aged 62 yrs., 3 mos., 12 dys.

Barnett, William, s. of ——, May 12, 1730.

Barron, Clara V., dau. of Thomas and Susan M. Vincent, 1880, aged 55 yrs.

Bartley, Lillian M., at Derry, Feb. 12, 1905, aged 13 mos.; bu. at Londonderry.
Louisa M., at Derry, Aug. 6, 1906; bu. at Londonderry.
Mary E., at Manchester, Sept. 19, 1906, aged 32 yrs.; bu. at Londonderry.

Beede, Florence Grace, dau. of George W. and Annie S. Moody, Oct. 22, 1905, aged 8 mos., 4 dys.
Hayzle May, dau. of George W. and Annie S. Moody, Jan. 6, 1901.
Helen Beatrice, dau. of George W. and Annie S. Moody, Dec. 4, 1907, aged 10 mos.
George E. S., s. of George W. and Annie S. Moody, Mar. 17, 1908, aged 1 mo., 19 dys.
Julius L., s. of David and —— Miler, Nov. 5, 1905, aged 68 yrs., 6 mos., 29 dys.

Belanger, Laura M., at Derry, Dec. 5, 1908, aged 3 mos.

Bell, Joseph, Oct. 14, 1779, aged 83 yrs.

Bellavance, Elmira Eva, at Derry, June 19, 1906, aged 4 yrs., 2 mos., 6 dys.; bu. at Londonderry.

Bennett, William J., s. of Andrew and Mary Hall, Dec. 8, 1893, aged 67 yrs., 7 mos., 12 dys.

Benson, George T., Apr. 5, 1899, aged 73 yrs.

Walter E., s. of George T. and Pendaice M., Apr. 29, 1907, aged 48 yrs., 7 mos., 16 dys.

Berg, Selma, dau. of Andea Anderson, Feb. 6, 1898, aged 39 yrs.

Bergeron, Arthur, s. of Joseph and Lizzie Archambault, Oct. 21, 1896, aged 11 yrs., 2 mos., 25 dys.

Dennis Francis, s. of Oliver and Minnie Keef, Apr., 29, 1908, aged 6 mos., 1 day.

Emma M., dau. of Joseph and Lizzie Archambault, Jan. 22, 1897, aged 9 yrs., 6 mos., 24 dys.

Infant, Apr. 3, 1908.

Berry, Joseph, Jan. 12, 1881, aged 54 yrs.

Rose A., dau. of Robert Andrews and Ellen Brudden, Sept. 25, 1891, aged 30 yrs., 3 mos.

Betts, Arthur Cabot, s. of Aliden W. and Maude A. Wheeler, Nov. 8, 1898, aged 1 yr., 5 mos., 2 dys.

Bienvenne, ———, at Amherst, N. H., Sept. 6, 1905, aged 46 yrs., 3 mos., 28 dys.; bu. at Londonderry.

Biron, Bernard J., s. of Joseph and Lillian I. Sutton, at Derry, N. H., Apr. 25, 1902, aged 1 yr., 9 mos., 11 dys.; bu. at Londonderry.

Blanchard, Delia, at Concord, N. H., Mar. 6, 1907, aged 23 yrs.; bu. at Londonderry.

Blood, Charles L., s. of Charles L. and Frances M. Smith, July 23, 1877, aged 2 yrs.

Charles L., s. of John L., Jan. 1, 1886, aged 45 yrs.

Emeline, dau. of John Greely, Oct. 27, 1893, aged 81 yrs., 11 mos., 3 dys.

George W., 8th N. H. Vol., at New Orleans, Apr., 1863.

Jane P., w. of Pliver, Nov. 4, 1895, aged 76 yrs., 1 mo., 26 dys.

John L., s. of Charles L. and Frances M. Smith, July 23, 1877, aged 9 yrs.

John L., s. of Jeremiah and Hannah, Feb. 4, 1882, aged 75 yrs.

John, s. of Oliver, Nov. 16, 1885.

Oliver, July 31, 1887, aged 69 yrs., 3 mos., 7 dys.

Sarah F. P., at Worcester, Mass., Apr. 19, 1902, aged 54 yrs., 9 mos., 29 dys.; bu. Londonderry.

Bolduc, Dorilda, at Derry, Aug. 12, 1906, aged 9 mos., 6 dys.; bu. at Londonderry.

Boles, Effie E., at Derry, Feb. 10, 1908, 16 yrs., 5 mos., 10 dys.; bu. at Londonderry.

George W., s. of Lewis and Eliza H. Whorf, Mar. 15, 1895, aged 40 yrs., 10 mos., 3 dys.

Lewis, s. of Greenleaf and Hannah Farmer, Mar. 14, 1905, aged 88 yrs., 8 mos.

Bollis, Phoebe Bell, dau. of Alvin and Etta Carpenter, Sept. 21, 1898, aged 30 dys.

Boulanger, Maria L., at Derry, Oct. 31, 1905, aged 4 mos., 15 dys.; bu. at Londonderry.

Bowles, Martin M., s. of Miles and Judith A. Cogswell, Aug. 9, 1896, aged 56 yrs.

Boyce, Alonzo (dwarf), Mar. 22, 1866.

Andros, ———, 1864.

Charles Tyler, s. of William and Wealthy Fling, Jan. 4, 1892, aged 52 yrs.

Ellen Louisa adopted dau. of Moses and Jane Alley, ———, 1865, aged 13 yrs.

Giles Ladd, s. of Lafayette, Aug. 2, 1883, aged 48 yrs.

Hugh, Feb. 10, 1856, aged 39 yrs.

James, at Stoneham, Mass., July 3, 1890, aged 78 yrs.; bu. at Londonderry.

Jenetta M., Feb. 21, 1855, aged 39 yrs.

John G., 7th N. H. Vol., Dec. 18, 1873.

John, May 11, 1868, aged 78 yrs.

Loomis, dau. of William and Ruth, Aug. 1, 1868, aged 78 yrs.

Mason V., s. of William and Wealthy Fling, Mar, 6. 1901. aged 51 yrs.

May Frances, Oct. 6, 1853, aged 2 yrs.

Nathaniel, Mar. 24, 1855, aged 54 yrs.

Rufus, s. of Nathaniel, May 20, 1858, aged 27 yrs.

Sarah F., w. of Charles F., June 13, 1905, aged 35 yrs.

Sarah, wid. of Benjamin, Aug. 1, 1874, aged 86 yrs.

Boyes, Clarissa M., dau. of Robert and Persis Garvin, Apr. 28, 1832.

Elisabeth, Sept. 4, 1723.

Jacob, s. of Robert and Persis Garvin, Dec. 31, 1831.

James, Senior, Apr. 8, 1724.

Mary Ann C., dau. of Robert and Persis Garvin, June 19, 1842.

Persis (Garvin), Mar. 5, 1875, aged 74 yrs.

Reuben, s. of Robert and Persis Garvin, Apr. 27, 1844.

Robert M., s. of Robert and Persis Garvin, ———, 1872, aged 27 yrs.

Boyes, Suel W., s. of Robert and Persis Garvin, Sept. 13, 1838.

Boyd, Charlotte W. (Sheppard), w. of Calvin Boyd, Jan. 10, 1900, aged 85 yrs., 9 mos., 16 dys.

Thomas, s. of Robert and Mary L. Towns, Jan. 22, 1892, aged 65 yrs., 11 mos., 12 dys.

Boyden, Joseph, soldier of civil war, July 7, 1893, aged 60 yrs.

Boynton, Edward P., hus. of Emma Morrison, at Cambridge, Mass., May 14, 1893, aged 48 yrs., 4 mos., 15 dys.; bu. at Londonderry.

Emma M., w. of Edward P., Dec. 27, 1907, aged 63 yrs.; bu. at Londonderry.

William, s. of William and Betsey, May 14, 1871, aged 74 yrs.

Brainerd, Henry H., s. of Timothy and Harriet, Feb. 5, 1848, aged 3 yrs.

Braley, Angeline (Boyce), dau. of Hannah Whidden, Oct. 8, 1870, aged 27 yrs.

Bresnan, Isabella, Sept. 14, 1884.

Theresa, dau. of William and Ellen Haggerty, July 11, 1897, aged 9 yrs., 9 mos., 20 dys.

Brickett, Annah H., w. of Henry, W., June 7, 1900, aged 68 yrs., 2 mos., 27 dys.

Brooks, Isaac, s. of Isaac and ———, Dec. 14, 1881, aged 64 yrs.

John W., s. of Edward W. and Anna M. Buck, Mar. 7, 1896.

Infant, July 30, 1898.

Brown, Bertha M., dau. of Arthur E. and Marilla York, Aug. 12, 1906, aged 3 mos., 11 dys.

Charles Louis, s. of Louis F. and Sarah Noble, Dec. 26, 1901, aged 10 yrs., 7 mos., 7 dys.

Nellie E., dau. of Joel Rogers and Sarah James, Jan. 11, 1902, aged 48 yrs., 11 mos., 11 dys.

Robert A., s. of Jacob and Hannah Emerson, Feb. 2, 1896, aged 64 yrs., 9 mos., 13 dys.

Walter C., s. of Alberto C. and Persis Anderson, Dec. 31, 1879.

Bryant, Ira, s. of Richard and Love Kimball, July 4, 1904, aged 65 yrs., 8 dys.

Bugbee, Ruth, dau. of Simon and Ruth Coburn, Mar. 22, 1881, aged 61 yrs.

Buker, Lucius T., s. of Silas and Edna Taylor, Oct. 4, 1907, aged 87 yrs., 9 mos., 26 dys.

Bullock, Elisabeth, dau. of Thomas, Mar. 13, 1873, aged 4 yrs.

Burbank, George M., s. of Frank A. and Bertha M. Towns, Sept. 15, 1909, aged 6 mos., 17 dys.

Burbank, John H., s. of Richard and Lucy Patten, Apr. 30, 1900, aged 78 yrs., 2 mos., 11 dys.
Nancy J., dau. of Trueworthy Chase and Lucy Emory, June 13, 1910, aged 82 yrs., 11 mos., 4 dys.

Burnham, Almira, July 30, 1886, aged 73 yrs.
Nathan, s. of Jacob and Mary, Feb. 9, 1881, aged 91 yrs.

Burns, Daniel H., s. of Daniel and Rachel Hunt, June 24, 1902, aged 71 yrs., 3 mos., 9 dys.
Eliza, Jan. 27, 1895.
Lydia C., Mar. 18, 1853.

Butler, Calvin G., Jan. 1, 1902.

Butterfield, Charles H., s. of Rufus and Mary J., Sept. 20, 1871.

Butterworth, Clayton A., s. of William A. and Edith B. Lowd, June 14, 1897, aged 18 dys.

Caldwell, Mary Nancy, dau. of Henry J. and Abbie Greeley, Apr. 11, 1900, aged 21 yrs., 5 mos., 6 dys.
Susan, Dec. 1, 1890, aged 96 yrs., 1 mo., 4 dys.

Call, George Edwin, s. of George M. and Allettie V. Simpson, Jan. 15, 1900, aged 6 mos., 24 dys.
Lewis W., s. of George M. and Allettie V. Simpson, Apr. 4, 1902, aged 1 yr., 5 mos.

Calwell, William, Nov. 2, 1724.

Campbell, Charlotte A. M., w. of Dr. William, Jan. 27, 1902, aged 71 yrs., 11 mos., 26 dys.
Infant s. of John E. and Mary J., Jan. 5, 1871.
Infant s. of John G. and Mary, May 21, 1872.
Infant s. of John G. and Mary, May 28, 1872.
Jane, w. of Alexander, May 2, 1776.
John, ———, 1863.
Luella A., dau. of Dr. William and w. Roswell Annis, June 24, 1883.
William J., Dr., Sept. 28, 1874, aged 54 yrs.
Winnefred J., dau. of Dr. William, Mar. 1, 1868, aged 2 yrs.

Carlton, Baby, July 25, 1904.
Infant ch. of William B., ———, 1867.

Carney, William, s. of William J. and Mary Wynne, June 15, 1899, aged 1 day.
———, s. of William J. and Mary Wynne, July 19, 1900.

Carpenter, Ellen, dau. of Charles Hardy and Eliza A. Robert, Jan. 28, 1904, aged 56 yrs., 5 mos., 10 dys.

Carson, Mertie M., dau. of Ira M. and Lucinda, July 14, 1871, aged 6 yrs.

Chaplin, Lizzie, at Derry, July 2, 1908, aged 64 yrs., 6 mos., 7 dys.; bu. at Londonderry.

Chase, Amasa K., s. of Simon and Huldah, May 20, 1883, aged 50 yrs.
Annis M., w. of John, Feb. 6, 1851, aged 20 yrs.
Charles H., s. of Fred E. and Alleta M. Young, at Manchester, N. H., Oct. 19, 1910, aged 16 yrs.; bu. at Londonderry.
Daniel, Feb. 18, 1845, aged 79 yrs.
Edmond A., Nov. 2, 1891, aged 63 yrs., 10 mos., 5 dys.
Elijah Gourdian, Apr. 19, 1893, aged 74 yrs.
Elisabeth U., ———, 1873, aged 50 yrs.
Elisabeth, w. of Isaac, Apr. 19, 1894, aged 78 yrs.
Eliza H., dau. of Leonard Page and Mary Austin, June 29, 1900, aged 21 yrs., 1 mo., 6 dys.
Emery M., s. of John M. and Hannah F. Clark, Aug. 21, 1860.
Emily A., dau. of Simon Jr. and Emily A., Apr. 28, 1851, aged 8 months.
Ephraim, s. of Isaac and Elizabeth, Aug. 4, 1846, aged 2 yrs., 3 mos., 20 dys.
Francis M., hus. of Lovinia, Nov. 15, 1869, aged 72 yrs.
George M., s. of Edmond J. and Lovinia Eaton, Feb. 14, 1892, aged 26 yrs., 8 mos., 30 dys.
Hannah F., w. of John M., Mar. 30, 1890, aged 57 yrs.
Huldah, Nov. 23, 1900.
Huldah E., dau. of Simon Jr. and Emily A., Mar. 21, 1851, aged 4 yrs.
Huldah E., w. of Simon, Apr. 11, 1878, aged 86 yrs.
Infant s. of Trueworthy D. and Nancy M. Pettingill, Dec. 2, 1868.
Isaac, Sept. 21, 1869, aged 59 yrs.
John, June —, 1844, aged 53 yrs
Lovinia, w. of Francis M., Mar. 12, 1856, aged 59 yrs.
Mary V., dau. of Joshua Blodgett and Sarah Vickery, Jan. 9, 1892, aged 87 yrs., 6 mos., 23 dys.
Mary W., Sept. 6, 1891, aged 78 yrs., 8 mos.
Molly, dau. of Jacob and Molly, ———.
Nathaniel, Nov. 17, 1902, aged 68 yrs.
Peaslee M., Jan. 15, 1854, aged 48 yrs.
Sarah, Apr. 3, 1840, aged 68 yrs.
Simon, Dec. 27, 1864, aged 73 yrs.
Simon F., s. of Simon Jr. and Emily A., Feb. 9, 1851, aged 5 mos.
Simon, Jr., Apr. 2, 1851, aged 27 years.
Sophia, dau. of Daniel and Elisabeth Howe, Sept. 8, 1879, aged 44 yrs.
Trueworthy D., Feb. 24, 1872, aged 43 yrs.
Trueworthy (Mrs.), ———, 1863.
Trueworthy, Nov. 17, 1902.

Chase, William C., s. of Francis and Lovinia, Nov. 1, 1898, aged 62 yrs., 27 dys.

Choat, George s. of William and Sukey, July 6, 1797.
Lydia, dau. of William and Sukey, May 12, 1792.

Chrispeen, Betsey (Cheney), w. of George W., July 12, 1893, aged 86 yrs., 2 mos.
George W., s. of Richard and Seviah Styles, Sept. 20, 1900, aged 91 yrs., 3 mos., 16 dys.
Hannah Woodlbury, Mrs., w. of George W., 1868.

Christie, Robert Leo, s. of John and Emma J. Finnegan, Mar. 3, 1905, aged 7 mos., 21 dys.

Clark, Carrie B. (Haselton), w. of Charles A. M., at Richmond, Va., Nov. 6, 1910, aged 49 yrs.; bu. at Londonderry.
Charles G., Dec. 15, 1854, aged 3 yrs.
Elisabeth, July 9, 1730.
James, Aug. 1, 1858, aged 67 yrs.
John, Feb. 17, 1855, aged 70 yrs.
Martha, Dec. 3, 1858, aged 57 yrs.
Matthew, drowned at Amoskeag Falls, May 28, 1731.
Myra J., dau. of James D. and Julia M. Page, Feb. 9, 1876, aged 29 yrs.
Quincy E., s. of Eli and Mary Morley, Oct. 12, 1891, aged 43 yrs., 6 mos., 22 dys.
Susan, Dec. 24, 1853, aged 58 yrs.
William, May 26, 1853, aged 15 yrs.

Clarke, John, Jan. 13, 1720–1.

Cleveland, Mabel, dau. of Rev. A. A., Dec. 15, 1869, aged 20 mos.

Clifford, Eugene, Aug. 2, 1875, aged 9 mos.

Clive, Lillian M., dau. of Thomas A. and Katherine Mahoir, Aug. 8, 1909, aged 3 mos.

Clough, Burtt, s. of Frank B. and Julia, Aug. 10, 1896, aged 24 yrs., 8 mos., 21 dys.
Lois May, Aug. 25, 1875, aged 8 mos.
Nancy M., Sept. 2, 1885, aged 85 yrs.

Coburn, Eliza C. (Nesmith), w. of Isaac, Feb. 25, 1896, aged 79 yrs., 8 mos., 8 dys.
Harriet (Flanders), w. of Joel, Oct. 11, 1877, aged 57 yrs.
Isaac, hus. of Sally, June 11, 1863.
Joel, Jan. 24, 1887, aged 75 yrs.
Sally, w. of Isaac, Mar. 11, 1866.

Cochran, Isaac, Jan. 11, 1853.
Lilly, dau. of Samuel, at Derry, May 2, 1884, aged 85 yrs., 10 mos.

Cochran, Mabelle, dau. of Isaac W. and Lucy Tilley, Aug. 1, 1901, aged 23 yrs., 9 mos., 26 dys.

Cody, Marion A., at Derry, Dec. 17, 1904, aged 2 yrs., 4 mos.; bu. in Londonderry.

Coffin, Abigail, Mrs., 1865, aged 96 yrs.
Eunice E., Dec. 24, 1896, aged 76 yrs., 6 mos.
Haskell P., Mar. 3, 1883, aged 46 yrs.

Cogswell, Aaron, s. of Joseph and Abigail, Mar. 25, 1803.
Moses, s. of Joseph and Abigail, June 20, 1802.

Colburn, Abigail H., dau. of Ralph and Clarrissa, May 24, 1910, aged 76 yrs., 5 mos., 24 dys.
Charles, s. of Ralph and Clarrissa, Apr. 8, 1910, aged 72 yrs., 2 dys.
Newton, s. of Joshua and Lydia Sawyer, Sept. 29, 1893, aged 80 yrs., 2 mos., 6 dys.

Colby, Arvilla (Nesmith), w. of Washington, Nov. 18, 1893, aged 57 yrs., 2 mos.
Charlotte M., dau. of John Emerson and w. of Albert P. Colby, May 13, 1907, aged 84 yrs., 3 mos.
Hattie, dau. of James Schwartz and Julia A. Cartner, Nov. 6, 1900, aged 59 yrs., 6 mos.
Henry, in Civil War, ———, 1864.
Isaac, in Civil War, ———, 1864.
Jacob Peavey, s. of Alfred and Almeady, July 20, 1881, aged 26 yrs.
Sally, w. of William, July 6, 1849, aged 48 yrs., 8 mos.
Sarah L., dau. of Benjamin E. Robinson, Nov. 7, 1903, aged 54 yrs., 9 mos.
Margaret (Miss), dau. of Ela and Jane, Oct. 28, 1878, aged 82 yrs., 3 mos.
William, ———, 1866, aged 40 yrs.

Comings, Ann, Nov. 16, 1770, aged 85 yrs.

Conant, Albert G., in Manchester, Jan. 13, 1897, aged 77 yrs., 9 mos.; bu. in Londonderry.
Antoinette dau. of William and Rachel, and w. of Edward P. Moore, Oct., 1881, aged 43 yrs.
Clara F., dau. of William and Rachel, and w. of Thomas Stevenson, Feb., 1906, aged 56 yrs.
Lyman A., s. of William and Rachel, Mar., 1903, aged 63 yrs.
Priscilla (Lawson), w. of Albert G., in Haverhill, Mass., Aug. 24, 1909, aged 77 yrs., 8 mos.; bu. in Londonderry.
Rachel Watts, w. of William, Nov. 17, 1877, aged 62 yrs.
William, s. of Nathaniel and Rhoda, Dec. 17, 1881, aged 73 yrs.

Conner, Charles H., s. of John H. and Ella F. Benson, Aug. 14, 1881.

Connor, Hester, w. of Stephen, Oct. 31, 1908, aged 43 yrs., 9 mos., 3 dys.

Stephen W., s. of Stephen and Philindia Morrill, Jan. 18, 1908, aged 69 yrs., 3 mos.

Cooley, Ann Augusta, in Rochester, Vt., Sept. 22, 1904, aged 61 yrs.; bu. in Londonderry.

Ellen A., dau. of Phoebe and Reuben, Dec. 16, 1901, aged 61 yrs., 6 mos.

George H., s. of Reuben, Aug. 6, 1891, aged 56 yrs., 9 mos.

Mary R., in Nashua, N. H., May 11, 1897, aged 63 yrs.; bu. in Londonderry.

Phoebe (Sterling), w. of Reuben, Feb. 2, 1899, aged 83 yrs., 6 mos.

Reuben, Dec. 24, 1883, aged 71 yrs.

Copp, Almira E., dau. of John A. Plimmer, and w. of Rev. H. B. Copp, d. at Epping, N. H., July 9, 1896, aged 56 yrs.; bu. in Londonderry.

Corliss, Elsie Viola, dau. of Harry C. and Marion B. Nugent, Sept. 11, 1906, aged 3 mos., 6 dys.

Harriet, in Concord, Feb. 22, 1892, aged 67 yrs.; bu. at Londonderry.

Infant dau. of Harry C. and Marion B. Nugent, Apr. 10, 1908, aged 1 day.

John F., s. of Absalom and Polly Farnum, Dec. 2, 1903, aged 67 yrs., 9 mos.

William Jr., s. of William and Phoebe McEwer, Oct. 14, 1894, aged 30 yrs., 2 mos.

Corning, Alfred A., hus. of Clara Rowell July 22, 1871, aged 39 yrs., 9 mos.

Charles F., ———, 1866, aged 57 yrs.

Esther F., Oct. 30, 1851.

Hannah, w. of Nathan, July 2, 1872, aged 65 yrs.

Lydia (Reed), w. of Peter, July 28, 1887, aged 80 yrs., 9 mos.

Mary Ann, dau. of Alexander Center and Sarah Nichols, Oct. 29, 1890, aged 82 yrs., 3 mos.

Mary M., dau. of Alexander McMurphy and Sarah Duncan, Apr. 1, 1893, aged 85 yrs.

Nathan, Nov. 1, 1869, aged 56 yrs., 3 mos.

Nathaniel, s. of Eleazer, Jan. 3, 1883, aged 80 yrs.

Nathaniel, s. of Nathaniel and Mary, June 9, 1878, aged 39 yrs.

Nettie J., dau. of Sylvester R. and Sarah Currier, Jan. 28, 1880, aged 5 yrs.

Peter, s. of John and Sally, Apr. 8, 1874, aged 80 yrs.

Corning, Samuel, Apr. 22, 1852.
Samuel A., s. of Sylvester R. and Sarah Currier, Dec. 21, 1872, aged 3 yrs.
Susan M., dau. of Sylvester R. and Sarah Currier, Dec. 13, 1883, aged 6 yrs.

Corthell, Henrietta R., in Derry, June 7, 1904, aged 28 dys.; bu. in Londonderry.
Jane S., dau. of George W. Crispeen and Hannah Barker, Nov. 30, 1910, aged 65 yrs., 6 mos., 25 dys.
Myron G., s. of Albin and A. A. Goodwin, Apr. 6, 1895.

Cote, Ernest F., Aug. 24, 1906; bu. in Londonderry.
Joseph, infant, in Windham, Feb. 3, 1906; bu. in Londonderry.
Joseph A., in Derry, May 23, 1906, aged 2 mos.; bu. in Londonderry.
Jonas, s. of Joseph and Marie, Nov. 1, 1906, aged 68 yrs.
Lillian, Dec. 9, 1907, aged 28 yrs.; bu. in Londonderry.
——— Telephone and Julia Jaques, Apr. 6, 1907; bu. in Londonderry.

Courteau, George, Feb. 8, 1892, aged 65 yrs.

Cowdrey, Clara, w. of Joseph, July 19, 1876.
Joseph, Oct. 9, 1877, aged 72 yrs.

Cressey, Elisabeth, dau. of John and Nancy Doloff, in Janwood, N. J., Jan. 31, 1908, aged 81 yrs.
Leonard F., in Plainfield, N. J., Aug. 28, 1907, aged 83 yrs., 2 mos.; bu. in Londonderry.

Cristy, Sarah, Aug. 28, 1763, aged 39 yrs.

Crosby, John, s. of Charles H. and Lizzie J. Stone, Jan. 21, 1899, aged 3 yrs.

Cross, John E., s. of William G. and Clara Colburn, Oct. 11, 1897, aged 17 yrs., 10 mos.
Mertena L., dau. of Levi E. and Mary J., Sept. 14, 1881.

Crowell, Eliza, Apr. 21, 1859.
George, in Springfield, Mass., Oct. 10, 1896, aged 40 yrs.; bu. in Londonderry.
George D., Sept. 10, 1853, aged 3 yrs.
Samuel, Feb. 20, 1864, aged 77 yrs.
Sarah E., dau. of Samuel, Oct. 4, 1844, aged 22 mos.
Sarah Frances, dau. of Henry, ———, 1865, aged 8 mos.
Sarah, w. of Samuel, Dec. 16, 1863, aged 77 yrs.

Cullin, Henry B., about July 10, 1886, aged 24 yrs.

Currier, Joshua P., Apr. 8, 1856.

Curtis, Annie J., May 16, 1907; bu. in Londonderry.
Mary Catherine, in Boston, Mass., Jan. 24, 1907; bu. in Londonderry.

Cutler, George W., s. of Lemuel and Betsey Paul, July 16, 1908, aged 72 yrs., 9 mos.
Hiram, s. of Lemuel and Betsey Paul, Dec. 31, 1902, aged 76 yrs., 10 mos.
Lemuel, s. of Isaac, May 24, 1881, aged 85 yrs.
Lucinda, w. of Hiram, Sept. 27, 1904, aged 69 yrs., 4 mos.

Cutter, Elisabeth B. S., dau. of William Shepard and Lucy, May 16, 1874, aged 66 yrs.
Rosa, Aug. 10, 1875, aged 27 yrs.

Dana, George, s. of Jonathan, Dec. 7, 1861, aged 22 yrs.
Jonathan, Jan. 4, 1894.
Lucinda Jane dau. of Jonathan Dana, and w. of Wallace Hall, in Salem, Mass., ———, 1872.
Lucinda, w. of Jonathan, Sept. 23, 1845, aged 39 yrs.
Maria D., w. of John, Apr. 2, 1878, aged 68 yrs.; bu. in Londonderry.
Mary E. Nov. 27, 1878, aged 33 yrs.

Davis, Helen C., dau. of Henry F. and Rebecca George, Oct. 7, 1892, aged 16 yrs., 3 mos.
Jonathan, Dec. 29, 1855, aged 64 yrs.
Paul, Jan. 23, 1859, aged 59 yrs., 2 mos.
Susan A. (Watts), w. of Paul, June 13, 1879, aged 82 yrs., 6 mos.

Day, Charles A., in Windham, N. H., June 21, 1904, aged 47 yrs.; bu. in Londonderry.
Frank, s. of Joseph L. and Laura Gould, June 26, 1884.

Dearborn, Asenath, dau. of Ezekiel Willey, Sept. 7, 1882, aged 67 yrs.

Delven, Mary Ann, dau. of Frederick F. and Anna F. Paquette, Jan. 27, 1909, aged 3 mos.

Desmarais, Idola, in Derry, N. H., Aug. 31, 1903, aged 8 yrs., 6 mos.; bu. in Londonderry.

Desrosiers, Hilda, dau. of Edmund and Lula Theis, Sept. 17, 1909, aged 5 yrs., 8 mos.

De Varney, Lillian E., dau. of David W. and Annie Beauregard, Oct. 11, 1901, aged 31 dys.

Dicey, Christopher C., Apr. 9, 1892, aged 68 yrs.

Dickey, Child, s. of John and Rhoda, Mar. 4, 1803.
Clarinda, dau. of James Annis and Dillia Dix, w. of Wallace Dickey, Feb. 14, 1872.
Elias, s. of William and Elisabeth, Feb. 27, 1755.
Elisabeth F., dau. of Warren Pettingill, Mar. 6, 1893, aged 65 yrs., 10 mos.

Dickey, Elisabeth White, in Groveland, Mass., Feb. 4, 1902, aged 78 yrs., 10 mos.
Elisabeth (White), w. of Joseph Jr., ——, 1878, aged 71 yrs.
Fanny, ——, 1873, aged 78 yrs.
Fanny D. (Montgomery), w. of Capt. Joseph, Apr. 3, 1872, aged 88 yrs., 10 mos.
Frances, dau. of Capt. Joseph and Fanny Montgomery, Mar. 25, 1855, aged 35 yrs., 6 mos.
Janet, dau. of Robert and Hannah, Jan. 2, 1879, aged 88 yrs.
Jannette, dau. of Samuel and Martha Taylor, deaf mute, June, 1811, aged 67 yrs.
James P., s. of Adam and Mariam, Aug. 13, 1878, aged 40 yrs.
Jennie, Jan. 2, 1880, aged 88 yrs.
John P. (Dea.), s. of John, Dec. —, 1875, at Genesee, N. Y.
Joseph, Capt., son of Robert and Hannah, Aug. 30, 1878, aged 94 yrs., 4 mos.
Joseph Jr., s. of Capt. Joseph and Fanny, July 24, 1866, aged 43 yrs.
Mary Ann Nancy, w. of Robert, Dec. 3, 1863, aged 54 yrs.
Mary, dau. of Capt. Joseph and Fanny Montgomery, Oct. 30, 1900, aged 82 yrs., 6 mos.
Margaret, dau. of Capt. Joseph and Fanny Montgomery, Aug., 1904, aged 82 yrs., 9 mos.
Montgomery, s. of Capt. Joseph and Fanny, Apr. 3, 1891, aged 75 yrs., 4 mos.
Rosanna (McDonald), w. of Elias, since date of will, Apr. 20, 1795.

Dill, James W. Jr., s. of James W. and Clara Dickey, May 23, 1900, aged 6 mos.

Dillingham, Sarah G., dau. of Perley Wallace and Mary, shot by a nephew, Feb. 10, 1880, aged 33 yrs.

Dinsmoor, James, Nov. 23, 1795, aged 52 yrs.
Mary, w. of James, Nov. 3, 1796, aged 50 yrs.

Dinsmor, Margaret, w. of Robert, June 2, 1733.
Robert, Oct. 14, 17—.

Dinsmore, Abiah, Sept. 12, 1859.
John, s. of Thomas and Fanny H., Aug. 6, 1874, aged 63 yrs.
Lucy, dau. of Timothy Barker and Abiah, Feb. 11, 1877, aged 72 yrs.
Thomas, at Morris Island, S. C., Aug. 11, 1863; civil war.

Dobbins, Thomas E., s. of Patrick and Margaret Broe, Mar. 13, 1910, aged 36 yrs., 6 mos., 24 dys.

Dodge, Benjamin, s. of Isaac and Mary, Aug. 7, 1883, aged 84 yrs.

Doherty, Dorothy L., dau. of Charles P. and Nellie A. Robie, July 31, 1905, aged 1 yr., 4 mos., 27 dys.

Doiron, Francis T., s. of Moses and Caroline Peters, Jan. 31, 1910, aged 10 dys.

Dolan, Patrick J., in Haverhill, Mass., Dec. 29, 1907, aged 31 yrs., 7 mos.; bu. in Londonderry.

Doran, Elisabeth, in Derry, N. H., Feb. 8, 1908, aged 1 day; bu. in Londonderry.

Dotey, William, Dec. 6, 1875, aged 70 yrs.

Dougan, ———, dau. of Alexander and Annie Bennett, Apr. 1, 1907.

Dow, Betsey E., sister of Isaac, Feb. 5, 1877, aged 76 yrs., 11 mos.
Elisabeth (Savory), w. of Isaac, Feb. 25, 1884, aged 73 yrs., 9 mos.
Hezekiah, June 4, 1827, aged 17 yrs.
Isaac, Apr. 22, 1878, aged 71 yrs., 1 mo.
Jacob, Sept. 29, 1841, aged 32 yrs.
John, Feb. 12, 1831, aged 68 yrs.
John C., adopted s. of Isaac, Aug. 1, 1875, aged 25 yrs., 3 mos.
Mary, w. of John, Nov. 21, 1845, aged 67 yrs.
Mary, w. of Samuel, Feb. 18, 1859, aged 66 yrs., 1 mo., 20 dys.
Samuel, July 25, 1859, aged 65 yrs., 1 mo., 13 dys.

Dowey, Anna L., Feb. 17, 1897, aged 75 yrs.

Drew, Amos W., s. of Samuel and Betsey, Jan. 18, 1873, aged 80 yrs.

Drucher, Lora Ann, dau. of Walter A. and Edith A. Cross, Sept. 8, 1883.
Lottie A., dau. of Walter A. and Edith A. Cross, Sept. 8, 1883.

Duncan, Abraham, Mar. 1, 1805, aged 64 yrs.
Jane, w. of Abraham, June 9, 1812, aged 65 yrs.
Jane, w. of John, Mar. 1, 1835, aged 68 yrs.
Mrs. Mary B., Jan. 28, 1870, aged 91 yrs.
Squire John, Jan. 24, 1852, aged 83 yrs.

Dusant, Leroy Onslow, s. of George W. and Anna F. Lund, Feb. 28, 1894, aged 23 yrs., 1 mo., 14 dys.

Dusette, Joseph L. A., Aug. 24, 1906, in Derry, N. H., aged 8 mos., 28 dys.; bu. in Londonderry.

Dwinels, Elisha, Mar. 26, 1855, aged 84 yrs.

Eames, Alzina C., dau. of William A. Nichols and Sarah H. Marsh, July 15, 1905, in Reading, Mass., aged 52 yrs., 6 mos.; bu. in Londonderry.

Eaton, Child of W. A., May 18, 1894.
James G., Dec. 28, 1856, aged 65 yrs.
Joseph H. (Mrs.), Dec. 9, 1870, aged 76 yrs.
Linda C., Sept. 14, 1853, aged 1 yr.

Ela, Edward, Sept. 3, 1812, aged 60 yrs.
Edward, Dec. 22, 1853, aged 74 yrs.
Edward P., s. of Edward and Sarah, Sept. 2, 1876, aged 64 yrs.
Elisabeth A., dau. of Joel D. Seaward and Lydia M., Aug. 21, 1903, aged 50 yrs., 7 mos.
Hannah, w. of Edward, May 21, 1804, aged 52 yrs.
Mary, dau. of Edward and Mary, Jan. 21, 1822, aged 2 yrs., 5 mos.
Mary, w. of Edward, May 26, 1880, aged 98 yrs.
Sarah, dau. of Daniel and Hannah, Sept. 29, 1778, aged 17 mos., 22 dys.
Sarah, dau. of Edward and Hannah, Sept. 29, 1778.
Sarah, w. of David, Dec. 26, 1879, aged 25 yrs., 3 mos., 21 dys.
Sarah, w. of ———, Jan. 3, 1812, aged 32 yrs.
———, s. of George E. and Mary E. Low, Oct. 23, 1906.

Elkins, Frank, s. of George and Mary Glidden, July 1, 1893, aged 22 yrs., 9 mos.

Emerson, Francis B., Aug. 31, 1854, aged 9 yrs.
Isaiah, s. of David and Eliza Califf, Oct. 16, 1907, aged 79 yrs.
Lucy A., dau. of John Bartlett and Myra Fisher, July 6, 1907, aged 66 yrs., 1 mo.
Mary Ann, w. of William P., dau. of Samuel Manter and Isabel Reid, Apr. 18, 1900, aged 76 yrs.
William P., s. of Charles, Oct. 27, 1902, aged 95 yrs.

Emery, Hannah D., dau. of Richard, July 6, 1898, aged 8 yrs., 6 mos., 23 dys.
A. J. (Miss), ———, 1866.
Nellie M., Dec. 23, 1897, in Lowell, Mass., aged 55 yrs., 7 mos., 28 dys.; bu. in Londonderry.
Sarah M., w. of Thomas, Dec. 31, 1891, aged 68 yrs., 6 mos.
Thomas W., s. of Joseph D. and Lavina, Mar. 6, 1890, aged 56 yrs.

Estey, Benjamin F., s. of John and Hannah Cochrane, Apr. 29, 1907, aged 53 yrs., 5 mos.
Charles H., s. of John and Hannah, Sept. 25, 1834, aged 15 yrs., 8 mos., 10 dys.

Estey, Eliza S., Nov. 24, 1886, aged 47 yrs.
Hannah, w. of John, Aug. 5, 1858, aged 47 yrs., 5 dys.
John H., ———, 1865.
John, s. of John and Hannah, July 12, 1865, at Washington, D. C., aged 24 yrs., 8 mos.
John, s. of John and ——— Peabody, Apr. 4, 1895, aged 87 yrs.
William E., Apr. 25, 1850, aged 1 yr., 1 mo., 10 dys.

Esty, Mary A., w. of Stephen A. Esty, and dau. of John Remington, Sept. 20, 1879, aged 20 yrs.
Richard, Jan. 5, 1853.

Fairfield, Henry W., s. of Benjamin, Mar. 25, 1902, aged 63 yrs., 4 mos., 13 dys.
Sabrina, dau. of Samuel Leach, Aug. 17, 1910, aged 63 yrs.

Farley, Augustus L., Apr. 13, 1877, aged 43 yrs.
George, ———, 1863.
Gilman, s. of Joseph and Susanna Eastman, Apr. 11, 1900, aged 91 yrs., 4 mos., 28 dys.
Hannah (Mrs.), ———, 1864.
Joseph, ———, 1863.
Sophia, w. of Gilman, and dau. of Timothy Barker and ——— Kimball, Mar. 22, 1900, aged 89 yrs., 17 dys.
Sophronia C., in Lynn, Mass., Mar. 22, 1899, aged 64 yrs., 5 mos.; bu. in Londonderry.

Farrell, Porter, Oct. 11, 1890, aged 60 yrs., 7 mos.

Favor, Frank W., hus. of Emily J. Flanders, Nov. 13, 1901.

Feagan, ——— C., s. ———, Sept. 1, 1861.

Fellows, Charles H., s. of Orrin P. and Helen M. Stickney, Mar. 24, 1901, aged 38 yrs., 10 mos., 21 dys.
Ethel, dau. of Augustus and Anna Willey, May 30, 1892, aged 7 yrs., 2 mos., 5 dys.

Ferrin, William, s. of John, b. in Ireland, Sept. 4, 1897, aged 74 yrs.

Fisher, Abigail, dau. of Lieut. Ebenezer, June 10, 1803, aged 4 yrs., 8 mos.
Agnes, w. of Samuel, Mar. 12, 1755, aged 27 yrs.
Caleb (Rev.), in Appleton, Wis., ———, 1875.
Ellis, s. of Lieut. Ebenezer, Sept. 16, 1804, aged 9 mos.
Marjorie D., in Derry, N. H., Oct. 25, 1906, aged 8 mos. 30 dys.; bu. in Londonderry.
Mary, w. of Lieut. Ebenezer, Nov. 28,, 1814, aged 45 yrs.
Samuel (Elder), Apr. 10, 1806, aged 84 yrs.
Samuel, s. of Lieut. Ebenezer, in Warsaw, N. Y., 1876, aged 74 yrs.
Sarah, w. of Samuel, Feb. 3, 1813, aged 80 yrs.
William, s. of Elder, Oct. 25, 1775, aged 14 yrs.

Fitzgerald, Susie A., dau. of George N. and Martha Watts, in Derry, N. H., July 29, 1891; bu. in Londonderry.

Flanders, David (Dr.), Nov. 5, 1850, aged 50 yrs.
Lucy B., w. of Dr. David, Aug. 19, 1881, aged 77 yrs.
Priscilla (Sawyer), 1st w. of Reuben Flanders, Apr. 16, 1869, aged 26 yrs., 4 mos.

Fletcher, Abel (Rev.), Aug. 13, 1874, aged 72 yrs.

Fling, Edmund, s. of William M. and Susanna Watts, Mar. 30, 1825, aged 18 yrs.
John W., s. of William M. and Susanna Watts, Apr. 23, 1898, aged 73 yrs., 9 mos.
Susanna (Watts), Dec. 7, 1840, aged 53 yrs.
William, June 21, 1825, aged 40 yrs.
William, s. of William M. and Susanna Watts, Nov. 26, 1845, aged 28 yrs.

Flint, Heman, hus., June 12, 1874, aged 89 yrs.
Rhoda, w., May 30, 1870, aged 84 yrs., 9 mos.

Floyd, Daniel, s. of James M. and Sarah Karr, Mar. 8, 1891, aged 51 yrs., 3 mos.
James B., s. of James K. and Harriet E. Crowell, Apr. 3, 1875, aged 3 yrs.
Sarah L., w. of James M. and dau. of James Karr and Sarah Huse, Aug. 2, 1891, aged 77 yrs., 7 mos., 10 dys.
James M., s. of Daniel and Esther Ashby, June 16, 1896, aged 86 yrs., 3 mos., 28 dys.

Fogarty, William O., s. of William and Ida Defoe, June 25, 1909, aged 16 yrs., 4 mos., 4 dys.

Follansbee, Edwin, s. of Edwin and Eliza Codwell, Apr. 20, 1905, aged 36 yrs., 7 mos., 20 dys.
Charles E., in civil war, ——, 1863.
Edwin, s. of John and Mary, Feb. 25, 1901, aged 83 yrs., 7 mos., 25 dys.
Eliza A., dau. of Nathan Caldwell, in Auburn, N. H., Jan. 19, 1910, aged 69 yrs., 10 mos., 3 dys.; bu. in Londonderry, N. H.
Esther, w. of Edwin, July 31, 1863.

Foster, Harriet M., dau. of Obediah R. and Harriet E. Smith, July 24, 1876, aged 32 yrs.
Herbert A., s. of Obediah R. and Harriet E. Smith, Aug. 29, 1873, aged 25 yrs.

Fountain, Joseph G. T., in Derry, N. H., May 28, 1908, aged 14 dys.; bu. in Londonderry.

Frappier, George, in Derry, N. H., Aug. 22, 1907, aged 4 mos., 6 dys.; bu. in Londonderry.

Freeze, Alice Elisabeth, dau. of Henry C. and ——— Trask, Aug. 24, 1902, aged 9 mos., 3 dys.

French, Jacob, father of Irene French (Stokes), at Manchester, N. H., Aug. 18, 1855, aged 80 yrs.; bu. in Valley Cemetery, Manchester, N. H.

Martha J., w. of Rev. S. F. French, and dau. of George Upton and Elisabeth Hardy, May 24, 1902, aged 70 yrs., 11 mos., 22 dys.

Friend, Vera P., dau. of George E. and Ina V. Fletcher, Feb. 24, 1901, aged 1 mo., 24 dys.

Frost, Edgar A., s. of Charles R. and Mary E., Apr. 30, 1873, aged 20 yrs.

Sarah E., dau. of Benjamin Russell and Eliza Batchelder, Feb. 23, 1903, aged 72 yrs., 7 mos., 18 dys.

Furber, Edwina E., dau. of Edward and Eliza Sprague, Sept. 27, 1909, aged 21 yrs., 11 mos., 27 dys.

Gage, Abigail, 1st w. of Billy R., Apr. 19, 1808, aged 23 yrs., 10 mos.

Billy R., Mar. 7, 1837, aged 54 yrs.

Jane R., w. of Richard, Jan. 13, 1859, aged 83 yrs.

Nancy A., 3d w. of Billy R., Aug. 19, 1865, aged 81 yrs.

Rebecca, 2d w. of Billy R., Nov. 30, 1816, aged 34 yrs.

Richard, Oct. 3, 1830, aged 60 yrs.

William H., June 3, 1873.

William W., at Somerville, Mass., Aug. 15, 1898, aged 76 yrs., 7 mos., 14 dys.; bu. in Londonderry.

Gagnon, B. L., in Derry, Apr. 25, 1906, aged 6 dys.; bu. in Londonderry.

May B. A., dau. of Alfred and Virginia Bourdon, in Derry, Apr. 22, 1906, aged 3 dys.; bu. in Londonderry.

Virginia, in Manchester, N. H., June 8, 1906, aged 31 yrs.; bu. in Londonderry.

Gale, John, s. of Ephraim, Feb. 19, 1877, aged 83 yrs.

Rachel J., dau. of Rodney Hadley and Lydia Brown, Mar. 12, 1891, aged 66 yrs.

Gallieu, ———, in Derry, May 5, 1906, aged 3 mos., 8 dys.; bu. in Londonderry.

Gardner, George H., s. of Lorenzo and S. Bancroft, Apr. 21, 1895, aged 22 yrs., 11 mos., 27 dys.

Lorenzo W., s. of Charles H. and Eliza, July 13, 1887, aged 5 mos., 20 dys.

Persis H., dau. of Lorenzo and S. Bancroft, June 8, 1895, aged 20 yrs., 1 mo., 23 dys.

Susan E., dau. of Savary Bancroft, Apr. 14, 1893, aged 50 yrs., 3 mos., 16 dys.

Garland, Joseph, s. of Nathaniel, May 5, 1894, aged 91 yrs., 6 mos., 1 day.

Garvin, Capt. George S., s. of Benjamin F. and Nancy Spinney, Oct. 25, 1907, aged 62 yrs., 7 mos., 7 dys.
Infant s. of Fred E. and Emma Provencher, June 22, 1896, aged 1 day.
Jane, Feb. 10, 1862, aged 80 yrs.
Laura J., 1st w. of Capt. George S., Mar. 17, 1896, aged 48 yrs.

Gerow, Hannah, Nov. 8, 1855.

Gibson, Eliza Ann, w. of Robert, Feb. 28, 1886, aged 84 yrs.
Robert, s. of Barnabas and Hannah, Aug. 22, 1881, aged 84 yrs.

Gilcreast, Annie L., dau. of Daniel Smith and Sophia Britton, in Hillsborough, N. H., May 10, 1905, aged 35 yrs., 11 mos., 26 dys.; bu. in Londonderry.
David, s. of David and Sally, Apr. 13, 1880, aged 73 yrs.
Frederick A., s. of David and Sally Holmes, Sept. 27, 1907, aged 72 yrs., 6 mos.
Infant dau. of John and Miranda, Apr. 17, 1867.
James Madison, s. of David and Sallie, ———, 1863.
John, s. of David and Sarah Davis, Nov. 20, 1891, aged 72 yrs., 4 mos., 7 dys.
Miranda P., w. of John, Feb. 19, 1874, aged 47 yrs.
Nancy (Proctor), w. of Samuel, May 1, 1903, aged 85 yrs., 26 dys.
Sallie (Mrs.), 1863.
Sallie H. (Mrs.), June 28, 1874, aged 64 yrs.
Samuel, s. of David and Sarah Davis, Jan. 13, 1903, aged 80 yrs., 2 mos., 6 dys.

Gill, Andrew, Mar. 17, 1861.

Gionet, Fred, s. ———, June 7, 1909, aged 30 yrs.
William R., s. of Fred and Catherine Gallieu, June 3, 1909, aged 11 mos., 10 dys.

Goff, Jane E., dau. ———, Jan. 8, 1899, aged 45 yrs., 4 mos.

Goodwin, Abbie C., dau. of J. C. Austin and Betsey Barker, and w. of Daniel Goodwin, Dec. 11, 1897, aged 67 yrs., 8 mos.
Albert V., s. of Daniel W. and Sarah A. Moody, July 19, 1891, aged 7 yrs., 6 mos.
Ann Maria, dau. of David and Mary, Aug. 14, 1873.
Anna M., 2d w. of Dea. Joshua, Dec. 29, 1869, aged 90 yrs.
Arthur W., s. of Henry, in Boston, Mass., ———, 1870, aged 6 yrs.
Caleb (Dea.), Nov. 14, 1851, aged 77 yrs.

Goodwin, Caroline, Mrs., 1867.
Carrie W., w. of John, June 18, 1867, aged 24 yrs.
Daniel, s. of Josiah and Esther, June 27, 1864, in civil war.
Daniel, Rev., Dec. 30, 1893, aged 84 yrs.
David, s. of Joshua, Jan. 21, 1881, aged 77 yrs.
David, June 20, 1822, aged 78 yrs.
Elisabeth, 1st w. of Dea. Joshua, Mar. 1, 1844, aged 74 yrs.
Enoch, Nov. 28, 1825, aged 40 yrs.
Esther Stone, dau. of Joseph S. and Maria S. Palmer, May 10, 1894.
Esther, w. of Josiah, Mar. 9, 1888, aged 78 yrs.
Fannie S., 1st w. of Joseph S., May 24, 1883, aged 33 yrs.
Infant s. of Joseph S. and Maria L.
John, s. of Josiah and Esther, in Lynn, Mass., Oct. 26, 1875; bu. in Londonderry.
Joshua (Dea.), June 25, 1873, aged 93 yrs.
Joshua, Jr., May 5, 1852, aged 50 yrs.
Josiah, s. of Joshua and Elisabeth, July 29, 1893, aged 86 yrs.
Martha, w. of Dea. Caleb, Mar. 3, 1850, aged 71 yrs., 6 mos.
Mary, dau. of David and Eliza, Oct. 3, 1861.
Mary, dau. of David and Mary, Oct. 3, 1861, aged 21 yrs., 5 mos.
Mary H., dau. of Joshua and Hannah Hilliard, Dec. 7, 1881, aged 77 yrs.
Mary L., dau. of Joseph S. and Maria L., May 5, 1887.
Mary, w. of Joshua Jr., Oct. 10, 1890.
Mehitable, dau. of Caleb and Martha, Apr. 28, 1873, aged 72 yrs.
Mehitable, w. of David, Dec. 12, 1822, aged 81 yrs.
Rebecca, w. of Dea. Joshua, May 27, 1806, aged 41 yrs., 4 mos.
Reuby, dau. of Dea. Caleb and Martha, Aug. 11, 1807, aged 3 yrs., 8 mos.
Rev. Daniel, Dec. 30, 1893, aged 84 yrs.
Sally, w. of Enoch, Sept. 17, 1825, aged 41 yrs.
Sarah A., infant dau. of Daniel W. and Sarah A. Moody, Mar. 24, 1888, aged 10 hours.
Sarah A., w. of Daniel, and dau. of J. B. Moody and Dolly McDonald, Mar. 23, 1888, aged 35 yrs.

Goss, Ann Augusta, dau. of Henry S. and Martha, burned to death Nov. 26, 1853, aged 7 yrs., 1 mo.
Henry S., s. of John and Rachel French, Jan. 21, 1903, aged 79 yrs., 1 mo., 8 dys.
John, Feb. 10, 1855, aged 64 yrs., 3 mos.
Rachel (French), May 8, 1858, aged 63 yrs., 8 mos., 11 dys.
Martha T. (Senter), w. of Henry Sullivan, Oct. 18, 1889, aged 65 yrs

Gould, Lena, dau. of John and Marielice Roy, Mar. 15, 1906, aged 11 mos., 3 dys.

Goyette, Germain, in Derry, May 25, 1908, aged 11 mos., 21 dys.; bu. in Londonderry.

Gravel, Louis H. A., in Derry, Apr. 24, 1906, aged 5 mos., 4 dys.; bu. in Londonderry.

Graves, Ebenezer, Dec. 10, 1724, aged 1 yr., 2 mos.
Minnie M., dau. of John and Ellen McAllister, Mar. 20, 1907, aged 17 yrs., 5 mos., 4 dys.
Sara, July 16, 1724, aged 1 yr., 2 mos.

Gregg, Abigail P., w. of William, Nov. 17, 1881, aged 68 yrs., 2 mos.
Horace D., May 23, 1873, aegd 30 yrs., 10 mos.
Lauraett, w. of Nathan Parker, Sept. 25, 1872, aged 27 yrs., 10 mos. (Soldier of Civil War.)
Mary J., dau. of Samuel Gregg and Janet Dickey, Mar. 2, 1904, aged 83 yrs., 2 mos., 23 dys.
Mary (Mrs.), ——, 1863.
Mary R., June 3, 1819.
Robert, Sept. 6, 1866, aged 40 yrs., 9 mos.
Samuel, Mar. 15, 1829, aged 42 yrs., 5 mos.
William, Nov. 13, 1866, aged 52 yrs., 8 mos.

Greeley, Abigail, w. of Franklin, Apr. 20, 1882, aged 74 yrs.
Arthur Henry, s. of John W. 2d and Carrie Osborne, Apr. 25, 1896, aged 1 day.
Charles Dustin, s. of Sarah, Feb. 19, 1862, aged 38 yrs., 11 mos.
Frank, ——, 1865.
Franklin, Aug. 2, 1864, aged 55 yrs.
George W., Aug. 3, 1888, 67 yrs., 10 mos.
John, May 14, 1872, aged 89 yrs.
John (Mrs.), ——, 1863.
Julia A., dau. of Oliver Blood and Sarah Dunn, June 16, 1899.
Martha, w. of John, soldier, Aug. 18, 1863, aged 78 yrs.
Phebe C., in Hudson, N. H., Jan. 13, 1904, aged 85 yrs.; bu. in Londonderry.
Philip, s. of Edward and Hannah M. Eaton, Sept. 5, 1904, aged 80 yrs., 1 mo., 12 dys.
Sanford, June 1, 1884, aged 71 yrs.

Greenleaf, Jabez L., s. ——, Dec. 15, 1903, aged 68 yrs.

Greenwood, Sophronia D., in Derry, N. H., Sept. 28, 1902, aged 9 yrs., 9 mos.; bu. in Londonderry.

Griffin, Benjamin, s. of Benjamin and Mary, Mar. 9, 1875, aged 48 yrs.

Griffin, Daniel, May 18, 1882.
Eleanor, Sept. 16, 1861.
Ella May, dau. of Daniel and Ella M. Nichols, Feb. 13, 1890, aged 10 yrs., 7 mos., 12 dys.
Hannah, w. of Dea. Jonathan, Mar. 14, 1820, aged 75 yrs.
Hannah, dau. of Dea. Jonathan, Feb. 27, 1827, aged 65 yrs.
James, s. of Frank and Margaret Drea, May 10, 1903, aged 1 yr., 4 mos., 6 dys.
John W., s. of Frank and Margaret, Apr. 9, 1908, aged 19 yrs., 4 mos., 22 dys.
Jonathan (Dea.), June 18, 1825, aged 86 yrs.
Josephine, dau. of Frank and Margaret, June 28, 1908, aged 2 yrs., 2 mos., 24 dys.
Mary, in Brentwood, N. H., Jan. 21, 1899, aged 83 yrs.; bu. in Londonderry.
Moses, Mar. 31, 1846, aged 83 yrs.
Moses, Jr., Jan. 22, 1841, aged 29 yrs.
William P., May 10, 1886, aged 77 yrs.

Groleau, Fred, in Derry, N. H., Oct. 9, 1907, aged 29 yrs., 9 mos.; bu. in Londonderry.

Guilbault, George, Feb. 9, 1903, in Derry, N. H., aged 3 mos., 3 dys.; bu. in Londonderry.
Mary, in Derry, N. H., Mar. 26, 1904, aged 73 yrs.; bu. in Londonderry.

Gutterson, Eli S., May 19, 1863, aged 44 yrs., 10 mos.

Hall, Sarah R., Oct. 31, 1861.
Bertha, dau. of William and Affie Cole, Oct. 30, 1889, aged 1 mo.

Hambeett, Joseph M., s. of Amos and Nancy P. Marsh, Dec. 20, 1904, aged 58 yrs., 10 mos.

Hamblet, Martha, ——, 1868.
W. N., ——, 1868.

Hamlet, Dustin, 1st N. H. H. Art., Jan. 10, 1865, aged 43 yrs., 8 mos.
Helen L., dau. of H. J. and L. D., Mar. 13, 1866, aged 1 yr., 3 mos.
Rosella M., June 29, 1863, aged 3 yrs., 11 mos.
Willie A., June 20, 1863, aged 1 yr., 6 mos., 25 dys.

Hamlin, Vallie Laborer, Apr., 17, 1906, aged 32 yrs.

Hamnett, Samuel, b. in England, Dec. 31, 1901, aged 67 yrs.

Hardy, Martha E., 2d w. of William G., and dau. of Heman Flint and Rhoda Cheever, Sept. 10, 1894, aged 72 yrs., 15 dys.
Sarah (Mrs.), Jan. 1, 1867, aged 89 yrs., 9 mos., 13 dys.

Hart, Charlotte, w. of Nicholas, and dau. of Michael Prout, July 3, 1901, aged 80 yrs., 8 mos.

Hartop, Annie E., dau. of Arthur and Annie Boles, Apr. 9, 1908, aged 1 yr., 7 mos., 9 dys.

George B., s. of Arthur and Annie Boles, Oct. 31, 1898, aged 12 yrs., 9 mos., 2 dys.

James B., s. of Arthur and Annie Boles, June 25, 1909, aged 21 yrs., 2 mos.

Harvell, Phebe, ———, 1873, aged 70 yrs.

Harvey, Ephraim W., s. of John and Rebecca Emerson, Apr. 11, 1910, aged 85 yrs., 3 mos., 29 dys.

Ginger (Miss), Apr. 30, 1865, aged 100 yrs. (Negro.)

Jerome B., s. of John and Rebecca Emerson, Aug. 12, 1897, aged 56 yrs., 6 mos.

John, Jan. 5, 1864.

Susanna (Stevens), w. of Ephraim W., June 9, 1910, aged 86 yrs., 4 mos., 11 dys.

Hastings, Fannie M., dau. of E. Merrill and Sophia Plummer, Oct. 17, 1906, aged 58 yrs., 2 mos., 22 dys.

Hayes, Sarah H., w. of Rev. Joseph Hayes and dau. of Abraham Mitchell, 1871, aged 52 yrs.

Haynes, John, M. D., s. of James and Sarah, May 3, 1874, aged 43 yrs., 5 mos.

Mary M., 1st w. of John, M. D., July 21, 1869.

Healey, Earle F., s. of Albert L. and Flora, in Manchester, N. H., Apr. 5, 1906, aged 1 mo., 21 dys.; bu. in Londonderry.

Josiah M., s. of Elliott, June 5, 1899, aged 88 yrs., 8 mos., 19 dys.

Walter, s. of Albert and Hattie Ladd, Somerville, Mass., July 21, 1890, aged 9 mos., 2 dys.; bu. at Londonderry.

Heath, Arthur, s. of Capt. George E., Apr. 17, 1869, aged 5 yrs.

Heroux, Joseph, in Derry, N. H., May 13, 1908, aged 56 yrs., 5 mos., 20 dys.; bu. in Londonderry.

Hicks, Charlie, s. of Charles P. and Mary, Sept. 7, 1876, aged 13 mos.

Hill, Abby J., dau. of George A., June 6, 1850, aged 1 yr., 3 mos., 16 dys.

George A., s. of Benjamin and Hannah, May 25, 1883, aged 61 yrs., 7 mos., 4 dys.

Joanna F., w. of George A., June 21, 1858, aged 34 yrs., 3 mos., 10 dys.

Hinckley, Owen, s. of Smith Hinckley and Relief Smith, Dec. 29, 1909, aged 77 yrs., 1 mo., 26 dys.

Hine, Joseph, in Concord, N. H., Sept. 8, 1901, aged 91 yrs.; bu. at Londonderry.

Hine, Lizzie R., dau. of Joseph V. Libbey and Mary A., Aug. 15, 1899, aged 61 yrs.

Hitchen, William, s. of Thomas and Mary A. Hallowell, Aug. 29, 1903, aged 59 yrs., 3 dys.

Hog, John, Aug. 13, 1755, aged 23 yrs.
Thomas, Jan. 8, 1748, aged 42 yrs.

Hogan, Ann, dau. of Patrick McGreeny and Catherine Lynch, June 28, 1910, aged 51 yrs.

Hogg, Mary, w. of Thomas, May 1, 1790, aged 24 yrs.

Holbrook, Martha (Langford), in Haverhill, Mass., Sept. 18, 1903.
Walter S., at Haverhill, Mass., Oct. 23, 1907.

Holden, Charles W., s. of Charles A. and Mary E., Jan. 10, 1873, aged 9 yrs.

Holmes, Abraham, May 20, 1753.
Anna B., Apr. 23, 1875, aged 76 yrs.
Betsey (Mrs.), ——, 1865, aged 79 yrs.
Charles M., s. of Robert and Elisabeth Anderson, July 30, 1897, aged 77 yrs., 3 mos.
Christopher N., s. of Charles and Mary A., Feb. 14, 1874, aged 22 yrs.
Elder Matthew, s. of Thomas and Margaret, Sept. 14, 1874, aged 79 yrs.
Elisabeth F., dau. of Matthew and Betsey F., in Chicago, Ill., Sept. 20, 1892, aged 63 yrs.; bu. in Londonderry.
Jane, w. of Robert, Dec. 10, 1871, aged 80 yrs.
John, s. of Stephen S. and Elisabeth Johnson, Dec. 20, 1897, aged 84 yrs., 8 mos., 7 dys.
Judith N., w. of William M., Oct. 2, 1885.
Mary, dau. of Robert and Jane, Nov. 3, 1860.
Mary J., in Derry, N. H., July 15, 1894, aged 73 yrs., 7 mos.; bu. in Londonderry.
Moses Noyes, in the West, June 12, 1909.
Robert, ——, 1825.
William A., Apr. 10, 1855, aged 42 yrs.
William M., May 11, 1885.

Hopkins, Marey, Jan. 12, 1745.

Houle, Angeline, dau. of Edward Pellerin and Maria Bergeron, Mar. 9, 1907, aged 38 yrs., 10 mos., 12 dys.
Vonne, in Derry, N. H., May 7, 1908, aged 3 yrs., 6 mos., 2 dys.; bu. in Londonderry.

Hovey, Abigail (Dustin), 3d w. of John, ——, 1883, in Ohio, aged 84 yrs.
Abby D., dau. of John and Abigail, ——, in Ohio.
Five other children living or dead in Ohio.

Hovey, Albert G., s. of John and Abigail, Nov. 27, 1898, aged 76 yrs.
Almira E., dau. of Elmira E. Boyce, in Hollis, N. H., Jan. 19, 1894, aged 68 yrs., 8 mos., 25 dys.; bu. in Londonderry.
Charlotte, dau. of Robert H. and Sarah Hadley, Apr. 6, 1908, in Manchester, N. H., aged 70 yrs.; bu. at Londonderry.
Eleinor (White), 1st w. of John, at Londonderry, Mar. 29, 1812, aged 23 yrs.
Elisabeth (White), 2d w. of John, at Londonderry, Mar. 27, 1819, aged 25 yrs.
Henry A., ———, 1865, aged 16 yrs. Disease contracted in civil war.
John.* in Marietta, O., about 1851. He had three wives.
Lucy Jane, dau. of John and Eleinor, aged 1 yr.
R. M., ———, 1863.
Walter, W., Aug. 16, 1890, aged 2 mos.
———, (Mrs.), ———, 1868, aged 77 yrs.

Huard, Edward E., in Derry, N. H., June 9, 1903, aged 20 dys.; bu. in Londonderry.

Huntee, Charles H., s. of Currier, June 21, 1869, aged 26 yrs., 6 mos.
James, s. of Currier, Aug. 10, 1849, aged 10 mos.
Lovilla, w. of William C., and dau. of Grafton Manter, Dec. 14, 1883.
Sally, w. of Currier, Mar. 8, 1849, aged 34 yrs., 7 mos.
Sarah Ann, dau. of William and Alta, June 25, 1840, aged 2 yrs., 8 mos.
Susan, dau. of Currier, July 13, 1853, aged 1 yr., 8 mos.
———, July 12, 1853.

Hunter, Fannie, 2d w. of Currier Huntee, in Derry, N. H., Jan. 6, 1892, aged 79 yrs., 5 mos.; bu. at Londonderry.
Joshua, Apr. 12, 1853, aged 11 yrs.

Huntress, Joseph E., s. of Edward L. and Ella, Aug. 29, 1881.

Hurd, Cora E., at Manchester, N. H., Feb. 17, 1897, aged 31 yrs., 1 mo., 6 dys.; bu. at Londonderry.
Mary F., at Haverhill, Mar. 31, 1910, aged 80 yrs., 2 mos., 3 dys.; bu. at Londonderry.

Huse, Eunice, Aug. 7, 1863, aged 66 yrs., 2 mos.

Hutchinson, Mabel H., in Manchester, N. H., May 5, 1906, aged 36 yrs., 4 mos., 23 dys.; bu. at Londonderry.

*John Hovey, a carpenter, built the Baptist Meeting House in Londonderry. He was a former owner of the land on which it stood. In 1839 he moved with his family to Ohio.

Jackson, Belinda, dau. of Betsey Coburn, Sept. 22, 1841, aged 19 yrs.
Betsey, w. of Joseph, Aug. 14, 1856, aged 63 yrs.
Clarinda, dau. of Joseph and Betsey, Mar. 7, 1849, aged 31 yrs.
Esther W., dau. of Joseph and Betsey, Apr. 23, 1855, aged 30 yrs.
Ephraim, Co. K, 13th N. H. Vol., Aug. 7, 1873, aged 42 yrs.
Hugh M., s. of Joseph and Betsey, July 3, 1849, aged 29 yrs.
James M., s. of William and Sophia, May 27, 1881.
Joseph, Feb. 17, 1845, aged 54 yrs.
Mary, w. of Samuel, Oct. 6, 1833, aged 69 yrs.
Mary, w. of John and dau. of John Duncan, Aug. 11, 1876, in Leroy, N. Y., aged 76 yrs.
Morrison, Aug. 26, 1843, aged 43 yrs.
Samuel, Oct. 12, 1842, aged 80 yrs.
——— from England, Aug. 8, 1871.
William W., s. of Joseph and Betsey, Dec. 23, 1854, aged 37 yrs.
Samuel, s. of James and Martha Emery, Mar. 28, 1905, aged 57 yrs., 2 mos., 28 dys.

James, Thomas, Mar. 2, 1818, aged 65 yrs.

Jameson, James, Nov. 11, 1877.

Jaques, Henry E., s. of Charles H. and Rebica Philbrook, May 26, 1898, aged 38 yrs., 6 mos.

Jeffers, Mrs. Christina, Jan. 10, 1799, aged 59 yrs.

Jenness, Annie R., dau. of Miah Clark, Dec. 20, 1906, at Windham, N. H., aged 67 yrs., 7 mos., 10 dys.; bu. at Londonderry.

Jililoty, Sadia, in Derry, N. H., Spet. 26, 1906, aged 23 yrs.; bu. in Londonderry.

Jodain, M. Maria, in Derry, N. H., Mar. 20, 1908, aged 13 dys.; bu. at Londonderry.

Johnson, George D., hus. of T. Jane Mullins, Oct. 12, 1863.
Georgie, dau. of James M. Gilcreast and Eveline, Aug. 2, 1881, aged 23 yrs.
Hannah, Dec. 23, 1856, aged 74 yrs.
Jane T., Jan. 25, 1886, aged 64 yrs.
John, b. in Sweden, June 5, 1907, in Londonderry, aged 66 yrs.
Melissa D., w. of John and dau. of George Hamlin and Lucinda Dow, Dec. 5, 1908, aged 70 yrs., 8 mos.

Jones, Josiah, Aug. 16, 1796, aged 65 yrs., 4 mos., 24 dys.
Lafe W., s. of Wells Jones and Mary J. Norton, Nov. 17, 1909, aged 54 yrs., 6 mos., 17 dys.

Jordan, Joseph, in Derry, N. H., Mar. 12, 1903, aged 45 yrs., 1 mo., 13 dys.; bu. at Londonderry.

Karr, ———, Jan. 9, 1856, aged 32 yrs.
Luther Bell, s. of William D. and Clarissa, Oct. 20, 1839, aged 5 yrs., 5 mos., 15 dys.
Mary, dau. of James and Sarah Huse, Dec. 9, 1905, aged 83 yrs., 9 mos., 11 dys.

Kelley, Edward, at Manchester, N. H., Jan. 31, 1905, aged 26 yrs., 7 mos., 11 dys.; bu. at Londonderry.
Michael, at Derry, N. H., Oct. 1, 1908, aged 59 yrs., 2 mos.; bu. at Londonderry.
William A., at Rockland, Vt., Nov. 9, 1901; bu. at Londonderry.

Kendall, Rachel H., w. of Everet C. and dau. of John Goss and Rachel, Mar. 2, 1882.
Robert S., 1865.

Kidder, Nora Francis, dau. of Frank A. and Abbie A., Sept. 17, 1883.

Kimball, Isaac, June 24, 1841, aged 55 yrs., 11 mos., 18 dys.
J. Maria, dau. of Isaac and Judith, July 6, 1865, aged 36 yrs., 10 mos., 11 dys.
Judith, w. of Isaac, Oct. 26, 1878, aged 87 yrs.
Wilfred, s. of Richard H., Dec. 21, 1896.

King, Hannah, Jan. 10, 1851, aged 15 yrs.

Knight, Helen, w. of Wesley B., soldier, and dau. of Dea. David Anderson, Apr. 18, 1896, aged 52 yrs., 9 mos., 4 dys.
Winnifred A., dau. of Franklin P. Carpenter and Evelyn Hitchens, Aug. 23, 1910, aged 38 yrs., 5 mos.

Kutz, Bertha L., dau. of ——— Sleeper and Jennie Gilcreast, Mar. 3, 1910, at Goffstown, N. H., aged 23 yrs.; bu. at Londonderry.

Labassiere, Emile, in Derry, Dec. 11, 1905, aged 30 yrs., 8 mos., 11 dys.; bu. in Londonderry.

Labranche, Celinda, at Derry, N. H., May 13, 1903, aged 55 yrs., 9 mos.

Lacroix, Homer, in Derry, N. H., Apr. 2, 1908, aged 17 dys.; bu. in Londonderry.

Ladd, Andrew J., s. of Timothy and Mary Laive, Aug. 3, 1905, in Epsom, N. H., aged 69 yrs., 3 dys.; bu. in Londonderry.
Ch. of Mrs. Ladd, Aug. 10, 1871, aged 10 mos.
Timothy, Sept. 18, ———, aged 81 yrs., 7 mos.

Lalliberte, Louis M., in Derry, Jan. 21, 1908, aged 53 yrs., 7 mos., 21 dys.; bu. at Londonderry.
Ullric J., in Derry, N. H., Mar. 26, 1908, aged 22 yrs., 4 mos., 2 dys.; bu. in Londonderry.

Lamb, Alexander, s. of Alexander and Mary Pacbella, in Derry, N. H., Aug. 6, 1905; bu. at Londonderry.
Mary R., in Derry, N. H., Oct. 21, 1905, aged 32 yrs.; bu. in Londonderry.

Lannier, Leo A., s. of Joseph and Maria Prosper, June 6, 1902. aged 32 yrs., 2 mos., 18 dys.

Laporte, Josephine, Sept. 12, 1907, aged 4 mos., 15 dys.; bu. at Londonderry.

Largesse, Nillie J., dau. of Napoleon, June 10, 1893, aged 6 mos.

Lary, George E., Sept. 3, 1906, aged 68 yrs., 8 mos., 25 dys.

Lasley, Mary, Apr. 8, 1722, aged 1 mo., 2 dys.

Lawrence, Christopher, in Derry, N. H., Feb. 27, 1908, aged 2 yrs., 1 mo., 5 dys.; bu. at Londonderry.
Nicholas, Oct. 26, 1877, aged 76 yrs.
Sarah H., in Manchester, N. H., June 9, 1891, aged 75 yrs ; bu. in Londonderry.

Laws, Loretta, in Derry, N. H., Jan. 16, 1907, aged 39 yrs., 4 mos., 29 dys.; bu. at Londonderry.

Lawson, Catherine, Jan. 21, 1885, aged 74 yrs.
Edward, from Nottingham, England, Jan. 1, 1870.
George H., Co. K, N. H. Infantry, Dec. 27, 1867.
Jemima, Apr. 4, 1854, aged 17 yrs.
Prescilla, dau. of Mehitable, July 16, 1867, aged 76 yrs.
William, s. of Edward and Sarah, Nov. 26, 1875, aged 35 yrs
William, Co. K, 4th N. H. Infantry, Nov. 26, 1875.

Leach, Betsey, 1877, aged 86 yrs.
Elisabeth P., Aug. 10, 1877, aged 86 yrs., 5 mos., 14 dys.
Joseph, Apr. 19, 1824, aged 70 yrs.
Olive, Jan. 31, 1839, aged 83 yrs.
Mary, May 24, 1848, aged 52 yrs., 4 mos., 10 dys.
Mrs. David R., Apr. 30, 1887, aged 69 yrs., 2 mos.

Le Branch, ———, dau. of William and Josie Gallant, Oct. 27, 1904.

Lee, Lewis, s. of Samuel, Apr. 20, 1887, aged 88 yrs., 7 mos., 5 dys.

Lemieux, George H., in Derry, N. H., Aug. 5, 1908, aged 4 mos., 16 dys.; bu. in Londonderry.

Lamireaux, Gobert, in Derry, N. H., June 13, 1903, aged 29 yrs., 2 mos., 10 dys.; bu. in Londonderry.

L'Etoile, Josephine L. P., in Derry, N. H., Feb. 20, 1903, aged 4 mos., 10 dys.; bu. in Londonderry.

Lewis, Mrs. Molly, 1863.
Nancy S., 1865.

Lezotte, Hazel, dau. of George, Mar. 18, 1900, aged 6 mos., 15 dys.

Libby, Mary A., dau. of Joseph and Elisabeth Phinney, May 2, 1897, aged 84 yrs.

Linton, John, in Concord, N. H., Feb. 8, 1904, aged 76 yrs.; bu. in Londonderry.

Loomis, Addie, May 24, 1868, aged 28 yrs.
Jane, dau. of William Holt, Mar. 9, 1895, aged 79 yrs., 1 mo., 1 day.

Loon, Mary, dau. of Mary Foster, Sept. 6, 1896, aged 61 yrs.

Lovigne, Wilfred, in Derry, N. H., July 27, 1908, aged 7 mos., 1 days; bu. at Londonderry.

Lowd, Nathan A., s. of Sedley A. and Julia M., Oct. 31, 1871.

Lund, Bridgett T., dau. of Michael Connolly and Hannah, June 6, 1899, aged 23 yrs., 5 mos.

Lunt, Charlie F., s. of Aaron and Susan, ———.

Lupier, James, in Derry, N. H., Sept. 22, 1908, aged 2 mos.; bu. in Londonderry.

Lurvey, Lulu, dau. of James M. and Sarah M. McConnell, Sept. 14, 1894, aged 16 yrs., 1 mo., 6 dys.

MacGregore,* Rev. James, Mar. 5, 1729, aged 52 yrs.

Mack, Andrew W., s. of Robert and Annie Clark, Feb. 7, 1877.
Annie (Clark), w. of Robert, Aug. 28, 1855, aged 63 yrs.
Frances A. (Preston), w. of Andrew W., May 17, 1908, aged 78 yrs., 9 mos., 13 dys.
Isabella, dau. of Robert and Annie, Mar. 20, 1827, aged 3 mos., 15 dys.
Jane D. (Patterson), w. of Robert C., Feb. 3, 1894.
Robert, Sept. 9, 1870, aged 86 yrs.
Robert C., s. of Robert and Annie Clark, Jan. 11, 1894.

MacMurphy, Alexander, Feb. 19, 1733.
Alexander, Oct. 10, 1788, aged 29 yrs.
Jane, w. of Robert, Dec. 31, 1804, aged 85 yrs.
Jane, w. of Robert, Jr., Jan. 13, 1806, aged 50 yrs.
Jean, Jan. 18, 1724.
William, Oct. 15, 1791, aged 6 yrs.
William, s. of Robert and Jane, Aug. 10, 1791, aged 35 yrs.

Maheir, Charles J., in Derry, N. H., Feb. 4, 1908, aged 50 yrs., 5 mos.; bu. at Londonderry.

Manning, Charles E., s. of Charles L. and Mary E., Dec. 9, 1878.
Hannah, Nov. 26, 1872, aged 45 yrs.

*Rev. James was the first minister of East Parish. He was born in Ireland, and died in Londonderry, in active service, Wednesday, March 5, 1729.

Manter, Daniel, 1866.
Harriet, July 4, 1858, aged 58 yrs.
Isabella, July 3, 1874.
Mary, 1877, aged 77 yrs.
Samuel, s. of George and Mary Center, Dec. 20, 1893, aged 94 yrs., 8 mos., 22 dys.

March, Albert Napoleon, soldier, in Maryland, Nov. 1, 1862.
Hannah C., Oct. 17, 1852.
Hannah C., dau. of John and Hannah C. Crowell, Jan. 27, 1892, aged 49 yrs., 1 mo.
John, s. of Morris and Sarah Kelley, Feb. 1, 1892, aged 86 yrs., 10 mos., 27 dys.
Mary (Mrs.), 1863.
Morris, in Civil War, Dec., 1864.

Marcotte, Cora Bertha, in Derry, N. H., Jan. 16, 1904, aged 3 mos., 20 dys.; bu. in Londonderry.

Marden, Laura F., dau. of Solomon and Charlotte, Feb. 12, 1881, aged 46 yrs.

Mars, Abby M., dau. of Stephen and Mary Young, Mar. 30, 1883, aged 50 yrs.

Marsh, Annie May, dau. of Winfield S. and Lizzie B. Prichard, July 29, 1892, aged 13 yrs., 4 mos., 1 day.
Lizzie B., w. of Winfield S., Nov. 29, 1902, aged 54 yrs., 9 mos., 7 dys.
Winfield S., s. of Winfield S. and Lizzie B. Prichard, Jan. 8, 1889, aged 7 yrs., 8 mos., 25 dys.

Marshall, John D. K., s. of Robert and Patience, Jan. 20, 1910, aged 72 yrs.
John N., July 22, 1886, aged 74 yrs.
Mary E., dau. of Eben and Mary Frost, July 19, 1899, aged 73 yrs.
Patience (Kilton), w. of Robert, Mar. 24, 1877, aged 82 yrs.
Robert, Feb. 8, 1886, aged 82 yrs.
William S., Sept., 1873, aged 60 yrs.

Martin, Peter, Jan. 17, 1856, aged 55 yrs., 4 mos., 23 dys.
Infant son, Feb. 28, 1876.

Masters, Lucy A., in Derry, N. H., Oct. 1, 1906, aged 70 yrs., 1 mo., 17 dys.; bu. at Londonderry.

Matthews, Hannah D., dau. of Nehemiah Lovejoy and Sarah D. Marshall, May 20, 1899, aged 81 yrs., 6 mos.
Heman O., s. of Hiram C. and Maria P. Clark, Jan. 27, 1909, aged 66 yrs., 11 mos., 24 dys.

McAffee, Alfred, s. of Samuel and Catherine Holmes, Apr. 9, 1877, aged 71 yrs., 4 mos., 22 dys.

McAllister, Bridgett, Mar. 22, 1895, aged 70 yrs., 8 dys.

McBallou, Alexander, June 12, 1854, aged 50 yrs.

McCabe, Thomas, b. in Ireland, Dec. 11, 1903, aged 77 yrs.

McCanby, John, s. of James and Ellen Roach, Sept. 21, 1907, aged 47 yrs.

McClary, David, 1866.

McCleary, Thomas, Oct. 15, 1787, aged 81 yrs.

McConnell, James, s. of James and Ruth Cogswell, Sept. 12, 1892, aged 74 yrs., 11 mos., 22 dys.
Lucretia R., dau. of Morris Mulliken and Annie Willoughby, Oct. 8, 1893, aged 81 yrs., 5 mos., 29 dys.

McDonough, Mary, dau. of Margaret Grennow, Sept. 28, 1909, aged 74 yrs., 1 mo., 14 dys.

McFaurn, Ann J., dau. of Thomas Orr and ——— Huston, Aug. 9, 1902, aged 78 yrs., 3 mos., 9 dys.

McGregor, William, Dec. 9, 1882, aged 50 yrs., 10 mos.

McKean, Elisabeth, Apr. 21, 17—.

McKenney, Andrew J., soldier, Oct. 30, 1865, aged 25 yrs.
Betsey, Oct., 1874, aged 66 yrs.

McMurphy, James, s. of Alexander and Sarah, Jan. 28, 1881, aged 83 yrs.
Miss Jane, dau. of Archibald, Nov. 25, 1872, aged 98 yrs., 27 dys.
Sarah R., Dec. 25, 1894, aged 85 yrs., 6 mos., 11 dys.

Melville, Betsey, Jan. 25, 1856, aged 83 yrs.

Merrill, Julia A., in Manchester, N. H., Jan. 9, 1907, aged 62 yrs., 3 mos., 22 dys.; bu. at Londonderry.
Ralph H., in Derry, N. H., July 27, 1903, aged 7 mos.; bu. at Londonderry.

Messer, George F., s. of Nathaniel and Mary Ann Lund, Nov. 26, 1900, aged 70 yrs., 6 mos.

Metcalf, Edward, s. of Daniel and Candice Stratton, Mar. 21, 1896, aged 75 yrs., 10 mos., 17 dys.
Elvira, sister of Edward, Mar. 6, 1899, aged 86 yrs.
Sybrena M., w. of Edward and dau. of Jonathan Holmes, Oct. 25, 1906, aged 76 yrs., 1 mo., 18 dys.

Miller, Seldon, Jan. 26, 1885.

Mills, Lyndon E., s. of Ernest L. and Allfe E. Hamlett, Sept. 2, 1892, aged 8 dys.
Wilhelmina J., in Nashua, N. H., July 7, 1896, aged 3 mos., 12 dys.; bu. at Londonderry.

Miner, George, s. of Amos and Fanny, July 21, 1879, aged 63 yrs.

Miner, Mary H., dau. of Matila Classe and Hugh Jenkins, Sept. 4, 1909, aged 68 yrs.

Mitchell, Cynthia A., dau. of Martin Pettingill and Angeline Barker, in Haverhill, Mass., June 14, 1903, aged 39 yrs., 4 mos.; bu. at Londonderry.

Moar, Edward P., in Civil War, Aug. 15, 1864.
Harriet Lovina, w. of Charles E. Perkins, July 30, 1862, aged 20 yrs., 10 mos.
Hattie E., dau. of Joshua, Aug. 31, 1865, aged 2 yrs.
John, 1868.
Joshua A., s. of Joshua and Betsey, Sept. 26, 1872, aged 58 yrs.
Lovina W., dau. of ——— Witherspoon, Dec. 26, 1882, aged 68 yrs., 8 mos.

Moody, Mary E., dau. of Charles Palmer and Mary E. Hamblett, July 29, 1889, aged 33 yrs., 1 mo., 6 dys.

Moore, Allis, June 9, 1859.
Annie G., w. of Joseph E. and dau. of John Brown and Mary Smith, Nov. 8, 1901, aged 99 yrs., 11 mos., 22 dys.
John A., s. of James and Jane Anderson, in Windham, N. H., Mar. 25, 1908, aged 77 yrs.; bu. at Londonderry.
Joseph E. (Spinner Joe), Dec. 26, 1891, aged 94 yrs., 5 mos., 11 dys.
Martha M., w. of Walter H. and dau. of William Scollay and Kate Frazer, Apr. 17, 1906, aged 63 yrs.
Martin Luther, at Derry, N. H., Dec. 30, 1908.
Nancy E., dau. of James Armstrong and Alice Ridder, at Windham, Jan. 12, 1900, aged 65 yrs., 8 mos., 16 dys.; bu. at Londonderry.
Thomas T., s. of Robert M. and Sally Dunlap, Nov. 25, 1898, aged 71 yrs., 1 mo., 23 dys.
Walter H., Dec. 17, 1899, aged 71 yrs.

Moran, Pierre, s. of Louis and Angelique Cote, Aug. 24, 1905, aged 6 yrs.; bu. at Londonderry.
Visnalda F., in Derry, N. H., Dec. 3, 1904, aged 37 yrs., 8 mos., 5 dys.; bu. at Londonderry.

Morin, Annie, in Derry, N. H., July 29, 1908; bu. in Londonderry.

Morison, John, Feb. 16, 1736, aged 108 yrs.

Morrison, Albert, Aug. 9, 1858, aged 2 yrs.
Charles, Aug. 11, 1858.
Miss Eliza, dau. of Rev. Mr. Morrison, Dec. 26, 1863, at Merrimack, N. H.
James, Dec. 25, 1821.
Joolan (Julian ?), Mar. 28, 1811.

Morrison, Sarah Ann, dau. of Robinson Bean, Aug. 2, 1883, aged 58 yrs.

Morren, Mamie, in Derry, N. H., Sept. 21, 1901, aged 6 yrs., 6 mos.; bu. at Londonderry.

Morse, Alice Grace, dau. of James and Lucy Burnham, July 3, 1876, aged 23 yrs.

Charles, Feb. 12, 1856.

Henry, s. of Stephen and Rebecca, Dec. 26, 1870, aged 21 yrs.

John, s. of Stephen and Rebecca, Mar. 23, 1871, aged 19 yrs.

John, Dec. 29, 1868, aged 75 yrs.

Johnson, June 21, 1872.

Newell, s. of Stephen and Rebecca, May 19, 1868, aged 18 yrs.

Rebecca J. (Page), in Haverhill, Mass., May 26, 1910, aged 88 yrs., 2 mos.; bu. at Londonderry.

Mottram, John, s. of John and Hannah Arudale, Sept. 25, 1899, aged 74 yrs., 7 mos.

Mary, dau. of James Howarth of England, Oct. 29, 1907, aged 83 yrs., 4 mos., 23 dys.; bu. at Londonderry.

Mary H., dau. of John and Mary, July 5, 1882, aged 15 yrs.

Mullins, infant of Charles William and Katie Freeley, June 3, 1894.

Murley, Edwin J., s. of John Murley, Aug. 13, 1898, aged 11 mos., 13 dys.

Murray, Mary B., dau. of Thomas McCabe and Mary Innis, Mar. 25, 1910, aged 53 yrs., 1 mo., 28 dys.

Nesmith, Cyrus, 1881, aged 80 yrs.

Dea. James, Mar. 1, 1796, aged 55 yrs.

James, July 15, 1793, aged 75 yrs.

James, Capt., June 24, 1847, aged 53 yrs.

Luzetah J., dau. of Cyrus and Lydia, 1842.

Lydiah (Huse), w. of Cyrus, 1876, aged 69 yrs.

Mary, w. of James, Feb. 27, 1805, aged 82 yrs.

Mary, w. of Capt. James, Mar. 7, 1866, aged 68 yrs., 10 mos.

Nancy B., w. of Capt. Thomas, 1880.

Sarah F., Mar. 8, 1849, aged 23 yrs.

Thomas, Capt., Apr. 7, 1861.

Nevins, Mrs. Betsey, 1867.

Mary P., w. of Dea. James and dau. of Abel Plummer and Mary Anderson, Feb. 11, 1890, aged 81 yrs., 5 mos., 19 dys.

Newhall, William H., s. of Samuel and Mary Lewis, Mar. 7, 1887, aged 68 yrs., 21 dys.

Nichardson, Margaret, b. in Nova Scotia, d. Mar. 23, 1891, aged 77 yrs.

Nichols, Charles F., s. of Charles F. and Cora, Aug. 30, 1879.
Hannah Willey, w. of Jacob, July 18, 1907.
Jacob, Sept. 11, 1878, aged 89 yrs., 5 mos., 14 dys.
William A., 1869.

Nicholson, George C., Aug. 20, 1853, aged 7 mos.

Nikels, James, Mar. 28, 1724.

Norman, Hordard, s. of L. P. and J. Miller, Feb. 8, 1895, aged 3 yrs.

Noyes, Hattie M. Corning, 1st w. of Joseph T. Noyes, Oct. 8, 1869, aged 34 yrs., 6 mos.
Henry M., in Manchester, N. H., July 12, 1904, aged 2 mos., 4 dys.; bu. at Londonderry.
Laura A., Jan. 12, 1884.
Miss Lucy, 1863.
Mary Ann (Richardson), 2d w. of Joseph T., Mar. 6, 1885, aged 47 yrs., 3 mos., 20 dys.
Warren W., s. of Carlos W. and Clara J. Richardson, Aug. 1, 1861, aged 1 yr., 3 mos., 13 days.

Oatley, Charles D., 1868, aged 35 yrs.

O'Connor, Madelin, in Manchester, N. H., Feb. 4, 1907, aged 36 yrs.; bu. at Londonderry.

Olsen, Elisabeth, dau. of George Glover and Caroline McAdams, Aug. 2, 1901, aged 67 yrs., 3 mos., 1 day.

Ordway, Peter, Mar. 5, 1855, aged 66 yrs.

Orterweil, Isaac, s. of Selig Orterweil and Eva Heigg, Sept. 7, 1910, aged 52 yrs., 10 mos., 4 dys.

O'Sullivan, John P., s. of Timothy and Mary, June 12, 1892, aged 74 yrs., 10 mos., 12 dys.

Oughterson, James, Mar. 3, 1761, aged 64 yrs.

Owens, John G., in Haverhill, Mass., Mar. 21, 1906, aged 79 yrs., 1 mo., 19 dys.; bu. at Londonderry.

Packer, Jennie, dau. of Joshua Moar, Dec. 21, 1909, in New York City, aged 68 yrs.; bu. at Londonderry.

Page, Mrs. Charles, 1864.
Darius, s. of Joel and Rachel, Apr. 5, 1842, aged 2 yrs., 3 mos.
Inez G., in Derry, Mar. 14, 1904, aged 11 yrs., 9 mos., 18 dys.; bu. at Londonderry.
Infant s. of Horace and Lucy A., 1877.
James D., s. of Joseph and Rhoda Davis, Dec. 29, 1887, aged 63 yrs., 6 mos., 20 dys.
John O., s. of James and Julia Moore, killed at railroad crossing, Feb. 16, 1893, aged 46 yrs., 11 mos., 11 dys.

Page, Julia (Moore), w. of James D. Page, in Derry, N. H., Nov. 23, 1910, aged 83 yrs., 6 mos.; bu. at Londonderry, N. H.
Leonard, June 15, 1886, aged 67 yrs., 12 dys.
Mary, dau. of Joshua Austin and Betsey Barker, Apr. 16, 1902, aged 77 yrs., 8 mos., 26 dys.; bu. at Londonderry.
Mary A., Sept. 12, 1851.
Mary E., dau. of Thomas Proctor, Oct. 16, 1902, aged 57 yrs., 9 mos., 16 dys.
Rebecca I., dau. of Joseph and Rhoda, in Haverhill, May 26, 1910, aged 88 yrs., 2 mos.; bu. at Londonderry.
Serena, Aug. 30, 1851.

Paige, Alfred H., s. of Andrew H. and Effie M. Marshall, July 26, 1906, aged 24 dys.

Pairie, Boselin, in Derry, July 3, 1906, aged 48 yrs.; bu. at Londonderry.

Paquette, Joseph, s. of Francis and ——— Croteau, in Manchester, N. H., Mar. 1, 1906, aged 31 yrs., 4 mos., 29 dys.; bu. at Londonderry.

Pare, Olive H., dau. of John S. Webster and Annie E. Moody, Apr. 23, 1906, aged 23 yrs., 2 mos., 24 dys.

Parker, Laura (Gregg), dau. of William Gregg, at Lowell, Mass., 1872.

Paro, Inez, dau. of Dominique Paro, Jan. 10, 1890, aged 3 yrs., 4 mos., 23 dys.
Dominique, Apr. 10, 1897, aged 50 yrs.

Patnode, Libby. dau. of David Rouillier and Maria Thibaudeau, Aug. 16, 1906, aged 34 yrs., 11 mos., 2 dys.

Patterson, Adeline, Sept. 9, 1899, aged 76 yrs.
Douglass R., Nov. 12, 1886, aged 70 yrs.
Elisabeth, w. of Peter, June 2, 1786, aged 23 yrs.
Hannah D., w. of Thomas, Nov. 12, 1869, aged 71 yrs.
Thomas, Oct. 27, 1869, aged 83 yrs.

Peabody, Asa A., Sept. 1, 1865, aged 37 yrs., 10 mos., 28 dys.
Ida, Apr. 19, 1864, aged 12 yrs., 5 mos., 16 dys.
James, 1864.
Mrs. Maria, Aug. 11, 1865, aged 37 yrs., 4 mos., 21 dys.

Peavey, Jacob, Mar. 5, 1872, aged 76 yrs.
Sarah, w. of Jacob, Aug. 15, 1884.

Pegnam, John, 1863.

Pelham, Charles, in Methuen, Mass., Oct. 22, 1875, aged about 54 yrs.

Peltier, Joseph A., s. of Adalate and Mary Willett, Nov. 28, 1904, aged 3 yrs., 21 dys.

Pelton, Amy M., w. of John C. Towns, Sept. 23, 1891, aged 52 yrs., 4 mos.
Sarah M., dau. of John Cross and Sally Bennett, Feb. 15, 1894, aged 86 yrs., 5 mos.

Perham, Mary A., dau. of Timothy Barker and Abiah Kimball, May 23, 1897, aged 84 yrs., 1 mo., 11 dys.

Perkins, Alice A., dau. of Winslow Richards and Rebecca Dean, Oct. 22, 1905, aged 50 yrs.
Hannah J., dau. of Morrill Currier and ——— Riddle, Jan. 6, 1890, aged 64 yrs., 11 mos., 6 dys.
Valencourt, in Lowell, Mass., Apr. 4, 1906, aged 48 yrs.; bu. in Londonderry.

Perrett, Virginia H., dau. of William and Mary Currier, Aug. 8, 1898, aged 1 yr., 2 mos.

Perron, Frederick, s. of Louis and Mary J., Dec., 1881.
Phebe, dau. of Louis and Mary J., Dec., 1881.

Perry, John, in Manchester, N. H., Sept. 30, 1905, aged 43 yrs.; bu. in Londonderry.

Pettingill, Almina, dau. of Daniel F. Hobbs and Betsey ———, Mar. 14, 1897, aged 73 yrs., 3 mos.
Elisabeth H., Feb. 2, 1890, aged 81 yrs., 11 mos.
Rachel, dau. of Margaret, Aug. 2, 1881, aged 77 yrs.
Warren, Feb. 6, 1860.
Warren, 1864.
William, Dec. 26, 1855, aged 84 yrs.
William, 1866, aged 57 yrs.

Pickering, Daniel, May 21, 1863, aged 65 yrs., 3 mos.

Pike, Chester, s. of Sylvester and Mehitable Underhill, Feb. 7, 1906, aged 68 yrs., 4 mos., 20 dys.
Eliza A., dau. of Edward Parker and Mary R. Kendall, July 4, 1909, aged 69 yrs., 10 mos., 22 dys.

Pinkerton, David, Mar. 8, 1808, aged 75 yrs.
John, Feb. 10, 1708, aged 80 yrs.

Plummer, Arley, Jan. 10, 1879, aged 80 yrs., 11 mos., 21 dys.
Isaac, Jan. 22, 1855, aged 84 yrs.
Lydia C., w. of Arley, Nov. 10, 1889, aged 81 yrs., 9 mos.
Olive, Aug. 5, 1871, aged 70 yrs.

Poisson, Ann M., dau. of Hector and Rebecca Michaud, Mar. 25, 1906, in Derry, N. H., aged 1 yr., 11 mos., 3 dys.; bu. in Londonderry.

Poland, Samuel W., s. of Samuel and Thankful Smith, Jan. 28, 1901, aged 67 yrs., 6 mos., 23 dys.

Pond, Persis, dau. of Fortinatus and Persis Wheeler, Apr. 17, 1877, aged 80 yrs.

Pond, Child of George W. and Lucy A. Merriam, Oct. 10, 1889, lived one hour.
William J., soldier, at Baton Rouge, June 29, 1863.

Poore, Albert H., s. of William C. and Juliette C. Johnson, Feb. 28, 1894, aged 16 yrs., 4 mos.

Porter, Lavisa, dau. of B. H. Sargent and Lavisa, Oct. 8, 1908, in Nashua, N. H., aged 61 yrs., 3 mos.; bu. in Londonderry.

Potter, Franklin L., s. of Albert and Alma, June 5, 1883.

Powers, Ansel B., s. of Isaac, July 9, 1907, aged 41 yrs., 11 mos., 29 dys.
Rebecca (Mrs.), 1864.

Prescott, G. Weston, s. of Seth B. and Sarah J. Emery, Aug. 8, 1902, aged 34 yrs., 11 mos., 2 days.

Pressey, John S., s. of John and Mary A. Colby, June 30, 1902, aged 30 yrs., 2 mos., 19 dys.

Priday, William, s. of Christopher and Margaret, Aug. 2, 1874, aged 54 yrs.

Prime, Annie F., dau. of Robert Gould and Mary Wiggin, Jan. 16, 1904, aged 50 yrs., 4 mos. 11 dys.
Lillian E., July 13, 1894, aged 45 yrs.

Prince, Charles L., in Derry, N. H., July 15, 1904; bu. in Londonderry.

Proctor, Sally Clark, wid. of James Proctor, July, 1875, aged 80 yrs.

Putnam, Miss Kate, 1863.
Willard A., s. of William H. and Susan Briggs, Aug. 23, 1899, aged 71 yrs., 8 mos., 18 dys.

Rainey, Mrs. J. T., dau. of Charles Rowell, Apr. 1, 1891, aged 23 yrs., 10 mos.
Lena, dau. of J. T. Rainey, Apr. 1, 1891.

Randall, Alfred, on way home from Civil War, 1863.
Hannah E., dau. of Alfred and Hannah, Jan. 15, 1859.
George, Nov. 8, 1870, aged 15 yrs.

Rattray, Alice F., w. of James W., in Londonderry, Aug. 1, 1885, b. in Lee, N. H.
James W., in Londonderry, Nov. 13, 1881; b. in Dundee, Scotland.
James W., s. of James W. and Alice F., in Londonderry, Aug. 7, 1854.

Reed, William C., s. of Joel and Joan Chandler, Jan. 17, 1895, aged 84 yrs., 1 mo.

Reid, George, s. of James and Mary, Sept., 1815, aged 82 yrs.
Wife of George, Apr. 7, 1823, aged 88 yrs.

Remington, John, s. of Henry and Elisabeth Lacey, Jan. 3, 1901, aged 70 yrs., 9 mos., 3 dys.
Justin M., s. of John and Mary S., Oct. 15, 1862, aged 2 yrs., 4 mos., 15 dys.
Marianna A., dau. of John and Mary S. and w. of S. A. Estey, Sept. 21, 1879, aged 20 yrs., 9 mos., 6 days.

Ricard, E. ———, dau. of ———, Dec. 9, 1901, at Manchester, N. H., aged 45 yrs.; bu. at Londonderry.

Richardson, Emily J., Nov. 16, 1874, aged 14 yrs., 3 mos.
Infant s. of S. Carlton and Regina Harvey, Dec. 30, 1867.

Ripley, Joseph, 1864.

Ritchie, Rose, in Derry, N. H., Aug. 18, 1906, aged 4 mos., 15 dys.; bu. in Londonderry.

Roberts, Mattie H., dau. of N. Roberts and P. F. Hussey, Sept. 29, 1891.

Robie, Elmira D., in Derry, N. H., Nov. 8, 1891, aged 18 yrs.; bu. in Londonderry.
Frank, Apr. 10, 1904.
Frank L., s. of Tappan R., Mar. 7, 1905, at Derry, N. H., aged 51 yrs., 11 mos., 24 dys.; bu. at Londonderry.
Loraine F., s. of Frank L. and Jennie, July 27, 1872.

Robinson, Catherine M., Oct. 6, 1906, in Derry, N. H., aged 16 yrs., 1 mo., 26 dys.; bu. at Londonderry.
Jane R., dau. of Benjamin French and Leafey A. Blodgett, Jan. 1, 1896, aged 54 yrs., 5 mos., 14 dys.

Robitaille, Delia, dau. of Joseph and Philomin Lemaireux, Mar. 25, 1906, aged 31 yrs., 1 mo.

Rogers, Abigail C., Dec. 19, 1886, aged 87 yrs.
Jeremiah, Apr. 27, 1877.

Rousseau, Marie Ann, dau. of Joseph Guilette, Jan. 8, 1896, aged 79 yrs., 8 mos., 14 dys.

Roy, Albert, s. of Honore and Georgiana Boucher, Mar. 6, 1906, aged 4 yrs., 7 mos., 24 dys.

Salner, Nelson, s. of Barney and Rebecca Shooper, Oct. 25, 1896, aged 6 yrs., 8 dys.

Sanborn, Cyrus, at Manchester, N. H., Jan. 28, 1871, aged 49 yrs.
John, killed at Port Hudson, June 2, 1863.

Savory, Betsey, dau. of Jonathan and Hannah, Aug. 4, 1818, aged 23 yrs.
Grisel, w. of Thomas, Apr. 10, 1832, aged 50 yrs.
Hannah, w. of Dea. Jonathan, Sept. 18, 1819, aged 58 yrs.
Hannah, Mar. 7, 1833, aged 48 yrs.
Dea. Jonathan, Feb. 25, 1841, aged 81 yrs.
Thomas, Dec. 16, 1867, aged 84 yrs.

Scobey, Martha, Oct. 6, 1754, aged 30 yrs.
Matthew, July 2, 1764, aged 31 yrs.
Samuel, Jan. 20, 1737, aged 3 years.

Scollay, Catherine, w. of William, Dec. 22, 1874, aged 58 yrs., 11 mos.
Catherine, dau. of William and Catherine, Dec. 27, 1855, aged 18 yrs., 4 mos.
Estellae E., dau. of William and Catherine, June 22, 1881, aged 24 yrs., 3 mos.
William, Dec. 17, 1890, aged 77 yrs., 3 mos.

Seaman, William H., hus. of Marianna P. (Clark), June, 1910, at Washington, D. C.

Senter, Joseph, s. of Abel and Sarah Leach, Mar. 29, 1897, aged 70 yrs., 3 mos., 20 dys.
Sophia, at Brentwood, N. H., Oct. 23, 1899, aged 83 yrs.; bu. in Londonderry.
Winfield S., s. of Benjamin and Abigail Whidden, in Manchester, N. H., Apr. 17, 1908, aged 54 yrs.; bu. at Londonderry.

Shattuck, Hattie E., dau. of John E. Merrill and J. A. Kendrick, Jan. 7, 1875, aged 20 yrs., 7 mos.

Shepard, Albert D., 1868.
Elisabeth Ann, w. of Isaac R. and dau. of Gilman Langdon and Sarah, Dec. 27, 1876.
William Blair, 1867, aged 87 yrs., 6 mos.
———, Feb. 7, 1862, aged 80 yrs.

Shipley, Mary Hyde, 1867, aged 1 yr., 8 mos.

Short, Rose, dau. of Hannah Jerome, June 14, 1899, aged 38 yrs.

Simonds, Aaron W., at Morris Island, Oct. 21, 1863.

Sing, Charles, at Derry, N. H., July 9, 1908, aged 85 yrs., 1 mo., 7 dys.; bu. at Londonderry.

Sirais, Michael, Apr. 16, 1906, at Derry, N. H., aged 36 yrs., 6 mos., 16 dys.; bu. at Londonderry.

Skinner, Edwin W., s. of George W. and Eliza, Sept. 12, 1858, aged 8 mos., 10 dys.
Eliza J. Goodwin, w. of George W., Sept. 12, 1858, aged 32 yrs., 4 mos.
George W., Apr. 9, 1863, aged 31 yrs.

Skogland, ———, s. of Alexander and Inez V. Bean, July 19, 1909, aged 6 hours.

Slate, Levenia Lettia, dau. of Lyman J. and L. B., Sept. 27, 1862, aged 10 mos., 4 dys.

Sleeper, Jennie M., dau. of John Gilcreast and Miranda Peabody, in Sutton, N. H., Aug. 25, 1899, aged 37 yrs., 3 mos., 21 dys.; bu. in Londonderry.

Small, Annie M., at Manchester, N. H., Mar. 1, 1903, aged 50 yrs., 8 mos., 14 dys.; bu. at Londonderry.

John N., soldier, Sept. 30, 1885.

Philip G., in Dover, N. H., Sept. 26, 1896; bu. at Londonderry.

Smart, Sarah A., Feb. 20, 1902.

Smith, Celia Jane, dau. of Robert Marshall and Patience Kilton, Mar. 1, 1904, aged 68 yrs., 3 mos.

Charles, in Nashua, N. H., Apr. 6, 1894, aged 62 yrs., 5 mos., 15 dys.; bu. at Londonderry.

Charles H., s. of John (?) Hermit, Aug. 18, 1906, aged 73 yrs.

Charles, Mrs., 1867.

Clara A. Hobbs, Mrs., 1908, at Acton, Me.

David, Aug. 13, 1839, aged 67 yrs.

David, Dea., Oct., 1871, aged 76 yrs.

Edward, s. of Timothy A. and Mary, July 27, 1861.

Harold C., s. of Louis and Margaret Bresnan, Oct. 20, 1908, aged 3 dys.

Huldah, dau. of Simon Chase and Huldah Emery, Nov. 21, 1900, aged 79 yrs.

Ichabod, Nov. 7, 1892, aged 68 yrs.

Jane, w. of John and dau. of Thomas McClary and Elisabeth, Mar. 5, 1779, aged 29 yrs.

Joseph, June 27, 1838, aged 23 yrs.

Lizzie A., in Salem, N. H., Jan. 15, 1891, aged 50 yrs., 4 mos., 2 dys.; bu. at Londonderry.

Lois, w. of David, Nov. 26, 1850, aged 78 yrs.

Lorenzo D., 1908, at Acton, Me.

Mary A. B., dau. of David and Ruth Whittemore, Aug. 15, 1891, aged 55 yrs., 11 mos., 30 dys.; unm.

May, dau. of Henry J. and Julia M., Jan. 22, 1890, aged 2 yrs., 2 mos., 22 dys.

Orrin A., at Boston, Mass., Feb. 5, 1901, aged 24 yrs., 5 mos., 15 dys.; bu. at Londonderry.

Samuel, at Lowell, Mass., Mar. 29, 1875, aged 74 yrs.

Samuel, Mrs., 1868.

Timothy A., soldier, at Beaufort, S. C., Sept. 11, 1862.

Snow, Freddie Lincoln, s. of George W. and Eliza Ann, July 27, 1877, aged 16 yrs.

Spinney, Alexander, Aug. 26, 1847, aged 63 yrs., 5 mos.

Hugh Bartley, s. of Alexander and Zillah, June 27, 1862, aged 39 yrs., 8 mos. Soldier in Civil War.

Spinney, Zillah Dow, w. of Alexander, Jan. 8, 1849, aged 63 yrs.

Stearns, Sarah W., Aug. 4, 1893, aged 56 yrs., 2 mos., 14 dys.

Stevens, Edwin R., s. of James and Mary Collins, Oct. 11, 1904, aged 58 yrs., 8 mos.

Mary W., dau. of Michael Moulton and Mary Willoughby, Jan. 28, 1897, aged 77 yrs., 6 mos., 28 dys.

Stewart, Fred C., Apr. 11, 1888, aged 24 yrs.

Stickney, Edwin N., June 12, 1885, aged 22 yrs., 6 mos., 12 dys.; bu. in Merrill Cemetery.

Stoddly, Joseph Henry, s. of Arthur and Mary L. Loudon, Jan. 20, 1907, aged 1½ dys.

Stokes, Eugene, s. of Moses D. and Irene French, at Manchester, N. H., Sept. 9, 1850, aged 8 mos.; bu. in Valley Cemetery.

Strong, Emma, Feb. 7, 1885.

Stuart, Flora, Aug. 17, 1868, aged 118 yrs.

George W., s. of Flora, Jan. 31, 1876, aged 65 yrs. Colored family.

Isaiah, s. of Flora, July 26, 1874, aged 70 yrs.

Salona, dau. of Flora, May 10, 1887, aged 78 yrs.

Suiens, John, in Derry, N. H., July 9, 1908, aged 9 mos.; bu. in Londonderry.

Swett, Martha Grace, dau. of Frank and Sarah J. Whittemore, Aug. 18, 1866, aged 2 yrs., 3 mos., 4 dys.

Tabor, Joseph, in Lynn, Mass., Mar. 24, 1905, aged 61 yrs., 4 dys.; bu. at Londonderry.

Tanswell, Jeremiah, Aug. 18, 1882.

Tates, Resasid, in Derry, N. H., Dec. 10, 1907, aged 15 yrs., 6 mos., 6 dys.; bu. at Londonderry.

Tebbetts, Nancy A., at Gilmanton, N. H., Jan. 10, 1910, aged 62 yrs., 8 mos., 2 dys.; bu. at Londonderry.

Tewksbury, Ora M., at Manchester, N. H., Nov. 13, 1904, aged 10 yrs., 17 dys.; bu. at Londonderry.

Theiss, Louise, dau. of Henry, at Goffstown, N. H., Dec. 2, 1901, aged 18 yrs., 8 mos., 17 dys.; bu. at Londonderry.

Theris, Clarence J., s. of Viris Theris and ——— Saylus, at Derry, N. H., Nov. 5, 1905, aged 4 mos.; bu. at Londonderry.

Dennis, Dec. 28, 1905, at Haverhill, Mass., aged 34 yrs., 7 mos.; bu. at Londonderry.

Thibault, John Baptist, at Derry, N. H., Jan. 21, 1907, aged 81 yrs., 3 mos., 10 dys.; bu. at Londonderry.

Thomas, Clifton Durrell, s. of Frank L. and Mabel V. Chick, Oct. 29, 1905, aged 6 dys.

Thompson, Frank, Apr. 4, 1871, aged 1 yr.
Thomas, Rev., Sept. 22, 1738.

Thurston, Nellie E., w. of Walter Thurston, Oct. 29, 1872, aged 26 yrs.

Towle, Dalledo, s. of John F. and Ella E., Aug. 27, 1876.

Towne, Susannah, at Manchester, N. H., Mar. 14, 1903, aged 87 yrs., 2 mos., 13 dys.; bu. at Londonderry.

Towns, Amy M., dau. of L. S. Pelton and w. of John C., Sept. 23, 1891, aged 56 yrs., 4 mos., 4 dys.; bu. at Londonderry.
Arthur J. C., s. of John C. and Amy J., Jan. 14, 1873, aged 2 yrs., 11 mos.
Betsey, 3d w. of Jabez, Feb. 10, 1875, aged 86 yrs.
Freddie, s. of Silas T., May 2, 1870.
Harry S., s. of Silas T. and Phebe A., July 20, 1872.
Jabez, s. of Moses and Charlotte, Dec. 18, 1879, aged 95 yrs.
James W., Aug. 23, 1870, aged 84 yrs.
James W., Mrs., Feb., 1875, aged 80 yrs. (?).
Jane, 2d w. of Jabez, Aug. 25, 1847, aged 52 yrs.
John C., s. of Jabez, at Manchester, N. H., Apr. 1, 1903, aged 65 yrs., 5 mos., 16 dys.; bu. at Londonderry.
Mary, 1st w. of Jabez, Jan. 1, 1828, aged 36 yrs.
Moses M., s. of Moses and Charlotte, Oct. 4, 1804.
Nellie J., dau. of John C. and Amy Pelton, Aug. 7, 1908, aged 43 yrs., 2 mos., 7 dys.; bu. at Londonderry.
Sarah E., dau. of John and Elisabeth, Aug. 24, 1825, aged 2 yrs., 6 mos.
Silas T., s. of Jabez and Mary Campbell, Apr. 27, 1904, aged 79 yrs., 10 mos.
Susannah, dau. of Moses and Charlotte, Oct. 10, 1804.

Trafton, Sarah J., dau. of Ebenezer Jameson and Sarah Pamers, Nov., 1905, aged 71 yrs., 4 mos., 29 dys.

Trappier, Henry, s. of J. B. Trappier and Fredoline Desmarias, Sept. 10, 1908, aged 15 yrs., 11 mos., 15 dys.; bu. at Londonderry.

Trask, James, in Litchfield, N. H., Aug. 23, 1891, aged 84 yrs., 11 mos.; bu. in Londonderry.
Phebe D. C., w. of James, Oct. 16, 1895, aged 86 yrs., 10 mos., 19 dys.; bu. in Londonderry.

Trombley, William J., at Derry, N. H., Aug. 1, 1908, aged 2 mos.; bu. at Londonderry.

Trudel, ———, Mar. 22, 1904; bu. at Londonderry.

Truell, Lizzie S., w. of George W. and dau. of George E. Fifield, July 6, 1870, aged 26 yrs.

Tucker, Albert G., s. of John and Abigail, Oct. 2, 1882, aged 65 yrs.
Alice, Mar. 3, 1792, aged 23 yrs.
Louis G., May 16, 1884.

Turcotte, Alma, dau. of Joseph and Ellen M., June 24, 1878, aged 1 yr.
Clara J., dau. of Joseph and Ellen M., Mar. 6, 1879, aged 4 yrs.
Obeline, dau. of Ludger and Luvina Jutras, Sept. 23, 1907, aged 22 yrs., 13 dys.
Elisabeth V., in Derry, N. H., July 16, 1906, aged 6 yrs., 2 mos., 24 dys.; bu. in Londonderry.
Ratlind R., in Derry, N. H., Apr. 15, 1903, aged 3 mos.; bu. at Londonderry.
Silome M., dau. of Joseph and Ellen M., Feb. 26, 1879, aged 6 yrs.

Twiss, Benjamin, 1864.

Upton, Sarah Jane, dau. of David Gilcreast and Sarah Holmes, Apr. 17, 1905, aged 73 yrs., 1 mo., 5 days.

Vezina, ———, dau. of Napoleon Vezina and Malvina Preva, Mar. 22, 1903.

Vickery, Armanda S., killed at Battle of Wilderness, June 10, 1864.
Charles, Lieut., killed at Gettysburg, 1863.
Roxanna Austen, w. of Calvin, Dec. 4, 1848, aged 59 yrs.

Villeux, ———, July 22, 1908, in Derry, N. H.; aged 7 mos.; bu. in Londonderry.

Vose, Relief Stearns, dau. of Jonathan Stearns, Apr. 5, 1892, aged 90 yrs.

Waldo, Mary Etta, dau. of James Annis, Sept. 12, 1903, aged 77 yrs.

Wallace, Addie, Apr. 5, 1886, aged 47 yrs.
Annas Barnard,* Jan. 6, 1761, aged 63 yrs.
Barbara, w. of Thomas,† Sept. 2, 1771, aged 95 yrs.
Charles, Sept., 1874, aged 11 mos.
Hannah G., Jan. 21, 1859, aged 74 yrs.
Harriet A., at Aberdeen, South Dakota, Dec. 10, 1906; bu. at Londonderry.
James, Oct. 30, 1791, aged 80 yrs.
James, Capt., Dec. 14, 1792, aged 71 yrs.
John,* Mar. 29, 1777, aged 82 yrs.
Mary, Aug. 9, 1853, aged 48 yrs.
Mary, dau. of Perley, June 20, 1876, aged 26 yrs.
Naomi, w. of Capt. Robert, May 10, 1791, aged 80 yrs.
Perley, 1878, aged 66 yrs.

*First couple married in Londonderry, May 18, 1721, by Rev. James MacGregore.
†The Thomas who died in 1754.

Wallace, Rebecca, Sept. 22, 1804, aged 81 yrs.
Robert, Capt., Oct. 10, 1782, aged 73 yrs.
Samuel, July 29, 1778, aged 41 yrs.
Thomas, Aug. 22, 1754, aged 82 yrs.
Thomas, May 7, 1789, aged 73 yrs.
Thomas, Jan. 26, 1790, aged 46 yrs.
Wife of Thomas,* Apr. 4, 1785, aged 31 yrs.
William,† Mar. 27, 1733, aged 26 yrs.
William M. A., s. of Thomas and Barbara, Mar. 27, 1733, aged 26 yrs.

Walters, Richard T., s. of John and Margaret O'Neil, Aug. 4, 1907, aged 55 yrs.

Wardwell, infant s. of Mary J., May 3, 1871.

Warmack, Willie A., June 17, 1895, aged 4 yrs., 6 mos., 2 dys.

Warren, Sarah, dau. of Francis Poff and Mary J., Mar. 13, 1880, aged 26 yrs.
Wealthy W., dau. of Reuben Wells and Sarah Haynes, Dec. 12, 1889, aged 46 yrs., 5 mos.

Watts, Daniel, Aug. 23, 1858, aged 73 yrs.
Elwin, s. of Herman L. and Alice J. Fitts, Apr. 22, 1905, aged 3 dys.
Esther, Apr. 19, 1832, aged 22 yrs.
Frank Elmer, s. of Herman L. and Alice J. Fitts, Sept. 10, 1905, aged 5 yrs., 4 mos., 29 dys.
Hugh, May 18, 1830, aged 28 yrs.
James, Capt., Sept. 12, 1831, aged 71 yrs.
James, Dec. 28, 1848, aged 54 yrs.
James, s. of James and Miriam, Mar. 14, 1840, aged 20 yrs.
Jenny, w. of Moses Garvin, Feb. 10, 1862, aged 80 yrs.
John, Dec. 20, 1812, aged 6 yrs.
John, Apr. 5, 1819, aged 71 yrs.
Leon Melvin, s. of Herman L. and Alice J. Fitts, Oct. 12, 1905, aged 2 yrs., 26 dys.
Lillian Frances, dau. of Charles H. and L. M. Nichols, Jan. 13, 1890, aged 4 yrs., 11 dys.
Martha J., Feb. 17, 1858, aged 33 yrs.
Moses, May 6, 1829, aged 31 yrs.
Peggy, w. of Moses, May 3, 1795, aged 64 yrs.
Peggy, Sept. 29, 1812, aged 4 yrs.
Polly, Sept. 27, 1850.
Susannah, w. of John, Apr. 16, 1826, aged 73 yrs.

Waugh, Cora M., dau. of John M. Chase and Hannah Clark, Nov. 6, 1898, aged 31 yrs., 8 mos., 23 dys.

*Thomas who died in 1790.
†First person buried in the "Hill Graveyard."

Webster, David, Dec. 7, 1859.

Weed, William, 1878, aged 79 yrs.

Welch, Thomas, Jan. 24, 1855, aged 56 yrs.

Welcome, Rosae Delman, dau. of William George and Mary L. Clouthier, Dec. 31, 1900, aged 3 mos., 1 dy.

Wells, Isabel, dau. of William Emerson, Nov. 14, 1870, aged 21 yrs.
Moses, Aug. 8, 1879, aged 87 yrs.

Westgate, Berthana G., dau. of Elzi R. and Ida M. Wilcox, Sept. 20, 1902, aged 1 yr., 9 mos., 11 dys.

Wheeler, Joseph J., s. of John F. and Etta M. Swinnington, Apr. 3, 1906.

Whidden, Mary F., Nov. 9, 1854, aged 2 yrs.
Mila A., dau. of ——, at Derry, N. H., Oct. 27, 1902, aged 53 yrs., 11 mos., 24 dys.; bu. at Londonderry.
Susie, Sept. 23, 1885, aged 38 yrs.
William K., s. of William H. and Nellie A. Kendall, July 21, 1903.

Whipple, Mary E., dau. of L. Gardner and S. Bancroft, Apr. 27, 1895, aged 37 yrs., 6 mos., 27 dys.

Whitcomb, Oliver, Apr. 1, 1870, aged 72 yrs.
Walter, s. of Peter, at Cambridge, Mass., Feb. 28, 1910.

White, Frank K., s. of William, 1865.
Isaac K., Sept. 17, 1854, aged 7 mos.
Lorenzo, soldier, at St. Augustine, Florida, Apr. 18, 1862.
Patrick J., in Derry, N. H., Apr. 1, 1907, aged 79 yrs., 6 mos., 8 dys.; bu. in Londonderry.

Whitney, Cora S., dau. of James Center and Sophia Plummer, Apr. 24, 1905, aged 54 yrs., 2 mos.
Maud, dau. of Robert M. and Cora Senter, Sept. 15, 1882.

Whittemore, David A., s. of David and Mary N., June 24, 1872, aged 69 yrs.
Orrin P., s. of David and Sally, Sept. 3, 1873, aged 40 yrs.

Whittendon, Irene A., Oct. 13, 1897, aged 42 yrs.

Whittier, Emily, w. of Ebenezer, Dec. 20, 1840.
George N., s. of Ebenezer, Aug. 27, 1844.
Maria R., Mar. 26, 1880, aged 72 yrs.
Miss Rachel, 1864.

Whittle, John W., hus. of Emily J. Flanders, Jan. 3, 1883.
Infant of J. W., July, 1868, aged 1 mo., 6 dys.

Whorf, Ella, Aug. 1, 1854, aged 3 yrs.
John Milton, killed by fall of elevator at Boston, 1876, aged 55 yrs.

Wiear, David, s. of Adam and Margaret, Feb. 15, 1765, aged 25 yrs.

Wilkins, Alice E., dau. of Asa A. Perley and Lucy A. Austin, Dec. 12, 1904, aged 54 yrs., 3 mos., 17 dys.

Willey, Benjamin L., s. of Vowell, Sept. 19, 1871.
Eliza Bachelder, July 26, 1872, aged 65 yrs.
Henry J., s. of Jacob, at Concord, N. H., Mar. 24, 1895, aged 41 yrs.; bu. at Londonderry.
Vowell, s. of Benjamin and Martha, June 1, 1874, aged 67 yrs.

Williams, Mary S., dau. of Austin Case and Julia Stevens, May 19, 1909, aged 78 yrs., 1 mo., 23 dys.

Wilson, Elisabeth, w. of Samuel, July 14, 1816, aged 85 yrs.
James, May 25, 1812, aged 10 wks.
James, Lieut., May 28, 1836, aged 70 yrs.
John, Mar. 19, 1872, aged 86 yrs.
Mary Adams, w. of John, d. with infant ch., Jan. 27, 1817, aged 26 yrs.
Mary Ann, w. of Lieut. James, Dec. 4, 1839, aged 70 yrs.
Nancy, w. of John, Nov. 29, 1869, aged 83 yrs.
Rebecca, w. of Joseph, May 25, 1770, aged 66 yrs.
Samuel, Feb. 19, 1805, aged 42 yrs.
Samuel, s. of Samuel and Mary, Sept. 11, 1804, aged 3 yrs.
Samuel, Dec. 4, 1801, aged 73 yrs.
Samuel, Oct. 10, 1829, aged 31 yrs.
Sophronia, dau. of James and Mary Ann, Apr. 17, 1839, aged 30 yrs.
———, dau. of Scotty and Nellie Ramkey, June 11, 1904.

Wing, Caroline B., dau. of Nelson Webber and Mary Dyer, Aug. 5, 1906, aged 63 yrs., 3 mos., 20 dys.
Hazel Elisabeth, dau. of Seth G. and Pearl C. Proctor, Aug. 2, 1910, aged 4 yrs., 7 mos., 12 dys.

Woodburn, David, Oct. 9, 1823, aged 85 yrs.
John, 1867, aged 72 yrs.
Lucinda, Oct. 12, 1886, aged 80 yrs.
Lucinda A., dau. of Hiram True, Dec. 9, 1897, aged 69 yrs., 10 mos., 13 dys.
Margaret, w. of David, Oct. 17, 1792, aged 39 yrs.

Woodbury, infant of Abram, at Haverhill, Mass., July 17, 1876.
Joel, s. of David A. and Ella R. Emery, Dec. 28, 1907, aged 6 yrs., 26 dys.
Mabel, dau. of David A. and Ella R. Emery, Jan. 14, 1908, aged 16 yrs., 6 mos., 3 dys.
Samuel, Mrs., Nov. 4, 1869.
Silas, at Derry, N. H., Oct. 5, 1899, aged 3 mos.; bu. at Londonderry.

Worcester, infant dau. of Charles and Ida M., Aug. 21, 1883.

Wright, Louise Eunice, dau. of Ralph W. and Edith L. Dustin, Jan. 28, 1909, aged 7 mos.

Phoebe, dau. of Frank Welcome and Kate Martin, Nov. 8, 1905, aged 41 yrs., 1 mo.

Young, Israel M., July 18, 1880, aged 44 yrs., 9 mos.

Izetta, dau. of Charles Gardner and Mary Whittaker, Aug. 24, 1894, aged 34 yrs., 11 mos., 8 dys.

Pauline O., at Nashua, N. H., Oct. 16, 1891, aged 31 yrs., 11 mos.; bu. at Londonderry.

DEATHS—ADDITIONAL NAMES.

Abbott, Harold V., Apr. 16, 1910.
Adams, Frank, July 26, 1908.
Gertrude, Nov. 19, 1883.
Janet (Taylor), w. William, Dec., 1828.
Jonathan, 1820.
Rowena, Aug., 1881, aged 4 mos., 13 dys.
William, Oct., 1828.
Alderson, Eld. David, May 11, 1905.
Eliza G., Mar. 18, 1875.
Francis D., Mar. 6, 1886, aged 59 yrs.
George Edward, Feb. 20, 1907.
George V., Feb. 2, 1892.
Helen F., Apr. 18, 1896.
James, Jan. 23, 1869.
Jane (Davidson), 1st w. Francis D., Mar. 13, 1880, aged 71 yrs.
Martha A. (Richards), May 8, 1908.
Martin E., killed by automobile, May 15, 1911.
Nancy (Campbell), Mar. 6, 1876.
Persis (Tenney), Sept. 26, 1906.
Rufus, May 3, 1904.
Rufus, Rev., Feb. 11, 1874.
Sarah A. (Lane), 1st w. George E., Sept. 3, 1868.
Sarah J. (Harvel), 2d w. George E., Feb. 20, 1894.
William Henry, Apr. 14, 1902.
Aldrich, Frederick Charles, July 14, 1883.
Alley, Alice Philips, Feb. 20, 1901.
Hannah, 1st w. Moses, Feb. 23, 1841.
Jane D. (Boyce), 2d w. Moses, Sept. 12, 1875.
Moses, at Lynn, Mass., Mar. 17, 1879.
Annis, Angie J., Dec. 23, 1863.
Augusta M., Apr. 11, 1889.
Charles U., Nov. 6, 1909.
Clarisa L., Jan. 1, 1839.
David L., Dec. 25, 1863.
Edith M., May 10, 1875.
Elmer E., Apr. 2, 1907.
Ernest H., Jan. 9, 1892.
George Walter, June 1, 1867.
George W., Mar. 25, 1910.
George W., Jr., Feb. 4, 1908 (killed under load wood).
Helen M., July 14, 1898.
Isaac B., Nov. 15, 1843.
James Monroe, July 11, 1855.
Martha, Sept. 23, 1895.
Mary Ann, Sept. 15, 1901.
Mary Etta, Sept. 12, 1903.
Mehitable (Page), w. Samuel W., Apr. 10, 1901.
Roxenna, Sept. 4, 1846.
Ayer, Benjamin F., Feb. 10, 1904.

Bailey, Fred Charles, May 8, 1882.
Grace Hunkins, Aug. 16, 1905.
Ruth Pike, May 14, 1900.
Baker, Doris Louise, Sept. 2, 1909.
Ballou, Alexander McGregor, Dec. 23, 1909.
Bancroft, David E., Apr. 1, 1851.
Barker, Herbert Arthur, May 28, 1886.
Eva Mildred, Jan. 23, 1888.
Bartley, Robert, M. D., Nov., 1820.
Bell, John, Nov. 30, 1825.
Mary A. (Gilmore), w. John, Apr. 21, 1822.
Benson, Ruth J. (Page), w. Andrew J., June 2, 1880.
Frank A., June 11, 1853.
George W., Dec. 20, 1862.
Ida M., Sept. 29, 1861.
Blodgett, Augusta Watts, June 6, 1903.
Bethiah (Reed), Sept. 10, 1904.
Celestia A., Oct. 14, 1863.
Elizabeth Vickery, Feb. 9, 1895.
Isaac, Jan. 11, 1858.
Isaac I., April 6, 1854.
Joshua S., June 10, 1843.
Sarah (Vickery), w. Joshua S., Sept. 19, 1863.
Boyce, Alphonse, Feb. 25, 1905.
Angeline W., Oct. 8, 1870.
Belinda J., May 3, 1871.
Boyce, Benjamin, Capt., Mar. 1, 1849.
Betsey M., Apr. 28, 1849.
Clarence A., Sept. 27, 1857.
Cylanda (Flanders), June 14, 1910.
Daniel, Aug. 28, 1853.
Daniel F., Nov. 3, 1883
David, Mar. 9, 1820.
Dervy M., Mar. 1, 1863.
Edgar N., Apr. 12, 1904.
Edwin H., Aug. 22, 1860.
Freeman C., July 11, 1831.
George C., Apr. 13, 1876.
George W., Feb. 27, 1898, in California.
Hannah (Whidden), w. William M., Feb. 20, 1893.
Hannah Jane, dau. Samuel and Susan, Jan. 15, 1907.
Hazen G., July 14, 1851.
Horatio Nelson, July 16, 1849, of cholera.
Hugh, Sept. 9, 1856.
Hugh, s. of Hugh, Jan. 20, 1889.
Jacob, Apr. 19, 1812.
James, Mar. 7, 1818.
James, s. Hugh, Feb. 28, 1837.
Jennette, July 14, 1862.
Jeremiah Mason, of cholera, July 15, 1849.
Maria, w. William P. Merrell, Feb. 1, 1901.
Nathan C., May 5, 1828.
Newell, Jan. 15, 1907.
Robert, Jan. 24, 1840.
Samuel, July 15, 1889.
Stephen M., Dec. 1, 1908, in California.
Susan P. (Dickey), w. Samuel, Aug. 24, 1878.
Susanna (Garvin), w. Hugh, Oct. 12, 1846.
Wealthy (Fling), w. William, May 26, 1866.
William, Feb. 26, 1875.
William M., Dec. 20, 1879.
Boyd, Calvin, Feb. 8, 1879.
George H., Sept. 2, 1892.
Frank F., s. of Calvin, Oct. 14, 1910.
Maria, Mar. 28, 1895.
Maria W., dau. Mason, Jan. 28, 1905.
Martha (Dickey), w. William, Apr. 27, 1879.
Mary, June 5, 1874.
Mason, Sept. 23, 1889.
William, Oct. 10, 1825.
Brickett, Alice, Aug. 30, 1813.
Charles Franklin, Nov. 28, 1855.
Charles Henry, s. Charles F., Nov. 29, 1913.
Delia Welch, Sept. 16, 1891.
Edward Clarence, s. Henry W., Apr. 14, 1876.
Elisabeth Poor, Jan. 28, 1876.
Emily (Spinney), w. Charles F., June 26, 1906.
Esther, Dec. 16, 1801.
Harriet Newell, Mar. 17, 1856.
Henry Welch, July 1, 1907.
Herbert Kimball, in California, Sept. 30, 1853.
James, Apr. 3, 1793.
James Kent, Sept. 25, 1862.
Jonathan, Dec. 19, 1872.
Lizzie A., Feb. 23, 1902.
Lydia (Kent), w. Jonathan, Mar. 24, 1870.
Nathaniel, Jan. 1, 1796.
Brooks, Charles E., Aug. 23, 1871.
Brown, Rev. Jonathan, Feb., 1838, aged 80 yrs.
Burgess, Jeffery, Sept. 7, 1910.
Burns, Daniel, Feb. 16, 1870, Salem, N. H.
Daniel Hardy, June 29, 1902.
Eliza A. S. (Goss), Jan. 6, 1895.
Lydia C. (Marsh), Aug. 12, 1852.
Rachel (Hunt), June 8, 1852.

Caldwell, Hattie N., Feb. 13, 1905.
Henry J., June 24, 1910.
Jefferson, s. of James, Apr. 14, 1882.
Joseph, Nov. 24, 1854.

Caldwell, Mary, w. Joseph, Sept. 2, 1845.
Nancy (Upton), 1st w. Jefferson, June 9, 1864.
Nancy, 2d w. Jefferson, Nov. 13, 1880.
Campbell, Francena E., dau. Dea. Samuel, Sept. 19, 1859.
Samuel, Dea., Apr. 17, 1902.
Carlton, George W., Sept. 8, 1862.
Mary Elisabeth, Mar. 30, 1867.
William B., Apr. 26, 1888.
Chase, Ann, July 11, 1883.
Esther, w. Edwin Follansbee, July 31, 1863.
Ethel May, May 21, 1890.
Frank Emery, Feb. 18, 1884.
John Henry, Aug. 29, 1864.
Lydia, w. Nathaniel, Jan. 9, 1872.
Nancy M. (Pettingill), w. Trueworthy D., Sept. 6, 1892.
Nathaniel, Nov. 21, 1879.
Phebe Maria (Hale), Dce. 20, 1903.
Clark, Alvina Nora, June 19, 1894.
Elizabeth (Perkins), w. Reed P., July 4, 1880.
John, Jan. 13, 1720–1. First death in Londonderry.
Joseph R., Feb. 7, 1903.
Matthew, Rev., successor to Rev. James McGregor, Jan. 25, 1735, aged 76 yrs. 76 yrs.
Ninian, Apr. 26, 1844, in Hancock, N. H.
Ralph Warner, July 22, 1887.
Reed P., Apr. 8, 1882.
Sally (Warner), w. Ninian, July 1, 1865, in Hancock, N. H.
Sarah Albina, Aug. 12, 1841.
Sarah Elizabeth, May 18, 1893.
Warren Dana, Apr. 2, 1911.
Coburn, Eld. Daniel G., Sept. 26, 1863.
Isaac, Jan. 13, 1883.
Roxanna (Blodgett), w. Daniel G., Jan. 5, 1895.
Cochran, Isaac Wallace, Aug. 4, 1887.
Lucy Woolner (Tilley), May 10, 1910.
Colby, Albert P., Sept. 3, 1905.
Daniel M., Aug. 15, 1885.
Ebenezer, May 1, 1886.
Sarah (Philbric), Apr. 14, 1891.
Washington, May 4, 1907.
Corning, Alexander M., Dec. 12, 1893.
Almira Newell, Jan. 22, 1857.
Anna Jane, Nov. 7, 1857.
Charles Freeman, Jan. 7, 1866.
Elias Randall, Oct. 12, 1835.
Esther (White), w. Freeman, Mar. 16, 1846.
Esther Ann, Sept. 23, 1847.
Esther Frances, Oct. 30, 1851.
Freeman, s. of Nathan, June 19, 1860.
George W., Sept. 5, 1844.
George W., Oct. 5, 1835.
Hannah, Jan. 30, 1907.
Hannah B., Jan. 30, 1907.
John, July 18, 1837.
John Anderson, Aug. 23, 1908.
Laura A. (Blaisdell), 2d w. Freeman, Oct. 26, 1883.
Lydia (Read), w. Peter, July 28, 1887.
Mary Esther, Jan. 23, 1879.
Nathaniel, Aug. 4, 1869.
Sally (Crowell), w. John, Aug. 18, 1840.
Sarah Elisabeth, Dec. 4, 1888.
Susie M., Dec. 13, 1883.
Sylvester R., Feb. 1, 1897.
Crowell, Charles Albert, Nov. 30, 1899.
Daniel Thurston, May 25, 1850, in California.
Elisabeth, dau. Peter and Harriet, May 26, 1853.
Hannah (Eastman), w. Samuel, Jr., Jan. 31, 1890.
Harriet (Hardy), Dec. 4, 1883.
Henry, Feb. 18, 1906.
James, July 24, 1855.
Judith (Plummer), dau. Dr. Plummer, Auburn, July 29, 1904.
Myron, Jan. 16, 1893.
Ora (Martin), with her infant son, Mar. 4, 1820.
Crowell, Peter, s. David, Sept. 7, 1869.
Samuel, Jr., Dec. 29, 1882.
Sarah A., June 23, 1854.

Daley, Daniel J., May 5, 1905.
John, May 30, 1901.
Davidson, Rev. William, Feb. 15, 1791, aged 77 yrs.
Dickey, Adam, June 17, 1817.
Caroline P. (Cogswell), 1st w. Eld. John, Dec. 14, 1888.
David Woodburn, Nov. 19, 1854.
Fannie Montgomery, Mar. 14, 1861.
George W., Oct. 8, 1911.
Hannah (Woodburn), July 12, 1845.
Harrison Tyler, Mar. 24, 1842.
Henry Clay, in Civil War, Oct., 1874.
Horace Greeley, Nov. 10, 1855 .
Dickey, Irvin Thornton, in Civil War, Apr. 1, 1864.
Isaac S., Aug. 18, 1907.
Isaiah, at Pittsburgh, Pa., 1872.
Jane, Feb. 20, 1830.
Jane (Nahor), w. Adam, June 13, 1815.
Jenny (Morrison), w. Robert, Sept. 4, 1862.
John, s. John and Margaret, July 25, 1894.
John, s. Robert, Aug. 26, 1852.
John, Elder, July 25, 1894.
Joseph, Nov. 26, 1746.
Laura S. (George), 2d w. Lyman A., Mar. 11, 1904.
Margaret Ann, Dec. 5, 1854.
Margaret (Pettingill), w. Isaac S., June 16, 1884.
Margaret (Woodburn), w. John, July 23, 1874.
Nancy (Humphrey), w. Samuel s. Robert, Nov. 26, 1851.
Ranson Flanders, Sept. 11, 1893.
Robert, s. Robert and Jenny, Oct. 3, 1825.
Robert, s. Robert and Margaret, July 2, 1809.
Robert, May 28, 1866.
Robert, June 19, 1805.
Samuel, s. Adam and Jane, July 26, 1824.
Samuel, s. Robert, Apr. 22, 1861.
Sarah Kendall, Sept. 12, 1877.
William, July 18, 1787.
Winfield Scott, Aug. 16, 1880.
Zoe Ann, dau. Robert and Jenny, May 27, 1886.
Doland, John, Sept. 5, 1860, at Manchester.
Dooley, Frank J., s. James and Martha, Mar. 22, 1894.
James, soldier, July 13, 1895.
Martha L., Feb. 14, 1899.

Ela, George E., Aug. 25, 1907.
Isabel (Gregg), Aug. 12, 1906.
John A., Aug. 2, 1880.
Mary, Jan. 21, 1822.
Samuel G., July 14, 1853.
Samuel D., s. Edward and Mary Dickey, Dec. 27, 1839.
Emerson, Isabel, Nov. 14, 1870.
Estey, Charles Enos, Aug. 11, 1864.
Daniel, Nov. 11, 1891.
Daniel Milton, s. Daniel, Dec. 25, 1841.
George Franklin, July 24, 1904.
Harriet Emeline, Nov. 4, 1869.
Horace Peabody, in Civil War, Jan. 24, 1865.
Rebecca (Hawkins), w. Daniel, June 26, 1887.
Evans, Oliver Dodge, Jan. 3, 1885.

Flanders, Clara E., May 12, 1884.
Emily (Colby), w. Samuel B., Jan. 29, 1885.
Emily J. (Whittle), Mar. 10, 1901.
Esther, Feb. 9, 1893.
Etta P., Mar. 30, 1892.
Hannah Frances, Mar. 5, 1859.
Nute Boyce, Mar. 17, 1887.
Paul B., May 22, 1899.
Ransom B., s. Zoe Ann, Sept. 11, 1893.
Reuben W., Aug. 20, 1898.

Flanders, Samuel B., b. in Dunbarton, N. H., Dec. 10, 1862.
Simeon D., Feb. 7, 1844.
Fling, Charles W., Oct. 21, 1889.
Daniel W., Jan. 11, 1893.
Edward, Apr. 30, 1826.
John W., Apr. 23, 1898.
Mary A. (Goodwin), w. John W., June 10, 1890.
Rachel, Aug. 7, 1869.
Rufus, Mar. 7, 1860.
Wealthy, May 26, 1866.
William M., June 21, 1826.
Furber, Elbridge Wallace, Sept. 12, 1881.
John S., Feb. 10, 1891.
John W., Nov. 29, 1885.
Laura J. (Wallace), w. John S., Oct. 18, 1910.
Laura Jane, Mar. 17, 1896.

Gage, Lydia T., May 4, 1865.
Gardner, Charles N., Aug. 30, 1879.
Garven, Benjamin F., June 23, 1903.
Elizabeth, Mar. 30, 1812.
Jacob, drowned Aug. 21, 1822.
John, May 17, 1815.
Margaret (Watts), w. Jacob, Dec. 24, 1846.
Perses, Mar. 5, 1875.
Tamar, Sept. 18, 1862.
Garvin, Eldora J., Apr. 17, 1910.
Elwyn W., Feb. 23, 1862.
Eva Dora, Oct. 18, 1892.
Nancy (Spinney), w. Benjamin F., July 29, 1903.
Norman C., May 31, 1851.
George, George W., Apr. 1, 1903.
Gibson, Alice Helen, Jan. 24, 1906.
Grace Harriet, Dec. 2, 1907.
John Calvin, Aug. 24, 1900.
Paul, Jan. 24, 1897.
Sarah Jane (White), w. John C., Mar. 18, 1892.
Gilchrist, George, Aug. 10, 1910.
Gilcreast, Carle E. Cressy, July, 1878.
Clara J., 1887.
Clarence W., 1882.
Ella Eliza, 1881.
Elwin A., Mar. 12, 1858.
Eugene M., 1873.
Georgie A., 1878.
Lafarest J., 1878.
Glidden, Abbie A., 1853.
A. Eugene, 1897.
James, 1864.
Goodhue, Elsie Christie, Jan. 24, 1875.
Juline F. (Miner), w. Ralph H., in Lawrence, Mass., Feb. 17, 1905.
Goodwin, Amos J., Feb. 13, 1897.
Arthur W., Sept., 1870.
George Newman, July 26, 1911.
Mary Ann, June 10, 1890.
Polly (Mary) (Jones), w. Joshua, Jr., Oct. 10, 1890.
Rebecca J., Mar. 3, 1892.
Greeley, Alfred D., Dec. 6, 1888.
Alice Phillips (Alley), w. George W., Feb. 20, 1901.
Ann (Dart), Dec. 25, 1909.
Elbridge G., Aug. 16, 1903.
Francis O., 1864.
Franklin Perham, Mar. 24, 1864.
George A., 1849.
George E., Sept. 5, 1883.
George W., Aug. 3, 1888.
Herbert Alley, Dec. 21, 1902.
Horace H., 1861.
John W., July 7, 1902.
Julia A. (Blood), w. Elbridge G., June 16, 1899.
Lucy (Senter), 1849.
Lucy M., 1889.
Phebe A., w. Charles E., Apr. 23, 1911.
Sarah A., 1902.
Sarah Arvilla, Jan. 3, 1882.
Gregg, Prof. Jarvis, June 28, 1836.
William, s. Capt. John, Sept. 16, 1815.
Griffin, Fidelia, w. Oscar, Jan. 26, 1894.
Harriet D. Major, w. Rufus, Aug. 21, 1886.
Griffin, Rufus, June 10, 1861.

Hale, Etta M., w. Samuel, Aug. 22, 1891.
Hall, Ella M. (Watts), 1st w. Henry R., July 18, 1890.
Elsie L., dau. Henry R. and Ella M. June 7, 1889.
Henry R., Nov. 2, 1904.
Lucinda R. (Wheeler), 2d w. Robert, June 7, 1896.
Mary Elizabeth, June 23, 1907.
Nancy E. (Wheeler), 1st w. Robert, Feb. 16, 1868.
Olive Marion, Apr. 25, 1908.
Robert, s. Samuel, Apr. 2, 1904.
Hardy, Aaron P., July 8, 1887.
Benjamin, May 16, 1870.
Benjamin, Jr., May 5, 1901.
Clarrissa Parker, 1875.
Daniel, May 25, 1859.
Delia W. (Brickett), Sept. 16, 1891.
Etter J. (Mooar), Jan. 20, 1881.
Fred Monroe, Nov. 13, 1875.
Freeman H., Feb. 26, 1906.
George A., June 13, 1906.
Harriet, dau. Daniel and Sarah, Dec. 4, 1883.
John, Dec. 19, 1893.
John G., Feb. 10, 1910.
Mary A., Sept. 6, 1853.
Mary (Whittier), w. William G., May 2 1860, aged 43 yrs.
Sarah, w. Daniel, Jan. 1, 1867.
Sylvester, 1866.
William D., Nov. 25, 1907.
William G., June 2, 1886.
Hart, dau. John D. and Abbie A., Sept. 30, 1882.
s. John D. and Abbie A., Dec. 29, 1885.
Hartford, Ella, Apr. 9, 1879.
Lizzie, July 22, 1879.
Harvell, Emeline (Miller), w. Joseph, Jr., Feb. 17, 1894.
James Erwing, Sept. 23, 1848.
Joseph, Lieut., Dec. 1, 1838.
Joseph, Jr., May 11, 1888.
Julia F., Oct. 1, 1854.
Marcia, Dec. 4, 1869.
Mary L. (Underwood), w. Lieut. Joseph, Sept., 1843.
Sarah H. (Manter), w. Joseph, Jr., Mar. 18, 1862.
Sarah J., Feb. 20, 1894.
Harvey, Gilman, 1840.
Gilman, 1874.
Jonas, 1853.
Jonas, May 18, 1862.
Jonas, Jr., May 23, 1873.
Jonathan, Dec. 27, 1863.
John, Jan. 5, 1864.
Josiah A., 1873.
Manas, Apr. 18, 1865.
Maria J., 1856.
Nancy, wife of Gilman, 1884.
Rachel, 2d wife Jonas, Nov. 16, 1826.
Rachel, 3d wife Jonas, Nov. 19, 1860.
Rebecca (Emerson) w. John, Sept. 11, 1864.
Rebekah, Oct. 16, 1847.
Salley, 1820.
Sarah Ann, Aug. 3, 1859.
Sophronia, wife Jonas, Jr., Nov. 25, 1873.
Susan, wife Jonathan, June 24, 1842.
Susanna (Stevens), w. Ephraim, June 8, 1910; Warren, 1904; Josephine L. Dustin, 1st w., 1881; Mary E. Cheever, 2d w., 1891; Gracie A., dau., 1873.—W. Harvey monument.
Hayes, Rev. Amasa A., Oct. 25, 1830.
Hicks, Henry J., Mar. 8, 1898.
Israel F., Jan. 17, 1911.
Susanna O. (Greve), w. Henry J., Jan. 4, 1880.
Holmes, Addie M., June 12, 1883.
David Coffin, drowned July 20, 1882.
Etta M., Feb. 11, 1881.
Gertrude, Sept. 21, 1867.
Georgia M. (Spalding), 1st w. Thomas, Oct. 15, 1875.

Holmes, Hannah T. (Rowe), Feb., 1908.
Joseph Matthew, Apr. 22, 1865.
Katie L., June 1, 1882.
M. Henry, June 13, 1883.
Hurd, Charles, May 23, 1873.
Charles, Jr., in Haverhill, Mass., Nov. 22, 1902.
Elmer E., Apr. 16, 1908.
George, June 10, 1875.
George A., Sept. 13, 1911.
Nancy M., Apr. 19, 1877.

Jones, Amos, May 10, 1843.
Hannah, Sept. 8, 1838.
Harriet, May 12, 1873.
Lorinda, Jan. 21, 1901.
Newman, July 9, 1836.
Polly, Oct. 10, 1890.
Jenkins, Martha C., Apr. 8, 1905.

Kendall, Emma R., Feb. 9, 1863, aged 8 yrs., 11 mos., 18 dys.
Everett C., Apr. 19, 1903.
R. Harriet (Goss), w. Everett C., Mar. 2, 1882.
Kimball, Isaac, Mar. 10, 1890.
Rebecca J. (Goodwin), 2d w. Isaac, May 3, 1892.
Sarah J. (Clough), 1st w. Isaac, Feb. 23, 1851.

Leach, David Rollins, Apr. 1, 1878.
Libby, Elvira (Hobbs), w. Richard, Mar. 14, 1897.
Richard, Mar. 29, 1848.
Lord, William Loren, June 17, 1886.
Lowd, Arabella, Dec. 19, 1895.
Charles E., Oct. 21, 1908.
Martha (Grant), w. William B., Mar. 6, 1907.
Susan F., Aug. 1, 1879.
William B., Dec. 14, 1891.
Lund, Robert J., Dec. 25, 1907.

McAllister, Alexander, s. David and Eleanor, about 1777.
Andrew, in 1812.
Archibald, 1778.
Benjamin, Dec. 14, 1887.
Caroline (Choate), Aug. 4, 1902.
Caroline (Savory), w. Benjamin, Oct. 25, 1883.
Charles, Oct. 22, 1905.
David, 1750, aged 46 yrs.
George, Sept. 9, 1899.
George, 4th, s. David and Eleanor, 1840, aged 94 yrs.
Henderson, drowned at sea, Jan. 30, 1825, aged 18 yrs.
Isaac, s. John and Rebekah, Aug. 30, 1858.
Isaac, Mar. 29, 1869.
Jonathan, Jan. 22, 1907.
John, Oct. 2, 1812, aged 31 yrs.
John, s. David and Eleanor, 1780, aged 36 yrs.
Rebecca (Henderson) (White), 1839, aged about 96 yrs.
Sarah, Sept., 1823.
Sarah (Harriman), w. Isaac, Feb. 16, 1854.
Thomas Savory, May 3, 1880.
William, s. Angus and Margaret, 1755, aged 55 yrs.
McClary, Charles, Sept. 21, 1877.
David, June 20, 1891.
Eleanor (Watts), w. Thomas, Aug. 30, 1829.
Eliza, Aug. 30, 1899.
Jane, July 15, 1907.
Jane H. (Russell), 1st w. John, June 26, 1862.
John, Feb. 22, 1905.
Hugh, lost at sea.
Thomas, Aug. 30, 1829.
McGregor, Alexander, Feb. 1, 1885.
Augusta W. (Blodgett), June 6, 1903.
Carrie E., Jan. 6, 1883.
David, May 17, 1891.
David, Rev., May 30, 1777.

McGregor, Emma N., 1875.
Etter R., 1881.
Francena N., 1864.
George F., Jan. 20, 189[illegible].
Gracie, Feb. 18, 1894.
Harriet L., 1886.
Lewis Aiken, Mar. 8, 1882.
Marietta (Nesmith), Jan. 25, 1884.
Mary (Boyd), w. Rev. David, Sept. 28, 1793.
Sarah, July 23, 1873.
Sarah (Wise), Mar. 25, 1887.
McKean, John R., July 15, 1901.
McKeen, James, Jr., about 1778, in Vermont.
McMurphy, John, Sept. 21, 1755.
Mary, w. John, Nov. 19, 1770.
McQuesten, George B., Feb. 10, 1905.
Lucy J. (Drew), 3d w. George B., Jan. 16, 1908.
Mack, John Preston, Sept. 10, 1873.
Mackay, Abbie M. (Thompson), w. James W., Dec. 25, 1876.
Arthur E., Apr. 12, 1882.
James W., Dce. 22, 1887.
Magoon, Charles Manfred, d. at 9 mos., in Dec., 1885.
Manter, Clarissa, Dec. 16, 1866.
David, Oct. 7, 1855.
David, 1858.
Elizabeth Ann Smith, 2d w. Col. Francis, May 29, 1883.
Francis, Col., Mar. 1, 1888. In War of 1812.
George, Mar. 3, 1860.
George, M. D., 3d N. H. Vol., July 7, 1870.
Harriet (Crowningshield), 1st w. Col. Francis, July 4, 1858, aged 58 yrs.
Harriet M., Apr. 1, 1900.
Isabel Reed, w. Capt. Samuel, July 3, 1874.
Isabel, Nov. 10, 1902.
James, Mar. 16, 1856.
Louisa A., Oct. 28, 1898.
Mary Ann, Apr. 18. 1900.
Mary B., about 1827.
Mary Florence, Jan. 3, 1889.
Mary Olena, Oct. 25, 1882.
Melena A. (Barker), 1st w. George F., dentist, Apr. 19, 1870, at Wellfleet, Mass.
Parvel Cathruf, 1837.
Phineas, July 25, 1855.
Polly or Mary (Senter), 2d w. George, Feb. 22, 1860.
Samuel, Capt., Dec. 20, 1893.
Samuel, Jr., Aug. 7, 1884.
Marshall, John D. K., Jan. 20, 1910.
Matthews, Hiram C., June 10, 1910.
Maxfield, Clyde Gould, Dec. 24, 1902.
Merrill, Calvin, Sept. 24, 1853.
Ella Eva, Apr. 27, 1897.
Ellen Frances, Apr. 3, 1881.
Eunice Emeline, Nov. 3, 1863.
Fannie (Gray), May 24, 1898.
Ida, Aug. 20, 1879.
John, Apr. 6, 1894.
John Edward, Aug. 4, 1902.
Messer, Bessie Isabel, Nov. 3, 1910.
Miller, George W., Dec. 2, 1902.
Mooar, Aretta Josephine, Jan. 20, 1881.
Maria Jane, Dec. 19, 1909.
Moody, Dolly B. (McDonald), July 12, 1904.
Jeremiah Bean, Mar. 11 1904.
Levi Jay, Feb. 3, 1861.
Mary Susan, Feb. 15, 1907.
Royce D., Sept. 20, 1904.
Morrison, Belinda C., Sept. 27, 1863.
Charles H., in Civil War, Dec. 22, 1864.
Emeline, Dec. 27, 1907.
Franklin G., Oct. 4, 1904.
James G., in army, May 27, 1863.
John, Sept. 12, 1870.
Margaret, May 5, 1853, aged 21 yrs.
Sally (Coburn), Jan. 16, 1899.
Sarah (Giles), Jan. 1, 1881.
Thomas, Sept. 1, 1852.
William, Rev., 2d pastor W. Parish, Mar. 9, 1818.
Morse, Andrew J., May 25, 1903.
Mullins, Augusta B., June 9, 1863.

Mullins, Betsey, Nov. 12, 1906.
Clara, Dec. 10, 1899.
Hason, drowned June 1, 1832.
Irael, Oct. 13, 1859.
Louise Ella, Mar. 25, 1908.
Mary (Garvin), w. Israel, May 17, 1864.
Robert, Sept. 6, 1830.
T. Jane, Jan. 25, 1880.

Nesmith, Arvilla (Colby), Nov. 18, 1893.
Cyrus, 1881.
Eva Marion, June 19, 1900.
Lydiah, 1876.
Luetah, 1842.
Louise E. (Mullins), Mar. 25, 1908.
Nancy B., w. Thomas, 1880.
Oreal, 1863.
Thomas, Capt., 1861.
Nevins, Charles Henry, Nov. 18, 1876.
Henry A., 1872.
James, Dea., 1873.
James E., 1853.
Sarah E., 1876.
Nichols, Abigail, w. William, Nov. 15, 1828.
Alexander, Jan. 21, 1775.
Alexander, Mar. 6, 1824.
Ann (Cochran), w. William, 1758.
Anna, dau. James and Dinah, Sept. 27, 1840.
David, Mar. 29, 1854.
Dinah, Nov. 7, 1835.
Hannah (Caldwell), June 25, 1818.
Hannah, Dec. 10, 1859.
James, May 10, 1818.
James, Nov. 5, 1826.
James, May 29, 1831.
James, Feb., 1833.
Margaret, 1799.
Margaret, w. James Kincaid, Mar. 11, 1823.
Margaret, Oct. 10, 1850.
Mary, 1838.
Nancy, June 1, 1853.
Samuel, June 20, 1859.
Samuel, Aug. 5, 1800.
Thomas, June 6, 1803.
William, Sept. 12, 1838.
Norcross, Frank E., Nov. 8, 1907.
George N., July 1, 1861.
Joshua L., Sept. 1, 1862.
Noyes, Andrew Warren, Feb. 19, 1909.
Benning, June 17, 1881.
Ella L., Nov. 11, 1869.
Eva F., Jan. 4, 1889.
Fred E., Sept. 29, 1896.
Martha C., Mar. 30, 1908.
Mary Barstow (Warren), w. Benning, July 22, 1892.
Myron E., Sept. 3, 1899.
Sylvester C., May 21, 1856.

Page, Armenia, June 26, 1866.
Darius, Aug. 5, 1842.
Eldusta M., Apr. 9, 1893.
Joel, 1890.
Olin W., July 17, 1907.
Orren L., Apr. 21, 1904.
Rachel (Fling), w. Joel, Aug. 7, 1869.
Randal, Feb. 6, 1877.
Sarah R., Apr. 25, 1868.
Parker, Celinda Perham, May 28, 1893.
Edward, Apr. 9, 1888.
Edward Lutwyche, Rev., July 14, 1850.
Eliza A., July 24, 1909.
Eldora M. (Dodge), w. John, Dec. 15, 1892.
Horatio Nelson, Oct. 21, 1901.
Jonathan, Dr., Sept., 1791.
John, Eld., Jan. 16, 1862.
John, Jan. 23, 1907.
Mary K., June 25, 1897.
Polly (Peabody), Jan. 23, 1846.
Parshley, Cora L., Mar. 8, 1885.
Enoch H., Mar. 20, 1894.
Kenneth M., Dec. 16, 1904.
Lauria D. (Hobbs), Feb. 14, 1906.
Laura W., Oct. 7, 1909.
Mary V., Aug. 20, 1904.
Warren S., Mar. 17, 1874.

Patterson, David, Feb. 12, 1793.
Elisabeth (Burns), 1848.
Elizabeth, June 6, 1875.
George Washington, Oct. 15, 1879.
Grisey, w. Peter, 1817.
Grisey (Barnett), 1850.
Grisey (Burns), 1845.
James, June 4, 1815.
James Betton, Feb. 23, 1788.
Jane (Frank), Feb. 19, 1867.
John, 1793.
John, Jan. 30, 1817.
Margaret (Holmes), 1838.
Margaret (Taylor), Nov. 24, 1858.
Mary (McNeill), Feb. 22, 1812.
Peter, Feb. 17, 1863.
Peter, 1800.
Rachel (McNeill), 1838.
Robert, 1828.
Robert, June 27, 1859.
Sarah (Melendy), 1820.
Thomas, May 20, 1834.
William, Aug. 14, 1838.
Payne, Charles Herbertson, Jan. 3, 1908.
Charles Wesley, s. Wesley W., Mar. 11, 1892.
George E., May 29, 1900.
Maroia (Wychoff), w. Wesley W., Jan. 25, 1891.
Nancy D. (Page), w. Samuel N., Nov. 21, 1899.
Nelson S., Oct. 6, 1905.
Roland. Mar. 11, 1892.
Samuel N., May 12, 1902.
Peabody, Elbridge W., Nov. 9, 1907.
Eliza. Jan. 7, 1905.
Henrietta, w. Joseph Roach, Feb. 27, 1904.
Orrville A,, July 1, 1899.
Maria, 1st w. Orrville A., Aug. 11, 1865.
Willie W., Oct. 1, 1863.
Perkins, Elizabeth. July 4, 1880.
Franklin. Feb. 26, 1843, at sea.
Harriet Louisa, Aug. 11, 1862.
James, Dea., Apr. 8. 1864.
Jane (Youngman), Dec. 27, 1887.
Joseph, Feb. 1. 1806.
Joseph, killed in Mexican war.
Mary (Foster), w. Joseph, Aug. 5, 1802.
Mary Poland, July 6, 1808.
Philemon Smith, July, 1790.
Sally, Nov. 15, 1810.
Sally Smith, w. Dea. James, Mar. 22, 1859.
Sarah, Aug. 5, 1827.
Washington, July 10, 1895.
Pettingill, Annie, May 30, 1871.
Betsey, w. Wm. Richardson, Jan. 4, 1889.
Cynthia A., June 14, 1903.
David, about 1868.
Edgar P., Feb. 24. 1880.
Elvira (Hobbs), Mar. 14, 1897.
George, Jan. 27, 1870.
Hannah B., Mar. 3, 1880.
Herbert. July 15, 1870.
Hugh, Nov. 1, 1846.
James, Feb. 27, 1876.
James F., Aug. 20, 1874.
Laura M., Mar. 17, 1900.
Margaret (Watts), 1st w. William, 1820.
Nathaniel, Jan. 3. 1892 or '93.
Warren Martin, Dec. 20, 1876.
Pillsbury, Adams Dix, May 3, 1877.
A. Judson, Sept. 18, 1851.
Ann Judson, Feb. 28, 1856.
Annie Sarah, July 30, 1861.
Arthur A., Nov. 30, 1873.
Charles S., Mar. 23, 1902.
Edwin, Oct. 27, 1888.
Grace Lillian, July 6, 1909.
Helen Iona, Mar. 9, 1895.
John Arthur, Jan. 17, 1873.
Josiah H., Nov. 5, 1879.
Lavinia H., Sept. 30, 1871.
Martha E., Oct. 11, 1874.
Lavinia (Hobart), w. Stephen, Oct. 29, 1871.
John Thurston, May 3, 1862.
Stephen, Jan. 22, 1851.
Stephen P., Sept. 7, 1869.
Ulyses G., Apr. 3, 1905.

Pillsbury, Vera Dix, May 25, 1897.
William S., Oct. 7, 1911.
May C. (Clough), w. Charles E., Nov. 27, 1903.
Pinkerton, Betsey, w. John Aiken, in 1837.
Elisabeth, Mar. 18, 1789.
John, 1780, aged 80 yrs.
John, June 4, 1795, aged 17 yrs., 7 mos., 22 dys.
John, Maj., May 1, 1816.
John Morrison, Feb. 6, 1881.
Naomi, May 4, 1790.
Polly (Tufts), 2d w. Maj. John, Feb. 19, 1844, aged 94 yrs.
Rachel (Duncan), Sept. 13, 1781.
Platts, Abigail, Apr. 10, 1878.
Charles Fremont, Dec. 25, 1859.
Egbert, Oct. 6, 1863.
Eliza, Mar. 30, 1830.
Ella Frances, Mar. 1, 1876.
Francis Manter, Mar. 25, 1880.
George Henry, Oct. 25, 1858.
George Manter, Apr. 24, 1894.
George W., May 20, 1907.
Harriet (Manter), Apr. 1, 1900.
Hattie S., Nov. 27, 1900.
Ida Florence, Mar., 1895.
James, Revolutionary soldier, d. Jan. 9, 1835.
James, soldier War 1812, 1828, Brasher, N. Y.
James Munroe, Jan. 17, 1892.
Mamie Edith, May 24, 1900.
Mary, Apr. 22, 1858.
Mary (Crowningshield), Mar. 19, 1862.
Mary (Manter), Jan., 1890.
Mary (Warner), Nov. 29, 1839.
Mehitable, Nov. 20, 1844.
Nancy, Mar. 15, 1873.
Sarah, Mar. 14, 1864.
Susan, June 22, 1829, at Fort Covington, N. Y.
Thomas B., June 15, 1874.
Plummer, Albert C., Mar. 25, 1873.
Charlotte Towns (Boyd), Dec. 19, 1898.
Elisabeth Hale, 1807.
Eliza P. (Coffin), w. John A., Feb. 15, 1880.
John Anderson, Capt., Apr. 7, 1904.
Kate E. (Hughes), w. Granville F., Feb. 28, 1911.
Nathan, Aug. 24, 1886.

Ray, Lewis Clark, Aug. 29, 1897.
Reid, Elisabeth (1st), Mar., 1847.
George, Gen., Sept., 1815.
George (5th), Jan. 30, 1848.
Harold Morrison, Jan. 1, 1892.
James, Nov., 1755.
John, Feb., 1803.
James (2d), in London, Eng., May, 1827.
John (4th), Dec., 1834.
Mary, Feb., 1775.
Mary (3d), June, 1834.
Mary Woodburn, w. Gen. George, Apr. 7, 1823.
Mercia Burnham, Sept. 28, 1890.
Walter Phineas, April, 1893.
Walter, Jan. 5, 1892.
Richardson, Abigail, 1749.
Addison K., July 15, 1908.
Caleb, Mar. 16, 1870.
Caleb, killed at Ticonderoga in French and Indian War (?).
Charles W., 1902.
Clara J., Oct. 22, 1877.
Harry, Jan. 22, 1892.
John W., Dec. 20, 1850.
Lydia (Messer), w. William, July 14, 1843.
Margaret, Sept. 4, 1859.
Mary Ann, Mar. 6, 1885.
Mary H., Feb. 19, 1839.
Mary Jane (Wilson), Jan. 10, 1902.
Nathaniel W., Sept., 1848.
Samuel, May 8, 1900.
Samuel R., Feb. 19, 1872.
Sarah B., Oct. 1, 1888.
Sarah Hale (Goodwin), w. William P., Jan. 3, 1903.
Richardson, Sophia S., Oct. 20, 1879.
Thomas J., Sept. 20, 1873.
Warren, Oct. 24, 1893.
Warren, Jr., Mar. 9, 1908.
William, Mar. 14, 1658.
William Messer, Jan. 4, 1889.
William M., May 19, 1871.
William Percy, July 2, 1897.
William Pettingill, May 13, 1893.
Ripley, George H., Apr. 4, 1904.
Susan M., Aug., 1908.
Joseph, Oct., 1864.
Rowell, Clara Jane, Jan. 31, 1897.
Jane P. (Spinney), Oct. 17, 1866.
Janette (Hall), w. Joseph M., Nov. 25, 1869.
John, Feb. 1, 1896.
Joseph M., Dec. 20, 1894.
Laura Z., Aug., 1875.

Sampson, Agnes, May 24, 1812.
Alice K. (Simonds), w. Branch, 2d, Jan. 11, 1890.
Branch, Jan. 11, 1852.
Branch, Apr. 8, 1893.
Carrie A. (Lord), w. Edward, Apr. 28, 1895.
Edward, s. Branch and Alice K., Apr. 19, 1895.
Eliza Holly, w. Turner, 1854.
Hannah W. (Colby), w. Edward, July 24, 1865.
Harriet, Oct. 21, 1852.
Huldah C., w. Phineas Frost, Oct. 1, 1893.
Ida E., July 16, 1872.
Jennie U. (Mudgett), w. Edward, Dec. 7, 1885.
Lucy A., July 18, 1843.
Lydia A., w. Albert V. Stevens, May 6, 1906.
Matilda, w. Joseph Ripley, Sept. 2, 1879.
Nancy, w. John J. Grant, Mar. 19, 1892.
Polly (Crocker), Nov. 7, 1848.
Turner, Jan. 21, 1880.
Sanborn, Eliza B., July 31, 1869.
Josiah, Dec. 23, 1881.
Martha A. (Dolan), w. Josiah, Jan. 24, 1910.
Eliza B., July 31, 1869.
Savery, Abigail (Coffin), Sept. 8, 1885.
Jonathan, Feb. 2, 1881.
Sawyer, Thomas J., Feb. 10, 1908.
Schwartz, Cordelia, w. Frederick, May 9, 1893.
Frederick L., Sept. 22, 1892.
Mary L., July 9, 1905.
Nellie, Mar. 13, 1909.
Shipley, John, Jan. 3, 1875.
Joseph Lucian, Dec. 17, 1894.
Mary Frances, Jan. 28, 1842.
Rebecca (Dickey), w. John, Apr. 10, 1880.
Sleeper, Hannah Jane (Dickey), w. Josiah, Dec. 27, 1897.
Josiah, Dec. 10, 1881.
Smith, Alexander, Mar. 5, 1858.
Alice B., Dec. 17, 1902.
Clarisa Melvin, May 28, 1832.
Elisha, May 26, 1887.
Elisabeth A., May 29, 1883.
Elisabeth M. (Selden), w. Nathaniel, Nov. 22, 1888.
Ella Nancy, May 26, 1903.
Ellen J., May 25, 1903.
Grace R., Aug. 12, 1902.
Halsey Dinsmore, Aug. 10, 1904.
Hannah L. (Colburn), w. Robert S., Sept. 4, 1910.
Harriet E., July 1, 1904.
Henry Leigh, Aug. 27, 1888.
Nellie A. (Annis), Sept. 24, 1910; 50 yrs., 6 mos., 23 dys.
Laura J. (Jones), w. Reuben A., Sept. 1, 1876.
Leigh, Aug., 1886.
Lizzie A. (Choate), Jan. 15, 1890, aged 50 yrs., 4 mos., 2 dys.
Mary Jane, June 28, 1904.
Mary P., Apr. 29, 1910.

Smith, Nancy Hodgman, w. Sherburn D., Nov. 23, 1909.
Nathan S., July 31, 1908.
Nathaniel, Mar. 17, 1861.
Rachel (Sanborn), w. Elisha, Mar. 28, 1893.
Reuben Alonzo, Feb. 16, 1904.
Robert Selden, Sept. 23, 1905.
Sarah Ann, June 8, 1905.
Sarah (Melvin), Jan. 31, 1889.
Sherburn Dana, Nov. 24, 1905.
Susan D. (Hazelton), w. Henry C., Apr. 14, 1903.
Walter Alexander, 1898.
Spinney, John D., Oct. 28, 1890.
Zilla M. (Taylor), Apr. 10, 1893.
Spofford, Albert, Jan. 7, 1887.
Stark, Gen. John, May 8, 1822.
Starrett, Sarah A., dau. Levi R. and Anna D. Sampson, Nov. 22, 1883.
Stevens, Albert V., Apr. 26, 1861.
Betsy Ann (Ambrose), w. Horace E., May 4, 1877.
Florence A., Oct. 30, 1894.
Harriet, Oct. 21, 1852.
Horace E., Dec. 25, 1886.
Stokes, Henry P., Apr. 16, 1908.
Irene A., Oct. 13, 1910.
Irene (French), w. Moses D., Apr. 10, 1885.
Jennie P. (Durrah), w. Orrin B., Oct. 27, 1890.
Moses D., July 17, 1882.
Orrin B., Apr. 15, 1895.
Stone, James G., Nov. 8, 1913.
Nancy Jane (Sanborn), Nov. 7, 1869.
Sweatt, Abby, Jan., 1837.
Lizzie, Aug. 9, 1905.
Mary L. Galencia, Sept. 11, 1905.
Mary M. Herbert, Mar. 26, 1903.
Moses, Jan. 11, 1863.
Sarah J. (Thompson), Dec. 5, 1882.

Taylor, James Calvin, Jan. 14, 1888.
Tewksbury, Dora M., w. Sumner, Nov. 11, 1909.
Era M., Aug. 23, 1895.
Sumner, Oct. 25, 1909.
Walter L., Sept. 8, 1897.
Tenney, Albert, Dec. 30, 1894.
Albert W., Oct. 26, 1860.
Ardelle L., Dec. 19, 1895.
Arley P., Mar. 14, 1842.
Arley P., soldier, Nov. 16, 1865.
Asa, Jan. 15, 1818.
Charles, Dec. 16, 1886.
Charles A., Oct. 11, 1906.
David, June 19, 1837.
David, May 8, 1880.
Eliza, Oct. 12, 1846.
Eliza C. (Peabody), w. Charles, Jan. 7, 1905.
George G., Feb. 9, 1908.
Lydia C., Nov. 4, 1910.
Martha, Oct. 8, 1891.
Mary, Aug. 31, 1888.
Mary Jane Dickey, g. dau. Gen. Stark, w. Albert, May 8, 1903.
Mollie, w. Asa, Aug. 27, 1831.
Nancy E. (Rowell), w. George G., Mar. 15, 1898.
Persis Plummer, w. David, Dec., 1887.
Persis, Sept. 26, 1906.
Thomas, Joseph D., Mar. 1, 1907.
Judith D. (Emmons), May 13, 1909.
Thorn, Dr. Isaac, July 13, 1825.
Titcomb, Albert O., Nov. 22, 1905.
Frank F., Aug. 15, 1856.
Sally H. (Webster), w. Simeon C., Mar. 29, 1903.
Simeon C., Sept. 27, 1856.

Walker, Reuben, May 20, 1815.
Wallace, Elisabeth (Patterson), Dec. 30, 1833.
James, 1794.
Mary Wilson (Ocean Mary), w. James, 1813.
Wallace, Robert, 1815.
William, 1824.
Watts, Anna C. (Palmer), w. Caleb M., Sept. 7, 1903.
Annie Eliza, Aug. 10, 1911.
Caleb M., Mar. 8, 1895.
Clayton E., May 3, 1893.
Daniel Mason, Mar. 9, 1847.
Deborah, Feb. 4, 1835.
Delia May, Nov. 5, 1910.
Elisabeh J. Wheeler, Apr. 30, 1867.
Ella M., July 18, 1890.
Esther Jane, m. Walter Boyce, Feb. 13, 1913.
Frank H., Oct. 1, 1875.
Freeman C., Mar. 17, 1903.
Hattie M., Mar. 4, 1852, aged 2 yrs.
Herman L., killed by electric car at Lawrence, Mass., June 11, 1907.
Henry P., Apr. 9, 1897.
Horace Perkins, Aug. 15, 1890.
Joshua C., Jan. 21, 1873.
Mariam E., Aug., 1888.
Mariam P. (Annis), w. Charles H., July 2, 1894.
Margaret, Aug. 19, 1840.
Maria (Boyd), w. Horace P., Mar. 28, 1895.
Martha Boyd, Feb. 21, 1877.
Martha (Goodwin), w. Joshua C., Dec. 16, 1869.
Martha M., July 12, 1861.
Webster, Amos, in Nashua, Sept. 22, 1906.
Amos C., July 11, 1895.
Betsey Ann, July 15, 1889.
Caleb, June 29, 1863; soldier.
Caroline (Chase), Nov. 14, 1861.
Charles Warren, Oct. 13, 1904.
Elisabeth K. (Whittaker), 2d w. Amos C., Nov. 2, 1888.
Hattie L., Jan. 8, 1905.
Jonathan, Oct. 10, 1865; 67 yrs.
Marion Louise, May 16, 1896.
Mary Ann (Everton), Feb. 13, 1881; 68½ yrs.
Oscar Dana, Dec. 20, 1897.
William Wallace, Mar. 8, 1863; soldier.
Wetherbee, Grace (Baker), w. Hezekiah, Feb. 9, 1865.
Hezekiah, Capt., Mar. 18, 1869.
John H., Apr. 24, 1897.
Sarah E. (Corning), w. Wm. B., Dec. 4, 1888.
Susan A., Sept. 10, 1864.
William B., Sept. 11, 1884.
Wheeler, Ann (Lincoln), 2d w. Tilly H., Mar. 14, 1900.
Charles H., drowned Aug. 8, 1890.
David Gooden, soldier, Sept. 11, 1867.
Elisabeth J., Apr. 30, 1867.
James Sumner, Mar. 30, 1867.
Nancy Ann, Jan. 20, 1910.
Rebecca (Goodwin), 1st w. Tilly H., May 28, 1850.
Sarah F., June 13, 1905.
Tilly H., Nov. 15, 1880.
Whidden, Adeline (baby), Feb. 14, 1862.
Adeline (Boyce), w. Joshua, Feb. 6, 1862.
Alice M., Mar. 21, 1904.
Caroline, Feb. 26, 1914.
Elbridge, 1848.
Ellen M., Dec. 2, 1857.
George M., June 25, 1864, in Civil War.
Hannah (Morrill), Sept. 2, 1881.
Hannah M., Feb. 20, 1893.
James Warren, Nov., 1909.
John P., July 20, 1897.
Joshua, Aug. 7, 1896.
Lillie, 1897.
Martha Ellen, June 9, 1884.
Mary Frances, Apr. 14, 1858.
Mary J., Oct. 21, 1908.
Mary Josephine, Sept. 7, 1863.
Michael, Nov. 2, 1861.
Rufus Monroe, Jan. 18, 1852.
Walter, Apr. 14, 1858.
William Henry, May 15, 1907.
Winfield Scott, Apr. 17, 1908.
Whitcomb, Harriet C., Feb. 11, 1892.

White, Edgar William, s. Iserach, Feb. 1, 1854.
Eliza Ann, Nov. 1, 1838.
Emily, in Boston, 1909.
Esther, Mar. 25, 1885.
Harriet M. B., Feb., 1901.
Henry Harrison, Oct. 26, 1904.
John, April 18, 1860.
Manella, 1890, aged 36 yrs.
Maria, July 3, 1829.
Nelson, May 24, 1851.
Rachel (Corning), May 25, 1885.
Reuben, Mar. 31, 1859.
Ruel Baldwin, Sept. 23, 1883.
Samuel C., Dec. 1, 1892.
Susanna (Dickey), w. John, Feb. 9, 1867.
Whittemore, Amy L. (Parry), w. Joshua, Nov. 6, 1866.
Elias J., Oct. 11, 1882.
Henry J., June 11, 1905.
Joshua Lewis, Jan. 18, 1891.
Lewis Goodwin, Apr. 27, 1883.
Zackariah K., June 28, 1901.
Whittle, Carrie J., Sept. 30, 1880.
Ernest W., Aug. 4, 1868.
Whorf, Benjamin, Sept. 10, 1842.
Benjamin F., Jan. 27, 1903.
Juliette A. B. (Page), Jan. 8, 1892.
Shuah, w. Benjamin, Oct. 7, 1874.
Wiley, Alverton, Oct. 13, 1874.
Ella A. (Gilcreast), w. George B., June 19, 1882.
Ephraim A., Jan. 17, 1897.
George B., Oct. 23, 1906.
Lucy E., Aug. 26, 1861.
Mary A., Feb. 21, 1892.
Nancy A. (Blood), w. Ephraim, Feb. 28, 1893.
Sarah E., Mar. 4, 1862.
Wilkins, Archibald McMurphy, Dec. 17, 1886.
Charles Wesley, Dec. 6, 1881.
Daniel, Sept. 30, 1872.
Daniel, Jr., June 7, 1894.
Daniel O., Aug. 22, 1832.
Edwin Oscar, May 28, 1905.
Elijah R. Sept. 30, 1908.
Elisabeth (Russell), Aug. 23, 1834.
Harriet N. (Davis), June 19, 1902.
Lillian (Lamprey), w. Herbert E., Sept. 12, 1905, in Keene, N. H.
Mary McMurphy (Thompson), Aug. 17, 1839.
Norman Stanley, Jan. 30, 1905.
William Wesley, Sept. 1, 1892.
Willey, Etta M., Aug. 22, 1891.
Jacob N., Jan. 29, 1867.
Rachel T., w. Jacob N., Aug. 31, 1886.
Wilson, Abigail (Jewett), 2d w. Thomas, Feb. 5, 1863.
Abbie Delia, Feb. 17, 1910.
Adeline (Annis), Oct. 27, 1903.
Wilson, Eva Dora, Oct. 18, 1892.
James, in Bradford, Vt., 1843.
John Eddy, Sept. 25, 1853
John Pinkerton, July 22, 1901.
Lilla J., 1865.
May Belinda, June 21, 1909.
Rebecca P., Sept. 27, 1853.
Rebecca (Pinkerton), 1st w. Thomas, Dec. 3, 1827.
Robert Henry, Oct. 18, 1884.
Thomas, Jan. 16, 1863.
Thomas H., Sept. 10, 1853.
Woodbury, Abram A., Sept. 14, 1903.
Alma Jane, Sept. 14, 1888.
Annah Augusta, Aug. 12, 1863.
Benjamin F., Jan. 8, 1865.
Charles W., Jan. 12, 1884.
Eben, killed by a falling tree in 1822.
Hannah (Barker), Apr. 7, 1912.
James G., June 1, 1842.
John Clayton, Oct. 3, 1909.
John G., June 18, 1909.
Louisa J. (Baker), w. Samuel, Oct. 25, 1908.
Samuel, June 3, 1878.
Samuel Leroy, Feb. 27, 1865.
Woods, Alice H. (Fellows), July 31, 1896.
Ensign C., Mar. 7, 1907.
Wychoff, Elizabeth, w. Joseph A., Sept. 25, 1900.
Emma A., Aug. 8, 1891.
Joseph A., 4th N. H. Vols., Oct. 22, 1862.
Julia E., May 20, 1863.
Maroia, Jan. 25, 1887.

Young, Charles Edward, Feb. 11, 1899.
Charles Franklin, Jan. 8, 1861.
Charles Wesley, Oct. 16, 1886.
Charlotte M. (Boyce), Sept. 6, 1875.
David Hamblett, July 24, 1902.
David William, May 4, 1909.
Emeline (Pettengill), 2d w. John P., Feb. 1, 1885.
Ephraim, Sept. 23, 1896.
Ephraim J., Aug. 28, 1849.
Esther (Stevens), w. Israel, Oct. 19, 1868.
Frederic Augustus, Aug. 14, 1899.
Israel, May 13, 1848.
James Franklin, Nov. 26, 1898.
Jane (Hall), 1st w. John P., Dec. 13, 1867.
Jonathan, Feb. 26, 1883.
John Herbert, Aug. 26, 1870.
John P., June 27, 1885.
Martha (Plummer), Jan. 15, 1887.
Mary Jane, Mar. 27, 1832.
Nathan P., May 1, 1867.
Rachel (Harvey), in Temple, N. H., Sept., 1908.
Sarah D. (Gilcreast), w. Charles E., Aug. 4, 1895.